For reference

DISCARD

CHAMBERS

FACT
FINDER

CHAMBERS

CHAMBERS
An imprint of Chambers Harrap Publishers Ltd
7 Hopetoun Crescent
Edinburgh, EH7 4AY

www.chambers.co.uk

This second edition published by Chambers Harrap Publishers Ltd 2006
Previous edition published 2004

A CIP catalogue record for this book is available from the British Library.

ISBN-13: 978 0550 10142 6
ISBN-10: 0550 10142 X

Image credits

Star images, p10
Copyright © 2002 by Houghton Mifflin Company. Reproduced by permission from
The American Heritage Student Science Dictionary.

Cloud images, pp36–7
Copyright © 2002 by Houghton Mifflin Company. Reproduced by permission from
The American Heritage Student Science Dictionary.

Electromagnetic spectrum image, p381
Copyright © 2002 by Houghton Mifflin Company. Reproduced by permission from
The American Heritage Student Science Dictionary.

Muscles diagram, p390
Copyright © www.arttoday.com

Designed and typeset by Chambers Harrap Publishers Ltd, Edinburgh
Printed and bound in Germany by Bercker

CONTRIBUTORS

Editor

Hazel Norris

Contributors

Gary Dexter
Alison Pickering
Camilla Rockwood

Editorial Assistance

Vicky Aldus
Katie Brooks

Publishing Manager

Patrick White

Prepress

Isla MacLean

Prepress Manager

Clair Simpson

INTRODUCTION

This new edition of *Chambers Factfinder* builds on the strengths that have seen the *Factfinder* series swiftly become a key part of the Chambers reference book range. The *Factfinder* is designed to be not only informative and reliable, but also easy to use and entertaining; the facts and figures have been specially chosen for their relevance, including some information often marginalized elsewhere, but which is nevertheless valuable for quizzes, crosswords, arguments and puzzles. This new edition has been extensively revised and updated, with several new sections added.

Amusing 'fascinating fact' boxes pepper the text; from providing additional interesting material on a subject, to dropping in quirky, little-known or intriguing snippets of information, these fact boxes are a browser's delight and bring the subject areas to life. Trivia lovers will be pleased to encounter yet more oddities and unusual facts in this new edition.

A 'one-stop' approach is taken, with careful and intuitive grouping of material so that all the data on a particular subject can be found in a single place. There are 28 major subject areas, within which are clearly-labelled individual subsections, arranged so as to take the user on a journey from the furthest realms of the universe to our own planet and the world around us, and then on to the world's people and the diverse fields of human culture and achievement.

Data is presented simply in tables and lists for clarity, aided by maps, diagrams, pie charts, pictures and boxes; introductory information is distinguished by background tints. Detailed contents pages at the front of the book and a handy index at the back guide the reader to the information sought.

Chambers Factfinder is designed to be accessible, user-friendly and full of the information that really matters. Whether you are hoping to win a pub quiz, prove a point in an argument, find a crossword solution or just browsing inquisitively for fun, this book should satisfy your curiosity.

ABBREVIATIONS

a	acre(s)	km	kilometre(s)
abbrev	abbreviation(s)	kph	kilometre(s) per hour
AD	Anno Domini	kW	kilowatt(s)
AU	astronomical unit(s)	l	litre(s)
BBC	British Broadcasting Corporation	lb	pound(s)
BC	Before Christ	lbm	pound(s) mass
bu	bushel(s)	m	metre(s)
C	Celsius (Centigrade)	MB	megabyte(s)
c	century	mg	milligram(s)
c.	circa	mi	mile(s)
cc	cubic centimetre(s)	ml	millilitre(s)
CIS	Commonwealth of Independent States	mm	millimetre(s)
		MP	Member of Parliament
cl	centilitre(s)	mph	mile(s) per hour
cm	centimetre(s)	Mt	Mount
Co	company	N	north
cu	cubic	n/a	not applicable
cwt	hundredweight(s)	NASA	National Aeronautics and Space Administration
dB	decibel(s)		
DC	District of Columbia	no.	number
dm	decimetre(s)	oz	ounce(s)
E	east	pk	peck(s)
e	estimate	pop	population
eg	for example	p(p)	page(s)
etc	and so on (et cetera)	Prot	Protestant
EU	European Union	pt	pint(s)
F	Fahrenheit	qt	quart(s)
fl.	floruit	RC	Roman Catholic
fl oz	fluid ounce(s)	S	south
ft	foot (feet)	sec	second(s)
g	gram(s)	SI	Système International (d'Unités)
gal	gallon(s)	sq	square
GB	gigabyte(s)	SS	Saints
GMT	Greenwich Mean Time	St	Saint
ha	hectare(s)	st	stone(s)
hl	hectolitre(s)	TV	television
HQ	headquarters	UK	United Kingdom
HRE	Holy Roman Empire	UN	United Nations
ie	that is (id est)	US	United States
in	inch(es)	USA	United States of America
ISO	International Organization for Standardization	USSR	Union of Soviet Socialist Republics
		UT	Unified Team
IVR	International Vehicle Registration	v	versus
		W	west
K	Kelvin	yd	yard(s)
KB	kilobyte(s)	ZIP	zone improvement plan
kg	kilogram(s)		

Months are abbreviated to the first three letters (26 Nov 1976).

Additional abbreviations can be found under individual sections in the text; for example, currency abbreviations are listed under **ECONOMICS**.

CONTENTS

HUMAN GEOGRAPHY

FACTFINDER

CONTENTS

CONTENTS

POLITICS, LAW AND ORDER

ANCIENT GREECE AND ROME

RELIGIONS, BELIEFS AND FOLKLORE

TIME

SCIENCE

HUMAN BODY

MATHEMATICS

ECONOMICS

MEASUREMENT, CONVERSION AND SIZE

INVENTIONS, DISCOVERIES AND FIRSTS

ARCHITECTURE AND ENGINEERING

SOCIETY AND LEARNING

LITERATURE

ART

FILM AND TELEVISION

MUSIC

FOOD AND DRINK

LANGUAGE

COMMUNICATION

TRANSPORT

SPORTS, COMPETITIONS AND GAMES

CONTENTS

THE SOLAR SYSTEM

SUN

Age	4.6 billion–4.7 billion years	**Predicted total lifespan**	10 billion years
Distance from Earth (mean)	150 million km/93 million mi	**Surface area**	6 087 billion sq km/ 2 350 billion sq mi
Diameter	1 392 500km/864 950mi	**Volume**	1.4122×10^{18} cu km/ 3.388×10^{17} cu mi
Mass	1.989×10^{30} kg/4.385×10^{30} lb		
Luminosity	3.83×10^{27} kW	**Density (mean)**	1.409g/cu cm/87.96 lb/cu ft
Temperature (core)	15 million K/15 million°C/ 27 million°F	**Surface gravity**	2.740×10^{4} cm/sq sec/10 787in/sq sec
Rotation	26.8 days (of solar equator, as seen from Earth)	**Temperature (surface)**	5 770 K/5 500°C/ 10 000°F

Composition of the Sun's photosphere

Element	% weight
Hydrogen	73.46
Helium	24.85
Oxygen	0.77
Carbon	0.29
Iron	0.16
Neon	0.12
Nitrogen	0.09
Silicon	0.07
Magnesium	0.05
Sulphur	0.04
Others	0.10

Exploding Energy

The Sun's energy comes from nuclear fusion. It consumes hundreds of millions of tonnes of hydrogen every second, which reactions convert into helium. This generates as much energy every second as almost 91 billion tonnes, or 100 billion tons, of TNT exploding.

- ☐ Hydrogen
- ▨ Helium
- ☐ Oxygen
- ☐ Carbon
- ▨ Others

Inside the Sun

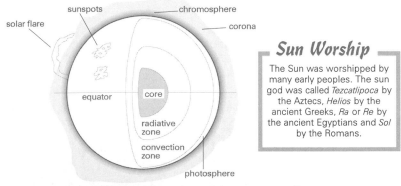

sunspots — chromosphere
solar flare — corona
equator — core
radiative zone
convection zone
photosphere

Sun Worship

The Sun was worshipped by many early peoples. The sun god was called *Tezcatlipoca* by the Aztecs, *Helios* by the ancient Greeks, *Ra* or *Re* by the ancient Egyptians and *Sol* by the Romans.

SOLAR SYSTEM

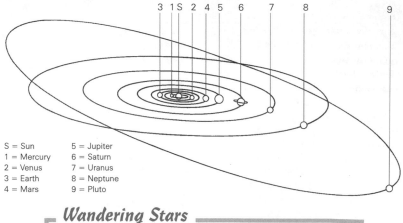

S = Sun
1 = Mercury
2 = Venus
3 = Earth
4 = Mars

5 = Jupiter
6 = Saturn
7 = Uranus
8 = Neptune
9 = Pluto

Wandering Stars

Planet comes from the Greek word *planētēs*, meaning *wanderer*. Planets were known by the ancient Greeks as *astéres planêtai*, or *wandering stars*, because it was believed that they meandered about the skies.

PLANETS

For satellites, the first figure gives the total number. The names of the major satellites are listed with those closest to the planet first; the year of discovery is given in parentheses. See separate section **The Earth** for information on the Earth.

Mercury

Diameter at equator	4 878km/3 031mi
Maximum distance from the Sun	69.4 million km/43 million mi
Minimum distance from the Sun	46.8 million km/29 million mi
Length of year	88 days
Length of day	58 days 16 hours
Atmosphere	Almost none; traces of oxygen, sodium, and helium
Surface gravity	370cm/sq sec/146in/sq sec
Rings	None
Satellites	None

Discovered

Known in prehistory; named after the Roman god of merchants, the messenger of the gods, possibly because of its fast movement.

Polar Planet

In 1991 radar observations indicated that Mercury may have water ice at its north and south poles.

Venus

Diameter at equator	12 104km/7 521mi
Maximum distance from the Sun	109 million km/67.6 million mi
Minimum distance from the Sun	107.6 million km/66.7 million mi
Length of year	224.7 days
Length of day	243 days
Atmosphere	Mainly carbon dioxide and nitrogen; clouds of sulphuric acid
Surface gravity	887cm/sq sec/349in/sq sec
Rings	None
Satellites	None

Discovered

Known in prehistory; named after the Roman goddess of love, because of its brightness. Most of its surface features are named after female figures.

Sultry Venus

Venus has an extreme greenhouse effect due to the high concentrations of carbon dioxide in its atmosphere. Temperatures on the surface are hot enough to melt lead.

Earth see separate section **THE EARTH**

Mars

Diameter at equator	6 794km/4 222mi
Maximum distance from the Sun	249.2 million km/154.5 million mi
Minimum distance from the Sun	207.3 million km/128.5 million mi
Length of year	687 days
Length of day	24 hours 37 minutes 23 seconds
Atmosphere	Carbon dioxide, nitrogen, argon
Surface gravity	371cm/sq sec/146in/sq sec
Rings	None
Satellites	2: Phobos (1877), Deimos (1877)

Discovered

Known in prehistory; named after the Roman god of war, because of its red colour.

Volcanic Mars

Mars is home to the largest volcano in the solar system, Olympus Mons. It is 624km/374mi in diameter, 25km/16mi high and has a crater 80km/50mi wide.

Jupiter

Diameter at equator	142 800km/88 700mi
Maximum distance from the Sun	817.4 million km/506.8 million mi
Minimum distance from the Sun	741.6 million km/459.8 million mi
Length of year	11.86 years
Length of day	9 hours 50 minutes 30 seconds
Atmosphere	Mainly hydrogen and helium
Surface gravity	2 312cm/sq sec/910in/sq sec
Rings	Yes
Satellites	Almost 60: Io (1610), Europa (1610), Ganymede (1610) and Callisto (1610)

Discovered

Known in prehistory; named after the Roman god of the sky and its attributes (Sun, Moon, thunder, rain, etc).

Almost a Star

Jupiter is a proto-star. If it had been 50–100 times more massive, hydrogen fusion in its interior would have caused it to shine like our Sun.

Saturn

Diameter at equator	120 536km/74 900mi
Maximum distance from the Sun	1.5 billion km/937.6 million mi
Minimum distance from the Sun	1.3 billion km/834.6 million mi
Length of year	29.46 years
Length of day	10 hours 14 minutes
Atmosphere	Mainly hydrogen and helium
Surface gravity	896cm/sq sec/353in/sq sec
Rings	Yes
Satellites	At least 30: Mimas (1789), Enceladus (1789), Tethys (1684), Dione (1684), Rhea (1672), Titan (1655), Hyperion (1848), Iapetus (1671)

Discovered

Known in prehistory; named after the Roman god of fertility and agriculture.

Titanic Aliens

Saturn's largest moon, Titan, is a little bigger than the planet Mercury. Scientists think there is a chance that the organic compounds in its atmosphere may indicate the presence of some form of life.

Uranus

Diameter at equator	51 118km/31 765mi
Maximum distance from the Sun	3 billion km/1.8 billion mi
Minimum distance from the Sun	2.7 billion km/1.7 billion mi
Length of year	84.01 years
Length of day	16–28 hours[1]
Atmosphere	Hydrogen, helium, methane
Surface gravity	869cm/sq sec/342in/sq sec
Rings	Yes
Satellites	At least 20: Ariel (1851), Umbriel (1851), Miranda (1948), Titania (1787), Oberon (1787)

Discovered

1781; its discoverer, William Herschel, wanted to name it *Georgium Sidus* ('the Georgian planet') after the reigning British monarch, but the name Uranus came into more common use in around 1850. In Greek mythology Uranus was the god of the heavens.

[1] *Different latitudes rotate at different speeds.*

Catastrophic Collision

Uranus orbits the Sun 'on its side' – that is, with its poles pointing toward the Sun. This may be the result of a catastrophic collision with a huge body such as a minor planet or asteroid.

Neptune

Diameter at equator	49 492km/30 754mi
Maximum distance from the Sun	4.5 million km/2.8 billion mi
Minimum distance from the Sun	4.4 billion km/2.7 billion mi
Length of year	164.79 years
Length of day	18–20 hours[1]
Atmosphere	Methane, hydrogen, helium
Surface gravity	1 100cm/sq sec/433in/sq sec
Rings	Yes
Satellites	11: Proteus (1989), Triton (1846), Nereid (1949)

Discovered

1846; the first planet to be discovered by mathematical calculations, rather than observation. Named after the Roman god of the sea.

[1] *Different latitudes rotate at different speeds.*

Far Out

Neptune is usually the eighth planet from the Sun, but for 20 of every 248 Earth years (most recently 1979–99) it becomes the ninth, the furthest planet, as Pluto's orbit takes it closer to the Sun.

Pluto

Diameter at equator	2 300km/1 429mi
Maximum distance from the Sun	7.3 billion km/4.5 billion mi
Minimum distance from the Sun	4.4 billion km/2.7 billion mi
Length of year	247.7 years
Length of day	6 days 9 hours
Atmosphere	Almost none; probably seasonal traces of methane, nitrogen and carbon monoxide
Surface gravity	60cm/sq sec/24in/sq sec
Rings	None
Satellites	1: Charon (1978)
Discovered	
1930; named after the Roman god of the underworld.	

Possible Planets

Pluto may not actually be a planet at all. Some scientists believe instead that it is just one of a large number of icy bodies known as the Kuiper belt. This orbiting belt is thought to be the origin of some of the solar system's comets. In 2003, a possible tenth planet was discovered to be orbiting the Sun, three times further away than Pluto. However, the 'planet', named Sedna after the Inuit goddess of the ocean, should probably be classified as a planetoid rather than a planet. A new candidate for tenth planet, larger and more distant than Sedna, was discovered in 2005.

MOON

Diameter	3 476km/2 160mi
Average distance from Earth	384 467km/238 908mi
Orbital period	27.32 days
Age	Approximately 4.6 billion years
Atmosphere	Trace elements only; water ice has however been detected at the poles
Mean surface temperature	107°C/225°F (day), −153°C/−245°F (night)
Surface gravity	162cm/sq sec/64in/sq sec
Mass	7.3483×10^{22} kg/16.2×10^{22} lb
Density	3.341g/cu cm/208.572 lb/cu ft

Moon Mystery

No one knows for certain where the Moon comes from. The most probable theory suggests that a body approximately the size of Mars once hit the Earth, and the Moon is part of the debris from that collision. Others suggest that it may originally have been part of the Earth that broke away, or perhaps that it was separate and just happened to be caught by the Earth's gravity, or even that it formed gradually in orbit over time.

Lunar seas

The Romans thought that the dark areas visible on the surface of the Moon were lunar 'maria', seas. Modern astronomy has shown instead that they are dry plains filled with volcanic rocks. However, how they formed is still unclear.

Latin name	English name	Latin name	English name
Lacus Mortis	Lake of Death	Mare Serenitatis	Sea of Serenity
Lacus Somniorum	Lake of Dreams	Mare Smythii	Smyth's Sea
Mare Australe	Southern Sea	Mare Spumans	Foaming Sea
Mare Crisium	Sea of Crises	Mare Tranquillitatis	Sea of Tranquillity
Mare Fecunditatis	Sea of Fertility	Mare Undarum	Sea of Waves
Mare Frigoris	Sea of Cold	Mare Vaporum	Sea of Vapours
Mare Humboldtianum	Humboldt's Sea	Oceanus Procellarum	Ocean of Storms
Mare Humorum	Sea of Moisture	Palus Epidemiarum	Marsh of Epidemics
Mare Imbrium	Sea of Showers	Palus Nebularum	Marsh of Mists
Mare Ingenii[1]	Sea of Geniuses	Palus Putredinis	Marsh of Decay
Mare Marginis	Marginal Sea	Palus Somnii	Marsh of Sleep
Mare Moscoviense[1]	Moscow Sea	Sinus Aestuum	Bay of Heats
Mare Nectaris	Sea of Nectar	Sinus Iridum	Bay of Rainbows
Mare Nubium	Sea of Clouds	Sinus Medii	Central Bay
Mare Orientale[1]	Eastern Sea	Sinus Roris	Bay of Dew

[1] *On the far side of the Moon.*

Phases of the Moon

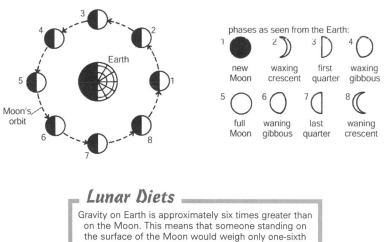

Earth

Moon's orbit

phases as seen from the Earth:

1 new Moon   2 waxing crescent   3 first quarter   4 waxing gibbous

5 full Moon   6 waning gibbous   7 last quarter   8 waning crescent

Lunar Diets

Gravity on Earth is approximately six times greater than on the Moon. This means that someone standing on the surface of the Moon would weigh only one-sixth of his or her usual weight on Earth.

STARS

The constellations

A constellation is composed of stars which form a group as seen from the Earth. There are 88 constellations in total.

Latin name	English name	Latin name	English name
Andromeda	Andromeda	Lacerta	Lizard
Antlia	Air Pump	Leo	Lion
Apus	Bird of Paradise	Leo Minor	Little Lion
Aquarius	Water Bearer	Lepus	Hare
Aquila	Eagle	Libra	Scales
Ara	Altar	Lupus	Wolf
Aries	Ram	Lynx	Lynx
Auriga	Charioteer	Lyra	Harp
Boötes	Herdsman	Mensa	Table
Caelum	Chisel	Microscopium	Microscope
Camelopardalis	Giraffe	Monoceros	Unicorn
Cancer	Crab	Musca	Fly
Canes Venatici	Hunting Dogs	Norma	Level
Canis Major	Great Dog	Octans	Octant
Canis Minor	Little Dog	Ophiuchus	Serpent Bearer
Capricornus	Sea Goat	Orion	Orion
Carina	Keel	Pavo	Peacock
Cassiopeia	Cassiopeia	Pegasus	Winged Horse
Centaurus	Centaur	Perseus	Perseus
Cepheus	Cepheus	Phoenix	Phoenix
Cetus	Whale	Pictor	Easel
Chamaeleon	Chameleon	Pisces	Fishes
Circinus	Compasses	Piscis Austrinus	Southern Fish
Columba	Dove	Puppis	Ship's Stern
Coma Berenices	Berenice's Hair	Pyxis	Mariner's Compass
Corona Australis	Southern Crown	Reticulum	Net
Corona Borealis	Northern Crown	Sagitta	Arrow
Corvus	Crow	Sagittarius	Archer
Crater	Cup	Scorpius	Scorpion
Crux	Southern Cross	Sculptor	Sculptor
Cygnus	Swan	Scutum	Shield
Delphinus	Dolphin	Serpens	Serpent
Dorado	Swordfish	Sextans	Sextant
Draco	Dragon	Taurus	Bull
Equuleus	Little Horse	Telescopium	Telescope
Eridanus	River Eridanus	Triangulum	Triangle
Fornax	Furnace	Triangulum Australe	Southern Triangle
Gemini	Twins	Tucana	Toucan
Grus	Crane	Ursa Major	Great Bear
Hercules	Hercules	Ursa Minor	Little Bear
Horologium	Clock	Vela	Sails
Hydra	Sea Serpent	Virgo	Virgin
Hydrus	Water Snake	Volans	Flying Fish
Indus	Indian	Vulpecula	Fox

Twinkle, Twinkle, Little Star

Because stars are so far away, starlight has to travel a great distance to reach Earth, and stars appear only as tiny points of light in the sky. They twinkle because of rapid changes in their brightness caused by moving air in the atmosphere through which their light rays pass. The scientific word for twinkling is *scintillation*. Planets are nearer to us, meaning that they appear larger in the sky and their light is stronger and less susceptible to atmospheric turbulence, so they don't twinkle.

Brightest stars

The apparent brightness of a star is represented by a number called its magnitude. The larger the number, the fainter the star. The faintest stars visible to the naked eye are slightly fainter than magnitude six. Only approximately 6 000 of the billions of stars in the sky are visible to the naked eye. The table lists the ten brightest stars visible from the Earth.

Star name	Distance (light years)	Apparent magnitude	Absolute magnitude
Sirius A	8.6	−1.46	+1.4
Canopus	98	−0.72	−8.5
Arcturus	36	−0.06	−0.3
Alpha Centauri A	4.3	−0.01	+4.4
Vega	26.5	+0.04	+0.5
Capella	45	+0.05	−0.7
Rigel	900	+0.14	−6.8
Procyon A	11.2	+0.37	+2.6
Betelgeuse	520	+0.41	−5.5
Achernar	118	+0.51	−1.0

Nearest stars

Star name	Distance (light years)	Apparent magnitude	Absolute magnitude
Proxima Centauri	4.3	+11.05	+15.5
Alpha Centauri A	4.3	−0.01	+4.4
Alpha Centauri B	4.3	+1.33	+5.7
Barnard's Star	5.9	+9.54	+13.3
Wolf 359	7.6	+13.53	+16.7
Lalande 21185	8.1	+7.50	+10.5
Sirius A	8.6	−1.46	+1.4
Sirius B	8.6	+8.68	+11.6
Luyten 726 8A	8.9	+12.45	+15.3
UV 726 8B	8.9	+12.95	+15.3

Biggest and Brightest Star

The Pistol Star is the largest and most powerful star known. Astronomers think it is approximately 100 times bigger than our Sun, and 10 million times brighter – it emits as much energy in just a few seconds as our Sun does in a whole year. The Pistol Star is only approximately 25 000 light years away from us, but it is hidden behind huge clouds of space dust, so despite its brightness isn't visible from the Earth.

Star life cycle

A star is a sphere of matter held together entirely by its own gravitational field, generating energy by means of nuclear fusion reactions deep in its interior. Stars shine as a result of the heat and light energy generated by these reactions. A star will go through several different stages during its lifetime, which can be billions of years.

nebula

A cloud of gas and dust. As this matter contracts under gravity, the beginnings of the star are created.

Dwarf Stars

As well as *white dwarf* and *black dwarf* stars, astronomers think that there may also be *brown dwarfs*, very large planets just below the critical mass needed to ignite a stellar nuclear reaction in their own interiors and turn them into stars.

main-sequence star

Eventually the star stops contracting and nuclear fusion reactions begin. The main reaction converts hydrogen into helium. The star begins to shine. Stars spend most of their life at this stage, during which their temperature and brightness will barely change. Our Sun is a main-sequence star.

red giant

Eventually reactions in the star's core stop as all the hydrogen is exhausted. The star expands, and swells up greatly. It becomes cooler but brighter.

supernova

The star explodes, radiating enormous amounts of energy into space. But the core of the star can collapse under its own gravitational field.

smaller, less massive stars

larger stars

white dwarf

The star implodes, collapsing into a small, very dense body. It is nearing the end of its life. The remains may eventually cool into a *black dwarf*, which no longer emits visible light.

neutron star

If a star has insufficient gravity to collapse entirely, it will become a tiny body, a mass of neutrons only a few miles across, but of very high density.

black hole

The core collapses in on itself to the point where its gravity is so strong that nothing, not even light, can escape.

COMETS

Origin

Short-period comets, those which take less than 200 years to orbit the Sun, come from the Kuiper Belt, a large ring of icy bodies orbiting the Sun just beyond Neptune.

Long-period comets take much longer to orbit the Sun (up to 30 million years) and originate in the Oort cloud, a cloud of frozen comet nuclei approximately 100 000 astronomical units[1] away from the Sun. It is estimated that the Oort cloud contains approximately 10 trillion (10 000 000 000 000) comets.

Number

Over 850 recorded to date; approximately ten new comets are discovered each year.

Size, structure and movement

The solid nucleus of a comet is usually several kilometres in diameter, but may be several hundred kilometres; it consists of ice, dust and solid particles like a large, dirty snowball. When the comet passes close to the Sun, a cloud of gas and dust is ejected from the nucleus, forming a huge head or coma, many thousands of kilometres in diameter. The radiations from the Sun elongate the gas and dust to form one or more tails, often extending millions of kilometres in space. These tails point away from the Sun, but as the comet recedes, the tail will decrease in length until the comet returns to its latent dirty snowball state.

Selected comets

The date given is the year in which the comet was first seen.

Halley: 240BC, 76.1 year orbit	**Daylight Comet:** 1910, orbit not known
Tycho: 1577, orbit not known	**Schwassmann-Wachmann 1:** 1925, 15 year orbit
Kirch[2]: 1680, 8 814 year orbit	
De Chéseaux: 1744, orbit not known	**Arend-Roland:** 1957, orbit not known
Lexell: 1770, 5.6 year orbit	**Mrkos:** 1957, orbit not known
Encke: 1786, 3.3 year orbit	**Humason:** 1961, 3 000 year orbit
Flauergues: 1811, 3 094 year orbit	**Seki-Lines:** 1962, orbit not known
Pons-Winnecke: 1819, 6.34 year orbit	**Ikeya-Seki:** 1965, 880 year orbit
Great Comet: 1843, 512.6 year orbit	**Tago-Sato-Kosaka:** 1969, 420 000 year orbit
Donati: 1858, 1 950 year orbit	**Bennett:** 1970, 1 680 year orbit
Tebbutt: 1861, 409.1 year orbit	**Kohoutek:** 1973, 75 000 year orbit
Swift-Tuttle: 1862, 125 year orbit	**West:** 1975, 500 000 year orbit
Cruls: 1882, 758.4 year orbit	**IRAS-Araki-Alcock:** 1983, orbit not known
Wolf: 1884, 8.4 year orbit	**Hale-Bopp:** 1995, 2 400 year orbit
Morehouse: 1908, orbit not known	**Hyakutake:** 1996, 18 000 year orbit

[1] *One astronomical unit is equal to the mean distance between the Earth and the Sun.*
[2] *Kirch is also known as Newton.*

Halley's Comet

One of the best-known and brightest comets is Halley's comet. First recorded in 240BC, when it was seen over China, the comet is visible from Earth approximately every 76 years. Most famously it was visible during the Battle of Hastings in 1066, an event depicted in the Bayeux Tapestry. The comet was named after the English astronomer Edmond Halley (1656–1742), who successfully predicted the years in which it would return. Halley's comet was last seen in 1986, and will not be visible from Earth again until 2061.

ASTEROIDS AND METEORS

Annual meteor showers

Meteors appear to radiate from the named star region.

Shower	Dates	Maximum activity
Quadrantids	1–6 Jan	3–4 Jan
Lyrids	19–25 Apr	22 Apr
Alpha-Scorpiids	20 Apr–19 May	28 Apr–10 May
Eta Aquariids	1–8 May	5 May
Delta Aquariids	15 Jul–10 Aug	28 Jul–5 Aug
Perseids	27 Jul–17 Aug	11–14 Aug
Orionids	15–25 Oct	21 Oct
Taurids	25 Oct–25 Nov	4–14 Nov
Leonids	14–20 Nov	17–18 Nov
Geminids	8–14 Dec	13–14 Dec
Ursids	19–24 Dec	22–23 Dec

Falling Stars

On the night of 16–17 Nov 1966, the Leonids put on a spectacular display between western North America and the eastern USSR. It is estimated that there were approximately 2 300 meteors every minute.

Meteoroids and meteorites

Origin
Interplanetary; some may originate from the Asteroid Belt, others may have cometary origins.

Average composition
Rocky and/or metallic.

Average size
From a few micrometres to many metres or even kilometres; smaller meteoroids that burn up in the Earth's atmosphere are known popularly as 'shooting stars'; larger meteoroids that reach the Earth's surface are scientifically termed meteorites.

Speed
Meteoroids can enter the Earth's atmosphere at speeds of up to 70km/sec, or 45mi/sec. They normally burn up at a height of approximately 100km/60mi.

First recorded human injury from a meteorite
Mrs Hewlett Hodges of Sylacauga, Alabama, USA, was badly bruised by a 3.5kg/8 lb meteorite which fell on her home on 30 Nov 1954.

Heaviest known meteorite
A meteorite found in Grootfontein, Namibia, in 1920 weighed 60 tonnes/59 tons. It was composed of nickel-rich iron and was almost 3m/9.8ft wide.

Asteroids

Origin
The Asteroid Belt orbiting the Sun between Mars and Jupiter. This region may contain millions of asteroids.

Number of catalogued asteroids
Approximately 20 000.

Largest asteroid
Ceres (1801); 940km/584mi in diameter.

Average composition
Metallic rock with possible addition of water ice.

First landing on an asteroid
2001, on the asteroid Eros, by the unmanned NEAR Shoemaker spacecraft.

ECLIPSES

Solar eclipses

The eclipse begins in the first country named. In an annular eclipse, the apparent size of the Moon is too small for a total eclipse and a bright ring of Sun remains visible. Eclipse data is given for the years 2001–11.

Date	Type of eclipse	Visibility path
21 Jun 2001	Total	southern Atlantic Ocean, southern Africa, Madagascar
14 Dec 2001	Annular	Pacific Ocean, Central America
10 Jun 2002	Annular	Indonesia, Pacific Ocean, Mexico
4 Dec 2002	Total	southern Africa, Indian Ocean, Australia
31 May 2003	Annular	Iceland, Greenland (Denmark), Scotland (UK)
23 Nov 2003	Total	Antarctica
8 Apr 2005	Annular/Total	Pacific Ocean, Panama, Venezuela
3 Oct 2005	Annular	Atlantic Ocean, Spain, Libya, Indian Ocean
29 Mar 2006	Total	Atlantic Ocean, Libya, Turkey, Russia
22 Sep 2006	Annular	Guyana, Atlantic Ocean, Indian Ocean
7 Feb 2008	Annular	Antarctica
1 Aug 2008	Total	Arctic, Siberia (Russia), China
26 Jan 2009	Annular	southern Atlantic Ocean, Indian Ocean, Borneo (Indonesia)
22 Jul 2009	Total	India, China, Pacific Ocean
15 Jan 2010	Annular	Africa, Indian Ocean, China
11 Jul 2010	Total	Pacific Ocean, southern Chile

Sun

total eclipse penumbra
visible here

Moon
umbra
Earth

partial eclipse
visible here

Lunar eclipses

Eclipse data is given for the years 2001–11.

Date	Type of eclipse	Time of mid-eclipse (UT¹)	Where visible
9 Jan 2001	Total	20.22	Europe, Asia, Africa
5 Jul 2001	Partial	14.57	Asia, Australia, Pacific Ocean
16 May 2003	Total	03.41	Americas, Europe, Africa
9 Nov 2003	Total	01.20	Americas, Europe, Africa, western Asia
4 May 2004	Total	20.32	Europe, Africa, Asia
28 Oct 2004	Total	03.05	Americas, Europe, Africa
17 Oct 2005	Partial	12.05	eastern Asia, Pacific Ocean, North America
7 Sep 2006	Partial	18.53	Australia, Asia, eastern Africa
3 Mar 2007	Total	23.22	Europe, Asia, Africa
28 Aug 2007	Total	10.39	Australia, Pacific Ocean, part of North America
21 Feb 2008	Total	03.27	Americas, Europe, Africa
16 Aug 2008	Partial	21.12	Europe, Africa, western Asia
31 Dec 2009	Partial	19.23	Asia, Africa, Europe
26 Jun 2010	Partial	11.39	Pacific Rim
21 Dec 2010	Total	08.17	North and South America
15 Jun 2011	Total	20.12	Asia, Africa, Europe
10 Dec 2011	Total	14.32	Pacific Ocean, Australia. eastern Asia

¹ *Universal Time, equivalent to Greenwich Mean Time (GMT).*

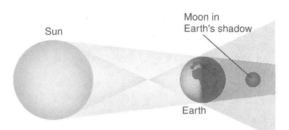

Sun

Moon in Earth's shadow

Earth

Moon-Eating Monsters

In many ancient cultures eclipses were viewed with great fear. It was believed that the Sun or Moon was being attacked and swallowed up by a huge monster or demon, often a dragon. People would make as much noise and commotion as possible during the eclipse to scare the savage beast away and return the Sun or Moon to them safely.

ASTRONOMY AND SPACE EXPLORATION

ASTRONOMERS ROYAL

Astronomer Royal is an honorary title awarded to a distinguished British astronomer. Until 1972, the director of the Royal Observatory at Greenwich automatically became the Astronomer Royal, but the two posts have since been separate.

Dates	Astronomer Royal	Dates	Astronomer Royal
1675–1719	John Flamsteed	1910–33	Sir Frank Dyson
1720–42	Edmond Halley	1933–55	Sir Harold Spencer Jones
1742–62	James Bradley	1956–71	Sir Richard Woolley
1762–4	Nathaniel Bliss	1972–82	Sir Martin Ryle
1765–1811	Nevil Maskelyne	1982–90	Sir Francis Graham-Smith
1811–35	John Pond	1991–5	Sir Arnold Wolfendale
1835–81	Sir George Airy	1995–	Sir Martin Rees
1881–1910	Sir William Christie		

Royal Raven Poo

The first Astronomer Royal, John Flamsteed, worked from the Tower of London until the building of the Royal Observatory at Greenwich was completed. Conditions at the Tower were not ideal for astronomy, however. The Tower's famous ravens found Flamsteed's telescopes to be excellent perches, and the unhappy astronomer had trouble gazing at the stars with his telescopes splattered with raven poo.

SPACE FIRSTS

Date	Event
4 Oct 1957	**First satellite** to orbit the Earth, Sputnik 1, is launched by the USSR.
3 Nov 1957	USSR's Sputnik 2 mission puts the **first living creature**, a dog called Laika, into space; Laika dies soon after launch from overheating and stress.
2 Jan 1959	USSR's Luna 1 mission **escapes Earth gravity**.
14 Sep 1959	USSR's Luna 2 mission makes a **lunar impact**.
4 Oct 1959	USSR's Luna 3 mission is launched and takes a **photo of the far side of the Moon**.
12 Aug 1960	**First communications satellite**, ECHO 1, is launched by the USA.
31 Jan 1961	**First 'chimponaut'**, a chimpanzee called Ham, enters space as part of the US Mercury programme. He survives. Previously monkeys, pigs, bears and mice had been used.
12 Apr 1961	Yuri Gagarin becomes the **first man in space**, making one orbit of the Earth aboard the USSR's Vostok 1 spacecraft. More than 400 people have since followed him.
20 Feb 1962	John Glenn becomes the **first American** to orbit the Earth.

Date	Event
16 Jun 1963	Valentina Tereshkova becomes the **first woman** in space aboard the USSR's Vostok 6 spacecraft.
18 Mar 1965	Alexei Leonov of the USSR's Voshkod 2 mission makes the **first spacewalk**.
1 Mar 1966	USSR robotic spacecraft Venera 3 lands on **Venus**.
30 May 1966	US spacecraft Surveyor 1 makes a soft landing on the **Moon**.
21–27 Dec 1968	Astronauts from the USA's Apollo 8 make the **first manned orbit** of the Moon (10 orbits).
20 Jul 1969	**First men set foot on the Moon**, landing at the Sea of Tranquillity; they are the USA's Apollo 11 crew members Neil Armstrong and Buzz Aldrin. Michael Collins remains on board the spacecraft.
19 Apr 1971	Salyut 1, the world's **first space station**, is launched by the USSR.
27 Nov 1971	Robotic probe from the USSR's Mars 2 mission makes the first crash landing on **Mars**.
3 Mar 1972	USA's Pioneer 10 spacecraft is launched; it later makes a Jupiter flyby, crosses Pluto's orbit and becomes the **first man-made object to escape the solar system**.
17 Jul 1975	Apollo (USA) and Soyuz (USSR) **spacecraft dock in space**.
20 Jul 1976	USA's Viking 1 spacecraft conducts operations on the surface of **Mars**.
12 Apr 1981	USA commences **space shuttle flights**.
13 Mar 1986	Robotic probe Giotto, launched by the European Space Agency, has a close-up rendezvous with **Halley's comet**.
19 Feb 1986	Main module of Mir, the **first space station designed for semi-permanent orbit**, is launched by the USSR.
24 Apr 1990	Hubble Space Telescope, the **first optical space-based telescope**, is launched.
2 Dec 1990	**First passenger pays to go into space** aboard a Russian Soyuz TM11 flight.
18 May 1991	Helen Sharman becomes the **first British person** in space with the Soyuz TM12 mission.
31 Oct 2000	**International Space Station** receives its first residents, from the USA, Russia, Europe, Canada and Japan.
28 Apr 2001	**First space tourist** visits the International Space Station.
21 Jun 2004	SpaceShipOne became the **first private manned spacecraft** to fly into space, reaching 100km/62mi above the Earth. Its pilot, Mike Melvill, became the **first commercial astronaut**.

Astronomy Gastronomy

During the eight days of the Apollo 11 mission in 1969, the astronauts had a choice of two meals. NASA says that 'Meal A was bacon squares, peaches, sugar cookie cubes, coffee and pineapple-grapefruit drink. Meal B included beef stew, cream of chicken soup, date fruitcake, grape punch and orange drink'.

MOON LANDINGS

Mission	Launch	Duration (hours:minutes)	Crew
Apollo 11	16–24 Jul 1969	195:18	Neil A Armstrong, Michael Collins, Edwin E 'Buzz' Aldrin, Jr

On 20 Jul the first human beings land on the Moon, at the Sea of Tranquillity. Scientific instruments are deployed and 20kg/44lbs of moon rock brought back to Earth.

Apollo 12	14–24 Nov 1969	244:36	Charles 'Pete' Conrad, Jr, Richard F Gordon, Jr, Alan L Bean

The second landing is made on 19 Nov at the Ocean of Storms. Geological studies are undertaken and parts of the unmanned Surveyor 3 craft retrieved.

Apollo 14	31 Jan–9 Feb 1971	216:02	Alan B Shepard, Jr, Stuart A Roosa, Edgar D Mitchell

The third mission lands on 5 Feb in the Fra Mauro area, the area scheduled for the failed Apollo 13 mission (see below). The first golf shot on the Moon is played by Alan Shepard.

Apollo 15	26 Jul–7 Aug 1971	295:12	David R Scott, James B Irwin, Alfred M Worden

On 30 Jul the fourth landing takes place. The Lunar Roving Vehicle is used for the first time. Improved spacesuits give astronauts the longest stay so far, at almost 67 hours.

Apollo 16	16–27 Apr 1972	265:51	John W Young, Charles M Duke, Jr Thomas K Mattingly II

The fifth Moon landing is made on 20 Apr in the Descartes Highlands area. The first studies of lunar highland geology are undertaken.

Apollo 17	7–19 Dec 1972	301:52	Eugene A Cernan, Ronald E Evans, Harrison H 'Jack' Schmitt

The final and longest of the Apollo missions touches down successfully on 11 Dec in the Taurus–Littrow highlands and valley area. Harrison Schmitt is the first scientist–astronaut to walk on the Moon.

Note: Apollo 13 (11–17 Apr 1970) was to have been the third Moon landing. Carrying James A Lovell, Jr, John L Swigert, Jr and Fred W Haise, Jr, the mission had to be aborted without landing on the Moon after an explosion in an oxygen tank. The mission lasted 142 hours and 54 minutes.

One Small Step

At 4:18pm (US Eastern Daylight Time) on 20 Jul 1969, the Apollo 11 lunar module touched down for the first time on the surface of the Moon and commander Neil Armstrong reported that 'the Eagle has landed'. At 10:56pm Armstrong stepped, left foot first, onto the Moon and declared 'That's one small step for a man, one giant leap for mankind'. He said the Moon has 'a stark beauty all its own'. The astronauts later spoke to the President in the White House, in what Nixon described as 'the most historic telephone call ever made', and left a plaque stating 'Here men from the planet Earth first set foot on the Moon. July 1969 AD. We came in peace for all mankind.'

SPACE RECORDS

Most time spent in space	Russian cosmonaut Sergei Krikalev spent a total of 803 days 9 hours 39 minutes in space between Nov 1988 and Oct 2005.
Most space flights	US astronaut Jerry Ross completed his seventh space mission in Apr 2002. He shares the record with fellow US astronaut Franklin Chang-Diaz, who completed his seventh space mission in Jun 2002.
First space walk	Russian cosmonaut Alexei Leonov made the first spacewalk from Voskhod 2 on 18 Mar 1965.
Longest space walk	US astronauts Susan Helms and Jim Voss both spent 8 hours 56 minutes in space outside the International Space Station on 11 Mar 2001.
Longest space shuttle flight	The space shuttle Columbia, with a crew of five, completed a mission of 17 days 15 hours 53 minutes between 19 Nov and 7 Dec 1996.
Shortest manned space flight	US astronaut Alan Shepard, aboard a Mercury–Redstone rocket, made a sub-orbital flight lasting 15 minutes 28 seconds on 5 May 1961.
Longest time spent on the surface of the Moon	During the Apollo 17 lunar mission (7–19 Dec 1972), the crew spent 74 hours 59 minutes on the Moon's surface.
Longest time spent in orbit around the Moon	During the Apollo 17 lunar mission (7–19 Dec 1972), Ronald E Evans spent 147 hours 41 minutes in orbit around the Moon.
Man-made object furthest from Earth	On 17 Feb 1998 Voyager 1, launched on 5 Sep 1977, became the most remote man-made object in the universe in its journey towards interstellar regions.
Fastest spacecraft speed	The Helios space probes, launched in 1974 and 1976, reached speeds of 252 800kph/158 000mph as they orbited the Sun.
Oldest person in space	John Glenn, aged 77, went into space aboard the space shuttle Discovery on 15 Jan 1998. On 20 Feb 1962 he had become the first American to orbit the Earth.
Most isolated space traveller	During the USA's Apollo 15 lunar mission between 30 Jul and 1 Aug 1971, Alfred M Worden stayed in orbit around the Moon while his fellow crew members explored its surface, and travelled 3 596.4km/2 234.75mi from the nearest human being.

Out of This World

Dennis Tito, a US businessman, became the first 'space tourist' in 2001. He reportedly paid the Russian space administration $20 million, the equivalent of £14 million, to visit the International Space Station. Tito described the experience as 'paradise'. South African millionaire Mark Shuttleworth became the second space tourist in 2002, and US businessman Gregory Olsen was the third to visit the space station in 2005.

THE EARTH

There are no universally agreed estimates of many of the natural phenomena given in this section. Surveys make use of different criteria for identifying natural boundaries, and use different techniques of measurement. The estimated sizes of continents, oceans, seas, deserts and rivers are particularly subject to variation.

EARTH

Age	4.6 billion years
Distance from Sun (mean)	150 million km/93 million mi
Surface area	510 069 120 sq km/196 938 800 sq mi
Mass	$5\,976 \times 10^{24}$ kg/$13\,175 \times 10^{24}$ lb
Surface gravity	980cm/sq sec/386in/sq sec
Land surface (approximate)	148 million sq km/57 million sq mi (approx 29% of total area)
Water surface (approximate)	361.6 million sq km/140 million sq mi (approx 71% of total area)
Circumference (equator)	40 076km/24 902mi
Circumference (meridian)	40 000km/24 860mi
Diameter (equator)	12 757km/7 927mi
Diameter (meridian)	12 714km/7 900mi
Period of axial rotation	23 hours 56 minutes 4.0966 seconds
Temperature at core	4 500°C/8 100°F

Ice Kingdom

Ice permanently covers approximately 10% of the land surface of the Earth, with the majority of the ice cover at the South Pole. But there have been several great ice ages in the past, when a much larger part of the Earth's surface was covered with ice. The most famous, commonly known as 'the Ice Age', was during the Pleistocene period from approximately 2 million years ago to approximately 10 000 years ago.

Composition of the Earth's crust

Element	% weight
Oxygen	46.60
Silicon	27.72
Aluminium	8.13
Iron	5.00
Calcium	3.63
Sodium	2.83
Potassium	2.59
Magnesium	2.09
Others	1.41

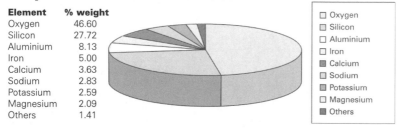

☐ Oxygen
☐ Silicon
☐ Aluminium
☐ Iron
■ Calcium
☐ Sodium
■ Potassium
☐ Magnesium
■ Others

Structure of the Earth

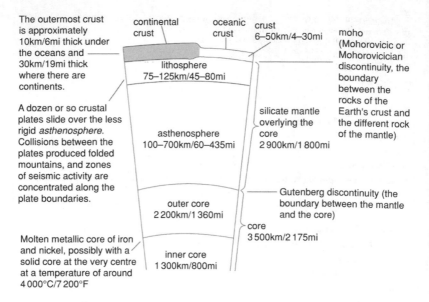

The outermost crust is approximately 10km/6mi thick under the oceans and 30km/19mi thick where there are continents.

A dozen or so crustal plates slide over the less rigid *asthenosphere*. Collisions between the plates produced folded mountains, and zones of seismic activity are concentrated along the plate boundaries.

Molten metallic core of iron and nickel, possibly with a solid core at the very centre at a temperature of around 4 000°C/7 200°F

continental crust

oceanic crust

crust 6–50km/4–30mi

lithosphere 75–125km/45–80mi

silicate mantle overlying the core 2 900km/1 800mi

moho (Mohorovicic or Mohorovicician discontinuity, the boundary between the rocks of the Earth's crust and the different rock of the mantle)

asthenosphere 100–700km/60–435mi

outer core 2 200km/1 360mi

Gutenberg discontinuity (the boundary between the mantle and the core)

core 3 500km/2 175mi

inner core 1 300km/800mi

Atmosphere

The Earth's atmosphere is composed of air, generally containing 78% nitrogen, 21% oxygen and 1% argon, together with carbon dioxide, hydrogen, ozone and methane, and traces of the other rare gases. The amount of water vapour present depends on the temperature and humidity.

Gas	% volume
Nitrogen	78.1
Oxygen	20.95
Argon	0.934
Carbon dioxide	0.031
Neon	0.00182
Helium	0.00052
Methane	0.0002
Krypton	0.00011
Hydrogen	0.00005
Nitrous oxide	0.00005
Ozone	0.00004
Xenon	0.000009

☐ Nitrogen
▧ Oxygen
☐ Argon
☐ Carbon dioxide
▧ Others

The atmosphere is divided into several layers.

Thermosphere

Air is very 'thin' (at low density) and atmospheric pressure is only a millionth of a billionth of that at sea level. Temperature increases with height, and may reach 2 000°C/3 600°F. Composed of the *ionosphere*, which reflects radio waves back to Earth enabling signals to be transmitted around the curved surface of the Earth, the *ionopause* transitional layer, and the *exosphere*, the outermost layer of the Earth's atmosphere, approximately 500km/300mi above the surface, from which light gases can escape into space.

Mesopause

Transitional layer between the mesosphere and the thermosphere, approximately 80–85km/50–55mi above the surface. The minimum atmospheric temperature, approximately –100°C/–150°F occurs in this layer, and atmospheric pressure is 100 000 times lower than at sea level.

Mesosphere

Middle atmosphere, up to approximately 85km/55mi above the surface. Temperature decreases with height.

Stratopause

Transitional layer, approximately 50–55km/30–35mi above the surface. The temperature is approximately 0°C/32°F.

Stratosphere

Contains very few clouds. Aircraft usually fly in this layer above the weather disturbances in the troposphere. Temperatures increase with height, and typical pressure is only a hundredth of that on the surface. Also includes the *ozone layer*, approximately 20–40km/12–25mi above the surface.

Tropopause

Transitional layer, approximately 10km/6mi above the surface. The temperature is approximately –60°C/–80°F.

Troposphere

Lower part of the atmosphere, from the surface up to a height varying from approximately 9km/5mi at the poles to 17km/10mi at the equator. Contains almost all of the clouds. Temperature decreases with height.

Note: Diagram not to scale.

EARTHQUAKE SEVERITY MEASUREMENT

Modified Mercalli intensity scale (1956 revision)

The Mercalli scale measures the intensity of earthquake shocks in terms of the damage they cause. It was named after the Italian geologist Giuseppe Mercalli (1850–1914).

Intensity value / description

I   Not felt; marginal and long-period effects of large earthquakes.

II   Felt by persons at rest, on upper floors or favourably placed.

III   Felt indoors; hanging objects swing; vibration like passing of light trucks; duration estimated; may not be recognized as an earthquake.

IV   Hanging objects swing; vibration like passing of heavy trucks, or sensation of a jolt like a heavy ball striking the walls; standing cars rock; windows, dishes, doors rattle; glasses clink; crockery clashes; in the upper range of IV, wooden walls and frames creak.

V   Felt outdoors; direction estimated; sleepers awoken; liquids disturbed, some spilled; small unstable objects displaced or upset; doors swing, close, open; shutters, pictures move; pendulum clocks stop, start, change rate.

VI   Felt by all; many frightened and run outdoors; persons walk unsteadily; windows, dishes, glassware break; knick-knacks, books, etc, fall off shelves; pictures fall off walls; furniture moves or overturns; weak plaster and masonry D crack; small bells ring (church, school); trees, bushes shake visibly, or heard to rustle.

VII   Difficult to stand; noticed by drivers; hanging objects quiver; furniture breaks; damage to masonry D, including cracks; weak chimneys broken at roof line; fall of plaster, loose bricks, stones, tiles, cornices, also unbraced parapets and architectural ornaments; some cracks in masonry C; waves on ponds, water turbid with mud; small slides and caving in along sand or gravel banks; large bells ring; concrete irrigation ditches damaged.

VIII   Steering of cars affected; damage to masonry C and partial collapse; some damage to masonry B; none to masonry A; fall of stucco and some masonry walls; twisting, fall of chimneys, factory stacks, monuments, towers, elevated tanks; frame houses move on foundations if not bolted down; loose panel walls thrown out; decayed piling broken off; branches broken from trees; changes in flow or temperature of springs and wells; cracks in wet ground and on steep slopes.

IX   General panic; masonry D destroyed; masonry C heavily damaged, sometimes with complete collapse; masonry B seriously damaged; general damage to foundations; frame structures, if not bolted, shift off foundations; frames racked; serious damage to reservoirs; underground pipes break; conspicuous cracks in ground; in alluviated areas sand and mud ejected, earthquake fountains, sand craters.

X   Most masonry and frame structures destroyed with their foundations; some well-built wooden structures and bridges destroyed; serious damage to dams, dykes, embankments; large landslides; water thrown on banks of canals, rivers, lakes, etc; sand and mud shifted horizontally on beaches and flat land; rails bent slightly.

XI   Rails bent greatly; underground pipelines completely out of service.

XII   Damage nearly total; large rock masses displaced; lines of sight and level distorted; objects thrown into the air.

Notes: Masonry types

A   *Good workmanship, mortar and design; reinforced, especially laterally, and bound together using steel, concrete, etc; designed to resist lateral forces.*

B   *Good workmanship and mortar; reinforced, but not designed in detail to resist lateral forces.*

C   *Ordinary workmanship and mortar; no extreme weakness like failing to tie in at corners, but neither reinforced nor designed against horizontal forces.*

D   *Weak materials, such as adobe; poor mortar; low standards of workmanship; weak horizontally.*

Richter scale

The Richter scale measures earthquake magnitude in terms of seismic energy released. It is logarithmic; a quake of magnitude 2 is barely perceptible, 5 is rather strong, and those over 7 are very strong. It was devised by US seismologist Dr Charles F Richter (1900–85).

Magnitude	Relative amount of energy released	Magnitude	Relative amount of energy released
1	1	6	29 million
2	31	7	890 million
3	960	8	28 billion
4	30 000	9	850 billion
5	920 000		

Whole Lotta Shakin'

The strongest earthquake ever recorded struck Chile on 22 May 1960, and measured 9.5 on the Richter Scale. Since 1900 there have only been three other earthquakes measuring 9 or above on the Richter Scale: Kamchatka, Russia (1952; 9.0), Alaska, USA (1964; 9.2) and coastal Sumatra, Indonesia (2004; 9.0).

CONTINENTS

A continent is any of the seven main land masses of the world, namely Africa, Antarctica, Asia, Australia and Oceania, Europe, North America and South America. A continent's area also includes the submerged continental shelf around the edge of the exposed land mass.

Continent	Area	Percentage of total land mass	Lowest point below sea level	Highest elevation
Africa	30 293 000 sq km/ 11 696 000 sq mi	20.2%	Lake Assal, Djibouti −156m/−512ft	Mt Kilimanjaro, Tanzania 5 895m/19 340ft
Antarctica	13 975 000 sq km/ 5 396 000 sq mi	9.3%	Bently sub-glacial trench −2 538m/−8 327ft	Vinson Massif 5 140m/16 864ft
Asia	44 493 000 sq km/ 17 179 000 sq mi	29.6%	Dead Sea, Israel/ Jordan/West Bank −400m/−1 312ft	Mt Everest, China/ Nepal 8 850m/29 035ft
Australia and Oceania[1]	8 945 000 sq km/ 3 454 000 sq mi	5.9%	Lake Eyre, Australia −15m/−49ft	Puncak Jaya, Indonesia 5 030m/16 503ft
Europe[2]	10 245 000 sq km/ 3 956 000 sq mi	6.8%	Caspian Sea, Iran/ Russia/Turkmenistan/ Kazakhstan/Azerbaijan −29m/−94ft	Mt Elbrus, Russia 5 642m/18 510ft
North America	24 454 000 sq km/ 9 442 000 sq mi	16.3%	Death Valley, California, USA −86m/−282ft	Mt McKinley, Alaska, USA 6 194m/20 322ft
South America	17 838 000 sq km/ 6 887 000 sq mi	11.9%	Península Valdés, Argentina −40m/−131ft	Aconcagua, Argentina 6 960m/22 835ft

[1] *The land mass of Australia plus the wider continental area.*   [2] *Including the former western USSR.*

Continental drift

Continental drift is the theory that the continents were formed as a result of the breaking up of a single land mass into several smaller land masses, which slowly drifted apart across the Earth's surface. Arrows indicate the direction of drift.

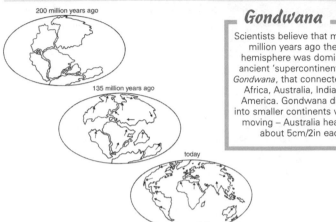

200 million years ago

135 million years ago

today

Gondwana

Scientists believe that more than 200 million years ago the southern hemisphere was dominated by an ancient 'supercontinent', known as *Gondwana*, that connected Antarctica, Africa, Australia, India and South America. Gondwana disintegrated into smaller continents which are still moving – Australia heads north at about 5cm/2in each year.

OCEANS

Water covers approximately 71% of the Earth's surface. Four oceans were traditionally recognized, with the International Hydrographic Organization (IHO) officially delimiting a fifth, the Southern Ocean, in 2000. However, the Atlantic Ocean and the Pacific Ocean are often divided (by the equator) into the North Atlantic and South Atlantic, and the North Pacific and South Pacific, leading to the recognition of seven oceans.

Ocean	Area	Average depth	Greatest depth
Arctic	14 056 000 sq km/ 5 427 021 sq mi	1 330m/4 400ft	Molloy Deep 5 680m/18 635ft
Atlantic	76 762 000 sq km/ 29 637 808 sq mi	3 700m/12 100ft	Puerto Rico Trench 8 648m/28 372ft
Indian	68 556 000 sq km/ 26 469 471 sq mi	3 900m/12 800ft	Java Trench 7 725m/25 344ft
Pacific	155 557 000 sq km/ 60 060 557 sq mi	4 300m/14 100ft	Mariana Trench 11 040m/36 220ft
Southern	20 327 000 sq km/ 7 848 254 sq mi	4 500m/14 800ft	South Sandwich Trench 7 235m/23 737ft

Water, Water, Everywhere

The Pacific Ocean alone covers approximately 28% of the Earth's surface, making this single ocean bigger than all the land mass of the Earth.

MAJOR OCEAN TRENCHES

Ocean trenches are long, narrow steep-sided depressions in an ocean floor. They are commonly found running parallel to a continent. There are more than 20 in total; the majority are found in the Pacific Ocean.

Trench	Ocean	Greatest depth
Cayman	Atlantic	7 686m/25 216ft
Japan	Pacific	8 513m/27 929ft
Java	Indian	7 725m/25 344ft
Kermadec	Pacific	10 047m/32 962ft
Kuril	Pacific	10 542m/34 587ft
Mariana (Marianas)	Pacific	11 040m/36 220ft
Middle America	Pacific	6 669m/21 880ft
Nansei Shoto (Ryukyu)	Pacific	7 507m/24 629ft
Palau	Pacific	7 986m/26 200ft
Peru-Chile (Atacama)	Pacific	8 065m/26 460ft
Philippine (Mindanao)	Pacific	10 539m/34 578ft
Puerto Rico	Atlantic	8 648m/28 372ft
Romanche	Atlantic	7 758m/25 453ft
South Sandwich	Southern	7 235m/23 737ft
Tonga	Pacific	10 882m/35 702ft
Yap (West Caroline)	Pacific	8 527m/27 976ft

Note: Other major trenches include the Aleutian, the Izu Bonin and the Bougainville, all in the Pacific Ocean.

LARGEST SEAS

Oceans are excluded.

Sea	Area[1]
Coral Sea	4 791 000 sq km/1 850 000 sq mi
Arabian Sea	3 863 000 sq km/1 492 000 sq mi
South China (Nan) Sea	3 685 000 sq km/1 423 000 sq mi
Mediterranean Sea	2 516 000 sq km/971 000 sq mi
Bering Sea	2 304 000 sq km/890 000 sq mi
Bay of Bengal	2 172 000 sq km/839 000 sq mi
Sea of Okhotsk	1 590 000 sq km/614 000 sq mi
Gulf of Mexico	1 543 000 sq km/596 000 sq mi
Gulf of Guinea	1 533 000 sq km/592 000 sq mi
Barents Sea	1 405 000 sq km/542 000 sq mi
Norwegian Sea	1 383 000 sq km/534 000 sq mi
Gulf of Alaska	1 327 000 sq km/512 000 sq mi
Hudson Bay	1 232 000 sq km/476 000 sq mi
Greenland Sea	1 205 000 sq km/465 000 sq mi
Arafura Sea	1 037 000 sq km/400 000 sq mi
Philippine Sea	1 036 000 sq km/400 000 sq mi
Sea of Japan (East Sea)	978 000 sq km/378 000 sq mi
East Siberian Sea	901 000 sq km/348 000 sq mi
Kara Sea	883 000 sq km/341 000 sq mi
East China Sea	664 000 sq km/256 000 sq mi

Sea	Area[1]
Andaman Sea	565 000 sq km/218 000 sq mi
North Sea	520 000 sq km/201 000 sq mi
Black Sea	508 000 sq km/196 000 sq mi
Red Sea	453 000 sq km/175 000 sq mi
Baltic Sea	414 000 sq km/160 000 sq mi
Arabian Gulf	239 000 sq km/92 000 sq mi
St Lawrence Gulf	238 000 sq km/92 000 sq mi

[1] *Areas are rounded to the nearest 1 000 sq km/sq mi.*

Seven Seas

The term 'Seven Seas' is frequently used to refer to all the seas and oceans of the world. There are many suggestions as to the seas it specifically refers to, but it is commonly thought to refer to the oceans: Arctic, Antarctic, North Atlantic, South Atlantic, North Pacific, South Pacific and Indian Ocean.

LARGEST ISLANDS

Island	Area[1]
Australia[2]	7 692 300 sq km/2 970 000 sq mi
Greenland	2 175 600 sq km/840 000 sq mi
New Guinea	790 000 sq km/305 000 sq mi
Borneo	737 000 sq km/285 000 sq mi
Madagascar	587 000 sq km/226 600 sq mi
Baffin	507 000 sq km/195 800 sq mi
Sumatra	425 000 sq km/164 100 sq mi
Honshu (Hondo)	228 000 sq km/88 000 sq mi
Great Britain	219 000 sq km/84 600 sq mi
Victoria, Canada	217 300 sq km/83 900 sq mi
Ellesmere, Canada	196 000 sq km/75 700 sq mi
Celebes	174 000 sq km/67 200 sq mi
South Island, New Zealand	151 000 sq km/58 300 sq mi
Java	129 000 sq km/49 800 sq mi
North Island, New Zealand	114 000 sq km/44 000 sq mi
Cuba	110 900 sq km/42 800 sq mi
Newfoundland	109 000 sq km/42 100 sq mi
Luzon	105 000 sq km/40 500 sq mi
Iceland	103 000 sq km/39 800 sq mi
Mindanao	94 600 sq km/36 500 sq mi
Novaya Zemlya (two islands)	90 600 sq km/35 000 sq mi
Ireland	84 100 sq km/32 500 sq mi
Hokkaido	78 500 sq km/30 300 sq mi
Hispaniola	77 200 sq km/29 800 sq mi
Sakhalin	75 100 sq km/29 000 sq mi
Tierra del Fuego	71 200 sq km/27 500 sq mi

[1] *Areas are rounded to the nearest 100 sq km/sq mi.*
[2] *Sometimes discounted, as a continent.*

LARGEST LAKES

Lake	Location	Area[1]
Caspian Sea	Iran/Russia/Turkmenistan/ Kazakhstan/Azerbaijan	371 000 sq km/143 240 sq mi[2]
Superior	USA/Canada	82 260 sq km/31 760 sq mi[3]
Aral Sea	Uzbekistan/Kazakhstan	64 500 sq km/24 900 sq mi[2]
Victoria	east Africa	62 940 sq km/24 300 sq mi
Huron	USA/Canada	59 580 sq km/23 000 sq mi[3]
Michigan	USA	58 020 sq km/22 400 sq mi
Tanganyika	east Africa	32 000 sq km/12 360 sq mi
Baikal	Russia	31 500 sq km/12 160 sq mi
Great Bear	Canada	31 330 sq km/12 100 sq mi
Great Slave	Canada	28 570 sq km/11 030 sq mi
Erie	USA/Canada	25 710 sq km/9 930 sq mi[3]
Winnipeg	Canada	24 390 sq km/9 420 sq mi
Malawi/Nyasa	east Africa	22 490 sq km/8 680 sq mi
Ontario	USA/Canada	19 270 sq km/7 440 sq mi[3]
Ladoga	Russia	18 130 sq km/7 000 sq mi
Balkhash	Kazakhstan	17 000–22 000 sq km/6 560–8 490 sq mi[2]
Maracaibo	Venezuela	13 010 sq km/5 020 sq mi[4]
Patos	Brazil	10 140 sq km/3 920 sq mi
Chad	west Africa	10 000–26 000 sq km/3 860–10 040 sq mi
Onega	Russia	9 800 sq km/3 780 sq mi
Rudolf	east Africa	9 100 sq km/3 510 sq mi
Eyre	Australia	8 800 sq km/3 400 sq mi[4]
Titicaca	Peru/Bolivia	8 300 sq km/3 200 sq mi

Note: The Caspian and Aral Seas, being entirely surrounded by land, are classified as lakes.

[1] *Areas are rounded to the nearest 10 sq km/sq mi.* [3] *Average of areas given by Canada and USA.*
[2] *Salt lakes.* [4] *Salt lagoons.*

GREAT LAKES

A group of five interconnected lakes, covering more than 244 000 sq km/94 000 sq mi, which separate eastern Canada from the USA. They contain approximately one-fifth of the Earth's fresh surface water.

Great Lake	Location	Area	Volume
Superior	USA/Canada	82 260 sq km/31 760 sq mi[1]	12 100 cu km/2 900 cu mi
Huron	USA/Canada	59 580 sq km/23 000 sq mi[1]	3 540 cu km/850 cu mi
Michigan	USA	58 020 sq km/22 400 sq mi	4 920 cu km/1 180 cu mi
Erie	USA/Canada	25 710 sq km/9 930 sq mi[1]	484 cu km/116 cu mi
Ontario	USA/Canada	19 270 sq km/7 440 sq mi[1]	1 640 cu km/393 cu mi

[1] *Average of areas given by Canada and USA.*

Lovely Lake

Lake Ontario's name is said to come from an Iroquois word meaning 'beautiful lake'.

LONGEST RIVERS

River	Outflow	Length[1]
Nile–Kagera–Ruvuvu–Ruvusu–Luvironza	Mediterranean Sea (Egypt)	6 690km/4 160mi
Amazon–Ucayali–Tambo–Ene–Apurimac	Atlantic Ocean (Brazil)	6 570km/4 080mi
Mississippi–Missouri–Jefferson–Beaverhead–Red Rock	Gulf of Mexico (USA)	6 020km/3 740mi
Chang Jiang (Yangtze)	East China Sea (China)	5 980km/3 720mi
Yenisey–Angara–Selenga–Ider	Kara Sea (Russia)	5 870km/3 650mi
Amur–Argun–Kerulen	Tartar Strait (Russia)	5 780km/3 590mi
Ob–Irtysh	Gulf of Ob, Kara Sea (Russia)	5 410km/3 360mi
Plata–Parana–Grande	Atlantic Ocean (Argentina/Uruguay)	4 880km/3 030mi
Huang He (Yellow)	Yellow Sea (China)	4 840km/3 010mi
Congo–Lualaba	South Atlantic Ocean (Angola/Democratic Republic of the Congo)	4 630km/2 880mi
Lena	Laptev Sea (Russia)	4 400km/2 730mi
Mackenzie–Slave–Peace–Finlay	Beaufort Sea (Canada)	4 240km/2 630mi
Mekong	South China Sea (Vietnam)	4 180km/2 600mi
Niger	Gulf of Guinea (Nigeria)	4 100km/2 550mi

[1] *Lengths are given to the nearest 10km/mi, and include the river plus tributaries comprising the longest watercourse.*

HIGHEST WATERFALLS

Waterfall	Location	Height[1]
Angel (upper fall)	Venezuela	807m/2 648ft
Itatinga	Brazil	628m/2 060ft
Cuquenán	Guyana/Venezuela	610m/2 001ft
Ormeli	Norway	563m/1 847ft
Tysse	Norway	533m/1 749ft
Pilao	Brazil	524m/1 719ft
Ribbon	USA	491m/1 611ft
Vestre Mardola	Norway	468m/1 535ft
Kaieteur	Guyana	457m/1 500ft
Cleve-Garth	New Zealand	450m/1 476ft

[1] *Height denotes individual leaps.*

Niagara Falls

Almost 170 000 cu m/6 million cu ft of water per minute crashes over Niagara Falls, on the US–Canadian border. But it isn't just water that has gone over the Falls. The first person to make the 52m/170ft drop over the Horseshoe Falls in a barrel was 63-year-old Annie Taylor, who pioneered the trip on 24 Oct 1901. She has been followed by 15 others in various contraptions, some of whom have perished. The only person to survive without any protection was Kirk Jones of Michigan, who took the plunge on 21 Oct 2003.

DEEPEST CAVES

Cave	Location	Depth
Jean Bernard	France	1 494m/4 902ft
Snezhnaya	Georgia	1 340m/4 396ft
Puertas de Illamina	Spain	1 338m/4 390ft
Pierre-Saint-Martin	France	1 321m/4 334ft
Sistema Huautla	Mexico	1 240m/4 068ft
Berger	France	1 198m/3 930ft
Vqerdi	Spain	1 195m/3 921ft
Dachstein-Mammuthöhle	Austria	1 174m/3 852ft
Zitu	Spain	1 139m/3 737ft
Badalona	Spain	1 130m/3 707ft
Batmanhöhle	Austria	1 105m/3 625ft
Schneeloch	Austria	1 101m/3 612ft
G E S Malaga	Spain	1 070m/3 510ft
Lamprechtsofen	Austria	1 024m/3 360ft

LARGEST DESERTS

Desert	Location	Area[1]
Sahara	north Africa	8 600 000 sq km/3 320 000 sq mi
Arabian	south-west Asia	2 330 000 sq km/900 000 sq mi
Gobi	Mongolia and north-east China	1 166 000 sq km/450 000 sq mi
Patagonian	Argentina	673 000 sq km/260 000 sq mi
Great Victoria	south-west Australia	647 000 sq km/250 000 sq mi
Great Basin	south-west USA	492 000 sq km/190 000 sq mi
Chihuahuan	Mexico	450 000 sq km/174 000 sq mi
Great Sandy	north-west Australia	400 000 sq km/154 000 sq mi
Sonoran	south-west USA	310 000 sq km/120 000 sq mi
Kyzyl Kum	Kazakhstan	300 000 sq km/116 000 sq mi
Takla Makan	northern China	270 000 sq km/104 000 sq mi
Kalahari	south-west Africa	260 000 sq km/100 000 sq mi
Kara Kum	Turkmenistan	260 000 sq km/100 000 sq mi
Kavir	Iran	260 000 sq km/100 000 sq mi
Syrian	Saudi Arabia/Jordan/Syria/Iraq	260 000 sq km/100 000 sq mi
Nubian	Sudan	260 000 sq km/100 000 sq mi
Thar	India/Pakistan	200 000 sq km/77 000 sq mi
Ust'-Urt	Kazakhstan	160 000 sq km/62 000 sq mi
Bet-Pak-Dala	southern Kazakhstan	155 000 sq km/60 000 sq mi
Simpson	central Australia	145 000 sq km/56 000 sq mi
Dzungaria	China	142 000 sq km/55 000 sq mi
Atacama	Chile	140 000 sq km/54 000 sq mi
Namib	south-east Africa	134 000 sq km/52 000 sq mi
Sturt	south-east Australia	130 000 sq km/50 000 sq mi
Bolson de Mapimi	Mexico	130 000 sq km/50 000 sq mi
Ordos	China	130 000 sq km/50 000 sq mi
Alashan	China	116 000 sq km/45 000 sq mi

[1] Desert areas are very approximate, because clear physical boundaries may not occur.

HIGHEST MOUNTAINS

Mountain[1]	Location	Height[2]
Everest	China/Nepal	8 850m/29 040ft
K2 (Qogir)	Jammu-Kashmir[3]/China	8 610m/28 250ft
Kanchenjunga	India/Nepal	8 590m/28 170ft
Lhotse	China/Nepal	8 500m/27 890ft
Kangchenjunga South Peak	India/Nepal	8 470m/27 800ft
Makalu I	China/Nepal	8 470m/27 800ft
Kangchenjunga West Peak	India/Nepal	8 420m/27 620ft
Lhotse East Peak	China/Nepal	8 380m/27 500ft
Dhaulagiri	Nepal	8 170m/26 810ft
Cho Oyu	China/Nepal	8 150m/26 750ft
Manaslu	Nepal	8 130m/26 660ft
Nanga Parbat	Kashmir-Jammu[3]	8 130m/26 660ft
Annapurna I	Nepal	8 080m/26 500ft
Gasherbrum I	Kashmir-Jammu[3]	8 070m/26 470ft
Broad Peak I	Kashmir-Jammu[3]	8 050m/26 400ft
Gasherbrum II	Kashmir-Jammu[3]	8 030m/26 360ft
Gosainthan	China	8 010m/26 290ft
Broad Peak Central	Kashmir-Jammu[3]	8 000m/26 250ft
Gasherbrum III	Kashmir-Jammu[3]	7 950m/26 090ft
Annapurna II	Nepal	7 940m/26 040ft
Nanda Devi	India	7 820m/25 660ft
Rakaposhi	Kashmir[3]	7 790m/25 560ft
Kamet	India	7 760m/25 450ft
Ulugh Muztagh	China (Tibet)	7 720m/25 340ft
Tirichmir	Pakistan	7 690m/25 230ft
Muz Tag Ata	China	7 550m/24 760ft
Peak Ismoili Somoni	Tajikistan	7 500m/24 590ft
Pobedy Peak	China/Kyrgyzstan	7 440m/24 410ft
Aconcagua	Argentina	6 960m/22 830ft
Ojos del Salado[4]	Argentina/Chile	6 910m/22 660ft

[1] *Mt and similar designations have not been included in the name.*
[2] *Heights are given to the nearest 10m/ft.*
[3] *Kashmir-Jammu is a disputed region on the border of India and Pakistan.*
[4] *Ojos del Salado is the world's highest volcano.*

LONGEST MOUNTAIN RANGES

Mountain ranges longer than 3 000km/1 900mi are given.

Mountains	Location	Length[1]
Andes	South America	7 200km/4 500mi
Rocky Mountains	North America	4 800km/3 000mi
Himalayas–Karakoram–Hindu Kush	Asia	3 800km/2 400mi
Great Dividing Range	Australia	3 600km/2 250mi
Trans-Antarctic Mountains	Antarctica	3 500km/2 200mi
Atlantic Coast Range South	America	3 000km/1 900mi

[1] *Lengths are given to the nearest 100km/mi.*

PHYSICAL EXTREMES

Highest mountain	Mt Everest, China/Nepal	8 850m/29 035ft
Longest mountain range	Andes, South America	7 200km/4 500mi
Highest cliffs	Near Molokai, Hawaii, USA	1 010m/3 300ft
Lowest point on Earth	Dead Sea, Israel/Jordan/ West Bank (Palestine)	400m/1 312ft below sea level
Deepest cave	Jean Bernard, France	1 494m/4 902ft
Largest cave	Sarawak Chamber (Lubang Nasib Bagus), Malaysia	700m/2 300ft long by 70m/230ft high by average 300m/985ft wide
Largest ocean	Pacific Ocean	155 55/ 000 sq km/ 60 060 557 sq mi
Deepest point in the ocean	Challenger Deep, Mariana Trench, Pacific Ocean	11 040m/36 220ft
Highest tides	Minas Basin, Bay of Fundy, Canada	16m/53ft difference between high and low tide
Largest sea	Coral Sea	4 791 000 sq km/ 1 850 000 sq mi
Largest lake	Caspian Sea, Iran/Russia/ Turkmenistan/Kazakhstan/ Azerbaijan	371 000 sq km/143 240 sq mi
Deepest lake	Lake Baikal, Russia	1 637m/5 371ft
Highest lake	In crater of Licancábur volcano, Chile/Bolivia	5 930m/19 455ft
Highest navigable lake	Titicaca, Peru/Bolivia	3 810m/12 500ft
Saltiest lake	Don Juan Pond, Antarctica	40.2% salt by weight *(the Dead Sea has 23.1% and the ocean just 3.38%)*
Longest river	River Nile, Africa	6 690km/4 160mi
Highest waterfall	Angel (upper fall), Venezuela	807m/2 648ft
Largest island	Australia[1]	7 692 300 sq km/2 970 000 sq mi
Largest desert	Sahara, north Africa	8 600 000 sq km/3 320 000 sq mi
Largest glacier	Lambert Glacier, Antarctica	1 000 000 sq km/386 102 sq mi

[1] *Sometimes discounted, as a continent.*

Mighty Mountain

The peak of Mauna Kea, Hawaii, USA reaches 4 205m/13 796ft above sea level. However, the base of the mountain is the seabed of the Pacific Ocean, and its full height from foot to summit is a mighty 10 205m/33 480ft – higher than Mt Everest.

Mt Everest

Sir George Everest (1790–1866) was a Welsh military engineer. He became Surveyor-General of India in 1830 and completed a trigonometrical survey of the Indian subcontinent in 1841, being knighted in 1861. Mt Everest was named after him in 1865. Interestingly, Everest himself would not have recognized the modern pronunciation *ev-uh-rest*. He pronounced the name *eve-rest*.

NATIONAL PARKS (UK)

England and Wales

The National Parks and Access to the Countryside Act (1949) provided for the creation of National Parks in England and Wales. The Environment Act (1995) states their purpose as 'a) conserving and enhancing the natural beauty, wildlife and cultural heritage of the areas, and b) promoting opportunities for the understanding and enjoyment of the special qualities of those areas by the public'.

National Park	Year designated (order)	Area	Terrain
Brecon Beacons	1957 (10th)	1 351 sq km/522 sq mi	Mountains/valleys
Broads	1989 (11th)	303 sq km/117 sq mi	Waterways/fens
Dartmoor	1951 (4th)	954 sq km/368 sq mi	Moorland
Exmoor	1954 (8th)	693 sq km/268 sq mi	Moorland/coastline
Lake District	1951 (2nd)	2 292 sq km/885 sq mi	Mountains/valleys/ glaciated lakes
New Forest	2005 (12th)	580 sq km/224 sq mi	Woodland/heath
Northumberland	1956 (9th)	1 049 sq km/405 sq mi	Hills
North York Moors	1952 (6th)	1 432 sq km/554 sq mi	Woodland/moorland
Peak District	1951 (1st)	1 438 sq km/555 sq mi	Moorland/dales
Pembrokeshire Coast	1952 (5th)	620 sq km/239 sq mi	Cliffs/islands/ moorland
Snowdonia	1951 (3rd)	2 142 sq km/827 sq mi	Mountains/valleys
Yorkshire Dales	1954 (7th)	1 769 sq km/682 sq mi	Dales

Note: The South Downs are currently in the process of being designated as a National Park.

Scotland

The National Parks (Scotland) Act (2000) provided for the creation of National Parks in Scotland. The Act states their purpose as being 'a) to conserve and enhance the natural and cultural heritage of the area, b) to promote sustainable use of the natural resources of the area, c) to promote understanding and enjoyment (including enjoyment in the form of recreation) of the special qualities of the area by the public, and d) to promote sustainable economic and social development of the area's communities'.

National Park	Year established (order)	Area	Terrain
Loch Lomond and The Trossachs	2002 (1st)	1 865 sq km/720 sq mi	Mountains/valleys/ lochs
Cairngorms	2003 (2nd)	3 800 sq km/1 467 sq mi	Mountains/moorland

High Places

England's highest mountain is Scafell Pike in the Lake District at 978m/3 209ft, the highest mountain in Wales is Snowdon at 1 085m/3 560ft, and Slieve Donard at 852m/2 795ft is Northern Ireland's highest point. All three are dwarfed by Scotland's highest mountain: Ben Nevis reaches a mighty 1 343m/4 406ft, but it is still a mere pimple compared to the world's highest peaks.

BEAUFORT SCALE

Beaufort number	Wind name	m/sec	Windspeed kph	Windspeed mph	Observable wind characteristics	Sea disturbance number	Average wave height m	Average wave height ft	Observable sea characteristics
0	Calm	1	<1	<1	Smoke rises vertically	0	0	0	Sea like a mirror
1	Light air	1	1–5	1–3	Wind direction shown by smoke drift, but not by wind vanes	0	0	0	Ripples like scales, without foam crests
2	Light breeze	2	6–11	4–7	Wind felt on face; leaves rustle; vanes moved by wind	1	0.3	0–1	More definite wavelets, but crests do not break
3	Gentle breeze	4	12–19	8–12	Leaves and small twigs in constant motion; wind extends light flag	2	0.3–0.6	1–2	Large wavelets; crests begin to break; scattered white horses
4	Moderate breeze	7	20–28	13–18	Raises dust, loose paper; small branches moved	3	0.6–1.2	2–4	Small waves become longer; fairly frequent white horses
5	Fresh breeze	10	29–38	19–24	Small trees in leaf begin to sway; crested wavelets on inland waters	4	1.2–2.4	4–8	Moderate waves with a more definite long form; many white horses; some spray possible
6	Strong breeze	12	39–49	25–31	Large branches in motion; difficult to use umbrellas; whistling heard in telegraph wires	5	2.4–4	8–13	Large waves form; more extensive white foam crests; some spray probable
7	Near gale	15	50–61	32–38	Whole trees in motion; inconvenience walking against wind	6	4–6	13–20	Sea heaps up; streaks of white foam blown along
8	Gale	18	62–74	39–46	Breaks twigs off trees; impedes progress	6	4–6	13–20	Moderately high waves of greater length; well-marked streaks of foam
9	Strong gale	20	75–8	47–54	Slight structural damage occurs	6	4–6	13–20	High waves; dense streaks of foam; sea begins to roll; spray affects visibility
10	Storm	26	89–102	55–63	Trees uprooted; considerable damage occurs	7	6–9	20–30	Very high waves with long overhanging crests; dense streaks of foam blown along; generally white appearance of surface; heavy rolling
11	Violent storm	30	103–117	64–72	Widespread damage	8	9–14	30–45	Exceptionally high waves; long white patches of foam; poor visibility; ships lost to view behind waves
12–17	Hurricane	≥30	≥118	≥73		9	14	>45	Air filled with foam and spray; sea completely white; very poor visibility

WIND

A *cyclone* is a circulation of winds in the atmosphere which rotates anticlockwise round a depression in the northern hemisphere and clockwise in the southern hemisphere.

A *hurricane* is a rotating windstorm originating over tropical oceans, with winds in excess of 119kph/74mph. Hurricanes may be up to 645km/400mi wide, and can move forwards at up to 48kph/30mph, travelling up to 4 830km/3 000mi before becoming exhausted. Hurricanes occur between Jul and Oct in the northern hemisphere and between Nov and Mar in the southern hemisphere. They are named by the National Hurricane Center, USA, in alphabetical sequence as they occur each year. Since 1978 names given have been alternately male/female. In the Pacific they are known as *typhoons*, and in the Indian Ocean as *tropical cyclones*.

A *tornado* is a column of air rotating rapidly around a very low pressure centre.

Tremendous Tornado

The largest tornado ever recorded struck northern Oklahoma, USA, in May 1999. It measured 1 600m/5 250ft in diameter.

WIND CHILL TEMPERATURE INDEX

Exposed skin cools more rapidly when exposed to wind than at the same temperature in still conditions. This means that people feel colder on a windy day than they would on a still day at the same temperature. The wind chill temperature index takes account of the temperature and the wind speed to produce the equivalent temperature. The US National Weather Service defines wind chill temperature as 'a measure of the combined cooling effect of wind and temperature'.

To convert Fahrenheit to Celsius, subtract 32, multiply by 5 and then divide the total by 9.

Outside temperature (°F)

	Calm	40	35	30	25	20	15	10	5	0	−5	−10	−15	−20	−25	−30	−35	−40	−45
5	36	31	25	19	13	7	1	−5	−11	−16	−22	−28	−34	−40	−46	−52	−57	−63	
10	34	27	21	15	9	3	−4	−10	−16	−22	−28	−35	−41	−47	−53	−59	−66	−72	
15	32	25	19	13	6	0	−7	−13	−19	−26	−32	−39	−45	−51	−58	−64	−71	−77	
20	30	24	17	11	4	−2	−9	−15	−22	−29	−35	−42	−48	−55	−61	−68	−74	−81	
25	29	23	16	9	3	−4	−11	−17	−24	−31	−37	−44	−51	−58	−64	−71	−78	−84	
30	28	22	15	8	1	−5	−12	−19	−26	−33	−39	−46	−53	−60	−67	−73	−80	−87	
35	28	21	14	7	0	−7	−14	−21	−27	−34	−41	−48	−55	−62	−69	−76	−82	−89	
40	27	20	13	6	−1	−8	−15	−22	−29	−36	−43	−50	−57	−64	−71	−78	−84	−91	
45	26	19	12	5	−2	−9	−16	−23	−30	−37	−44	−51	−58	−65	−72	−79	−86	−93	
50	26	19	12	4	−3	−10	−17	−24	−31	−38	−45	−52	−60	−67	−74	−81	−88	−95	
55	25	18	11	4	−3	−11	−18	−25	−32	−39	−46	−54	61	−68	−75	−82	−89	−97	
60	25	17	10	3	−4	−11	−19	−26	−33	−40	−48	−55	−62	−69	−76	−84	−91	−98	

Wind speed (mph)

Data source: US National Weather Service, Wind Chill Temperature Index (2001 revision).

WEATHER AND CLIMATE EXTREMES

Hottest place	Dallol, Ethiopia, at 34.4°C/93.9°F (annual mean temperature).
Highest recorded temperature in the shade	58°C/136.4°F at Al'Aziziyah, Libya, on 13 Sep 1922.
Coldest place	Plateau Station, Antarctica, at −56.6°C/−69.8°F (annual mean temperature).
Coldest recorded temperature	−89.2°C/−128.6°F at Vostok, Antarctica, on 21 Jul 1983.
Greatest temperature range	Verkhoyansk, Siberia, Russia, where temperatures can range from −68°C/−90.4°F to 37°C/98°F, a difference of 105°C/221°F.
Driest place	Atacama desert near Calama, Chile, where no rainfall was recorded in over 400 years to 1972. Today, the desert's average annual rainfall is just 0.1mm/0.0039in.
Most rain to fall in 24 hours	1 870mm/74in which fell on Cilaos, Réunion, in the Indian Ocean, on 15–16 Mar 1952.
Most intense rainfall	38.1mm/1.8in which fell in one minute at Basse Terre, Guadeloupe, Caribbean on 26 Nov 1970.
Most rainy days in a year	Mt Wai'ale'ale, Kauai, Hawaii, USA has an average of 350 days of rain each year.
Wettest place	Mawsynram, Meghalaya State, India, where the annual average rainfall is 11 870mm/467in; in Tutunendo, Colombia, the annual average rainfall is 11 770mm/464in.
Least amount of sunshine	North and South Poles, where the Sun does not rise for 182 days of winter.
Greatest amount of sunshine	Yuma, Arizona, USA, with a mean average of 4 055 hours of sun per year, or 91% of the possible hours of sunshine.
Greatest amount of snow to fall in a year	31 102mm/1 225in, at Paradise, Mt Rainier, Washington, USA, in 1971–2.
Greatest amount of snow to fall in a day	193cm/76in at Silver Lake, Colorado on 14 Apr 1921.
Highest recorded surface wind speed	371.75kph/231mph, at Mt Washington, New Hampshire, USA, on 12 Apr 1934.
Most days of thunder in a year	Tororo, Uganda, had an average of 251 days of thunder per year between 1967 and 1976.
Most hail in a year	Keriche, Kenya has an average of 132 days of hail each year.
Heaviest hailstones	On 14 Apr 1986 hailstones weighing up to 1kg/2.2 lb fell in Gopalganj, Bangladesh, killing 92 people. On 5 Sep 1958 a hailstone weighing 142g/5oz fell at Horsham, West Sussex, the largest hailstone ever recorded in the UK.

Stormy Weather

Just one thunderstorm can produce 500 million litres, or 110 million gallons, of rain.

CLOUDS

Clouds are formed by the condensation or freezing of water vapour on minute particles in the atmosphere when air masses move upward as a result of convection currents, unstable conditions, etc, and in so doing cool rapidly. Clouds are usually classified into ten main types according to their height and shape.

Meteorologists use feet to measure cloud height; to convert to metres, multiply by 0.3048.

The Language of Clouds

The scientific study of clouds is called *nephology*, from the Greek word for cloud, *nephos*. The names of cloud types come from Latin: *cirrus* means a tuft or curl, *cumulus* means a heap, *stratus* means something spread out, *alto* means high and *nimbus* was the word for a rain-cloud.

Low clouds

The base of low clouds is usually surface–7 000ft.

Stratus (St)

Cloud base: usually surface–1 500ft.
Colour: usually grey.

Cumulonimbus (Cb)

Cloud base: usually 1 000–5 000ft.
Colour: white above with dark underside.

Cumulus (Cu)

Cloud base: usually 1 200–6 000ft.
Colour: white in sunlight but dark underside.

Stratocumulus (Sc)

Cloud base: usually 1 200–7 000ft.
Colour: grey or white, with shading.

Medium clouds

The base of medium clouds is usually 7 000–17 000ft, although Nimbostratus may be much lower.

Nimbostratus (Ns)

Cloud base: usually 1 500–10 000ft.
Colour: dark grey.

Altocumulus (Ac)

Cloud base: usually 7 000–17 000ft.
Colour: grey or white, with shading.

Altostratus (As)
Cloud base: usually 8 000–17 000ft.
Colour: greyish or bluish.

High clouds

The base of high clouds is usually 17 000–35 000ft. High clouds are composed of ice crystals.

Cirrus (Ci)

Cloud base: usually 17 000–35 000ft.
Colour: white.

Cirrocumulus (Cc)

Cloud base: usually 17 000–35 000ft.
Colour: white.

Cirrostratus (Cs)

Cloud base: usually 17 000–35 000ft.
Colour: white.

On Cloud Nine

Someone who is extremely pleased or happy has long been described as being 'on cloud nine'. The phrase is thought to come from the classification system used by the old US Weather Bureau, which divided clouds into nine types: 'cloud nine' was the dramatic cumulonimbus, towering many kilometres into the sky. Hence to be on cloud nine was to be magnificently high up.

ICEBERGS

Icebergs can pose a significant hazard to shipping and as a result are reported, tracked and monitored. They are divided into two shape categories: tabular, those with a flat top and steep vertical sides, and non-tabular, which is subdivided into groups including pinnacled, domed, drydocked and wedged.

Iceberg	Height[1] (above water)	Length
growler	<1m	<5m
bergybit	1–4m	5–14m
small	5–15m	15–60m
medium	16–45m	61–120m
large	46–75m	121–200m
very large	>75m	>200m

[1] To convert metres to feet, multiply by 3.2808.

SHIPPING FORECAST AREAS

* Formerly Finisterre (renamed 2002)   *Reproduced with data supplied by the Met Office.*

Roaring Forties

The 'Roaring Forties' is a sailors' term referring to the tract of stormy west winds and high seas south of 40°S latitude. There is also the 'Furious Fifties', a similarly turbulent stretch of ocean.

POINTS OF THE COMPASS

Naming the 32 compass points in order, in either or both directions, is called 'boxing the compass'.

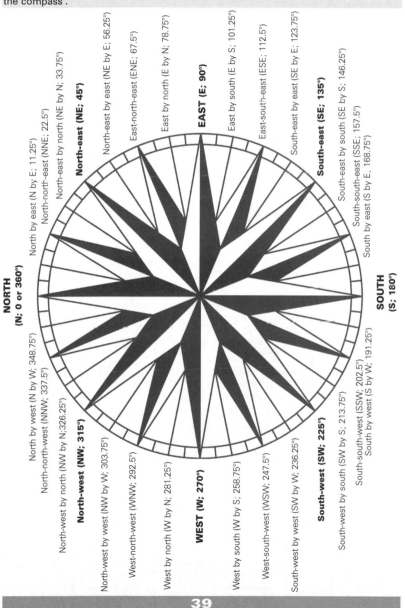

PLANTS AND ANIMALS

CLASSIFICATION

There are seven major levels of classification in taxonomy.

kingdom
phylum (*plural* phyla)
class
order
family
genus (*plural* genera)
species

MRS GREN

Scientists identify seven characteristics of living things, which can be remembered by the acronym MRS GREN: Movement, Respiration, Sensitivity, Growth, Reproduction, Excretion, Nutrition.

FISH RECORDS

Fastest	Over short distances, the sailfish can reach a speed of 110kph/68mph; however marlins are the fastest over longer distances, and can reach a burst speed of 68–80kph/40–50mph.
Largest	The whale shark is said to reach over 18m/59ft, with the largest on record being 12.65m/41ft 6in, weighing an estimated 21.5 tonnes/21.1 tons.
Smallest	The dwarf pygmy goby, found in the streams and rivers of Luzon in the Philippines, measures 7.5–9.9mm/0.3–0.4in and weighs 4–5mg/0.00014–0.00018oz. The smallest fish found in British waters is the Guillet's goby, which reaches a maximum length of 24mm/0.95in.
Largest predatory	The great white shark reaches an average of 4.3–4.6m/14–15ft in length, and a weight of 520–770kg/1 150–1 700 lb. There are some reports of larger specimens up to 10m/33ft.
Most widespread	The distribution of the bristlemouths of genus *Cyclothone* is worldwide with the exception of the Arctic.
Most restricted	The devil's hole pupfish inhabits only a small area of water above a rock shelf in a spring-fed pool in Ash Meadows, Nevada, USA.
Deepest dweller	In 1970 a brotulid *Bassogigas profundissimus* was recovered from a depth of 8 299m/27 230ft, making it the deepest living vertebrate.
Longest lived	Some specimens of the sturgeon are thought to be over 80 years old.
Shortest lived	Tooth carp of the suborder *Cyprinodontidae* live for only 8 months in the wild.
Most eggs	The ocean sunfish can lay up to 30 million eggs at a time. Each egg measures approximately 1.3mm/0.05in in diameter.

BIRD RECORDS

Largest	The ostrich can reach 2.75m/9ft in height and 156kg/345 lb in weight.
Smallest	The bee hummingbird of Cuba is under 6cm/2.4in long and weighs 3g/0.1oz.
Highest flier	Ruppell's griffon, a vulture, has been measured at 11 275m/36 991ft above sea level.
Fastest flier	The peregrine falcon can dive through the air at speeds up to 185kph/115mph. The fastest bird in level flight is the eider duck, which can reach 80kph/50mph.
Fastest animal on two legs	The ostrich can maintain a speed of 50kph/31mph for 15 minutes or more, and it may reach 65–70kph/40–43mph in short bursts, for example when escaping from predators.
Greatest wingspan	The wandering albatross can reach 3.65m/12ft.
Heaviest flying bird	The great bustard and the kori bustard both weigh up to 18kg/40 lb, with swans not far behind at approximately 16kg/35 lb.
Heaviest bird of prey	The Andean condor can reach 9–12kg/20–27lb.
Deepest diver	The emperor penguin can reach a depth of 265m/870ft. The great northern diver or loon can dive to approximately 80m/262ft – deeper than any other flying bird.
Furthest migrator	The arctic tern travels up to 36 000km/22 400mi each year, flying from the Arctic to the Antarctic and back again.
Most abundant	Africa's red-billed quelea is the most numerous wild bird, with an estimated population of approximately 1.5 billion. The domestic chicken is the most abundant of all birds, numbering over 4 billion.
Largest egg	The ostrich lays the largest egg, with the heaviest specimen on record weighing 2.35kg/5 lb 2oz.

Feathered Friends

The greatest number of feathers ever counted on a bird was 25 216, on a swan.

MAMMAL RECORDS

Largest	The blue whale, up to 30m/98ft long and weighing up to 150 tonnes/148 tons, is the largest known mammal. The largest land mammal is the male African elephant, standing up to 3.3m/11ft at the shoulder and weighing up to 7 tonnes/6.89 tons.
Tallest	The giraffe stands up to 5.5m/18ft high.
Smallest	The pygmy white-toothed shrew, also called the Etruscan shrew, has a body approximately 5cm/2in long and weighs up to 2.5g/0.1oz. Some bats weigh even less.
Longest lived	Bowhead whales may be the oldest living mammals, with some specimens estimated at 177 to 245 years old at death. The next oldest are fin whales, at 114 years, and blue whales, at 110 years.

Loudest	Blue whales and fin whales can make calls that have been measured at 188 decibels and can travel for hundreds of kilometres through water.
Fastest on land	The cheetah can reach 100kph/62mph, but only in short bursts. The pronghorn can maintain speeds of 50kph/31mph for several kilometres.
Largest land carnivore	The Kodiak bear averages 2.4m/7.8ft in length and can weigh 680kg/1 500 lb.
Most prolific breeder	A North American meadow mouse can produce up to 17 litters in a single year (4–9 babies per litter).
Longest gestation period	The Asiatic elephant has the longest pregnancy, at 650–760 days.
Most widespread	Humans are the most widely distributed mammals, closely followed by the house mouse, which has accompanied humans to all parts of the world.

Monkey Around

The wonderful world of monkeys includes the sun-tailed monkey, purple-faced leaf monkey, greater white-nosed monkey, red-bellied monkey, yellow-tailed woolly monkey, moustached monkey, black-bearded saki, bald-faced saki, owl-faced monkey and red-handed howler.

AMPHIBIAN RECORDS

Largest	The Chinese giant salamander can grow up to 1.8m/5ft 11in long.
Smallest	The world's smallest amphibian is the frog *Eleutherodactylus limbatus* of Cuba, which is only 8.51mm/0.33–0.47in long when it reaches adulthood.
Largest frog	The Goliath frog can weigh up to 3.25kg/7.16 lb, and reach 32cm/12.6in in length.
Longest lived	The Japanese giant salamander, *Andrias japonicus*, has reached 55 years in captivity.

REPTILE RECORDS

Largest	The estuarine or saltwater crocodile, which lives throughout tropical regions in Asia and the Pacific, can grow to over 7m/23ft long, although some eyewitness reports suggest crocodiles up to 10m/33ft in length.
Longest snake	The reticulated python of south-east Asia grows to an average of 6m/20ft, but the greatest length on record is 10m/32ft 9.5in.
Largest snake	The largest snake is probably the anaconda, which may not grow as long as the reticulated python but is thicker and heavier. Specimens have been known to reach 249kg/550 lb.

Smallest lizard	Two lizards are considered to be the smallest in the world: *Sphaerodactylus ariasiae* and the *Sphaerodactylus parthenopion*, which both measure an average of 16mm/0.6in.
Longest lived tortoise	Tortoises can reach ages of more than 100 years. The oldest specimen on record is a Madagascar giant tortoise that reputedly lived to 188 years, dying in 1965.

INSECT RECORDS

Longest	The stick insect *Pharnacia serratipes*, living in Indonesia, can grow to 33cm/13in long.
Most massive	Females of the goliath beetle of the Congo in Africa can grow to 100g/0.25 lb and are around the same size as a clenched fist.
Greatest wingspan	The white witch moth, living in the rainforests of South and Central America, has a wingspan of up to 36cm/14in.
Fastest flying	Some dragonflies can fly at speeds of up to 75kmph/45mph.
Largest egg	The Malaysian stick insect lays eggs around 1.3cm/0.5in long, the size of a large jelly bean. Other insects lay even larger eggs, but these are cases containing a number of individual eggs.
Loudest	The African cicada produces a call that registers up to 106.7 decibels.
Shortest lived	Mayflies live for as little as an hour as adults with wings, although they may previously have lived for 2–3 years as nymphs in bodies of water.

SPIDER RECORDS

Largest	Male goliath bird-eating spiders, found in some rainforest regions of South America, can grow to have a leg span of 28cm/11in.
Smallest	Among the smallest spiders in the world are symphytognathid spiders from central Africa. Adult individuals reach an average of 0.5mm/0.02in across.
Largest web	The golden orb web spider, living in tropical areas worldwide, makes webs which can extend to 6m/19ft 8in in height and 2m/6ft 7in in width.

WORM RECORDS

Longest	The bootlace worm can reach 40m/131ft.
Longest tapeworm	The human tapeworm can grow as long as 15m/49ft 2in.

CRUSTACEAN RECORDS

Largest	The Japanese spider crab can achieve a claw span of 3m/9ft 10in.
Heaviest	The American or North Atlantic lobster can weigh up to 20.14kg/44 lb 6oz.
Lightest	Water fleas are the smallest crustaceans, weighing as little as 0.00025g/0.0000088oz.

MOLLUSC RECORDS

Largest cephalopod   The giant squid has been measured up to 18m/59ft in length and 900kg/1 980 lb in weight. It has never been observed in the wild and scientists have so far relied on measuring dead specimens.

Largest snail   The African giant snail is the largest land gastropod. The biggest specimen on record was 39.3cm/15.5in long and weighed 900g/2 lb.

Largest bivalve   The giant clam can measure more than 1.4–1.5m/4ft 7in–4ft 11in across and weigh up to 295kg/650 lb.

JELLYFISH RECORDS

Largest   The Arctic giant jellyfish is reckoned to be the largest, with a body diameter of up to 2.2m/7ft 3in and a tentacle length of 35m/115ft.

Smallest   Polyp forms of various species of jellyfish may measure only around 1mm/0.039in across.

Venomous Jelly

The jellyfish with the deadliest venom is the box jellyfish, *Chironex fleckeri*. Also known as the sea wasp, it is found in the coastal waters of northern Australia from Nov to May. The 'bell' of the jellyfish can reach 30cm/12in across, while each of the sixty thick stinging tentacles trail up to 3m/10ft behind it; the translucent jellyfish is often almost impossible to spot in the water. Each one carries enough poison to kill 60 human adults; the venom not only attacks the nerves and heart but also destroys the skin, causing intense and excruciating pain before an agonizing death.

PLANT RECORDS

Largest living tree   The largest tree in terms of mass is the giant sequoia. The largest individual specimen is the 'General Sherman' in Sequoia National Park, California, USA, and is 83.82m/275ft tall. It is more than 10 times as massive as a blue whale.

Tallest living tree   The tallest tree is the coast redwood. The tallest individual specimen is the 'Stratosphere Giant' in the Humboldt Redwoods State Park, California, USA, and is 112.6m/369ft 4.8in tall.

Most massive plant   The largest individual plant in terms of mass so far discovered is a group of quaking aspen trees growing in the Wasatch Mountains, Utah, USA. Its roots extend over an area of 43ha/106 acres.

Largest fungus   A fungus known as the honey mushroom can extend over hundreds of hectares. The largest individual fungus of this type is thought to grow in the Malheur National Forest in the Blue Mountains of eastern Oregon, USA, and covers around 820ha/2 028 acres.

Oldest living tree   The tree that lives longest is estimated to be the bristlecone pine. The oldest individual yet found is named 'Methuselah' and grows in the White Mountains on the California–Nevada border in the USA. It is reckoned to be 4 767 years old.

Fastest growing plant   Bamboo can grow faster than any other plant, at up to 91cm/3ft per day.

Largest flower	The parasitic *Rafflesia arnoldi*, which grows on cissus vines in the south-east Asian rainforest, has the largest flowers. They can measure up to 91cm/3ft in width, with a weight of 11kg/24lb.
Largest leaf	The largest leaves of any plant belong to the raffia palm of the Mascarene Islands, Indian Ocean, and the Amazonian bamboo palm of South America and Africa; both measure up to 20m/65ft 7in in length.
Largest seed	The giant fan palm, known as the double coconut or coco de mer, produces the largest seed, weighing up to 20kg/44lb.
Longest root	Winter rye has been shown to have one of the most extensive yet tightly-packed root systems of any plant, with a single specimen producing 622.8km/387mi of roots in only 0.051cu m/1.8 cu ft of soil.

MOST POISONOUS ANIMALS

Deadliest snake	The hook-nosed sea snake of seas and coastal waters in the Middle East, Asia and Australasia may be the world's deadliest snake. Its venom is 60 times more poisonous than a rattlesnake's.
Snake with most venom	The inland taipan, or fierce snake, of central Australia can deliver the greatest amount of venom per bite; 110mg/0.0038oz has been recorded, although 44mg/0.0015oz is more common. It is thought to be the most venomous land snake.
Snake responsible for most deaths	Russell's viper lives in habitats worldwide and is notably aggressive, with a deadly venom. It has probably killed more people than any other snake.
Most poisonous fish	The puffer fish of the Indian and Pacific oceans and Red Sea secretes a deadly poison that is present in its blood, organs and skin. A dose of less than 0.1g/0.004oz is sufficient to kill an adult human.
Most poisonous frog	The golden poison dart frog, living in western Colombia, secretes a poison which is the most toxic of any known land animal. Just 1g/0.035oz of it could kill 100 000 people.

MOST POISONOUS PLANTS

Most poisonous in the world	The seeds of the castor bean plant, the source of castor oil, are highly toxic. Just 1mg/0.00004oz of their main toxin, ricin, can be enough to kill a human adult. Ricin is considered internationally to be a chemical and biological weapon.
Most poisonous in Europe	Monk's hood, also called wolfsbane, may be Europe's most poisonous plant. It was formerly used in traps to kill wolves.
Most poisonous in the USA	Western water hemlock is often cited as the most poisonous plant in the USA, and is a particular hazard to livestock. Small amounts of it are sufficient to kill a horse.
Most poisonous fungus	The death cap is the cause of most fatal poisonings from fungi. Whitish in colour, it is often mistaken for an edible mushroom.
Most poisonous edible fruit	The pith surrounding the ackee fruit is commonly cooked and eaten in Jamaica. The unripe pith, however, can be highly toxic, and may lead to serious illness, coma and death if ingested.

ANIMAL AGES

Animal	Average age reached in captivity (years)	Animal	Average age reached in captivity (years)
bear	15–30	horse	20–25
camel	12	kangaroo	4–7
cat	10–12	lion	10–15
chimpanzee	20	monkey	12–15
cow	9–15	mouse	3
dog	10–12	pig	10
elephant	30–40	pigeon	10–12
fox	7–10	rabbit	5–8
giraffe	10	rhinoceros	15–20
goat	8	sheep	12
gorilla	20	squirrel	8–10
guinea pig	4	tiger	16
hippopotamus	25–30	zebra	15

CLOSE SEASONS (UK)

The close season is the time of the year when it is illegal to kill certain game or fish. Dates given are inclusive; for birds, the first dates refer to England, Scotland and Wales and the second to Northern Ireland, while for deer the first dates refer to England, Wales and Northern Ireland, the second to Scotland. Where only one set of dates is given the close season is the same across the UK.

Fish

Close season dates vary locally, according to bylaws, species of fish and type of water (lake, river, canal, etc).

Birds

Capercailzie	1 Feb–30 Sep	Woodcock	1 Feb–30 Sep; 1 Feb–30 Sep
Partridge	2 Feb–31 Aug; 1 Feb–31 Aug	Grouse[1]	11 Dec–11 Aug; 1 Dec–11 Aug
Pheasant	2 Feb–30 Sep; 1 Feb–30 Sep	Black game[2]	11 Dec–19 Aug[3]
Common snipe	1 Feb–11 Aug; 1 Feb–31 Aug		

[1] Includes red grouse and ptarmigan.
[2] Black grouse.
[3] To 31 Aug in Somerset, Devon and the New Forest.

Deer

Female		Male	
Red deer	1 Mar–31 Oct; 16 Feb–20 Oct	Red deer	1 May–31 Jul; 21 Oct–30 Jun
Fallow deer	1 Mar–31 Oct; 16 Feb–20 Oct	Fallow deer	1 May–31 Jul
Sika deer	1 Mar–31 Oct; 16 Feb–20 Oct	Sika deer	1 May–31 Jul; 21 Oct–30 Jun
Roe deer	1 Mar–31 Oct; 1 Apr–20 Oct	Roe deer	1 Nov–31 Mar; 21 Oct–31 Mar

Note: There is no statutory close season for muntjak or Chinese water deer.

HUMAN GEOGRAPHY

COUNTRIES A–Z

Introduction

Data given in this section is subject to frequent change.

Names of countries and cities
The official name of the country is given in English. Where appropriate the short form of the local name is given first, followed by the long form. English names of capital cities are given first, followed by the local name(s). Any notable names by which a country has been previously known in the 20c are listed with relevant dates.

Area
Area figures are for land mass only and do not include territorial waters (eg Kiribati covers c.3 million sq km/1.2 million sq mi but land area is only 717 sq km/277 sq mi).

Chief towns
If no chief towns are given the country is too small or sparsely populated to have major settlements.

Population
Unless otherwise indicated, population statistics are from the United Nations Population Division, 'World Population Prospects: The 2004 Revision'.

Nationality
Nationality gives the usual adjective form; exceptions are clearly marked.

Time zone
No allowance is made for Daylight Saving Time.

Currency
The three-letter ISO currency code is given alongside any commonly-used abbreviations.

Country codes
Country codes are from the official ISO list.

Climate
Temperature figures are given in degrees Celsius. To convert to Fahrenheit multiply by 9, divide by 5 and add 32.

National holidays
The first part of each listing gives the holidays that occur on fixed dates. Most dates are accompanied by an indication of the purpose of the day, eg Independence = Independence Day; dates which have no gloss are either fixed dates within the Christian calendar (for which see below) or bank holidays. The second part of the listing gives holidays that vary, usually depending on religious factors. The most common of these are given in abbreviated form (see list below).

Where national holidays last for more than one day, the number of days devoted to the holiday is shown in parentheses. The listings do not include holidays that affect only certain parts of a country, half-day holidays or Sundays.

The following fixed dates are shown without gloss:

Jan 1	New Year's Day	Nov 1	All Saints' Day
Jan 6	Epiphany	Nov 2	All Souls' Day
Mar 21	Novrus (Persian New Year;	Dec 8	Immaculate Conception
	various spellings)	Dec 24	Christmas Eve
May 1	Labour Day (often known by a	Dec 25	Christmas Day
	different name, such as	Dec 26	Boxing Day/St Stephen's Day
	Workers' Day)	Dec 31	New Year's Eve
Aug 15	Assumption of Our Lady		

The following abbreviations are used for variable religious feast days:

A	Ascension Thursday
Ad	Id-ul-Adha (also found with other spellings, especially Eid-ul-Adha; various names relating to this occasion are used in different countries, such as Tabaski, Id el-Kebir, Hari Raja Haji)
Ar	Arafa
As	Ashora (found with various spellings)
C	Carnival (immediately before Christian Lent, unless specified)
CC	Corpus Christi
D	Diwali/Deepavali
EM	Easter Monday
ER	End of Ramadan (known generally as Id/Eid-ul-Fitr, but various names relating to this occasion are used in different countries, such as Karite, Hari Raja Puasa)
ES	Easter Sunday
GF	Good Friday
HS	Holy Saturday
HT	Holy Thursday
NY	New Year
PB	Prophet's Birthday (known generally as Maul-id-al-Nabi in various forms and spellings)
R	First day of Ramadan
WM	Whit Monday

Dependencies

Dependencies and other territories are listed by type then alphabetically.

Political leaders

Countries and organizations are listed alphabetically, with former or alternative names given in parentheses. Rulers are named chronologically since 1900 or (for new nations) since independence. For some major English-speaking nations, relevant details are also given of pre-20c rulers, along with a note of any political affiliation. Relevant details are also given of pre-20c rulers for some major monarchies, and other useful information, for example dynasties, is also included where appropriate. The list does not distinguish successive terms of office by a single ruler. Listings are complete to Aug 2005.

There is no universally agreed way of transliterating proper names in non-Roman alphabets; variations from the spellings given are therefore to be expected, especially in the case of Arabic rulers. Minor variations in the titles adopted by Chiefs of State, or in the name of an administration, are not given; these occur most notably in countries under military rule.

ABU DHABI see **UNITED ARAB EMIRATES**

AFGHANISTAN

Official name	Islamic Republic of Afghanistan	**Languages**	Dari, Pashto
Local name	Afqânestân (Dari), Afğānistãn (Pashto)	**Ethnic groups**	Pashtun 38%, Tajik 25%, Hazara 19%, Uzbek 6%, others 12%
Former name	*as listed below under Political leaders*	**Religions**	Islam 99% (Sunni 74%, Shia 25%), others 1%
Independence	1919	**Time zone**	GMT +4.5
Area	647 497 sq km/249 934 sq mi	**Currency**	1 Afghani (AF/AFN) = 100 puls
Capital	Kabul; Kābul, Kãbol	**Telephone**	+93
Chief towns	Herat, Kandahar	**Internet**	.af
Population	29 863 000 (2005e)	**Country code**	AFG
Nationality	Afghan		

Location
A republic in south-central Asia, bounded to the north by Turkmenistan, Uzbekistan and Tajikistan; to the extreme north-east by China and the disputed area of Jammu and Kashmir; to the east and south by Pakistan; and to the west by Iran.

Physical description
Landlocked and mountainous, centred on the Hindu Kush system which reaches over 7 000m/23 000ft in centre and north-east; highest point is Nowshak (7 485m/24 557ft); north-west is the fertile valley of Herat; arid uplands in south; desert in south-west.

Climate
Continental climate with winter severity increased by altitude; summers are warm everywhere except on the highest peaks; protected from summer monsoons by the southern mountains; lower levels have a desert or semi-arid climate.

National holidays
Mar 21, Apr 28 (Victory of the Muslim Nation), May 1, 4 (Remembrance for Martyrs and Disabled), Aug 19 (Independence); Ad (3), Ar, As, ER (3), NY (Muslim), PB, R.

Political leaders

Afghan Empire

Monarch

1881–1901	Abdur Rahman Khan	1929	Habibullah Ghazi
1901–19	Habibullah Khan	1929–33	Nadir Shah
1919–29	Amanullah Khan	1933–73	Zahir Shah

Republic of Afghanistan

President
1973–8   Mohammad Daoud Khan

Democratic Republic of Afghanistan

President of Revolutionary Council
1978–9   Nour Mohammad Taraki
1979   Hafizullah Amin

Soviet invasion

1979–86	Babrak Karmal	1987–92	Mohammad Najibullah
1986–7	Haji Mohammad Chamkani	1992	Sebghatullah Mojaddedi
	Acting President		*Acting President*

General Secretary

1978–86	*As President*	1986–92	Mohammad Najibullah

Prime Minister

1929–46	Sardar Mohammad Hashim Khan	1967–71	Nour Ahmad Etemadi
1946–53	Shah Mahmoud Khan Ghazi	1972–3	Mohammad Mousa Shafiq
1953–63	Mohammad Daoud	1973–9	*As President*
1963–5	Mohammad Yousef	1979–81	Babrak Karmal
1965–7	Mohammad Hashim Maiwandwal	1981–8	Sultan Ali Keshtmand

Republic of Afghanistan

1988–9	Mohammad Hasan Sharq	1992–3	Abdul Sabour Fareed
1989–90	Sultan Ali Keshtmand	1993–6	Gulbuddin Hekmatyar
1990–2	Fazal Haq Khaliqyar		

Islamic State of Afghanistan

President
1992–2001 Burhanuddin Rabbani[1]

Chairman of Interim Government
2001–2 Hamid Karzai

Islamic Republic of Afghanistan[2]

President
2002– Hamid Karzai

[1] *Ousted by the Taliban in 1996, but remained titular head of state; Taliban de facto rulers 1996–2001.*
[2] *Islamic Transitional State of Afghanistan until 2004.*

AJMAN *see* **UNITED ARAB EMIRATES**

ALBANIA

Official name	Republic of Albania	**Population**	3 130 000 (2005e)
Local name	Shqipëria; Republika e Shqipërisë	**Nationality**	Albanian
		Languages	Albanian
Former name	Kingdom of Albania (1928–39), People's Republic of Albania (1946–76), People's Socialist Republic of Albania (until 1991)	**Ethnic groups**	Albanian 95%, Greek 3%, others 2%
		Religions	Islam 60% (Sunni), none/ unaffiliated 28%, Christianity 12% (Orthodox 8%, RC 4%)
Independence	1912	**Time zone**	GMT +1
Area	28 748 sq km/11 097 sq mi	**Currency**	1 Lek (plural Lekë) (Lk/ALL) = 100 qindarka
Capital	Tirana; Tiranë	**Telephone**	+355
Chief towns	Shkodër, Durrës, Vlorë, Korçë, Elbasan	**Internet**	.al
		Country code	ALB

Location
A republic in the western part of the Balkan Peninsula, bounded to the north by Serbia and Montenegro; to the north-east by Macedonia; to the south-east by Greece; and to the west by the Adriatic Sea.

Physical description
Mountainous, relatively inaccessible and untravelled; highest point is Maja e Korabit (Golem Korab; 2 753m/9 032ft) on the Macedonian border; northern Albanian Alps rise to 2 692m/8 832ft; 50% of the population live in 25% of the area (the low-lying west).

Climate
A Mediterranean-type climate: hot and dry on the plains in summer (average Jul temperature 24–25°C); winters are mild and damp (average Jan temperature 8–9°C), but often severe in the mountains.

National holidays
Jan 1, Mar 21, May 1, Nov 28 (Independence), 29 (Liberation), Dec 25; Ad, ER, ES, NY (Albanian), Orthodox Easter (Apr/May).

Political leaders

Monarch

1928–39	Zog I (Ahmed Zogu)
1939–44	*Italian rule*

President

1944–85	Enver Hoxha	1997–2002	Rexhep Mejdani
1985–92	Ramiz Alia	2002–	Alfred Moisiu
1992–7	Sali Berisha		

Prime Minister

1914	Turhan Pashë Permëti	1943	*Provisional Executive Committee* (Ibrahim Biçakçlu)
1914	Esad Toptani		
1914–18	Abdullah Rushdi		
1918–20	Turhan Pashë Permëti	1943	*Council of Regents* (Mehdi Frashëri)
1920	Sulejman Deluina		
1920–1	Iljaz Bej Vrioni	1943–4	Rexhep Mitrovica
1921	Pandeli Evangeli	1944	Fiori Dine
1921	Xhafer Ypi	1944–54	Enver Hoxha
1921–2	Omer Vrioni	1954–81	Mehmed Shehu
1922–4	Ahmed Zogu	1981–91	Adil Carcani
1924	Iljaz Bej Vrioni	1991	Ylli Buffi
1924–5	Fan Noli	1991	Fatos Nano
1925–8	Ahmed Zogu	1991–2	Vilson Ahmeti
1928–30	Koço Kota	1992–7	Aleksander Meksi
1930–5	Pandeli Evangeli	1997	Bashkim Fino
1935–6	Mehdi Frashëri	1997–8	Fatos Nano
1936–9	Koço Kota	1998–9	Pandeli Majko
1939–41	Shefqet Verlaci	1999–2002	Ilir Meta
1941–3	Mustafa Merlika-Kruja	2002	Pandeli Majko
1943	Eqrem Libohova	2002–5	Fatos Nano
1943	Maliq Bushati	2005–	Sali Berisha
1943	Eqrem Libohova		

ALGERIA

Official name	People's Democratic Republic of Algeria	**Population**	32 854 000 (2005e)
		Nationality	Algerian
Local name	Al-Jazā'ir; Al-Jumhūriyya al-Jazā'iriyya ad-Dimuqratiyya ash-Sha'biyya (Arabic), Algérie; République Algérienne Démocratique et Populaire (French)	**Languages**	Arabic, Tamazight; French is also spoken
		Ethnic groups	Arab 74%, Berber 25%, European 1%
		Religions	Islam 99% (Sunni), others 1%
Independence	1962	**Time zone**	GMT +1
Area	2 460 500 sq km/949 753 sq mi	**Currency**	1 Algerian Dinar (AD, DA/DZD) = 100 centimes
Capital	Algiers; Alger, El Djazâir, Al-Jazā'ir	**Telephone**	+213
		Internet	.dz
Chief towns	Constantine, Oran, Skikda, Annaba, Mostaganem, Blida, Tlemcen	**Country code**	DZA

Location
A republic in North Africa, bounded to the north by the Mediterranean Sea; to the north-east by Tunisia; to the east by Libya; to the south-east by Niger; to the south-west by Western Sahara, Mauritania and Mali; and to the west by Morocco.

Physical description
From the Mediterranean coast, where 91% of the population are located on the narrow coastal plain, the mountains rise to the Atlas Saharien; the Sahara Desert lies to the south; the Hoggar Mountains in the far south rise to 2 918m/9 573ft at Mt Tahat.

Climate
Typical Mediterranean climate on the north coast; snow on the higher ground; Algiers, representative of the coastal region, has average maximum daily temperatures of 15–29°C; elsewhere an essentially rainless Saharan climate.

National holidays
Jan 1, May 1, Jun 19 (Revolutionary Readjustment), Jul 5 (Independence), Nov 1 (Revolution); Ad (2), As, ER (2), NY (Muslim), PB.

Political leaders

President

1962–5	Ahmed Ben Bella	1992–4	Ali Kafi
1965–78	Houari Boumédienne	1994–9	Liamine Zeroual
1979–92	Chandli Benjedid	1999–	Abdelaziz Bouteflika
1992	*High Commission of State: Chair* Mohamed Boudiaf		

Prime Minister

1962–3	Ahmed Ben Bella	1992–3	Belaid Abdessalam
1963–79	*No Prime Minister*	1993–4	Redha Malek
1979–84	Mohamed Ben Ahmed Abdelghani	1994–5	Mokdad Sifi
		1995–8	Ahmed Ouyahia
1984–8	Abdelhamid Brahimi	1998–9	Ismail Hamdani
1988–9	Kasdi Merbah	1999–2000	Ahmed Benbitour
1989–91	Mouloud Hamrouche	2000–3	Ali Benflis
1991–2	Sid Ahmed Ghozali	2003–	Ahmed Ouyahia

AMERICAN SAMOA *see* **UNITED STATES OF AMERICA**

ANDORRA

Official name	Principality of Andorra; also sometimes known as The Valleys of Andorra	**Ethnic groups**	Spanish 61%, Andorran 30%, French 6%, others 3%
Local name	Andorra; Principat d'Andorra	**Religions**	Christianity 95% (RC 94%, Prot 1%), none/ unaffiliated 5%
Area	468 sq km/181 sq mi		
Capital	Andorra la Vella; Andorra la Vieja (Spanish), Andorre la Vielle (French), Andorra la Vella (Catalan)	**Time zone**	GMT +1
		Currency	1 Euro (€/EUR) = 100 cents
		Telephone	+376
Population	67 000 (2005e)	**Internet**	.ad
Nationality	Andorran	**Country code**	AND
Languages	Catalan; French and Spanish are also spoken		

Location
A semi-independent neutral state in the central Pyrenees between France and Spain.

Physical description
A small, mountainous country, reaching 2 947m/9 669ft at Coma Pedrosa, occupying two valleys (del Norte and del Orient) of the River Valira.

Climate
Winters are cold but dry and sunny; the midsummer months are slightly drier than spring and autumn.

National holidays
Jan 1, 6, Mar 14 (Constitution), May 1, Jun 24 (People's Festival), Aug 15, Sep 8 (Our Lady of Meritxell), Nov 1, Dec 8, 21 (St Thomas), 25, 26; EM, GF, WM.

Political leaders

There are two heads of state, called Co-Princes: the President of France (see entry for France) and the Bishop of Urgell, Spain (Joan Enric Vives i Sicília since 2003).

President of the Executive Council

1982–4	Óscar Ribas Reig		1994–2005	Marc Forné Molné
1984–90	Josep Pintat Solens		2005–	Albert Pintat Santolària
1990–4	Óscar Ribas Reig			

In the High Pyrenees

Andorra, nestled among the mountains of the eastern Pyrenees, proudly claims to be Europe's highest inhabited country. The lowest point is a still-respectable 840m/2 756ft above sea level, while the highest mountain, Coma Pedrosa, reaches a sizeable 2 947m/9 669ft. Andorra manages to pack 65 peaks that reach higher than 2 500m/8 202ft into just 468 sq km/181 sq mi of land.

ANGOLA

Official name	Republic of Angola	**Languages**	Portuguese; many Bantu languages are also spoken
Local name	Angola; República de Angola		
Former name	People's Republic of Angola (until 1992)	**Ethnic groups**	Ovimbundu 37%, Mbundu 25%, Bakongo 13%, others 25%
Independence	1975	**Religions**	Christianity 81% (RC 69%, Prot 12%), traditional beliefs 19%
Area	1 245 790 sq km/480 875 sq mi		
Capital	Luanda	**Time zone**	GMT +1
Chief towns	Huambo, Benguela, Lobito, Namibe (Moçâmedes), Cabinda, Malanje, Lubango	**Currency**	1 Kwanza (Kz/AOA) = 100 lwei
		Telephone	+244
Population	15 941 000 (2005e)	**Internet**	.ao
Nationality	Angolan	**Country code**	AGO

Location
A republic in south-west Africa, bounded to the north by Democratic Republic of the Congo; to the east by Zambia; to the south by Namibia; and to the west by the southern Atlantic Ocean; the separate province of Cabinda is enclosed by Congo and Democratic Republic of the Congo, and bounded to the west by the southern Atlantic Ocean.

Physical description
A narrow coastal plain, widening in the north towards the Congo Delta; high plateau inland with an average elevation of 1 200m/3 937ft; highest point is Serro Môco (2 619m/8 592ft); numerous rivers rise in the plateau but few are navigable for any length.

Climate
Mostly a tropical plateau climate; a single wet season Oct–Mar and a long dry season; average daily temperatures of 24–29°C in upland region; temperature and rainfall much reduced on the coast, which is semi-desert as far north as Luanda.

National holidays
Jan 1, 4 (Martyrs of the Colonial Repression), Feb 4 (Beginning of the Armed Struggle), Mar 8 (Women), May 1, Jun 1 (Children), Sep 17 (Nation's Founder/National Hero), Nov 2, 11 (Independence), Dec 25.

Political leaders

President
1975–9	Antonio Agostinho Neto
1979–	José Eduardo dos Santos

Prime Minister
1975–8	Lopo do Nasciemento	1996–97	Fernando José de França van Dúnem
1978–91	*No Prime Minister*	1999–2002	*No Prime Minister*
1991–2	Fernando José de França van Dúnem	2002–	Fernando da Piedade Dias dos Santos
1992–6	Marcolino José Carlos Moco		

ANGUILLA *see* **UNITED KINGDOM**

ANTARCTIC TERRITORY, BRITISH *see* **UNITED KINGDOM**

ANTIGUA AND BARBUDA

Official name	State of Antigua and Barbuda	**Religions**	Christianity 96% (Prot 87%, RC 9%), Rastafarianism 1%, none/unaffiliated 1%, others 2%
Local name	Antigua and Barbuda		
Independence	1981		
Area	442 sq km/171 sq mi	**Time zone**	GMT −4
Capital	St John's	**Currency**	1 East Caribbean Dollar (EC$/XCD) = 100 cents
Chief towns	Codrington (on Barbuda)		
Population	81 000 (2005e)	**Telephone**	+1 268
Nationality	Antiguan, Barbudan	**Internet**	.ag
Languages	English	**Country code**	ATG
Ethnic groups	African descent 92%, British 4%, others 4%		

Location
An independent group of three islands in the Leeward group of the Lesser Antilles in the eastern Caribbean Sea: Antigua, Barbuda and the uninhabited Redonda.

Physical description
The western part of Antigua rises to 402m/1 319ft at Boggy Peak; Barbuda is a flat, coral island reaching only 44m/144ft at its highest point, with a large lagoon on its western side.

Climate
Tropical, with temperatures ranging from 24°C in Jan to 27°C in Aug–Sep.

National holidays
Jan 1, Nov 1 (Independence), Dec 25, 26; EM, GF, WM, Labour (1st Mon in May), Emancipation (1st Mon and Tue in Aug).

Political leaders

Head of State: British monarch, represented by Governor General (Sir James Carlisle since 1993).

Prime Minister
1981–94	Vere Cornwall Bird
1994–2004	Lester Bryant Bird
2004–	Baldwin Spencer

Kings of Redonda

Although uninhabited and covering barely 1 sq km/0.4 sq mi, the tiny island of Redonda is claimed as a sovereign state by several self-styled 'kings'. The monarchy was supposedly instituted in 1865 by one Matthew Dowdy Shiell, a Caribbean trader who proclaimed himself king of the island to celebrate the birth of his first son. While the following two 'kings' were commonly acknowledged, thereafter the succession to the title 'King of Redonda' has been hotly disputed and jealously defended. Today, the two principal rivals – both with a national anthem, and both quick to denounce the other as an impudent impostor – are the British King Leo I and the Antiguan King Bob.

ARGENTINA

Official name	Argentine Republic	**Languages**	Spanish
Local name	Argentina; República Argentina	**Ethnic groups**	European 85%, mestizo 14%, others 1%
Independence	1816	**Religions**	Christianity 92% (RC
Area	3 761 274 sq km/ 1 451 852 sq mi		90%, Prot 2%), Judaism 2%, others 6%
Capital	Buenos Aires	**Time zone**	GMT –3
Chief towns	Córdoba, Rosario, Mendoza, La Plata, Mar del Plata, San Miguel de Tucumán	**Currency**	1 Argentine Peso ($/ARS) = 100 centavos
		Telephone	+54
		Internet	.ar
Population	38 747 000 (2005e)	**Country code**	ARG
Nationality	Argentine, Argentinian		

Location
A republic in south-eastern South America, bounded to the north by Bolivia and Paraguay; to the north-east by Brazil and Uruguay; to the south-east by the southern Atlantic Ocean; and to the west and south by Chile.

Physical description
The Andes stretch the entire length, north to south, forming the boundary with Chile; the highest peak is Aconcagua (6 960m/22 835ft); the *pampa*, a grassy, treeless plain is to the east, with uneven, arid steppes to the south.

Climate
Most of Argentina lies in the rainshadow of the Andes; temperatures range from tropical to moderately cool (average annual temperature 16°C at Buenos Aires), with some desert; the south is directly influenced by strong prevailing westerlies.

National holidays
Jan 1, Apr 2 (Malvinas), May 1, 25 (National), Jun 20 (Flag), Jul 9 (Independence), Aug 17 (Death of General San Martín), Oct 12 (Americas Discovery), Dec 8, 25; GF, HT.

Silver Country

The name *Argentina* comes from the Latin word *argentum*, meaning 'silver'. When Spanish explorers first reached the area in the early 16c the local people gave them silver gifts, and they returned home with tales of a mountain supposedly composed of silver. The main river estuary was christened *Río de la Plata*, or 'River of Silver'.

Political leaders

President

1898–1904	Julio Argentino Roca	1940–3	Ramón S Castillo
1904–6	Manuel Quintana	1943–4	Pedro P Ramírez
1906–10	José Figueroa Alcorta	1944–6	Edelmiro J Farrell
1910–14	Roque Sáenz Peña	1946–55	Juan Perón
1914–16	Victorino de la Plaza	1955–8	Eduardo Lonardi
1916–22	Hipólito Yrigoyen	1958–62	Arturo Frondizi
1922–8	Marcelo T de Alvear	1962–3	José María Guido
1928–30	Hipólito Yrigoyen	1963–6	Arturo Illia
1930–2	José Félix Uriburu	1966–70	Juan Carlos Onganía
1932–8	Augustin Pedro Justo	1970–1	Roberto Marcelo Levingston
1938–40	Roberto M Ortiz	1971–3	Alejandro Agustin Lanusse

1973	Héctor J Cámpora	1982–3	Reynaldo Bignone
1973–4	Juan Perón	1983–8	Raúl Alfonsín
1974–6	Martínez de Perón	1988–99	Carlos Saúl Menem
1976–81	*Military Junta* (Jorge Rafaél Videla)	1999–2001	Fernando de la Rúa
1981	*Military Junta* (Roberto Eduardo Viola)	2001	*Three Interim Presidents*
		2002–3	Eduardo Duhalde
1981–2	*Military Junta* (Leopoldo Galtieri)	2003–	Nestor Kirchner

ARMENIA

Official name	Republic of Armenia	**Chief towns**	Vanadzor, Gyumri
Local name	Hayastan; Hayastany Hanrapetoutyun	**Population**	3 016 000 (2005e)
		Nationality	Armenian
Former name	Transcaucasian Soviet Federated Socialist Republic (with Azerbaijan and Georgia, 1922–36), Armenian Soviet Socialist Republic (1920–2, 1936–90), within the Union of Soviet Socialist Republics (USSR; 1922–91)	**Languages**	Armenian; Russian is also widely spoken
		Ethnic groups	Armenian 93%, Azeri 3%, Russian 2%, others 2%
		Religions	Christianity 94% (Orthodox), others 6%
		Time zone	GMT +4
		Currency	1 Armenian Dram (Drm/AMD) = 100 lumas
Independence	1991	**Telephone**	+374
Area	29 800 sq km/11 500 sq mi	**Internet**	.am
Capital	Yerevan; Erevan	**Country code**	ARM

Location
A republic in southern Transcaucasia, bounded to the north by Georgia; to the east and south-west by Azerbaijan; to the south by Iran; and to the west by Turkey.

Physical description
Mountainous, rising to 4 090m/13 418ft at Mt Aragats in the west; largest lake is Sevan.

Climate
Dry and cold in the summer, cold in the winter.

National holidays
Jan 1, 6 (Armenian Christmas), Apr 24 (Day of Remembrance of the Victims of the Genocide), May 28 (Declaration of the First Armenian Republic, 1918), Sep 21 (Independence), Dec 7 (Day of Remembrance of the Victims of the Earthquake); EM, ES, GF, HS.

Political leaders

President

1991–8	Levon Ter-Petrossian	1998–	Robert Kocharyan

Prime Minister

1991–2	Gagik Haroutunian	1998–9	Armen Darbinian
1992–3	Khosrov Haroutunian	1999	Vazgen Sarkissian
1993–6	Hrand Bagratian	1999–2000	Aram Sarkissian
1996–7	Armen Sarkissian	2000–	Andranik Markarian
1997–8	Robert Kocharyan		

ARUBA see **NETHERLANDS, THE**

AUSTRALIA

Official name	Commonwealth of Australia	**Ethnic groups**	European 95%, Asian 4%, Aboriginal and others 1%
Local name	Australia		
Independence	1901	**Religions**	Christianity 73% (Prot 47%, RC 26%), none/ unaffiliated 17%, others 10%
Area	7 692 300 sq km/ 2 969 228 sq mi		
Capital	Canberra	**Time zone**	GMT +8/10.5
Chief towns	Melbourne, Brisbane, Perth, Adelaide, Sydney	**Currency**	1 Australian Dollar ($A/AUD) = 100 cents
Population	20 155 000 (2005e)	**Telephone**	+61
Nationality	Australian	**Internet**	.au
Languages	English; Aboriginal languages are also spoken	**Country code**	AUS

Location
An independent country, entirely in the southern hemisphere; separated from Indonesia, East Timor and Papua New Guinea to the north by the Timor Sea, Arafura Sea and Torres Strait; to the east is the Pacific Ocean and Tasman Sea; to the south the Southern Ocean; and to the west the Indian Ocean.

Physical description
The largest island and the smallest continent in the world; consists largely of plains and plateaux; the West Australian plateau occupies nearly half the whole area; most of the plateau is desert; Great Dividing Range parallel to the eastern seaboard rises to 2 228m/7 310ft at Mt Kosciusko (Australia's highest point); the island of Tasmania lies to the south; fertile land is limited to the coastal east and south-east and to a small part of the south-west, and the population is concentrated in these two regions.

Climate
Half the country has a rainfall variability of more than 30%, with many areas experiencing prolonged drought; Darwin's average daily temperature is 26–34°C in Nov and 19–31°C in Jul; Melbourne's average daily temperature is 6–13°C in Jul and 14–26°C in Jan–Feb.

National holidays
Jan 1, 26 (Australia), Apr 25 (Anzac), Dec 25, 26; Queen's Birthday (Jun, *except Western Australia, Sept/Oct*), EM, GF, HS; *additional days vary between states*.

Australian states and territories

Name	Population (2005e)[1]	Area	Capital
Australian Capital Territory (ACT)	325 100	2 432 sq km/939 sq mi	Canberra
New South Wales (NSW)	6 764 600	801 427 sq km/309 431 sq mi	Sydney
Northern Territory (NT)	201 800	1 346 200 sq km/519 768 sq mi	Darwin
Queensland (QLD)	3 945 800	1 732 700 sq km/668 995 sq mi	Brisbane
South Australia (SA)	1 540 200	984 376 sq km/380 070 sq mi	Adelaide
Tasmania (TAS)	484 700	68 331 sq km/26 383 sq mi	Hobart
Victoria (VIC)	5 012 700	227 600 sq km/87 876 sq mi	Melbourne
Western Australia (WA)	2 003 800	2 525 500 sq km/975 096 sq mi	Perth

[1] *Population figures are from the Australian Bureau of Statistics.*

Overseas territories

Norfolk Island

Location	An island in the western Pacific Ocean, lying 1 488km/925mi north-east of Sydney, eastern Australia.		
Area	35 sq km/14 sq mi	Internet	.nf
Capital	Kingston	Country code	NFK
Population	1 800 (2005e)		

Heard and McDonald Islands

Location	An island group comprising Heard Island, Shag Island and the McDonald Islands in the Southern Ocean, approximately 4 000km/2 500mi south-west of Fremantle, western Australia.		
Area	412 sq km/159 sq mi	Internet	.hm
Population	uninhabited	Country code	HMD

Christmas Island

Location	An island in the Indian Ocean, approximately 360km/224mi south of the Indonesian island of Java.		
Area	135 sq km/52 sq mi	Internet	.cx
Capital	The Settlement	Country code	CXR
Population	350 (2005e)		

Cocos (Keeling) Islands

Location	Two separate groups of atolls in the Indian Ocean, 3 685km/2 290mi west of Darwin, northern Australia, comprising 27 islands; the main islands are West Island and Home Island.		
Area	14.2 sq km/5.5 sq mi	Internet	.cc
Capital	West Island	Country code	CCK
Population	630 (2005e)		

Note: Australia also possesses the uninhabited Ashmore and Cartier Islands in the Indian Ocean and the Coral Sea Islands in the Coral Sea north-east of Australia.

Political leaders

Head of State: British monarch, represented by Governor General (Michael Jeffery since 2003).

Prime Minister

1901–3	Edmund Barton *Prot*	1913–14	Joseph Cook *Lib*
1903–4	Alfred Deakin *Prot*	1914–15	Andrew Fisher *Lab*
1904	John Christian Watson *Lab*	1915–17	William Morris Hughes
1904–5	George Houston Reid *Free*		*Nat Lab*
1905–8	Alfred Deakin *Prot*	1917–23	William Morris Hughes *Nat*
1908–9	Andrew Fisher *Lab*	1923–9	Stanley Melbourne Bruce *Nat*
1909–10	Alfred Deakin *Fus*	1929–32	James Henry Scullin *Lab*
1910–13	Andrew Fisher *Lab*	1932–9	Joseph Aloysius Lyons *Un*

1939	Earle Christmas Page *Co*	1968–71	John Grey Gorton *Lib*
1939–41	Robert Gordon Menzies *Un*	1971–2	William McMahon *Lib*
1941	Arthur William Fadden *Co*	1972–5	Edward Gough Whitlam
1941–5	John Joseph Curtin *Lab*		*Lab*
1945	Francis Michael Forde *Lab*	1975–83	John Malcolm Fraser *Lib*
1945–9	Joseph Benedict Chifley *Lab*	1983–91	Robert James Lee Hawke
1949–66	Robert Gordon Menzies *Lib*		*Lab*
1966–7	Harold Edward Holt *Lib*	1991–6	Paul Keating *Lab*
1967–8	John McEwen *Co*	1996–	John Howard *Lib*

Co = Country		*Lab = Labor*		*Nat Lab = National Labor*	
Con = Conservative		*Lib = Liberal*		*Prot = Protectionist*	
Free = Free Trade		*Nat = Nationalist*		*Un = United*	
Fus = Fusion					

AUSTRIA

Official name	Republic of Austria	**Languages**	German
Local name	Österreich; Republik Österreich	**Ethnic groups**	Austrian 98%, others 2%
Former name	formerly part of Austria–Hungary (until 1918)	**Religions**	Christianity 84% (RC 77%, Prot 7%), none/unaffiliated 8%, Islam 2%, others 6%
Independence	1955		
Area	83 854 sq km/32 368 sq mi	**Time zone**	GMT +1
Capital	Vienna; Wien	**Currency**	1 Euro (€/EUR) = 100 cents
Chief towns	Graz, Linz, Salzburg, Innsbruck, Klagenfurt	**Telephone**	+43
		Internet	.at
Population	8 189 000 (2005e)	**Country code**	AUT
Nationality	Austrian		

Location
A republic in central Europe, bounded to the north-west by Germany; to the north by the Czech Republic; to the north-east by Slovakia; to the south-east by Hungary; to the south by Slovenia and Italy; and to the west by Switzerland and Liechtenstein.

Physical description
Situated at the eastern end of the Alps, the country is almost entirely mountainous; highest point is Grossglockner, at 3 797m/12 457ft; most of the country is in the drainage basin of the River Danube.

Climate
Three climatic regions: the Alps (often sunny in winter but cloudy in summer); the Danube valley and the Vienna basin (the driest region); and the south-east, a region of heavy thunderstorms; most rain in summer; winters are cold.

National holidays
Jan 1, 6, May 1, Aug 15, Oct 26 (National), Nov 1, Dec 8, 25, 26; A, CC, EM, WM.

Political leaders

Monarch (Habsburg Dynasty)

1440–93	Frederick III	1519–58	Karl V
1493–1519	Maximilian I	1558–64	Ferdinand I

1564–76	Maximilian II	1742–5	Karl VII
1576–1612	Rudolf II	1745–65	Franz I
1612–19	Matthias	1765–90	Josef II
1619–37	Ferdinand II	1790–2	Leopold II
1637–57	Ferdinand III	1792–1835	Franz II
1658–1705	Leopold I	1835–48	Ferdinand I
1705–11	Josef I	1848–1916	Franz Josef
1711–40	Karl VI	1916–18	Karl I
1740–2	*Interregnum*		

President

1918–20	Karl Sätz	1957–65	Adolf Schärf
1920–8	Michael Hainisch	1965–74	Franz Jonas
1928–38	Wilhelm Miklas	1974–86	Rudolf Kirchschläger
1938–45	*German rule*	1986–92	Kurt Waldheim
1945–50	Karl Renner	1992–2004	Thomas Klestil
1950–7	Theodor Körner	2004–	Heinz Fischer

Chancellor

1918–20	Karl Renner	1932–4	Engelbert Dollfus
1920–1	Michael Mayr	1934–8	Kurt von Schuschnigg
1921–2	Johann Schober	1938–45	*German rule*
1922	Walter Breisky	1945	Karl Renner
1922	Johann Schober	1945–53	Leopold Figl
1922–4	Ignaz Seipel	1953–61	Julius Raab
1924–6	Rudolph Ramek	1961–4	Alfons Gorbach
1926–9	Ignaz Seipel	1964–70	Josef Klaus
1929–30	Ernst Streeruwitz	1970–83	Bruno Kreisky
1930	Johann Schober	1983–6	Fred Sinowatz
1930	Carl Vaugoin	1986–97	Franz Vranitzky
1930–1	Otto Ender	1997–2000	Viktor Klima
1931–2	Karl Buresch	2000–	Wolfgang Schüssel

AZERBAIJAN

Official name	Azerbaijani Republic	**Population**	8 411 000 (2005e)
Local name	Azərbaycan Respublikası	**Nationality**	Azerbaijani
Former name	Azerbaijan People's Republic (1918–20), Transcaucasian Soviet Federated Socialist Republic (with Armenia and Georgia, 1922–36), Azerbaijan Soviet Socialist Republic (1920–2, 1936–90), within the Union of Soviet Socialist Republics (USSR; 1922–91)	**Languages**	Azeri
		Ethnic groups	Azeri 83%, Russian 6%, Armenian 6%, Dagestani 3%, others 2%
		Religions	Islam 93% (Shia), Christianity 5% (Orthodox), others 2%
		Time zone	GMT +4
		Currency	1 Azerbaijani Manat (AZM) = 100 gopik
Independence	1991	**Telephone**	+994
Area	86 600 sq km/33 428 sq mi	**Internet**	.az
Capital	Baku; Bakı	**Country code**	AZE
Chief towns	Gäncä, Sumqayit		

Location
A republic in eastern Transcaucasia, bounded to the north by Georgia and Russia; to the east by the Caspian Sea; and to the south by Iran; Armenia splits the country in the south-west.

Physical description
Crossed by the Greater Caucasus in the north and the Lesser Caucasus in the south-west; they are separated by the plain of River Kura; the highest peak is Mt Bazar-Dyuzi (4 480m/14 698ft) in the north-east; 10.5% of total area is forested.

Climate
Continental; hot in summer, cold in winter.

National holidays
Jan 1, 20 (Martyrs), 8 Mar (Women), May 9 (Victory), 28 (Republic), Jun 15 (National Salvation), 26 (Army and Navy), Oct 18 (Independence), Nov 12 (Constitution), 17 (National Revival), Dec 31 (Azerbaijani Solidarity Worldwide); Ad, ER, NY (Muslim) (2).

Political leaders

President

1991–2	Ayaz Mutalibov	1993–2003	Heydar Aliyev
1992	Yakub Mamedov *Acting President*	2003–	Ilham Aliyev
1992–3	Abul Faz Elchibey		

Prime Minister

1991–2	Hassan Hasanov	1993	Panakh Guseinov
1992	Feirus Mustafayev	1993–4	Surat Guseinov
	Acting Prime Minister	1994–6	Fuad Kuliyev
1992–3	Rakhim Guseinov	1996–2003	Artur Rasizade
1993	Ali Masimov	2003	Ilham Aliyev
	Acting Prime Minister	2003–	Artur Rasizade

Azeri Proverbs

Azerbaijan's many proverbs, known as 'father's words', include 'it's impossible to hold two watermelons in one hand' and 'don't tie garlic on your head if you don't have a headache'.

AZORES *see* **PORTUGAL**

THE BAHAMAS

Official name	Commonwealth of the Bahamas	**Ethnic groups**	black 85%, white 15%
Local name	Bahamas	**Religions**	Christianity 95% (Prot and others 74%, RC 21%), none/unaffiliated 3%, others 2%
Independence	1973		
Area	13 934 sq km/5 379 sq mi	**Time zone**	GMT –5
Capital	Nassau	**Currency**	1 Bahamian Dollar (BA$, B$/BSD) = 100 cents
Chief towns	Freeport		
Population	323 000 (2005e)	**Telephone**	+1 242
Nationality	Bahamian	**Internet**	.bs
Languages	English	**Country code**	BHS

Location
An independent country lying south-east of the coast of the US state of Florida in the northern Atlantic Ocean.

Physical description
An archipelago of c.700 low-lying islands and over 2 000 cays; the coralline limestone islands of the Bahamas comprise the two oceanic banks of Little Bahama and Great Bahama; the highest point on the low-lying islands, Mt Alvernia on Cat Island, is only 63m/207ft above sea level.

Climate
Subtropical, with average temperatures of 21°C in winter and 27°C in summer; hurricanes are frequent in Jun–Nov.

National holidays
Jan 1, Jul 10 (Independence), Oct 12 (Discovery), Dec 25, 26; EM, GF, WM; Labour (1st Mon in Jun), Emancipation (1st Fri in Aug).

Political leaders

Head of State: British monarch, represented by Governor General (Dame Ivy Dumont since 2001).

Prime Minister
1973–92   Lynden O Pindling
1992–2002   Hubert A Ingraham
2002–   Perry Christie

Islands of the Shallow Seas

The Bahamas were first discovered by Europeans when Christopher Columbus arrived in 1492. The sailors were supposedly struck by the depth of the surrounding waters, and remarked *'baja mar'* – the Spanish for 'low water' or, loosely, 'shallow seas' – inadvertently christening the islands.

BAHRAIN

Official name	Kingdom of Bahrain	**Languages**	Arabic
Local name	Al-Bahrayn; Mamlakat al-Bahrayn	**Ethnic groups**	Bahraini 63%, Asian 13%, other Arab 10%, Iranian 8%, others 6%
Former name	State of Bahrain (until 2002)	**Religions**	Islam 95% (Shia 73%, Sunni 22%), others 5%
Independence	1971		
Area	678 sq km/262 sq mi	**Time zone**	GMT +3
Capital	Manama; Al Manāmah	**Currency**	1 Bahraini Dinar (BD/BHD) = 1 000 fils
Chief towns	Al Muharraq		
Population	727 000 (2005e)	**Telephone**	+973
Nationality	Bahraini	**Internet**	.bh
		Country code	BHR

Location
A monarchy in the Arabian Gulf, midway between the Qatar Peninsula and mainland Saudi Arabia; a causeway (25km/16mi in length) connects Bahrain to Saudi Arabia.

Physical description
A group of 35 islands; the island of Bahrain is c.48km/30mi long and 13–16km/8–10mi wide; highest point is Jabal Dukhan (135m/443ft); largely bare and infertile, though helped by many major drainage schemes since 1973.

Climate
Cool north/north-east winds, with a little rain in Dec–Mar; rest of the year dominated by either a moist north-east wind (the *Shamal*) or the hot, sand-bearing *Qaws* from the south; average temperature 36°C in summer, 19°C in Jan.

National holidays
Jan 1, Dec 16 (National); Ad (3), As, ER (3), NY (Muslim), PB.

Political leaders

Emir

1971–99	Isa Bin Salman Al-Khalifah
1999–2002	Hamad Bin Isa Al-Khalifah

Monarch

2002–	Hamad Bin Isa Al-Khalifah

Prime Minister

1970–	Khalifah Bin Salman Al-Khalifah

Land of Immortality

In the third millennium BC Bahrain was known as *Dilmun*, and was described in an ancient tale as the 'land of immortality' where the 'flower of eternal youth' might be found. The later name *Bahrain* comes from Arabic and means 'two seas'.

BALEARIC ISLANDS *see* **SPAIN**

BANGLADESH

Official name	People's Republic of Bangladesh	**Population**	141 822 000 (2005e)
		Nationality	Bangladeshi
Local name	Gana Prajatantri Bangladesh	**Languages**	Bangla (Bengali); English is the second language
Former name	Part of the Indian states of Bengal (until 1905) and East Bengal (until 1947), then part of Pakistan as East Pakistan (until 1971)	**Ethnic groups**	Bengali 98%, others 2%
		Religions	Islam 87% (mostly Sunni), Hinduism 12%, others 1%
		Time zone	GMT +6
Independence	1971	**Currency**	1 Taka (TK/BDT) = 100 poisha
Area	143 998 sq km/55 583 sq mi		
Capital	Dhaka (formerly known as Dacca)	**Telephone**	+880
		Internet	.bd
Chief towns	Chittagong, Khulna, Narayanganj	**Country code**	BGD

Location
A republic in southern Asia, bounded to the north, east and west by India; to the south-east by Myanmar; and to the south by the Bay of Bengal.

Physical description
Mainly a vast, low-lying alluvial plain, cut by a network of rivers and marshes; main rivers (including the Ganges and the Brahmaputra) join in the south to form the world's largest delta; frequent flooding; highest point is Keokradong (1 230m/4 035ft).

Climate
Tropical monsoon climate; hot season in Mar–Jun with heavy thunderstorms; very humid, with higher temperatures inland; main rainy season is Jun–Sep; cyclones in the Bay of Bengal cause widespread flooding of coastal areas.

National holidays
Feb 21 (Shaheed Dibash/International Mother Language), Mar 26 (Independence/National), May 1, Nov 7 (National Revolution and Solidarity), Dec 16 (Victory), 25; Ad (3), As, Buddha Purnima (Apr/May), Durgapuja (Jijaya Dashami), ER (3), Jamatul Wida, Janmashtami, NY (Bengali), PB, Shab-e-Barat, Shab-e-Qadr.

Political leaders

President

1971–2	Sayed Nazrul Islam *Acting President*	1982–3	Abdul Fazal Mohammad Ahsanuddin Chowdhury
1972	Mujibur Rahman	1983–90	Hossain Mohammad Ershad
1972–3	Abu Saeed Chowdhury	1990–1	Shehabuddin Ahmed *Acting President*
1973–5	Mohammad Mohammadullah		
1975	Mujibur Rahman	1991–6	Abdur Rahman Biswas
1975	Khondaker Mushtaq Ahmad	1996–2001	Shehabuddin Ahmed
1975–7	Abu Saadat Mohammad Sayem	2001–2	A Q M Badruddoza Chowdhury
1977–81	Zia Ur-Rahman	2002–	Iajuddin Ahmed
1981–2	Abdus Sattar		

Prime Minister

1971–2	Tajuddin Ahmed	1986–8	Mizanur Rahman Chowdhury
1972–5	Mujibur Rahman	1988–90	Kazi Zafar Ahmed
1975	Mohammad Monsur Ali	1991–6	Khaleda Zia
1975–9	*Martial Law*	1996	Mohammad Habibur Rahman
1979–82	Mohammad Azizur Rahman	1996–2001	Sheikh Hasina Wajed
1982–4	*Martial Law*	2001–	Khaleda Zia
1984–5	Ataur Rahman Khan		

Water Lilies and Jackfruit

The national symbol of Bangladesh is the water lily, known in Bangla as the *shapla*, and the national fruit is the huge and distinctive jackfruit, called *kathal*. The little magpie robin, or *doel*, is the national bird. Bangladesh's national sport is *kabaddi*, a team game that's popular across India and south-east Asia; it is a version of tag played barefoot by two teams of seven.

BARBADOS

Official name	Barbados	**Religions**	Christianity 71% (Prot and others 67%, RC 4%), none/unaffiliated 17%, others 12%
Local name	Barbados		
Independence	1966		
Area	430 sq km/166 sq mi	**Time zone**	GMT −4
Capital	Bridgetown	**Currency**	1 Barbados Dollar (BD$/BBD) = 100 cents
Chief towns	Speightstown		
Population	270 000 (2005e)	**Telephone**	+1 246
Nationality	Barbadian or Bajan (informal)	**Internet**	.bb
		Country code	BRB
Languages	English		
Ethnic groups	black 80%, others 16%, white 4%		

Location
An independent state and the most easterly of the Caribbean Islands, situated in the northern Atlantic Ocean to the north of Guyana.

Physical description
A small, triangular island, 32km/20mi long (north-west to south-east); it rises to 340m/1 115ft at Mt Hillaby and is ringed by a coral reef.

Climate
Tropical, with an average annual temperature of 27°C.

National holidays
Jan 1, 21 (Errol Barrow), Apr 28 (National Heroes), May 1, Aug 1 (Emancipation), Dec 1 (Independence), Dec 25, 26; EM, GF, WM, Kadooment (Aug).

Political leaders

Head of State: British monarch, represented by Governor General (Sir Clifford Husbands since 1996).

Prime Minister

1966–76	Errol Walton Barrow	1986–7	Errol Walton Barrow
1976–85	J M G (Tom) Adams	1987–94	L Erskine Sandiford
1985–6	H Bernard St John	1994–	Owen Arthur

Bearded Ones

Bearded fig trees (*Ficus citrifolia*) used to be common in Barbados. When the Portuguese explorer Pedro a Campos visited in 1536, he named the island *Los Barbados*, meaning 'the bearded ones', in recognition of these trees. The tree is still featured on the national coat of arms, along with the national flower, the Pride of Barbados. The coat of arms also features a dolphin, a pelican, sugar cane and the motto 'Pride and Industry'. The national flag's ultramarine stripes represent the sea and sky and the golden centre represents the island's beautiful beaches. It also features the trident of Neptune, the ancient sea god.

BARBUDA *see* **ANTIGUA AND BARBUDA**

BELARUS

Official name	Republic of Belarus		Bobruysk, Grodno, Brest
Local name	Belarus; Respublika Belarus	**Population**	9 755 000 (2005e)
		Nationality	Belarussian
Former name	Belorussian People's Republic (1918–19), Byelorussian or Belorussian Soviet Socialist Republic (until 1991), within the Union of Soviet Socialist Republics (USSR; 1922–91); sometimes also formerly known as Byelorussia, Belorussia, Byelarus or White Russia	**Languages**	Belarussian, Russian
		Ethnic groups	Belarussian 78%, Russian 13%, Polish 4%, Ukrainian 3%, others 2%
		Religions	Christianity 72% (Orthodox 60%, RC 8%, Prot 4%), others 28% (including Islam and Judaism)
		Time zone	GMT +2
Independence	1991	**Currency**	1 Belarussian Rouble (BR/BYR) = 100 kopeks
Area	207 600 sq km/80 134 sq mi	**Telephone**	+375
Capital	Minsk	**Internet**	.by
Chief towns	Gomel, Vitebsk, Mogilev,	**Country code**	BLR

Location
A republic in eastern Europe, bounded to the north by Latvia; to the north and east by Russia; to the south by Ukraine; to the west by Poland; and to the north-west by Lithuania.

Physical description
Largely flat, with low hills in the north-west rising to 345m/1 132ft at Dzyarzhynskaya Hara; c.11 000 lakes; one-third of the country is covered by forests.

Climate
Mild winters and cool summers.

National holidays
Jan 1, 7 (Orthodox Christmas), Mar 8 (Women), May 1, 6 (Memorial/Radounitsa), 9 (Victory), Jul 3 (Independence), Nov 7 (Oct Revolution), Dec 25; ES, Orthodox Easter Sunday.

Political leaders

Chair of Supreme Soviet
1991–4	Stanislav Shushkevich
1994–6	Mecheslav Grib

President
1994–	Alexander Lukashenko

Prime Minister
1990–4	Vyacheslav Kebich	2000–1	Uladzimir Yarmoshyn
1994–6	Mikhail Chigir	2001–3	Gennady Vasilyevich Novitsky
1996–2000	Sergei Ling	2003–	Sergey Sidorsky

BELAU *see* **PALAU**

BELGIUM

Official name	Kingdom of Belgium	**Languages**	Flemish (Dutch), French, German (mainly on the eastern border); Brussels is officially a bilingual city (French and Flemish)
Local name	Belgique; Royaume de Belgique (French), België; Koninkrijk België (Flemish), Belgien; Königreich Belgien (German)		
		Ethnic groups	Fleming 55%, Walloon 33%, Italian 2%, Moroccan 1%, others 9%
Independence	1830		
Area	32 545 sq km/12 562 sq mi	**Religions**	Christianity 85% (RC 75%, Prot 10%), none/ unaffiliated 10%, Islam 2%, others 3%
Capital	Brussels; Bruxelles (French), Brussel (Flemish), Brüssel (German)		
		Time zone	GMT +1
Chief towns	Antwerp, Ghent, Charleroi, Liège, Bruges, Namur, Mons	**Currency**	1 Euro (€/EUR) = 100 cents
		Telephone	+32
Population	10 419 000 (2005e)	**Internet**	.be
Nationality	Belgian	**Country code**	BEL

Location
A kingdom in north-western Europe, bounded to the north by the Netherlands; to the east by Germany; to the south-east by Luxembourg; to the south by France; and to the north-west by the North Sea.

Physical description
Mostly low-lying fertile agricultural land, with some hills in the south-east (Ardennes); highest point is Signal de Botrange (694m/2 277ft); low-lying dune-fringed coastline; main rivers drain across the Dutch border and are linked by a network of canals.

Climate
Cool and temperate with strong maritime influences.

National holidays
Jan 1, May 1, Jul 21 (Independence), Aug 15, Nov 1, 11 (Armistice), Dec 25; A, EM, ES, WM; *also community holidays (Jul 11 Flemish, Sep 27 French, Nov 15 German).*

Political leaders

Belgium became an independent kingdom in 1831. A national congress elected Prince Leopold of Saxe-Coburg as king.

Monarch

1831–65	Léopold I		1944–50	Prince Charles *Regent*
1865–1909	Léopold II		1950–93	Baudouin *Regent 1950–2*
1909–34	Albert I		1993–	Albert II
1934–51	Léopold III			

Prime Minister

1899–1907	Paul de Smet de Nayer		1918	Gerhard Cooreman
1907–8	Jules de Trooz		1918–20	Léon Delacroix
1908–11	Frans Schollaert		1920–1	Henri Carton de Wiart
1911–18	Charles de Broqueville		1921–5	Georges Theunis

1925	Alois van de Vyvere	1950–2	Joseph Pholien
1925–6	Prosper Poullet	1952–4	Jean van Houtte
1926–31	Henri Jaspar	1954–8	Achille van Acker
1931–2	Jules Renkin	1958–61	Gaston Eyskens
1932–4	Charles de Broqueville	1961–5	Théodore Lefèvre
1934–5	Georges Theunis	1965–6	Pierre Harmel
1935–7	Paul van Zeeland	1966–8	Paul Vanden Boeynants
1937–8	Paul Émile Janson	1968–73	Gaston Eyskens
1938–9	Paul Spaak	1973–4	Edmond Leburton
1939–45	Hubert Pierlot	1974–8	Léo Tindemans
1945–6	Achille van Acker	1978	Paul Vanden Boeynants
1946	Paul Spaak	1979–81	Wilfried Martens
1946	Achille van Acker	1981	Marc Eyskens
1946–7	Camille Huysmans	1981–91	Wilfried Martens
1947–9	Paul Spaak	1992–9	Jean-Luc Dehaene
1949–50	Gaston Eyskens	1999–	Guy Verhofstadt
1950	Jean Pierre Duvieusart		

BELIZE

Official name	Belize		Creole languages are also spoken
Local name	Belize		
Former name	British Honduras (until 1973)	**Ethnic groups**	mestizo 44%, Creole 30%, Maya 11%, Garifuna 7%, others 8%
Independence	1981	**Religions**	Christianity 92% (RC 62%, Prot 30%), none/ unaffiliated 2%, others 6%
Area	22 963 sq km/8 864 sq mi		
Capital	Belmopan		
Chief towns	Belize City, Dangriga, Punta Gorda, San Ignacio	**Time zone**	GMT –6
Population	270 000 (2005e)	**Currency**	1 Belize Dollar (BZ$/BZD) = 100 cents
Nationality	Belizean	**Telephone**	+501
Languages	English; Spanish and local Mayan, Carib and	**Internet**	.bz
		Country code	BLZ

Location
An independent state in Central America, bounded to the north by Mexico; to the east by the Caribbean Sea; and to the south and west by Guatemala.

Physical description
An extensive coastal plain, swampy in the north, more fertile in the south; Maya Mountains extend almost to the east coast, rising to 1 120m/3 674ft at Victoria Peak; inner coastal waters are protected by the world's second longest barrier reef.

Climate
Generally subtropical but tempered by trade winds; coastal temperatures vary between 10°C and 36°C, with a greater range in the mountains; variable rainfall; dry season in Feb–May; hurricanes can cause severe damage.

National holidays
Jan 1, Mar 9 (Baron Bliss), May 1, 24 (Commonwealth), Sep 10 (St George's Caye), 21 (Independence), Oct 12 (Columbus), Nov 19 (Garifuna Settlement), Dec 25, 26; EM, GF, HS.

Political leaders

Head of State: British Monarch, represented by Governor General (Sir Colville Young since 1993).

Prime Minister

1981–4	George Cadle Price	1993–8	Manuel Esquivel
1985–9	Manuel Esquivel	1998–	Said Wilbert Musa
1989–93	George Cadle Price		

Flourishing in the Shade

The national motto of Belize is *Sub Umbra Florero*, which means 'Under the shade I flourish'. Belize's national tree is the mahogany and its national flower is the black orchid. The colourful keel-billed toucan is the national bird.

BENIN

Official name	Republic of Benin	**Nationality**	Beninese
Local name	Bénin; République du Bénin	**Languages**	French; local languages are also spoken
Former name	Dahomey (until 1975); People's Republic of Benin (1975–90)	**Ethnic groups**	Fon 39%, Bariba 21%, Yoruba 10%, others 30%
Independence	1960	**Religions**	traditional beliefs 61%, Christianity 22% (RC 19%, Prot 3%), Islam 17%
Area	112 622 sq km/43 472 sq mi		
Capital	Porto Novo (administrative and constitutional) and Cotonou (economic and seat of government)	**Time zone**	GMT +1
		Currency	1 CFA Franc (CFAFr/XOF) = 100 centimes
		Telephone	+229
Chief towns	Ouidah, Abomey, Kandi, Parakou, Natitingou	**Internet**	.bj
		Country code	BEN
Population	8 439 000 (2005e)		

Location
A republic in West Africa, bounded to the north by Niger; to the east by Nigeria; to the south by the Bight of Benin in the Gulf of Guinea; to the west by Togo; and to the north-west by Burkina Faso.

Physical description
Rises from a 100km/62mi sandy coast with lagoons, to low-lying plains, then to a savannah plateau at c.400m/1 300ft; the Atakora Mountains rise to over 500m/1 640ft in the north-west; highest point is Mt Sokbaro (658m/2 159ft); several rivers.

Climate
Tropical climate, with three zones; south has rain throughout year, especially during the 'Guinea Monsoon' (May–Oct); centre has two rainy seasons (peaks in May–Jun and Oct); north has one (Jul–Sep).

National holidays
Jan 1, 10 (Traditional religions), May 1, Aug 1 (National), 15, Nov 1, Dec 25; A, Ad, EM, WM.

Political leaders

Dahomey

President

1960–3	Hubert Coutoucou Maga	1968–9	Émile Derlin Zinsou
1963–4	Christophe Soglo	1969–70	*Presidential Committee*
1964–5	Sourou Migan Apithy		(Maurice Kouandété)
1965	Justin Tométin Ahomadegbé	1970–2	*Presidential Committee* (Hubert
1965	Tairou Congacou		Coutoucou Maga)
1965–7	Christophe Soglo	1972–5	Mathieu Kérékou
1967–8	Alphonse Amadou Alley		

Prime Minister

1958–9	Sourou Migan Apithy	1965–7	*As President*
1959–60	Hubert Coutoucou Maga	1967–8	Maurice Kouandété
1960–4	*As President*	1968–75	*As President*
1964–5	Justin Tométin Ahomadegbé		

People's Republic of Benin

President and Prime Minister

1975–90   Mathieu (from 1980, sometimes called Ahmed) Kérékou

Republic of Benin

President

1990–1	Mathieu Kérékou
1991–6	Nicéphore Soglo
1996–	Mathicu Kćrékou

Prime Minister

1990–1	Nicéphore Soglo	1996–8	Adrien Houngbedgi
1991–6	*As President*	1998	*Post abolished*

BERMUDA *see* **UNITED KINGDOM**

BHUTAN

Official name	Kingdom of Bhutan		35%, others 15%
Local name	Druk Yul	**Religions**	Buddhism 73%,
Area	46 600 sq km/18 000 sq		Hinduism 22%, Islam 5%
	mi	**Time zone**	GMT +6
Capital	Thimphu	**Currency**	1 Ngultrum (Nu/BTN) =
Chief towns	Phuntsholing		100 chetrum; the Indian
Population	2 163 000 (2005e)		rupee is also used.
Nationality	Bhutanese	**Telephone**	+975
Languages	Dzongkha	**Internet**	.bt
Ethnic groups	Bhote 50%, Nepalese	**Country code**	BTN

Location
A state in the eastern Himalayas, bounded to the north by China and to the south by India.

Physical description
High peaks of the east Himalayas, reaching over 7 000m/22 966ft in the north; highest point is Kula Kangri (7 553m/24 780ft); forested mountain ridges with fertile valleys descend to low foothills in the south; many rivers flow to meet the River Brahmaputra.

Climate
Permanent snowfields and glaciers in the mountains; subtropical forest in the south; torrential rain is common.

National holidays
May 2 (Birthday of Jigme Dorji Wangchuk), Jun 2 (Coronation of Fourth Hereditary King), Jul 21 (First Sermon of Lord Buddha, Death of Jigme Dorji Wangchuk), Nov 11–13 (Birthday of HM Jigme Singye Wangchuk), Dec 17 (National).

Political leaders

Monarch (Druk Gyalpo)

1907–26	Uggyen Wangchuk	1952–72	Jigme Dorji Wangchuk
1926–52	Jigme Wangchuk	1972–	Jigme Singye Wangchuk

Prime Minister

1952–64	Jigme Palden Dorji	2000–1	Lyonpo Yeshey Zimba
1964	Lhendup Dorji	2001–2	Lyonpo Khandu
	Acting Prime Minister		Wangchuk
1964–98	*No Prime Minister*	2002–3	Lyonpo Kinzang Dorji
1998–99	Lyonpo Jigme Yozer Thinley	2003–4	Lyonpo Jigme Thinley
1999–2000	Lyonpo Sangye Ngedup	2004–	Lyonpo Yeshey Zimba

Land of the Thunder Dragon

The name Bhutan is thought to come from the Sanskrit word *Bhu-uttan*, meaning 'high land'. However, the Bhutanese people call their country *Druk Yul*, meaning 'Land of the Thunder Dragon'.

BOLIVIA

Official name	Republic of Bolivia	**Languages**	Spanish, Quechua, Ayamará
Local name	Bolivia; República de Bolivia	**Ethnic groups**	mestizo 30%, Quechua 30%, Aymará 25%, European 10%, others 5%
Independence	1825		
Area	1 098 580 sq km/424 052 sq mi		
Capital	La Paz (administrative) and Sucre (official and legislative)	**Religions**	Christianity 97% (RC 92%, Prot 5%), Baha'i 3%
		Time zone	GMT –4
Chief towns	Cochabamba, El Alto, Oruro, Potosí, Santa Cruz	**Currency**	1 Boliviano ($b/BOB) = 100 centavos
Population	9 182 000 (2005e)	**Telephone**	+591
Nationality	Bolivian	**Internet**	.bo
		Country code	BOL

Location
A republic in western South America, bounded to the north and east by Brazil; to the south-east by Paraguay; to the south by Argentina; to the south-west by Chile; and to the west by Peru.

Physical description
Bounded to the west by the Andes, rising to 6 542m/21 463ft at Nevado Sajama; flat 400km/250mi Altiplano Plateau in the east which lies at 3 600m/11 811ft above sea level; major lakes are Titicaca on the Peruvian border and Poopó; several rivers.

Climate
Varies, according to altitude; humid and tropical in the lowlands, cold and semi-arid in the mountains.

National holidays
Jan 1, May 1, Aug 6 (Independence), Nov 2, Dec 25; C, CC, GF.

Political leaders

President

1899–1904	José Manuel Pando		*and* Alfredo Ovando Candía
1904–9	Ismael Montes	1966	Alfredo Ovando Candía
1909–13	Heliodoro Villazón	1966–9	René Barrientos Ortuño
1913–17	Ismael Montes	1969	Luis Adolfo Siles Salinas
1917–20	José N Gutiérrez Guerra	1969–70	Alfredo Ovando Candía
1920–5	Bautista Saavedra	1970	Rogelio Mirando
1925–6	José Cabina Villanueva	1970–1	Juan José Torres Gonzales
1926–30	Hernando Siles	1971–8	Hugo Banzer Suárez
1930	Roberto Hinojusa *President of*	1978	Juan Pereda Asbún
	Revolutionaries	1978–9	*Military Junta* (David
1930–1	Carlos Blanco Galindo		Padilla Arericiba)
1931–4	Daniel Salamanca	1979	Walter Guevara Arze
1934–6	José Luis Tejado Sorzano	1979–80	Lydia Gueiler Tejada
1936–7	David Toro	1980–1	*Military Junta* (Luis García
1937–9	Germán Busch		Meza)
1939–40	Carlos Quintanilla *(provisional)*	1981–2	*Military Junta* (Celso
1940–3	Enrique Peñaranda y del Castillo		Torrelio Villa)
1943–6	Gualberto Villaroel	1982	Guido Vildoso Calderón
1946	Nestor Guillen	1982–5	Hernán Siles Suazo
1946–7	Tomas Monje Gutiérrez	1985–9	Víctor Paz Estenssoro
1947–9	Enrique Hertzog	1989–93	Jaime Paz Zamora
1949–51	Mamerto Urriolagoitía	1993–7	Gonzalo Sánchez de Lozada
1951–2	Hugo Ballivián	1997–2001	Hugo Bánzer Suárez
1952	Hernán Siles Suazo	2001–2	Jorge Quiroga Ramírez
1952–6	Víctor Paz Estenssoro	2002–3	Gonzalo Sánchez de Lozada
1956–60	Hernán Siles Suazo	2003–5	Carlos Mesa
1960–4	Víctor Paz Estenssoro	2005–	Eduardo Rodríguez *Acting*
1964–5	René Barrientos Ortuño		*President*
1965–6	René Barrientos Ortuño		

Highest Capital

La Paz is the highest capital city in the world, with an altitude of 3 665 m/12 024ft. However, it is itself dwarfed by Mt Illimani, which at 6 402m/21 004ft towers above the city to the south-east. La Paz was founded in 1548 by the Spanish.

BOSNIA AND HERZEGOVINA

Official name	Republic of Bosnia and Herzegovina; sometimes also known as Bosnia-Herzegovina	**Chief towns**	Banja Luka, Zenica, Tuzla, Mostar
Local name	Bosna i Hercegovina; Republika Bosna i Hercegovina	**Population**	3 907 000 (2005e)
		Nationality	Bosnian, Herzegovinian
		Languages	Bosnian, Serbian, Croatian
Former name	formerly part of the Kingdom of Serbs, Croats and Slovenes (until 1929), Kingdom of Yugoslavia (1929–41), Federal People's Republic of Yugoslavia (1945–63), Socialist Federal People's Republic of Yugoslavia (1963–92)	**Ethnic groups**	Bosniak 40%, Serb 31%, Croat 19%
		Religions	Christianity 50% (Orthodox 31%, RC 15%, Prot 4%), Islam 40%, none/unaffiliated 1%, others 9%
		Time zone	GMT +1
Independence	1992	**Currency**	1 Convertible Mark (KM/BAM) = 100 pfennige
Area	51 129 sq km/19 736 sq mi	**Telephone**	+387
Capital	Sarajevo	**Internet**	.ba
		Country code	BIH

Location
A republic in central Europe; bounded to the north and west by Croatia; and to the east and south by Serbia and Montenegro.

Physical description
Mountainous and includes part of the Dinaric Alps; highest point is Maglic (2 386m/7 828ft); it is noted for its limestone gorges.

Climate
Continental, with hot summers and cold winters.

National holidays
Jan 9 (Republic), Mar 1 (Independence), May 1, Nov 25 (Republic).

Political leaders

See **Serbia and Montenegro** for political leaders of the former Yugoslavia.

Republic

Chairman of the Presidency

1990–8	Alija Izetbegović	2002–3	Mirko Šarović
1998–9	Živko Radišić	2003	Borislav Paravac
1999–2000	Ante Jelavić	2003–4	Dragan Čović
2000	Alija Izetbegović	2004	Sulejman Tihić
2000–1	Živko Radišić	2004–5	Borislav Paravac
2001–2	Jozo Križanović	2005–	Ivo Miro Jovic
2002	Beriz Belkić		

Note: Tripartite presidency rotates every eight months; at the time of going to press, Borislav Paravac (Serb), Sulejman Tihić (Muslim) and Ivo Miro Jovic (Croat).

Prime Minister

1990–2	Jure Pelivan		2000	Spasoje Tusevljak
1992–3	Mile Akmadzic		2000–1	Martin Raguz
1993–6	Haris Silajdžic		2001	Bozidar Matic
1996–7	Hasan Muratovic		2001–2	Zlatko Lagumdzija
1997–9	Boro Bosic *co-Prime Minister*		2002	Dragan Mikerevic
1997–2000	Haris Silajdžic *co-Prime Minister*		2002–	Adnan Terzic
1999–2000	Svetozar Mihajlovic *co-Prime Minister*			

Federation[1]

President

1994–7	Krešimir Zubak		2000–1	Ejup Ganić
1997	Vladimir Šoljić		2001–2	Karlo Filipović
1997–8	Ejup Ganić		2002–3	Safet Halilović
1999–2000	Ivo Andrić-Lužanski		2003–	Niko Lozančić

Prime Minister

1994–6	Haris Silajdžic		2001–3	Alija Behmen
1996	Izudin Kapetanovic		2003–	Ahmet Hadžipašić
1996–2001	Edhem Bicakcić			
2001	Dragan Čović *Acting Prime Minister*			

Republika Srpska[2]

President

1992–6	Radovan Karadzic		2000–2	Mirko Šarović
1996–8	Biljana Plavšic		2002–	Dragan Čavić
1998–9	Nikola Poplašen			

Prime Minister

1992–3	Branko Djeric		1998–2001	Milorad Dodik
1993–4	Vladimir Lukic		2001–3	Mladen Ivanic
1994–5	Dusan Kozic		2003–5	Dragan Mikerevic
1995–6	Rajko Kasagic		2005–	Pero Bukejlovic
1996–8	Gojko Klickovic			

[1] *Bosnian Croat Federation.*   [2] *Bosnian Serb Republic.*

BOTSWANA

Official name	Republic of Botswana		noun), Tswana (adjective)
Local name	Botswana	**Languages**	Setswana, English
Former name	Bechuanaland (until 1966)	**Ethnic groups**	Tswana 80%, Shona
Independence	1966		12%, San 3%, others 5%
Area	582 096 sq km/224 689 sq mi	**Religions**	traditional beliefs 50%, Christianity 50% (predominantly Prot)
Capital	Gaborone		
Chief towns	Francistown, Lobatse, Selebi-Phikwe, Orapa, Jwaneng	**Time zone**	GMT +2
		Currency	1 Pula (P/BWP) = 100 thebe
Population	1 765 000 (2005e)	**Telephone**	+267
Nationality	Motswana (singular noun), Batswana (plural	**Internet**	.bw
		Country code	BWA

Location
A republic in southern Africa, bounded to the north and west by Namibia; to the north by Zambia; to the east by Zimbabwe; and to the south by South Africa.

Physical description
Kalahari desert covers 84% of the land, at an average elevation of c.1 100m/3 609ft; most people live in the fertile east, bordered by the River Limpopo; highest point is Otse Mountain (1 491m/4 892ft); rich Okavango River delta in the north-west.

Climate
Largely subtropical, increasingly arid in the south and west; rainfall in the north and east falls almost totally in summer (Oct–Apr); average maximum daily temperatures 23–32°C; annual rainfall is erratic in the Kalahari Desert.

National holidays
Jan 1, 2, May 1, Jul 1 (Sir Seretse Khama), Sep 30 (Botswana), Dec 25, 26; A, EM, GF, HS, President's Day (Jul); Jul, Oct Public Holidays.

Political leaders

President

1966–80	Seretse Khama
1980–98	Ketumile Masire
1998–	Festus Mogae

Kalahari Country

The Kalahari desert covers 84% of Botswana. Known as 'Kgalagadi' in the Setswana language, the desert landscape varies from sand dunes and salt pans to mile upon mile of scrubland and stunted trees. The Central Kalahari Game Reserve covers 52 800 sq km/20 400 sq mi – an area larger than Switzerland.

BOUVET ISLAND *see* **NORWAY**

BRAZIL

Official name	Federative Republic of Brazil	**Languages**	Portuguese
Local name	Brasil; República Federativa do Brasil	**Ethnic groups**	white 55%, mixed 22%, black 12%, others 11%
Independence	1822	**Religions**	Christianity 94% (RC 87%, Prot 7%), none 3%, others 3%
Area	8 511 965 sq km/ 3 285 618 sq mi	**Time zone**	GMT –2/5
Capital	Brasília	**Currency**	1 Brazilian Real (R$/BRL) = 100 centavos
Chief towns	São Paulo, Rio de Janeiro, Belo Horizonte, Recife, Salvador	**Telephone**	+55
		Internet	.br
Population	186 405 000 (2005e)	**Country code**	BRA
Nationality	Brazilian		

Location
A republic in eastern and central South America, bounded to the north-west by Colombia; to the north by Venezuela, Guyana, Suriname and French Guiana; to the east by the Atlantic Ocean; to the south by Uruguay; to the south-west by Argentina and Paraguay; and to the west by Peru and Bolivia.

Physical description
The low-lying Amazon basin in the north is drained by rivers that carry one fifth of the earth's running water; the highest peak is Pico da Neblina (3 014m/9 888ft) in the south; 30% of the population live on a narrow coastal strip c.100km/62mi wide.

Climate
Almost entirely tropical; the Equator passes through the north, and the Tropic of Capricorn through the south-east; the Amazon basin has no dry season, with average midday temperatures of 27–32°C; long droughts in the north-east with daily temperatures 21–36°C; hot and tropical on the coast; seasonal, temperate climate in the far south.

National holidays
Jan 1, Apr 21 (Tiradentes), May 1, Sep 7 (Independence), Oct 12 (Our Lady of Aparecida), Nov 2, 15 (Proclamation of the Republic), Dec 25; C (5), CC, GF; *much local variation*.

Political leaders

President

1898–1902	Manuel Ferraz de Campos Sales	1956–61	Juscelino Kubitschek de Oliveira
1902–6	Francisco de Paula Rodrigues Alves	1961	Jânio da Silva Quadros
		1961–3	João Belchior Marques Goulart
1906–9	Alfonso Pena	1963	Pascoal Ranieri Mazilli
1909–10	Nilo Peçanha	1963–4	João Belchior Marques Goulart
1910–14	Hermes Rodrigues da Fonseca	1964	Pascoal Ranieri Mazilli
1914–18	Venceslau Brás Pereira Gomes	1964–7	Humberto de Alencar Castelo Branco
1918–19	Francisco de Paula Rodrigues Alves	1967–9	Artur da Costa e Silva
1919–22	Epitácio Pessoa	1969–74	Emílio Garrastazu Médici
1922–6	Artur da Silva Bernardes	1974–9	Ernesto Geisel
1926–30	Washington Luís Pereira de Sousa	1979–85	João Baptista de Oliveira Figueiredo
1930–45	Getúlio Dorneles Vargas	1985–90	José Sarney
1945–51	Eurico Gaspar Dutra	1990–2	Fernando Collor de Mello
1951–4	Getúlio Dorneles Vargas	1992–4	Itamar Franco
1954–5	João Café Filho	1994–2002	Fernando Henrique Cardoso
1955	Carlos Coimbra da Luz	2003–	Luiz Inacio Lula da Silva
1955–6	Nereu de Oliveira Ramos		

South American Giant

Brazil is the largest country in South America, and covers almost half the total area of the continent. It is crossed by both the equator and the Tropic of Capricorn, has North Atlantic and South Atlantic coasts, and borders every other South American country except Ecuador and Chile.

BRITISH ANTARCTIC TERRITORY *see* **UNITED KINGDOM**

BRITISH INDIAN OCEAN TERRITORY *see* **UNITED KINGDOM**

BRITISH VIRGIN ISLANDS *see* **UNITED KINGDOM**

BRUNEI DARUSSALAM

Official name	State of Brunei, Abode of Peace	Chinese are widely spoken
Local name	Brunei; Negara Brunei Darussalam	**Ethnic groups**	Malay 64%, Chinese 20%, others 16%
Independence	1984	**Religions**	Islam 65%, traditional beliefs and others 15%, Buddhism 12%, Christianity 8%
Area	5 765 sq km/2 225 sq mi	
Capital	Bandar Seri Begawan	**Time zone**	GMT +8
Chief towns	Kuala Belait, Seria, Muara, Bangar, Pekan Tutong	**Currency**	1 Brunei Dollar (B$/BND) = 100 cents
Population	374 000 (2005e)	**Telephone**	+673
Nationality	Bruneian	**Internet**	.bn
Languages	Malay; English and	**Country code**	BRN

Location

A state on the north-west coast of Borneo, south-eastern Asia, bounded by the South China Sea in the north-west, and on all other sides by Malaysia's Sarawak and Sabah states.

Physical description

Swampy coastal plain rising through foothills to a mountainous region on the Malaysian border; highest point is Bukit Pagon (1 850m/6 098ft); 75% is equatorial rainforest; the Limbang River Valley in Sarawak divides the state into two.

Climate

Tropical climate, with high temperatures and humidity, and no marked seasons; average daily temperature 24–30°C; rainfall in the interior is twice as high as on the coast.

National holidays

Jan 1, Feb 23 (National), May 31 (Royal Brunei Armed Forces), Jul 15 (Sultan's Birthday), Dec 25; Ad, ER (2), Isra' Me'raj, NY (Chinese), NY (Muslim), PB, R, Revelation of the Koran.

Political leaders

Monarch (Sultan)

1967–   Muda Hassanal Bolkiah Mu'izzadin Waddaulah

The Royal Umbrella

The red national crest of Brunei Darussalam is a striking feature in the centre of the state's yellow, white and black flag. The crest was developed from ancient royal symbols, and each element has a particular significance. At the top are the *bendera*, a small pennant, and the *payung ubor-ubor*, or royal umbrella, symbolizing the monarchy. Beneath is the *sayap*, two wings each with four feathers that represent the 'protection of justice, tranquillity, prosperity and peace', followed by the *bulan*, the crescent symbol of Islam, with the state's motto: 'always in service with God's guidance'. Finally, on each side of the crest is a *tangan* or *kimhap*, an outstretched hand, which the government explains as representing their 'pledge to promote welfare, peace and prosperity'. Beneath the crest is a scroll inscribed with the name Brunei Darussalam.

BULGARIA

Official name	Republic of Bulgaria	**Languages**	Bulgarian
Local name	Bălgarija; Republika Bălgarija	**Ethnic groups**	Bulgarian 85%, Turk 9%, others 6%
Former name	*as listed below under Political leaders*	**Religions**	Christianity 80% (Orthodox), Islam 13%, none/unaffiliated 5%, Judaism 1%, others 1%
Independence	1908		
Area	110 912 sq km/42 812 sq mi	**Time zone**	GMT +2
Capital	Sofia; Sofija	**Currency**	1 Bulgarian Lev (Lv/BGN) = 100 stotinki
Chief towns	Plovdiv, Varna, Ruse, Burgas, Stara Zagora, Pleven	**Telephone**	+359
		Internet	.bg
Population	7 726 000 (2005e)	**Country code**	BGR
Nationality	Bulgarian		

Location
A republic in south-eastern Europe, bounded to the north by Romania; to the east by the Black Sea; to the south-east by Turkey; to the south by Greece; to the south-west by Macedonia; and to the west by Serbia and Montenegro.

Physical description
Traversed west to east by the Balkan Mountains, rising to over 2 000m/6 562ft; Rhodope Mountains in the south-west rise to nearly 3 000m/9 842ft; highest point is Musala (2 925m/9 596ft); comparatively narrow lowlands stretch south from the River Danube.

Climate
Largely continental, with hot summers and cold winters, but to the south the climate is increasingly Mediterranean; winters are slightly warmer on the Black Sea coast.

National holidays
Jan 1, Mar 3 (National), May 1, 24 (Slavonic Script and Bulgarian Culture), Sep 6 (Unification), 22 (Independence), Dec 24, 25, 26; Orthodox Easter (Apr/May).

Political leaders

Tsardom of Bulgaria

Monarch

1887–1908	Ferdinand *Prince*	1918–43	Boris III
1908–18	Ferdinand I	1943–6	Simeon II

People's Republic of Bulgaria

President

1946–7	Vasil Kolarov	1964–71	Georgi Traikov
1947–50	Mincho Naichev	1971–89	Todor Zhivkov
1950–8	Georgi Damianov	1989–90	Petar Mladenov
1958–64	Dimitro Ganev		

Premier

1946–9	Georgi Dimitrov	1956–62	Anton Yugov
1949–50	Vasil Kolarov	1962–71	Todor Zhivkov
1950–6	Vulko Chervenkov	1971–81	Stanko Todorov

| 1981–6 | Grisha Filipov | 1990 | Andrei Lukanov |
| 1986–90 | Georgy Atanasov | 1990–1 | Dimitur Popov |

First Secretary

| 1946–53 | Vulko Chervenkov | 1989–90 | Petar Mladenov |
| 1953–89 | Todor Zhivkov | 1990 | Alexander Lilov |

Republic of Bulgaria

President

1990–7	Zhelyu Zhelev
1997–2002	Petar Stoyanov
2002–	Georgi Parvanov

Prime Minister

1991–2	Filip Dimitrov	1997	Stefan Sofiyanski
1992–4	Lyuben Berov		*Acting Prime Minister*
1994–5	Renate Indzhova	1997–2001	Ivan Kostov
	Acting Prime Minister	2001–5	Simeon Saxe-Coburg Gotha
1995–7	Zhan Videnov		(Simeon II)
		2005–	Sergey Stanishev

Return of the King

King Simeon II went into exile in 1946 when Bulgaria became a republic, and lived in Spain for more than 50 years. After the fall of communism he returned to Bulgaria in 2001 and was elected Prime Minister, becoming the first eastern European former monarch to return to power.

BURKINA FASO

Official name	Burkina Faso	**Ethnic groups**	Mossi 45%, Mande 10%, Fulani 9%, Bobo 7%, others 29%
Local name	Burkina Faso		
Former name	Upper Volta (until 1984)	**Religions**	traditional beliefs 45%, Islam 44%, Christianity 11% (RC 10%, others 1%)
Independence	1960		
Area	274 540 sq km/105 972 sq mi		
Capital	Ouagadougou	**Time zone**	GMT
Chief towns	Bobo-Dioulasso, Koudougou, Ouahigouya, Tenkodogo	**Currency**	1 CFA Franc (CFAFr/XOF) = 100 centimes
		Telephone	+226
Population	13 228 000 (2005e)	**Internet**	.bf
Nationality	Burkinabé	**Country code**	BFA
Languages	French; many local languages are also spoken		

Location
A republic in West Africa, bounded to the north by Mali; to the east by Niger; to the south-east by Benin; to the south by Togo and Ghana; and to the south-west by Côte d'Ivoire.

Physical description
Low-lying plateau, falling away to the south; highest point is Tena Kourou (749m/2 457ft); many rivers (tributaries of the Volta or Niger) are unnavigable in the dry season; wooded savannas in the south; semi-desert in the north.

Climate
Tropical climate; average temperature 27°C in the dry season (Dec–May); rainy season (Jun–Oct), with violent storms (Aug); the *harmattan* wind blows from the north-east (Dec–Mar); rainfall decreases from south to north.

National holidays
Jan 1, 3 (1966 Revolution), Mar 8 (Women), May 1, Aug 5 (Independence), 15, Nov 1, Dec 11 (National), 25; A, Ad, EM, ER, PB.

Political leaders

Upper Volta

President

1960–6	Maurice Yaméogo	1983–4	Thomas Sankara *Chairman of National Revolutionary Council*
1966–80	Sangoulé Lamizana		
1980	Saye Zerbo		
1982–3	Jean-Baptiste Ouedraogo *Chairman of People's Salvation Council*		

Burkina Faso

President

1984–7	Thomas Sankara *Chairman*
1987–	Blaise Compaoré

Prime Minister

1992–4	Youssouf Ouedraogo	1996–2000	Kadré Désiré Ouedraogo
1994–6	Roch Christian Kaboré	2000–	Paramanga Ernest Yonli

> ## Land of Honest Men
>
> Previously known as Upper Volta, after the upper reaches of the River Volta, Burkina Faso was renamed in 1984 by the politician Thomas Sankara (1950–87). The new name came from the local languages and means 'Land of Honest Men' or 'Land of Upright Men'.

BURMA *see* **MYANMAR**

BURUNDI

Official name	Republic of Burundi	Population	7 548 000 (2005e)
Local name	Burundi; République du Burundi (French), Republika y'UBurundi (Kirundi)	Nationality	Burundian
		Languages	French, Kirundi; Swahili is also spoken
Former name	Urundi, as part of Ruanda-Urundi (with Rwanda, until 1962), Kingdom of Burundi (1962–6)	Ethnic groups	Hutu 85%, Tutsi 14%, others 1%
		Religions	Christianity 70%, traditional beliefs 29%, Islam 1%
Independence	1962	Time zone	GMT +2
Area	27 834 sq km/10 744 sq mi	Currency	1 Burundi Franc (BuFr, FBu/BIF) = 100 centimes
Capital	Bujumbura	Telephone	+257
Chief towns	Bubanza, Ngozi, Muyinga, Muramvya, Gitega, Bururi, Rutana	Internet	.bi
		Country code	BDI

Location
A republic in central Africa, bounded to the north by Rwanda; to the east and south by Tanzania; to the south-west by Lake Tanganyika; and to the west by Democratic Republic of the Congo.

Physical description
Lies across the Nile–Congo watershed; bounded to the west by the narrow River Ruizi plain and Lake Tanganyika; River Akanyaru forms northern border; interior plateau at average height of c.1 500m/4 921ft; highest point is Mt Heha (2 670m/8 760ft).

Climate
Equatorial climate, varying with altitude and season; moderately wet, except during the dry season (Jun–Sep).

National holidays
Jan 1, May 1, Jul 1 (Independence), Aug 15, Sep 18 (Victory of Uprona), Nov 1, Dec 25; A.

Political leaders

Monarch
1962–6	Mwambutsa IV
1966	Ntare V

President
1966–77	Michel Micombero	1994–6	Sylvestre Ntibantunganya
1977–87	Jean-Baptiste Bagaza	1996–2003	Pierre Buyoya
1987–93	Military Junta (Pierre Buyoya)	2003–5	Domitien Ndayizeye
1993	Melchior Ndadaye	2005–	Pierre Nkurunziza
1994	Cyprien Ntaryamira		

Prime Minister
1961	Joseph Cimpaye	1964–5	Albin Nyamoya
1961	Louis Rwagasore	1965	Pierre Ngendandumwe
1962–3	André Muhirwa	1965	Pie Masumbuko Acting Prime Minister
1963–4	Pierre Ngendandumwe		

1965	Joseph Bamina	1988–93	Adrien Sibomana
1965–6	Léopold Biha	1993–4	Sylvie Kinigi
1966–76	Michel Micombero	1994–5	Anatole Kanyenkiko
1976–8	Edouard Nzambimana	1995–6	Antoine Nduwayo
1978–87	*No Prime Minister*	1996–8	Pascal-Firmin Ndimira
1987–8	Pierre Buyoya	1998–	*No Prime Minister*

Swiss Africa

Burundi's government has dubbed the country 'the heart of Africa', a 'Swiss Africa', the 'country of the thousand and one hills' and the 'country of eternal spring'.

CAICOS ISLANDS *see* **UNITED KINGDOM**

CAMBODIA

Official name	Kingdom of Cambodia	**Chief towns**	Battambang, Kâmpŏng Som, Kâmpŏng Chhnăng
Local name	Kâmpuchéa; Preăh Réaché 'Anachâkr Kâmpuchéa	**Population**	14 071 000 (2005e)
		Nationality	Cambodian
Former name	formerly part of Indochina (until 1953), Kingdom of Cambodia (1953–70), Khmer Republic (1970–6), Democratic Kampuchea (1976–9), People's Republic of Kampuchea (1979–89), State of Cambodia (1989–93)	**Languages**	Khmer; French is also widely spoken
		Ethnic groups	Khmer 93%, Chinese 3%, Vietnamese 2%, others 2%
		Religions	Buddhism 95%, Islam 2%, others 3%
		Time zone	GMT +7
Independence	1953	**Currency**	1 Riel (CRI/KHR) = 100 sen
Area	181 035 sq km/69 880 sq mi	**Telephone**	+855
		Internet	.kh
Capital	Phnom Penh; Phnum Pénh	**Country code**	KHM

Location
A republic in south-east Asia, bounded to the north-west by Thailand; to the north by Laos; to the east by Vietnam; and to the south and south-west by the Gulf of Thailand.

Physical description
Surrounds the Tonlé Sap (lake) on the Cambodian Plain, which is crossed by the floodplain of the Mekong River; Cardamom Mountains stretch 160km/100mi across the Thailand border, rising to 1 813m/5 948ft at Phnom Aural.

Climate
Tropical monsoon climate, with a wet season in May–Sep; heavy rainfall in the south-western mountains; high temperatures in the lowland region throughout the year.

National holidays
Jan 1, 7 (Victory over Genocide), Mar 8 (Women), Apr 3 (Culture), May 1, Jun 1 (Children), 18 (Queen's Birthday), Sep 24 (Constitution and Coronation), Oct 23 (Paris Peace Agreement), 30 (King's Birthday) (3), Nov 9 (Independence), Dec 10 (Human Rights); Cambodian New Year (Apr) (3), Pchum Ben (Sep) (3), Royal Ploughing Ceremony (May), Visakha Bochea (May), Water/Moon Festival (Nov) (3).

Political leaders

Monarch

1941–55	Norodom Sihanouk II
1955–60	Norodom Suramarit

Chief of State

1960–70	Prince Norodom Sihanouk

Khmer Republic Chief of State

1970–2	Cheng Heng *Acting Chief of State*	1976–81	Khieu Samphan
1972–5	Lon Nol	1981–91	Heng Samrin
1975–6	Prince Norodom Sihanouk		

President of Government in exile (until 1991)

1970–5	Prince Norodom Sihanouk
1982–93	Prince Norodom Sihanouk

Monarch

1993–2004	King Norodom Sihanouk
2004–	King Norodom Sihamoni

Prime Minister

1945–6	Son Ngoc Thanh	1956–7	Prince Norodom Sihanouk
1946–8	Prince Monireth	1957–8	Sim Var
1948–9	Son Ngoc Thanh	1958	Ek Yi Oun
1949–51	Prince Monipong	1958	Samdech Penn Nouth *Acting Prime Minister*
1951	Son Ngoc Thanh		
1951–2	Huy Kanthoul	1958	Sim Var
1952–3	Norodom Sihanouk II	1958–60	Prince Norodom Sihanouk
1953	Samdech Penn Nouth	1960–1	Pho Proung
1953–4	Chan Nak	1961	Samdech Penn Nouth
1954–5	Leng Ngeth	1961–3	Prince Norodom Sihanouk
1955–6	Prince Norodom Sihanouk	1963–6	Prince Norodom Kantol
1956	Oum Chheang Sun	1966–7	Lon Nol
1956	Prince Norodom Sihanouk	1967–8	Prince Norodom Sihanouk
1956	Khim Tit	1968–9	Samdech Penn Nouth
1956	Prince Norodom Sihanouk	1969–72	Lon Nol
1956	Sam Yun		

Khmer Republic Prime Minister

1972	Sisovath Sivik Matak	1975–6	Samdech Penn Nouth
1972	Son Ngoc Thanh	1976–9	Pol Pot
1972–3	Hang Thun Hak	1979–81	Khieu Samphan
1973	In Tam	1981–5	Chan Si
1973–5	Long Boret	1985–93	Hun Sen

Prime Minister (Government in exile until 1991)

1970–3	Samdech Penn Nouth	1997	Ung Huot *First Prime Minister*
1982–91	Son Sann		Hun Sen *Second Prime Minister*
1993–7	Norodom Ranariddh *First Prime Minister* Hun Sen *Second Prime Minister*	1998–	Hun Sen

CAMEROON

Official name	Republic of Cameroon	**Population**	16 322 000 (2005e)
Local name	Cameroun; République du Cameroun	**Nationality**	Cameroonian
		Languages	French, English; many local languages are also spoken
Former name	Kamerun (until 1919), French Cameroon (until 1960) and British Cameroon (until 1961, when south part joined new Republic of Cameroon, north part joined Nigeria), Federal Republic of Cameroon (1961–72), United Republic of Cameroon (1972–84)	**Ethnic groups**	Fang 21%, Bamileke and Bamum 19%, Douala, Luanda and Bassa 15%, Fulani 10%, others 35%
		Religions	Christianity 53% (RC 35%, Prot 18%), traditional beliefs 25%, Islam 22%
		Time zone	GMT +1
Independence	1960	**Currency**	1 CFA Franc (CFAFr/XAF) = 100 centimes
Area	475 439 sq km/183 519 sq mi	**Telephone**	+237
Capital	Yaoundé	**Internet**	.cm
Chief towns	Douala	**Country code**	CMR

Location
A republic in West Africa, bounded to the north-west by Nigeria; to the north-east by Chad; to the east by the Central African Republic; to the south-east by Congo; to the south by Gabon and Equatorial Guinea; and to the west by the Gulf of Guinea.

Physical description
Equatorial forest on the coastal plain rising to a central plateau of over 1 300m/4 265ft; west is forested and mountainous; active volcano Mt Cameroon (4 070m/13 352ft) is the highest peak in West Africa; savanna and semi-desert towards Lake Chad.

Climate
North has a wet season in Apr–Sep, dry the rest of the year; northern plains are semi-arid; equatorial south has rain throughout the year, with two wet seasons and two dry seasons; maximum daily temperatures in the south average 27–30°C.

National holidays
Jan 1, Feb 11 (Youth), May 1, 20 (National), Aug 15, Dec 25; A, Ad, ER, GF.

Political leaders

President
1960–82	Ahmadun Ahidjo
1982–	Paul Biya

Prime Minister
1960	Ahmadou Ahidjo
1960–1	Charles Assalé
1961–75	*No Prime Minister*
1975–82	Paul Biya
1982–3	Bello Bouba Maigari
1983–4	Luc Ayang
1984–91	*No Prime Minister*
1991–2	Sadou Hayatou
1992–6	Simon Achidi Achu
1996–2004	Peter Mafany Musonge
2004–	Ephraïm Inoni

Prawn River

In 1472 the Portuguese sailor Fernando Po sailed up the River Wouri in Douala. He was amazed at the number of prawns in the river, and so named the place *Rio dos Camarões*, or 'River of Prawns'. From *camarões* the name Cameroon evolved.

HUMAN GEOGRAPHY

CANADA

Official name	Canada		13%, Amerindian 4%, others 7%
Local name	Canada		*Percentages add to more than 100% as some people identify with more than one ethnicity.*
Area	9 970 610 sq km/ 3 848 655 sq mi		
Capital	Ottawa		
Chief towns	Calgary, Edmonton, Montréal, Québec, Toronto, Vancouver, Victoria, Winnipeg	**Religions**	Christianity 77% (RC 43%, Prot 29%, Orthodox 2%, other 3%), none 16%, others 7%
Population	32 268 000 (2005e)	**Time zone**	GMT –3.5/8
Nationality	Canadian	**Currency**	1 Canadian Dollar (C$, Can$/CAD) = 100 cents
Languages	English, French		
Ethnic groups	British origin 39%, Canadian 31%, other European 25%, French origin 20%, Irish origin	**Telephone**	+1
		Internet	.ca
		Country code	CAN

Location
An independent country in North America, bounded to the north-west by the US state of Alaska; to the north by the Arctic Ocean, Beaufort Sea and Baffin Bay; to the north-east by the Davis Strait; to the east by the Labrador Sea and the Atlantic Ocean; to the south by the United States of America; and to the west by the Pacific Ocean.

Physical description
North-east is dominated by the Canadian Shield; mountains of Nova Scotia and New Brunswick in the east; fertile lowlands in south Québec and Ontario; flat prairie country south and west of the Shield, stretching to the Western Cordillera, which includes the Rocky, Cassiar and Mackenzie mountains; Coast Mountains flank a rugged, heavily-indented coastline, rising to 5 950m/19 520ft at Mt Logan (highest peak); c.45% is forested; Great Lakes in south-east Ontario.

Climate
North coast is permanently ice-bound or obstructed by ice floes, except for Hudson Bay (frozen for c.9 months each year); cold air from the Arctic sweeps south and east in winter and spring; mild winters and warm summers on the west coast and some inland valleys of British Columbia; winter temperatures on the Atlantic shores are warmer than those of the interior, but summer temperatures are lower; much of the southern interior has warm summers and long, cold winters.

National holidays
Jan 1, Jul 1 (Canada), Nov 11 (Remembrance), Dec 25, 26; EM, GF, Labour (1st Mon in Sep), Thanksgiving (2nd Mon in Oct), Victoria (Mon preceding May 25).

Misdirected Names

Canada gained its name when early 16c explorers were directed by local indigenous people to the nearest village: *kanata* was the Huron-Iroquois word for 'settlement'. The explorers later used *kanata* to refer to the whole of the local area, and then to the larger region, and finally to everywhere north of the St Lawrence River. By the 1700s the name referred to a vast swathe of the continent.

Provinces of Canada

Name	Population (2005e)[1]	Area	Capital
Alberta (AB)	3 256 800	661 848 sq km/255 472 sq mi	Edmonton
British Columbia (BC)	4 254 500	944 735 sq km/364 667 sq mi	Victoria
Manitoba (MB)	1 177 600	647 797 sq km/250 050 sq mi	Winnipeg
New Brunswick (NB)	752 000	72 908 sq km/28 142 sq mi	Fredericton
Newfoundland and Labrador (NL)	516 000	405 212 sq km/156 412 sq mi	St John's
Northwest Territories (NT)	43 000	1 346 106 sq km/519 597 sq mi	Yellowknife
Nova Scotia (NS)	937 900	55 284 sq km/21 340 sq mi	Halifax
Nunavut (NU)	30 000	2 093 190 sq km/807 971 sq mi	Iqaluit
Ontario (ON)	12 541 400	1 076 395 sq km/415 488 sq mi	Toronto
Prince Edward Island (PE)	138 100	5 660 sq km/2 185 sq mi	Charlottetown
Québec (QC)	7 598 100	1 542 056 sq km/595 234 sq mi	Québec City
Saskatchewan (SK)	994 100	651 036 sq km/251 300 sq mi	Regina
Yukon Territory (YT)	31 000	482 443 sq km/186 223 sq mi	Whitehorse

[1] *Population figures are from Statistics Canada.*

Political leaders

Head of State: British monarch, represented by Governor General (Adrienne Clarkson since 1999).

Prime Minister

1867–73	John A Macdonald *Con*	1930–5	Richard Bedford Bennett *Con*
1873–8	Alexander Mackenzie *Lib*	1935–48	William Lyon Mackenzie King *Lib*
1878–91	John A Macdonald *Con*	1948–57	Louis St Laurent *Lib*
1891–2	John J C Abbot *Con*	1957–63	John George Diefenbaker *Con*
1892–4	John S D Thompson *Con*	1963–8	Lester Bowles Pearson *Lib*
1894–6	Mackenzie Bowell *Con*	1968–79	Pierre Elliott Trudeau *Lib*
1896	Charles Tupper *Con*	1979–80	Joseph Clark *Con*
1896–1911	Wilfrid Laurier *Lib*	1980–4	Pierre Elliott Trudeau *Lib*
1911–20	Robert Borden *Con/Un*	1984	John Turner *Lib*
1920–1	Arthur Meighen *Un/Con*	1984–93	Brian Mulroney *Con*
1921–6	William Lyon Mackenzie King *Lib*	1993	Kim Campbell *Con*
1926	Arthur Meighen *Con*	1993–2004	Jean Chrétien *Lib*
1926–30	William Lyon Mackenzie King *Lib*	2004–	Paul Martin *Lib*

Con = Conservative *Un = Unionist* *Lib = Liberal*

Long and Winding Road

The Trans-Canada Highway is the world's longest national highway. It runs 7 821km/ 4 860mi from St John's in Newfoundland and Labrador to Victoria in British Columbia.

Maple Leaves

The maple tree is the national tree of Canada, and the maple leaf its internationally recognized symbol. Ten species of maple tree grow in Canada: the *bigleaf, black, Douglas, Manitoba, mountain, red, silver, striped, sugar* and *vine maple*.

CANARY ISLANDS *see* **SPAIN**

CAPE VERDE

Official name	Republic of Cape Verde	**Ethnic groups**	mestizo 61%, African 29%, European 1%, others 9%
Local name	Cabo Verde; República de Cabo Verde		
Independence	1975	**Religions**	Christianity 98% (RC), none/unaffiliated 1%, others 1%
Area	4 033 sq km/1 557 sq mi		
Capital	Praia	**Time zone**	GMT −1
Chief towns	Mindelo	**Currency**	1 Cape Verde Escudo (CVEsc/CVE) = 100 centavos
Population	507 000 (2005e)		
Nationality	Cape Verdean		
Languages	Portuguese; Crioulo, a Creole language blending Portuguese and West African words, is spoken widely	**Telephone**	+238
		Internet	.cv
		Country code	CPV

Location
An island group in the Atlantic Ocean off the coast of West Africa.

Physical description
Islands are of volcanic origin, mostly mountainous; highest peak is Pico do Cano (2 829m/ 9 281ft), an active volcano on Fogo Island; coastal plains are semi-desert; savanna or thin forest lies on the mountains; fine, sandy beaches on most islands.

Climate
Located at the northern limit of the tropical rain belt; low and unreliable rainfall mainly in Aug and Sep; cooler and damper in the uplands; severe drought can occur; tropical heat; average temperatures at Praia range between 21°C (Jan) and 27°C (Oct).

National holidays
Jan 1, 13 (Democracy and Freedom), 20 (National Heroes), May 1, Jul 5 (Independence), Aug 15, Sep 12 (National), Nov 1, Dec 25; ES, GF, Ash Wednesday.

Political leaders

President

1975–91	Arístides Pereira
1991–2001	Antonio Mascarenhas Monteiro
2001–	Pedro Pires

Prime Minister

1975–91	Pedro Pires	2000–1	António Gualberto do Rosário
1991–2000	Carlos Wahnon Veiga	2001–	José Maria Neves

Black Sands

Cape Verde is renowned for its black sand beaches, such as that at Faja d'Agua on the small island of Brava. The black volcanic sand is rich in minerals, and is reputed to have beneficial medicinal qualities.

CAYMAN ISLANDS *see* **UNITED KINGDOM**

CENTRAL AFRICAN REPUBLIC

Official name	Central African Republic (CAR)	**Nationality**	Central African
Local name	République Centrafricaine (French), Ködörösêse tî Bêafrîka (Sango)	**Languages**	French, Sango
		Ethnic groups	Baya 34%, Banda 27%, Mandjia 21%, Sara 10%, others 8%
Former name	Ubangi Shari (until 1958), Central African Republic (1958–76), Central African Empire (1976–9)	**Religions**	Christianity 50% (Prot 25%, RC 25%), traditional beliefs 22%, Islam 14%, none/unaffiliated 13%, others 1%
Independence	1960		
Area	626 780 sq km/241 937 sq mi	**Time zone**	GMT +1
		Currency	1 CFA Franc (CFAFr/XAF) = 100 centimes
Capital	Bangui		
Chief towns	Berbérati, Bouar, Bossangoa	**Telephone**	+236
		Internet	.cf
Population	4 038 000 (2005e)	**Country code**	CAF

Location
A republic in central Africa, bounded to the north-west by Chad; to the north-east by Sudan; to the south by Democratic Republic of the Congo and Congo; and to the west by Cameroon.

Physical description
On a plateau forming the watershed between the Chad and Congo river basins; highest ground is in the north-east (Massif des Bongos) and north-west; highest point is Mont Ngaoui (1 420m/4 659ft).

Climate
Single rainy season in the north between May and Sep; more equatorial climate in the south; average temperatures at Bangui are 24–27°C.

National holidays
Jan 1, Mar 29 (Death of President Boganda), May 1, Jun 1 (Mothers), Aug 13 (Independence), 15, Sep 1 (Arrival of the Military Committee for National Recovery), Nov 1, Dec 1 (Republic), 25; A, EM, WM.

Political leaders

President

1960–6	David Dacko	1981–93	André Kolingba
1966–79	Jean-Bédel Bokassa	1993–2003	Ange-Félix Patasse
	(*from 1977,* Emperor Bokassa I)	2003–	François Bozizé

Prime Minister

1991–2	Edouard Frank	1997–9	Michel Gbezera-Bria
1992–3	Thimothée Malendoma	1999–2001	Anicet Georges Dologuélé
1993	Enoch Derant Lakoué	2001–3	Martin Ziguélé
1993–5	Jean-Luc Mandaba	2003	Abel Goumba
1995–6	Gabriel Koyambounou	2003–5	Célestin Gaombalet
1996–7	Jean-Paul Ngoupandé	2005–	Élie Doté

CHAD

Official name	Republic of Chad		spoken
Local name	Tchad; République du Tchad	**Ethnic groups**	Arab 26%, Sara 25%, Teda 18%, others 31%
Independence	1960	**Religions**	Islam 50%, Christianity 25% (RC 20%, Prot 5%), traditional beliefs 25%
Area	1 284 640 sq km/495 871 sq mi		
Capital	N'Djamena (also Ndjamena)	**Time zone**	GMT +1
		Currency	1 CFA Franc (CFAFr/XAF) = 100 centimes
Chief towns	Moundou, Sarh, Abéché		
Population	9 749 000 (2005e)	**Telephone**	+235
Nationality	Chadian	**Internet**	.td
Languages	French, Arabic; many local languages are also	**Country code**	TCD

Location
A republic in north central Africa, bounded to the north by Libya; to the east by Sudan; to the south by Central African Republic; and to the west by Cameroon, Nigeria and Niger.

Physical description
A mostly arid, semi-desert plateau at the edge of the Sahara Desert; Lake Chad lies in the south-west; Tibesti Mountains rise to 3 415m/11 204ft at Emi Koussi; vegetation is generally desert scrub or steppe; most people live in the tropical south.

Climate
Moderately wet in the south between May and Oct, but dry for the rest of the year; hot and arid north is almost rainless; central plain is hot and dry, with a brief rainy season during Jun–Sep.

National holidays
Jan 1, May 1, 25 (OAU Foundation), Aug 11 (Independence), Nov 1, 28 (Republic), Dec 25; Ad, EM, ES, ER.

Political leaders

President

1960–75	François Tombalbaye	1979	Mohammed Shawwa
1975–9	Supreme Military Council (Félix Malloum)	1979–82	Goukouni Oueddi
		1982–90	Hissène Habré
1979	Goukouni Oueddi	1990–	Idriss Déby

Prime Minister

1991–2	Jean Alingue Bawoyeu	1997–9	Nassour Ouaidou Guelendouksia
1992–3	Joseph Yodemane	1999–2002	Negoum Yamassoum
1993	Fidèle Moungar	2002–3	Haroun Kabadi
1993–5	Delwa Kassire Koumakoye	2003–5	Moussa Faki Mahamat
1995–7	Koibla Djimasta	2005–	Pascal Yoadimnadji

CHANNEL ISLANDS *see* **UNITED KINGDOM**

CHILE

Official name	Republic of Chile	**Ethnic groups**	mestizo 94%, Amerindian 6%
Local name	Chile; República de Chile		
Independence	1818	**Religions**	Christianity 88% (RC 80%, Prot 8%), none/unaffiliated 11%, others 1%
Area	756 626 sq km/292 058 sq mi		
Capital	Santiago	**Time zone**	GMT –4
Chief towns	Valparaíso, Concepción, Talcahuano, Antofagasta, Viña del Mar	**Currency**	1 Chilean Peso (Ch$/CLP) = 100 centavos
Population	16 295 000 (2005e)	**Telephone**	+56
Nationality	Chilean	**Internet**	.cl
Languages	Spanish	**Country code**	CHL

Location
A republic in south-western South America, bounded to the north by Peru and Bolivia; to the east by Argentina; and to the west by the Pacific Ocean.

Physical description
Narrow coastal belt, backed by Andean mountains rising in the north to 6 723m/22 057ft at Llullaillaco; highest point is Ojos del Salado (6 910m/22 660ft); lower mountains in the centre and south; fertile central valley; Atacama Desert lies in the far north-west.

Climate
Highly varied (spans 37° of latitude; altitudes from the Andean peaks to the coastal plain); extreme aridity in the Atacama Desert; cold, wet and windy in the far south; Mediterranean climate in centre, with warm, wet winters and dry summers.

National holidays
Jan 1, May 1, 21 (Navy), Aug 15, Sep 18 (Independence), 19 (Armed Forces), Oct 12 (Americas), Dec 8, 25, 26; CC, GF, EM, Aug public holiday, May public holiday.

Political leaders

President

1900–1	Federico Errázuriz Echaurren	1925–7	Emiliano Figueroa
1901	Aníbal Zañartu *Vice President*	1927–31	Carlos Ibáñez
1901–3	Germán Riesco	1931	Pedro Opaso Letelier *Vice President*
1903	Ramón Barros Luco *Vice President*		
1903–6	Germán Riesco	1931	Juan Esteban Montero *Vice President*
1906–10	Pedro Montt		
1910	Ismael Tocornal *Vice President*	1931	Manuel Trucco Franzani *Vice President*
1910	Elías Fernández Albano *Vice President*		
		1931–2	Juan Esteban Montero
1910	Emiliano Figueroa Larraín *Vice President*	1932	*Military Juntas*
		1932	Carlos G Dávila *Provisional President*
1910–15	Ramón Barros Luco		
1915–20	Juan Luis Sanfuentes	1932	Bartolomé Blanche *Provisional President*
1920–4	Arturo Alessandri		
1924–5	*Military Juntas*	1932	Abraham Oyanedel *Vice President*
1925	Arturo Alessandri		
1925	Luis Barros Borgoño *Vice President*	1932–8	Arturo Alessandri Palma
		1938–41	Pedro Aguirre Cerda

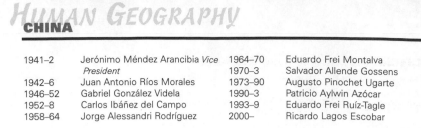

1941–2	Jerónimo Méndez Arancibia *Vice President*	1964–70	Eduardo Frei Montalva
1942–6	Juan Antonio Ríos Morales	1970–3	Salvador Allende Gossens
1946–52	Gabriel González Videla	1973–90	Augusto Pinochet Ugarte
1952–8	Carlos Ibáñez del Campo	1990–3	Patricio Aylwin Azócar
1958–64	Jorge Alessandri Rodríguez	1993–9	Eduardo Frei Ruíz-Tagle
		2000–	Ricardo Lagos Escobar

CHINA

Official name	People's Republic of China (PRC)		Yue (Cantonese), Wu, Minbei, Minnan, Xiang, Gan, Hakka; minority languages
Local name	Zhong Guo; Zhonghua Renmin Gongheguo		
Area	9 597 000 sq km/ 3 704 000 sq mi	**Ethnic groups**	Han 92%, others 8%
Capital	Beijing (formerly known as Peking)	**Religions**	none/unaffiliated 59%, Chinese folk religion 20%, Buddhism 6%, Islam 2%, others 13%
Chief towns	Shanghai, Tianjin, Shenyang, Wuhan, Guangzhou	**Time zone**	GMT +8
		Currency	1 Yuan ($, Y/CNY) = 10 jiao = 100 fen
Population	1 315 844 000 (2005e)		
Nationality	Chinese	**Telephone**	+86
Languages	standard Chinese (Putonghua) or Mandarin, also	**Internet**	.cn
		Country code	CHN

Location
A state in central and eastern Asia, bounded to the north-west by Kyrgyzstan and Kazakhstan; to the north by Mongolia and Russia; to the east by North Korea, the Yellow Sea and the East China Sea; to the south by the South China Sea, Vietnam, Laos, Myanmar, India, Bhutan and Nepal; and to the west by India, the disputed region of Jammu and Kashmir, Pakistan, Afghanistan and Tajikistan.

Physical description
Over two-thirds is upland, mountain and plateau; highest mountains are in the west, where the Tibetan Plateau rises to an average altitude of 4 000m/13 123ft; highest point is Mt Everest 8 850m/29 035ft; land descends to desert or semi-desert in Sinkiang and Inner Mongolia; broad fertile plains of Manchuria in the north-east and the densely forested Changpai Shan uplands; fertile southern plains and east coast are heavily populated.

Climate
Varied, with seven zones: (1) north-east has cold winters, with strong north winds and warm, humid summers; in Manchuria, the rivers are frozen for four to six months each year, and snow lies for 100–150 days; (2) centre has warm and humid summers, sometimes typhoons or tropical cyclones on the coast; (3) south, partly within the tropics, is the wettest area in summer; frequent typhoons (especially during Jul–Oct); (4) south-west has summer temperatures moderated by altitude, winters are mild with little rain; summers are wet on the mountains; (5) Tibet autonomous region, a high plateau surrounded by mountains, has severe winters with frequent light snow and hard frost, summers are warm, but nights are cold; (6) Xinjiang and the western interior has an arid desert climate with cold winters; (7) Inner Mongolia has an extreme continental-type climate, with cold winters and warm summers, and strong winds in winter and spring.

National holidays
Jan 1, May 1, Oct 1 (National) (2); Spring Festival (4) (Jan/Feb).

Special Administrative Regions
Hong Kong (HK)

Location	Comprises the Kowloon/New Territories peninsula and more than 200 islands in the South China Sea.

Local name	Xianggang; Xianggang Tebie Xingzhengqu	**Population**	7 041 000 (2005e)
		Internet	.hk
Area	16 sq km/6 sq mi	**Country code**	HGK

Macao

Location	Macao peninsula is linked by bridge and causeway to two islands in the South China Sea.

Local name	Aomen; Aomen Tebie Xingzhengqu; Macau (Portuguese)	**Population**	460 000 (2005e)
		Internet	.mo
		Country code	MAC
Area	1 067 sq km/412 sq mi		

Note: China also occupies the Paracel Islands in the South China Sea.

Political leaders

Dynasties

c.22–18cBC	Hsia	AD317–420	Eastern Chin
c.18–12cBC	Shang or Yin	AD420–589	Northern and Southern Dynasties
c.1111–256BC	Chou		
c.1111–770BC	Western Chou	581–618	Sui
770–256BC	Eastern Chou	618–907	Tang
770–476BC	Ch'un Ch'iu Period	907–960	Five Dynasties and Ten Kingdoms Period
475–221BC	Warring States Period		
221–206BC	Ch'in	960–1279	Sung
206BC–AD220	Han	960–1127	Northern Sung
206BC–AD9	Western Han	1127–1279	Southern Sung
AD9–23	Hsin Interregnum	1115–1234	Chin (Jurchen Tartars)
AD25–220	Eastern Han	1279–1368	Yuan (Mongol)
AD220–265	Three Kingdoms Period	1368–1644	Ming
AD265–420	Chin	1644–1912	Ch'ing or Qing (Manchu)
AD265–317	Western Chin		

Qing (Ch'ing) dynasty

Emperor

1875–1908	Guangxu (Kuang-hsü)
1908–12	Xuantong (Hsüan-t'ung)

Prime Minister

1901–3	Ronglu (Jung-lu)	1912	Lu Zhengxiang (Lu Cheng-hsiang)
1903–11	Prince Qing (Ch'ing)	1912	Yuan Shikai (Yüan Shih-k'ai)

Republic of China

President

1912	Sun Yat-sen (Sun Yixian) *Provisional*	1926–7	*Civil Disorder*
		1927–8	Zhang Zuolin (Chang Tso-lin)
1912–16	Yuan Shikai (Yüan Shih-k'ai)	1928–31	Chiang K'ai-shek (Jiang Jieshi)
1916–17	Li Yuanhong (Li Yüan-hung)	1931–2	Cheng Minxu (Ch'eng Ming-hsü) *Acting President*
1917–18	Feng Guozhang (Feng Kuo-chang)		
1918–22	Xu Shichang (Hsü Shih-ch'ang)	1932–43	Lin Sen (Lin Sen)
1921–5	Sun Yat-sen (Sun Yixian) *Canton Administration*	1940–4	Wang Jingwei (Wang Ching-wei) *in Japanese-occupied territory*
1922–3	Li Yuanhong (Li Yüan-hung)	1943–9	Chiang K'ai-shek (Jiang Jieshi)
1923–4	Cao Kun (Ts'ao K'un)	1945–9	*Civil War*
1924–6	Duan Qirui (Tuan Ch'i-jui)	1949	Li Zongren (Li Tsung-jen)

Premier

1912	Tang Shaoyi (T'ang Shao-i)	1922–3	Wang Daxie (Wang Ta-hsieh)
1912–13	Zhao Bingjun (Chao Ping-chün)	1923	Zhang Shaozeng (Chang Shao-ts'eng)
1912–13	Xiong Xiling (Hsiung Hsi-ling)		
1914	Sun Baoyi (Sun Pao-chi)	1923–4	Gao Lingwei (Kao Ling-wei)
1915–16	*no Premier*	1924	Sun Baoyi (Sun Pao-ch'i)
1916–17	Duan Qirui (Tuan Ch'i-jui)	1924	Gu Weijun (Ku Wei-chün) *Acting Premier*
1917–18	Wang Shizhen (Wang Shih-chen)		
1918	Duan Qirui (Tuan Ch'i-jui)	1924	Yan Huiqing (Yen Hui-ch'ing)
1918–19	Qian Nengxun (Ch'ien Neng-hsün)	1924–5	Huang Fu (Huang Fu) *Acting Premier*
1919	Gong Xinzhan (Kung Hsin-chan)		
1919–20	Jin Yunpeng (Chin Yün-p'eng)	1925	Duan Qirui (Tuan Ch'i-jui)
1920	Sa Zhenbing (Sa Chen-ping)	1925–6	Xu Shiying (Hsü Shih-ying)
1920–1	Jin Yunpeng (Chin Yün-p'eng)	1926	Jia Deyao (Chia Te-yao)
1921–2	Liang Shiyi (Liang Shih-i)	1926	Hu Weide (Hu Wei-te)
1922	Zhou Ziqi (Chow Tzu-ch'i) *Acting Premier*	1926	Yan Huiqing (Yen Hui-ch'ing)
		1926	Du Xigui (Tu Hsi-kuei)
1922	Yan Huiqing (Yen Hui-ch'ing)	1926–7	Gu Weijun (Ku Wei-chün)
1922	Wang Chonghui (Wang Ch'ung-hui)	1927	*Civil Disorder*

President of the Executive Council

1928–30	Tan Yankai (T'an Yen-k'ai)		Ch'ung-hui) *Acting President*
1930	T V Soong (Sung Tzu-wen) *Acting President*	1938–9	Kong Xiangxi (K'ung Hsiang-hsi)
		1939–44	Chiang K'ai-shek (Jiang Jieshi)
1930	Wang Jingwei (Wang Ching-wei)	1944–7	T V Soong (Sung Tzu-wen)
1930–1	Chiang K'ai-shek (Jiang Jieshi)	1945–9	*Civil War*
1931–2	Sun Fo (Sun Fo)	1948	Wang Wenhao (Wong Wen-hao)
1932–5	Wang Jingwei (Wang Ching-wei)	1948–9	Sun Fo (Sun Fo)
1935–7	Chiang K'ai-shek (Jiang Jieshi)	1949	He Yingqin (Ho Ying-ch'in)
1937–8	Wang Chonghui (Wang	1949	Yan Xishan (Yen Hsi-shan)

People's Republic of China

President

1949–59	Mao Zedong (Mao Tse-tung)	1978–83	Ye Jianying
1959–68	Liu Shaoqi	1983–8	Li Xiannian
1968–75	Dong Biwu	1988–93	Yang Shangkun
1975–6	Zhu De	1993–2003	Jiang Zemin
1976–8	Sung Qingling	2003–	Hu Jintao

Premier/Prime Minister

1949–76	Zhou Enlai (Chou En-lai)	1987–98	Li Peng
1976–80	Hua Guofeng	1998–2003	Zhu Rongji
1980–7	Zhao Ziyang	2003–	Wen Jiabao

Chairman of the Communist Party

1935–76	Mao Zedong (Mao Tse-tung)
1976–81	Hua Guofeng
1981–2	Hu Yaobang

General Secretary of the Communist Party

1982–7	Hu Yaobang	1989–2002	Jiang Zemin
1987–9	Zhao Ziyang	2002–	Hu Jintao

Note: Names are listed only in Pinyin transliterations for recent leaders.

Red for Go

The colour red is associated with the Communist party in China. During the Cultural Revolution (1966–76) it was reported that some over-zealous revolutionaries wanted the red traffic light to mean 'go', to symbolize the forward-thinking nature of the Communist regime.

CHINA, REPUBLIC OF *see* **TAIWAN**

CHINESE TAIPEI *see* **TAIWAN**

CHRISTMAS ISLAND *see* **AUSTRALIA**

CIS *see* **ARMENIA, AZERBAIJAN, BELARUS, GEORGIA, KAZAKHSTAN, KYRGYZSTAN, MOLDOVA, RUSSIA, TAJIKISTAN, TURKMENISTAN, UKRAINE, UZBEKISTAN** *and separate entry in* **POLITICS, LAW AND ORDER**

COCOS ISLANDS *see* **AUSTRALIA**

COLOMBIA

Official name	Republic of Colombia		mulatto 14%, black 4%,
Local name	Colombia; República de Colombia		mixed black and Amerindian 3%, Amerindian 1%
Independence	1810 (declared), 1819 (full)	**Religions**	Christianity 95% (RC), others 5%
Area	1 140 105 sq km/440 080 sq mi	**Time zone**	GMT –5
Capital	Bogotá; Santa Fé de Bogotá	**Currency**	1 Colombian Peso (Col$/COP) = 100 centavos
Chief towns	Medellín, Cali, Barranquilla		
Population	45 600 000 (2005e)	**Telephone**	+57
Nationality	Colombian	**Internet**	.co
Languages	Spanish	**Country code**	COL
Ethnic groups	mestizo 58%, white 20%,		

Location
A republic in north-western South America, bounded to the north-west by Panama; to the north by the Caribbean Sea; to the east by Venezuela; to the south-east by Brazil; to the south by Ecuador and Peru; and to the west by the Pacific Ocean.

Physical description
Caribbean and Pacific coastlines, with several islands; Andes run north to south, branching into three dividing narrow coastal plains from forested Amazon basin lowlands; highest peaks are Pico Cristóbal Colón and Pico Simón Bolívar (both 5 775m/18 947ft) and Nevado del Huila (5 750m/18 864ft).

Climate
Hot and humid coastal plains in the north-west and west; drier period on the Caribbean coast (Dec–Apr); in the Andes rainfall is even throughout the year; hot and humid tropical lowlands in the east.

National holidays
Jan 1, 6, Mar 19 (St Joseph), May 1, Jun 29 (SS Peter and Paul), Jul 20 (Independence), Aug 7 (Battle of Boyacá), 15, Oct 12 (Columbus), Nov 1, 11 (Independence of Cartagena), Dec 8, 25; A, CC, GF, HT, Sacred Heart (Jun).

Political leaders

President

1900–4	José Manuel Marroquín *Vice President*	1946–50	Mariano Ospina Pérez
		1950–3	Laureano Gómez
1904–9	Rafael Reyes	1953–7	Gustavo Rojas Pinilla
1909–10	Ramón González Valencia	1957	*Military Junta*
1910–14	Carlos E Restrepo	1958–62	Alberto Lleras Camargo
1914–18	José Vicente Concha	1962–6	Guillermo León Valencia
1918–21	Marco Fidel Suárez	1966–70	Carlos Lleras Restrepo
1921–2	Jorge Holguín *President Designate*	1970–4	Misael Pastrana Borrero
1922–6	Pedro Nel Ospina	1974–8	Alfonso López Michelsen
1926–30	Miguel Abadía Méndez	1978–82	Julio César Turbay Ayala
1930–4	Enrique Olaya Herrera	1982–6	Belisario Betancur
1934–8	Alfonso López	1986–90	Virgilio Barco Vargas
1938–42	Eduardo Santos	1990–4	César Gaviria Trujillo
1942–5	Alfonso López	1994–8	Ernesto Samper Pizano
1945–6	Alberto Lleras Camargo *President Designate*	1998–2002	Andrés Pastrana Arango
		2002–	Álvaro Uribe Vélez

Orchids and Condors

The national flower of Colombia is the orchid, while the national tree is the wax palm, which only grows in the Colombian Andes and is the world's tallest palm tree, reaching up to 70m/230ft. The mighty condor is the national bird, a creature of great historical and cultural significance for the people. It lives high in the Andes and is known as the 'eternal bird' for its long lifespan.

COMOROS

Official name	Union of the Comoros		a local Arabic-Swahili
Local name	Comores; Union des		dialect, is also spoken
	Comores	**Ethnic groups**	Comorian 97%, others
Former name	Federal Islamic Republic		3%
	of the Comoros (until	**Religions**	Islam 86% (Sunni),
	2001)		Christianity 14% (RC)
Independence	1975	**Time zone**	GMT +3
Area	1 862 sq km/719 sq mi	**Currency**	1 Comoran Franc (KMF)
Capital	Moroni; Môrônî		= 100 centimes
Population	798 000 (2005e)	**Telephone**	+269
Nationality	Comoran	**Internet**	.km
Languages	French, Arabic;	**Country code**	COM
	Shikomoro, or Comoran,		

Location
An island group at the northern end of the Mozambique Channel in the Indian Ocean, between Mozambique and Madagascar.

Physical description
Three volcanic islands, Grand Comore (Njazídja), Anjouan (Nzwani) and Mohéli (Mwali); interiors vary from steep mountains to low hills; highest point is the active volcano Le Karthala (2 360m/7 743ft) on Grand Comore.

Climate
Tropical; May Oct is the dry season and Nov–Apr is the hot, humid season; average temperatures are 20°C in Jul and 28°C in Nov.

National holidays
May 9 (Islamic New Year), 18 (Ashoura), Jul 6 (Independence), 18 (Mouloud/Prophet's Birthday), Nov 17 (President Abdallah's Assassination), 28 (Leilat al-Meiraj/Ascension of the Prophet); Ad, ER, R.

Political leaders

President

1976–78	Ali Soilih	1999–2002	Azali Assoumani
1978–89	Ahmed Abdallah Abderemane	2002	Hamada Madi Boléro *Interim*
1989–96	Said Mohammed Djohar		*President*
1996–8	Mohammed Taki Abdoulkarim	2002–	Azali Assoumani
1998–9	Tadjiddine Ben Said Massounde		
	Interim President		

Prime Minister

1976–8	Abdallah Mohammed	1994–5	Halifa Houmadi
1978–82	Salim Ben Ali	1995–6	Caambi el-Yachourtu
1982–4	Ali Mroudjae	1996	Tadjiddine Ben Said Massounde
1984–92	*No Prime Minister*	1996–7	Ahmed Abdou
1992	Mohammed Taki Abdoulkarim	1997–8	Nourdine Bourhane
1993	Ibrahim Abdermane Halidi	1998–9	Abbas Djoussouf
1993	Said Ali Mohammed	1999–2000	Bianrifi Tarmidi
1993–4	Ahmed Ben Cheikh Attoumane	2000–2	Hamada Madi Boléro
1994	Mohammed Abdou Madi	2002–	*No Prime Minister*

CONGO

Official name	Republic of Congo; also sometimes known as Congo (Brazzaville) or Congo-Brazzaville	**Population**	3 999 000 (2005e)
		Nationality	Congolese, Congo
		Languages	French, Kikongo, Lingala
Local name	Congo; République du Congo	**Ethnic groups**	Kongo 49%, Sangha 20%, Teke 17%, Mbosi 11%, others 3%
Former name	Middle Congo (until 1960), Republic of Congo (1960–70), People's Republic of Congo (1970–92)	**Religions**	Christianity 50% (RC), traditional beliefs 48%, Islam 2%
		Time zone	GMT +1
Independence	1960	**Currency**	1 CFA Franc (CFAFr/XAF) = 100 centimes
Area	341 945 sq km/131 990 sq mi	**Telephone**	+242
Capital	Brazzaville	**Internet**	.cg
Chief towns	Pointe-Noire, Loubomo, Nkayi	**Country code**	COG

Location
A west central African republic, bounded to the north-west by Cameroon; to the north by the Central African Republic; to the east and south by Democratic Republic of the Congo; to the south-east by the Angolan province of Cabinda; to the south-west by the southern Atlantic Ocean; and to the west by Gabon.

Physical description
Short Atlantic coastline fringes a broad mangrove plain that rises inland to mountains reaching 900m/2 953ft; River Congo flows south-west to the coast; Monts de la Lékéti reach 1 040m/3 412ft; mainly covered by dense grassland, mangrove and forest.

Climate
Hot, humid, equatorial climate; rainfall decreases near the Atlantic coast and in the south; temperatures vary little, with average daily maximum temperatures at Brazzaville 28–33°C; dry season is Jun–Sep.

National holidays
Jan 1, Mar 18 (Day of the Supreme Sacrifice), May 1, Jul 31 (Revolution), Aug 13–15 (The Three Glorious Days), Nov 1 (Day of the Dead), Dec 25 (Children), 31 (Foundation of the Party and People's Republic).

Political leaders

President

1960–3	Abbé Fulbert Youlou	1969–77	Marien Ngouabi
1963–8	Alphonse Massemba-Debat	1977–9	Joachim Yhomby Opango
1968	Marien Ngouabi	1979–92	Denis Sassou-Nguesso
1968	Alphonse Massemba-Debat	1992–7	Pascal Lissouba
1968–9	Alfred Raoul	1997–	Denis Sassou-Nguesso

Prime Minister

1958	Jacques Opangault	1968–9	Alfred Raoul
1958–60	Fulbert Youlou	1969–73	*No Prime Minister*
1960–3	*No Prime Minister*	1973–5	Henri Lopès
1963–6	Pascal Lissouba	1975–84	Louis Sylvain Goma
1966–8	Ambroise Noumazalaye	1984–9	Ange-Édouard Poungui

1989–90	Alphonse Poaty-Souchlaty		1992–3	Claude Antoine Dacosta
1990–1	Pierre Moussa *Acting Prime Minister*		1993–6	Joachim Yhombi-Opango
			1996–7	Charles David Ganao
1991	Louis Sylvain Goma		1997	Bernard Kolelas
1991–2	André Milongo		1997–2005	*No Prime Minister*
1992	Stéphane Maurice Bongho-Nouarra		2005–	Isidore Mvouba

Free French

During World War II Brazzaville served as the headquarters of the Free French forces led by General Charles de Gaulle. In the film *Casablanca* (1942), Rick and Captain Louis Renault head for the Free French garrison in Brazzaville at the end of the film and at the start of 'a beautiful friendship'.

CONGO, DEMOCRATIC REPUBLIC OF THE

Official name	Democratic Republic of the Congo (DR Congo, DRC or DROC); also sometimes known as Congo (Kinshasa) or Congo-Kinshasa	**Chief towns**	Lubumbashi, Kisangani, Mbuji-Mayi, Kananga	
		Population	57 549 000 (2005e)	
		Nationality	Congolese, Congo	
		Languages	French, Kikongo, Lingala	
Local name	Congo; République Démocratique du Congo	**Ethnic groups**	Bantu and Hamitic 44%, others 56%	
Former name	Congo Free State (until 1908), Belgian Congo (until 1960), Republic of the Congo (1960–4), Democratic Republic of Congo (1964–71), Zaïre (1971–97)	**Religions**	Christianity 60% (RC 45%, Prot 15%), traditional beliefs 30%, Islam 10%	
		Time zone	GMT +1/2	
		Currency	1 Congolese Franc (CF/CDF) = 100 centimes	
Independence	1960	**Telephone**	+243	
Area	2 343 950 sq km/904 765 sq mi	**Internet**	.cd	
		Country code	COD	
Capital	Kinshasa			

Location
A central African republic, bounded to the north by the Central African Republic; to the north-east by Sudan; to the east by Uganda, Rwanda, Burundi and Tanzania; to the south-east by Zambia; to the south-west by Angola; and to the west by Congo and the Atlantic Ocean.

Physical description
Rises in the east from a low-lying basin to a densely-forested plateau; Ruwenzori Mountains in the north-east rise to 5 110m/16 765ft at Pic Marguerite on Mt Ngaliema (Mt Stanley); chain of lakes in the Rift Valley; short 43km/27mi Atlantic coastline.

Climate
Crossed by the Equator and has a hot and humid climate; average maximum daily temperatures range between 28°C and 31°C.

National holidays
Jan 1, 4 (Martyrs of Independence), May 1, 20 (Mouvement Populaire de la Révolution), Jun 24 (Anniversary of Currency, Promulgation of the 1967 Constitution and Day of the Fishermen), 30 (Independence), Dec 25.

Political leaders

President

1960–5	Joseph Kasavubu	1997–2001	Laurent Kabila
1965–97	Mobutu Sese Seko (*formerly* Joseph Mobutu)	2001–	Joseph Kabila

Prime Minister

1960	Patrice Lumumba	1986–8	*No Prime Minister*
1960	Joseph Ileo	1988	Sambura Pida Nbagui
1960–1	*College of Commissioners*	1988–90	Léon Kengo Wa Dondo
1961	Joseph Ileo	1990–1	Lunda Bululu
1961–4	Cyrille Adoula	1991	Mulumba Lukeji
1964–5	Moïse Tshombe	1991	Etienne Tshisekedi
1965	Evariste Kimba	1991	Bernardin Mungul Diaka
1965–6	Mulamba Nyungu wa Kadima	1991–2	Karl I Bond
1966–77	*As President*	1992–3	Etienne Tshisekedi
1977–80	Mpinga Kasenga	1993–4	Faustin Birindwa
1980	Bo-Boliko Lokonga Monse Mihambu	1994–7	Léon Kengo Wa Dondo
1980–1	Nguza Karl I Bond	1997	Etienne Tshisekedi
1981–3	Nsinga Udjuu	1997	Likulia Bolongo
1983–6	Léon Kengo Wa Dondo	1997–	*No Prime Minister*

Mighty River

The River Congo is the second longest river in Africa, and the tenth longest in the world, at a massive 4 630km/2 880mi. It rises as the River Lualaba, crosses the Equator and becomes known as the River Congo, then flows in an arc across central Africa. The first European discovery of the river mouth was in 1482, but its extent was appreciated only in the 19c, with explorations by Stanley, Livingstone and others.

COOK ISLANDS *see* **NEW ZEALAND**

COSTA RICA

Official name	Republic of Costa Rica	**Ethnic groups**	white and mestizo 95%, black and mulatto 3%, Amerindian 1%, Chinese 1%
Local name	Costa Rica; República de Costa Rica		
Independence	1821	**Religions**	Christianity 85% (RC), others 15%
Area	51 022 sq km/19 694 sq mi		
Capital	San José	**Time zone**	GMT –6
Chief towns	Cartago, Heredia, Liberia, Puntarenas, Limón	**Currency**	1 Costa Rican Colón (CR¢/CRC) = 100 céntimos
Population	4 327 000 (2005e)	**Telephone**	+506
Nationality	Costa Rican	**Internet**	.cr
Languages	Spanish	**Country code**	CRI

Location
A republic in Central America, bounded to the north by Nicaragua; to the east by the Caribbean; to the south-east by Panama; and to the west by the Pacific Ocean.

Physical description
A series of volcanic ridges form the backbone (some volcanoes active); highest peak is Chirripó Grande (3 819m/12 529ft); central plateau lies at an altitude of 800–1 400m/ 2 600–4 600ft; swampy near the coast, with tropical forest inland; some lowland savanna.

Climate
Tropical climate, with a small temperature range and abundant rainfall; more temperate in the central uplands; dry season is Dec–May; average annual temperature is 26–28°C.

National holidays
Jan 1, Mar 19 (St Joseph), Apr 11 (Battle of Rivas), May 1, Aug 15 (Mothers), 31 (International Black People), Sep 15 (Independence), Oct 12 (Culture), Nov 2, Dec 24, 25, 31; Holy Week.

Political leaders

President

1894–1902	Rafael Yglesias y Castro	1948–9	*Civil Junta* (José Figueres Ferrer)
1902–6	Ascención Esquivel Ibarra	1949–52	Otilio Ulate Blanco
1906–10	Cleto González Víquez	1952–3	Alberto Oreamuno Flores
1910–12	Ricardo Jiménez Oreamuno	1953–8	José Figueres Ferrer
1912–14	Cleto González Víquez	1958–62	Mario Echandi Jiménez
1914–17	Alfredo González Flores	1962–6	Francisco José Orlich Bolmarcich
1917–19	Federico Tinoco Granados	1966–70	José Joaquín Trejos Fernández
1919	Julio Acosta García	1970–4	José Figueres Ferrer
1919–20	Juan Bautista Quiros	1974–8	Daniel Oduber Quirós
1920–4	Julio Acosta García	1978–82	Rodrigo Carazo Odio
1924–8	Ricardo Jiménez Oreamuno	1982–6	Luis Alberto Monge Álvarez
1928–32	Cleto González Víquez	1986–90	Oscar Arias Sánchez
1932–6	Ricardo Jiménez Oreamuno	1990–4	Rafael Ángel Calderón Fournier
1936–40	León Cortés Castro	1994–8	José Maria Figueres Olsen
1940–4	Rafael Ángel Calderón Guardia	1998–2002	Miguel Angel Rodríguez
1944–8	Teodoro Picado Michalski		Echevarría
1948	Santos Léon Herrera	2002–	Abel Pacheco de la Espriella

Pacifists on the Pacific

Costa Rica is one of very few countries not to have an army. The military was abolished in 1948, and the government claims to have since invested the money saved into improving the quality of life and living standards of its people. But what Costa Rica lacks in military muscle, it makes up for in wildlife; the country estimates that it covers just 0.03% of the Earth's land surface, but contains approximately 6% of the world's biodiversity.

CÔTE D'IVOIRE

Official name	Republic of Côte d'Ivoire	**Languages**	French; many local languages are also spoken
Local name	Côte d'Ivoire; République de la Côte d'Ivoire		
Former name	Ivory Coast (until 1986)	**Ethnic groups**	Akan 40%, Kru 17%, Voltaic 15%, Malinke 15%, Southern Mande 11%, others 2%
Independence	1960		
Area	320 633 sq km/123 764 sq mi		
Capital	Yamoussoukro (official) and Abidjan (administrative and economic)	**Religions**	Islam 45%, traditional beliefs 30%, Christianity 25%
		Time zone	GMT
Chief towns	Bouaké, Daloa, Man, Korhogo, Gagnoa	**Currency**	1 CFA Franc (CFAFr/XOF) = 100 centimes
		Telephone	+225
Population	18 154 000 (2005e)	**Internet**	.ci
Nationality	Ivorian	**Country code**	CIV

Location
A republic in West Africa, bounded to the north-west by Guinea; to the north by Mali and Burkina Faso; to the east by Ghana; to the south by the Gulf of Guinea; and to the west by Liberia.

Physical description
Sandy beaches and lagoons, backed by a broad forest-covered coastal plain; land rises towards savanna at 300–350m/980–1 150ft; Mt Nimba massif in the north-west reaches 1 752m/5 748ft (highest point); rivers generally flow north to south.

Climate
Tropical, varying with distance from the coast; rainfall decreases towards the north; average temperatures are 25–27°C.

National holidays
Jan 1, May 1, Aug 15, Nov 1, Dec 7 (Independence), 24, 25, 31; A, Ad, EM, ER, GF, WM.

Political leaders

President

1960–93	Félix Houphouët-Boigny		1999–2000	Robert Guëi
1993–9	Henri Konan-Bédié		2000–	Laurent Gbagbo

Prime Minister

1958–9	Auguste Denise		1999	Robert Guëi
1959–60	Félix Houphouët-Boigny		2000	Seydou Diarra
1960–90	*No Prime Minister*		2000–3	Pascal Affi N'Guessan
1990–3	Alassane Dramane Ouattara		2003–	Seydou Diarra
1993–9	Daniel Kablan Duncan			

Cocoa Kings

Côte d'Ivoire is the world's largest producer of cocoa. In 2003–4 it produced approximately 1.4 million tonnes/1 382 800 tons of cocoa beans, dwarfing its nearest competitor, Ghana, which produced only 736 000 tonnes/724 300 tons.

CROATIA

Official name	Republic of Croatia	**Chief towns**	Rijeka, Cakovec, Split, Zadar
Local name	Hrvatska; Republika Hrvatska	**Population**	4 551 000 (2005e)
Former name	formerly part of Kingdom of Serbs, Croats and Slovenes (until 1929), Kingdom of Yugoslavia (1929–41), Independent State of Croatia (1941–45), Federal People's Republic of Yugoslavia (1945–63), Socialist Federal People's Republic of Yugoslavia (1963–91)	**Nationality**	Croatian
		Languages	Croatian
		Ethnic groups	Croat 78%, Serb 12%, Bosniak 1%, others 9%
		Religions	Christianity 88% (RC 77%, Orthodox 11%), Islam 1%, others 11%
		Time zone	GMT +1
		Currency	1 Kuna (Kn/HRK) = 100 lipa
Independence	1991	**Telephone**	+385
Area	56 542 sq km/21 831 sq mi	**Internet**	.hr
Capital	Zagreb	**Country code**	HRV

Location
A republic in central Europe, bounded to the north by Slovenia; to the north-east by Hungary; to the east by Serbia and Montenegro; to the south-east by Bosnia and Herzegovina; and to the south-west by the Adriatic Sea.

Physical description
Mountainous, with islands on the Adriatic coast; highest point is Dinara (1 831m/6 007ft); inland terrain includes fertile plains.

Climate
Continental; hot summers and cold winters.

National holidays
Jan 1, May 1, 30 (National), Jun 22 (Antifascism), Aug 5 (National Thanksgiving), 15, Nov 1, Dec 25, 26; EM, GF.

Political leaders

See **Serbia and Montenegro** for political leaders of the former Yugoslavia.

President

1992–9	Franjo Tudjman	2000	Zlatko Tomčić *Acting President*
1999–2000	Vlatko Pavletić *Acting President*	2000–	Stjepan Mesić

Prime Minister

1990	Stjepan Mesić	1993–5	Nikica Valentić
1990–1	Josip Manolić	1995–2000	Zlatko Mateša
1991–2	Franjo Gregurić	2000–3	Ivica Račan
1992–3	Hrvoje Šarinić	2003–	Ivo Sanader

CUBA

Official name	Republic of Cuba	**Ethnic groups**	white 66%, mulatto 23%, black 11%
Local name	Cuba; República de Cuba		
Independence	1902	**Religions**	none/unaffiliated 55%, Christianity 43% (RC 40%, Prot 3%), traditional beliefs 2%
Area	110 860 sq km/42 792 sq mi		
Capital	Havana; La Habana	**Time zone**	GMT −5
Chief towns	Santiago de Cuba, Camagüey, Holguín, Santa Clara, Guantánamo	**Currency**	1 Cuban Peso (Cub$/CUP) = 100 centavos
Population	11 269 000 (2005e)	**Telephone**	+53
Nationality	Cuban	**Internet**	.cu
Languages	Spanish	**Country code**	CUB

Location
An island republic lying between the Gulf of Mexico and the Caribbean Sea, south of the US state of Florida.

Physical description
An archipelago, comprising the island of Cuba, Isla de la Juventud and c.1 600 islets and cays; heavily indented coastline; highest peak is Pico Turquino (2 005m/6 578ft); mostly flat, with wide, fertile valleys and plains.

Climate
Subtropical, warm and humid; average annual temperature is 25°C; dry season is Nov–Apr; hurricanes usually occur between Jun and Nov.

National holidays
Jan 1 (Day of Liberation), May 1, Jul 25 (National Rebellion) (2), Oct 10 (Beginning of the Independence Wars).

Political leaders

President

1902–6	Tomas Estrada Palma	1936–40	Federico Laredo Bru
1906–9	*US rule*	1940–4	Fulgencio Batista
1909–13	José Miguel Gómez	1944–8	Ramón Grau San Martín
1913–21	Mario García Menocal	1948–52	Carlos Prío Socarrás
1921–5	Alfredo Zayas y Alfonso	1952–9	Fulgencio Batista
1925–33	Gerardo Machado y Morales	1959	Manuel Urrutia
1933	Carlos Manuel de Céspedes	1959–76	Osvaldo Dorticós Torrado
1933–4	Ramón Grau San Martín	1959–76	Fidel Castro Ruz *Prime Minister and First Secretary*
1934–5	Carlos Mendieta		
1935–6	José A Barnet y Vinagres	1976–	Fidel Castro Ruz *President*
1936	Miguel Mariano Gómez y Arias		

Chatty Castro

Cuban President Fidel Castro holds the world record for the longest continuous speech at the United Nations. On 26 Sep 1960 Castro's speech denouncing imperialism and colonialism lasted an exhausting four and a half hours. He prefaced the speech by assuring those present that he would endeavour to be brief.

CYPRUS

Official name	Republic of Cyprus	**Languages**	Greek, Turkish, with English widely spoken
Local name	Kipros; Kypriaki Dimokratía (Greek), Kibris; Kibris Çumhuriyeti (Turkish)	**Ethnic groups**	Greek 78%, Turkish 18%, others 4%
Independence	1960	**Religions**	Christianity 78% (Orthodox), Islam 18%, others 4%
Area	9 251 sq km/3 571 sq mi		
Capital	Nicosia; Lefkosía (Greek), Lefkoşa (Turkish)	**Time zone**	GMT +2
Chief towns	Larnaca, Limassol, Kyrenia; Famagusta (formerly the chief port) is under Turkish occupation and has been declared closed by the Cyprus government	**Currency**	1 Cyprus Pound (C£/CYP) = 100 cents; Turkish lira are used in the northern part under Turkish occupation
		Telephone	+357
		Internet	.cy
		Country code	CYP
Population	835 000 (2005e)		
Nationality	Cypriot		

Location
An island republic in the eastern Mediterranean Sea, south of Turkey and west of Syria.

Physical description
Kyrenia Mountains extend along the north coast; forest-covered Troödos Mountains in the south-west rise to 1 951m/6 401ft at Mt Olympus; fertile plain across the island centre; indented coastline with several long, sandy beaches.

Climate
Typical Mediterranean climate with hot, dry summers and warm, wet winters; average daily temperatures (Jul–Aug) 22–29°C; winters are mild (average temperature 4°C in the mountains, 10°C on the plain); snow on higher land in winter.

National holidays
Jan 1, 6, Mar 25 (Greek National), Apr 1 (Greek Cypriot National), May 1, Aug 15, Oct 1 (Independence), 28 (Greek National Ochi), Dec 24, 25, 26; ES, Green Monday, Kataklysmos, Orthodox Easter (Apr/May) (3).

Political leaders

President

1960–77	Archbishop Makarios III	1993–2003	Glafcos Clerides
1977–88	Spyros Kyprianou	2003–	Tassos Papadopoulos
1988–93	Georgios Vassiliou		

Note: Turkey has occupied the northern third of Cyprus since 1974. It declared this area to be the Turkish Federated State of Cyprus in 1975 and the Turkish Republic of Northern Cyprus in 1983; the state is recognized only by Turkey. Since inception it has been led by Rauf Denktaş.

HUMAN GEOGRAPHY
CZECH REPUBLIC

CZECH REPUBLIC

Official name	Czech Republic	Languages	Czech
Local name	České Republiky, Česká Republika, Cesko	Ethnic groups	Czech 82%, Moravian 13%, Slovak 3%, others 2%
Former name	formerly part of Czechoslovakia (until 1993)	Religions	Christianity 48% (RC 40%, Prot 5%, Orthodox 3%), none/unaffiliated 40%, others 12%
Independence	1993		
Area	78 864 sq km/30 441 sq mi		
Capital	Prague; Praha	Time zone	GMT +1
Chief towns	Brno, Plzen, Ostrava, Olomouc	Currency	1 Koruna (Kč/CZK) = 100 haléřů
Population	10 220 000 (2005e)	Telephone	+420
Nationality	Czech	Internet	.cz
		Country code	CZE

Location
A republic in central Europe, bounded to the north and west by Germany; to the north and east by Poland; to the south-east by Slovakia; and to the south by Austria.

Physical description
Bohemia and West Moravia are separated from East Moravia and Slovakia by the River Morava valley; western range of the Carpathians rise in the east; highest point is Sněžka (1 602m/5 256ft); many lakes and rivers; richly wooded.

Climate
Continental, with warm, humid summers and cold, dry winters.

National holidays
Jan 1, May 1, 8 (Liberation), Jul 5 (SS Cyril and Methodius), 6 (Martyrdom of Jan Hus), Sep 28 (Statehood), Oct 28 (Independence), Nov 17 (Fight for Freedom and Democracy), Dec 24, 25, 26; EM.

Political leaders

Czechoslovakia

President

1918–35	Tomáš Garrigue Masaryk	1945–8	Edvard Beneš
1935–8	Edvard Beneš	1948–53	Klement Gottwald
1938	Emil Hácha	1953–7	Antonín Zápotocký
1938–45	Edvard Beneš *President in Exile (German Occupation)*	1957–68	Antonín Novotný
		1968–75	Ludvík Svoboda
1939–45	Emil Hácha *State President (German Occupation)*	1975–89	Gustáv Husák
		1989–93	Václav Havel
1939–45	Jozef Tiso *Slovak Republic President (German Occupation)*		

Prime Minister

1918–19	Karel Kramář	1926	Jan Černý
1919–20	Vlastimil Tusar	1926–9	Antonín Švehla
1920–1	Jan Černý	1929–32	František Udržal
1921–2	Edvard Beneš	1932–5	Jan Malypetr
1922–6	Antonín Švehla	1935–8	Milan Hodža

1938	Jan Syrový	1963–8	Josef Lenárt
1938–9	Rudolf Beran	1968–70	Oldřich Černik
1940–5	Jan Šrámek *in exile*	1970–88	Lubomír Štrougal
1945–6	Zdeněk Fierlinger	1988–9	Ladislav Adamec
1946–8	Klement Gottwald	1989–92	Marian Calfa
1948–53	Antonín Zápotocký	1992	Jan Strasky
1953–63	Viliám Široký		

First Secretary of the Communist Party

1948–52	Rudolf Slánsky	1987–9	Miloš Jakeš
1953–68	Antonín Novotný	1989	Karel Urbánek
1968–9	Alexander Dubček	1989–93	Ladislav Adamec
1969–87	Gustáv Husák		

In 1993 Czechoslovakia divided into two separate states, the Czech Republic and **Slovakia** (see separate entry).

Czech Republic

President

1993–2003	Václav Havel
2003–	Václav Klaus

Prime Minister

1993–7	Václav Klaus	2002–4	Vladimír Špidla
1997–8	Josef Tosovsky	2004–5	Stanislav Gross
1998–2002	Miloš Zeman	2005–	Jirí Paroubek

Bohemians

The term 'Bohemian', meaning someone who sets social conventions aside, derives its name from the Czech region of Bohemia. It came into English from French, where it meant 'Gypsy', in the belief that these wanderers came from Bohemia (then an independent kingdom).

DENMARK

Official name	Kingdom of Denmark	**Nationality**	Dane, Danish
Local name	Danmark; Kongeriget Danmark; also sometimes known as Rigsfællesskabet, the United Kingdom of Denmark, including the Faroe Islands and Greenland	**Languages**	Danish
		Ethnic groups	Danish 96%, Faroese and Inuit 1%, others 3%
		Religions	Christianity 93% (Prot 92%, RC 1%), none/ unaffiliated 2%, others 5%
Area	43 076 sq km/16 627 sq mi	**Time zone**	GMT +1
Capital	Copenhagen; København	**Currency**	1 Danish Krone (Dkr/DKK) = 100 øre
Chief towns	Århus, Odense, Ålborg, Esbjerg, Randers, Kolding	**Telephone**	+45
		Internet	.dk
Population	5 431 000 (2005e)	**Country code**	DNK

Location
A kingdom in northern Europe, comprising most of the Jutland Peninsula, bounded to the south by Germany, and more than 400 islands in the Baltic Sea and the North Sea.

Physical description
The smallest of the Scandinavian countries; uniformly low-lying; highest point (Ejer Bavnehøj) is only 173m/567ft; no large rivers and few lakes; shoreline is indented by many lagoons and fjords, the largest of which is Lim Fjord.

Climate
Much modified by the Gulf Stream, giving cold and cloudy winters, and warm, sunny summers.

National holidays
Jan 1, Jun 5 (Constitution), Dec 25, 26; A, EM, GF, HT, WM, General Prayer (Apr/May).

Danish self-governing territories

Faroe Islands

Location
The group of 18 islands and smaller islets lying between the Shetland Islands and Iceland, and subject to the Danish crown. Also spelt Faeroe Islands.

Local name	Føroyar (Faroese)/ Færøerne (Danish)	**Population**	47 000 (2005e)
		Internet	.fo
Area	1 399 sq km/540 sq mi	**Country code**	FRO
Capital	Tórshavn (1999e)		

Sheep Islands

The local name for the Faroes is *Føroyar*, which comes from an old Norse word meaning 'Sheep Islands'.

Glacier to Iceberg

The world's most active glacier is found at Ilulissat on Greenland's west coast. 'Ilulissat' means 'the icebergs' and the town lies on a fjord full of bergs created by the glacier. Moving at 25–30m/80–100ft a day, the glacier 'calves' across a 10km/6mi long front and produces 20 million tons of ice every 24 hours.

Greenland

Location
The second-largest island in the world (after Australia), lying north-east of North America in the North Atlantic and Arctic oceans; autonomous with limited self-government but subject to the Danish crown.

Local name	Kalaallit Nunaat (Inuit)/ Grønland (Danish)	**Population**	57 000 (2005e)
		Internet	.gl
Area	2 175 600 sq km/ 839 780 sq mi	**Country code**	GRL
Capital	Nuuk (Inuit), Godthåb (Danish)		

Political leaders

Monarch

1448–81	Kristian I	1746–66	Frederik V
1481–1513	Johan	1766–1808	Kristian VII
1513–23	Kristian II	1808–39	Frederik VI
1523–34	Frederik I	1839–48	Kristian VIII
1534–59	Kristian III	1848–63	Frederik VII
1559–88	Frederik II	1863–1906	Kristian IX
1588–1648	Kristian IV	1906–12	Frederik VIII
1648–70	Frederik III	1912–47	Kristian X
1670–99	Kristian V	1947–72	Frederik IX
1699–1730	Frederik IV	1972–	Margrethe II
1730–46	Kristian VI		

Prime Minister

1900–1	Hannibal Sehested	1945	Wilhelm Buhl
1901–5	J H Deuntzer	1945–7	Knud Kristensen
1905–8	J C Christensen	1947–50	Hans Hedtoft
1908–9	Niels Neergaard	1950–3	Erik Eriksen
1909	Ludvig Holstein-Ledreborg	1953–5	Hans Hedtoft
1909–10	C Th Zahle	1955–60	Hans Christian Hansen
1910–13	Klaus Berntsen	1960–2	Viggo Kampmann
1913–20	C Th Zahle	1962–8	Jens Otto Krag
1920	Otto Liebe	1968–71	Hilmar Baunsgaard
1920	M P Friis	1971–2	Jens Otto Krag
1920–4	Niels Neergaard	1972–3	Anker Jørgensen
1924–6	Thorvald Stauning	1973–5	Poul Hartling
1926–9	Thomas Madsen-Mygdal	1975–82	Anker Jørgensen
1929–42	Thorvald Stauning	1982–93	Poul Schlüter
1942	Wilhelm Buhl	1993–2001	Poul Nyrup Rasmussen
1942–3	Erik Scavenius	2001–	Anders Fogh Rasmussen
1943–5	*No government*		

DJIBOUTI

Official name	Republic of Djibouti	**Nationality**	Djiboutian
Local name	Djibouti; République de Djibouti (French), Jumhūriyya Jibūt (Arabic)	**Languages**	Arabic, French
		Ethnic groups	Issa 53%, Afar 36%, Arab 6%, others 5%
Former name	French Somaliland (until 1967), French Territory of the Afars and Issas (1966–77)	**Religions**	Islam 94% (Sunni), Christianity 6% (RC 4%, Prot 2%)
Independence	1977	**Time zone**	GMT +3
Area	23 310 sq km/8 998 sq mi	**Currency**	1 Djibouti Franc (DF, DjFr/DJF) = 100 centimes
Capital	Djibouti; Djīboûtî	**Telephone**	+253
Chief towns	Tadjoura, Dikhil, Obock, Ali-Sabieh	**Internet**	.dj
Population	793 000 (2005e)	**Country code**	DJI

Location
A republic in north-east Africa, bounded to the north by Eritrea and the Gulf of Aden; to the east by Somalia;and to the west and south by Ethiopia.

Physical description
A series of plateaux dropping down from mountains to flat low-lying rocky desert; 350km/220mi of fertile coastal strip around the Gulf of Tadjoura, which juts deep into the country; highest point, Moussa Ali, rises to 2 020m/6 627ft in the north.

Climate
Semi-arid with a hot season (May–Sep); very hot on coastal plains, maximum average daily temperature dropping below 30°C for only three months (Dec–Feb); slightly lower temperatures in the interior highlands.

National holidays
Jan 1, May 1, Jun 27 (Independence) (2), Dec 25; Ad (2), ER (2), NY (Muslim), PB, Al-Isra Wal-Mira'age (Mar/Apr).

Political leaders

President
1977–99   Hassan Gouled Aptidon
1999–   Ismaïl Omar Guelleh

Prime Minister
1977–8   Abdallah Mohammed Kamil
1978–2001   Barkat Gourad Hamadou
2001–   Dileïta Mohamed Dileïta

Low-Lying Lake

Djibouti's Lake Assal is the lowest point in Africa, at −156m/ −512ft. It lies in a rift valley, separated from the Gulf of Tadjourah that leads into the Gulf of Aden only by rocks made of ancient lava flows. These form a natural barrier and stop the lake being flooded by the salt waters of the Gulf.

DOMINICA

Official name	Commonwealth of Dominica		European 97%, Amerindian 2%, others 1%
Local name	Dominica		
Independence	1978	**Religions**	Christianity 93% (RC 77%, Prot 16%), others 7%
Area	751 sq km/290 sq mi		
Capital	Roseau	**Time zone**	GMT −4
Chief towns	Portsmouth, Grand Bay	**Currency**	1 East Caribbean Dollar (EC$/XCD) = 100 cents
Population	79 000 (2005e)		
Nationality	Dominican	**Telephone**	+1 767
Languages	English; French Creole is also spoken	**Internet**	.dm
		Country code	DMA
Ethnic groups	African/mixed African-		

Location
An independent island republic located in the Windward Islands, in the east Caribbean Sea.

Physical description
Roughly rectangular in shape, with a deeply-indented coastline; c.50km/30mi long and 26km/16mi wide, rising to 1 447m/4 747ft at Morne Diablotin; volcanic origin, with many fumaroles and sulphur springs; forestry covers 67% of its area.

Climate
Warm and humid; average monthly temperatures are 26–32°C; subject to hurricanes.

National holidays
Jan 1, May 1, Nov 3 (Independence), 4 (Community Service), Dec 25, 26; C (2), EM, GF, WM, August Monday (Aug).

Political leaders

President

1978–9	Louis Cools-Lartigue *Interim President*	1983–93	Clarence Augustus Seignoret
		1993–8	Crispin Anselm Sorhaindo
1979–80	Frederick Degazon[1]	1998–2003	Vernon Shaw
1979–80	Jenner Armour *Acting President*	2003–	Nicholas Liverpool
1980–3	Aurelius Marie		

Prime Minister

1978–9	Patrick Roland John	2000	Rosie Douglas
1979–80	Oliver Seraphine	2000–4	Pierre Charles
1980–95	Mary Eugenia Charles	2004–	Roosevelt Skerrit
1995–2000	Edison James		

[1] *Left Dominica Jun 1979 but did not officially resign until Feb 1980.*

Tall is Her Body

Dominica was first inhabited by the Igneri tribe from Orinoco about 3 000BC. Four thousand years later it was colonized by the Kalinago people, who christened the island *Wai tukubuli*, meaning 'tall is her body' in their Carib language.

DOMINICAN REPUBLIC

Official name	Dominican Republic (DR)	**Ethnic groups**	mulatto 74%, white 16%, black 10%
Local name	República Dominicana		
Independence	1844	**Religions**	Christianity 92% (RC), none/unaffiliated 7%, others 1%
Area	48 442 sq km/18 699 sq mi		
		Time zone	GMT –4
Capital	Santo Domingo	**Currency**	1 Dominican Peso (RD$, DR$/DOP) = 100 centavos
Chief towns	Santiago, La Vega, San Juan, San Francisco de Macorís, La Romana		
		Telephone	+1 809
Population	8 895 000 (2005e)	**Internet**	.do
Nationality	Dominican	**Country code**	DOM
Languages	Spanish		

Location
A republic in the West Indies, comprising the eastern two-thirds of the island of Hispaniola in the Caribbean Sea, and bounded by Haiti to the west.

Physical description
Crossed by the Cordillera Central, a heavily-wooded range with many peaks over 3 000m/9 840ft; Pico Duarte (3 175m/10 417ft) is the highest peak in the Caribbean; Lake Enriquillo lies in a broad valley in the south-west; wide coastal plain to the east.

Climate
Tropical maritime with a rainy season from May to Nov; average temperature at Santo Domingo ranges between 24°C (Jan) and 27°C (Jul); hurricanes may occur in Jun–Nov.

National holidays
Jan 1, 6, 21 (Our Lady of Altagracia), 26 (Duarte), Feb 27 (Independence), May 1, Aug 16 (Restoration of the Republic), Sep 24 (Our Lady of Mercy), Dec 25; CC, GF.

Political leaders

President

1899–1902	Juan Isidro Jiménez	1952–60	Hector Bienvenido Trujillo
1902–3	Horacio Vásquez	1960–2	Joaquín Videla Balaguer
1903	Alejandro Wos y Gil	1962	Rafael Bonnelly
1903–4	Juan Isidro Jiménez	1962	*Military Junta* (Huberto Bogaert)
1904–6	Carlos Morales	1962–3	Rafael Bonnelly
1906–11	Ramon Cáceres	1963	Juan Bosch Gavino
1911–12	Eladio Victoria	1963	*Military Junta* (Emilio de los
1912–13	Adolfo Nouel y Bobadilla		Santos)
1913–14	José Bordas y Valdés	1963–5	Donald Reid Cabral
1914	Ramon Báez	1965	*Civil War*
1914–16	Juan Isidro Jiménez	1965	Elias Wessin y Wessin
1916–22	*US occupation* (Francisco Henríquez y Carrajal)	1965	Antonio Imbert Barreras
		1965	Francisco Caamaño Deñó
1922–4	*US occupation* (Juan Batista Vicini Burgos)	1965–6	Héctor Garcia Godoy Cáceres
		1966–78	Joaquín Videla Balaguer
1924–30	Horacio Vásquez	1978–82	Antonio Guzmán Fernández
1930	Rafael Estrella Urena	1982–6	Salvador Jorge Blanco
1930–8	Rafael Leónidas Trujillo y Molina	1986–96	Joaquín Videla Balaguer
1938–40	Jacinto Bienvenudo Peynado	1996–2000	Leonel Fernández Reyna
1940–2	Manuel de Jesus Troncoso de la Concha	2000–4	Hipólito Mejía
1942–52	Rafael Leónidas Trujillo y Molina	2004–	Leonel Fernández Reyna

Hispaniola

The Dominican Republic comprises the east of the island of Hispaniola, an island first discovered by Europeans when Christopher Columbus visited it in 1492. It became the first Spanish colony in the Caribbean under the name Santo Domingo. The name Hispaniola is derived from *La Isla Española*, 'the Spanish island'.

DUBAI *see* **UNITED ARAB EMIRATES**

EAST TIMOR

Official name	Democratic Republic of East Timor	**Population**	947 000 (2005e)
		Nationality	Timorese
Local name	Timor-Leste; República Democrática de Timor-Leste (Portuguese), Timor Lorosa'e; Republika Demokratika Timor Lorosa'e (Tetum)	**Languages**	Portuguese, Tetum; English and Indonesian are also spoken
		Ethnic groups	Malay, Papuan
		Religions	Christianity 93% (RC 90%, Prot 3%), Islam 4%, others 3%
Former names	Portuguese Timor (until 1975), part of Indonesia (1976–2002)		
		Time zone	GMT +8
Independence	2002	**Currency**	1 US dollar ($/USD) = 100 cents
Area	14 874 sq km/5 743 sq mi	
		Telephone	+670
Capital	Dili	**Internet**	.tp
Chief towns	Baucau, Pante Macassar	**Country code**	TLS

Location
A republic in south-east Asia, comprising the eastern half of the island of Timor and bounded by Indonesia to the west; also includes the enclave of Oecusse in the west of the island; separated from Australia by the Timor Sea.

Physical description
Mountainous, with numerous rivers; highest peak is Tata Mailau (2 950m/9 678ft); also includes the smaller islands of Pulau Atauro and Jaco.

Climate
Hot and humid equatorial climate; dry season (Jun–Sep), rainy season (Dec–Mar); average temperature is 27°C on the coast, falling inland and with altitude.

National holidays
Jan 1, May 1, 20 (Independence), Aug 15, 30 (Constitution), Sep 20 (Liberation), Nov 1, 12 (Santa Cruz), Dec 8, 25; GF.

Political leaders

President
2002–   Xanana Gusmão

Prime Minister
2002–   Mari Alkatiri

A New Country

East Timor gained its independence on 20 May 2002, becoming the world's newest independent state and newest democracy. It became a member of the United Nations the same year.

ECUADOR

Official name	Republic of Ecuador	**Ethnic groups**	mestizo 50%, Amerindian 35%, white 10%, black 5%
Local name	Ecuador; República del Ecuador		
Independence	1822	**Religions**	Christianity 96% (RC 94%, Prot 2%), others 4%
Area	270 699 sq km/104 490 sq mi		
Capital	Quito	**Time zone**	GMT –5
Chief towns	Guayaquil, Cuenca, Riobamba, Esmeraldas	**Currency**	1 US dollar ($/USD) = 100 cents
Population	13 228 000 (2005e)	**Telephone**	+593
Nationality	Ecuadorean or Ecuadorian	**Internet**	.ec
		Country code	ECU
Languages	Spanish; Quechua is also spoken		

Location
A republic in north-west South America, bounded to the north by Colombia; to the south and east by Peru; and to the west by the Pacific Ocean; also includes the Galápagos Islands.

Physical description
Coastal plain in west; Andean uplands in the centre, three main ranges which include Cotopaxi (5 896m/19 344ft), the world's highest active volcano; highest point is Mt Chimborazo (6 267m/20 560ft); forested alluvial plains in east; frequent earthquakes; the Galápagos Islands include six main volcanic islands.

Climate
Hot and humid coast, rain throughout the year (especially Dec–Apr); temperatures are much reduced by altitude; Quito has warm days and chilly nights, with frequent heavy rain in the afternoon; hot and wet equatorial climate in the east.

National holidays
Jan 1, May 1, 24 (Battle of Pichincha), Aug 10 (Independence), Oct 9 (Independence of Guayaquil), Nov 2, 3 (Independence of Cuenca), Dec 25; GF.

Political leaders

President

1895–1901	Eloy Alfaro	1934–5	José María Velasco Ibarra
1901–5	Leónides Plaza Gutiérrez	1935	Antonio Pons
1905–6	Lizardo García	1935–7	Federico Páez
1906–11	Eloy Alfaro	1937–8	Alberto Enríquez Gallo
1911	Emilio Estrada	1938	Manuel María Borrero
1911–12	Carlos Freile Zaldumbide	1938–9	Aurelio Mosquera Narváez
1912–16	Leónides Plaza Gutiérrez	1939–40	Julio Enrique Moreno
1916–20	Alfredo Baquerizo Moreno	1940–4	Carlos Alberto Arroya del Río
1920–4	José Luis Tamayo	1944–7	José María Velasco Ibarra
1924–5	Gonzálo S Córdova	1947	Carlos Mancheno
1925–6	*Military Juntas*	1947–8	Carlos Julio Arosemena Tola
1926–31	Isidro Ayora	1948–52	Galo Plaza Lasso
1931–2	*Four Acting Presidents*	1952–6	José María Velasco Ibarra
1932–3	Juan de Dios Martínez Mera	1956–60	Camilo Ponce Enríquez
1933–4	Abelardo Montalvo	1960–1	José María Velasco Ibarra

1961–3	Carlos Julio Arosemena Monroy	1988–92	Rodrigo Borja Cevallos
1963–6	*Military Junta*	1992–6	Sixto Durán Ballén
1966	Clemente Yerovi Indaburu	1996–7	Abdalá Bucaram Ortiz
1966–8	Otto Arosemena Gómez	1997	Rosalia Arteaga *Acting President*
1968–72	José María Velasco Ibarra	1997–8	Fabián Alarcón Rivero
1972–6	Guillermo Rodríguez Lara	1998–2000	Jamil Mahuad Witt
1976–9	*Military Junta*	2000–3	Gustavo Noboa Bejerano
1979–81	Jaime Roldós Aguilera	2003–5	Lucio Gutiérrez
1981–4	Oswaldo Hurtado Larrea	2005–	Alfredo Palacio
1984–8	León Febres Cordero		

Incas and Volcanoes

Quito sits at an altitude of 2 850m/9 350ft at the foot of Guagua Pichincha, an active volcano prone to showering the city with clouds of ash. Quito was an Inca capital, but was destroyed by followers of the Inca leader Atahualpa when it became clear that it would be captured by the Spanish in the early 1530s. It was refounded in 1534.

EGYPT

Official name	Arab Republic of Egypt	**Nationality**	Egyptian
Local name	Misr; Al-Jumhūriyya al-Miṣriyya al-'Arabiyya	**Languages**	Arabic
Former name	formerly part of the United Arab Republic, with Syria (1958–61; name retained until 1971)	**Ethnic groups**	Eastern Hamitic 91%, others 9%
		Religions	Islam 94% (mostly Sunni), Christianity 6% (mostly Coptic)
Independence	1922	**Time zone**	GMT +2
Area	1 001 449 sq km/386 559 sq mi	**Currency**	1 Egyptian Pound (£E, LE/EGP) = 100 piastres
Capital	Cairo; El Qāhirah	**Telephone**	+20
Chief towns	Alexandria, Port Said, Aswan, Suez, El Gîza	**Internet**	.eg
Population	74 033 000 (2005e)	**Country code**	EGY

Location
A republic in north-east Africa, bounded to the north by the Mediterranean Sea; to the north-east by Israel; to the east by the Red Sea; to the south by Sudan; and to the west by Libya.

Physical description
River Nile flows north, dammed to create Lake Nasser; huge delta north of Cairo; Western Desert covers over two-thirds of the country; highest point is Gebel Katherîna (2 637m/ 8 651ft); 90% of the population live on the Nile floodplain (c.3% of the country's area).

Climate
Mainly desert, except for an 80km/50mi wide Mediterranean coastal fringe; very hot on the coast when the dust-laden *khamsin* wind blows north from the Sahara (Mar–Jun).

National holidays
Apr 25 (Sinai Liberation), May 1, 23 (Revolution), Oct 6 (Armed Forces); Ad (2), Ar, ER (2), NY (Muslim), PB, Sham El Nessim (Apr/May).

Political leaders

Khedive

1895–1914   Abbas Helmi II

Sultan
1914–17   Hussein Kamel
1917–22   Ahmed Fouad

Kingdom of Egypt

Monarch
1922–36   Fouad I
1936–7   Farouk *Trusteeship*
1937–52   Farouk I

Republic of Egypt

President

1953–4	Mohammed Najib	1970–81	Mohammed Anwar El-Sadat
1954–70	Gamal Abdel Nasser	1981–	Mohammed Hosni Mubarak

Prime Minister

1895–1908	Mustafa Fahmy	1948–9	Ibrahim Abdel Hadi
1908–10	Butros Ghali	1949–50	Hussein Sirry
1910–14	Mohammed Said	1950–2	Mustafa An-Nahass
1914–19	Hussein Rushdi	1952	Ali Maher
1919	Mohammed Said	1952	Najib El-Hilali
1919–20	Yousuf Wahba	1952	Hussein Sirry
1920–1	Mohammed Tewfiq Nazim	1952	Najib El-Hilali
1921–2	Adli Yegen	1952	Ali Maher
1922	Abdel Khaliq Tharwat	1952–4	Mohammed Najib
1922–3	Mohammed Tewfiq Nazim	1954	Gamal Abdel Nasser
1923–4	Yehia Ibrahim	1954	Mohammed Najib
1924	Saad Zaghloul	1954–62	Gamal Abdel Nasser
1924–6	Ahmed Zaywan	1958–61	*United Arab Republic*
1926–7	Adli Yegen	1962–5	Ali Sabri
1927–8	Abdel Khaliq Tharwat	1965–6	Zakariya Mohyi Ed-Din
1928	Mustafa An-Nahass	1966–7	Mohammed Sidqi Soliman
1928–9	Mohammed Mahmoud	1967–70	Gamal Abdel Nasser
1929–30	Adli Yegen	1970–2	Mahmoud Fawzi
1930	Mustafa An-Nahass	1972–3	Aziz Sidki
1930–3	Ismail Sidqi	1973–4	Mohammed Anwar El-Sadat
1933–4	Abdel Fattah Yahya	1974–5	Abdel Aziz Hijazy
1934–6	Mohammed Tewfiq Nazim	1975–8	Mamdouh Salem
1936	Ali Maher	1978–80	Mustafa Khalil
1936–7	Mustafa An-Nahass	1980–1	Mohammed Anwar El-Sadat
1937–9	Mohammed Mahmoud	1981–2	Mohammed Hosni Mubarak
1939–40	Ali Maher	1982–4	Fouad Monyi Ed-Din
1940	Hassan Sabri	1984	Kamal Hassan Ali
1940–2	Hussein Sirry	1985–6	Ali Lotfi
1942–4	Mustafa An-Nahass	1986–96	Atif Sidqi
1944–5	Ahmed Maher	1996–1999	Ahmed Kamal Al-Ganzouri
1945–6	Mahmoud Fahmy El-Nuqrashi	1999–2004	Atef Muhammed Ebeid
1946	Ismail Sidqi	2004–	Ahmed Nazif
1946–8	Mahmoud Fahmy El-Nuqrashi		

Ancient Egyptian dynasties

All dates are BC.

c.3100–2890	I	*Early Dynastic Period*
c.2890–2780	II	(First use of stone in building; hieroglyphic script developed.)
c.2780–2613	III	*Old Kingdom*
c.2613–2494	IV	(The age of the great pyramid builders. Longest reign in history: Pepi II, 90 years.)
c.2494–2345	V	
c.2345–2181	VI	
c.2181–2173	VII	*First Intermediate Period*
c.2173–2160	VIII	(Social order upset; few monuments built.)
c.2160–2130	IX	
c.2130–2040	X	
c.2133–1991	XI	
1991–1786	XII	*Middle Kingdom*
1786–1633	XIII	(Golden age of art and craftsmanship.)
1786–c.1603	XIV	*Second Intermediate Period*
1674–1567	XV	(Country divided into principalities.)
c.1684–1567	XVI	
c.1660–1567	XVII	
1567–1320	XVIII	*New Kingdom*
1320–1200	XIX	(Began with colonial expansion, ended in divided rule.)
1200–1085	XX	
1085–945	XXI	*Third Intermediate Period*
945–745	XXII	(Revival of prosperity and restoration of cults.)
745–718	XXIII	
718–715	XXIV	
715–668	XXV	
664–525	XXVI	*Late Period*
525–404	XXVII	(Completion of Nile–Red Sea canal. Alexander the Great reached Alexandria in 332BC.)
404–399	XXVIII	
399–380	XXIX	
380–343	XXX	
343–332	XXXI	

See also **EGYPTIAN GODS** *under* **RELIGIONS, BELIEFS AND FOLKLORE** *and*
SEVEN WONDERS OF THE WORLD *under* **ANCIENT GREECE AND ROME**

ÉIRE *see* **IRELAND**

EL SALVADOR

Official name	Republic of El Salvador		Amerindian 8%, white 1%
Local name	El Salvador; República de El Salvador	Religions	Christianity 97% (RC 77%, Prot 20%), others 3%
Independence	1841		
Area	21 476 sq km/8 290 sq mi	Time zone	GMT −6
Capital	San Salvador	Currency	1 El Salvador Colón (¢/SVC) = 100 centavos/1 US Dollar ($, US$/USD) = 100 cents
Chief towns	Santa Ana, San Miguel, Mejicanos		
Population	6 881 000 (2005e)	Telephone	+503
Nationality	Salvadoran	Internet	.sv
Languages	Spanish	Country code	SLV
Ethnic groups	mestizo 91%,		

Location
A republic in Central America, bounded to the north and east by Honduras; to the south by the Pacific Ocean; and to the west by Guatemala.

Physical description
Two volcanic ranges running east to west; highest volcano is Santa Ana (Ilamatepec) at 2 362m/7 749ft; terrain ranges from a narrow coastal belt in the south through upland valleys and plateaus to mountains in the north; highest point is Cerro El Pital (2 730m/ 8 957ft); many volcanic lakes; earthquakes are common.

Climate
Varies greatly with altitude; hot and tropical on the coastal lowlands; single rainy season (May–Oct); temperate uplands; average annual temperature at San Salvador is 23°C.

National holidays
Jan 1, May 1, 10 (Mothers), Aug 6 (El Salvador del Mundo) (2), Sep 15 (Independence), Nov 2, Dec 25, 31; GF, HT; *some local variation; public and private sector holidays may differ.*

Political leaders

President

1899–1903	Tomás Regalado	1931	*Military Administration*
1903–7	Pedro José Escalon	1931–4	Maximiliano H Martinez *Vice President*
1907–11	Fernando Figueroa		
1911–13	Manuel Enrique Araujo	1934–5	Andrés I Menéndez *Provisional President*
1913–14	Carlos Meléndez *President Designate*		
		1935–44	Maximiliano H Martinez
1914–15	Alfonso Quiñónez Molina *President Designate*	1944	Andrés I Menéndez *Vice President*
1915–18	Carlos Meléndez		
1918–19	Alfonso Quiñónez Molina *Vice President*	1944–5	Osmin Aguirre y Salinas *Provisional President*
		1945–8	Salvador Castaneda Castro
1919–23	Jorge Meléndez	1948–50	*Revolutionary Council*
1923–7	Alfonso Quiñónez Molina	1950–6	Oscar Osorio
1927–31	Pio Romero Bosque	1956–60	José María Lemus
1931	Arturo Araujo	1960–1	*Military Junta*

1961–2	*Civil-Military Administration*		1982–4	*Government of National*
1962	Rodolfo Eusebio Cordón			*Unanimity* (Alvaro Magaña)
	Provisional President		1984–9	José Napoleón Duarte
1962–7	Julio Adalberto Rivera		1989–94	Alfredo Cristiani
1967–72	Fidel Sánchez Hernández		1994–9	Armando Calderón Sol
1972–7	Arturo Armando Molina		1999–2004	Francisco Flores Perez
1977–9	Carlos Humberto Romero		2004–	Elias Antonio Saca
1979–82	*Military Juntas*			

ENGLAND *see* **UNITED KINGDOM**

EQUATORIAL GUINEA

Official name	Republic of Equatorial Guinea			Equatoguinean
		Languages	Spanish, French; pidgin English and Fang are also spoken	
Local name	Guinea Ecuatorial; República de Guinea Ecuatorial			
Former name	Spanish Guinea (until 1968)	**Ethnic groups**	Fang 82%, Bubi 11%, Ndowe 4%, others 3%	
Independence	1968	**Religions**	Christianity 89% (RC), traditional beliefs 4%, none/unaffiliated 6%, Islam 1%	
Area	26 016 sq km/10 042 sq mi			
Capital	Malabo	**Time zone**	GMT +1	
Chief towns	Bata and Evinayong on the mainland, Luba and Riaba on Bioko	**Currency**	1 CFA Franc (CFAFr/XAF) = 100 centimes	
		Telephone	+240	
Population	504 000 (2005e)	**Internet**	.gq	
Nationality	Equatorial Guinean or	**Country code**	GNQ	

Location
A republic in western central Africa, comprising a mainland area (Río Muni), bounded to the north by Cameroon; to the east and south by Gabon; and to the west by the Gulf of Guinea; and several islands (notably Bioko and Annabón) in the Gulf of Guinea.

Physical description
Mainland rises sharply from a narrow coast of mangrove swamps towards the heavily-forested African plateau; Bioko Island, about 160km/100mi north-west of the mainland, is of volcanic origin, rising to 3 007m/9 865ft at Pico de Basilé.

Climate
Hot and humid equatorial; average maximum daily temperature is 29–32°C.

National holidays
Jan 1, May 1, Jun 5 (President's Birthday), Aug 3 (Armed Forces), Oct 12 (Independence), Dec 10 (Human Rights), 25; CC, GF, Constitution (Aug).

Political leaders

President
1968–79	Francisco Macias Nguema
1979–	Teodoro Obiang Nguema Mbasogo

Prime Minister

1963–8	Bonifacio Ondó Edu	1996–2001	Ángel Serafín Seriche Dougan
1968–82	*No Prime Minister*	2001–4	Cándido Muatetema Rivas
1982–92	Cristino Seriche Bioko	2004–	Miguel Abia Biteo Boricó
1992–6	Silestre Siale Bileka		

ERITREA

Official name	State of Eritrea	**Languages**	Arabic, Tigrinya
Local name	Hagere Eretra, al-Dawla al-Iritra	**Ethnic groups**	Tigrinya 50%, Tigrean and Kunama 40%, Afar 4%, Saho 3%, others 3%
Former name	formerly part of Ethiopia (until 1993)	**Religions**	Islam 50%, Christianity 50% (Coptic)
Independence	1993		
Area	93 679 sq km/36 160 sq mi	**Time zone**	GMT +3
		Currency	1 Nakfa (Nfa/ERN) = 100 cents
Capital	Asmara; Asmera		
Chief towns	Assab, Massawa, Keren, Tessenai	**Telephone**	+291
		Internet	.er
Population	4 401 000 (2005e)	**Country code**	ERI
Nationality	Eritrean		

Location
A country in north-east Africa, bounded to the north and west by Sudan; to the north-east by the Red Sea; to the south-east by Djibouti; and to the south by Ethiopia.

Physical description
Low-lying coastline stretching 1 000km/620mi along the Red Sea, rising to an inland plateau; highest point is Soira (3 018m/9 901ft).

Climate
Hot and dry along the Red Sea desert coast; cooler and wetter in the central highlands; semi-arid in the western hills and lowlands.

National holidays
Jan 1, 7 (Eritrean Christmas), 19 (Eritrean Epiphany), May 24 (Freedom), Jun 20 (Martyrs), Sep 1 (Start of the Armed Struggle), 11 (Eritrean Orthodox Church NY), 27 (Feast of the Cross); Eritrean Easter (Mar/Apr) (2), Eritrean Whit Sunday (Mar/Apr).

Political leaders

President
1993–   Isaias Afewerki

Four Villages

It is believed that Asmara, the Eritrean capital, was originally four small villages. The original name was *Arbate Asmere*, meaning 'four united into one'.

ESTONIA

Official name	Republic of Estonia	**Languages**	Estonian
Local name	Eesti; Eesti Vabariik (Estonian), Estonskaya (Russian)	**Ethnic groups**	Estonian 68%, Russian 26%, Ukrainian 2%, Belarussian 1%, Finnish 1%, others 2%
Former name	Estonian Soviet Socialist Republic (1940–90), within the Union of Soviet Socialist Republics (USSR; 1940–91)	**Religions**	Christianity 100%, predominantly Lutheran Protestant, also Orthodox, Baptist, Methodist and Pentecostal; Judaism
Independence	1991		
Area	45 100 sq km/17 409 sq mi	**Time zone**	GMT +2
Capital	Tallinn	**Currency**	1 Kroon (KR/EEK) = 100 sents
Chief towns	Tartu, Narva, Kohtla-Järve, Pärnu	**Telephone**	+372
Population	1 330 000 (2005e)	**Internet**	.ee
Nationality	Estonian	**Country code**	EST

Location
A republic in north-eastern Europe, bounded to the north by the Gulf of Finland; to the east by Russia; to the south by Latvia; and to the west by the Baltic Sea.

Physical description
Over 1 500 lakes in a fairly flat terrain; highest point is Suur Munamagi (318m/1 043ft); there are many islands on the coast, notably Saaremaa, Hiiumaa and Muhu; 36% of the area is forested.

Climate
Cool summers, wet winters.

National holidays
Jan 1, Feb 24 (Independence), May 1 (Spring), Jun 23 (Victory), 24 (St John/Midsummer), Aug 20 (Restoration of Independence), Dec 25, 26; GF, ES, Whit Sunday.

Political leaders

President

1990–2	Arnold Rüütel
1992–2001	Lennart Meri
2001–	Arnold Rüütel

Prime Minister

1990–2	Edgar Savisaar	1997–9	Mart Siimann
1992	Tiit Vähi	1999–2002	Mart Laar
1992–4	Mart Laar	2002–3	Siim Kallas
1994–5	Andres Tarand	2003–5	Juhan Parts
1995–7	Tiit Vähi	2005–	Andrus Ansip

ETHIOPIA

Official name	Federal Democratic Republic of Ethiopia	**Languages**	Amharic; 70 local languages are also spoken
Local name	Ityopya; Ya'Ityopya Federalawi Dimokrasyawi Repeblik	**Ethnic groups**	Oromo 40%, Amhara and Tigrean 32%, Sidamo 9%, Shankella 6%, Somali 6%, others 7%
Former name	Abyssinia (until 1936), part of Italian East Africa (1936–41), People's Democratic Republic of Ethiopia (1987–91)	**Religions**	Christianity 42% (Coptic), Islam 40%, traditional beliefs 14%, others 4%
Area	1 128 497 sq km/435 600 sq mi	**Time zone**	GMT +3
Capital	Addis Ababa; Ādīs Ābeba, Addis Abeba	**Currency**	1 Ethiopian Birr (EB/ETB) = 100 cents
Chief towns	Dire Dawa, Harer	**Telephone**	+251
Population	77 431 000 (2005e)	**Internet**	.et
Nationality	Ethiopian	**Country code**	ETH

Location
A republic in north-east Africa, bounded to the north by Djibouti and Eritrea; to the north-east and east by Somalia; to the south by Kenya; and to the west and south-west by Sudan.

Physical description
Dominated by a mountainous central plateau; split diagonally by the Great Rift Valley; highest point is Ras Dashen (4 620m/15 157ft); plateau is crossed east to west by the Blue Nile, which has its source in Lake Tana; north and east are relatively low-lying; in the north-east the Danakil Depression dips to 116m/381ft below sea level; the country is landlocked, having lost about 10% of its territory and all of its Red Sea coastline when the former province of Eritrea gained its independence in 1993.

Climate
Tropical, moderated by higher altitudes; distinct wet season (Apr–Sep); temperatures warm, but rarely hot all year round; hot, semi-arid north-east and south-east lowlands; severe droughts in the 1980s caused widespread famine.

National holidays
Jan 7 (Ethiopian Christmas), 19 (Ethiopian Epiphany), Feb 18 (President), Mar 2 (Victory of Adwa), May 1, 28 (Downfall of the Dergue), Sep 27 (Finding of the True Cross); Ad, ER, NY (Ethiopian) (Sep), PB, Ethiopian Good Friday and Easter Sunday.

Political leaders

Monarch

1889–1911	Menelik II		1928–74	Haile Selassie *Emperor from 1930*
1911–16	Lij Iyasu (Joshua)			
1916–28	Zawditu			

Chairman of Provisional Military Administrative Council

1974–7	Teferi Benti
1977–87	Mengistu Haile Mariam

President

1987–91	Mengistu Haile Mariam	1991–5	Meles Zenawi
1991	Tesfaye Gebre Kidan *Acting President*	1995–2001	Negasso Gidada
		2001–	Girma Wolde-Giorgis

Prime Minister

1987–9	Fikre Selassie Wogderess	1991–5	Tamirat Layne *Acting Prime Minister*
1989–91	Haile Yimenu *Acting Prime Minister*	1995–	Meles Zenawi
1991	Tesfaye Dinka *Acting Prime Minister*		

FALKLAND ISLANDS *see* **UNITED KINGDOM**

FAROE ISLANDS *see* **DENMARK**

FIJI

Official name	Republic of the Fiji Islands	**Ethnic groups**	Fijian 51%, Indian 44%, others 5%
Local name	Matanitu Ko Viti	**Religions**	Christianity 46% (Prot 37%, mainly Methodist, RC 9%), Hinduism 38%, Islam 8%, Sikhism 1%, others 7%
Former name	Republic of Fiji (1987–98)		
Independence	1970		
Area	18 333 sq km/7 076 sq mi		
		Time zone	GMT +12
Capital	Suva	**Currency**	1 Fiji Dollar (F$/FJD) = 100 cents
Chief towns	Lautoka, Ba, Labasa, Nadi, Nausori		
		Telephone	+679
Population	848 000 (2005e)	**Internet**	.fj
Nationality	Fijian	**Country code**	FJI
Languages	Fijian, Hindi		

Location
An independent republic in the south-west Pacific Ocean.

Physical description
A Melanesian island group of 844 islands and islets, of which c.100 are permanently inhabited; larger islands are generally mountainous; highest peak, Tomaniivi, is on Viti Levu (1 324m/4 348ft); smaller islands consist of limestone, with little vegetation; extensive coral reef (Great Sea Reef) stretches for 500km/300mi along western fringe.

Climate
Winds are variable in the wet season between Nov and Apr, with tropical cyclonic storms likely; temperatures average 23–27°C; humidity on the windward slopes averages 74%.

National holidays
Jan 1, Dec 25, 26; D, EM, GF, HS, PB, Queen's Birthday (Jun), National Youth (Apr/May), Ratu Sir Lala Sukuna (1st Mon in Jun), Fiji (Oct).

Political leaders

Head of State until 1987: British monarch, represented by Governor General.

Governor General
1970–3	Robert Sidney Foster
1973–83	George Cakobau
1983–7	Penaia Ganilau
1987	*Military Administration* (Sitiveni Rabuka)

President
1987–93	Penaia Ganilau	2000–	Ratu Josefa Iloilo
1993–2000	Kamisese Mara		*Interim President until 2001*
2000	*Interim Military Government* (Frank Bainimarama)		

Prime Minister
1970–87	Kamisese Mara	2000	Epeli Nailatika *Interim Prime Minister*
1987	Timoci Bavadra		
1987–92	Kamisese Mara	2000–1	Laisenia Qarase
1992–9	Sitiveni Rabuka	2001	Tevita Momoedonu
1999–2000	Mahendra Chaudhry	2001–	Laisenia Qarase
2000	Tevita Momoedonu *Acting Prime Minister*		

Whales' Teeth

One of the national symbols of Fiji is the *tabua*, a whale's tooth. Historically very rare, the tabua is of supreme importance in Fijian traditions. Highly prized in ceremonies, it is regarded as a symbol of peace, understanding and love.

FINLAND

Official name	Republic of Finland	**Nationality**	Finnish
Local name	Suomi; Suomen Tasavalta (Finnish), Republiken Finland (Swedish)	**Languages**	Finnish, Swedish
		Ethnic groups	Finnish 93%, Swedish 6%, others 1%
Independence	1917	**Religions**	Christianity 91% (Prot 89%, Orthodox 1%, RC 1%), none/unaffiliated 9%
Area	338 145 sq km/130 524 sq mi		
		Time zone	GMT +2
Capital	Helsinki (Finnish), Helsingfors (Swedish)	**Currency**	1 Euro (€/EUR) = 100 cents
Chief towns	Tampere, Turku, Espoo, Vantaa	**Telephone**	+358
		Internet	.fi
Population	5 249 000 (2005e)	**Country code**	FIN

Location
A republic in northern Europe, bounded to the north by Norway; to the east by Russia; to the south by the Gulf of Finland; and to the west by the Gulf of Bothnia and Sweden.

Physical description
A low-lying glaciated plateau; over one-third of the country is north of the Arctic Circle; highest peak is Halti (1 328m/4 356ft); over 60 000 shallow lakes in the south-east; Saaristomeri archipelago has over 17 000 islands; 65% is forest and 10% water.

Climate
Northern location is ameliorated by the Baltic Sea; western winds bring warm air currents in summer; Eurasian winds bring cold spells in winter and heatwaves in summer; during summer the sun stays above the horizon for over 70 days.

National holidays
Jan 1, 6, May 1, Nov 1, Dec 6 (Independence), 24, 25, 26; A, EM, ES, GF, Midsummer Day (Jun), Whitsun (May/Jun).

Political leaders

Monarch

Finland was under Swedish control from the 13c until it was ceded to Russia in 1809. Russian rulers then assumed the title of Grand Duke of Finland. In 1917 it became an independent monarchy. However in Nov 1918, after initially accepting the throne the previous month, Landgrave Frederick Charles of Hesse, the brother-in-law of the German Emperor Wilhelm II, withdrew his acceptance because of the Armistice and the ensuing abdication of Wilhelm II. The previous regent remained in power until a Republic was declared in Jul 1919.

1918	Dr Pehr Evind Svinhufvud *Regent*
1918	Landgrave Frederick Charles of Hesse *(withdrew acceptance)*
1918–19	Dr Pehr Evind Svinhufvud *Regent*

President

1919–25	Kaarlo Ståhlberg	1946–56	Juho Paasikivi
1925–31	Lauri Relander	1956–82	Urho Kekkonen
1931–7	Pehr Svinhufvud	1982–94	Mauno Koivisto
1937–40	Kyösti Kallio	1994–2000	Martti Ahtisaari
1940–4	Risto Ryti	2000–	Tarja Halonen
1944–6	C G E Mannerheim		

Prime Minister

1917–18	Pehr Svinhufvud	1925–6	Kyösti Kallio
1918	Juho Paasikivi	1926–7	Väinö Tanner
1918–19	Lauri Ingman	1927–8	Juho Sunila
1919	Kaarlo Castrén	1928–9	Oskari Mantere
1919–20	Juho Vennola	1929–30	Kyösti Kallio
1920–1	Rafael Erich	1930–1	Pehr Svinhufvud
1921–2	Juho Vennola	1931–2	Juhu Sunila
1922	Aino Cajander	1932–6	Toivo Kivimäki
1922–4	Kyösti Kallio	1936–7	Kyösti Kallio
1924	Aino Cajander	1937–9	Aino Cajander
1924–5	Lauri Ingman	1939–41	Risto Ryti
1925	Antti Tulenheimo	1941–3	Johann Rangell

1943–4	Edwin Linkomies		1964–6	Johannes Virolainen
1944	Andreas Hackzell		1966–8	Rafael Paasio
1944	Urho Castrén		1968–70	Mauno Koivisto
1944–5	Juho Paasikivi		1970	Teuvo Aura
1946–8	Mauno Pekkala		1970–1	Ahti Karjalainen
1948–50	Karl Fagerholm		1971–2	Teuvo Aura
1950–3	Urho Kekkonen		1972	Rafael Paasio
1953–4	Sakari Tuomioja		1972–5	Kalevi Sorsa
1954	Ralf Törngren		1975	Keijo Liinamaa
1954–6	Urho Kekkonen		1975–7	Martti Miettunen
1956–7	Karl Fagerholm		1977–9	Kalevi Sorsa
1957	Väinö Sukselainen		1979–82	Mauno Koivisto
1957–8	Rainer von Fieandt		1982–7	Kalevi Sorsa
1958	Reino Kuuskoski		1987–91	Harri Holkeri
1958–9	Karl Fagerholm		1991–5	Esko Aho
1959–61	Väinö Sukselainen		1995–2003	Paavo Lipponen
1961–2	Martti Miettunen		2003	Anneli Jäätteenmäki
1962–3	Ahti Karjalainen		2003–	Matti Vanhanen
1963–4	Reino Lehto			

Curious Contests

Finland hosts some of the world's strangest competitions. The most famous is perhaps the Wife Carrying World Championships, which take place annually in Sonkajärvi. Contestants must carry a woman (although not necessarily their own wife) over a 253m/830ft track, with the fastest couple winning the wife's weight in beer. But while this contest is believed to have its roots in a traditional Finnish custom, some of the other competitions are of rather more recent vintage. The World Air Guitar Championships take place in Oulu, and the Mobile Phone Throwing World Championships in Savonlinna; both attract thousands of spectators and media attention from around the world.

FRANCE

Official name	French Republic		African 5%, Breton 1%, German 1%, others 1%
Local name	France; République Française	**Religions**	Christianity 84% (RC 80%, Prot 4%), none/ unaffiliated 8%, Islam 6%, Judaism 1%, Buddhism 1%
Area	551 000 sq km/213 000 sq mi		
Capital	Paris		
Chief towns	Marseilles, Lyons, Toulouse, Nice, Strasbourg	**Time zone**	GMT +1
		Currency	1 Euro (€/EUR) = 100 cents
Population	60 496 000 (2005e)	**Telephone**	+33
Nationality	French	**Internet**	.fr
Languages	French	**Country code**	FRA
Ethnic groups	French 92%, North		

Location
A republic in western Europe, bounded to the north and north-east by the English Channel, Belgium, Luxembourg and Germany; to the east by Germany, Switzerland, Italy and Monaco; to the south by the Mediterranean Sea, Spain and Andorra; and to the west by the Bay of Biscay; also includes the island of Corsica in the Mediterranean Sea.

Physical description
A country of low and medium-sized hills and plateaux deeply cut by rivers; bounded to the south and east by large mountain ranges; the Alps rise to 4 807m/15 771ft at Mont Blanc (the highest point) in the east, and the Pyrenees lie to the south; many major rivers.

Climate
South has a Mediterranean climate, with warm, moist winters and hot, dry summers; climate is maritime in the north-west; east has a continental climate.

National holidays
Jan 1, May 1, 8 (Victory), Jul 14 (Bastille), Aug 15, Nov 1, 11 (Armistice), Dec 25; A, EM, WM.

Overseas departments

French Guiana

Location	Situated on the north-eastern coast of South America, it is bounded to the west by Suriname; to the east and south by Brazil; and to the north by the Atlantic Ocean.		
Local name	Guyane	**Population**	187 000 (2005e)
Area	90 909 sq km/35 091 sq mi	**Internet**	.gf
Capital	Cayenne	**Country code**	GUF

Guadeloupe

Location	A group of seven islands in the central Lesser Antilles, in the east Caribbean Sea.		
Local name	Guadeloupe	**Population**	448 000 (2005e)
Area	1 779 sq km/687 sq mi	**Internet**	.gp
Capital	Basse-Terre	**Country code**	GLP

Martinique

Location	An island in the Windward group of the Lesser Antilles, in the east Caribbean Sea, between Dominica and St Lucia.		
Local name	Martinique	**Population**	396 000 (2005e)
Area	1 079 sq km/416 sq mi	**Internet**	.mq
Capital	Fort-de-France	**Country code**	MTQ

Réunion

Location	An island in the Indian Ocean, to the east of Madagascar.		
Local name	Réunion	**Population**	785 000 (2005e)
Area	2 510 sq km/969 sq mi	**Internet**	.re
Capital	St Denis	**Country code**	REU

Overseas territories

French Polynesia

Location	An island grouping of five scattered archipelagoes in the south-east Pacific Ocean, between the Cook Islands in the west and the Pitcairn Islands in the east.		
Local name	Polynésie Française	**Population**	257 000 (2005e)
Area	3 941 sq km/1 521 sq mi	**Internet**	.pf
Capital	Papeete	**Country code**	PYF

New Caledonia

Location	A group of islands in the south-west Pacific Ocean, 1 100km/680mi east of Australia.		
Local name	Nouvelle-Calédonie	**Population**	237 000 (2005e)
Area	18 575 sq km/7 170 sq mi	**Internet**	.nc
Capital	Nouméa	**Country code**	NCL

French Southern and Antarctic Territories

Location	A group of islands in the southern Indian Ocean and Adélie Land in Antarctica.		
Local name	Terres australes et antarctiques françaises	**Population**	Scientific staff only
		Internet	.tf
Area	507 781 sq km/196 003 sq mi	**Country code**	ATF

Wallis and Futuna Islands

Location	An island grouping (consisting principally of Wallis Island (Uvéa), Futuna and Alofi) in the south-central Pacific Ocean, lying north-east of Fiji.		
Local name	Îles de Wallis et Futuna	**Population**	15 000 (2005e)
Area	274 sq km/106 sq mi	**Internet**	.wf
Capital	Mata-Utui; Matâ'utu	**Country code**	WLF

DOM-TOM

French overseas departments and territories are collectively known as the *DOM-TOM*, *Départements d'outre-mer* and *Territoires d'outre-mer*. In contrast, the mainland of France is often known as *l'Hexagone*, a reference to its roughly hexagonal shape.

Territorial collectivities

Mayotte

Location	A small island group of volcanic origin, east of Comoros, in the west Indian Ocean.		
Local name	Mayotte	**Population**	193 600 (2005e)
Area	374 sq km/144 sq mi	**Internet**	.yt
Capital	Mamoudzou	**Country code**	MYT

St Pierre and Miquelon

Location	Two islands in the North Atlantic Ocean, south of Newfoundland (Canada).		
Local name	St-Pierre-et-Miquelon	**Population**	6 000 (2005e)
Area	240 sq km/93 sq mi	**Internet**	.pm
Capital	St Pierre	**Country code**	SPM

Note: France also possesses Bassas da India, Europa Island, the Glorioso Islands, Juan de Nova and Tromelin Island in the Indian Ocean and Clipperton Island in the Pacific Ocean, all largely uninhabited.

Political leaders

Monarch

987–996	Hugh Capet	1461–83	Louis XI
996–1031	Robert II	1483–98	Charles VIII
1031–60	Henry I	1498–1515	Louis XII
1060–1108	Philip I	1515–47	Francis I
1108–37	Louis VI	1547–59	Henry II
1137–80	Louis VII	1559–60	Francis II
1180–1223	Philip II Augustus	1560–74	Charles IX
1223–6	Louis VIII	1574–89	Henry III
1226–70	Louis IX	1589–1610	Henry IV (of Navarre)
1270–85	Philip III	1610–43	Louis XIII
1285–1314	Philip IV	1643–1715	Louis XIV
1314–16	Louis X	1715–74	Louis XV
1316	John I	1774–92	Louis XVI
1316–22	Philip V	1793–1804	*Republic*
1322–8	Charles IV	1804–14	*Empire* (Napoleon Bonaparte)
1328–50	Philip VI	1814–24	Louis XVIII
1350–64	John II	1824–30	Charles X
1364–80	Charles V	1830–48	Louis-Philippe
1380–1422	Charles VI	1848	*monarchy dissolved*
1422–61	Charles VII		

Royal Nicknames

Derogatory nicknames for early French kings include the *Bald* (Charles I, 823–77), the *Fat* (Charles II, 839–88) and the *Simple* (Charles III, 879–929). But they weren't all bad. There was also the *Fair* (Charles IV, 1294–1328), the *Wise* (Charles V, 1338–80), the *Victorious* (Charles VII, 1403–61), the *Affable* (Charles VIII, 1470–98), the *Well-Beloved* (Louis XV, 1710–74) and, of course, the *Sun King* himself, Louis XIV (1638–1715).

Third Republic

President

1899–1906	Emile Loubet	1920–4	Alexandre Millerand
1906–13	Armand Fallières	1924–31	Gaston Doumergue
1913–20	Raymond Poincaré	1931–2	Paul Doumer
1920	Paul Deschanel	1932–40	Albert Lebrun

Prime Minister

1899–1902	Pierre Waldeck-Rousseau	1926–9	Raymond Poincaré
1902–5	Emile Combes	1929	Aristide Briand
1905–6	Maurice Rouvier	1929–30	André Tardieu
1906	Jean Sarrien	1930	Camille Chautemps
1906–9	Georges Clemenceau	1930	André Tardieu
1909–11	Aristide Briand	1930–1	Théodore Steeg
1911	Ernest Monis	1931–2	Pierre Laval
1911–12	Joseph Caillaux	1932	André Tardieu
1912–13	Raymond Poincaré	1932	Édouard Herriot
1913	Aristide Briand	1932–3	Joseph Paul-Boncour
1913	Jean Louis Barthou	1933	Édouard Daladier
1913–14	Gaston Doumergue	1933	Albert Sarrault
1914	Alexandre Ribot	1933–4	Camille Chautemps
1914–15	René Viviani	1934	Édouard Daladier
1915–17	Aristide Briand	1934	Gaston Doumergue
1917	Alexandre Ribot	1934–5	Pierre-Étienne Flandin
1917	Paul Painlevé	1935	Fernand Bouisson
1917–20	Georges Clemenceau	1935–6	Pierre Laval
1920	Alexandre Millerand	1936	Albert Sarrault
1920–1	Georges Leygues	1936–7	Léon Blum
1921–2	Aristide Briand	1937–8	Camille Chautemps
1922–4	Raymond Poincaré	1938	Léon Blum
1924	Frédéric François-Marsal	1938–40	Édouard Daladier
1924–5	Édouard Herriot	1940	Paul Reynaud
1925	Paul Painlevé	1940	Philippe Pétain
1925–6	Aristide Briand		
1926	Édouard Herriot		

Vichy Government

President and Prime Minister
1940–4	Philippe Pétain

Provisional Government of the French Republic

President and Prime Minister
1944–6	Charles de Gaulle
1946	Félix Gouin
1946	Georges Bidault

Fourth Republic

President
1947–54	Vincent Auriol
1954–8	René Coty

Prime Minister

1946–7	Léon Blum	1947–8	Robert Schuman
1947	Paul Ramadier	1948	André Marie

1948	Robert Schuman	1953	René Mayer
1948–9	Henri Queuille	1953–4	Joseph Laniel
1949–50	Georges Bidault	1954–5	Pierre Mendès-France
1950	Henri Queuille	1955–6	Edgar Faure
1950–1	René Pleven	1956–7	Guy Mollet
1951	Henri Queuille	1957	Maurice Bourgès-Maunoury
1951–2	René Pleven	1957–8	Félix Gaillard
1952	Edgar Faure	1958	Pierre Pfimlin
1952–3	Antoine Pinay	1958–9	Charles de Gaulle

Fifth Republic

President

1958–69	Charles de Gaulle	1981–95	François Mitterrand
1969–74	Georges Pompidou	1995–	Jacques Chirac
1974–81	Valéry Giscard d'Estaing		

Prime Minister

1959–62	Michel Debró	1986–8	Jacques Chirac
1962–8	Georges Pompidou	1988–91	Michel Rocard
1968–9	Maurice Couve de Murville	1991–2	Édith Cresson
1969–72	Jacques Chaban Delmas	1992–3	Pierre Bérégovoy
1972–4	Pierre Mesmer	1993–5	Édouard Balladur
1974–6	Jacques Chirac	1995–7	Alain Juppé
1976–81	Raymond Barre	1997–2002	Lionel Jospin
1981–4	Pierre Mauroy	2002–5	Jean-Pierre Raffarin
1984–6	Laurent Fabius	2005–	Dominique de Villepin

FRENCH GUIANA *see* **FRANCE**

FRENCH POLYNESIA *see* **FRANCE**

FRENCH SOUTHERN AND ANTARCTIC TERRITORIES *see* **FRANCE**

FUJAIRAH *see* **UNITED ARAB EMIRATES**

GABON

Official name	Gabonese Republic		are widely spoken
Local name	Gabon; République Gabonaise	**Ethnic groups**	Fang 35%, Mpongwe 16%, Mbete 14%, Punu 11%, others 24%
Former name	French West Africa (1910–60)	**Religions**	Christianity 95% (RC 65%, Prot and others 30%), traditional beliefs 4%, Islam 1%
Independence	1960		
Area	267 667 sq km/103 319 sq mi		
		Time zone	GMT +1
Capital	Libreville	**Currency**	1 CFA Franc (CFAFr/XAF) = 100 centimes
Chief towns	Lambaréné, Franceville, Port Gentil		
		Telephone	+241
Population	1 384 000 (2005e)	**Internet**	.ga
Nationality	Gabonese	**Country code**	GAB
Languages	French; local languages		

Location
A republic in west Africa, bounded to the north by Equatorial Guinea and Cameroon; to the east and south by Congo; and to the west by the Atlantic Ocean.

Physical description
On the Equator for 880km/550mi west to east; lagoons and estuaries on the coast; land rises towards the African central plateau, cut by several rivers, notably the Ogooué; highest point is Mont Iboundji (1 575m/5 167ft).

Climate
Typical equatorial climate, hot, wet and humid; Libreville has an average maximum daily temperature of 33–37°C.

National holidays
Jan 1, May 1, Aug 15, 16 (Independence) (2), Nov 1, Dec 25; Ad, EM, ER, WM.

Political leaders

President
| 1960–7 | Léon M'ba |
| 1967– | Omar (*to 1973* Bernard-Albert) Bongo |

Prime Minister
1960–75	*As President*	1993–8	Paulin Obame-Nguema
1975–90	Léon Mébiame (Mébiane)	1999–	Jean-François Ntoutoume-
1991–3	Casimir Oyé M'ba		Emane

Hooded Cloak

The name Gabon is thought to come from the Portuguese word *gabão*, meaning a hooded cloak with sleeves, coined in reference to the shape of the coast and river estuary by Portuguese explorers in the late 15c.

THE GAMBIA

Official name	Republic of the Gambia	**Ethnic groups**	Mandinka 40%, Fulani 18%, Wolof 16%, Dyola 10%, Soninke 8%, others 8%
Local name	Gambia		
Former name	Senegambia (with Senegal, 1982–9)		
		Religions	Islam 95%, Christianity 4%, traditional beliefs 1%
Independence	1965		
Area	10 402 sq km/4 015 sq mi		
		Time zone	GMT
Capital	Banjul	**Currency**	1 Dalasi (D/GMD) = 100 butut
Chief towns	Serrekunda, Brikama, Bakau, Georgetown		
		Telephone	+220
Population	1 517 000 (2005e)	**Internet**	.gm
Nationality	Gambian	**Country code**	GMB
Languages	English; Mandinka, Fula and Wolof are also spoken		

Location
A republic situated in west Africa, bounded by the Atlantic Ocean in the west and on all other sides by Senegal.

Physical description
A strip of land stretching 322km/200mi east to west along the River Gambia; flat country, not rising above 90m/295ft.

Climate
Tropical; rainy season Jun–Sep with rainfall decreasing inland; high humidity in the wet season with high night temperatures; average temperatures range from 23°C (Jan) to 27°C (Jul), rising inland to over 40°C.

National holidays
Jan 1, Feb 18 (Independence), May 1, Aug 15 (St Mary), Dec 25; Ad, As, ER (2), GF, PB.

Political leaders

President

1965–94	Dawda Kairaba Jawara
1994–	Yahya Jammeh *Head of military junta 1994–6*

GAZA STRIP *see* **PALESTINIAN AUTONOMOUS AREAS** *under* **ISRAEL**

GEORGIA

Official name	Georgia	**Nationality**	Georgian
Local name	Sak'art'velos Respublikis	**Languages**	Georgian, Russian; Abkhazia is an official language in that province
Former name	Georgian Democratic Republic (1918–21), Transcaucasian Soviet Federated Socialist Republic (with Armenia and Azerbaijan, 1922–36), Georgian Soviet Socialist Republic (1936–90), within the Union of Soviet Socialist Republics (USSR; 1922–91)	**Ethnic groups**	Georgian 70%, Armenian 8%, Russian 6%, Azeri 6%, Ossetian 3%, others 7%
		Religions	Christianity 83% (Georgian Orthodox 65%, Russian Orthodox 10%, Armenian Orthodox 8%), Islam 11%, others 6%
Independence	1991		
Area	69 700 sq km/26 900 sq mi	**Time zone**	GMT +3
		Currency	1 Lari (GEL) = 100 tetri
Capital	T'bilisi or Tbilisi; also sometimes called Tiflis	**Telephone**	+995
		Internet	.ge
Chief towns	Kutaisi, Rustavi, Batumi, Sukhumi, Poti	**Country code**	GEO
Population	4 474 000 (2005e)		

Location
A republic in central and western Transcaucasia, bounded to the north by Russia; to the east by Azerbaijan; to the south by Armenia; to the south-west by Turkey; and to the west by the Black Sea.

Physical description
Contains the Greater Caucasus in the north and the Lesser Caucasus in the south; forest covers c.39% of the land; highest point is Mt Shkhara (5 608m/18 399ft).

Climate
Subtropical, warm and humid in the west; continental in the east with hot summers and cold winters.

National holidays
Jan 1, 7 (Orthodox Christmas), 19 (Orthodox Epiphany), Mar 3 (Mothers), Apr 9 (National), May 9 (National), 26 (Independence), Aug 28 (St Mary), Oct 14 (Mtskhetoba), Nov 23 (St Georgi); ES, EM.

Political leaders

President

1991–2	Zviad Gamsakhurdia	2003–4	Nino Burjanadze *Acting President*
1992	*Military Council*		
1992–2003	Eduard Shevardnadze	2004–	Mikheil Saakashvili

Prime Minister

1990–1	Tengiz Sigua	1992–3	Tengiz Sigua
1991	Murman Omanidze *Acting Prime Minister*	1993	Eduard Shevardnadze *Acting Prime Minister*
1991–2	Bessarion Gugushvili	1993–5	Otar Patsatsia

State Minister

1995–8	Niko Lekishvili	2003–5	Zurab Zhvania
1998–2000	Vazha Lordkipanidze	2005	Mikheil Saakashvili *Acting Prime Minister*
2000–1	Giorgi Arsenishvili		
2001–3	Avtandil Jorbenadze	2005–	Zurab Nogaideli

Mkhedruli ABC

The Georgian language has its own unique alphabet, called Mkhedruli, which has been in use since the eleventh century. Each letter of this alphabet corresponds to a sound in the language. While the Georgian language was threatened during the Soviet era, today it is protected; there are a number of official state organizations devoted to its promotion and preservation.

GEORGIA, SOUTH *see* **UNITED KINGDOM**

GERMANY

Official name	Federal Republic of Germany	**Nationality**	German
Local name	Deutschland; Bundesrepublik Deutschland	**Languages**	German; Sorbian (a Slavic language) is spoken by a few
Former name	*as listed below under Political leaders*	**Ethnic groups**	German 92%, Turkish 2%, others 6%
Area	357 868 sq km/138 137 sq mi	**Religions**	Christianity 76% (Prot 39%, RC 37%), none/unaffiliated 15%, Islam 3%, others 6%
Capital	Berlin	**Time zone**	GMT +1
Chief towns	Bonn, Hamburg, Munich, Cologne, Essen, Leipzig, Frankfurt (am Main)	**Currency**	1 Euro (€/EUR) = 100 cents
		Telephone	+49
		Internet	.de
Population	82 689 000 (2005e)	**Country code**	DEU

Location
An independent republic in central Europe, bounded to the north by the North Sea, Denmark and the Baltic Sea; to the east by Poland and the Czech Republic; to the south-east by Austria; to the south-west by Switzerland; and to the west by France, Luxembourg, Belgium and the Netherlands.

Physical description
Baltic coastline is backed by a fertile low-lying plain, low hills, and many glacial lakes; central uplands include the Black Forest; land rises in the south in several ranges, notably the Bavarian Alps; highest peak is the Zugspitze (2 962m/9 717ft); many major rivers.

Climate
Winters are mild but stormy in the north-west; elsewhere, the climate is continental (more temperate in the east); average winter temperatures 2°C (north) to –3°C (south); average summer temperature 16°C (north), slightly higher in the south.

National holidays
Jan 1, May 1, Oct 3 (Unity), Dec 25, 26; A, EM, GF, WM; *much regional variation*.

Political leaders

German Empire

Emperor

Modern Germany was united under Prussia in 1871.

1871–88	Wilhelm I
1888	Friedrich
1888–1918	Wilhelm II *abdicated 1918*

Chancellor

1909–17	Theobald von Bethmann Hollweg	1918	Prince Max von Baden
1917	Georg Michaelis	1918	Friedrich Ebert
1917–18	Georg Graf von Hertling		

German Republic

President

1919–25	Friedrich Ebert	1925–34	Paul von Hindenburg

Reich Chancellor

1919	Philipp Scheidemann		1925–6	Hans Luther
1919–20	Gustav Bauer		1926–8	Wilhelm Marx
1920	Hermann Müller		1928–30	Hermann Müller
1920–1	Konstantin Fehrenbach		1930–2	Heinrich Brüning
1921–2	Karl Joseph Wirth		1932	Franz von Papen
1922–3	Wilhelm Cuno		1932–3	Kurt von Schleicher
1923	Gustav Stresemann		1933	Adolf Hitler
1923–4	Wilhelm Marx			

Chancellor and Führer

1933–45	Adolf Hitler *Führer from 1934*
1945	Karl Dönitz

Allied Occupation

1945–9	*Military Governors*

German Democratic Republic (East Germany)

President

1949–60	Wilhelm Pieck

Chairman of the Council of State

1960–73	Walter Ernst Karl Ulbricht		1989	Egon Krenz
1973–6	Willi Stoph		1989–90	Gregor Gysi *General Secretary as*
1976–89	Erich Honecker			*Chairman*

Premier

1949–64	Otto Grotewohl		1976–89	Willi Stoph
1964–73	Willi Stoph		1989–90	Hans Modrow
1973–6	Horst Sindermann		1990	Lothar de Maizière

German Federal Republic (West Germany)

President

1949–59	Theodor Heuss		1974–9	Walter Scheel
1959–69	Heinrich Lübke		1979–84	Karl Carstens
1969–74	Gustav Heinemann		1984–90	Richard von Weizsäcker

Chancellor

1949–63	Konrad Adenauer		1969–74	Willy Brandt
1963–6	Ludwig Erhard		1974–82	Helmut Schmidt
1966–9	Kurt Georg Kiesinger		1982–90	Helmut Kohl

Germany

President

1990–4	Richard von Weizsäcker
1994–9	Roman Herzog
1999–2004	Johannes Rau
2004–	Horst Köhler

Chancellor

1990–8	Helmut Kohl
1998–2005	Gerhard Schröder

German Feast

The German authorities estimate that there are over 550 sources of natural mineral water in Germany, and more than 1 200 breweries that produce over 5 000 different beers. German bakers have come up with more than 300 kinds of bread and over 1 200 types of biscuit and cake.

GHANA

Official name	Republic of Ghana	**Ethnic groups**	Akan 53%, Mossi 17%, Ewe 12%, Ga-Adangame 8%, Gurma 2%, others 8%
Local name	Ghana		
Former name	British Gold Coast and British Togoland (until 1957)		
		Religions	Christianity 50% (Prot 32%, RC 18%), traditional beliefs 34%, Islam 10%, others 6%
Independence	1960		
Area	238 686 sq km/92 133 sq mi		
		Time zone	GMT
Capital	Accra	**Currency**	1 Cedi (¢/GHC) = 100 pesewas
Chief towns	Sekondi-Takoradi, Kumasi, Tamale		
		Telephone	+233
Population	22 113 000 (2005e)	**Internet**	.gh
Nationality	Ghanaian	**Country code**	GHA
Languages	English; almost 50 African languages are also spoken		

Location
A republic in West Africa, bounded to the north by Burkina Faso; to the east by Togo; to the south by the Gulf of Guinea; and to the west by Côte d'Ivoire.

Physical description
Coastline of sand bars and lagoons; low-lying plains inland, leading to the Ashanti plateau in the west and the River Volta basin in the east, dammed to form Lake Volta; mountains rise in the east to 885m/2 904ft at Afadjato.

Climate
Tropical climate, including a warm, dry coastal belt in the south-east, a hot, humid south-west corner, and hot, dry savanna in the north.

National holidays
Jan 1, Mar 6 (Independence), May 1, Jun 4 (Revolution), Jul 1 (Republic), Dec 1 (National Farmers), 25, 26; EM, GF.

Political leaders

President
1960–6   Kwame Nkrumah

Chairman of National Liberation Council
1966–9   Joseph Arthur Ankrah
1969   Akwasi Amankwa Afrifa
1969–70   *Presidential Committee*

President
1970–2   Edward Akufo-Addo

Chairman
1972–8   *National Redemption Council* (Ignatius Kuti Acheampong)
1978–9   *Supreme Military Council* (Fred W Akuffo)
1979   *Armed Forces Revolutionary Council* (Jerry John Rawlings)

President
1979–81   Hilla Limann

Chairman of Provisional National Defence Council
1981–2001   Jerry John Rawlings *President from 1992*

President
2001–   John Agyekum Kufuor

Prime Minister

1960–9	*As President*	1972–8	*As President*
1969–72	Kufi Abrefa Busia	1978–	*No Prime Minister*

Adinkra and Kente

The Asante people of Ghana have become famous for their beautiful fabrics.
'Kente' are hand-woven strips joined together to make larger cloths, while
'Adinkra' fabrics are distinguished by ceremonial and symbolic signs.

GIBRALTAR *see* **UNITED KINGDOM**

GREECE

Official name	Hellenic Republic	**Population**	11 120 000 (2005e)
Local name	Ellas, Ellada; Elliniki Dimokratia	**Nationality**	Greek
		Languages	Greek
Former name	Kingdom of Greece (until 1924 and 1935–73), Republic of Greece (until 1935)	**Ethnic groups**	Greek 98%, others 2%
		Religions	Christianity 98% (Orthodox), Islam 1%, others 1%
Independence	1832		
Area	131 957 sq km/50 935 sq mi	**Time zone**	GMT +2
		Currency	1 Euro (€/EUR) = 100 cents
Capital	Athens; Athína		
Chief towns	Thessaloniki, Patras, Heraklion, Volos, Larisa, Piraieus	**Telephone**	+30
		Internet	.gr
		Country code	GRC

Location
A republic in south-eastern Europe, occupying the southern part of the Balkan Peninsula and numerous islands in the Aegean and Ionian seas; bounded to the north by Albania and Macedonia; to the north-east by Bulgaria and to the east by Turkey.

Physical description
A large area of mainland, including the Peloponnese peninsula in the south, linked to the rest of the mainland by the narrow Isthmus of Corinth; over 6 000 islands, notably Crete, Euboea, Lesbos, Rhodes, Chios, Cephalonia, Lemnos, Samos, Naxos and Corfu; nearly 80% is mountainous or hilly; highest point is Mt Olympus (2 917m/9 570ft); several rivers and smaller lakes.

Climate
Mediterranean on the coast and islands, with mild, rainy winters and hot, dry summers; rainfall occurs almost entirely in the winter months.

National holidays
Jan 1, 6, Mar 25 (Independence), May 1, Aug 15, Oct 28 (Ochi), Dec 25, 26; GF, EM, ES, WM, Whit Sunday, Shrove Monday.

Political leaders

Monarch

1832–62	Otto of Bavaria		1920–2	Constantine I
1863–1913	George I		1922–3	George II
1913–17	Constantine I		1923–4	Paul Koundouriotis *Regent*
1917–20	Alexander			

President

1924–6	Paul Koundouriotis		1926–9	Paul Koundouriotis
1926	Theodore Pangalos		1929–35	Alexander T Zaïmis

Monarch

1935	George Kondylis *Regent*		1964–7	Constantine II
1935–47	George II		1967–73	*Military Junta*
1947–64	Paul		1973	George Papadopoulos *Regent*

President

1973	George Papadopoulos		1985–90	Christos Sartzetakis
1973–4	Phaedon Gizikis		1990–5	Constantine Karamanlis
1974–5	Michael Stasinopoulos		1995–2005	Constantine Stephanopoulos
1975–80	Constantine Tsatsos		2005–	Karolos Papoulias
1980–5	Constantine Karamanlis			

Prime Minister

1899–1901	George Theotokis		1924	Alexander Papanastasiou
1901–2	Alexander T Zaïmis		1924	Themistocles Sophoulis
1902–3	Theodore Deligiannis		1924–5	Andreas Michalakopoulos
1903	George Theotokis		1925–6	Alexander N Chatzikyriakos
1903	Demetrius G Rallis		1926	Theodore Pangalos
1903–4	George Theotokis		1926	Athanasius Eftaxias
1904–5	Theodore Deligiannis		1926	George Kondylis
1905	Demetrius G Rallis		1926–8	Alexander T Zaïmis
1905–9	George Theotokis		1928–32	Eleftherios K Venizelos
1909	Demetrius G Rallis		1932	Alexander Papanastasiou
1909–10	Kyriakoulis P Mavromichalis		1932	Eleftherios K Venizelos
1910	Stephen N Dragoumis		1932–3	Panagiotis Tsaldaris
1910–15	Eleftherios K Venizelos		1933	Eleftherios K Venizelos
1915	Demetrius P Gounaris		1933	Nicholas Plastiras
1915	Eleftherios K Venizelos		1933	Alexander Othonaos
1915	Alexander T Zaïmis		1933–5	Panagiotis Tsaldaris
1915–16	Stephen Skouloudis		1935	George Kondylis
1916	Alexander T Zaïmis		1935–6	Constantine Demertzis
1916	Nicholas P Kalogeropoulos		1936–41	John Metaxas
1916–17	Spyridon Lambros		1941	Alexander Koryzis
1917	Alexander T Zaïmis		1941	George II *Chairman of Ministers*
1917–20	Eleftherios K Venizelos		1941	*German Occupation* (Emmanuel
1920–1	Demetrius G Rallis			Tsouderos)
1921	Nicholas P Kalogeropoulos		1941–2	George Tsolakoglou
1921–2	Demetrius P Gounaris		1942–3	Constantine Logothetopoulos
1922	Nicholas Stratos		1943–4	John Rallis
1922	Peter E Protopapadakis		1941–4	Emmanuel Tsouderos
1922	Nicholas Triandaphyllakos			*Government in exile*
1922	Sortirios Krokidas		1944	Sophocles Venizelos
1922	Alexander T Zaïmis			*Government in exile*
1922–3	Stylianos Gonatas		1944–5	George Papandreou
1924	Eleftherios K Venizelos			*Government in exile*
1924	George Kaphandaris		1945	Nicholas Plastiras

1945	Peter Voulgaris	1963	Panagiotis Pipinellis
1945	Damaskinos, Archbishop of Athens	1963	Stylianos Mavromichalis
		1963	George Papandreou
1945	Panagiotis Kanellopoulos	1963–4	John Parskevopoulos
1945–6	Themistocles Sophoulis	1964–5	George Papandreou
1946	Panagiotis Politzas	1965	George Athanasiadis-Novas
1946–7	Constantine Tsaldaris	1965	Elias Tsirimokos
1947	Demetrius Maximos	1965–6	Stephen C Stefanopoulos
1947	Constantine Tsaldaris	1966–7	John Paraskevopoulos
1947–9	Themistocles Sophoulis	1967	Panagiotis Kanellopoulos
1949–50	Alexander Diomedes	1967–74	*Military Junta*
1950	John Theotokis	1967	Constantine Kollias
1950	Sophocles Venizelos	1967–73	George Papadopoulos
1950	Nicholas Plastiras	1973	Spyridon Markezinis
1950–1	Sophocles Venizelos	1973–4	Adamantios Androutsopoulos
1951	Nicholas Plastiras	1974–80	Constantine Karamanlis
1952	Demetrius Kiusopoulos	1980–1	George Rallis
1952–5	Alexander Papagos	1981–9	Andreas Papandreou
1955	Stephen C Stefanopoulos	1989	Tzannis Tzannetakis
1955–8	Constantine Karamanlis	1989–90	Xenofon Zolotas
1958	Constantine Georgakopoulos	1990–3	Constantine Mitsotakis
1958–61	Constantine Karamanlis	1993–6	Andreas Papandreou
1961	Constantine Dovas	1996–2004	Kostas Simitis
1961–3	Constantine Karamanlis	2004–	Kostas Karamanlis

Greek Islands

Greece includes around 6,000 islands, but just 227 are inhabited.

GREENLAND *see* **DENMARK**

GRENADA

Official name	State of Grenada		mixed 13%, East Indian 3%, European 1%
Local name	Grenada		
Independence	1974	**Religions**	Christianity 90% (RC 52%, Prot 38%), others 10%
Area	344 sq km/133 sq mi		
Capital	St George's	**Time zone**	GMT –4
Chief towns	Gouyave, Victoria, Grenville	**Currency**	1 East Caribbean Dollar (EC$/XCD) = 100 cents
Population	103 000 (2005e)	**Telephone**	+1 473
Nationality	Grenadian or Grenadan	**Internet**	.gd
Languages	English	**Country code**	GRD
Ethnic groups	African descent 83%,		

Location
An independent country of the West Indies, the most southerly of the Windward Islands in the eastern Caribbean Sea, comprising the main island of Grenada and the South Grenadines.

Physical description
Main island of Grenada is 34km/21mi long and 19km/12mi wide, of volcanic origin, with a ridge of mountains along its entire length; highest point is Mt St Catherine, which rises to 843m/2 766ft.

Climate
Subtropical; the average annual temperature is 23°C.

National holidays
Jan 1, 2, Feb 7 (Independence), May 1, Aug 3 (Emancipation) (2), Oct 25 (Thanksgiving), Dec 25, 26; CC, EM, GF, WM.

Political leaders

Head of State: British monarch, represented by Governor General (Sir Daniel Williams since 1996).

Prime Minister

1974–9	Eric M Gairy		1984–9	Herbert A Blaize
1979–83	Maurice Bishop		1989–90	Ben Jones
1983–4	Nicholas Brathwaite *Chairman of Interim Council*		1990–5	Nicholas Brathwaite
			1995–	Keith Mitchell

GRENADINES *see* **ST VINCENT AND THE GRENADINES**

GUADELOUPE *see* **FRANCE**

GUAM *see* **UNITED STATES OF AMERICA**

GUATEMALA

Official name	Republic of Guatemala		also spoken
Local name	Guatemala; República de Guatemala	**Ethnic groups**	Amerindian 44%, mestizo (Ladino) 40%, white 5%, black 2%, others 9%
Independence	1839		
Area	108 889 sq km/42 031 sq mi	**Religions**	Christianity 95% (RC 73%, Prot 22%), traditional beliefs (Mayan) 5%
Capital	Guatemala City; La Ciudad de Guatemala		
Chief towns	Quetzaltenango, Escuintla, Antigua, Mazatenango	**Time zone**	GMT –6
		Currency	1 Quetzal (Q/GTQ) = 100 centavos
Population	12 599 000 (2005e)	**Telephone**	+502
Nationality	Guatemalan	**Internet**	.gt
Languages	Spanish; many indigenous languages are	**Country code**	GTM

Location

A republic in central America, bounded to the north and west by Mexico; to the east by Belize and the Caribbean Sea; to the south-east by Honduras and El Salvador; and to the south-west by the Caribbean Sea.

Physical description

Over two-thirds mountainous with large forests; narrow Pacific coastal plain; highlands rise to 2 500–3 000m/8 200–9 840ft, with volcanoes on the southern edge; highest point is Tajumulco (4 220m/13 845ft); low undulating tableland in north.

Climate

Humid and tropical in the lowlands and on the Caribbean coast; rainy season from May to Oct; higher rainfall on exposed slopes; Guatemala City average temperatures are 17°C (Jan) and 21°C (Jul); subject to severe hurricanes and earthquakes.

National holidays

Jan 1, May 1, 10 (Mothers), Jun 30 (Army), Sep 15 (Independence), Oct 20 (Revolution), Nov 1, Dec 25, 31; GF, HT, Assumption (*date varies locally*).

Political leaders

President

1898–1920	Manuel Estrada Cabrera	1957–8	*Military Junta* (Guillermo Flores Avendaño)
1920–2	Carlos Herrera y Luna		
1922–6	José María Orellana	1958–63	Miguel Ydígoras Fuentes
1926–30	Lázaro Chacón	1963–6	*Military Junta* (Enrique Peralta Azurdia)
1930	Baudillo Palma		
1930–1	Manuel María Orellana	1966–70	Julio César Méndez Montenegro
1931	José María Reyna Andrade	1970–4	Carlos Araña Osorio
1931–44	Jorge Ubico Castañeda	1974–8	Kyell Eugenio Laugerua García
1944	Federico Ponce Vaidez	1978–82	Romeo Lucas García
1944–5	Jacobo Arbenz Guzmán	1982	Angel Aníbal Guevara
1945–51	Juan José Arévalo	1982–3	Efraín Rios Montt
1951–4	Jacobo Arbenz Guzmán	1983–6	Oscar Humberto Mejía Victores
1954	*Military Junta* (Carlos Díaz)	1986–91	Marco Vinicio Cerezo Arévalo
1954	Elfego J Monzón	1991–3	Jorge Serrano Elias
1954–7	Carlos Castillo Armas	1993–6	Ramiro de León Carpio
1957	*Military Junta* (Oscar Mendoza Azurdia)	1996–2000	Álvaro Arzú Irigoyen
		2000–4	Alfonso Portillo Cabrera
1957	Luis Arturo González López	2004–	Óscar Berger Perdomo

Resplendent Quetzal

The national bird of Guatemala is the quetzal, also known as the resplendent trogon. The quetzal has beautiful shimmering golden-green feathers, a crimson breast and brilliant iridescent tail feathers that may be up to 90cm/3ft long. It is steeped in myth and folklore, linked to the ancient Aztec god *Quetzalcoatl* and associated with freedom and liberty. The quetzal is immensely symbolic in Guatemala and has not only given its name to the national currency and to the major town of Quetzaltenango, but is depicted on the flag and the coat of arms and has appeared on postage stamps.

GUIANA, FRENCH *see* **FRANCE**

GUINEA

Official name	Republic of Guinea	**Languages**	French is the official language; eight local languages are also widely spoken
Local name	Guinée; République de Guinée		
Former name	French Guinea (until 1958), Republic of Guinea (1958–79), People's Revolutionary Republic of Guinea (1979–84)	**Ethnic groups**	Fulani 40%, Malinke 30%, Soussou 12%, Kissi 9%, others 9%
		Religions	Islam 85%, Christianity 8%, traditional beliefs 7%
Independence	1958	**Time zone**	GMT
Area	246 048 sq km/94 974 sq mi	**Currency**	1 Guinea Franc (GFr/GNF) = 100 centimes
Capital	Conakry	**Telephone**	+224
Chief towns	Kankan, Kindia, Labé	**Internet**	.gn
Population	9 402 000 (2005e)	**Country code**	GIN
Nationality	Guinean		

Location
A republic in West Africa, bounded to the north-west by Guinea-Bissau; to the north by Senegal and Mali; to the east by Côte d'Ivoire; to the south by Liberia and Sierra Leone; and to the south-west by the Atlantic Ocean.

Physical description
Coastal mangrove forests, rising to a forested and cultivated narrow coastal plain; massif beyond at c.900m/2 952ft; highest point is Mt Nimba (1 752m/5 748ft); savanna plains in the east; forested Guinea Highlands in the south rise above 1 000m/3 280ft.

Climate
Tropical climate (wet season May–Oct); average temperature in the dry season on the coast is 32°C, dropping to 23°C in the wet season; cooler inland.

National holidays
Jan 1, Apr 3 (Second Republic), May 1, Aug 15, Oct 2 (Independence), Dec 25; Ad, ER, PB.

Political leaders

President

1961–84	Ahmed Sékou Touré	1984–	Lansana Conté

Prime Minister

1958–72	Ahmed Sékou Touré	1996–9	Sidia Toure
1972–84	Louis Lansana Beavogui	1999–2004	Lamine Sidime
1984–5	Diarra Traore	2004	François Lonseny Fall
1985–96	*No Prime Minister*	2004–	Cellou Dalein Diallo

Local Languages

Although French is the official language of Guinea, the government estimates that only 15–20% of the country's people speak it. Instead, most people speak one of eight major national languages, of which the most important are Soussou, Malinke, Kissi, Peulh, Toma and Guerze.

GUINEA-BISSAU

Official name	Republic of Guinea-Bissau		Creole (Crioulo); many African languages are also spoken
Local name	Guiné-Bissau; República da Guiné-Bissau	**Ethnic groups**	Balante 26%, Fulani 24%, Malinke 13%, Mandyako 10%, Pepel 10%, others 17%
Former name	Portuguese Guinea (1952–74)		
Independence	1973 (proclaimed), 1974 (recognized)	**Religions**	traditional beliefs 52%, Islam 42%, Christianity 6%
Area	36 260 sq km/14 000 sq mi		
Capital	Bissau	**Time zone**	GMT
Chief towns	Bafatá, Bolama, Mansôa	**Currency**	1 CFA Franc (CFAFr/XOF) = 100 centimes
Population	1 586 000 (2005e)	**Telephone**	+245
Nationality	Guinea-Bissauan	**Internet**	.gw
Languages	Portuguese, Guinean	**Country code**	GNB

Location
A republic in West Africa, bounded to the north by Senegal; to the south-east by Guinea; and to the south-west by the Atlantic Ocean.

Physical description
Indented coast with islands (including the heavily-forested Bijagós Archipelago) and mangrove-lined estuaries, backed by forested coastal plains; low-lying, with savanna-covered plateaux in the south and east, rising to 310m/1 017ft.

Climate
Tropical climate with a wet season (Jun–Oct); average annual temperature range at Bissau is 24–27°C.

National holidays
Jan 1, 20 (National Heroes), Feb 8 (BNG Anniversary and Monetary Reform), Mar 8 (Women), May 1, Aug 3 (Martyrs of Colonialism), Sep 12 (National), 24 (Establishment of the Republic), Nov 14 (Readjustment), Dec 25.

Political leaders

President

1974–80	Luis de Almeida Cabral	2000–3	Kumba Yalla
1980–4	*Revolutionary Council* (João Bernardo Vieira)	2003	Veríssimo Correia Seabra *Interim President*
1984–99	João Bernardo Vieira	2003–5	Henrique Rosa *Interim President*
1999–2000	Malai Bacai Sanhá *Interim President*	2005	João Bernardo Vieira

Prime Minister

1992–4	Carlos Correia	2001	Faustino Imbali
1994–7	Manuel Saturnino da Costa	2001–2	Alamara Nhassé
1997–8	Carlos Correia	2002–3	Mário Pires
1998–2000	Francisco Fadul	2003–4	Artur Sanhá
2000–1	Caetano N'Tchama	2004–	Carlos Gomes Júnior

GUYANA

Official name	Co-operative Republic of Guyana	**Ethnic groups**	East Indian 49%, black 32%, mixed 12%, Amerindian 6%, Chinese 1%
Local name	Guyana		
Former name	British Guiana (until 1966)	**Religions**	Christianity 55% (Prot 36%, RC 19%), Hinduism 35%, Islam 9%, others 1%
Independence	1966		
Area	214 969 sq km/82 978 sq mi		
Capital	Georgetown	**Time zone**	GMT –4
Chief towns	Linden, New Amsterdam	**Currency**	1 Guyana Dollar (G$/GYD) = 100 cents
Population	751 000 (2005e)		
Nationality	Guyanese	**Telephone**	+592
Languages	English; Hindi, Urdu and local dialects are also spoken	**Internet**	.gy
		Country code	GUY

Location
A republic on the northern coast of South America, bounded to the north by the Atlantic Ocean; to the east by Suriname; to the south by Brazil; and to the west by Venezuela.

Physical description
Inland forest covers c.85% of the land area; grass-covered savanna in the hinterland; coastal plain, below sea level at high tide, is protected by sea defences, canals and dams; highest peak is Mt Roraima (2 810m/9 219ft) in the Pakaraima Mountains.

Climate
Equatorial climate in the lowlands, hot, wet, with constant high humidity; temperatures of 23–34°C in coastal lowlands with two seasons of high rainfall (May–Jul, Nov–Jan); lower temperatures on the high plateau inland.

National holidays
Jan 1, Feb 23 (Republic), May 1, 26 (Independence), Aug 1 (Freedom), Dec 25, 26; Ad, D, EM, GF, PB, Phagwah (Mar), Caribbean (Jul).

Political leaders

President

1970	Edward A Luckhoo	1992–7	Cheddi Bharrat Jagan
1970–80	Arthur Chung	1997	Samuel Hinds
1980–5	Linden Forbes Sampson Burnham	1997–9	Janet Jagan
1985–92	Hugh Desmond Hoyte	1999–	Bharrat Jagdeo

Prime Minister

1966–85	Linden Forbes Sampson Burnham	1997	Janet Jagan
1985–92	Hamilton Green	1997–	Samuel Hinds
1992–7	Samuel Hinds		

Land of Many Waters

The Atlantic Ocean pounds the coastline of northern Guyana and the country is criss-crossed by many rivers. Guyana also boasts the world's longest single-drop waterfall, Kaieteur Falls, where the Potaro River plunges 226m/741ft in one leap before continuing downward for another 231m/759ft. The name *Guyana* is believed to come from an Amerindian word meaning 'land of many waters'.

HAITI

Official name	Republic of Haiti	**Religions**	Christianity 95% (RC 80%, Prot 15%), none/unaffiliated 1%, others 4%
Local name	Haïti; République d'Haïti		
Independence	1804		
Area	27 750 sq km/10 712 sq mi		*Note: Around half the population practise voodoo*
Capital	Port-au-Prince	**Time zone**	GMT −5
Chief towns	Port-de-Paix, Cap-Haïtien, Gonaïves, Les Cayes, Jacmel, Jérémie	**Currency**	1 Gourde (G, Gde/HTG) = 100 centimes
		Telephone	+509
Population	8 528 000 (2005e)	**Internet**	.ht
Nationality	Haitian	**Country code**	HTI
Languages	French, Creole		
Ethnic groups	black 95%, mulatto and white 5%		

Location
A republic in the West Indies, comprising the western third of the island of Hispaniola in the Caribbean Sea and bounded by the Dominican Republic to the east; also includes the islands of Gonâve off the west coast and Tortue off the north coast.

Physical description
Consists of two mountainous peninsulas separated by a deep structural depression; to the east is the Massif de la Selle, with Haiti's highest peak, La Selle (2 680m/8 792ft).

Climate
Tropical maritime; average monthly temperatures range from 24°C to 29°C; the wet season is May–Sep; hurricanes are common.

National holidays
Jan 1 (Independence), 2 (Ancestors), Apr 14 (Americas), May 1, 18 (Flag/University), Aug 15, Oct 17 (Death of Dessalines), 24 (United Nations), Nov 1, 2, 18 (Battle of Vertières), Dec 25; A, C, CC, GF.

Political leaders

President

1896–1902	P A Tirésias Simon Lam	1946–50	Dumarsais Estimé
1902	Boisrond Canal	1950	*Military Junta* (Frank Lavaud)
1902–8	Alexis Nord	1950–6	Paul E Magloire
1908–11	Antoine Simon	1956–7	François Sylvain
1911–12	Michel Cincinnatus Leconte	1957	*Military Junta*
1912–13	Tancrède Auguste	1957	Léon Cantave
1913–14	Michael Oreste	1957	Daniel Fignolé
1914	Oreste Zamor	1957	Antoine Kebreau
1914–15	Joseph Davilmare Théodore	1957–71	François Duvalier ('Papa Doc')
1915	Jean Velbrun-Guillaume	1971–86	Jean-Claude Duvalier ('Baby Doc')
1915–22	Philippe Sudre Dartiguenave	1986–8	Henri Namphy
1922–30	Joseph Louis Bornó	1988	Leslie Manigat
1930	Étienne Roy	1988	Henri Namphy
1930–41	Sténio Joseph Vincent	1988–90	Prosper Avril
1941–6	Élie Lescot	1990–1	Ertha Pascal-Trouillot
1946	*Military Junta* (Frank Lavaud)	1991	Jean-Bertrand Aristide

1991	Raoul Cédras	1994–6	Jean-Bertrand Aristide
1991–2	Joseph Nérette	1996–2000	René Préval
1992–3	Marc-Louis Bazin	2000–4	Jean-Bertrand Aristide
1993–4	Jean-Bertrand Aristide	2004–	Boniface Alexandre *Interim*
1994	Émile Jonassaint		*President*

Prime Minister

1988	Martial Célestin	1994–5	Smarck Michel
1988–91	*No Prime Minister*	1995–6	Claudette Werleigh
1991	René Préval	1996–7	Rosny Smarth
1991–2	Jean-Jacques Honorat *Interim*	1998–2001	Jacques-Édouard Alexis
	Prime Minister	2001–2	Jean-Marie Cherestal
1992–3	Marc Bazin	2002–4	Yvon Neptune
1993–4	Robert Malval	2004–	Gérard Latortue *Interim Prime*
			Minister

Slave Revolution

The Haitian Revolution of 1791–1804 was the only successful slave revolution in the New World. It created the world's first black-led republic, and meant that Haiti became the first Caribbean state to achieve independence. The revolution began in Aug 1791 with a slave revolt led by Toussaint L'Ouverture and culminated in the independence of Haiti in 1804 when a slave named Dessalines proclaimed himself Emperor of the independent country.

HEARD AND MACDONALD ISLANDS *see* **AUSTRALIA**

HERZEGOVINA *see* **BOSNIA AND HERZEGOVINA**

HOLLAND *see* **THE NETHERLANDS**

HOLY SEE *see* **VATICAN**

HONDURAS

Official name	Republic of Honduras	**Languages**	Spanish; English is also spoken
Local name	Honduras; República de Honduras	**Ethnic groups**	mestizo 90%, Amerindian 7%, black 2%, white 1%
Independence	1821 (from Spain), 1838 (as sovereign state)		
Area	112 088 sq km/43 266 sq mi	**Religions**	Christianity 97% (RC 94%, Prot 3%), others 3%
Capital	Tegucigalpa		
Chief towns	San Pedro Sula, Choluteca, La Ceiba, El Progreso	**Time zone**	GMT –6
		Currency	1 Lempira (L, La/HNL) = 100 centavos
Population	7 205 000 (2005e)	**Telephone**	+504
Nationality	Honduran	**Internet**	.hn
		Country code	HND

Location
A republic in Central America, bounded to the north by the Caribbean Sea; to the south-east by Nicaragua; to the south by the Pacific Ocean; to the south-west by El Salvador; and to the west by Guatemala; also comprises the Bay Islands in the Caribbean Sea and a group of nearly 300 islands in the Gulf of Fonseca.

Physical description
Southern coastal lands are separated from those of the Caribbean by mountains running north-west to south-east; southern plateau rises to 2 870m/9 416ft at Cerro Las Minas; Laguna Caratasca lies in the extreme north-east.

Climate
Tropical climate in coastal areas, temperate in the centre and west; two wet seasons in upland areas (May–Jul, Sep–Oct); variable temperatures in the interior, 15–24°C; on the coastal plains the average temperature is 30°C.

National holidays
Jan 1, May 1, Sep 15 (Independence), Oct 3 (Soldiers), 12 (Americas), 21 (Armed Forces), Dec 25; GF, HT.

Political leaders

President

1900–3	Terencio Sierra	1920–4	Rafael López Gutiérrez
1903	Juan Angel Arias	1924–5	Vicente Tosta Carrasco
1903–7	Manuel Bonilla Chirinos	1925–8	Miguel Paz Barahona
1907–11	Miguel R Dávila	1929–32	Vicente Mejía Clindres
1912–15	Manuel Bonilla Chirinos	1932–49	Tiburcio Carías Andino
1915–20	Francisco Bertrand	1949–54	Juan Manuel Gálvez

Head of State
1954–6	Julio Lozano Diaz
1956–7	*Military Junta*

President
1958–63	José Ramón Villeda Morales

Head of State
1963–5	Oswaldo López Arellano

President
1965–71	Oswaldo López Arellano
1971–2	Ramón Ernesto Cruz

Head of State
1972–5	Oswaldo López Arellano
1975–8	Juan Alberto Melgar Castro
1978–82	Policarpo Paz García

President
1982–6	Roberto Suazo Córdova	1993–7	Carlos Roberto Reina
1986–9	José Azcona Hoyo	1997–2002	Carlos Roberto Flores Facussé
1989–93	Rafael Leonardo Callejas	2002–	Ricardo Maduro

Deep Blue Sea
Christopher Columbus arrived on the Caribbean coast of Honduras in 1502. He is reported to have exclaimed at how deep the coastal waters were, thus naming the country: *honduras* is the Spanish word for 'depths'. This was not the first time that Columbus's comments on the sea had resulted in a country name that would still be used 500 years later (see the fact box at the Bahamas).

HONG KONG *see* **CHINA**

HUNGARY

Official name	Republic of Hungary	**Population**	10 098 000 (2005e)
Local name	Magyarorszag; Magyar Köztársaság	**Nationality**	Hungarian
		Languages	Magyar (Hungarian)
Former name	formerly part of Austria-Hungary (until 1918), Hungarian People's Republic (1918, 1919, 1949–89), Hungarian Soviet Republic (1919), Hungarian State (1919–20, 1944–6), Hungarian Kingdom (1920–44), Hungarian Republic (1946–9)	**Ethnic groups**	Magyar 90%, Romany 4%, German 3%, Serb 2%, others 1%
		Religions	Christianity 79% (RC 58%, Prot 21%), none/unaffiliated 18%, Judaism 1%, others 2%
		Time zone	GMT +1
		Currency	1 Forint (Ft/HUF) = 100 fillér
Independence	1918	**Telephone**	+36
Area	93 030 sq km/35 910 sq mi	**Internet**	.hu
Capital	Budapest	**Country code**	HUN
Chief towns	Debrecen, Miskolc, Szeged, Pécs, Györ		

Location
A republic in central Europe, bounded to the north by Slovakia; to the east by Ukraine and Romania; to the south by Serbia and Montenegro and Croatia; and to the west by Slovenia and Austria.

Physical description
Drained by the River Danube and its tributaries (flowing north to south); frequent flooding; low spur of the Alps in the west, separating the Little Hungarian Plain from the Transdanubian downlands; highest peak is Kékes (1 014m/3 327ft).

Climate
Fairly extreme continental climate with a marked difference between summer and winter; wettest in spring and early summer; winters are cold and the Danube sometimes freezes over for long periods; frequent fog in settled winter weather.

National holidays
Jan 1, Mar 15 (Independence), May 1, Aug 20 (National/St Stephen), Oct 23 (Republic), Nov 1, Dec 25, 26; EM, WM.

Political leaders

Monarch

1900–16	Franz Josef I
1916–18	Charles IV

President

1919	Mihály Károlyi	1952–67	István Dobi
1919	*Revolutionary Governing Council* (Sándor Garbai)	1967–87	Pál Losonczi
		1987–8	Károly Németh
1920–44	Miklós Horthy *Regent*	1988–9	Brunó Ferenc Straub
1944–5	*Provisional National Assembly*	1989–90	Mátyás Szúrös
1946–8	Zoltán Tildy	1990–2000	Árpád Göncz
1948–50	Árpád Szakasits	2000–5	Ferenc Mádl
1950–2	Sándor Rónai	2005–	László Sólyom

Premier

1899–1903	Kálmán Széll	1944		Géza Lakatos
1903	Károly Khuen-Héderváry	1944		Ferenc Szálasi
1903–5	István Tisza	1944–5		*Provisional National Assembly*
1905–6	Géza Fejérváry			(Béla Dálnoki Miklós)
1906–10	Sándor Wekerle	1945–6		Zoltán Tildy
1910–12	Károly Khuen-Héderváry	1946–7		Ferenc Nagy
1912–13	Lázló Lukács	1947–8		Lajos Dinnyés
1913–17	István Tisza	1948–52		István Dobi
1917	Móric Esterházy	1952–3		Mátyás Rákosi
1917–18	Sándor Wekerle	1953–5		Imre Nagy
1918–19	Mihály Károlyi	1955–6		András Hegedüs
1919	Dénes Berinkey	1956		Imre Nagy
1919	*Revolutionary Governing Council*	1956–8		János Kádár
1919	Gyula Peidl	1958–61		Ferenc Münnich
1919	István Friedrich	1961–5		János Kádár
1919–20	Károly Huszár	1965–7		Gyula Kállai
1920	Sándor Simonyi-Semadam	1967–75		Jenő Fock
1920–1	Pál Teleki	1975–87		György Lázár
1921–31	István Bethlen	1987–8		Károly Grosz
1931–2	Gyula Károlyi	1988–90		Miklás Németh
1932–6	Gyula Gömbös	1990–3		József Antall
1936–8	Kálman Darányi	1993–4		Péter Boross
1938–9	Béla Imrédy	1994–8		Gyula Horn
1939–41	Pál Teleki	1998–2002		Viktor Orban
1941–2	Lázló Bárdossy	2002–4		Peter Medgyessy
1942–4	Miklós Kállay	2004–		Ferenc Gyurcsány
1944	Döme Sztójay			

First Secretary

1949–56	Mátyás Rákosi	1956–88	János Kádár
1956	Ernö Gerö	1988–90	Károly Grosz

ICELAND

Official name	Republic of Iceland	**Nationality**	Icelandic
Local name	Ísland; Lyðveldið Ísland	**Languages**	Icelandic
Former name	formerly part of Denmark (to 1918), Kingdom of Iceland (1918–44)	**Ethnic groups**	Icelandic 94%, Danish 1%, others 5%
Independence	1944	**Religions**	Christianity 94% (Prot 93%, RC 1%), none/unaffiliated 6%
Area	103 000 sq km/40 000 sq mi	**Time zone**	GMT
Capital	Reykjavík	**Currency**	1 Iceland Króna (IKr/ISK) = 100 aurar
Chief towns	Akureyri, Húsavík, Akranes, Keflavík, Ísafjördur	**Telephone**	+354
		Internet	.is
Population	295 000 (2005e)	**Country code**	ISL

Location
An island state lying between the northern Atlantic Ocean and the Arctic Ocean, south-east of Greenland and 900km/550mi west of Norway across the Norwegian Sea.

Physical description
A volcanic island, with several active volcanoes; heavily indented coastline, with many long fjords; high ridges rise to 2 119m/6 952ft at Hvannadalshnúkur; large snowfields and glaciers cover much of the land area.

Climate
Changeable climate, with relatively mild winters; average daily temperatures are minimum –2°C (Jan), maximum 14°C (Jul–Aug); Reykjavík is generally ice-free throughout the year; summers are cool and cloudy.

National holidays
Jan 1, May 1, Jun 17 (National), Dec 25, 26; A, EM, ES, GF, HT, WM, Whit Sunday, First Day of Summer (Apr), Aug Holiday Monday.

Political leaders

President

1944–52	Sveinn Björnsson	1980–96	Vigdís Finnbogadóttir
1952–68	Ásgeir Ásgeirsson	1996–	Ólafur Ragnar Grimsson
1968–80	Kristján Eldjárn		

Prime Minister

1900–1	C Goos	1950–3	Steingrímur Steinþórsson
1901–4	P A Alberti	1953–6	Ólafur Thors
1904–9	Hannes Hafstein	1956–8	Hermann Jónasson
1909–11	Björn Jónsson	1958 9	Emil Jónsson
1911–12	Kristján Jónsson	1959–61	Ólafur Thors
1912–14	Hannes Hafstein	1961	Bjarni Benediktsson
1914–15	Sigurður Eggerz	1961–3	Ólafur Thors
1915–17	Einar Arnórsson	1963–70	Bjarni Benediktsson
1917–22	Jón Magnússon	1970–1	Jóhann Hafstein
1922–4	Sigurður Eggerz	1971–4	Ólafur Jóhannesson
1924–6	Jón Magnússon	1974–8	Geir Hallgrímsson
1926–7	John þorláksson	1978–9	Ólafur Jóhannesson
1927–32	Tryggvi þórhallsson	1979	Benedikt Gröndal
1932–4	Ásgeir Ásgeirsson	1980–3	Gunnar Thoroddsen
1934–42	Hermann Jónasson	1983–7	Steingrímur Hermannsson
1942	Ólafur Thors	1987–8	Thorsteinn Pálsson
1942–4	Björn þórðarsson	1988–91	Steingrímur Hermannsson
1944–7	Ólafur Thors	1991–2004	Davíd Oddsson
1947–9	Stefán Jóhann Stefánsson	2004–	Halldór Ásgrímsson
1949–50	Ólafur Thors		

Geysers Galore

Iceland is famous for geysers – springs that periodically spout hot water and steam into the air. The most well-known is *Geysir*, meaning 'the gusher', which was first recorded in the year 1294 and from which the term *geyser* is derived. Others include *Strokkur* ('the churn'), *Smiður* ('the carpenter'), *Fata* ('the bucket') and *Óþerrishola* ('the rainmaker').

INDIA

Official name	Republic of India	**Ethnic groups**	Indo-Aryan 72%, Dravidian 25%, others 3%
Local name	Bhārat (Hindi)		
Independence	1947	**Religions**	Hinduism 82%, Islam 12% (Sunni), Sikhism 2%, Christianity 2%, Jainism 1%, Buddhism 1%
Area	3 166 829 sq km/ 1 222 396 sq mi		
Capital	New Delhi; Nī Dillī		
Chief towns¹	Ahmadabad, Bangalore, Chennai, Hyderabad, Jaipur, Kanpur, Kolkata, Lucknow, Mumbai, Nagpur, Poona	**Time zone**	GMT +5.5
		Currency	1 Indian Rupee (Re, Rs/INR) = 100 paise
		Telephone	+91
Population	1 103 371 000 (2005e)	**Internet**	.in
Nationality	Indian	**Country code**	IND
Languages	Hindi, English and 17 others		

Location
A federal republic in southern Asia, bounded to the north-west by Pakistan and the disputed region of Jammu and Kashmir; to the north by China, Nepal and Bhutan; to the east by Myanmar and Bangladesh; to the south-east by the Bay of Bengal; and to the south-west by the Arabian Sea.

Physical description
The second largest state in Asia, bordered to the north by the Himalayas; highest peaks are over 7 000m/22 966ft; Kanchenjunga (8 598m/28 298ft) on the Nepalese border is the highest point; central river plains to the south (including the Ganges and Brahmaputra); best agricultural land is in the east; plateau in the southern peninsula; Thar Desert in the north-west is bordered by semi-desert; coastal plains are important areas of rice cultivation.

Climate
Dominated by the Asiatic monsoon; rains come from the south-west (Jun–Oct); rainfall decreases (Dec–Feb) with winds from the north, followed by drought until Mar or May; temperatures in the mountains vary greatly with altitude; desert conditions in the extreme west; south of the plateau is tropical, even in the cool season; west coast is subject to rain throughout the year, with high humidity in the south; cyclones and storms on the south-east coast (especially Oct–Dec), with high temperatures and humidity during the monsoon season.

National holidays
Jan 1 (*some states*), 26 (Republic), May 1 (*some states*), Jun 30, Aug 15 (Independence), Oct 2 (Mahatma Gandhi's Birthday), Dec 25, 31; NY (Parsi, Aug, *some states*).

¹ *India has renamed several of its cities and states in recent years, reverting to pre-colonial names. Thus, Bombay is now known as Mumbai, Calcutta as Kolkata and Madras as Chennai. Other such changes may follow.*

Political leaders

President

1950–62	Rajendra Prasad	1969	Mohammed Hidayatullah *Acting President*
1962–7	Sarvepalli Radhakrishnan		
1967–9	Zakir Husain	1969–74	Varahagiri Venkatagiri
1969	Varahagiri Venkatagiri *Acting President*	1974–7	Fakhruddin Ali Ahmed
		1977	B D Jatti *Acting President*

1977–82	Neelam Sanjiva Reddy	1992–7	Shankar Dayal Sharma
1982–7	Giani Zail Singh	1997–2002	Kocheril Raman Narayanan
1987–92	Ramaswami Venkataraman	2002–	A P J Abdul Kalam

Prime Minister

1947–64	Jawaharlal Nehru	1984–9	Rajiv Gandhi
1964	Gulzari Lal Nanda *Acting Prime Minister*	1989–90	Vishwanath Pratap Singh
		1990–1	Chandra Shekhar
1964–6	Lal Bahadur Shastri	1991–6	P V Narasimha Rao
1966	Gulzari Lal Nanda *Acting Prime Minister*	1996	Atal Behari Vajpayee
		1996–7	H D Deve Gowda
1966–77	Indira Gandhi	1997	Inder Kumar Gujral
1977–9	Morarji Desai	1998–2004	Atal Behari Vajpayee
1979–80	Charan Singh	2004–	Manmohan Singh
1980–4	Indira Gandhi		

INDONESIA

Official name	Republic of Indonesia	**Languages**	Bahasa Indonesia; English, Dutch and Javanese are also widely spoken, and 300 regional languages
Local name	Indonesia; Republik Indonesia		
Former name	Netherlands East Indies, Dutch East Indies (until 1949), Republic of the United States of Indonesia (1949–50)	**Ethnic groups**	Javanese 45%, others 25%, Sudanese 14%, Coastal Malays 8%, Madurese 8%
		Religions	Islam 87%, Christianity 9% (Prot 6%, RC 3%), Hinduism 2%, Buddhism 1%, others 1%
Independence	1945 (declared), 1949		
Area	1 906 240 sq km/735 809 sq mi		
		Time zone	GMT +7/9
Capital	Jakarta	**Currency**	1 Rupiah (Rp/IDR) = 100 sen
Chief towns	Jayapura, Bandung, Semarang, Surabaya, Medan, Palembang		
		Telephone	+62
		Internet	.id
Population	222 781 000 (2005e)	**Country code**	IDN
Nationality	Indonesian		

Location
A republic in south-east Asia, bounded to the north of the island of Borneo by Malaysia; to the east of the island of Timor by East Timor; and to the east of the island of New Guinea by Papua New Guinea; the Indian Ocean lies to the west; the Java Sea, Banda Sea, Arafura Sea and Timor Sea surround some of its islands; the Pacific Ocean lies to the north.

Physical description
The world's largest island group; five main islands and 30 smaller archipelagoes totalling 13 677 islands and islets, of which c.6 000 are inhabited; over 100 volcanic peaks on Java, of which 15 are active; highest point is Puncak Jaya (5 030m/16 503ft).

Climate
Hot and humid equatorial climate; dry season (Jun–Sep), rainy season (Dec–Mar), apart from the Moluccas (Jun–Sep); average temperature is 27°C on island coasts, falling inland and with altitude.

National holidays
Jan 1, Aug 17 (Independence), Dec 25; A, Ad, ER (2), GF, NY (Chinese), NY (Muslim), NY (Balinese Hindu), PB, Ascension of the Prophet, Waisak (May).

Political leaders

President

1945–9	Ahmed Sukarno	1999–2001	Abdurrahman Wahid
1949–66	Ahmed Sukarno	2001–4	Megawati Sukarnoputri
1966–98	T N J Suharto	2004–	Susilo Bambang Yudhoyono
1998–9	B J Habibie		

Prime Minister

1945	R A A Wiranatakusumah	1951–2	Sukiman Wirjosandjojo
1945–7	Sutan Sjahrir	1952–3	Dr Wilopo
1947–8	Amir Sjarifuddin	1953–5	Ali Sastroamidjojo
1948	Mohammed Hatta	1955–6	Burhanuddin Harahap
1948–9	Sjarifuddin Prawiraranegara	1956–7	Ali Sastroamidjojo
1949	Susanto Tirtoprodjo	1957–9	Raden Haji Djuanda Kurtawidjaja
1949	Mohammed Hatta	1959–63	Ahmed Sukarno
1950	Dr Halim	1963–6	S E Subandrio
1950–1	Mohammed Natsir	1966–	*No Prime Minister*

IRAN

Official name	Islamic Republic of Iran		several minority languages spoken
Local name	Îrân; Jomhûri-ye-Eslâmi-ye-Îrân	**Ethnic groups**	Persian 51%, Azeri 24%, Gilaki and Mazandarani 8%, Kurdish 7%, others 10%
Former name	Persia (until 1935)		
Independence	1925		
Area	1 648 000 sq km/636 128 sq mi	**Religions**	Islam 99% (Shia 91%, Sunni 8%), others 1%
Capital	Tehran; Tehrân	**Time zone**	GMT +3.5
Chief towns	Mashhad, Isfahan, Tabriz, Shiraz, Abadan	**Currency**	Iranian Rial (Rls/IRR)
Population	69 515 000 (2005e)	**Telephone**	+98
Nationality	Iranian	**Internet**	.ir
Languages	Farsi (Persian), with	**Country code**	IRN

Location
A republic in south-west Asia, bounded to the north by Armenia, Azerbaijan, the Caspian Sea and Turkmenistan; to the east by Afghanistan and Pakistan; to the south by the Gulf of Oman and the Arabian Gulf; to the south-west by Iraq; and to the north-west by Turkey.

Physical description
A vast arid central plateau, average elevation 1 200 m/3 936ft, with many salt and sand basins; rimmed by mountain ranges that drop to narrow coastal lowlands; Elburz Mountains in the north rise to 5 670m/18 602ft at Mt Damavand.

Climate
Mainly a desert climate; average temperatures at Tehran are 2°C (Jan), 29°C (Jul); Caspian coast is wetter than interior; hot and humid around Arabian Gulf; frequent earthquakes.

National holidays
Feb 11 (Islamic Revolution), Mar 19 (Nationalization of Oil), 21, 31 (Islamic Republic), Apr 2 (13th Day of New Year), Jun 3 (Death of Imam Khomeini), 4 (Uprising); Ad, As, ER, PB, Eid Ghadir Khom, Tasooah, Arbaeen, Death of the Prophet, Martyrdom of Imam Reza, Birthday of Imam Ali, Ascension of the Prophet, Birthday of Imam Hussein, Birthday of the 12th living Imam, Martyrdom of Imam Ali, Death of Hadrath Zahra.

Political leaders

Shah

1896–1907	Muzaffar Ad-Din		1925–41	Mohammed Reza Khan
1907–9	Mohammed Ali		1941–79	Mohammed Reza Pahlavi
1909–25	Ahmad Mirza			

Leader of the Islamic Republic

1979–89	Ayatollah Ruhollah Khomeini
1989–	Ayatollah Sayyed Ali Khamenei

President

1980–1	Abolhassan Bani-Sadr		1989–97	Ali Akbar Hashemi Rafsanjani
1981	Mohammed Ali Rajai		1997–2005	Mohammad Khatami
1981–9	Sayyed Ali Khamenei		2005–	Mahmoud Ahmadinejad

Prime Minister

1979	Shahpur Bakhtiar		1981	Mohammed Javad Bahonar
1979–80	Mehdi Bazargan		1981	Mohammed Reza Mahdavi-Kani
1980–1	Mohammed Ali Rajai		1981–9	Mir Hossein Moussavi

IRAQ

Official name	Republic of Iraq	**Languages**	Arabic; Kurdish is also spoken
Local name	Al-Jumhūriyya al-'Iraqiyya		
Former name	part of the Ottoman Empire (until 1916), State of Iraq (1920–21), Iraqi Kingdom (1921–32), Kingdom of Iraq (1932–58)	**Ethnic groups**	Arab 77%, Kurdish 18%, Turkmen, Assyrian and others 5%
		Religions	Islam 96% (Shia 54%, Sunni 42%), Christianity 3%, others 1%
Independence	1932	**Time zone**	GMT +3
Area	434 925 sq km/167 881 sq mi	**Currency**	1 Iraqi Dinar (ID/IQD) = 1 000 fils
Capital	Baghdad	**Telephone**	+964
Chief towns	Basra, Kirkuk, Mosul	**Internet**	.iq
Population	28 807 000 (2005e)	**Country code**	IRQ
Nationality	Iraqi		

Location
A republic in western Asia, bounded to the north by Turkey; to the east by Iran; to the south-east by Kuwait and the Arabian Gulf; to the south by Saudi Arabia; to the west by Jordan; and to the north-west by Syria.

Physical description
Largely comprises the vast alluvial tract of the Tigris–Euphrates lowland; the rivers join about 190km/118mi from the Arabian Gulf; lowland has swamp vegetation; mountains in the north-east rise to over 3 000m/9 840ft; highest point is Haji Ibrahim (3 600m/11 810ft); desert in other areas.

Climate
Mainly arid; summers are very hot and dry; winters are often cold; average temperatures at Baghdad are 10°C (Jan) and 35°C (Jul); rainfall is highest in the north-east.

National holidays
Jan 1, 6 (Army), Feb 8 (8 Feb Revolution), Mar 21, May 1, Jul 14 (14 Jul Revolution), 17 (17 Jul Revolution); Ad (4), As, ER (3), NY (Muslim), PB.

Political leaders

Monarch
1921–33	Faisal I
1933–9	Ghazi I
1939–58	Faisal II (*Regent* 1939–53, Abdul Illah)

Commander of the National Forces
1958–63	Abdul Karim Qassem

Head of Council of State
1958–63	Mohammed Najib Ar-Rubai

President
1963–6	Abd as-Salam Arif
1966–8	Abd ar-Rahman Arif
1968–79	Ahmad Hassan al-Bakr
1979–2003	Saddam Hussein
2003–4	*US-Controlled Transitional Administration*
2004–5	Ghazi Yawer *Interim President*
2005–	Jalal Talabani *Interim President*

Prime Minister
1958–63	Abdul Karim Qassem
1963	Ahmad Hassan al-Bakr
1963–5	Tahir Yahya
1965	Arif Abd ar-Razzaq
1965–6	Abd ar-Rahman al-Bazzaz
1966–7	Naji Talib
1967	Abd ar-Rahman Arif
1967–8	Tahir Yahya
1968	Abd ar-Razzaq an-Naif
1968–79	Ahmad Hassan al-Bakr
1979–91	Saddam Hussein
1991	Sadun Hammadi
1991–3	Mohammed Hamzah az-Zubaydi
1993–4	Ahmad Hussein Khudayir as-Samarrai
1994–2003	Saddam Hussein[1]
2003–4	*US-controlled transitional administration*
2004–5	Iyad Allawi *Interim Prime Minister*
2005–	Ibrahim Jaafari *Interim Prime Minister*

[1] *Overthrown by a US-led military coalition.*

IRELAND

Official name	Ireland		Gaelic-speaking areas, mostly in the west, are known as the *Gaeltacht*
Local name	Éire		
Independence	1921 (treaty), 1922 (Irish Free State)	**Ethnic groups**	Irish 95%, others 5%
Area	70 282 sq km/27 129 sq mi	**Religions**	Christianity 91% (RC 88%, Prot 3%), none/unaffiliated 5%, others 4%
Capital	Dublin; Baile Átha Cliath		
Chief towns	Cork, Limerick, Waterford, Galway, Drogheda, Dundalk, Sligo	**Time zone**	GMT
		Currency	1 Euro (€/EUR) = 100 cents
Population	4 148 000 (2005e)	**Telephone**	+353
Nationality	Irish	**Internet**	.ie
Languages	Irish, English; the Irish	**Country code**	IRL

Location
A republic occupying all but north-eastern Ireland, separated from Great Britain by the Irish Sea and St George's Channel, and bounded to the north-east by Northern Ireland, part of the United Kingdom.

Physical description
Mountainous landscapes in the west with quartzite peaks weathered into conical mountains; highest point is Carrantuohill (1 041m/3 415ft); mountains in the south create a landscape of ridges and valleys; eastern lowlands drained by slow-moving rivers.

Climate
Mild and equable, with few extremes of temperature; rainfall is heaviest in the west.

National holidays
Jan 1, Mar 17 (St Patrick), Dec 25, 26; EM, 1st Mon in May, 1st Mon in Jun, 1st Mon in Aug, last Mon in Oct public holidays.

Political leaders

Governor General

1922–7	Timothy Michael Healy	1936–7	Frank Fahy *and* Éamon de
1927–32	James McNeill		Valera *Acting heads of state*
1932–6	Donald Buckley		

President

1937–8	*Presidential Commission*	1974–6	Carroll Daly
1938–45	Douglas Hyde	1976–90	Patrick J Hillery
1945–59	Sean Thomas O'Kelly	1990–7	Mary Robinson
1959–73	Éamon de Valera	1997–	Mary McAleese
1973–4	Erskine H Childers		

Prime Minister

1919–21	Éamon de Valera	1966–73	John Lynch
1922	Arthur Griffiths	1973–7	Liam Cosgrave
1922–32	William Cosgrave	1977–9	John Lynch
1932–48	Éamon de Valera	1979–82	Charles Haughey
1948–51	John Aloysius Costello	1982–7	Garrett Fitzgerald
1951–4	Éamon de Valera	1987–92	Charles Haughey
1954–7	John Aloysius Costello	1992–4	Albert Reynolds
1957–9	Éamon de Valera	1994–7	John Bruton
1959–66	Sean Lemass	1997–	Bertie Ahern

Green, White and Orange

The green, white and orange Irish national flag was first seen in the mid-1800s, but became popular after 1916. According to the Irish government, 'the green represents the older Gaelic and Anglo-Norman element in the population, the orange the Protestant supporters of William of Orange, while the white represents the lasting peace between the two traditions'.

IRELAND, NORTHERN *see* **UNITED KINGDOM**

ISLE OF MAN *see* **UNITED KINGDOM**

ISRAEL

Official name	State of Israel	**Ethnic groups**	Jewish 81%, Arab and others 19%
Local name	Medinat Yisra'el, Dawlat Isrā'īl	**Religions**	Judaism 82%, Islam 14%, Druze 2%, Christianity 2%
Independence	1948		
Area	20 770 sq km/8 017 sq mi	**Time zone**	GMT +2
Capital[1]	Tel Aviv-Jaffa	**Currency**	1 New Israeli Shekel[2] (NIS/ILS) = 100 agorot
Chief towns	Jerusalem, Haifa, Beersheba, Acre, Holon	**Telephone**	+972
Population	6 725 000 (2005e)	**Internet**	.il
Nationality	Israeli	**Country code**	ISR
Languages	Hebrew, Arabic		

Location
A republic in the Middle East, bounded to the north by Lebanon; to the north-east by Syria; to the east by Jordan; to the south-west by Egypt; and to the west by the Mediterranean Sea.

Physical description
Extends 420km/260mi north to south; narrow coastal plain; mountainous interior, rising to 1 208m/3 963ft at Mt Meron; drops below sea level in the Jordan–Red Sea Rift Valley; Negev Desert in the south occupies c.60% of the country's area.

Climate
Typically Mediterranean in the north and centre, with hot, dry summers and warm, wet winters; average temperatures at Tel Aviv-Jaffa are 14°C (Jan) to 27°C (Jul); rainfall is heavier inland, with occasional snow; low rainfall in Negev Desert.

National holidays
Rosh Hashanah (Jewish NY; Sep/Oct), Yom Kippur (Sep/Oct), Sukkot (Sep/Oct), Hanukkah (Nov/Dec), Tu B'Shevat (Jan/Feb), Purim (Feb/Mar), Passover (Mar/Apr), Holocaust Martyrs and Heroes Remembrance (Apr/May), Remembrance for the Fallen of Israel's Wars (Apr/May), Independence (Apr/May), Lag B'omer (Apr/May), Jerusalem (May/Jun), Shavuot (May/Jun), Tisha B'Av (Jul/Aug); *Israel's national holidays have fixed dates in the Jewish calendar; for example Hanukkah begins on 25 Kislev.*

[1] *Israel claims Jerusalem as its capital, but this is not recognized internationally.*
[2] *Also sometimes transliterated as sheqel.*

Political leaders

President

1948–52	Chaim Weizmann	1978–83	Yitzhak Navon
1952–63	Itzhak Ben-Zvi	1983–93	Chaim Herzog
1963–73	Zalman Shazar	1993–2000	Ezer Weizman
1973–8	Ephraim Katzair	2000–	Moshe Katsav

Prime Minister

1948–53	David Ben-Gurion	1969–74	Golda Meir
1954–5	Moshe Sharett	1974–7	Yitzhak Rabin
1955–63	David Ben-Gurion	1977–83	Menachem Begin
1963–9	Levi Eshkol	1983–4	Yitzhak Shamir

1984–8	Shimon Peres	1996–9	Binyamin Netanyahu
1988–92	Yitzhak Shamir	1999–2001	Ehud Barak
1992–5	Yitzhak Rabin	2001–	Ariel Sharon
1995–6	Shimon Peres *Acting Prime Minister*		

Palestinian autonomous areas

Local name	Palestine; Qita Ghazzah (Gaza Strip), Daffah al-Gharbiyah (West Bank)		(West Bank); Palestinian Arab and other 99.4%, Jewish 0.6% (Gaza Strip)
Former name	Palestine (under British mandate 1920–48)	**Religions**	Islam 75% (Sunni), Jewish 17%, Christian and other 8% (West Bank); Islam (Sunni) 98.7%, Christian 0.7%, Jewish 0.6% (Gaza Strip)
Area[1]	6 231 sq km/2 406 sq mi (total)		
Capital[2]	Gaza City		
Chief towns	Nablus, Hebron, Jericho, Ramallah, Bethlehem (West Bank); Khan Yunis, Rafah (Gaza Strip)	**Time zone**	GMT +2
		Currency	1 Jordanian Dinar (JD) = 1 000 fils, 1 New Israeli Shekel[3] (NIS/ILS) = 100 agorot
Population	3 702 000 (2005e)		
Nationality	Palestinian	**Telephone**	+970
Languages	Arabic; Hebrew, English	**Internet**	.ps
Ethnic groups	Palestinian Arab and other 83%, Jewish 17%	**Country code**	PSE

Location
A disputed territory in the Middle East. It comprises the Gaza Strip, bordering the Mediterranean Sea to the west, Egypt to the south-west and otherwise surrounded by Israel; and the West Bank, a region separated from Jordan to the west by the River Jordan and the Dead Sea and otherwise surrounded by Israel.

Physical description
Gaza Strip is a low-lying, sandy coastal plain; highest point is Abu 'Awdah (105m/344ft); West Bank has a mountainous interior, dropping to below sea level (–400m/–1 312ft) at the Dead Sea; highest point is Tall Asur (1 022m/3 353ft).

Climate
Typically Mediterranean temperate climate, with hot, dry summers and warm, wet winters.

[1] 412 sq km/159 sq mi is fully autonomous (352 sq km/136 sq mi Gaza Strip and 60 sq km/23 sq mi Jericho area of West Bank); 5 819 sq km/2 247sq mi is partially autonomous (West Bank).
[2] Palestine claims East Jerusalem as its capital, but this is under Israeli occupation; Gaza City is the administrative capital.
[3] Also sometimes transliterated as sheqel.

Ancient Jericho

The West Bank city of Jericho is the site of the world's earliest known town, continuously occupied from c.9000BC–1850BC.

Political leaders

The West Bank was administered by Jordan until Israel took control after the Six Day War in 1967; Jordan's claims were ceded to the Palestine Liberation Organization (PLO) in 1974 and its legal and administrative links were cut in 1988. The Gaza Strip was administered by Egypt from 1949 until it was lost to the Israelis in 1967; the Israeli military administered it until 1994. In 1993 negotiations between Israel and the PLO resulted in a 'Declaration of Principles on Interim Self Government Arrangements' concerning Palestinian self-rule in the occupied territories, and in May 1994 a transitional period of self-rule began in the Gaza Strip and the Jericho area of the West Bank under the Palestinian National Authority.

Leader of the Palestinian National Authority

1994–2004	Yasser Arafat	2004	Rauhi Fattouh *Acting*
2004	Ahmed Qureia *Acting for Arafat*	2005–	Mahmoud Abbas (Abu Mazen)

Prime Minister

2003	Mahmoud Abbas (Abu Mazen)
2003–	Ahmed Qureia (Abu Ala)

ITALY

Official name	Italian Republic	**Languages**	Italian; German, French and Slovene are also spoken in some parts
Local name	Italia; Repubblica Italiana		
Former name	*as listed below under Political leaders*	**Ethnic groups**	Italian 94%, others 6%
Area	301 225 sq km/116 273 sq mi	**Religions**	Christianity 85% (RC), none/unaffiliated 14%, others 1%
Capital	Rome; Roma		
Chief towns	Milan, Turin, Genoa, Naples, Bologna, Palermo, Florence, Venice	**Time zone**	GMT +1
		Currency	1 Euro (€/EUR) = 100 cents
		Telephone	+39
Population	58 093 000 (2005e)	**Internet**	.it
Nationality	Italian	**Country code**	ITA

Location
A republic in southern central Europe, bounded to the north-west by France; to the north by Switzerland and Austria; to the north-east by Slovenia; the south is surrounded by the Adriatic, Ionian, Tyrrhenian and Mediterranean seas.

Physical description
Peninsula extends c.800km/500mi south-east; Alps in the north form an arc, with the highest peaks along the Swiss–French frontier at Mont Blanc (Monte Bianco; 4 807m/15 771ft) and the Matterhorn (4 477m/14 688ft); broad, fertile Lombardo–Venetian plain; several lakes at the foot of the Alps; three active volcanoes: Mt Etna (3 323m/10 902ft), Vesuvius (1 277m/4 190ft) and Stromboli (926m/3 038ft); also includes Sicily, Sardinia and some smaller islands; it completely encloses San Marino.

Climate
Great variation; north has hot, sunny summers and short, cold winters; higher areas are cold, wet, often snowy; coastal regions have a Mediterranean climate (warm, wet winters and hot, dry summers); long hours of summer sunshine in the extreme south.

National holidays
Jan 1, 6, Apr 25 (Liberation), May 1, Jun 2 (National), Aug 15, Nov 1, Dec 8, 25, 26; EM; *much local variation*.

Political leaders

Kingdom of Italy

Monarch

1861–78	Victor-Emmanuel II	1900–46	Victor-Emmanuel III
1878–1900	Humbert I	1946	Humbert II

Prime Minister

1900–1	Giuseppe Saracco	1917–19	Vittorio Emmanuele Orlando
1901–3	Giuseppe Zanardelli	1919–20	Francesco Saverio Nitti
1903–5	Giovanni Giolitti	1920–1	Giovanni Giolitti
1905–6	Alessandro Fortis	1921–2	Ivanoe Bonomi
1906	Sydney Sonnino	1922	Luigi Facta
1906–9	Giovanni Giolitti	1922–43	Benito Mussolini
1909–10	Sydney Sonnino	1943–4	Pietro Badoglio
1910–11	Luigi Luzzatti	1944–5	Ivanoe Bonomi
1911–14	Giovanni Giolitti	1945	Ferrucio Parri
1914–16	Antonio Salandra	1945	Alcide de Gasperi
1916–17	Paolo Boselli		

Italian Republic

President

1946–8	Enrico de Nicola	1971–8	Giovanni Leone
1948–55	Luigi Einaudi	1978–85	Alessandro Pertini
1955–62	Giovanni Gronchi	1985–92	Francesco Cossiga
1962–4	Antonio Segni	1992–9	Oscar Luigi Scalfaro
1964–71	Giuseppe Saragat	1999–	Carlo Azeglio Ciampi

Prime Minister

1946–53	Alcide de Gasperi	1979–80	Francisco Cossiga
1953–4	Giuseppe Pella	1980–1	Arnaldo Forlani
1954	Amintore Fanfani	1981–2	Giovanni Spadolini
1954–5	Mario Scelba	1982–3	Amintore Fanfani
1955–7	Antonio Segni	1983–7	Bettino Craxi
1957–8	Adone Zoli	1987	Amintore Fanfani
1958–9	Amintore Fanfani	1987–8	Giovanni Goria
1959–60	Antonio Segni	1988–9	Ciriaco de Mita
1960	Fernando Tambroni	1989–92	Giulio Andreotti
1960–3	Amintore Fanfani	1992–3	Giuliano Amato
1963	Giovanni Leone	1993–4	Carlo Azeglio Ciampi
1963–8	Aldo Moro	1994	Silvio Berlusconi
1968	Giovanni Leone	1995–6	Lamberto Dini
1968–70	Mariano Rumor	1996–8	Romano Prodi
1970–2	Emilio Colombo	1998–2000	Massimo D'Alema
1972–4	Giulio Andreotti	2000–1	Giuliano Amato
1974–6	Aldo Moro	2001–	Silvio Berlusconi
1976–8	Giulio Andreotti		

IVORY COAST *see* **CÔTE D'IVOIRE**

JAMAICA

Official name	Jamaica	**Religions**	Christianity 61% (Prot 25%, Church of God 21%, RC 6%, others 9%), none/unaffiliated 18%, Rastafarianism 6%, others 15%
Local name	Jamaica		
Independence	1962		
Area	10 957 sq km/4 229 sq mi		
Capital	Kingston		
Chief towns	Montego Bay, Spanish Town	**Time zone**	GMT –5
		Currency	1 Jamaican Dollar (J$/JMD) = 100 cents
Population	2 651 000 (2005e)		
Nationality	Jamaican	**Telephone**	+1 876
Languages	English; Jamaican Creole is also spoken	**Internet**	.jm
		Country code	JAM
Ethnic groups	black 90%, mixed 7%, East Indian 2%, others 1%		

Location
An island country in the West Indies in the Caribbean Sea.

Physical description
The third-largest island in the Caribbean Sea with a maximum length of 234km/145mi; mountainous and rugged particularly in the east, where the Blue Mountains rise to 2 256m/7 401ft at Blue Mountain Peak; more than 100 small rivers.

Climate
Humid and tropical climate at sea level, more temperate at higher altitudes; coastal temperatures range from 21°C to 34°C; virtually no rainfall on the south and south-west plains; lies within the hurricane belt.

National holidays
Jan 1, May 23 (Labour), Aug 1 (Emancipation), 6 (Independence), Oct 21 (National Heroes), Dec 25, 26; Ash Wednesday, EM, GF.

Political leaders

Head of State: British monarch, represented by Governor General (Sir Howard Cooke since 1991).

Prime Minister

1962–7	William Alexander Bustamante	1980–9	Edward Phillip George Seaga
1967	Donald Burns Sangster	1989–92	Michael Norman Manley
1967–72	Hugh Lawson Shearer	1992–	Percival James Patterson
1972–80	Michael Norman Manley		

Land of Wood and Water

Jamaica's name comes from *Xaymaca*, the name given to the island by its first inhabitants, the Taino people. In their language the name meant 'land of wood and water'.

JAN MAYEN ISLAND *see* **NORWAY**

JAPAN

Official name	Japan	**Languages**	Japanese
Local name	Nihon	**Ethnic groups**	Japanese 99%, others 1%
Area	381 945 sq km/147 431 sq mi	**Religions**	Shintoism and Buddhism 84%, others 15%, Christianity 1%
Capital	Tokyo; Tōkyō, Tôkyô		
Chief towns	Yokohama, Osaka, Nagoya, Sapporo, Kyoto, Kobe	**Time zone**	GMT +9
		Currency	1 Yen (Y, ¥/JPY) = 100 sen
		Telephone	+81
Population	128 085 000 (2005e)	**Internet**	.jp
Nationality	Japanese	**Country code**	JPN

Location
An island state off the east coast of Asia, comprising the four large islands of Hokkaido (the northernmost island), Honshu (the largest island), Kyushu and Shikoku (in the southwest), and many small islands; the country tails off to the south into the Ryukyu chain of volcanic islands, of which Okinawa is the largest.

Physical description
Consists mainly of steep mountains with many volcanoes; Hokkaido has a central range rising to over 2 000m/6 562ft, falling to coastal uplands and plains; Honshu comprises parallel arcs of mountains bounded by narrow coastal plains and includes Mt Fuji (3 776m/12 388ft), Japan's highest point; heavily populated Kanto plain lies in the east; frequent earthquakes.

Climate
Oceanic climate, influenced by the Asian monsoon; short, warm summers, and severe winters with heavy snow in the north; average daily temperature at Akita (north Honshu) ranges from –5°C to 2°C (Jan), 19°C to 28°C (Aug); variable winter weather throughout; typhoons occur in summer and early autumn; mild, almost subtropical winters with light rainfall in south Honshu, Shikoku and Kyushu; summer heat is often oppressive.

National holidays
Jan 1, Feb 11 (National Foundation), Apr 29 (Greenery), May 3 (Constitution Memorial), 5 (Children), Sep 15 (Respect for the Aged), Nov 3 (Culture), 23 (Labour Thanksgiving), Dec 23 (Emperor's Birthday); Autumnal Equinox, Coming-of-Age (2nd Mon in Jan), Marine Day (Jul), Sports (2nd Mon in Oct), Vernal Equinox.

Political leaders

Chief of State (Emperor)

660–585BC	Jimmu[1]	29BC–70AD	Suinin[1]
581–549BC	Suizei[1]	AD71–130	Keiko[1]
549–511BC	Annei[1]	AD131–190	Seimu[1]
510–477BC	Itoku[1]	AD192–200	Chuai[1]
475–393BC	Kosho[1]	AD270–310	Ojin[2]
392–291BC	Koan[1]	AD313–399	Nintoku[2]
290–215BC	Korei[1]	AD400–405	Richu[2]
214–158BC	Kogen[1]	AD406–410	Hanzei[2]
158–98BC	Kaika[1]	AD412–453	Ingyo[2]
97–30BC	Sujin[1]	AD453–456	Anko[2]

AD456–479	Yuryaku[2]
AD480–484	Seinei[2]
AD485–487	Kenzo[2]
AD488–498	Ninken[2]
AD498–506	Buretsu[2]
507–531	Keitai[2]
531–535	Ankan[2]
535–539	Senka[2]
539–571	Kimmei
572–585	Bidatsu
585–587	Yomei
587–592	Sushun
592–628	Suiko (Empress)
629–641	Jomei
642–645	Kogyoku (Empress)
645–654	Kotuko
655–661	Saimei (Empress)
662–671	Tenji
671–672	Kobun
673–686	Temmu
686–697	Jito (Empress)
697–707	Mommu
707–715	Gemmei (Empress)
715–724	Gensho (Empress)
724–749	Shomu
749–758	Koken (Empress)
758–764	Junnin
764–770	Shotoku (Empress)
770–781	Konin
781–806	Kammu
806–809	Heizei
809–823	Saga
823–833	Junna
833–850	Nimmyo
850–858	Montoku
858–876	Seiwa
876–884	Yozei
884–887	Koko
887–897	Uda
897–930	Daigo
930–946	Suzaku
946–967	Murakami
967–969	Reizei
969–984	En-yu
984–986	Kazan
986–1011	Ichijo
1011–16	Sanjo
1016–36	Go-Ichijo
1036–45	Go-Suzaku
1045–68	Go-Reizei
1068–72	Go-Sanyo
1072–86	Shirakawa
1086–1107	Horikawa
1107–23	Toba
1123–41	Sutoku
1141–55	Konoe
1155–8	Go-Shirakawa
1158–65	Nijo
1165–8	Rokujo
1168–80	Takakura
1180–3	Antoku
1183–98	Go-Toba
1198–1210	Tsuchimikado
1210–21	Juntoku
1221	Chukyo
1221–32	Go-Horikawa
1232–42	Shijo
1242–6	Go-Saga
1246–59	Go-Fukakusa
1259–74	Kameyama
1274–87	Go-Uda
1287–98	Fushimi
1298–1301	Go-Fushimi
1301–8	Go-Nijo
1308–18	Hanazono
1318–39	Go-Daigo
1339–68	Go-Murakami
1368–83	Chokei
1383–92	Go-Kameyama

Northern Court

1331–3	Kogon
1336–48	Komyo
1348–51	Suko
1352–71	Go-Kogon
1371–82	Go-Enyu
1382–1412	Go-Komatsu
1412–28	Shoko
1428–64	Go-Hanazono
1464–1500	Go-Suchimikado
1500–26	Go Kashiwabara
1526–57	Go-Nara
1557–86	Ogimachi
1586–1611	Go-Yozei
1611–29	Go-Mizuno-o
1629–43	Meisho (Empress)
1643–54	Go-Komyo
1654–63	Go-Sai
1663–87	Reigen
1687–1709	Higashiyama
1709–35	Nakamikado
1735–47	Sakuramachi
1747–62	Momozono
1762–70	Go-Sakuramachi
1770–9	Go-Momozono
1779–1817	Kokaku
1817–46	Ninko

1846–66	Komei	1926–89	Hirohito (Showa Era)
1867–1912	Mutsuhito (Meiji Era)	1989–	Akihito (Heisei Era)
1912–26	Yoshihito (Taisho Era)		

[1] The first 14 emperors (to Chuai) are regarded as legendary.
[2] The regnal dates for the 15th to the 28th emperor (Senka), taken from the early Japanese chronicle, 'Nihon shoki', are not considered to be authentic.

Prime Minister

1900–1	Hirobumi Ito	1945	Kantaro Suzuki
1901–6	Taro Katsura	1945	Naruhiko Higashikuni
1906–8	Kimmochi Saionji	1945–6	Kijuro Shidehara
1908–11	Taro Katsura	1946–7	Shigeru Yoshida
1911–12	Kimmochi Saionji	1947–8	Tetsu Katayama
1912–13	Taro Katsura	1948	Hitoshi Ashida
1913–14	Gonnohyoe Yamamoto	1948–54	Shigeru Yoshida
1914–16	Shigenobu Okuma	1954–6	Ichiro Hatoyama
1916–18	Masatake Terauchi	1956–7	Tanzan Ishibashi
1918–21	Takashi Hara	1957–60	Nobusuke Kishi
1921–2	Korekiyo Takahashi	1960–4	Hayato Ikeda
1922–3	Tomosaburo Kato	1964–72	Eisaku Sato
1923–4	Gonnohyoe Yamamoto	1972–4	Kakuei Tanaka
1924	Keigo Kiyoura	1974–6	Takeo Miki
1924–6	Takaaki Kato	1976–8	Takeo Fukuda
1926–7	Reijiro Wakatsuki	1978–80	Masayoshi Ohira
1927–9	Giichi Tanaka	1980–2	Zenko Suzuki
1929–31	Osachi Hamaguchi	1982–7	Yasuhiro Nakasone
1931	Reijiro Wakatsuki	1987–9	Noburu Takeshita
1931–2	Tsuyoshi Inukai	1989	Sasuke Uno
1932–4	Makoto Saito	1989–91	Toshiki Kaifu
1934–6	Keisuke Okada	1991–93	Kiichi Miyazawa
1936–7	Koki Hirota	1993	Morihiro Hosokawa
1937	Senjuro Hayashi	1994	Tsutoma Hata
1937–9	Fumimaro Konoe	1994–6	Tomiichi Murayama
1939	Kiichiro Hiranuma	1996–8	Ryutaro Hashimoto
1939–40	Nobuyuki Abe	1998–2000	Keizo Obuchi
1940	Mitsumasa Yonai	2000	Mikio Aoki *Acting Prime Minister*
1940–1	Fumimaro Konoe	2000–1	Yoshiro Mori
1941–4	Hideki Tojo	2001–	Junichiro Koizumi
1944–5	Kuniaki Koiso		

Growing Old Gracefully

Japan has the highest life expectancy in the world, at an average of 81.9 years. By 2050, life expectancy at birth for the Japanese is forecast to rise to 88.3 years. In 2003 the Japanese government announced that the country has more than 20 000 centenarians.

JORDAN

Official name	Hashemite Kingdom of Jordan		Aqaba
		Population	5 703 000 (2005e)
Local name	Al'Urdunn; Al-Mamlaka al-Urdunniyya al-Hashimiyya	**Nationality**	Jordanian
		Languages	Arabic
Former name	Emirate of Transjordan (until 1946), Hashemite Kingdom of Transjordan (1946–9)	**Ethnic groups**	Arab 98%, others 2%
		Religions	Islam 94% (Sunni), Christianity 6%
		Time zone	GMT +2
Independence	1946	**Currency**	1 Jordanian Dinar (JD/JOD) = 1 000 fils
Area	96 188 sq km/37 129 sq mi		
		Telephone	+962
Capital	Amman; 'Ammān	**Internet**	.jo
Chief towns	Irbid, Zarqa, Salt, Karak,	**Country code**	JOR

Location
A kingdom in the Middle East, bounded to the north by Syria; to the north-east by Iraq; to the east and south by Saudi Arabia; and to the west by Israel.

Physical description
Divided by the Red Sea–Jordan rift valley; lowest point is –400m/–1 312ft at the Dead Sea; sides of the rift rise through undulating hills; Syrian desert in the east, sandy in the south, hard and rocky further north; highest point is Jabal Rum (1 754m/5 755ft).

Climate
Desert covers c.90% of the country; summers are uniformly hot and sunny; typically Mediterranean climate elsewhere, with hot, dry summers and cool, wet winters; temperatures at Amman are 7°C (Jan), 25°C (Jul).

National holidays
Jan 1, May 1, 25 (Independence), Jun 9 (Accession of King Abdullah),10 (Great Arab Revolt), Nov 14 (late King Hussein's Birthday); Ad (4), R, ER (3), NY (Muslim), PB, Al-Isra' wal mi'raj.

Political leaders

Monarch

1921–51	Abdullah ibn Hussein I	1952–99	Hussein ibn Talal
1951–2	Talal I	1999–	Abdullah ibn Hussein II

Prime Minister

1921	Rashid Tali	1951–3	Taufiq Abul-Huda
1921	Muzhir Ar-Raslan	1953–4	Fauzi Al-Mulqi
1921–3	Rida Ar-Riqabi	1954–5	Taufiq Abul-Huda
1923	Muzhir Ar-Raslan	1955	Said Al-Mufti
1923–4	Hassan Khalid	1955	Hazza Al-Majali
1924–33	Rida Ar-Riqabi	1955–6	Ibrahim Hashim
1933–8	Ibrahim Hashim	1956	Samir Ar-Rifai
1938–44	Taufiq Abul-Huda	1956	Said Al-Mufti
1944–5	Samir Ar-Rifai	1956	Ibrahim Hashim
1945–7	Ibrahim Hashim	1956–7	Suleiman Nabulsi
1947–50	Taufiq Abul-Huda	1957	Hussein Fakhri Al-Khalidi
1950	Said Al-Mufti	1957–8	Ibrahim Hashim
1950–1	Samir Ar-Rifai	1958	Nuri Pasha Al-Said

1958–9	Samir Ar-Rifai	1976–9	Mudar Badran
1959–60	Hazza Al-Majali	1979–80	Sharif Abdul Hamid Sharaf
1960–2	Bahjat Talhuni	1980	Kassem Rimawi
1962–3	Wasfi At-Tall	1980–4	Mudar Badran
1963	Samir Ar-Rifai	1984–5	Ahmad Ubayat
1963–4	Sharif Hussein Bin Nasir	1985–9	Zeid Ar-Rifai
1964–5	Bahjat Talhuni	1989	Sharif Zaid ibn Shaker
1965–7	Wasfi At-Tall	1989–91	Mudar Badran
1967	Sharif Hussein Bin Nasir	1991	Taher Al-Masri
1967	Saad Jumaa	1991–3	Sharif Zaid ibn Shaker
1967–9	Bahjat Talhuni	1993–5	Abdel Salam Al-Majali
1969	Abdul Munem Rifai	1995–7	Abdul Karim Kabariti
1969–70	Bahjat Talhuni	1997–8	Abdel Salam Al-Majali
1970	Abdul Munem Rifai	1998–9	Fayez Tarawneh
1970	*Military Junta* (Mohammed Daud)	1999–2000	Abdul Raouf Rawabdeh
1970	Mohamed Ahmed Tugan	2000–3	Ali Abu Al-Ragheb
1970–1	Wasfi At-Tall	2003–5	Faisal Al-Fayez
1971–3	Ahmad Lozi	2005–	Adnan Badran
1973–6	Zeid Rifai		

KAMPUCHEA *see* **CAMBODIA**

KAZAKHSTAN

Official name	Republic of Kazakhstan	**Nationality**	Kazakhstani
Local name	Qazaqstan Respūblīkasy	**Languages**	Kazakh; Russian is also widely spoken
Former name	Kazakh Soviet Socialist Republic (until 1991), within the Union of Soviet Socialist Republics (USSR; 1922–91)	**Ethnic groups**	Kazakh 46%, Russian 35%, Ukrainian 5%, German 4%, others 10%
Independence	1991	**Religions**	Islam 48%, Christianity 46% (Orthodox 44%, Prot 2%), others 6%
Area	2 717 300 sq km/ 1 048 878 sq mi	**Time zone**	GMT +4/6
Capital	Astana	**Currency**	1 Tenge (KZT) = 100 tiyn
Chief towns	Karaganda, Semipalatinsk, Chimkent, Petropavlovsk	**Telephone**	+7
		Internet	.kz
Population	14 825 000 (2005e)	**Country code**	KAZ

Location
A republic in western Asia, bounded to the north by Russia; to the east by China; to the south by Kyrgyzstan, Uzbekistan and Turkmenistan; and to the west by the Caspian Sea.

Physical description
Steppeland in the north gives way to desert in the south; mountain ranges in the east and south-east; highest point is Khan Tengri (6 995m/22 949ft) in the Tien Shan mountains; largest lake is Lake Balkhash; Aral Sea lies on the south border with Uzbekistan.

Climate
Continental; hot summers and cold winters.

National holidays
Jan 1, Mar 8 (Women), 21, May 1, 9 (Victory), Aug 30 (Constitution), Oct 25 (State Sovereignty), Dec 16 (Independence), 31.

Political leaders

President
1991–   Nursultan Nazarbayev

Prime Minister

1991–4	Sergei Tereshchenko	1999–2002	Kasymzhomart Tokaev
1994–7	Akezhan Kazhageldin	2002–3	Imangali Tasmagambetov
1997–9	Nurlan Balgimbayev	2003–	Daniyal Akhmetov

KEELING ISLANDS *see* **AUSTRALIA**

KENYA

Official name	Republic of Kenya	**Ethnic groups**	Kikuyu 22%, Luhya 14%, Luo 13%, Kalenjin 12%, Kamba 11%, others 28%
Local name	Jamhuri ya Kenya		
Former name	British East Africa Protectorate (until 1920)	**Religions**	Christianity 66% (Prot 38%, RC 28%), traditional beliefs 26%, Islam 7%, others 1%
Independence	1963		
Area	564 162 sq km/217 766 sq mi		
Capital	Nairobi	**Time zone**	GMT +3
Chief towns	Mombasa, Kisumu, Nakuru, Malindi	**Currency**	1 Kenyan Shilling (Ksh/KES) = 100 cents
Population	34 256 000 (2005e)	**Telephone**	+254
Nationality	Kenyan	**Internet**	.ke
Languages	English and Swahili, with many tribal languages spoken	**Country code**	KEN

Location
A republic in East Africa, bounded to the north by Ethiopia; to the north-east by Somalia; to the east by the Indian Ocean; to the south by Tanzania; to the west by Uganda and Lake Victoria; and to the north-west by Sudan.

Physical description
Crossed by the Equator; highest point is Mt Kenya (5 200m/17 060ft); Great Rift Valley in the west runs north to south; dry, arid semi-desert in the north; largest body of water is Lake Turkana in the north; Chalbi Desert lies south-east of the lake.

Climate
Tropical climate on the coast, with high temperatures and humidity; in Mombasa the average daily temperatures are 27–31°C; annual rainfall decreases from south to the far north; frost and snow lie in the high mountains.

National holidays
Jan 1, May 1, Jun 1 (Madaraka), Oct 10 (Moi), 20 (Kenyatta) (2), Dec 12 (Jamhuri), 25, 26; EM, ER, GF.

Political leaders

President

1963–78	Mzee Jomo Kenyatta
1978–2002	Daniel arap Moi
2002–	Mwai Kibaki

KIRIBATI

Official name	Republic of Kiribati	**Ethnic groups**	Micronesian 98%, others 2%
Local name	Kiribati; Ribaberikin Kiribati	**Religions**	Christianity 91% (RC 53%, Prot 38%), Baha'i 3%, others 6%
Former name	Gilbert Islands, as part of the Gilbert and Ellice Islands (until 1979)		
		Time zone	GMT +12/14
Independence	1979	**Currency**	1 Australian Dollar ($A/AUD) = 100 cents
Area	717 sq km/277 sq mi		
Capital	Tarawa	**Telephone**	+686
Population	99 000 (2005e)	**Internet**	.ki
Nationality	I-Kiribati	**Country code**	KIR
Languages	English, I-Kiribati		

Location
An island republic in the central Pacific Ocean.

Physical description
A group of 33 low-lying coral islands scattered over c.3 million sq km/1.2 million sq mi of the central Pacific Ocean; islands seldom rise to more than 4m/13ft and usually consist of a reef enclosing a lagoon; Banaba, a solid coral outcrop with a fringing reef, rises to 87m/285ft.

Climate
Maritime equatorial climate in the central islands; islands further north and south are tropical; average annual temperature is 27°C; rainy season from Nov to Apr; some islands suffer from periodic drought.

National holidays
Jan 1, Mar 8 (Women), Apr 17 (National Health), Jul 11 (Gospel), 12 (Independence) (3), Aug 6 (Youth), Dec 10 (Human Rights), 25, 26; GF, HS, EM, ES; *length of holidays varies locally*.

Political leaders

President

1979–82	Ieremia T Tabai	1994–2003	Teburoro Tito
1982–3	*Council of State* (Rota Onorio)	2003	*Council of State* (Tion Otang)
1983–91	Ieremia T Tabai	2003–	Anote Tong
1991–4	Teatao Teannaki		
1994	*Council of State* (Tekire Tameura/Ata Teaotai)		

It's a Date

The International Date Line runs through the middle of Kiribati, meaning that the time difference between its easternmost and westernmost islands should be 24 hours. However, in 1995 the government 'bent' the Date Line to make the date the same everywhere, moving the line hundreds of kilometres east in a bulge big enough to include all the islands. An additional benefit of this was that Kiribati's Caroline Island, renamed Millennium Island, was the first place to see the sunrise on 1 Jan 2000, drawing attention and tourists from around the world.

KOREA, NORTH

Official name	Democratic People's Republic of Korea (DPRK)	**Languages**	Korean
		Ethnic groups	Korean 100%
Local name	Chosun; Chosun Minchu-chui In'min Kongwa-guk	**Religions**	none/unaffiliated 67%, traditional beliefs 16%,
Independence	1948		Chondogyo 14%,
Area	122 098 sq km/47 130 sq mi		Buddhism 2%, Christianity 1%
Capital	Pyongyang; P'yŏngyang	**Time zone**	GMT +9
Chief towns	Chongjin, Sinuiju, Wonsan, Kaesong	**Currency**	1 North Korean Won (NKW/KPW) = 100 chon
Population	22 488 000 (2005e)	**Telephone**	+850
Nationality	North Korean	**Internet**	.kp
		Country code	PRK

Location
A state in eastern Asia, comprising the northern half of the Korean Peninsula, bounded to the north by China; to the north-east by Russia; to the east by the Sea of Japan (the East Sea); to the south by South Korea, from which it is separated by a demilitarized zone; and to the west by Korea Bay.

Physical description
On a high plateau occupying the north of a mountainous peninsula which projects south-east from China; many areas rise to over 2 000m/6 562ft; highest point is Mt Paektu (2 744m/9 003ft); lower mountains in the south descend to coastal plains.

Climate
Temperate, with warm summers and severely cold winters; rivers freeze for 3–4 months, and ice blocks harbours; daily temperatures at Pyongyang in the west range from –3°C to –13°C (Jan), and from 20°C to 29°C (Jul–Aug).

National holidays
Jan 1, Feb 16 (Kim Jong Il's Birthday), Mar 8 (Women), Apr 15 (Kim Il Sung's Birthday), Apr 25 (Army Foundation), May 1, Jul 27 (Fatherland Liberation War Victory), Aug 15 (Liberation), Sep 9 (Foundation of the Republic), Oct 10 (Foundation of the Workers' Party), Dec 27 (Constitution).

Political leaders

President
1948–57	Kim Doo-bong	1994–7	*Position vacant*
1957–72	Choi Yong-kun	1998–	Kim Il Sung (deceased)
1972–94	Kim Il Sung		*Eternal President*

Chairman of National Defence Commission
1993–	Kim Jong Il

Prime Minister
1948–76	Kim Il Sung	1988–92	Yon Hyong-muk
1976–7	Park Sung-chul	1992–7	Kang Song-san
1977–84	Li Jong-ok	1997–2003	Hong Song-nam
1984–6	Kang Song-san	2003–	Pak Pong-ju
1986–8	Yi Kun-mo		

KOREA, SOUTH

Official name	Republic of Korea (ROK)	**Ethnic groups**	Korean 100%
Local name	Hanguk; Dae-han-min-guk	**Religions**	Christianity 51% (Prot 39%, RC 12%), Buddhism 47%, others 2%
Independence	1948		
Area	98 913 sq km/38 180 sq mi	**Time zone**	GMT +9
Capital[1]	Seoul; Sŏul	**Currency**	1 Won (W/KRW) = 100 jeon
Chief towns	Inchon, Pusan, Taegu		
Population	47 817 000 (2005e)	**Telephone**	+82
Nationality	South Korean	**Internet**	.kr
Languages	Korean	**Country code**	KOR

Location
A republic in eastern Asia, comprising the southern half of the Korean Peninsula and about 3 000 islands off its west and south coasts, bounded to the north by North Korea, from which it is separated by a demilitarized zone; to the east by the Sea of Japan (the East Sea); to the south by the Korean Strait; and to the west by the Yellow Sea.

Physical description
Taebaek Sanmaek Range runs north to south along the east coast, reaching heights of over 900m/2 953ft; it descends through a series of ridges to broad, undulating coastal lowlands; highest peak is Halla-san (1 950m/6 398ft) on the island of Cheju-do.

Climate
Extreme continental climate, with cold winters and hot summers; typhoons possible in the wettest months (Jun–Sep); average daily temperatures at Seoul range from –9°C to 0°C (Jan), 22°C to 31°C (Aug).

National holidays
Jan 1–3, Mar 1 (Independence Movement), 10 (Labour), Apr 5 (Arbor), May 5 (Children), Jun 6 (Memorial), Jul 17 (Constitution), Aug 15 (Liberation), Oct 1 (Armed Forces), 3 (National Foundation), 9 (Korean Alphabet), Dec 25; NY (Chinese) (Jan/Feb), Lord Buddha's Birthday (May), Moon Festival (Sep/Oct).

[1] *In 2004 plans were announced to transfer the capital to the Yeongi-Kongju area by 2012; whether this will be put into effect remains uncertain.*

Political leaders

President
1948–60	Syngman Rhee	1980	Park Choong-hoon *Acting President*
1960	Ho Chong *Acting President*	1980–8	Chun Doo-hwan
1960	Kwak Sang-hun *Acting President*	1988–93	Roh Tae-woo
1960	Ho Chong *Acting President*	1993–7	Kim Young-sam
1960–3	Yun Po-sun	1997–2003	Kim Dae-jung
1963–79	Park Chung-hee	2003–	Roh Moo-hyun
1979–80	Choi Kyu-hah	2004	Ko Kun *Acting President for suspended President Roh*

Prime Minister
1948–50	Lee Pom-sok	1952	Lee Yun-yong *Acting Prime Minister*
1950	Shin Song-mo *Acting Prime Minister*		
		1952	Chang Taek-sang
1950–1	John M Chang	1952–4	Paik Too-chin
1951–2	Ho Chong *Acting Prime Minister*	1954–6	Pyon Yong-tae

1956–60	Syngman Rhee		1988	Lee Hyun-jae
1960	Ho Chong		1988–90	Kang Young-hoon
1960–1	John M Chang		1990–1	Ro Jai-bong
1961	Chang To-yong		1991–2	Chung Won-shik
1961–2	Song Yo-chan		1992–3	Hyun Soong-jong
1962–3	Kim Hyun-chul		1993	Hwang In-sung
1963–4	Choe Tu-son		1993–4	Lee Hoi-chang
1964–70	Chung Il-kwon		1994	Lee Yung-duck
1970–1	Paik Too-chin		1994–5	Yi Hong-ku
1971–5	Kim Jong-pil		1995–7	Lee Soo-sung
1975–9	Choi Kyu-hah		1997–8	Koh Kun
1979–80	Shin Hyun-hwak		1998–2000	Kim Jong-pil
1980	Park Choong-hoon *Acting Prime Minister*		2000	Park Tae-joon
			2000	Lee Hun-jai *Acting Prime Minister*
1980–2	Nam Duck-woo		2000–2	Lee Han-dong
1982	Yoo Chang-soon		2002–3	Kim Suk-soo
1982–3	Kim Sang-hyup		2003–4	Ko Kun
1983–5	Chin Lee-chong		2004–	Lee Hae-chan
1985–8	Lho Shin-yong			

KUWAIT

Official name	State of Kuwait	**Ethnic groups**	Kuwaiti 47%, other Arab 36%, South Asian 8%, Iranian 4%, others 5%
Local name	Dawlat al-Kuwayt		
Independence	1961		
Area	17 818 sq km/6 878 sq mi	**Religions**	Islam 85% (Sunni 45%, Shia 40%), Hinduism 2%, others 13%
Capital	Kuwait City; Al Kuwayt	**Time zone**	GMT +3
Chief towns	Shuwaikh, Mina al Ahmadi	**Currency**	1 Kuwaiti Dinar (KD/KWD) = 1 000 fils
Population	2 687 000 (2005e)	**Telephone**	+965
Nationality	Kuwaiti	**Internet**	.kw
Languages	Arabic; English is also widely spoken	**Country code**	KWT

Location
An independent state at the head of the Arabian Gulf, bounded to the north and west by Iraq; to the east by the Arabian Gulf; and to the south by Saudi Arabia.

Physical description
Consists of the mainland and nine offshore islands; terrain is flat or gently undulating, rising in the south-west to 271m/889ft; Wadi al Batin runs along the western border with Iraq; terrain is generally stony with sparse vegetation.

Climate
Hot, dry climate; summer temperatures are very high, often above 45°C (Jul–Aug); winter daytime temperatures often exceed 20°C; humidity is generally high; sandstorms are common throughout the year.

National holidays
Jan 1, Feb 25 (National), 26 (Liberation); Mt Ararat and Ad (4), ER (3), NY (Muslim), PB, Ascension of the Prophet.

Political leaders

Emir
Family name: Al-Sabah

1896–1915	Mubarak	1950–65	Abdallah Al-Salem
1915–17	Jaber II	1965–77	Sabah Al-Salem
1917–21	Salem Al-Mubarak	1978–	Jaber Al-Ahmed Al-Jaber
1921–50	Ahmed Al-Jaber		

Prime Minister
Family name: Al-Sabah

1962–3	Jaber Al-Ahmed Al-Jaber	1978–2003	Saad Al-Abdallah Al-Salem
1963 5	Sabah Al-Salem	2003–	Sabah Al-Ahmed Al-Jaber
1965–78	Jaber Al-Ahmed Al-Jaber		

KYRGYZSTAN

Official name	Kyrgyz Republic	**Languages**	Kyrgyz, Russian
Local name	Kyrgyz Respublikasy	**Ethnic groups**	Kyrgyz 55%, Russian 21%, Uzbek 13%, Ukrainian 3%, German 2%, Tatar 2%, others 4%
Former name	Kyrgyz Soviet Socialist Republic (until 1990), within the Union of Soviet Socialist Republics (USSR; 1922–91)	**Religions**	Islam 75%, Christianity 20% (Orthodox), others 5%
Independence	1991		
Area	198 500 sq km/76 621 sq mi	**Time zone**	GMT +5
		Currency	1 Som (Kgs/KGS) = 100 tyjyn[1]
Capital	Bishkek; Biškek		
Chief towns	Osh, Przhevalsk, Kyzyl-Kiya	**Telephone**	+996
		Internet	.kg
Population	5 264 000 (2005e)	**Country code**	KGZ
Nationality	Kyrgyz		

Location
A republic in central Asia, bounded to the north by Kazakhstan; to the south-east by China; to the south by Tajikistan; and to the west by Uzbekistan.

Physical description
Largely occupied by the Tien Shan Mountains; highest point is Pobedy Peak (7 439m/24 406ft); Lake Issyk-Kul is the largest lake.

Climate
Varies according to location; sub-tropical in the south-west, dry in the north and west, continental to polar in the mountainous east.

National holidays
Jan 1, 7 (Russian Orthodox Christmas), Mar 8 (Women), 21, May 1, 5 (Constitution), 9 (Victory), Aug 31 (Independence); Ad, ER, Navroos.

[1] *Also sometimes transliterated as tyin or tyiyn.*

Political leaders

President

1991–2005	Askar Akayev
2005–	Kurmanbek Bakiyev

Prime Minister

1991	Nasirdin Isanov	1999	Boris Silayev *Acting Prime Minister*
1991–2	Andrey Andreyevich Yordan *Acting Prime Minister*	1999–2000	Amangeldy Muraliyev
		2000–2	Kurmanbek Bakiyev
1992–3	Tursunbek Chyngyshev	2002–5	Nikolai Tanayev
1993–8	Apas Jumagulov	2005	Kurmanbek Bakiyev
1998	Kubanychbek Djumaliyev	2005	Medetbek Kerimkulov *Acting Prime Minister*
1998	Boris Silayev *Acting Prime Minister*		
1998–9	Jumabek Ibraimov	2005–	Feliks Kulov *Acting Prime Minister*

Yurts in the Sun

The national flag of Kyrgyzstan has a red background, symbolizing courage and audacity. In its centre is a golden sun, representing peace and wealth. Within the sun is a *tunduk*, the roof of a yurt, symbolizing home within the big wide world.

LAOS

Official name	Lao People's Democratic Republic	**Languages**	Lao
Local name	Lao; Sathalanalat Paxathipatai Paxaxôn Lao	**Ethnic groups**	Lao Loum 68%, Lao Theung 22%, Lao Soung 9%, others 1%
Former name	Kingdom of Laos (1945–75)	**Religions**	Buddhism 76%, traditional beliefs 20%, Christianity 2% (Prot 1%, RC 1%), Islam 1%, Chinese folk religion 1%
Independence	1949		
Area	236 800 sq km/91 405 sq mi		
Capital	Vientiane; Viangchan	**Time zone**	GMT +7
Chief towns	Luang Prabang, Pakse, Savannakhét	**Currency**	1 Kip (Kp/LAK) = 100 at
		Telephone	+856
Population	5 924 000 (2005e)	**Internet**	.la
Nationality	Lao or Laotian	**Country code**	LAO

Location
A republic in south-east Asia, bounded to the north by China; to the east by Vietnam; to the south by Cambodia; and to the west by Thailand and Myanmar.

Physical description
On the Indochinese Peninsula; dense jungle and rugged mountains in the east; highest point is Phu Bia (2 820m/9 252ft); Mekong River flows north-west–south-east, following much of the west frontier with Thailand.

Climate
Monsoonal with heavy rain in May–Sep; hot and dry Feb–Apr; average annual temperatures in Vientiane are 14–34°C.

National holidays
Jan 1, 20 (Foundation of the Lao People's Revolutionary Army), Mar 8 (Women), 22 (Foundation of the Lao People's Revolutionary Party), May 1, Jun 1 (Children), Aug 23 (Declaration of Power), Oct 7 (Teachers), 12 (Independence), Dec 2 (National Foundation); New Year/Water Festival (Apr) (3), Boat Racing Festival (Oct), That Luang Festival (Nov), Makhabouxa (Feb), Visakhabouxa (May), Hokhaopadabdine (Aug), Hokhaosalak (Sep), Buddhist days (2).

Political leaders

Monarch

1904–59	Sisavang Vong
1959–75	Savang Vatthana

President

1975–87	Souphanouvong	1992–8	Nouhak Phoumsavan
1987–91	Phoumi Vongvichit	1998–	Khamtai Siphandon
1991–2	Kaysone Phomvihane		

Prime Minister

1951–4	Souvanna Phouma	1960	Sunthone Patthamavong
1954–6	Katay Don Sasorith	1960	Quinim Pholsena
1956–8	Souvanna Phouma	1960–2	Boun Oum Na Champassac
1958–9	Phoui Sahanikone	1962–75	Souvanna Phouma
1959–60	Sunthone Patthamavong	1975–91	Kaysone Phomvihane
1960	Kou Abhay	1991–8	Khamtai Siphandon
1960	Somsanith	1998–2001	Sisavath Keobounphan
1960	Souvana Phouma	2001–	Boungnang Vorachit

Land of a Million Elephants

In 1353 King Fa Ngum unified various settlements along the Mekong River into a single state, which he named *Lane Xang*, the 'Land of a Million Elephants'. The nation's capital was at Luang Prabang, then called Xiengdong Xiengthong, but in 1560 the capital was moved to Vientiane where it was fortified. *Vientiane* means 'rampart of sandalwood'.

LATVIA

Official name	Republic of Latvia	**Ethnic groups**	Latvian 57%, Russian 31%, Belarussian 5%, Ukrainian 4%, others 3%
Local name	Latvija; Latvijas Republika		
Former name	Latvian Soviet Socialist Republic (1940–90), within the Union of Soviet Socialist Republics (USSR; 1940–91)	**Religions**	Christianity, predominantly Lutheran Protestant, with Roman Catholic and Orthodox minorities
Independence	1991	**Time zone**	GMT +2
Area	63 700 sq km/24 600 sq mi	**Currency**	1 Lat (Ls/LVL) = 100 santims
Capital	Riga; Rīga		
Chief towns	Daugavpils, Liepaja	**Telephone**	+371
Population	2 307 000 (2005e)	**Internet**	.lv
Nationality	Latvian	**Country code**	LVA
Languages	Latvian		

Location
A republic in north-eastern Europe, bounded to the north-west by the Gulf of Riga; to the north by Estonia; to the east by Russia; to the south-east by Belarus and Lithuania; and to the west by the Baltic Sea.

Physical description
A flat, glaciated area; north-west coast is indented by the Gulf of Riga; highest point is Gaizinkalns (312m/1 024ft); over 40% is forested.

Climate
Moderate winters; cool, rainy summers.

National holidays
Jan 1, May 1 (Convocation of the Constituent Assembly), Jun 23 (Ligo), 24 (Jani/Summer Solstice), Nov 18 (Proclamation of the Republic), Dec 25, 26, 31; EM, ES, GF, Mothers (2nd Sun in May).

Political leaders

President

1990–3	Anatolijs Gorbunovs
1993–9	Guntis Ulmanis
1999–	Vaira Vike-Freiberga

Prime Minister

1990–3	Ivars Godmanis		1999–2000	Andris Skele
1993–4	Valdis Birkavs		2000–2	Andris Berzins
1994–5	Maris Gailis		2002–4	Einars Repse
1995–7	Andris Skele		2004	Indulis Emsis
1997–8	Guntars Krasts		2004–	Aigars Kalvitis
1998–9	Vilis Kristopans			

Crocodile Dundee?

In the small village of Dundaga, north-east of Riga, is a huge statue of a crocodile. It commemorates local man Arvids von Blumenfelds, who emigrated to Australia in the 1940s and lived in the outback. It is said that the film *Crocodile Dundee* (1986) was inspired by his exploits.

LEBANON

Official name	Republic of Lebanon	**Languages**	Arabic, French; English and Armenian are also spoken
Local name	Al-Lubnān; Al-Jumhŭriyya al-Lubnaniyya (Arabic), Liban; République Libanaise (French)		
		Ethnic groups	Arab 95%, Armenian 4%, others 1%
Independence	1943	**Religions**	Islam 69%, Christianity 30%, Druze 1%
Area	10 452 sq km/4 034 sq mi	**Time zone**	GMT +2
		Currency	1 Lebanese Pound (LP, L£/LBP) = 100 piastres
Capital	Beirut; Bayrŭt		
Chief towns	Tripoli, Saida, Zahle	**Telephone**	+961
Population	3 577 000 (2005e)	**Internet**	.lb
Nationality	Lebanese	**Country code**	LBN

Location
A republic on the eastern coast of the Mediterranean Sea, bounded to the north and east by Syria, and to the south by Israel.

Physical description
Narrow Mediterranean coastal plain rises to the Lebanon Mountains, which extend along most of the country; peaks include the Qornet es-Sauda (3 090m/10 137ft); arid eastern slopes fall to the fertile El Beqaa plateau; Anti-Lebanon range lies in the east.

Climate
Mediterranean, varying with altitude, with hot, dry summers and warm, moist winters; average temperatures at Beirut are 13–27°C; much cooler and drier in the Beqaa valley and irrigation is essential.

National holidays
Jan 1, Feb 9 (St Maron), May 1, 6 (Martyrs), 25 (Resistance and Liberation), Aug 15, Nov 1, 22 (Independence), Dec 25; Ad (3), As, EM, GF, ER (3), NY (Muslim), PB.

Political leaders

President

1943–52	Bishara Al-Khoury	1982	Bashir Gemayel
1952–8	Camille Shamoun	1982–8	Amin Gemayel
1958–64	Fouad Shehab	1988–9	*No President*
1964–70	Charle Hilo	1989	Rene Muawad
1970–6	Suleiman Frenjieh	1989–98	Elias Hrawi
1976–82	Elias Sarkis	1998–	Émile Lahoud

Prime Minister

1943	Riad Solh	1964–5	Hussein Oweini
1943–4	Henry Pharaon	1965–6	Rashid Karami
1944–5	Riad Solh	1966	Abdullah Yafi
1945	Abdul Hamid Karame	1966–8	Rashid Karami
1945–6	Sami Solh	1968–9	Abdullah Yafi
1946	Saadi Munla	1969–70	Rashid Karami
1946–51	Riad Solh	1970–3	Saeb Salam
1951	Hussein Oweini	1973	Amin al-Hafez
1951–2	Abdullah Yafi	1973–4	Takieddine Solh
1952	Sami Solh	1974–5	Rashid Solh
1952	Nazem Accari	1975	Noureddin Rifai
1952	Saeb Salam	1975–6	Rashid Karami
1952	Fouad Chehab	1976–80	Selim al-Hoss
1952–3	Khaled Chehab	1980	Takieddine Solh
1953	Saeb Salam	1980–4	Chafiq al-Wazan
1953–5	Abdullah Yafi	1984–8	Rashid Karami
1955	Sami Solh	1988–90	Michel Aoun/Selim al-Hoss
1955–6	Rashid Karami	1990–2	Umar Karami
1956	Abdullah Yafi	1992–8	Rafiq al-Hariri
1956–8	Sami Solh	1998–2000	Selim al-Hoss
1958–60	Rashid Karami	2000–4	Rafiq al-Hariri
1960	Ahmad Daouq	2004–5	Umar Karami
1960–1	Saeb Salam	2005	Najib Mikati
1961–4	Rashid Karami	2005–	Fouad Siniora

LESOTHO

Official name	Kingdom of Lesotho		and Xhosa are also spoken
Local name	Lesotho; Mmuso wa Lesotho	**Ethnic groups**	Sotho 99%, others 1%
Former name	Basutoland (until 1966)	**Religions**	Christianity 94% (RC
Independence	1966		45%, Prot 41%, others
Area	30 460 sq km/11 758 sq mi		8%), traditional beliefs 6%
		Time zone	GMT +2
Capital	Maseru	**Currency**	1 Loti (plural Maloti) (M,
Chief towns	Mafeteng, Quthing		LSM/LSL) = 100 lisente;
Population	1 795 000 (2005e)		the South African Rand is
Nationality	Mosotho (singular), Basotho (plural)		also used
		Telephone	+266
Languages	Sesotho, English; Zulu	**Internet**	.ls
		Country code	LSO

Location
An African kingdom completely bounded by South Africa.

Physical description
Drakensberg Mountains in north-east and east include the highest peak, Thabana Ntlenyana (3 482m/11 424ft); Mulati Mountains running south to west form a steep escarpment; population mainly lives west of the highlands at altitude of 1 500–1 800m/4 920–5 900ft.

Climate
Mild, dry winters; warm summer season is Oct–Apr; lowland summer maximum temperature is 32°C, winter minimum is 7°C.

National holidays
Jan 1, Mar 11 (Moshoeshoe), Apr 4 (Heroes), May 1, Jul 17 (King's Birthday), Oct 4 (Independence), Dec 25, 26; A, EM, GF.

Political leaders

Monarch
1966–70   Moshoeshoe II

Head of State
1970   Leabua Jonathan

Monarch

1970	'MaMohato Lerotholi *Queen Regent*	1990–5	Letsie III
		1995–6	Moshoeshoe II
1970–90	Moshoeshoe II	1996	'MaMohato Lerotholi *Queen Regent*
1990	'MaMohato Lerotholi *Queen Regent*	1996–	Letsie III

Prime Minister
1966–86   Leabua Jonathan

Chairman of Military Council
1986–91   Justin Metsing Lekhanya
1991–3   Elias Tutsoane Ramaema

Prime Minister

1993–4	Ntsu Mokhehle	1994–8	Ntsu Mokhehle
1994	Hae Phoofolo (*interim*)	1998–	Pakalitha Mosisili

LIBERIA

Official name	Republic of Liberia	**Ethnic groups**	Kpelle 19%, Bassa 16%, Grebo 8%, Gio 8%, Kru 6%, Mano 6%, others 37%
Local name	Liberia		
Independence	1847		
Area	113 370 sq km/43 760 sq mi	**Religions**	Christianity 68%, Islam 14%, traditional beliefs 10%, others 8%
Capital	Monrovia		
Chief towns	Harper, Greenville, Buchanan, Robertsport	**Time zone**	GMT
		Currency	1 Liberian Dollar (L$/LRD) = 100 cents
Population	3 283 000 (2005e)		
Nationality	Liberian	**Telephone**	+231
Languages	English; many local languages are also spoken	**Internet**	.lr
		Country code	LBR

Location
A republic in West Africa, bounded to the north-west by Sierra Leone; to the north by Guinea; to the east by Côte d'Ivoire; and to the south by the Atlantic Ocean.

Physical description
Low coastal belt with lagoons, beaches, and mangrove marshes; rolling plateau (500–800m/1 640–2 624ft) with grasslands and forest; land rises inland to mountains; highest point is Mt Wuteve (1 380m/4 528ft); rivers cut south-west down through the plateau.

Climate
Equatorial climate, with high temperatures and abundant rainfall; rainfall declines from south to north; high humidity during the rainy season (Apr–Sep), especially on the coast.

National holidays
Jan 1, Feb 11 (Armed Forces), Mar 15 (J J Roberts), Apr 12 (Redemption), May 14 (National Unification), Jul 26 (Independence), Aug 24 (National Flag), Nov 29 (President Tubman's Birthday), Dec 25; Decoration (Mar), National Fast and Prayer (Apr), Thanksgiving (Nov).

Political leaders

President

1900–4	Garretson Wilmot Gibson	1930–43	Edwin J Barclay
1904–12	Arthur Barclay	1943–71	William V S Tubman
1912–20	Daniel Edward Howard	1971–80	William Richard Tolbert
1920–30	Charles Dunbar Burgess King		

Chairman of People's Redemption Council
1980–6   Samuel K Doe

President
1986–90   Samuel K Doe
1991–4   Amos Sawyer *Interim President*

Chairman of Council of State
1994–5   David Kpormakor
1995–6   Wilton Sankawulo
1996–7   Ruth Perry

President

1997–2003	Charles Taylor
2003	Moses Zeh Blah *Interim President*[1]
2003–	Gyude Bryant

[1] *Charles Taylor went into exile in Aug 2003; Moses Zeh Blah handed power to a transitional government in Oct 2003.*

LIBYA

Official name	Great Socialist People's Libyan Arab Jamahiriya	**Population**	5 853 000 (2005e)
Local name	Lībyā; Al-Jamāhīriyya Al-'Arabiyya Al-Lībyya Ash-Sha'biyya Al-Ishtirākiyya	**Nationality**	Libyan
		Languages	Arabic
		Ethnic groups	Arab and Berber 94%, others 6%
Former name	United Libyan Kingdom (1951–63), Libyan Kingdom (1963–9), Libyan Arab Republic (1969–77)	**Religions**	Islam 97% (Sunni), others 3%
		Time zone	GMT +2
Independence	1951	**Currency**	1 Libyan Dinar (LD/LYD) = 1 000 dirhams
Area	1 758 610 sq km/678 823 sq mi	**Telephone**	+218
		Internet	.ly
Capital	Tripoli; Tarābulus	**Country code**	LBY
Chief towns	Misratah, Benghazi, Tobruk		

Location

A state in North Africa, bounded to the north-west by Tunisia; to the north by the Mediterranean Sea; to the east by Egypt; to the south-east by Sudan; to the south by Chad; to the south-west by Niger; and to the west by Algeria.

Physical description

Mainly low-lying Saharan desert or semi-desert; land rises in the south to over 2 000m/6 561ft in the Tibesti Massif; highest point, Pic Bette (2 286m/7 500ft), lies on the Chad frontier; surface water is limited to infrequent oases.

Climate

Mediterranean climate on the coast; Tripoli, representative of the coastal region, has average maximum daily temperatures of 16–30°C; temperatures in the south are over 40°C for three months of the year.

National holidays

Mar 2 (Declaration of Establishment of Authority of People), 8 (National), 28 (Evacuation of British Troops), Jun 11 (Evacuation of US Troops), Jul 23 (National), Sep 1 (National), Oct 7 (Evacuation of Italian Fascists); Ad (4), ER (3), PB.

Political leaders

Monarch

1951–69	Idris I (Sidi Muhammad Idris Al-Mahdi As-Sanusi)

Chairman of Revolutionary Command Council

1969–77	Muammar Al-Gaddafi

General Secretary of the General People's Congress

1977–9	Muammar Al-Gaddafi	1979–81	Abdul Ati Al-Ubaidi

| 1981–4 | Muhammad Az-Zaruq Rajab | 1990–2 | Abdul Razzaq as-Sawsa |
| 1984–90 | Mifta al-Usta Umar | 1992– | Zintani Muhammad az-Zintani |

Leader of the Revolution
1969–   Muammar Al-Gaddafi

Prime Minister

1951–4	Mahmud al-Muntasir	1965–7	Hussein Mazzek
1954	Muhammad Sakizli	1967	Abdul Qadir al-Badri
1954–7	Mustafa Ben Halim	1967–8	Abdul Hamid al-Bakkoush
1957–60	Abdul Majid Kubar	1968–9	Wanis al-Qaddafi
1960–3	Muhammad Osman Said	1969–70	Mahmud Sulayman al-Maghribi
1963–4	Mohieddin Fikini	1972–7	Abdul Salam Jalloud
1964–5	Mahmud al-Muntasir		

General Secretary of the General People's Committee

1977–9	Abdul Ati al-Ubaidi	1994–7	Abdul Majid al-Qaud
1979–84	Jadallah Azzuz at-Talhi	1997–2000	Muhammad Ahmad al-Mangoush
1984–6	Muhammad az-Zaruq Rajab	2000–3	Mubarak Abdallah al-Shamikh
1986–7	Jadallah Azzuz at-Talhi	2003–	Shukri Muhammad Ghanim
1987–90	Umar Mustafa al-Muntasir		
1990–4	Abu Zayd Umar Durda		

LIECHTENSTEIN

Official name	Principality of Liechtenstein		form of an Alemannic dialect
Local name	Liechtenstein; Fürstentum Liechtenstein	**Ethnic groups**	Liechtensteiner 62%, Swiss 17%, Austrian 8%, German 5%, others 8%
Independence	1719 (part of Holy Roman Empire to 1806)	**Religions**	Christianity 88% (RC 80%, Prot 8%), others 12%
Area	160 sq km/62 sq mi	**Time zone**	GMT +1
Capital	Vaduz	**Currency**	1 Swiss Franc (SFr, SwF/CHF) = 100 centimes = 100 rappen
Chief towns	Schaan, Triesen, Balzers		
Population	35 000 (2005e)		
Nationality	Liechtensteiner, Liechtenstein	**Telephone**	+423
Languages	German, spoken in the	**Internet**	.li
		Country code	LIE

Location
An independent principality in central Europe, bounded by Austria to the east and Switzerland to the west.

Physical description
Bounded to the west by the River Rhine, its valley occupying c.40% of the country; much of the rest consists of forested mountains, rising to 2 599m/8 527ft in the Grauspitz.

Climate
Mild, influenced by a warm south wind (the *Föhn*); average maximum temperature of 20–28°C in summer.

National holidays
Jan 1, 2 (Berchtold), 6, Feb 2 (Candlemas), Mar 19 (St Joseph), May 1, Aug 15, Sep 8 (Nativity of Our Lady), Nov 1, Dec 8, 24, 25, 26, 31; A, C, CC, EM, ES, GF, WM, Whit Sunday.

Political leaders

Prince

1858–1929	Johann II	1938–89	Franz Josef II
1929–38	Franz von Paula	1989–	Hans Adam II

Prime Minister

1928–45	Franz Josef Hoop	1978–93	Hans Brunhart
1945–62	Alexander Friek	1993	Markus Büchel
1962–70	Gérard Batliner	1993–2001	Mario Frick
1970–4	Alfred J Hilbe	2001–	Otmar Hasler
1974–8	Walter Kieber		

LITHUANIA

Official name	Republic of Lithuania	**Nationality**	Lithuanian
Local name	Lietuva; Lietuvos Respublika	**Languages**	Lithuanian
		Ethnic groups	Lithuanian 81%, Russian 9%, Polish 7%, others 3%
Former name	Lithuanian Soviet Socialist Republic (1940–90), within the Union of Soviet Socialist Republics (USSR; 1940–91)	**Religions**	Christianity (predominantly RC, with Lutheran Prot, Baptist and Orthodox minorities); also Judaism and Islam
Independence	1990 (declared), 1991 (recognized)	**Time zone**	GMT +2
Area	65 200 sq km/25 167 sq mi	**Currency**	1 Litas (Lt/LTL) = 100 centas
Capital	Vilnius	**Telephone**	+370
Chief towns	Kaunas, Klaipėda, Šiauliai	**Internet**	.lt
Population	3 431 000 (2005e)	**Country code**	LTU

Location
A republic in north-eastern Europe, bounded to the north by Latvia; to the east by Belarus; to the south by Poland; to the south-west by Russia; and to the west by the Baltic Sea.

Physical description
Glaciated plains cover much of the area; highest point is Juozapine Hill (294m/965ft).

Climate
Varies between maritime and continental; wet, with moderate winters and summers.

National holidays
Jan 1, Feb 16 (Independence), Mar 11 (Restoration of Statehood), Jul 6 (Coronation of Mindaugas/Statehood), Aug 15, Nov 1, Dec 25, 26; ES; Mother's Day (1st Sun in May).

Political leaders

President

1990–3	Vytautas Landsbergis	2004	Arturas Paulauskas
1993–8	Algirdas Brazauskas		*Acting President*
1998–2003	Valdas Adamkus	2004–	Valdas Adamkus
2003–4	Rolandas Paksas		

Prime Minister

1990–1	Kazimiera Prunskienë	1999	Rolandas Paksas
1991	Albertas Simenas	1999	Irena Degutienë *Acting Prime Minister*
1991–2	Gediminas Vagnorius		
1992	Aleksandras Abisala	1999–2000	Andrius Kubilius
1992–3	Bronislovas Lubys	2000–1	Rolandas Paksas
1993–6	Adolfas Slezevicius	2001	Eugenijus Gentvilas *Acting Prime Minister*
1996	Laurynas Stankevicius		
1996–9	Gediminas Vagnorius	2001–	Algirdas Brazauskas
1999	Irena Degutienë *Acting Prime Minister*		

Amber Gold

Amber was known as 'Lithuania's gold' and was collected and traded for centuries.

LUXEMBOURG

Official name	Grand Duchy of Luxembourg	**Population**	465 000 (2005e)
Local name	Luxembourg; Grand-Duché de Luxembourg (French), Luxemburg; Grossherzogtum Luxemburg (German), Lëtzebuerg; Groussherzogtom Lëtzebuerg (Lëtzebuergesch)	**Nationality**	Luxembourger, Luxembourg
		Languages	French, German, Lëtzebuergesch
		Ethnic groups	Luxembourger 72%, Portuguese 9%, Italian 5%, French 3%, Belgian 2%, German 2%, others 7%
Independence	1867	**Religions**	Christianity 99% (RC 97%, Prot 2%), Judaism 1%
Area	2 586 sq km/998 sq mi		
Capital	Luxembourg; Luxembourg (French), Luxemburg (German), Lëtzebuerg (Lëtzebuergesch)	**Time zone**	GMT +1
		Currency	1 Euro (€/EUR) = 100 cents
		Telephone	+352
		Internet	.lu
Chief towns	Esch-sur-Alzette, Dudelange, Differdange	**Country code**	LUX

Location
An independent constitutional monarchy in north-western Europe, bounded to the north-east and east by Germany; to the south by France; and to the north-west and west by Belgium.

Physical description
Divided into two natural regions: Ösling in the north (wooded, hilly land) and flatter, more fertile Gutland; highest point is Buurgplaatz (559m/1 833ft); water resources developed by canalization of the River Mosel, hydroelectric dams on the River Our and reservoirs on the River Sûre.

Climate
Drier and sunnier in the south, but winters can be severe; summers and autumns are warm enough for cultivation of vines in the sheltered Mosel Valley.

National holidays
Jan 1, May 1, Jun 23 (National), Aug 15, Nov 1, 2, Dec 25, 26, 31; A, EM, WM, Shrove Monday.

Political leaders

Grand Dukes and Duchesses

1890–1905	Adolf of Nassau	1919–64	Charlotte (*in exile* 1940–4)
1905–12	William IV	1964–2000	Jean
1912–19	Marie Adelaide	2000–	Henri

Prime Minister

1889–1915	Paul Eyschen	1937–53	Pierre Dupong (*in exile* 1940–4)
1915	Mathias Mongenast	1953–8	Joseph Bech
1915–16	Hubert Loutsch	1958–9	Pierre Frieden
1916–17	Victor Thorn	1959–69	Pierre Werner
1917–18	Léon Kaufmann	1969–79	Gaston Thorn
1918–25	Emil Reuter	1979–84	Pierre Werner
1925–6	Pierre Prum	1984–95	Jacques Santer
1926–37	Joseph Bech	1995–	Jean-Claude Juncker

Grand Cuisine

Luxembourg has more Michelin-starred restaurants per square mile than any other country in the world.

MACAO *see* **CHINA**

MACEDONIA

Official name	Former Yugoslav Republic of Macedonia (FYRM or FYR Macedonia; *international name*); Republic of Macedonia (*local name*)	**Capital**	Skopje
		Chief towns	Bitola, Gostivar, Tetovo, Kumanovo
		Population	2 034 000 (2005e)
		Nationality	Macedonian
Local name	Makedonija; Republika Makedonija, Poranesna Jugoslovenska Republika Makedonija	**Languages**	Macedonian, Albanian
		Ethnic groups	Macedonian 66%, Albanian 23%, Turkish 4%, others 7%
Former name	formerly part of Kingdom of Serbs, Croats and Slovenes (until 1929), Kingdom of Yugoslavia (1929–41), Federal People's Republic of Yugoslavia (1945–63), Socialist Federal People's Republic of Yugoslavia (1963–91)	**Religions**	Christianity 67% (Orthodox), Islam 30%, others 3%
		Time zone	GMT +1
		Currency	1 Denar (D, den/MKD) = 100 deni
		Telephone	+389
		Internet	.mk
Independence	1991	**Country code**	MKD
Area	25 713 sq km/9 925 sq mi		

Location
A republic in southern Europe, bounded to the north by Serbia and Montenegro; to the east by Bulgaria; to the south by Greece; and to the west by Albania.

Physical description
Mountainous, covered with deep basins and valleys; bisected by the River Vardar; highest point is Golem Korab (Maja e Korabit; 2 753m/9 032ft) on the Albanian border.

Climate
Cold winters and warm, dry summers.

National holidays
Jan 1, 6 (Orthodox Christmas) (2), Mar 8 (Women), May 1, 24 (SS Cyril and Methodius), Aug 2 (St Elijah's Uprising), Sep 8 (Independence), Dec 25, 26; Ad, EM, ER, Old NY.

See **Serbia and Montenegro** for political leaders of the former Yugoslavia.

Political leaders

President

1991–5	Kiro Gligorov	2004	Ljupco Jordanovski *Interim President*
1995–8	Stojan Andov *Acting President*		
1998–9	Kiro Gligorov	2004–	Branko Crvenkovski
1999–2004	Boris Trajkovski		

Prime Minister

1991–2	Branko Crvenkovski	2002–4	Branko Crvenkovski
1992–6	Petar Gosev	2004	Hari Kostov
1996–8	Branko Crvenkovski	2004–	Vlado Buckovski
1998–2002	Ljubco Georgievski		

MADAGASCAR

Official name	Republic of Madagascar	**Population**	18 606 000 (2005e)
Local name	Madagasikara; Repoblikan'i Madagasikara (Malagasy), Madagascar; République du Madagascar (French)	**Nationality**	Malagasy
		Languages	Malagasy, French
		Ethnic groups	Merina 26%, Betsimisaraka 16%, Betsileo 12%, Tsimihety 7%, Sakalava 7%, others 32%
Former name	Malagasy Republic (1958–75), Democratic Republic of Madagascar (until 1992)	**Religions**	traditional beliefs 52%, Christianity 42% (RC 24%, Prot 18%), Islam 6%
Independence	1960		
Area	592 800 sq km/228 821 sq mi	**Time zone**	GMT +3
		Currency	1 Ariary (A/MGA) = 5 Iraimbilanja
Capital	Antananarivo		
Chief towns	Toamasina, Mahajanga, Fianarantsoa, Antsiranana, Toliara	**Telephone**	+261
		Internet	.mg
		Country code	MDG

Location
An island republic in the Indian Ocean, separated from Mozambique by the Mozambique Channel.

Physical description
Ridge of mountains runs north to south, rising to 2 876m/9 436ft at Maromokotra; cliffs to the east drop down to a coastal plain through tropical forest; a terraced descent to the west through savanna to the coast, which is heavily indented in the north.

Climate
Temperate climate in the highlands; tropical coastal region.

National holidays
Jan 1, Mar 29 (Memorial), May 1, Jun 26 (Independence), Aug 15, Nov 1, Dec 25, 30 (National); A, EM, GF, WM.

Political leaders

President

1960–72	Philibert Tsiranana		1975–93	Didier Ratsiraka
1972–5	Gabriel Ramanantsoa		1993–7	Albert Zafy
1975	Richard Ratsimandrava		1997–2002	Didier Ratsiraka
1975	Gilles Andriamahazo		2002–	Marc Ravalomanana

Prime Minister

1960–75	*As President*		1995–6	Emmanuel Rakotovahiny
1975–6	Joël Rakotomala		1996–7	Norbert Ratsirahonana
1976–7	Justin Rakotoriaina		1997–8	Paskal Rakotmavo
1977–88	Désiré Rakotoarijaona		1998–2002	Tantely Andrianarivo
1988–91	Victor Ramahatra		2002–	Jacques Sylla
1991–3	Guy Willy Razanamasy			
1993–5	Francisque Ravony			

MADEIRA *see* **PORTUGAL**

MALAWI

Official name	Republic of Malawi	**Languages**	English, Chichewa
Local name	Dziko la Malawi	**Ethnic groups**	Maravi 59%, Lomwe 20%, Yao 13%, Ngoni 6%, others 2%
Former name	Nyasaland (until 1964), part of the Federation of Rhodesia and Nyasaland (1953–63)	**Religions**	Christianity 70% (Prot 50%, RC 20%), Islam 21%, traditional beliefs 9%
Independence	1964		
Area	118 484 sq km/45 735 sq mi	**Time zone**	GMT +2
Capital	Lilongwe	**Currency**	1 Kwacha (MK/MWK) = 100 tambala
Chief towns	Blantyre, Zomba, Limbe, Salima	**Telephone**	+265
Population	12 884 000 (2005e)	**Internet**	.mw
Nationality	Malawian	**Country code**	MWI

Location
A republic in south-eastern Africa, bounded to the north by Tanzania; to the east by Lake Nyasa (Lake Malawi); to the south-west and south-east by Mozambique; and to the west by Zambia.

Physical description
Crossed north to south by the Great Rift Valley in which lies Africa's third-largest lake, Lake Nyasa (Lake Malawi); high plateaux on either side (900–1 200m/2 950–3 937ft); highlands in the south rise to 3 000m/9 840ft at Sapitwa Peak on Mt Mulanje.

Climate
Tropical climate in the south, with high year-round temperatures, 28–37°C; more moderate temperatures in centre; higher rainfall in the mountains overlooking Lake Nyasa.

National holidays
Jan 1, 15 (Chilembwe), Mar 3 (Martyrs), May 1, Jun 14 (Freedom), Jul 6 (Independence), Dec 25, 26; EM, ER, GF, Mothers (2nd Mon in Oct).

Political leaders

President

1966–94	Hastings Kamuzu Banda
1994–2004	Bakili Muluzi
2004–	Bingu wa Mutharika

Get By in Chichewa

The Chichewa word for *hello* is *moni*, and *how are you?* is *muli bwanji?* Other useful words include *madzi* for *water*, *chakudya* for *food* and *chimbudzi* for *toilet*. If you hear a shout of *mkango*, it is either time to grab your camera or run for your life – it means *lion*.

MALAYSIA

Official name	Federation of Malaysia		and local languages are also spoken
Local name	Malaysia		
Independence	1957	**Ethnic groups**	Malay and indigenous 58%, Chinese 26%, Indian 7%, others 9%
Area	329 749 sq km/127 283 sq mi		
Capital	Kuala Lumpur (official) and Putrajaya (administrative and seat of government)	**Religions**	Islam 53%, Buddhism 17%, Chinese folk religion 12%, Hinduism 7%, Christianity 6%, others 5%
Chief towns	George Town, Ipoh, Malacca, Johor Baharu, Kuching, Kota Kinabalu	**Time zone**	GMT +8
		Currency	1 Malaysian Ringgit (M$/MYR) = 100 cents
Population	25 347 000 (2005e)		
Nationality	Malaysian	**Telephone**	+60
Languages	Bahasa Malaysia (Malay); Chinese, English, Tamil	**Internet**	.my
		Country code	MYS

Location

An independent federation of states in south-east Asia, including mainland peninsular Malaysia, bounded to the north by Thailand and linked by a causeway to Singapore in the south; also includes the northern part of the island of Borneo, bounded to the south by Indonesia and completely surrounding Brunei Darussalam.

Physical description

Mainland peninsula (700km/435mi long) of mountains with narrow coastal plains; mostly tropical rainforest and mangrove swamp; Sarawak has a narrow, swampy coastal belt and mountainous interior; Sabah has a deeply indented coastline and narrow coastal plain, rising sharply into mountains reaching 4 094m/13 431ft at Mt Kinabalu, Malaysia's highest peak.

Climate

Tropical climate, with highest temperatures in coastal areas; strongly influenced by monsoon winds; high humidity.

National holidays

Jan 1 (*most states*), May 1, Jun 7 (Head of State's Birthday), Aug 31 (National), Dec 25; Ad (2), D (*most states*), ER (2), NY (Chinese) (Jan/Feb), NY (Muslim), PB, Wesak; *several local festivals*.

Political leaders

Chief of State (Yang di-Pertuan Agong)

1957–63	Abdul Rahman	1989–94	Azlan Muhibuddin Shah
1963–5	Syed Putra Jamalullah	1994–9	Jaafar Ibni Abdul Rahman
1965–70	Ismail Nasiruddin Shah	1999–2001	Salehuddin Abdul Aziz Shah
1970–5	Abdul Halim Muadzam Shah	2001	Mizal Zainal Abidin *Acting Chief of State*
1975–9	Yahya Petra Ibrahim		
1979–84	Haji Ahmad Shah Al-Mustain Billah	2001–	Syed Sirajuddin Syed Putra Jamalullail
1984–9	Mahmood Iskandar Shah		

Prime Minister

1957–70	Abdul Rahman Putra Al-Haj	1997	Anwar Ibrahim *Acting Prime Minister*
1970–6	Abdul Razak bin Hussein		
1976–9	Haji Hussein bin Onn	1997–2003	Mahathir bin Mohamad
1979–97	Mahathir bin Mohamad	2003–	Abdullah Ahmad Badawi

Malaysian Mud

The name of Malaysia's capital city, *Kuala Lumpur*, comes from Malay words meaning 'muddy estuary'.

MALDIVES

Official name	Republic of Maldives	**Ethnic groups**	Sinhalese majority; Arab and African minorities
Local name	Dhivehi Raajje; Dhivehi Rājjē Jumhūriyyā	**Religions**	Islam 100% (Sunni)
Former name	Maldive Islands	**Time zone**	GMT +5
Independence	1965	**Currency**	1 Rufiyaa (MRf, Rf/MVR) = 100 laarees
Area	300 sq km/120 sq mi		
Capital	Malé; Daviyani	**Telephone**	+960
Population	329 000 (2005e)	**Internet**	.mv
Nationality	Maldivian	**Country code**	MDV
Languages	Dhivehi; English is spoken widely		

Location
An archipelago republic in the Indian Ocean.

Physical description
Small, low-lying islands, no more than 1.8m/6ft above sea level, with sandy beaches fringed with coconut palms. Of the 1 190 islands, spread over 26 coral atolls, fewer than 200 are inhabited; Fua Mulaku Island is the largest island, while Huvadhoo Atoll is the largest atoll.

Climate
Generally warm and humid; affected by south-west monsoons from Apr to Oct; average daily temperature is 22°C.

National holidays
Jan 1, May 3 (National), Jul 26 (Independence) (2), Nov 3 (Victory), 11 (Republic); Ad (4), Ar, ER (3), NY (Muslim), PB, R, Day the Maldives Embraced Islam.

Political leaders

Monarch (Sultan)
1954–68   Mohammed Farid Didi

President
1968–78   Ibrahim Nasir
1978–   Maumoon Abdul Gayoom

Maldives in the Dictionary

The Maldives have contributed just one word to the English language: *atoll*, meaning a coral island with a circular belt of coral enclosing a central lagoon. The language of the Maldives, Dhivehi, is unusual in that it has no word for *hello* or *goodbye*. *Kihineh* is used instead of *hello*, meaning *how are you?*, while *dhanee!* or *I'm going!* is often used instead of *goodbye*.

MALI

Official name	Republic of Mali		are spoken widely
Local name	Mali; République du Mali	Ethnic groups	Bambara 34%, Fulani 17%, Senufo 12%, Soninke 8%, Songhai 7%, Tuareg 7%, Malinke 6%, others 9%
Former name	French Sudan (until 1959), Mali Federation (until 1960)		
Independence	1960	Religions	Islam 85% (mostly Sunni), traditional beliefs 14%, Christianity 1%
Area	1 240 192 sq km/478 714 sq mi		
Capital	Bamako	Time zone	GMT
Chief towns	Ségou, Mopti, Sikasso, Kayes, Gao, Timbuktu	Currency	1 CFA Franc (CFAFr/XOF) = 100 centimes
Population	13 518 000 (2005e)	Telephone	+223
Nationality	Malian	Internet	.ml
Languages	French; Bambara and other local languages	Country code	MLI

Location
A republic in West Africa, bounded to the north-west by Mauritania; to the north-east by Algeria; to the east by Niger; to the south-east by Burkina Faso; to the south by Côte d'Ivoire; to the south-west by Guinea; and to the west by Senegal.

Physical description
On the fringe of the Sahara; lower part of the Hoggar massif is located in the north; arid plains between 300m/984ft and 500m/1 640ft; featureless desert land in the north with sand dunes; highest point is Hombori Tondo (1 155m/3 789ft); mainly savanna in the south.

Climate
Hot, dry climate with rainfall increasing from north to south; in the south the rainfall season lasts for five months (Jun–Oct); almost no annual average rainfall in the Saharan north.

National holidays
Jan 1, 20 (Memorial), Mar 26 (Martyrs), May 1, 25 (African Unity), Sep 22 (National), Dec 25; Ad, ER, PB, R.

Political leaders

President
1960–8	Modibo Keita	1992–2002	Alpha Oumar Konaré
1968–91	Moussa Traoré[1]	2002–	Amadou Toumani Touré
1991–2	Amadou Toumani Touré[2]		

Prime Minister
1986–88	Mamadou Dembelé	1994–2000	Ibrahim Boubacar Keita
1988–91	*No Prime Minister*	2000–2	Mande Sidibe
1991–2	Soumana Sacko	2002–4	Ahmed Mohamed ag Hamani
1992–3	Younoussi Touré	2004–	Ousmane Issoufi Maiga
1993–4	Abdoulaye Sekou Sow		

[1] *Chairman of Military Committee for the National Liberation until 1969; Head of State until 1979; President from 1979.*
[2] *Chairman of Military Committee for the Salvation of the People.*

MALTA

Official name	Republic of Malta		are many Arabic words in the local vocabulary
Local name	Malta; Repubblika ta' Malta	**Ethnic groups**	Maltese 98%, British 2%
Independence	1964	**Religions**	Christianity 98% (RC 97%, Prot 1%), others 1%, none/unaffiliated 1%
Area	316 sq km/122 sq mi		
Capital	Valletta	**Time zone**	GMT +1
Chief towns	Sliema, Birkirkara, Qormi, Rabat, Victoria	**Currency**	1 Maltese Lira (LM/MTL) = 100 cents = 1 000 mils
Population	402 000 (2005e)	**Telephone**	+356
Nationality	Maltese	**Internet**	.mt
Languages	English, Maltese; there	**Country code**	MLT

Location
An archipelago republic in the central Mediterranean Sea.

Physical description
Generally low-lying, rising to 253m/830ft; no rivers or mountains; well-indented coastline.

Climate
Dry summers and mild winters; average daily winter temperature is 13°C.

National holidays
Jan 1, Feb 10 (St Paul's Shipwreck), Mar 19 (St Joseph), 31 (Freedom), May 1, Jun 7 (Sette Giugno), 29 (SS Peter and Paul), Aug 15, Sep 8 (Our Lady of the Victories), 21 (Independence), Dec 8, 13 (Republic), 25; GF.

Political leaders

President

1974–6	Anthony Mamo	1989–94	Vincent Tabone
1976–81	Anton Buttigieg	1994–9	Ugo Mifsud Bonnici
1981–2	Albert Hyzler *Acting President*	1999–2004	Guido de Marco
1982–7	Agatha Barbara	2004–	Edward Fenech-Adami
1987–9	Paul Xuereb *Acting President*		

Prime Minister

1962–71	G Borg Olivier	1996–8	Alfred Sant
1971–84	Dom Mintoff	1998–2004	Edward Fenech-Adami
1984–7	Carmelo Mifsud Bonnici	2004–	Lawrence Gonzi
1987–96	Edward Fenech-Adami		

Maltese Medal

In 1942 Malta was awarded the George Cross for its resistance to heavy air attacks in World War II.

MALVINAS *see* **FALKLAND ISLANDS** *under* **UNITED KINGDOM**

MAN, ISLE OF *see* **UNITED KINGDOM**

MARIANA ISLANDS, NORTHERN *see* **UNITED STATES OF AMERICA**

MARSHALL ISLANDS

Official name	Republic of the Marshall Islands (RMI)	**Languages**	Marshallese, English
Local name	Marshall Islands, Majol	**Ethnic groups**	Micronesian 97%, others 3%
Former name	formerly part of the Trust Territory of the Pacific Islands (1947–79)	**Religions**	Christianity 97% (Prot 90%, RC 7%), others 3%
Independence	1986	**Time zone**	GMT +12
Area	c.180 sq km/70 sq mi	**Currency**	1 US Dollar ($, US$/USD) = 100 cents
Capital	Majuro	**Telephone**	+692
Population	62 000 (2005e)	**Internet**	.mh
Nationality	Marshallese	**Country code**	MHL

Location
An archipelago republic in the central Pacific Ocean.

Physical description
Coral limestone and sand islands, atolls and reefs, with few natural resources; low-lying, rising to no more than 10m/33ft.

Climate
Hot and humid; wet season is from May to Nov; occasional typhoons.

National holidays
Jan 1, Mar 1 (Nuclear Victims), May 1 (Constitution), Nov 17 (President), Dec 25; Fishermen (1st Fri in Jul), Workers (1st Fri in Sep), Customs (last Fri in Sep), Thanksgiving (3rd Thur in Nov), Gospel (1st Fri in Dec).

Political leaders

President

1979–96	Amata Kabua	1997–2000	Imata Kabua
1996–7	Kunio Lemari *Acting President*	2000–	Kessai Note

The Real Bikini

The bikini swimsuit was named after Bikini Atoll in the Marshall Islands. The atoll was the scene of atom-bomb experiments in the late 1940s, and the bikini's effects on men were reputed to be similar. The real Bikini Atoll covers 6 sq km/2.3 sq mi of land and 594 sq km/229 sq mi of lagoon, and has 36 islets. The atoll's name is slightly different in Marshallese – had the word come into English in its original form, people might now be wearing a *pikinni* instead.

MARTINIQUE *see* **FRANCE**

MAURITANIA

Official name	Islamic Republic of Mauritania	**Languages**	Arabic; French is also widely spoken
Local name	Mauritanie; République Islamique de Mauritanie (French), Mūrītāniyā; Al-Jumhūriyya al-Islāmiyya al-Mawrītāniyya (Arabic)	**Ethnic groups**	Arab and Berber 72%, Wolof 6%, Tukulor 5%, Soninke 3%, Fulani 1%, others 13%
		Religions	Islam 99%, others 1%
Independence	1960	**Time zone**	GMT
Area	1 029 920 sq km/397 549 sq mi	**Currency**	1 Ouguiya (U, UM/MRO) = 5 khoums
Capital	Nouakchott	**Telephone**	+222
Chief towns	Nouadhibou, Atar	**Internet**	.mr
Population	3 069 000 (2005e)	**Country code**	MRT
Nationality	Maurltanlan		

Location
A republic in north-west Africa, bounded to the north by Western Sahara; to the north-east by Algeria; to the south and east by Mali; to the south-west by Senegal; and to the west by the Atlantic Ocean.

Physical description
Saharan zone covers two-thirds of the country with sand dunes, mountainous plateaux and occasional oases; coastal area has minimal rainfall and little vegetation; Senegal River is the chief agricultural region; highest point is Kediet Idjill (915m/3 002ft).

Climate
Dry and tropical with sparse rainfall; temperatures can rise to over 49°C in the Sahara.

National holidays
Jan 1, May 1, 25 (Celebration of the African Union), Nov 28 (National); Ad, ER, NY (Muslim), PB.

Political leaders

President

1961–78	Mokhtar Ould Daddah	1980–4	Mohammed Khouna Ould Haydallah
1978–9	Mustapha Ould Mohammed Salek		
1979–80	Mohammed Mahmoud Ould Ahmed Louly	1984–2005	Maaouya Ould Sid'Ahmed Taya

Chairman of the Military Council for Justice and Democracy
2005–   Ely Ould Mohammed Vall

Prime Minister

1992–6	Sidi Mohammed Ould Boubaker
1996–7	Cheikh el Avia Ould Mohammed Khouna
1997–8	Mohammed Lemine Ould Guig
1998–2003	Cheikh el Avia Ould Mohammed Khouna
2003–5	Sghaïr Ould M'Bareck
2005–	Sidi Mohammed Ould Boubaker

Place of Winds

When Mauritania became independent in 1960 it lacked a capital, so a new city was built on the coast. It was named Nouakchott, supposedly meaning 'place of winds'.

MAURITIUS

Official name	Republic of Mauritius		Creole 27%, others 5%
Local name	Mauritius	**Religions**	Hinduism 52%,
Independence	1968		Christianity 28% (RC
Area	1 865 sq km/720 sq mi		26%, Prot 2%), Islam
			17%, others 3%
Capital	Port Louis	**Time zone**	GMT +4
Population	1 245 000 (2005e)	**Currency**	1 Mauritius Rupee (MR,
Nationality	Mauritian		MauRe/MUR) = 100 cents
Languages	English; French is also	**Telephone**	+230
	spoken	**Internet**	.mu
Ethnic groups	Indo-Mauritian 68%,	**Country code**	MUS

Location
An island republic in the Indian Ocean, east of Madagascar.

Physical description
Volcanic, with a central plateau; highest peak is Piton de la Petite Rivière Noire (828m/2 717ft); dry, lowland coast, with wooded savanna, mangrove swamp and bamboo; surrounded by coral reefs enclosing lagoons and sandy beaches.

Climate
Tropical-maritime, with temperatures averaging 22–26°C; wide variation in rainfall with most rain falling in the central plateau.

National holidays
Jan 1, 2, Feb 1 (Abolition of Slavery), Mar 12 (National), May 1, Nov 1, 2 (Arrival of Indentured Labourers), Dec 25; D, Chinese Spring Festival (Jan/Feb), ER, Ganesh Chathurti (Aug/Sep), Maha Shivaratree (Feb/Mar), Ougadi (Mar/Apr), Thaipoosam Cavadee (Jan/Feb).

Political leaders

Head of State until 1992: British monarch, represented by Governor General.

President

1992	Veerasamy Ringadoo	2002–3	Karl Offmann
1992–2002	Cassam Uteem	2003	Raouf Bundhun *Acting President*
2002	Angidi Chettiar *Acting President*	2003–	Anerood Jugnauth
2002	Arianga Pillay *Acting President*		

Prime Minister

1968–82	Seewoosagur Ramgoolam	2000–3	Anerood Jugnauth
1982–95	Anerood Jugnauth	2003–5	Paul Berengér
1995–2000	Navin Ramgoolam	2005–	Navin Ramgoolam

Dead as a Dodo

Perhaps the most famous native of Mauritius was the dodo, a clumsy flightless bird about the size of a turkey. The dodo amused early explorers, but when permanent settlements were set up its demise was swift; hunting and newly-introduced animal predators meant it became extinct about the end of the 17c. *Dodo* comes from the Portuguese word *doudo*, meaning silly.

MAYOTTE *see* **FRANCE**

MEXICO

Official name	United Mexican States	**Ethnic groups**	mestizo 60%, Amerindian 25%, European 12%, others 3%
Local name	México; Estados Unidos Méxicanos		
Independence	1821	**Religions**	Christianity 96% (RC 93%, Prot 3%), others 3%, none/unaffiliated 1%
Area	1 978 800 sq km/763 817 sq mi		
Capital	Mexico City; Ciudad de México	**Time zone**	GMT –6/8
		Currency	1 Mexican Peso (Mex$/MXN) = 100 centavos
Chief towns	Guadalajara, Léon, Monterrey, Ciudad Juárez		
Population	107 029 000 (2005e)	**Telephone**	+52
Nationality	Mexican	**Internet**	.mx
Languages	Spanish; Native American languages are also spoken	**Country code**	MEX

Location
A federal republic in southern North America, bounded to the north by the United States of America; to the east by the Gulf of Mexico; to the south by Guatemala and Belize; to the west and south-west by the Pacific Ocean; and to the west by the Gulf of California.

Physical description
Narrow coastal plains rise steeply to a central plateau, reaching a height of c.2 400m/7 874ft around Mexico City; volcanic peaks to the south, notably Citlaltépetl (also called Volcan Pico de Orizaba; 5 699m/18 697ft); Yucatán peninsula lowlands in south-east; subject to very severe earthquakes.

Climate
Great climatic variation between the coastlands and mountains; desert or semi-desert conditions in the north-west; typically tropical climate on the east coast; generally wetter on the south coast; extreme temperature variations in the north.

National holidays
Jan 1, Feb 5 (Constitution), Mar 21 (Birthday of Benito Juárez), May 1, 5 (Puebla Battle), Sep 1 (Presidential Report), 16 (Independence), Oct 12 (Columbus), Nov 2, 20 (Mexican Revolution), Dec 12 (Our Lady of Guadaloupe), 25, 31; HT, GF.

Political leaders

President

1876–1911	Porfirio Diaz	1915–20	Venustiano Carranza
1911	Francisco León de la Barra	1920	Adolfo de la Huerta
1911–13	Francisco I Madero	1920–4	Alvaro Obregón
1913–14	Victoriano Huerta	1924–8	Plutarco Elías Calles
1914	Francisco Carvajal	1928–30	Emilio Portes Gil
1914	Venustiano Carranza	1930–2	Pascual Ortíz Rubio
1914–15	Eulalio Gutiérrez *Provisional President*	1932–4	Abelardo L Rodríguez
		1934–40	Lazaro Cardenas
1915	Roque González Garza *Provisional President*	1940–6	Manuel Avila Camacho
		1946–52	Miguel Alemán
1915	Francisco Lagos Chazaro *Provisional President*	1952–8	Adolfo Ruiz Cortines
		1958–64	Adolfo López Mateos

1964–70	Gustavo Díaz Ordaz	1988–94	Carlos Salinas de Gortari
1970–6	Luis Echeverría	1994–2000	Ernesto Zedillo Ponce de León
1976–82	José López Portillo	2000–	Vincente Fox Quesada
1982–8	Miguel de la Madrid Hurtado		

Aztec Capital

Mexico City is the oldest capital in continental America, and is built on the site of the Aztec capital, Tenochtitlán.

MICRONESIA

Official name	Federated States of Micronesia (FSM)		Pohnpeian, Yapese
Local name	Micronesia	**Languages**	English; eight major indigenous languages are also spoken
Former name	formerly part of the Trust Territory of the Pacific Islands (1947–79)	**Ethnic groups**	Chuukese 42%, Pohnpeian 27%, others 31%
Independence	1991	**Religions**	Christianity 97% (RC 50%, Prot 47%), others 3%
Area	700 sq km/270 sq mi		
Capital	Palikir (on Pohnpei)	**Time zone**	GMT +10/11
Chief towns	Kolonia, Colonia, Weno, Lelu	**Currency**	1 US Dollar (US$/USD) = 100 cents
Population	110 000 (2005e)	**Telephone**	+691
Nationality	Micronesian; also Chuukese, Kosraen,	**Internet**	.fm
		Country code	FSM

Location
An archipelago republic of 607 islands divided into four states – Yap, Chuuk (formerly Truk), Pohnpei (formerly Ponape) and Kosrae (formerly Kosaie) – in the western Pacific Ocean.

Physical description
Islands vary geologically, from low, coral atolls to high mountainous islands; Pohnpei, Kosrae and Chuuk have volcanic outcroppings; highest point is Totolom (791m/2 595ft).

Climate
Tropical; heavy rainfall all year round, especially in the eastern islands; subject to typhoons.

National holidays
Jan 1, May 10 (Proclamation of the Federated States of Micronesia), Oct 24 (United Nations Day), Nov 4 (National Day), Dec 25; *additional days vary between states*.

Political leaders

President

1979–87	Tosiwo Nakayama	1997–9	Jacob Nena
1987–91	John Haglelgam	1999–2003	Leo Falcam
1991–7	Bailey Olter	2003–	Joseph Urusemal

Stone Money

The islanders of Yap still use traditional stone money as legal tender as well as the US dollar. The 'coins' are huge, doughnut-shaped stone discs, some taller than a person.

MOLDOVA

Official name	Republic of Moldova	**Nationality**	Moldovan
Local name	Moldova; Republica Moldova	**Languages**	Moldovan
Former name	formerly part of Romania (1918–40), Moldavia or Moldavian Soviet Socialist Republic (until 1991), within the Union of Soviet Socialist Republics (USSR; 1922–91)	**Ethnic groups**	Moldovan 65%, Ukrainian 14%, Russian 13%, Gagauzi 4%, Jewish 2%, others 2%
		Religions	Christianity 98% (Orthodox), Judaism 2%
		Time zone	GMT +2
Independence	1991	**Currency**	1 Moldovan Leu (Mld/MDL) = 100 bani
Area	33 700 sq km/13 000 sq mi	**Telephone**	+373
Capital	Chisinau, Chisinau	**Internet**	.md
Chief towns	Tiraspol, Bendery, Beltsy	**Country code**	MDA
Population	4 206 000 (2005e)		

Location
A republic in eastern Europe, bounded to the west by Romania, and on all other sides by Ukraine.

Physical description
Terrain consists of a hilly plain, reaching a height of 429m/1 407ft at Mt Balanesti in the centre.

Climate
Moderate winters; warm summers.

National holidays
Jan 1, 7 (Orthodox Christmas) (2), Mar 8 (Women), May 1, 9 (Victory), Aug 27 (Independence), 31 (Limba Noastra/Our Language); EM, ES; 1st Mon after Easter.

Political leaders

President
1991–6	Mircea Snegur
1996–2001	Petru Lucinschi
2001–	Vladimir Voronin

Prime Minister
1991–2	Valery Muravsky	1999	Ion Sturza
1992–7	Andrei Sangheli	1999–2001	Dumitru Barghis
1997–9	Ion Ciubuc	2001–	Vasile Tarlev

Spring City

The Moldovan capital, Chisinau, takes its name from a word meaning 'spring', 'pump' or 'pipe' in the Moldovan language.

MONACO

Official name	Principality of Monaco	Ethnic groups	French 59%, Monégasque 17%, Italian 16%, others 8%
Local name	Monaco; Principauté de Monaco		
Area	1.9 sq km/0.75 sq mi	Religions	Christianity 95% (RC 90%, Prot 5%), others 5%
Capital	Monaco		
Chief towns	Monte Carlo	Time zone	GMT +1
Population	35 000 (2005e)	Currency	1 Euro (€/EUR) = 100 cents
Nationality	Monégasque or Monacan	Telephone	+377
		Internet	.mc
Languages	French	Country code	MCO

Location
A principality bounded to the south-east by the Mediterranean Sea and on all other sides by France, close to the Italian frontier.

Physical description
Hilly, rugged and rocky, rising to 63m/206ft; almost entirely urban.

Climate
Warm, dry summers and mild winters.

National holidays
Jan 1, 27 (St Devote), May 1, Aug 15, Nov 1, 19 (National), Dec 8, 25; A, CC, EM, WM.

Political leaders

Head of State (Monarch)

1889–1922	Albert	1949–2005	Rainier III
1922–49	Louis II	2005–	Albert II

MONGOLIA

Official name	State of Mongolia	Nationality	Mongolian
Local name	Mongol Uls	Languages	Khalkha Mongolian
Former name	Outer Mongolia (until 1924); People's Republic of Mongolia (1924–92)	Ethnic groups	Mongol 90%, Kazakh 4%, Chinese 2%, Russian 2%, others 2%
Independence	1911 (declared), 1924 (republic)	Religions	Mainly Buddhism
		Time zone	GMT +8
Area	1 564 619 sq km/604 099 sq mi	Currency	1 Tugrik (T/MNT) = 100 möngö
Capital	Ulan Bator; Ulaanbaatar	Telephone	+976
Chief towns	Darhan, Erdenet	Internet	.mn
Population	2 646 000 (2005e)	Country code	MNG

Location
A republic in eastern central Asia, bounded to the north by Russia and on all other sides by China.

Physical description
Mountainous, at an average height of 1 580m/5 184ft; highest point is Tavan Bogd (4 374m/14 350ft); high ground is mainly in the west, with mountains north-west to south-east, running into the Gobi Desert; lowland plains are mainly arid grasslands.

Climate
Continental, with hard and long-lasting frosts in winter; average temperature at Ulan Bator is 27°C in Jan and 9–24°C in Jul; rainfall is generally low; arid desert conditions prevail in the south.

National holidays
Jan 1, 2, Mar 8 (Women), May 1, Jul 10 (People's Revolution) (3), Nov 7 (Oct Revolution).

Political leaders

Prime Minister

1924–8	Tserendorji	1936–8	Amor
1928–32	Amor	1939–52	Korloghiin Choibalsan
1932–6	Gendun	1952–74	Yumsjhagiin Tsedenbal

Chairman of the Presidium

1948–53	Gonchighlin Bumatsende	1974–84	Yumsjhagiin Tsedenbal
1954–72	Jamsarangiin Sambu	1984–90	Jambyn Batmunkh
1972–4	Sonomyn Luvsan		

President

1990–7	Punsalmaagiyn Ochirbat
1997–2005	Natsagiyn Bagabandi
2005–	Nambaryn Enkhbayar

Premier

1974–84	Jambyn Batmunkh	1998–9	Janlaviyn Narantsatsralt
1984–90	Dumaagiyn Sodnom	1999–2000	Rinchinnyamiyn Amarjagal
1990–2	Dashiyn Byambasuren	2000–4	Nambaryn Enkhbayar
1992–6	Puntsagiyn Jasray	2004	Chultern Ulaan *Acting Prime*
1996–8	Mendsaihany Enkhsahan		*Minister*
1998	Tsahiagiyin Elbegdorj	2004–	Tsakhia Elbegdorj

Outer Mongolia

Outer Mongolia is sometimes used light-heartedly to describe anywhere very far away and isolated. But it is actually the official former name of Mongolia. Mongolia was originally the homeland of nomadic tribes, which united under Ghengis Khan in the 13c to become part of a great Mongol Empire. Mongolia was later assimilated into China, and divided into Inner and Outer Mongolia. Inner Mongolia remains an autonomous region of China, but Outer Mongolia declared itself independent in 1911.

MONTENEGRO *see* **SERBIA AND MONTENEGRO**

MONTSERRAT *see* **UNITED KINGDOM**

MOROCCO

Official name	Kingdom of Morocco	**Languages**	Arabic; Berber and French are also spoken
Local name	Al-Mamlaka Al-Maghribiyya	**Ethnic groups**	Arab and Berber 99%, European 1%
Independence	1956		
Area	409 200 sq km/157 951 sq mi	**Religions**	Islam 99% (mostly Sunni), Christianity 1%
Capital	Rabat; Ar Ribāt, Er Ribât	**Time zone**	GMT
Chief towns	Casablanca, Fez, Marrakesh, Tangier, Meknès, Kenitra, Tétouan, Oujda, Agadir	**Currency**	1 Moroccan Dirham (DH/MAD) = 100 centimes
		Telephone	+212
Population	31 478 000 (2005e)	**Internet**	.ma
Nationality	Moroccan	**Country code**	MAR

Location
A kingdom in North Africa, bounded to the north-east by the Mediterranean Sea; to the east and south-east by Algeria; to the south by Western Sahara, over which it claims sovereignty; and to the west by the Atlantic Ocean.

Physical description
Dominated by a series of mountain ranges, rising in the High Atlas in the south to 4 165m/13 665ft at Mt Toubkal; Atlas Mountains descend south-east to the north-west edge of the Sahara Desert; has a broad coastal plain.

Climate
Mediterranean climate on the north coast; settled and hot in May–Sep; Sahara is virtually rainless, with extreme heat in summer but chilly winter nights; average maximum temperatures of 17–28°C on Atlantic coast; heavy winter snowfall in the High Atlas.

National holidays
Jan 1, 11 (Independence Manifest), May 1, Jul 30 (Feast of the Throne), Aug 14 (Qued-ed-Dahab Allegiance), Aug 21 (King and People), Nov 6 (Green Mar), 18 (Independence); Ad, ER, NY (Muslim), PB.

Political leaders

Monarch
1927–61	Mohammed V
1961–99	Hassan II
1999–	Mohammed VI

Prime Minister
1955–8	Si Mohammed Bekkai	1972–9	Ahmed Othman
1958	Ahmad Balfrej	1979–83	Maati Bouabid
1958–60	Abdullah Ibrahim	1983–6	Mohammed Karim Lamrani
1960–3	*As Monarch*	1986–92	Izz Id-Dien Laraki
1963–5	Ahmad Bahnini	1992–4	Mohammed Karim Lamrani
1965–7	*As Monarch*	1994–8	Abdellatif Filali
1967–9	Moulay Ahmed Laraki	1998–2002	Abderrahmane el-Yousifi
1969–71	Mohammed Ben Hima	2002–	Driss Jettou
1971–2	Mohammed Karim Lamrani		

MOZAMBIQUE

Official name	Republic of Mozambique		are widely spoken
Local name	Moçambique; República de Moçambique	**Ethnic groups**	Makua 47%, Tsonga 23%, Malawi 12%, Shona 11%, Yao 4%, others 3%
Former name	People's Republic of Mozambique (1975–90)		
Independence	1975	**Religions**	traditional beliefs 55%, Christianity 28% (RC 25%, others 3%), Islam 17%
Area	789 800 sq km/304 863 sq mi		
Capital	Maputo	**Time zone**	GMT +2
Chief towns	Nampula, Beira, Pemba	**Currency**	1 Metical (Mt/MZM) = 100 centavos
Population	19 792 000 (2005e)		
Nationality	Mozambican	**Telephone**	+258
Languages	Portuguese; Swahili and other African languages	**Internet**	.mz
		Country code	MOZ

Location
A republic in south-eastern Africa, bounded to the north-west by Zambia and Malawi; to the north by Tanzania; to the east by the Mozambique Channel and the Indian Ocean; to the south by Swaziland; to the south and south-west by South Africa; and to the west by Zimbabwe.

Physical description
South of the Zambezi River the low-lying coast has sandy beaches and mangroves; low hills of volcanic origin inland; coast north of the Zambezi is more rugged, with savanna plateau inland; highest peak is Mt Binga (2 436m/7 992ft).

Climate
Tropical, with relatively low rainfall in the coastal lowlands; maximum daily temperatures of 25–32°C in the central coast zone; rainfall decreases in the drier areas of the interior lowlands; one rainy season in Dec–Mar.

National holidays
Jan 1, Feb 3 (Heroes), Apr 7 (Mozambican Women), May 1, Jun 25 (Independence), Sep 7 (Victory), 25 (Armed Forces), Oct 4 (Peace and Reconciliation), Dec 25 (Christmas/Family).

Political leaders

President
1975–86	Samora Moïses Machel
1986–2005	Joaquim Alberto Chissano
2005–	Armando Guebuza

Prime Minister
1986–94	Mario de Graça Machungo
1994–2004	Pascoal Mocumbi
2004–	Luisa Diogo

First Lady of Africa

The first president of Mozambique, Samora Machel, was killed in an air crash in 1986. His widow, Graça Machel, is internationally respected for her work for women's and children's rights. She later married the former president of South Africa, Nelson Mandela.

MYANMAR (BURMA)

Official name	Union of Myanmar; still often referred to internationally as Burma	**Nationality**	Burmese or Myanmarese
		Languages	Burmese; several minority languages are also spoken
Local name	Myanmar; Pyidaungsu Myanmar Naingngandaw		
Former name	Union of Burma (1948–74); Socialist Republic of the Union of Burma (1974–88), Union of Burma (1988–9)	**Ethnic groups**	Burman 68%, Shan 9%, Karen 7%, Rakhine 4%, Chinese 3%, Mon 2%, Kachin 1%, others 6%
		Religions	Buddhism 89%, Christianity 6%, Islam 4%, Hindu 1%
Independence	1948		
Area	678 576 sq km/261 930 sq mi	**Time zone**	GMT +6.5
		Currency	1 Kyat (K/MMK) = 100 pyas
Capital¹	Rangoon; Yangon	**Telephone**	+95
Chief towns	Mandalay, Henzada, Pegu, Myingyan	**Internet**	.mm
		Country code	MMR
Population	50 519 000 (2005e)		

Location
A republic in south-east Asia, bounded to the north-west by India; to the north-east by China; to the east by Laos and Thailand; to the south and west by the Bay of Bengal and the Andaman Sea; and to the west by Bangladesh.

Physical description
Mountains in the north, east and west rise to Hkakabo Razi (5 881m/19 294ft) and descend in a series of ridges and valleys; Irrawaddy River delta extends over 240km/150mi.

Climate
Tropical monsoon climate, with a marked change between the cooler, dry season (Nov–Apr) and the hotter, wet season (May–Sep); lowlands are very hot all year; high coastal humidity.

National holidays
Jan 4 (Independence), Feb 12 (Union), Mar 2 (Peasants), 27 (Armed Forces), May 1, Jul 19 (Martyrs), Dec 25; Ad, D, 4 Full Moon days, National (Nov), NY (Burmese), NY (Kayin), Tazaungdaing Festival (Nov), Thingyan (Apr) (3–5).

¹ In 2005 the seat of government moved to Pyinmana; the new capital will be officially called Yanlon.

Political leaders

President
1948–52	Sao Shwe Thaik	1957–62	U Wing Maung
1952–7	Agga Maha Thiri Thudhamma Ba U	1962	Sama Duwa Sinwa Nawng

Chairman of Revolutionary Council
1962–74   Ne Win

President
1974–81	Ne Win	1988	U Sein Lwin
1981–8	U San Yu	1988	Maung Maung

Chairman of State Law and Order Restoration Council
1988–92	Saw Maung
1992–7	Than Shwe

Chairman of State Peace and Development Council
1997–	Than Shwe

Prime Minister
1948–56	U Nu	1977–8	U Maung Maung Ka
1956–7	U Ba Swe	1988	U Tun Tin
1957–8	U Nu	1988–92	Saw Maung
1958–60	Ne Win	1992–2003	Than Shwe
1960–2	U Nu	2003–4	Khin Nyunt
1962–74	Ne Win	2004–	Soe Win
1974–7	U Sein Win		

NAMIBIA

Official name	Republic of Namibia		widely spoken
Local name	Namibia	**Ethnic groups**	Ovambo 50%, Kavango 9%, Damara 8%, Herero 8%, white 6%, Nama 5%, others 14%
Former name	South West Africa (until 1968)		
Independence	1990	**Religions**	Christianity 90%, traditional beliefs 10%
Area	823 144 sq km/317 734 sq mi		
		Time zone	GMT +1
Capital	Windhoek	**Currency**	1 Namibian Dollar (N$/NAD) = 100 cents; the South African Rand is also used.
Chief towns	Lüderitz, Keetmanshoop, Grootfontein		
Population	2 031 000 (2005e)		
Nationality	Namibian	**Telephone**	+264
Languages	English; Afrikaans, German and local languages are also	**Internet**	.na
		Country code	NAM

Location
A republic in south-western Africa, bounded to the north by Angola; to the north-east by Zambia and Zimbabwe; to the east by Botswana; to the south by South Africa; and to the west by the Atlantic Ocean.

Physical description
Namib Desert runs along the Atlantic Ocean coast; inland plateau has a mean elevation of 1 500m/4 921ft; highest point is Konigstein peak on Brandberg (2 574m/8 445ft); Kalahari Desert lies to the east and south; Orange River forms the frontier with South Africa.

Climate
Low rainfall on the coast, higher in the interior; the average maximum daily temperature range at Windhoek, representative of the interior, is 20–30°C.

National holidays
Jan 1, Mar 21 (Independence), May 1, 4 (Cassinga), Aug 26 (Heroes), Dec 10 (Human Rights), Dec 25, 26 (Family); A, GF, EM.

Political leaders

President
1990–2005	Sam Daniel Nujoma	2005–	Hifikepunye Pohamba

Prime Minister
1990–2002	Hage Geingob	2005–	Nahas Angula
2002–5	Theo-Ben Gurirab		

NAURU

Official name	Republic of Nauru	**Ethnic groups**	Nauruan 58%, other Pacific Islanders 26%, Chinese and Vietnamese 8%, European 8%
Local name	Naoero (Nauruan), Nauru (English)		
Independence	1968		
Area	21 sq km/8 sq mi	**Religions**	Christianity (predominantly Prot, with RC minority); also Buddhism
Capital	There is no capital as such, but government offices are situated in Yaren District		
		Time zone	GMT +12
Population	14 000 (2005e)	**Currency**	1 Australian Dollar ($A/AUD) = 100 cents
Nationality	Nauruan	**Telephone**	+674
Languages	Nauruan; English is also widely understood	**Internet**	.nr
		Country code	NRU

Location
An independent republic in the west-central Pacific Ocean, 4 000km/2 500mi north-east of Sydney, Australia.

Physical description
A small, isolated island; ground rises from sandy beaches to form a fertile coastal belt, c.100–300m/330–980ft wide, the only cultivable soil; central plateau inland, which reaches 65m/213ft at its highest point, composed largely of phosphate-bearing rocks.

Climate
Tropical, with average daily temperatures of 24–34°C, and average humidity between 70% and 80%; rainfall mainly in the monsoon season from Nov to Feb, with marked yearly deviations.

National holidays
Jan 1, 31 (Independence), Feb 1, May 17 (Constitution), Oct 26 (Angam), Dec 25, 26; GF, EM (2).

Political leaders

President

1968–76	Hammer de Roburt	1997–8	Kinza Clodumar
1976–8	Bernard Dowiyogo	1998–9	Bernard Dowiyogo
1978	Lagumot Harris	1999–2000	René Harris
1978–86	Hammer de Roburt	2000–1	Bernard Dowiyogo
1986	Kennan Adeang	2001–3	René Harris
1986–9	Hammer de Roburt	2003	Bernard Dowiyogo
1989	Kenas Aroi	2003	René Harris
1989–95	Bernard Dowiyogo	2003	Bernard Dowiyogo
1995–6	Lagumot Harris	2003	Derog Gioura *Acting President*
1996	Bernard Dowiyogo	2003	Ludwig Scotty
1996	Kennan Adeang	2003–4	René Harris
1996–7	Rueben Kun	2004–	Ludwig Scotty

NEPAL

Official name	Kingdom of Nepal		Tamang 3%, Tharu 3%,
Local name	Nepāl Adhirājya		Newar 3%, others 12%
Area	145 391 sq km/56 121 sq mi	**Religions**	Hinduism 90%, Buddhism 5%, Islam 3%, others 2%
Capital	Kathmandu		
Chief towns	Patan, Bhadgaon	**Time zone**	GMT +5.75
Population	27 133 000 (2005e)	**Currency**	1 Nepalese Rupee (NRp, NRs/NPR) = 100
Nationality	Nepalese		paise/pice
Languages	Nepali; around 70 local dialects and languages are also spoken	**Telephone**	+977
		Internet	.np
Ethnic groups	Nepali 59%, Bihari 20%,	**Country code**	NPL

Location
An independent kingdom in central Asia, bounded to the north by the Tibet region of China, and on all other sides by India.

Physical description
Rises steeply from the Ganges Basin; high fertile valleys in the hill country at 1 300m/4 265ft, such as the Vale of Kathmandu, are enclosed by mountain ranges; dominated by the glaciated peaks of the Himalayas; highest point is Mt Everest (8 850m/29 035ft).

Climate
Varies from subtropical lowland, with hot, humid summers and mild winters, to an alpine climate over 3 300m/10 827ft, with permanently snow-covered peaks; average temperatures at Kathmandu from 23°C (May–Aug) to 9°C (Jan); monsoon season during summer (Jun–Sep).

National holidays
Feb 19 (Democracy), Jul 8 (King's Birthday), Nov 8 (Constitution); NY (Nepalese) (Apr), Vijaya Dashami (Oct), Bhai Tika (Nov).

Political leaders

Monarch

1881–1911	Prithvi Bir Bikram Shah	1956–72	Mahendra Bir Bikram Shah
1911–50	Tribhuvan Bir Bikram Shah	1972–2001	Birendra Bir Bikram Shah Dev
1950–2	Bir Bikram	2001	Dipendra Bir Bikram Shah Dev
1952–5	Tribhuvan Bir Bikram Shah	2001–	Gyanendra Bir Bikram Shah Dev

Prime Minister

1901–29	Chandra Sham Sher Jang Bahadur Rana	1955–6	Mahendra Bir Bikram Shah
		1956–7	Tanka Prasad Acharya
1929–31	Bhim Cham Sham Sher Jang Bahadur Rana	1957–9	*King also Prime Minister*
		1959–60	Sri Bishawa Prasad Koirala
1931–45	Juddha Sham Sher Rana	1960–3	*No Prime Minister*
1945–8	Padma Sham Sher Jang Bahadur Rana	1963–5	Tulsi Giri
		1965–9	Surya Bahadur Thapa
1948–51	Mohan Sham Sher Jang Bahadur Rana	1969–70	Kirti Nidhi Bista
		1970–1	*King also Prime Minister*
1951–2	Matrika Prasad Koirala	1971–3	Kirti Nidhi Bista
1952–3	*King also Prime Minister*	1973–5	Nagendra Prasad Rijal
1953–5	Matrika Prasad Koirala	1975–7	Tulsi Giri

1977–9	Kirti Nidhi Bista	1997	Surya Bahadur Thapa
1979–83	Surya Bahadur Thapa	1998–9	Girija Prasad Koirala
1983–6	Lokendra Bahadur Chand	1999–2000	Krishna Prasad Bhattari
1986–91	Marich Man Singh Shrestha	2000–1	Girija Prasad Koirala
1991–4	Girija Prasad Koirala	2001–2	Sher Bahadur Deuba
1994–5	Man Mohan Adhikari	2002–3	Lokendra Bahadur Chand
1995–7	Sher Bahadur Deuba	2003–4	Surya Bahadur Thapa
1997	Lokendra Bahadur Chand	2004–5	Sher Bahadur Deuba

Note: In February 2005 the king took over direct rule.

Nepalese Peoples

Nepal is home to a diverse range of peoples, with more than 60 ethnic groups. These include the Sherpas, famous for their mountaineering skill, the Dolpa people, who live in probably the world's highest human settlements at around 4 000m/13 123ft, and the Gurungs, whose traditions include a colourful dancing season.

THE NETHERLANDS

Official name	Kingdom of the Netherlands; often known as Holland	**Languages**	Dutch; Frisian is spoken in Friesland, and English is widely spoken
Local name	Nederlanden; Koninkrijk der Nederlanden	**Ethnic groups**	Dutch 94%, others 6%
Area	33 929 sq km/13 097 sq mi	**Religions**	Christianity 63% (RC 36%, Prot 27%), none/unaffiliated 32%, Islam 3%, others 2%
Capital	Amsterdam; The Hague (Den Haag) is the seat of government	**Time zone**	GMT +1
Chief towns	Rotterdam, Utrecht, Haarlem, Eindhoven, Arnhem, Groningen	**Currency**	1 Euro (€/EUR) = 100 cents
		Telephone	+31
Population	16 299 000 (2005e)	**Internet**	.nl
Nationality	Dutch	**Country code**	NLD

Location
A kingdom in north-western Europe, bounded to the north and west by the North Sea; to the east by Germany; and to the south by Belgium.

Physical description
Generally low and flat, except in the south-east where hills rise to 321m/1 053ft; 24% of the land is below sea level, including much of the coast, which is protected by dunes and artificial dykes; many canals, totalling 6 340km/3 940mi in length.

Climate
Cool, temperate, maritime; average temperatures 1.7°C (Jan) and 17°C (Jul); rainfall is distributed fairly evenly throughout the year.

National holidays
Jan 1, Apr 30 (Queen), May 5 (Liberation), Dec 25, 26; A, EM, GF, WM.

Netherlands overseas territories

Aruba

Location	An island in the Caribbean Sea, about 30km/19mi north of Venezuela, and 70km/44mi west of Curaçao (The Netherlands).		
Area	193 sq km/75 sq mi	**Internet**	.aw
Capital	Oranjestad	**Country code**	ABW
Population	99 000 (2005e)		

Netherlands Antilles (Dutch Antilles)

Location	A group of islands in the Caribbean Sea, comprising the southern group of Curaçao and Bonaire north of the Venezuelan coast, and the northern group of St Maarten, St Eustatins and Saba, lying east of Puerto Rico (USA).		
Local name	Nederlandse Antillen	**Population**	183 000 (2005e)
Area	960 sq km/371 sq mi	**Internet**	.an
Capital	Willemstad	**Country code**	ANT

Political leaders

Monarch (House of Orange-Nassau)

1572–84	William the Silent	1806–10	Louis Bonaparte
1584–1625	Maurice	1813–40	William I
1625–47	Frederick Henry	1840–9	William II
1647–50	William II	1849–90	William III
1672–1702	William III	1890–1948	Wilhelmina
1747–51	William IV	1948–80	Juliana
1751–95	William V	1980–	Beatrix

Prime Minister

1897–1901	Nicholas G Pierson	1946–8	Louis J M Beel
1901–5	Abraham Kuyper	1948–51	Willem Drees/Josephus R H van
1905–8	Theodoor H de Meester		Schaik
1908–13	Theodorus Heemskerk	1951–8	Willem Drees
1913–18	Pieter W A Cort van der Linden	1958–9	Louis J M Beel
1918–25	Charles J M Ruys de Beerenbrouck	1959–63	Jan E de Quay
		1963–5	Victor G M Marijnen
1925–6	Hendrikus Colijn	1965–6	Joseph M L T Cals
1926	Dirk J de Geer	1966–7	Jelle Zijlstra
1926–33	Charles J M Ruys de Beerenbrouck	1967–71	Petrus J S de Jong
		1971–3	Barend W Biesheuvel
1933–9	Hendrikus Colijn	1973–7	Joop M Den Uyl
1939–40	Dirk J de Geer	1977–82	Andreas A M van Agt
1940–5	Pieter S Gerbrandy (in exile)	1982–94	Ruud F M Lubbers
1945–6	Willem Schemerhorn/Willem Drees	1994–2002	Wim Kok
		2002–	Jan Peter Balkenende

NEVIS see **ST KITTS AND NEVIS**

NEW CALEDONIA see **FRANCE**

NEW ZEALAND

Official name	New Zealand (NZ)		15%, Pacific Islanders 6%, Asian 5%
Local name	New Zealand (English), Aotearoa (Maori)		*Percentages add to more than 100% as some people identify with more than one ethnicity*
Independence	1907 (from Britain), 1947 (full)		
Area	268 812 sq km/103 761 sq mi	**Religions**	Christianity 67% (Prot 52%, RC 15%), none/unaffiliated 16%, others 17%
Capital	Wellington; Te Whanganui-a-Tara		
Chief towns	Auckland, Christchurch, Dunedin, Hamilton	**Time zone**	GMT +12
Population	4 028 000 (2005e)	**Currency**	1 New Zealand Dollar (NZ$/NZD) = 100 cents
Nationality	Kiwi (*informal*), New Zealand	**Telephone**	+64
		Internet	.nz
Languages	English, Maori	**Country code**	NZL
Ethnic groups	European 83%, Maori		

Location
An independent state comprising a group of islands in the Pacific Ocean to the south-east of Australia, from which it is separated by the Tasman Sea; the two principal islands are North Island and South Island, separated by the Cook Strait.

Physical description
North Island is mountainous in the centre, with many hot springs; peaks rise to 2 797m/ 9 176ft at Mt Ruapehu; South Island is mountainous for its whole length, rising in the Southern Alps to 3 753m/12 312ft at Mt Cook, New Zealand's highest point; many glaciers and mountain lakes.

Climate
Highly changeable weather, with all months moderately wet; almost subtropical in the north and on the east coast, with mild winters and warm, humid summers; Auckland daily temperatures are 8–13°C (Jul), 16–23°C (Jan); generally cooler in South Island.

National holidays
Jan 1, 2, Feb 6 (Waitangi), Apr 25 (Anzac), Dec 25, 26; EM, GF, Queen's Birthday (Jun), Labour (Oct).

Self-governing territories

Cook Islands

Location	A widely scattered group of 15 volcanic and coral islands in the South Pacific Ocean, c.3 200km/2 000mi north-east of New Zealand.		
Area	238 sq km/92 sq mi	**Internet**	.ck
Chief town	Avarua	**Country code**	COK
Population	18 000 (2005e)		

Niue

Location	A small island in the South Pacific Ocean, 2 140km/1 330mi north-east of New Zealand.
Area	263 sq km/101 sq mi **Internet** .nu
Chief town	Alofi **Country code** NIU
Population	1 000 (2005e)

Non-self-governing territories

Tokelau

Location	Comprises three small atolls (Atafu, Nukunonu, Fakaofo) in the South Pacific Ocean, c.3 500km/2 200mi north-east of New Zealand.
Area	10.1 sq km/3.9 sq mi **Internet** .tk
Population	1 000 (2005e) **Country code** TKL

Ross Dependency

Location	A territory in Antarctica.
Area	413 540 sq km/159 626 sq mi (land); 336 770 sq km/129 993 sq mi (permanent shelf ice)
Population	Populated solely by scientists.

Political leaders

Head of State: British monarch, represented by Governor General (Dame Silvia Cartwright since 2001).

Prime Minister

1893–1906	Richard John Seddon *Lib*	1957–60	Walter Nash *Lab*
1906	William Hall-Jones *Lib*	1960–72	Keith Jacka Holyoake *Nat*
1906–12	Joseph George Ward *Lib/Nat*	1972	John Ross Marshall *Nat*
1912	Thomas Mackenzie *Nat*	1972–4	Norman Eric Kirk *Lab*
1912–25	William Ferguson Massey *Ref*	1974–5	Wallace Edward Rowling *Lab*
1925	Francis Henry Dillon Bell *Ref*	1975–84	Robert David Muldoon *Nat*
1925–8	Joseph Gordon Coates *Ref*	1984–89	David Russell Lange *Lab*
1928–30	Joseph George Ward *Lib/Nat*	1989–90	Geoffrey Palmer *Lab*
1930–5	George William Forbes *Un*	1990	Mike Moore *Lab*
1935–40	Michael Joseph Savage *Lab*	1990–7	James Bolger *Nat*
1940–9	Peter Fraser *Lab*	1997–9	Jenny Shipley *Nat*
1949–57	Sidney George Holland *Nat*	1999–	Helen Clark *Lab*
1957	Keith Jacka Holyoake *Nat*		

Lab = Labor
Lib = Liberal
Nat = National
Ref = Reform
Un = United

Votes for Women

In 1893 New Zealand became the first country to give women the vote in national elections.

NICARAGUA

Official name	Republic of Nicaragua		local languages in Caribbean coastal areas
Local name	Nicaragua; República de Nicaragua	**Ethnic groups**	mestizo 69%, white 17%, black 9%, Amerindian 5%
Independence	1821		
Area	130 668 sq km/50 451 sq mi	**Religions**	Christianity 100% (RC 95%, Prot 5%)
Capital	Managua	**Time zone**	GMT −6
Chief towns	León, Granada, Masaya, Chinandega, Matagalpa, Corinto	**Currency**	1 Córdoba (C$/NIO) = 100 centavos = 10 reales
Population	5 487 000 (2005e)	**Telephone**	+505
Nationality	Nicaraguan	**Internet**	.ni
Languages	Spanish; English and	**Country code**	NIC

Location
A republic in Central America, bounded to the north by Honduras; to the east by the Caribbean Sea; to the south by Costa Rica; and to the west by the Pacific Ocean.

Physical description
Mountainous west with volcanic ranges rising to over 2 000m/6 562ft in the north-west; highest point is the Dipilto-Jalapa ridge (2 107m/6 913ft); two large lakes behind the coastal mountains; rolling uplands and forested plains to the east; many short rivers.

Climate
Tropical, with average annual temperatures ranging from 15–35°C according to altitude; there is a rainy season from May to Nov when humidity is high; subject to devastating hurricanes.

National holidays
Jan 1, May 1, Jul 19 (Sandinista Revolution), Sep 14 (Battle of San Jacinto), 15 (Independence), Dec 8, 25; GF, HT.

Political leaders

President

1893–1909	José Santos Zelaya	1937–47	Anastasio Somoza García
1909–10	José Madriz	1947	Leonardo Argüello
1910–11	José Dolores Estrada	1947	Benjamin Lascayo Sacasa
1911	Juan José Estrada	1947–50	Victor Manuel Román y Reyes
1911–17	Adolfo Díaz	1950–6	Anastasio Somoza García
1912	Luis Mena *rival President*	1956–63	Luis Somoza Debayle
1917–21	Emiliano Chamorro Vargas	1963–6	René Schick Gutiérrez
1921–3	Riego Manuel Chamorro	1966–7	Lorenzo Guerrero Gutiérrez
1923–4	Martínez Bartolo	1967–72	Anastasio Somoza Debayle
1925–6	Carlos Solórzano	1972–4	*Triumvirate*
1926	Emiliano Chamorro Vargas	1974–9	Anastasio Somoza Debayle
1926–8	Adolfo Díaz	1979–84	*Government Junta of National Reconstruction*
1926	Juan Bautista Sacasa *rival President*	1984–90	Daniel Ortega Saavedra
1928–32	José Marcia Moncada	1990–7	Violeta Barrios de Chamorro
1933–6	Juan Bautista Sacasa	1997–2002	Arnoldo Alemán Lacayo
1936	Carlos Brenes Jarquin	2002–	Enrique Bolaños

NIUE *see* **NEW ZEALAND**

NIGER

Official name	Republic of Niger	**Ethnic groups**	Hausa 56%, Djerma and Songhai 22%, Fulani 9%, Tuareg 8%, others 5%
Local name	Niger; République du Niger		
Independence	1960	**Religions**	Islam 80%, Christianity and traditional beliefs 20%
Area	1 186 408 sq km/ 457 953 sq mi		
		Time zone	GMT +1
Capital	Niamey	**Currency**	1 CFA Franc (CFAFr/XOF) = 100 centimes
Chief towns	Agadès, Diffa, Dosso, Maradi, Tahoua, Zinder		
		Telephone	+227
Population	13 957 000 (2005e)	**Internet**	.ne
Nationality	Nigerien	**Country code**	NER
Languages	French; Hausa and Djerma are spoken widely		

Location
A republic in West Africa, bounded to the north-west by Algeria; to the north-east by Libya; to the east by Chad; to the south by Nigeria and Benin; to the south-west by Burkina Faso; and to the west by Mali.

Physical description
Lies on the southern fringe of the Sahara Desert, on a high plateau; deserts in the east, centre and north; water in quantity is found only in the south-west around the River Niger and in the south-east around Lake Chad; highest point is Mt Greboun (2 310m/7 580ft).

Climate
One of the hottest countries in the world; marked rainy season in the south Jun–Oct; rainfall decreases in the north to almost negligible levels in desert areas; drought can occur.

National holidays
Jan 1, Apr 24 (Concord), May 1, Aug 3 (Independence), Dec 18 (Republic), 25; Ad, EM, ER, PB, Leilat-ul-kadr.

Political leaders

President

1960–74	Hamani Diori	1996–9	Ibrahim Baré Maïnassara
1974–87	Seyni Kountché	1999	Daouda Malam Wanke
1987–93	Ali Saibou	1999–	Mamadou Tandja
1993–6	Mahamane Ousmane		

Prime Minister

1957–8	Djibo Bakary	1990–1	Aliou Mahamidou
1958–60	Hamani Diori	1991–3	Amadou Cheiffou
1960–83	*No Prime Minister*	1993–4	Mahamadou Issoufou
1983	Mamane Oumarou	1994–5	Abdoulaye Souley
1983–8	Ahmid Algabid	1995	Amadou Boubacar Cissé
1988–9	Mamane Oumarou	1995–6	Hama Amadou

| 1996 | Boukary Adji | 1997–2000 | Ibrahim Assane Mayaki |
| 1996–7 | Amadou Boubacar Cissé | 2000– | Hama Amadou |

Nomads of Niger

Northern Niger is home to several nomadic peoples, including the Bororo Fulani. In their traditional marriage rituals a young man must seduce his beloved, then 'kidnap' her, elope and travel widely. People gather at the annual Guérewol festival for – according to the Embassy of Niger – 'celebrations, engagements, kidnappings of wives and baptisms'.

NIGERIA

Official name	Federal Republic of Nigeria		Edo and Igbo are also spoken
Local name	Nigeria	**Ethnic groups**	Yoruba 21%, Hausa 21%, Igbo 19%, Fulani 11%, Ibibio 6%, others 22%
Independence	1960		
Area	923 768 sq km/356 574 sq mi	**Religions**	Islam 50%, Christianity 40%, traditional beliefs 10%
Capital	Abuja		
Chief towns	Lagos, Ibadan, Ogbomosho, Kano, Oshogbo, Ilorin, Abeokuta, Port Harcourt	**Time zone**	GMT +1
		Currency	1 Naira (N,₦/NGN) = 100 kobo
Population	131 530 000 (2005e)	**Telephone**	+234
Nationality	Nigerian	**Internet**	.ng
Languages	English; Hausa, Yoruba,	**Country code**	NGA

Location
A republic in West Africa, bounded to the north by Niger; to the north-east by Chad; to the east by Cameroon; to the south by the Gulf of Guinea and the Bight of Benin; and to the west by Benin.

Physical description
Coastal strip dominated by the River Niger delta; tropical rainforest and oil palm bush lie north; dry central plateau of open woodland and savanna; edge of the Sahara Desert in the far north; numerous rivers; highest point is Mt Vogel (2 024m/6 640ft).

Climate
Two rainy seasons in the coastal areas; wettest part is the Niger delta and mountainous south-eastern frontier; Ibadan has an average daily maximum temperature of 31°C; only one rainy season in the north; dry season extends from Oct to Apr.

National holidays
Jan 1, May 1, 29 (Democracy), Oct 1 (National), Dec 25, 26; Ad, EM, ER, GF.

Political leaders

President
1960–6 Nnamdi Azikiwe

Prime Minister
1960–6 Abubakar Tafawa Balewa

Military Government

1966	J T U Aguiyi-Ironsi	1975–6	Murtala R Mohamed
1966–75	Yakubu Gowon	1976–9	Olusegun Obasanjo

President
1979–83 Alhaji Shehu Shagari

Military Government

1983–5	Mohammadu Buhari	1993	Ernest Shonekan *Interim*
1985–93	Ibrahim B Babangida		*President*

Chairman of Provisional Ruling Council
1993–8 Sani Abacha
1998–9 Abdulsalami Abubakar

President
1999– Olusegun Obasanjo

Agriculture, Peace and Unity

The Nigerian flag has two green stripes, representing agriculture, and a white centre that symbolizes peace and unity. The flag is accorded the utmost respect; the government states that 'next to Mother Earth, it is the only national symbol worth dying for'.

NORFOLK ISLAND see **AUSTRALIA**

NORTHERN IRELAND see **UNITED KINGDOM**

NORTHERN MARIANA ISLANDS see **UNITED STATES OF AMERICA**

NORTH KOREA see **KOREA, NORTH**

NORWAY

Official name	Kingdom of Norway	**Ethnic groups**	Norwegian 96%, Lapp 1%, others 3%
Local name	Norge; Kongeriket Norge		
Independence	1905	**Religions**	Christianity 89% (Prot 88%, RC 1%), others and none/unaffiliated 11%
Area	323 895 sq km/125 023 sq mi		
		Time zone	GMT +1
Capital	Oslo	**Currency**	1 Norwegian Krone (NKr/NOK) = 100 øre
Chief towns	Bergen, Trondheim, Stavanger, Kristiansand		
		Telephone	+47
Population	4 620 000 (2005e)	**Internet**	.no
Nationality	Norwegian	**Country code**	NOR
Languages	Norwegian, in the varieties of Bokmål and Nynorsk		

Location
A kingdom in north-west Europe, bounded to the north by the Arctic Ocean; to the east by Russia, Finland and Sweden; to the south by the Skagerrak; and to the west by the North Sea and Norwegian Sea.

Physical description
Mountainous, with many ranges and extensive plateau regions, especially in the south-west and centre; much of the interior rises above 1 500m/4 921ft; highest point is Galdhøpiggen (2 469m/8 100ft); numerous lakes; irregular coastline with many small islands and long deep fjords.

Climate
Arctic winter climate in the interior highlands, with snow, strong winds and severe frosts; comparatively mild winter conditions on the coast; heavy rainfall on the west coast; colder winters and warmer, drier summers in southern lowlands.

National holidays
Jan 1, May 1, 17 (Constitution), Dec 25, 26; A, EM, GF, HT, WM.

Bouvet Island

Location	An inaccessible and uninhabited ice-covered island of volcanic origin in the South Atlantic ocean, lying approximately 1 370km/850mi to the south-west of the Cape of Good Hope, South Africa.

Local name	Bouvetøya	**Internet**	.bv
Area	59 sq km/23 sq mi	**Country code**	BVT

Svalbard and Jan Mayen islands

Location	Svalbard Islands lie to the north of Norway and to the east of Greenland (Denmark) at the eastern edges of the Barents Sea, south of the Arctic Ocean; Jan Mayen Island lies to the north-east of Iceland and east of Greenland between the Norwegian Sea and the Greenland Sea.

Area	62 049 sq km/23 957 sq mi (Svalbard); 373 sq km/144 sq mi (Jan Mayen)	**Population**	2 700 (Svalbard; 2005e); uninhabited (Jan Mayen)
		Internet	.sj
Capital	Longyearbyen	**Country code**	SJM

Political leaders

Monarch

1872–1905	Oscar II *union with Sweden*	1957–91	Olav V
1905–57	Haakon VII	1991–	Harald V

Prime Minister

1898–1902	Johannes Steen	1920–1	Otto Bahr Halvorsen
1902–3	Otto Albert Blehr	1921–3	Otto Albert Blehr
1903–5	George Francis Hagerup	1923	Otto Bahr Halvorsen
1905–7	Christian Michelsen	1923–4	Abraham Berge
1907–8	Jørgen Løvland	1924–6	Johan Ludwig Mowinckel
1908–10	Gunnar Knudsen	1926–8	Ivar Lykke
1910–12	Wollert Konow	1928	Christopher Hornsrud
1912–13	Jens Bratlie	1928–31	Johan Ludwig Mowinckel
1913–20	Gunnar Knudsen	1931–2	Peder L Kolstad

1932–3	Jens Hundseid	1973–6	Trygve Bratteli
1933–5	Johan Ludwig Mowinckel	1976–81	Odvar Nordli
1935–45	Johan Nygaardsvold	1981	Gro Harlem Brundtland
1945–51	Einar Gerhardsen	1981–6	Kåre Willoch
1951–5	Oscar Torp	1986–9	Gro Harlem Brundtland
1955–63	Einar Gerhardsen	1989–90	Jan P Syse
1963	John Lyng	1990–6	Gro Harlem Brundtland
1963–5	Einar Gerhardsen	1996–7	Thorbjørn Jagland
1965–71	Per Borten	1997–2000	Kjell Magne Bondevik
1971–2	Trygve Bratteli	2000–1	Jens Stoltenberg
1972–3	Lars Korvald	2001–	Kjell Magne Bondevik

Midnight Sun and Northern Lights

In the far north of Norway the sun never sets in summer, earning it the nickname 'the Land of the Midnight Sun', while in the winter the same area witnesses the Aurora Borealis or Northern Lights – luminous and shimmering colours and streamers of light in the dark night sky.

OMAN

Official name	Sultanate of Oman	**Ethnic groups**	Arab 74%, Pakistani 22%, others 4%
Local name	'Umān; Saltanat 'Umān	**Religions**	Islam 86%, Hinduism 13%, others 1%
Former name	Sultanate of Muscat and Oman (until 1970)		
Area	300 000 sq km/115 800 sq mi	**Time zone**	GMT +4
		Currency	1 Omani Rial (RO/OMR) = 1 000 baisas
Capital	Muscat; Masqat		
Chief towns	Matrah, Nazwa, Salalah	**Telephone**	+968
Population	2 567 000 (2005e)	**Internet**	.om
Nationality	Omani	**Country code**	OMN
Languages	Arabic		

Location
An independent state in the south-east of the Arabian Peninsula, bounded to the north-west by the United Arab Emirates; to the north-east by the Gulf of Oman; to the east by the Arabian Sea; to the south-west by Yemen; and to the west by Saudi Arabia; the tip of the Musandam peninsula in the Strait of Hormuz is separated from the rest of the country by an 80km/50mi strip of the United Arab Emirates.

Physical description
Hajar range runs north-west to south-east parallel to the coast; several peaks in the Jebal al Akhdar are over 3 000m/9 842ft; highest point is Jebel Shams (3 075m/10 088ft); alluvial plain of the Batinah lies east and north of the Hajar; a vast sand desert is to the north-east.

Climate
Desert climate with much regional variation; summer (Apr–Oct) is hot and humid on the coast (maximum temperature 47°C), hot and dry in the interior; relatively temperate in mountains; light monsoon rains in the south from Jun to Sep.

National holidays
Nov 18 (National) (2), Dec 31; Ad (5), ER (4), NY (Muslim), PB, Lailat al-Miraj (Mar/Apr).

Political leaders

Sultan

1888–1913	Faisal Bin Turki	1932–70	Said Bin Taimur
1913–32	Taimur Bin Faisal	1970–	Qaboos Bin Said

Prime Minister

1970–2	Tariq Bin Taimur
1972–	*As sultan*

Fragrant Oman

Incense-burning is an Omani tradition, and many villages will have a specialized craftsman who makes incense, known as *bokhur*, from local ingredients including ambergris, frankincense, myrrh, rosewater and sandalwood.

PAKISTAN

Official name	Islamic Republic of Pakistan	**Languages**	Urdu; English and several local languages are also spoken
Local name	Pākistān; Islāmī Jamhūriya e Pākistān	**Ethnic groups**	Punjabi 55%, Sindhi 14%, Pashtun 14%, Mohajir 8%, Baluch 6%, others 3%
Former name	formerly part of India (until 1947), Dominion of Pakistan (1947–56); known as West Pakistan (until 1971)		
		Religions	Islam 97% (Sunni 77%, Shia 20%), Hinduism 2%, Christianity 1%
Independence	1947		
Area	803 943 sq km/310 322 sq mi	**Time zone**	GMT +5
		Currency	1 Pakistan Rupee (PRs, Rp/PKR) = 100 paisa
Capital	Islamabad; Islāmābād		
Chief towns	Karachi, Lahore, Faisalabad, Rawalpindi	**Telephone**	+92
		Internet	.pk
Population	157 935 000 (2005e)	**Country code**	PAK
Nationality	Pakistani		

Location
A republic in Asia, bounded to the north by China and the disputed area of Jammu and Kashmir; to the east by India; to the south by the Arabian Sea; and to the west by Afghanistan and Iran.

Physical description
Largely centred on the alluvial floodplain of the River Indus; bounded to the north and west by mountains rising to 8 610m/28 251ft at K2 in the disputed Kashmir-Jammu region; mostly flat plateaux, low-lying plains, and arid desert to the south of the Karakoram range.

Climate
Dominated by the Asiatic monsoon; hottest season is Mar–Jun, with highest temperatures in south; rainy season is late Jun–early Oct; climate varies in the mountains and upland plateaux; Indus Valley is extremely hot in summer.

National holidays
Jan 1, Feb 5 (Kashmir), Mar 23 (Pakistan), May 1, Jul 1, Aug 14 (Independence), Nov 9 (Iqbal), Dec 25 (Christmas/Birthday of Quaid-e-Azam); Ad (2), As (2), ER (3), PB, R; *additional religious optional holidays*.

Political leaders

President

1956–8	Iskander Mirza	1988–93	Ghulam Ishaq Khan
1958–69	Mohammad Ayoub Khan	1993	Wasim Sajjad *Acting President*
1969–71	Agha Mohammad Yahya Khan	1993–7	Farooq Ahmad Khan Leghari
1971–3	Zulfikar Ali Bhutto	1997–8	Wasim Sajjad *Acting President*
1973–8	Fazal Elahi Chawdry	1998–2001	Muhammed Rafiq Tarar
1978–88	Mohammad Zia Ul-Haq	2001–	Pervez Musharraf

Prime Minister

1947–51	Liaqat Ali Khan	1988	Mohammad Aslam Khan Khattak
1951–3	Khawaja Nazimuddin	1988–90	Benazir Bhutto
1953–5	Mohammad Ali	1990	Ghulam Mustafa Jatoi
1955–6	Chawdry Mohammad Ali	1990–3	Mian Mohammad Nawaz Sharif
1956–7	Hussein Shahid Suhrawardi	1993–6	Benazir Bhutto
1957	Ismail Chundrigar	1996–7	Meraj Khalid *Acting Prime Minister*
1957–8	Malik Feroz Khan Noon	1997–9	Mian Mohammad Nawaz Sharif
1958	Mohammad Ayoub Khan	1999–2002	*No Prime Minister*
1958–73	*No Prime Minister*	2002–4	Mir Zafarullah Khan Jamali
1973–7	Zulfikar Ali Bhutto	2004	Chaudhry Shujaat Hussain
1977–85	*No Prime Minister*	2004–	Shaukat Aziz
1985–8	Mohammad Khan Junejo		

PALAU

Official name	Republic of Palau	**Ethnic groups**	A composite of Polynesian, Malaysian and Melanesian peoples
Local name	Belau; Belu'u era Belau		
Former name	formerly part of the Trust Territory of the Pacific Islands (1917–79)	**Religions**	Christianity 66% (mostly RC), traditional beliefs (Modekngei) 34%
Independence	1994		
Area	494 sq km/191 sq mi	**Time zone**	GMT +10
Capital	Koror	**Currency**	1 US Dollar ($, US$/USD) = 100 cents
Population	20 000 (2000e)		
Nationality	Palauan	**Telephone**	+680
Languages	Palauan, English	**Internet**	.pw
		Country code	PLW

Location
An island republic in the western Pacific Ocean, 960km/600mi east of the Philippines.

Physical description
A group of c.350 small islands and islets; varies from the mountainous main island of Babelthuap to low-lying coral islands often surrounded by coral reefs; highest point is Mt Ngerchelchauus (242m/794ft).

Climate
Warm all year, with high humidity; average annual temperature is 27°C; typhoons are rare.

National holidays
Jan 1, Mar 15 (Youth), May 5 (Senior Citizens), Jun 1 (President), Jul 9 (Constitution), Oct 1 (Independence), 24 (United Nations), Dec 25; Labour Day (1st Mon in Sep), Thanksgiving (last Thurs in Nov).

Political leaders

President

1981–5	Haruo Remeliik	1988–9	Thomas Remengesau
1985	Thomas Remengesau *Acting*	1989–93	Ngiratkel Etpison
	President	1993–2000	Kuniwo Nakamura
1985	Alfonso Oiterong	2001–	Tommy Remengesau
1985–8	Lazarus Salii		

Get By in Palauan

The Palauan word for *hello* is *alii*, and *how are you?* is *ke ua ngerang? Goodbye* is *ak morolung*, while other useful phrases include *ngtecha ngklem?* for *what is your name?* and *bo momengur!* which means *have something to eat!*

PALESTINE, PALESTINIAN AUTONOMOUS AREAS *see* **ISRAEL**

PANAMA

Official name	Republic of Panama	**Ethnic groups**	mestizo 62%, black 13%, white 12%, mulatto 8%, Amerindian 5%
Local name	Panamá; República de Panamá		
Independence	1821 (from Spain), 1903 (from Gran Colombia union)	**Religions**	Christianity 89% (RC 84%, Prot 5%), Islam 5%, Baha'i 1%, others 5%
Area	77 082 sq km/29 753 sq mi	**Time zone**	GMT –5
Capital	Panama City; La Ciudad de Panamá	**Currency**	1 Balboa (B, Ba/PAB) = 100 centésimos; the US dollar is also used
Chief towns	David, Colón, Santiago	**Telephone**	+507
Population	3 232 000 (2005e)	**Internet**	.pa
Nationality	Panamanian	**Country code**	PAN
Languages	Spanish		

Location
A republic in Central America, bounded to the north by the Caribbean Sea; to the east by Colombia; to the south by the Pacific Ocean; and to the west by Costa Rica.

Physical description
Mostly mountainous; Serranía de Tabasará in the west rises to over 2 000m/6 562ft; highest point is Barú volcano in Chiriqui (3 475m/11 400ft); Azuero peninsula lies to the south; lake-studded lowland cuts across the isthmus; dense tropical forests on the Caribbean coast; Panama Canal (c.80km/50mi long) links the Pacific and Caribbean coasts.

Climate
Tropical, with a mean annual temperature of 32°C.

National holidays
Jan 1, 9 (Martyrs), May 1, Nov 3 (Independence), 10 (First Call of Independence), 28 (Independence from Spain), Dec 8 (Mothers), 25; C, GF; *some local variation*.

Political leaders

President

1904–8	Manuel Amador Guerrero	1945–8	Enrique Adolfo Jiménez Brin
1908–10	José Domingo de Obaldia	1948–9	Domingo Diaz Arosemena
1910	Federico Boyd	1949	Daniel Chanis
1910	Carlos Antonio Mendoza	1949	Roberto Francisco Chiari
1910–12	Pablo Arosemena	1949–51	Arnulfo Arias Madrid
1912	Rodolfo Chiari	1951–2	Alcibiades Arosemena
1912–16	Belisario Porras	1952–5	José Antonio Remón
1916–18	Ramón Maximiliano Valdés	1955	José Ramón Guizado
1918	Pedro Antonio Diaz	1955–6	Ricardo Manuel Arias Espinosa
1918	Cirilo Luis Urriola	1956–60	Ernesto de la Guardia
1918–20	Belisario Porras	1960–4	Roberto Francisco Chiari
1920	Ernesto T Lefevre	1964–8	Marco A Robles
1920–4	Belisario Porras	1968	Arnulfo Arias Madrid
1924–8	Rodolfo Chiari	1968	*Military Junta*
1928	Tomás Gabriel Duque	1968–9	Omar Torrijos Herrera
1928–31	Florencio Harmodio Arosemena	1969–78	Demetrio Basilio Lakas
1931	Harmodio Arias	1978–82	Aristides Royo
1931–2	Ricardo Joaquín Alfaro	1982–4	Ricardo de la Esoriella
1932–6	Harmodio Arias	1984	Jorge Enrique Illueca Sibauste
1936–9	Juan Demóstenes Arosemena	1984–5	Nicolás Ardito Barletta
1939	Ezequiel Fernández Jaén	1985–8	Eric Arturo Delvalle
1939–40	Augusto Samuel Boyd	1988–9	Manuel Solís Palma
1940–1	Arnulfo Arias Madrid	1989–94	Guillermo Endara Galimany
1941	Ernesto Jaén Guardia	1994–9	Ernesto Pérez Balladares
1941	José Pezet	1999–2004	Mireya Elisa Moscoso Rodriguez
1941 5	Ricardo Adolfo de la Guardia	2004–	Martin Torrijos

Fish and Butterflies

The name *Panama* is widely believed to mean 'an abundance of fish'
or 'an abundance of butterflies' in the local Amerindian language.

PAPUA NEW GUINEA

Official name	Independent State of Papua New Guinea (PNG)		languages are spoken
Local name	Papua New Guinea; Gau Hedinarai ai Papua–Matamata Guinea	**Ethnic groups**	Papuan 85%, Melanesian 1%, others 14%
		Religions	Christianity 66% (Prot and others 44%, RC 22%), traditional beliefs 34%
Independence	1975		
Area	462 840 sq km/178 656 sq mi	**Time zone**	GMT +10
Capital	Port Moresby	**Currency**	1 Kina (K/PGK) = 100 toea
Chief towns	Lae, Madang, Rabaul		
Population	5 887 000 (2005e)	**Telephone**	+675
Nationality	Papua New Guinean	**Internet**	.pg
Languages	Pidgin English; approximately 800 other	**Country code**	PNG

Location
An independent state in the south-western Pacific Ocean, comprising the eastern half of the island of New Guinea, bounded by Indonesia to the west, and many smaller islands; separated from Australia to the south by the Torres Strait.

Physical description
Complex mountain system, with snow-covered peaks rising above 4 000m/13 123ft; highest point is Mt Wilhelm (4 509m/14 793ft); mainly covered with tropical rainforest; coastal mangrove swamps; other islands are also mountainous and mostly volcanic.

Climate
Typically monsoonal, with temperatures and humidity constantly high; the average temperature range is 22–33°C; high rainfall.

National holidays
Jan 1, Jul 23 (Remembrance), Sep 16 (Independence), Dec 25, 26; EM, ES, GF, HS, Queen's Birthday (Jun).

Political leaders

Head of State: British monarch, represented by Governor General (Sir Paulias Matane since 2004).

Prime Minister

1975–80	Michael T Somare	1994–7	Julius Chan
1980–2	Julius Chan	1997	John Giheno *Acting Prime Minister*
1982–5	Michael T Somare	1997	Julius Chan
1985–8	Paias Wingti	1997–9	Bill Skate
1988–92	Rabbie Namaliu	1999–2002	Mekere Morauta
1992–4	Paias Wingti	2002–	Michael T Somare

Birds of Paradise

The beautiful feathers of the bird of paradise are used for decoration and in cultural and religious ceremonies across Papua New Guinea. A yellow bird of paradise with trailing plumes is shown in flight on the national flag, while the national crest shows a striking crimson and gold bird with spread wings sitting on a ceremonial drum, with a traditional spear behind it.

PARAGUAY

Official name	Republic of Paraguay	**Ethnic groups**	mestizo 92%, white 2%, Amerindian 2%, others 4%
Local name	Paraguay; República del Paraguay		
Independence	1811	**Religions**	Christianity 99% (RC 90%, Prot 9%, mostly Mennonite), others 1%
Area	406 750 sq km/157 000 sq mi		
Capital	Asunción	**Time zone**	GMT –4
Chief towns	Villarrica, Concepción	**Currency**	1 Guaraní (Gs/PYG) = 100 céntimos
Population	6 158 000 (2005e)	**Telephone**	+595
Nationality	Paraguayan	**Internet**	.py
Languages	Spanish, Guaraní	**Country code**	PRY

Location
A republic in central South America, bounded to the north-west by Bolivia; to the north and east by Brazil; and to the south and south-west by Argentina.

Physical description
Divided into two regions by the River Paraguay, lying mostly at altitudes below 450m/ 1476ft; west is mostly cattle country or scrub forest; more fertile in the east; higher Paraná Plateau is mainly wet, treeless savanna; highest point is Cerro Pero (842m/2 762ft).

Climate
Tropical in the north-west, with hot summers and warm winters; temperate in the south-east; temperature at Asunción ranges from 12°C in winter to 35°C in summer.

National holidays
Jan 1, Mar 1 (Battle of Cerro Corá), May 1, 15 (Independence), Jun 12 (Chaco Peace), Aug 15 (Foundation of Asunción), Dec 8, 25; GF, HT.

Political leaders

President

1898–1902	Emilio Aceval	1928–31	José Particio Guggiari
1902	Héctor Carvallo	1931–2	Emiliano González Navero
1902–4	Juan Antonio Escurra	1932	José Particio Guggiari
1904–5	Juan Gaona	1932–6	Eusebio Ayala
1905–6	Cecilio Baez	1936–7	Rafael Franco
1906–8	Benigno Ferreira	1937–9	Félix Paiva
1908–10	Emiliano González Navero	1939–40	José Félix Estigarribia
1910–11	Manuel Gondra	1940–8	Higino Moríñigo
1911	Albino Jara	1948	Juan Manuel Frutos
1911	Liberato Marcial Rojas	1948–9	Juan Natalicio González
1912	Pedro Peña	1949	Raimundo Rolón
1912	Emiliano González Navero	1949	Felipe Molas López
1912–16	Eduardo Schaerer	1949–54	Federico Chaves
1916–19	Manuel Franco	1954	Tomás Romero Pareira
1919–20	José P Montero	1954–89	Alfredo Stroessner
1920–1	Manuel Gondra	1989–93	Andrés Rodríguez
1921	Félix Paiva	1993–8	Juan Carlos Wasmosy
1921–3	Eusebio Ayala	1998–9	Raúl Cubas Grau
1923–4	Eligio Ayala	1999–2003	Luis González Mácchi
1924	Luis Alberto Riart	2003–	Nicanor Duarte Frutos
1924–8	Eligio Ayala		

Pleistocene Peccary

The Chacoan peccary is a hairy, pig-like creature that lives in the Gran Chaco, a vast area of arid scrublands, cacti and thorny vegetation in north-west Paraguay. The Chacoan peccary was thought to be extinct but had been described from fossil records of the Pleistocene period; the creature was discovered alive, to great scientific astonishment, in the 1970s.

PERU

Official name	Republic of Peru	**Ethnic groups**	Quechua 46%, mestizo 34%, white 12%, Aymara 5%, others 3%
Local name	Perú; República del Perú		
Independence	1821	**Religions**	Christianity 96% (RC 89%, Prot 7%), others 4%
Area	1 284 640 sq km/ 495 871 sq mi		
Capital	Lima	**Time zone**	GMT –5
Chief towns	Arequipa, Chiclayo, Cuzco, Trujillo	**Currency**	1 Nuevo Sol (Pes/PEN) = 100 cénts
Population	27 968 000 (2005e)	**Telephone**	+51
Nationality	Peruvian	**Internet**	.pe
Languages	Spanish, Quechua; Aymara is also widely spoken	**Country code**	PER

Location
A republic on the west coast of South America, bounded to the north by Ecuador; to the north-east by Colombia; to the east by Brazil and Bolivia; to the south by Chile; and to the west by the Pacific Ocean.

Physical description
Arid plains and foothills on the coast, with desert areas and fertile river valleys; 50% of the population live on the central sierra, at an average altitude of 3 000m/9 842ft; highest point is Huascarán (6 768m/22 204ft); forested Amazon basin lies to the east; major rivers flow to the Amazon; Lake Titicaca lies on the Bolivian border.

Climate
Mild temperatures on the coast; dry, arid desert in the south; northern coastal region is affected by El Niño; Andean temperatures never rise above 23°C with a large daily range; the climate is typically wet and tropical in the Amazon basin.

National holidays
Jan 1, May 1, Jun 24 (Peasants), 29 (SS Peter and Paul), Jul 28 (Independence) (2), Aug 30 (St Rose of Lima), Oct 8 (Battle of Angamos), Nov 1, Dec 8, 25; GF, HT.

Political leaders

President

1899–1903	Eduardo López de Romaña	1931	David Samanez Ocampo
1903–4	Manuel Candamo	1931–3	Luis M Sánchez Cerro
1904	Serapio Calderón	1933–9	Oscar R Benavides
1904–8	José Pardo y Barreda	1939–45	Manuel Prado
1908–12	Augusto B Leguía	1945–8	José Luis Bustamante y Rivero
1912–14	Guillermo Billinghurst	1948–56	Manuel A Odría
1914–15	Oscar R Benavides	1956–62	Manuel Prado
1915–19	José Pardo y Barreda	1962–3	*Military Junta*
1919–30	Augusto B Leguía	1963–8	Fernando Belaúnde Terry
1930	Manuel Ponce	1968–75	*Military Junta* (Juan Velasco Alvarado)
1930–1	Luis M Sánchez Cerro		
1931	Leoncio Elías	1975–80	*Military Junta* (Francisco Morales Bermúdez)
1931	Gustavo A Jiménez		

1980–5	Fernando Belaúnde Terry	2000–1	Valentín Paniagua *Interim*
1985–90	Alan García Pérez		*President*
1990–2000	Alberto Keinya Fujimori	2001–	Alejandro Toledo Manrique

Prime Minister

1900	Enrique Coronel Zegarra y Cortés	1935–6	Manuel Esteban Rodríguez
1900–1	Domingo M Almenara Butler	1936–9	Ernesto Montagne Markholz
1901–2	Cesáreo Chacaltana Reyes	1939	Alberto Rey de Castro y Romaña
1902	Cesáreo Octavio Deustua Escarza	1939–44	Alfredo Solf y Muro
1902–3	Eugenio Larrabure y Unanue	1944–5	Manuel Cisneros Sánchez
1903–4	José Pardo y Barreda	1945–6	Rafael Belaúnde y Diez Canseco
1904	Alberto Elmore Fernández de	1946–7	Julio Ernesto Portugal Escobedo
	Córdoba	1947	José Alcamora
1904–7	Augusto B Leguía y Salcedo	1948	Roque Augusto Saidías Maninat
1907	Agustín Tovar	1948	Armando Revoredo Iglesias
1907–8	Carlos A Washburn Salas	1948–54	*No Prime Minister*
1908–9	Eulogio Romero Salcedo	1954–6	Roque Augusto Saldías Maninat
1909–10	Rafael Fernández de Villanueva	1956–7	Manuel Cisneros Sánchez
	Cortez	1958–9	Luis Gallo Porras
1910	Javier Prado y Ugarteche	1959–61	Pedro Gerardo Beltrán Espantos
1910	Germán Schreiber Waddington	1961–2	Carlos Moreyra y Paz Soldán
1910	José Salvador Cavero	1962–3	Nicolás Lindley López
1910–11	Enrique C Basadre Stevenson	1963	Julio Óscar Trelles Montes
1911–12	Agustín G Ganoza Cavero	1963–5	Fernando Schwalb López Aldana
1912	Elías Malpartida	1965–7	Daniel Becerra de la Flor
1912–13	Enrique Varela	1967	Edgardo Seoane Corrales
1913	Federico Luna y Peralta	1967–8	Raúl Ferrero Rebagliati
1913	Aurelio Sousa Matute	1968	Oswaldo Hercelles García
1913–14	Enrique Varela	1968	Miguel Mujica Gallo
1914	Pedro E Muñiz	1968–73	Ernesto Montagne Sánchez
1914	Manuel Melitón Carvajal	1973–5	Edgardo Mercado Jarrín
1914	Aurelio Sousa Matute	1975	Francisco Morales Bermúdez
1914–15	Germán Schreiber Waddington	1975–6	Óscar Vargas Prieto
1915	Carlos Isaac Abrill	1976	Jorge Fernández Maldonado
1915–17	Enrique de la Riva-Agüero y Looz		Solari
	Corswaren	1976–8	Guillermo Arbulú Galliani
1917–18	Francisco Tudela y Varela	1978–9	Óscar Molina Pallochia
1918–19	Germán Arenas y Loayza	1979–80	Pedro Richter Prada
1919	Juan Manuel Zuloaga	1980–3	Manuel Ulloa Elías
1919–22	Germán Leguía y Martínez	1983–4	Fernando Schwalb López Aldana
	Jakeway	1984	Sandro Mariátegui Chiappe
1922–4	Julio Enrique Ego Aguirre	1984–5	Luis Pércovich Roca
1924–6	Alejandrino Maguiña	1985–7	Luis Alva Castro
1926–9	Pedro José Rada y Gamio	1987–8	Guillermo Larco Cox
1929–30	Benjamín Huamán de los Heros	1988–9	Armando Villanueva del Campo
1930–1	Fernando Sarmiento	1989	Luis Alberto Sánchez
1931–2	Germán Arenas y Loayza	1989–90	Guillermo Larco Cox
1932	Francisco R Lanatta	1990–1	Juan Carlos Hurtado Miller
1932	Luis A Flores	1991	Carlos Torres y Torres Lara
1932	Ricardo Rivadeneira	1991–2	Alfonso de los Heros
1932–3	José Matías Manzanilla	1992–3	Óscar de la Puente Raygada
	Barrientos	1993–4	Alfonso Bustamante y
1933	Jorge Prado y Ugarteche		Bustamante
1933–4	José de la Riva-Agüero y Osma	1994–5	Efraín Goldenberg Schreiber
1934–5	Carlos Arenas y Loayza	1995–6	Dante Córdova Blanco

1996–8	Alberto Pandolfi	2001	Javier Perez de Cuellar
1998	Javier Valle Riestra	2001–2	Roberto Daniño Zapata
1998–9	Alberto Pandolfi	2002–3	Luis Solari de la Fuente
1999	Víctor Joy Way	2003	Beatriz Merino
1999–2000	Alberto Bustamante Belaúnde	2003–5	Carlos Ferrero Costa
2000	Federico Salas Guevara	2005–	Pedro Pablo Kuczynski

Peruvian Pisco

Peru's national drink is *pisco*, an alcoholic grape liqueur made nowhere else in the world which is named after the Quechua word for 'bird'. Grape vines were introduced to Peru during Spanish colonization of South America in the 16c, but the Peruvians proved so adept at winemaking that worried Spanish vineyards banned the trade. The Peruvian producers therefore switched from wines to liqueurs, using ancient Inca earthenware, and created pisco.

PHILIPPINES

Official name	Republic of the Philippines		many local dialects are also spoken
Local name	Pilipinas; Repúblika Ñg Pilipinas	**Ethnic groups**	Tagalog 30%, Cebuano 23%, Ilocano 9%, Ilongo 9%, Bicol 6%, Samar-Leyte 3%, others 20%
Independence	1946		
Area	299 679 sq km/115 676 sq mi	**Religions**	Christianity 92% (RC 83%, Prot 9%), Islam 5%, others 3%
Capital	Manila		
Chief towns	Quezon City, Basilan, Cebu, Bacolod, Davao, Iloilo	**Time zone**	GMT +8
		Currency	1 Philippine Peso (PHP) = 100 centavos
Population	83 054 000 (2005e)		
Nationality	Filipino (masculine), Filipina (feminine), Philippine	**Telephone**	+63
		Internet	.ph
		Country code	PHL
Languages	Pilipino; English and		

Location
An archipelago republic between the South China Sea to the west and the Pacific Ocean to the east, lying north of Indonesia, west of Vietnam and China; and to the south of Taiwan.

Physical description
More than 7 100 islands and islets; largely mountainous, with north to south ridges rising to over 2 500m/8 200ft; highest point is Mt Apo (2 954m/9 691ft); narrow coastal margins and broad interior plateaux; forests cover half the land area; some islands are ringed by coral reefs.

Climate
Lowlands have a warm and humid tropical climate throughout the year, with an average temperature of 27°C; lying astride the typhoon belt, the Philippines are affected by c.15 cyclonic storms annually.

National holidays
Jan 1, Apr 9 (Araw Ng Kagitingan), May 1, Jun 12 (Independence), Aug 30 (National Heroes), Nov 1, 2, 30 (Bonifacio), Dec 25, 30 (Rizal), 31; GF, HT.

Political leaders

President

1935–44	Manuel L Quezon (*in exile from 1942*)	1957–61	Carlos P Garcia
		1961–5	Diosdado Macapagal
1943–4	José P Laurel (*Japanese occupation*)	1965–86	Ferdinand E Marcos (*Martial law 1972–81*)
1944–6	Sergio Osmeña	1986–92	Corazon C Aquino
1946–8	Manuel A Roxas	1992–8	Fidel V Ramos
1948–53	Elpidio Quirino	1998–2001	Joseph Estrada
1953–7	Ramon Magsaysay	2001–	Gloria Macapagal-Arroyo

Seashells and Volcanoes

The Philippines Department of Tourism proudly reports that 488 of the world's 500 species of coral are found in its waters, along with seven of the eight known species of giant clam, five of the eight species of marine turtle and approximately 12 000 types of seashell. It adds that the province of Camiguin not only has more volcanoes per square kilometre than any other island in the world, but is 'the only place in the Philippines which has more volcanoes (seven) than towns (five)'.

PITCAIRN ISLANDS *see* **UNITED KINGDOM**

POLAND

Official name	Republic of Poland	**Languages**	Polish
Local name	Polska; Rzeczpospolita Polska	**Ethnic groups**	Polish 98%, German 1%, others 1%
Former name	People's Republic of Poland (1952–89)	**Religions**	Christianity 96% (RC 93%, Orthodox 2%, Prot 1%), none/unaffiliated 2%, others 2%
Independence	1918		
Area	312 612 sq km/120 668 sq mi	**Time zone**	GMT +1
Capital	Warsaw; Warszawa	**Currency**	1 Złoty (Zl/PLN) = 100 groszy
Chief towns	Łódz, Kraków, Wrocław, Poznań, Gdańsk, Katowice, Lublin	**Telephone**	+48
		Internet	.pl
Population	38 530 000 (2005e)	**Country code**	POL
Nationality	Pole, Polish		

Location
A republic in central Europe, bounded to the north by the Baltic Sea and Russia; to the north-east by Lithuania and Belarus; to the south-east by Ukraine; to the south by Slovakia; to the south-west by the Czech Republic; and to the west by Germany.

Physical description
Mostly part of the great European plain; mountains in the south rise in the High Tatra to 2 499m/8 199ft at Mt Rysy; Europe's richest coal basin lies in the west (Silesia); lowlands with many lakes in the north.

Climate
Continental climate, with severe winters and hot summers; rain falls chiefly in summer.

National holidays
Jan 1, May 1, 3 (National), Aug 15, Nov 1, 11 (Independence), Dec 25, 26; CC, EM.

Political leaders

Republic of Poland

President

1945–52	Bolesław Bierut *Acting President until 1947*	1972–85	Henryk Jablonski
1952–64	Aleksander Zawadzki	1985–90	Wojciech Jaruzelski
1964–8	Edward Ochab	1990–5	Lech Wałesa
1968–70	Marian Spychalski	1995–	Aleksander Kwaśniewski
1970–2	Józef Cyrankiewicz		

Prime Minister

1947–52	Józef Cyrankiewicz	1991	Jan Krzysztof Bielecki
1952–4	Bolesław Bierut	1991–2	Jan Olszewski
1954–70	Józef Cyrankiewicz	1992	Waldemar Pawlak
1970–80	Piotr Jecoszewicz	1992–3	Hanna Suchocka
1980	Edward Babiuch	1993–5	Waldemar Pawlak
1980–1	Józef Pinkowski	1995–6	Józef Oleksy
1981–5	Wojciech Jaruzelski	1996–7	Wlodzimierz Cimoszewicz
1985–8	Zbigniew Messner	1997–2001	Jerzy Buzek
1988–9	Mieczyslaw Rakowski	2001–4	Leszek Miller
1989	Czeslaw Kiszczak	2004–	Marek Belka
1989–90	Tadeusz Mazowiecki		

First Secretary

1945–8	Władysław Gomułka	1970–80	Edward Gierek
1948–56	Bolesław Bierut	1980–1	Stanisław Kania
1956	Edward Ochab	1981–9	Wojciech Jaruzelski
1956–70	Władysław Gomułka	1989	Mieczyslaw Rakowski

Polish Pines

Forests cover about 27% of Poland, with pine trees the most abundant species.

POLYNESIA, FRENCH *see* **FRANCE**

PORTUGAL

Official name	Portuguese Republic	**Languages**	Portuguese
Local name	Portugal; República Portuguesa	**Ethnic groups**	Portuguese 99%, others 1%
Former name	Kingdom of Portugal (until 1910)	**Religions**	Christianity 96% (RC 94%, Prot 2%), none/unaffiliated 3%, others 1%
Independence	1668		
Area	88 500 sq km/34 200 sq mi	**Time zone**	GMT
Capital	Lisbon; Lisboa	**Currency**	1 Euro (€/EUR) = 100 cents
Chief towns	Oporto, Setúbal, Coimbra	**Telephone**	+351
Population	10 495 000 (2005e)	**Internet**	.pt
Nationality	Portuguese	**Country code**	PRT

Location
A republic in south-western Europe on the western side of the Iberian Peninsula, bounded to the north and east by Spain; and to the south and west by the Atlantic Ocean.

Physical description
Several mountain ranges formed by the west spurs of the Spanish mountain system; chief range is the Serra da Estrêla in the north, rising to 1 991m/6 532ft; highest point is Mt Pico on Ilha do Pico (Pico Island) in the Azores (2 351m/7 713ft).

Climate
Basically a maritime climate, with increased variation between summer and winter temperatures inland; west coast is relatively cool in summer; most rainfall in winter.

National holidays
Jan 1, Apr 25 (Liberty), May 1, Jun 10 (Camões-Portugal), Aug 15, Oct 5 (Republic), Nov 1, Dec 1 (Independence), Dec 8, 24, 25; C, CC, GF.

Azores

Location	An island archipelago of volcanic origin in the North Atlantic ocean, lying 1 400–1 800km/870–1 100mi to the west of the Cabo da Roca on mainland Portugal.		
Area	2 300 sq km/900 sq mi	**Capital**	Ponta Delgada

Madeira

Location	The main island in a Portuguese archipelago off the coast of North Africa, 990km/615mi south-west of Lisbon.		
Area	796 sq km/307 sq mi	**Capital**	Funchal

Political leaders

Monarch

1095–1112	Henry of Burgundy	1245–79	Alfonso III
1112–85	Alfonso I	1279–1325	Diniz
1185–1211	Sancho I	1325–57	Alfonso IV
1211–23	Alfonso II	1357–67	Peter I
1223–45	Sancho II	1367–83	Ferdinand

1383–5	disputed by John of Castile and John of Aviz		1683–1706	Peter II
			1706–50	John V
1385–1433	John I of Aviz		1750–77	Joseph
1433–8	Edward		1777–1816	Maria I
1438–81	Alfonso V		1777–86	Peter III (King Consort)
1481–95	John II		1816–26	John VI
1495–1521	Manuel I		1826	Peter IV (I of Brazil)
1521–57	John III		1826–8	Maria II
1557–78	Sebastian		1828–34	Miguel
1578–80	Henry		1834–53	Maria II
1580–98	Philip I (II of Spain)		1853–61	Peter V
1598–1621	Philip II (III of Spain)		1861–89	Luis
1621–40	Philip III (IV of Spain)		1889–1908	Charles
1640–56	John IV of Braganza		1908–10	Manuel II
1656–83	Alfonso VI			

First Republic

President

1910–11	Teófilo Braga		1918–19	Joâo do Canto e Castro
1911–15	Manuel José de Arriaga		1919–23	António José de Almeida
1915	Teófilo Braga		1923–5	Manuel Teixeira Gomes
1915–17	Bernardino Machado		1925–6	Bernardino Machado
1917–18	Sidónio Pais			

New State

President

1926	Military Junta (José Mendes Cabeçadas)		1926–51	António Oscar Fragoso Carmona
			1951–8	Francisco Craveiro Lopes
1926	Military Junta (Manuel de Oliveira Gomes da Costa)		1958–74	Américo de Deus Tomás

Prime Minister

1932–68	António de Oliveira Salazar
1968–74	Marcelo Caetano

Second Republic

President

1974	Military Junta (António Spínola)
1974–6	Military Junta (Francisco da Costa Gomes)

Prime Minister

1974	Adelino da Palma Carlos
1974–5	Vasco Gonçalves
1975–6	José Pinheiro de Azevedo

Third Republic

President

1976–86	António dos Santos Ramalho Eanes
1986–96	Mário Soares
1996–	Jorge Sampaio

Prime Minister

1976–8	Mário Soares	1983–5	Mário Soares
1978	Alfredo Nobre da Costa	1985–95	Aníbal Cavaço Silva
1978–9	Carlos Alberto de Mota Pinto	1995–2001	António Guterres
1979	Maria de Lurdes Pintasilgo	2002–4	José Manuel Durão Barroso
1980–1	Francisco de Sá Carneiro	2004–5	Pedro Santana Lopes
1981–3	Francisco Pinto Balsemão	2005–	José Sócrates

PRÍNCIPE *see* **SÃO TOMÉ AND PRÍNCIPE**

PUERTO RICO *see* **UNITED STATES OF AMERICA**

QATAR

Official name	State of Qatar	**Ethnic groups**	Arab 40%, Pakistani 18%, Indian 18%, Iranian 10%, others 14%
Local name	Qatar; Dawlat Qatar		
Independence	1971	**Religions**	Islam 95%, others 5%
Area	11 437 sq km/4 415 sq mi	**Time zone**	GMT +3
Capital	Doha; Ad Dawhah	**Currency**	1 Qatari Riyal (QR/QAR) = 100 dirhams
Chief towns	Dukhan, Al Khawr, Umm Sai'd, Al Wakrah		
Population	813 000 (2005e)	**Telephone**	+974
Nationality	Qatari	**Internet**	.qa
Languages	Arabic	**Country code**	QAT

Location
A state on the east coast of the Arabian Peninsula, comprising the Qatar Peninsula and numerous small offshore islands, bounded to the south by Saudi Arabia and the United Arab Emirates, and on all other sides by the Arabian Gulf.

Physical description
The peninsula, 160km/100mi long and 55–80km/34–50mi wide, slopes gently from the Dukhān Heights (98m/322ft) to the east shore; highest point is Qurayn Abu al Bawl (103m/338ft); barren terrain, mainly sand and gravel; coral reefs offshore.

Climate
Desert climate with average temperatures of 23°C in the winter and 35°C in the summer; high humidity; sparse annual rainfall.

National holidays
Sep 3 (Independence), Dec 31; Ad (4), ER (4).

Political leaders

Emir
Family name: al-Thani

1971–2	Ahmad Bin Ali
1972–95	Khalifa Bin Hamad
1995–	Hamad Bin Khalifah

Prime Minister

1971–95	*As emir*
1995–6	*As emir*
1996–	Abdullah Bin Khalifah

RAS AL-KHAIMAH *see* **UNITED ARAB EMIRATES**

REPUBLIC OF CHINA *see* **TAIWAN**

RÉUNION *see* **FRANCE**

ROMANIA

Official name	Romania	**Nationality**	Romanian
Local name	Romănia	**Languages**	Romanian
Former name	Kingdom of Romania (until 1947), People's Republic of Romania (1947–65), Socialist Republic of Romania (1965–89); known as Rumania in English until 1966	**Ethnic groups**	Romanian 89%, Magyar 9%, Romany 1%, others 1%
		Religions	Christianity 94% (Orthodox 82%, RC 6%, Prot 6%), none/unaffiliated 4%, Islam 1%, others 1%
Independence	1878	**Time zone**	GMT +2
Area	237 500 sq km/91 675 sq mi	**Currency**	1 Leu (L/RON) = 100 bani
Capital	Bucharest; Bucureşti	**Telephone**	+40
Chief towns	Braşov, Constanţa, Iaşi, Timişoara, Cluj-Napoca	**Internet**	.ro
		Country code	ROU
Population	21 711 000 (2005e)		

Location
A republic in south-eastern Europe, bounded to the north by Ukraine; to the east by Moldova, Ukraine and the Black Sea; to the south by Bulgaria; and to the west by Serbia and Montenegro and Hungary.

Physical description
Carpathian Mountains separate Old Romania from Transylvania, and form the heart of the country; highest peak is Mt Moldoveanu (2 544m/8 349ft); Romanian Plain in the south includes the richest arable area; over 25% of the land is forested.

Climate
Continental, with cold, snowy winters and warm summers; mildest area in winter is along the Black Sea coast; plains of the north and east can suffer from drought; average rainfall is higher in the mountains than in the Danube delta.

National holidays
Jan 1, 2, May 1, Dec 1 (National), 25, 26; Orthodox Easter (Apr/May) (2); *other major religions each have 2 days for festivals*.

Political leaders

Monarch
1881–1914	Carol I	1930–40	Carol II
1914–27	Ferdinand I	1940–7	Michael I
1927–30	Michael *Prince*		

President
1947–8	Mihai Sadoveanu *Interim President*	1952–8	Petru Groza
1948–52	Constantin I Parhon	1958–61	Ion Georghe Maurer

1961–5	Georghe Gheorghiu-Dej	1996–2000	Emil Constantinescu
1965–7	Chivu Stoica	2000–4	Ion Iliescu
1967–89	Nicolae Ceaușescu	2004–	Traian Basescu
1989–96	Ion Iliescu		

General Secretary

| 1955–65 | Georghe Gheorghiu-Dej | 1965–89 | Nicolae Ceaușescu |

Prime Minister

1900–1	Petre P Carp	1934–7	Gheorghe Tătărescu
1901–6	Dimitrie A Sturdza	1937	Octavian Goga
1906–7	Gheorge Grigore Cantacuzino	1937–9	Miron Cristea
1907–9	Dimitrie A Sturdza	1939	Armand Călinescu
1909	Ionel Brătianu	1939	Gheorghe Argeșanu
1909–10	Mihai Pherekyde	1939	Constantine Argetoianu
1910–11	Ionel Brătianu	1939–40	Gheorghe Tătărescu
1911–12	Petre P Carp	1940	Ion Gigurtu
1912–14	Titu Maiorescu	1940–4	Ion Antonescu
1914–18	Ionel Brătianu	1944	Constantin Savbnătescu
1918	Alexandru Averescu	1944–5	Nicolae Rădescu
1918	Alexandru Marghiloman	1945–52	Petru Groza
1918	Constantin Coandă	1952–5	Gheorghe Gheorghiu-Dej
1918	Ionel Brătianu	1955–61	Chivu Stoica
1919	Artur Văitoianu	1961–74	Ion Gheorghe Maurer
1919–20	Alexandru Vaida-Voevod	1974–80	Manea Mănescu
1920–1	Alexandru Averescu	1980–3	Ilie Verdet
1921–2	Take Ionescu	1983–9	Constantin Dăscălescu
1922–6	Ionel Brătianu	1989–91	Petre Roman
1926–7	Alexandru Averescu	1991–2	Theodor Stolojan
1927	Ionel Brătianu	1992–6	Nicolae Vacaroiu
1927–8	Vintila I C Brătianu	1996–8	Victor Ciorbea
1928–30	Juliu Maniu	1998	Gavril Dejeu *Interim Prime Minister*
1930	Gheorghe C Mironescu	1998–9	Radu Vasile
1930	Juliu Maniu	1999	Alexandru Athanesiu *Interim Prime Minister*
1930–1	Gheorghe C Mironescu		
1931–2	Nicolae Iorga	1999–2000	Mugur Isarescu
1932	Alexandru Vaida-Voevod	2000–4	Adrian Nastase
1932–3	Juliu Maniu	2004	Eugen Bejinariu *Interim Prime Minister*
1933	Alexandru Vaida-Voevod		
1933	Ion G Duca	2004–	Calin Popescu Tariceanu
1933–4	Constantin Angelescu		

Count Dracula's Castle

The classic vampire story *Dracula* (1897) by Bram Stoker is famed for its Transylvanian vampire. Transylvania is a real region of northern and central Romania, separated from the capital by the high Carpathian Mountains. The character of Dracula was inspired by one *Vlad Dracula*, a ruler of Romania in the mid-15c, whose nickname was Vlad the Impaler. Today the area thrives on the Dracula legend, with 'Dracula tours' taking in the real Dracula's birthplace in Sighisoara and his home at Castle Bran.

ROSS DEPENDENCY *see* **NEW ZEALAND**

RUSSIA

Official name	Russian Federation		Novosibirsk, Chelyabinsk, Kazan, Samara, Omsk
Local name	Rossiya; Rossiiskaya Federatsiya	**Population**	143 202 000 (2005e)
Former name	Russian Empire (until 1917), Russian Republic (1917), Russian Socialist Federal Soviet Republic (until 1991), within the Union of Soviet Socialist Republics (USSR; 1922–91)	**Nationality**	Russian
		Languages	Russian
		Ethnic groups	Russian 82%, Tatar 4%, Ukrainian 3%, Chuvash 1%, others 10%
		Religions	Christianity 75% (Orthodox), others including Islam 25%
Independence	1991		
Area	17 075 400 sq km/ 6 591 104 sq mi	**Time zone**	GMT +2/12
		Currency	1 Russian Rouble (R/RUB) = 100 kopeks
Capital	Moscow; Moskva		
Chief towns	St Petersburg, Nizhniy Novgorod, Rostov-on-Don, Volgograd, Yekaterinburg,	**Telephone**	+7
		Internet	.ru
		Country code	RUS

Location
A republic occupying much of eastern Europe and northern Asia, bounded to the north by the Arctic Ocean; to the east by the Sea of Okhotsk and the Bering Sea; to the south-east by North Korea, Mongolia and China; to the south-west by Kazakhstan and the Caspian Sea; to the west by Azerbaijan, Georgia and the Black Sea; and to the north-west by Ukraine, Belarus, Latvia, Estonia, Finland and Norway.

Physical description
Vast plains dominate the western half; Ural Mountains separate the East European Plain in the west from the West Siberian Lowlands in the east; Central Siberian Plateau lies east of the River Yenisei; further east lies the North Siberian Plain; over 20 000 lakes, the largest being the Caspian Sea, Lake Taymyr and Lake Baikal; highest point is Mt Elbrus (5 642m/18 510ft).

Climate
Several different climate regions; variable weather in the north and the centre; winter temperatures are increasingly severe in the east and north; Moscow average temperature is 9°C (Jan) and 18°C (Jul); Siberia has a continental climate, with very cold and prolonged winters and short, often warm summers.

National holidays
Jan 1, 2, 7 (Russian Orthodox Christmas), Feb 23 (Soldiers), Mar 8 (Women), May 1 (Spring and Labour) (2), 9 (Victory), Jun 12 (Independence), Aug 22 (Flag), Nov 7 (Accord and Conciliation), Dec 12 (Constitution); Russian Orthodox Easter (Apr/May).

Political leaders

Monarch (Tsar)

1283–1303	Daniel	1389–1425	Vasili I
1303–25	Yuri	1425–62	Vasili II
1325–41	Ivan I	1462–1505	Ivan III (the Great)
1341–53	Semeon	1505–33	Vasili III
1353–9	Ivan II	1533–84	Ivan IV (the Terrible)
1359–89	Dimitri Donskoy	1584–98	Feodor I

1598–1605	Boris Godunov	1727–30	Peter II
1605	Feodor II	1730–40	Anne
1605–6	Dimitri II	1740–1	Ivan VI
1606–10	Vasili IV Shuisky	1741–62	Elizabeth
1610–13	*no Tsar*	1762	Peter III
1613–45	Michael Romanov	1762–96	Catherine II (the Great)
1645–76	Alexei	1796–1801	Paul
1676–82	Feodor III	1801–25	Alexander I
1682–96	Ivan V *joint Tsar*	1825–55	Nicholas I
1682–1725	Peter I (the Great) *joint Tsar until 1696*	1855–81	Alexander II
		1881–94	Alexander III
1725–7	Catherine I	1894–1917	Nicholas II

See separate entry for the **USSR** for the period 1917–91.

President
1991–9	Boris Yeltsin
2000–	Vladimir Putin

Prime Minister
1991–2	Boris Yeltsin	1998–9	Yevgeny Primakov
1992	Yegor Gaidar *Acting Prime Minister*	1999	Sergei Stepashin
1992–8	Viktor Chernomyrdin	1999–2000	Vladimir Putin
1998	Sergei Kiriyenko	2000–4	Mikhail Kasyanov
1998	Viktor Chernomyrdin *Acting Prime Minister*	2004	Viktor Khristenko
		2004–	Mikhael Fradkov

White, Blue and Red

Russia has had several flags – the Tsar's flag in the 19c, the Soviet flag and the current white, blue and red striped flag. The latter flag was first used in 1705 by Peter the Great, was used several times in the intervening centuries, and finally officially declared to be the modern Russian flag in 1993.

RWANDA

Official name	Republic of Rwanda		Kinyarwanda; Swahili is widely used in commerce
Local name	Rwanda; République Rwandaise, Republika y'u Rwanda	**Ethnic groups**	Hutu 90%, Tutsi 9%, others 1%
Former name	Ruanda, as part of Ruanda-Urundi (with Burundi, until 1962)	**Religions**	Christianity 74% (RC 65%, Prot 9%), Islam 1%, traditional beliefs and others 25%
Independence	1962		
Area	26 338 sq km/10 166 sq mi	**Time zone**	GMT +2
Capital	Kigali	**Currency**	1 Rwanda Franc (RF, RWFr/RWF) = 100 centimes
Chief towns	Butare, Ruhengeri		
Population	9 038 000 (2005e)	**Telephone**	+250
Nationality	Rwandan	**Internet**	.rw
Languages	English, French,	**Country code**	RWA

Location
A republic in central Africa, bounded to the north by Uganda; to the east by Tanzania; to the south by Burundi; and to the west by Democratic Republic of the Congo and Lake Kivu.

Physical description
Situated at a relatively high altitude; highest point is Karisimbi volcano (4 507m/14 787ft) in the Virunga range; western third of the country drains into Lake Kivu and then the River Congo, remainder drains towards the River Nile; many lakes.

Climate
A highland tropical climate; the two wet seasons run from Oct to Dec and Mar to May, with the highest rainfall in the west, decreasing in the central uplands and to the north and east.

National holidays
Jan 1, 28 (Democracy), May 1, Jul 1 (Independence), 5 (Peace), Aug 1 (Harvest), 15, Sep 25 (Referendum), Oct 26 (Armed Forces), Nov 1, Dec 25; A, EM, WM.

Political leaders

President

1962–73	Grégoire Kayibanda	1994–2000	Pasteur Bizimungu
1973–94	Juvénal Habyarimana	2000–	Paul Kagame
1994	Theodore Sindikubgabo *Interim President*		

Prime Minister

1991–2	Sylvestre Nsanzimana	1994–5	Faustin Twagiramungu
1992–4	Dismas Nsengiyaremye	1995–2000	Pierre-Célestin Rwigyema
1994	Jean Kambanda *Acting Prime Minister*	2000–	Bernard Makuza

SAHARA, WESTERN *see* **WESTERN SAHARA**

ST HELENA *see* **UNITED KINGDOM**

ST KITTS AND NEVIS

Official name	Federation of St Kitts and Nevis; also known as St Christopher and Nevis	**Ethnic groups**	black 93%, mulatto 4%, white 1%, others 2%
Local name	St Kitts and Nevis	**Religions**	Christianity 78% (Prot 71%, RC 7%), others 22%
Independence	1983		
Area	269 sq km/104 sq mi	**Time zone**	GMT –4
Capital	Basseterre	**Currency**	1 East Caribbean Dollar (EC$/XCD) = 100 cents
Population	43 000 (2005e)		
Nationality	Kittitian, Nevisian	**Telephone**	+1 869
Languages	English	**Internet**	.kn
		Country code	KNA

Location
An independent state comprising the islands of St Kitts and Nevis in the North Leeward Islands, in the eastern Caribbean Sea.

Physical description
St Kitts is 37km/23mi long and has an area of 168 sq km/65 sq mi; a mountain range rises to 1 156m/3 793ft at Mt Liamuiga; Nevis, 3km/2mi south-east, has an area of 93 sq km/36 sq mi and is dominated by a central peak rising to 985m/3 232ft.

Climate
Warm, with an average annual temperature of 26°C; low humidity; subject to hurricanes.

National holidays
Jan 1, 2, Sep 19 (Independence), Dec 25, 26; EM, GF, WM, Labour (May), August Monday (Aug).

Political leaders

Head of State: British monarch, represented by Governor General (Sir Cuthbert Sebastian since 1996).

Prime Minister
1983–95	Kennedy A Simmonds
1995–	Denzil Douglas

Nelson on Nevis

Lord Horatio Nelson (1758–1805), the British admiral, is popularly known for his exploits in naval battles in Europe. However, he spent much of his early career with the British navy in the Caribbean, and it was on Nevis that he met and married Frances Nisbet (1761–1831). Today there is a Nelson Museum on Nevis, which boasts 'the largest collection of Nelson memorabilia in the Americas'.

ST LUCIA

Official name	St Lucia	**Ethnic groups**	black 90%, mixed 6%, East Indian 3%, white 1%
Local name	St Lucia		
Area	616 sq km/238 sq mi	**Religions**	Christianity 100% (RC 90%, Prot 10%)
Independence	1979		
Capital	Castries	**Time zone**	GMT –4
Chief towns	Vieux Fort, Soufrière	**Currency**	1 East Caribbean Dollar (EC$/XCD) = 100 cents
Population	161 000 (2005e)		
Nationality	St Lucian	**Telephone**	+1 758
Languages	English; French patois is also spoken	**Internet**	.lc
		Country code	LCA

Location
An independent country in the Windward Islands, in the eastern Caribbean Sea north of South America.

Physical description
The island is 43km/27mi long and 23km/14mi wide; mountainous centre, rising to 950m/3 117ft at Mt Gimie; twin volcanic peaks of Gros and Petit Piton rise steeply from the sea on the south-west coast of the island.

Climate
Tropical; annual temperatures range from 18°C to 34°C; wet season is Jun–Dec.

National holidays
Jan 1, 2, Feb 22 (Independence), May 1, Dec 13 (National), Dec 25, 26; Emancipation (Aug).

Political leaders

Head of State: British monarch, represented by Governor General (Dame Pearlette Louisy since 1997).

Prime Minister

1979	John Compton	1983–96	John Compton
1979–81	Allan Louisy	1996–7	Vaughan Lewis
1981–3	Winston Francis Cenac	1997–	Kenny Anthony

Saints and Iguanas

The Arawak Indians and Caribs were the first inhabitants of St Lucia, and knew the island as *Ioüanalao* and *Hewanorra*, meaning 'place where the iguana is found'. The island was renamed St Lucia by explorers in the late 16c, probably because it was first sighted on St Lucia's day (13 Dec).

ST PIERRE AND MIQUELON *see* **FRANCE**

ST VINCENT AND THE GRENADINES

Official name	St Vincent and the Grenadines	**Ethnic groups**	black 81%, mixed 15%, others 4%
Local name	St Vincent and the Grenadines	**Religions**	Christianity 81% (Prot 62%, RC 19%), others 19%
Independence	1979		
Area	390 sq km/150 sq mi	**Time zone**	GMT –4
Capital	Kingstown	**Currency**	1 East Caribbean Dollar (EC$/XCD) = 100 cents
Population	119 000 (2005e)		
Nationality	St Vincentian or Vincentian	**Telephone**	+1 784
		Internet	.vc
Languages	English; French patois is also spoken	**Country code**	VCT

Location
An island country in the Windward Islands, situated in the eastern Caribbean Sea north of South America.

Physical description
Comprises the island of St Vincent (length 29km/18mi; width 16km/10mi) and the northern Grenadine Islands; St Vincent is volcanic in origin; highest peak is Soufrière, an active volcano rising to a height of 1 234m/4 049ft.

Climate
Tropical, with an average annual temperature of 25°C.

National holidays
Jan 1, Mar 14 (National Heroes), May 1, Oct 27 (Independence), Dec 25, 26; C (Jul), EM, GF, WM, Caricom (Jul), Emancipation (Aug).

Political leaders

Head of State: British monarch, represented by Governor General (Sir Frederick Ballantyne since 2002).

Prime Minister

1979–84	Milton Cato	2000–1	Arnhim Eustace
1984–2000	James Fitz-Allen Mitchell	2001–	Ralph Gonsalves

SAMOA

Official name	Independent State of Samoa	**Languages**	Samoan, English
Local name	Samoa; 'O la Malo Tu To'atasi o Samoa	**Ethnic groups**	Samoan 92.6%, mixed 7%, European 0.4%
Former name	Western Samoa (until 1997)	**Religions**	Christianity 100%
		Time zone	GMT −11
Independence	1962	**Currency**	1 Tala (ST$/WST) = 100 sene
Area	2 842 sq km/1 097 sq mi		
Capital	Apia	**Telephone**	+685
		Internet	.ws
Population	185 000 (2005e)	**Country code**	WSM
Nationality	Samoan		

Location
An island state in the south-west Pacific Ocean, 2 600km/1 600mi north-east of Auckland, New Zealand.

Physical description
Formed from ranges of mainly extinct volcanoes; many dormant volcanoes (last activity was between 1905 and 1911); highest point is Mt Silisili (1 857m/6 092ft); thick tropical vegetation; several coral reefs along the coast.

Climate
Tropical; rainy season is Dec–Apr; average annual temperatures are 22–30°C; hurricanes occur.

National holidays
Jan 1, May 12 (Anzac), Jun 1 (Mothers of Samoa), Aug 4 (Labour), Oct 12 (White Sunday) (2), Nov 7 (Arbor), Dec 25, 26; EM, GF.

Political leaders

President
1962–3	Tupua Tamesehe Mea'ole *and* Malietoa Tanumafili II *Joint Presidents*
1963–	Malietoa Tanumafili II

Prime Minister
1962–1970	Fiame Mata'afa Faumuina Mulinu'u II	1982	Tupuola Taisi Efi
		1982–6	Tofilau Eti Alesana
1970–6	Tupua Tamasese Leolofi IV	1986–8	Va'ai Kolone
1976–82	Tupuola Taisi Efi	1988–98	Tofilau Eti Alesana
1982	Va'ai Kolone	1998–	Tuilaepa Sailele Malielegaoi

SAMOA, AMERICAN *see* **UNITED STATES OF AMERICA**

SANDWICH ISLANDS, SOUTH *see* **UNITED KINGDOM**

SAN MARINO

Official name	Republic of San Marino		Italian 11%, others 1%
Local name	San Marino; Repubblica di San Marino	**Religions**	Christianity 93% (RC), others and none/ unaffiliated 7%
Area	61 sq km/24 sq mi		
Capital	San Marino	**Time zone**	GMT +1
Chief towns	Serravalle	**Currency**	1 Euro (€/EUR) = 100 cents
Population	28 000 (2005e)		
Nationality	Sammarinese	**Telephone**	+378
Languages	Italian	**Internet**	.sm
Ethnic groups	Sammarinese 88%,	**Country code**	SMR

Location
A republic completely surrounded by eastern central Italy, lying 12mi/20km from the Adriatic Sea.

Physical description
Ruggedly mountainous, centred on the limestone ridges of Mt Titano (755m/2 477ft) and the valley of the River Ausa.

Climate
Temperate climate, with cool winters and warm summers (20–30°C); rainfall is moderate.

National holidays
Jan 1, 6, Feb 5 (Liberation and St Agatha), Mar 25 (Arengo), Apr 1 (Captain Regents' Ceremony), May 1, Jul 28 (Fall of Fascism), Aug 15, Sep 3 (San Marino and Republic), Oct 1 (Investiture of the New Captains Regent), Nov 1, 2 (Commemoration of the Dead), Dec 8, 25, 26.

Political leaders

Regent

Heads of state are two *capitani reggenti* or 'Captain Regents' appointed every 6 months.

SÃO TOMÉ AND PRÍNCIPE

Official name	Democratic Republic of São Tomé and Príncipe	**Ethnic groups**	black 90%, Portuguese and Creole 10%
Local name	São Tomé e Príncipe; República Democrática de São Tomé e Príncipe	**Religions**	Christianity 90% (RC 80%, Prot 5%, others 5%), others 10%
Independence	1975	**Time zone**	GMT
Area	1 001 sq km/386 sq mi	**Currency**	1 Dobra (Db/STD) = 100 céntimos
Capital	São Tomé		
Chief towns	Santo António	**Telephone**	+239
Population	157 000 (2005e)	**Internet**	.st
Nationality	São Toméan, Santoméan	**Country code**	STP
Languages	Portuguese		

Location
An island republic in the Gulf of Guinea, off West Africa; São Tomé lies c.440km/275mi and Príncipe c.200km/125mi off the north coast of Gabon.

Physical description
Volcanic islands, heavily forested; São Tomé has an area of 860 sq km/332 sq mi and reaches a height of 2 024m/6 640ft at Pico de São Tomé; Príncipe, the smaller of the two islands, covers 140 sq km/54 sq mi and has similar terrain.

Climate
Tropical; average annual temperature is 27°C on the coast, 20°C in the mountains; rainy season from Oct to May.

National holidays
Jan 1, Feb 3 (Liberty Heroes), May 1, Jul 12 (National Independence), Sep 6 (Armed Forces), 30 (Agricultural Reform), Dec 21 (Power of the People), 25 (Family).

Political leaders

President
1975–91	Manuel Pinto da Costa
1991–2001	Miguel Trovoada
2001–	Fradique de Menezes

Prime Minister
1974–5	Leonel Maria d'Alva	1995–6	Armindo Vaz d'Almeida
1975–8	Miguel Trovoada	1996–9	Raul Bragança
1978–88	*No Prime Minister*	1999–2002	Guilherme Posser da Costa
1988–91	Celestino Rocha da Costa	2002	Gabriel Costa
1991–2	Daniel Lima dos Santos Daio	2002–4	Maria das Neves
1992–4	Norberto José d'Alva Costa Alegre	2004–5	Damião Vaz d'Almeida
1994	Evaristo Carvalho	2005–	Maria do Carmo Silveira
1994–5	Carlos da Graça		

Saints and Princes

Portuguese explorers arrived in São Tomé on 21 Dec 1470, St Thomas's day – hence the name *São Tomé*, or St Thomas. They named the smaller island nearby *Príncipe* – 'prince' – after a member of the Portuguese royal family.

SAUDI ARABIA

Official name	Kingdom of Saudi Arabia	**Ethnic groups**	Arab 90%, Afro-Asian 10%
Local name	Al-Mamlaka al-'Arabiyya as-Sa'ūdiyya	**Religions**	Islam 99% (mostly Sunni), Christianity and others 1%
Area	2 331 000 sq km/ 899 766 sq mi	**Time zone**	GMT +3
Capital	Riyadh; Ar Riyād	**Currency**	1 Saudi Riyal (SR, SRIs/SAR) = 20 qursh = 100 halala
Chief towns	Jeddah, Mecca, Medina, Ta'if, Ad Dammam, Abha		
Population	24 573 000 (2005e)	**Telephone**	+966
Nationality	Saudi or Saudi Arabian	**Internet**	.sa
Languages	Arabic	**Country code**	SAU

Location
A kingdom comprising about four-fifths of the Arabian Peninsula, bounded to the north-west by Jordan; to the north by Iraq; to the north-east by Kuwait; to the east by the Arabian Gulf, Qatar and the United Arab Emirates, and Bahrain to which it is connected by a causeway; to the south-east by Oman; to the south-west by Yemen; and to the west by the Red Sea.

Physical description
Red Sea coastal plain is bounded to the east by mountains; south-west highlands include Jabal Sawda', the highest peak (3 133m/10 278ft); Arabian Peninsula slopes north and east to the oil-rich Al Hasa plain on the Arabian Gulf; large areas of sand desert in the interior; numerous salt flats in the eastern lowlands.

Climate
Hot and dry, with average temperatures from 21°C (north) to 26°C (south); day temperatures may rise to 50°C in the interior deserts; night frosts are common in the north and highlands; Red Sea coast is hot and humid; average rainfall is low.

National holidays
Sep 23 (National); Ad (4), ER (3).

Political leaders

Monarch
Family name: al-Saud

1932–53	Abdulaziz Bin Abdur-Rahman	1996	Abdullah Bin Abdulaziz *Acting Monarch*
1953–64	Saud Bin Abdulaziz		
1964–75	Faisal Bin Abdulaziz	1996–2005	Fahd Bin Abdulaziz
1975–82	Khalid Bin Abdulaziz	2005–	Abdullah Bin Abdulaziz
1982–96	Fahd Bin Abdulaziz		

Heart of Islam

Saudi Arabia is famed as the birthplace of Islam. The holy cities of Mecca, the birthplace of Muhammad, and Medina, where his tomb lies, are both in Saudi Arabia. The Saudi king traditionally holds the title 'Custodian of the Two Holy Mosques' in recognition of the country's role in protecting and supporting the holy shrines there.

SCOTLAND *see* **UNITED KINGDOM**

SENEGAL

Official name	Republic of Senegal	**Nationality**	Senegalese
Local name	Sénégal; République du Sénégal	**Languages**	French, Wolof
		Ethnic groups	Wolof 43%, Fulani 24%, Serer 15%, Diola 4%, others 14%
Former name	part of the Federation of Mali (1959–60); Senegambia (with The Gambia, 1982–9)	**Religions**	Islam 92% (Sunni), traditional beliefs 6%, Christianity 2% (RC)
Independence	1960		
Area	196 840 sq km/75 980 sq mi	**Time zone**	GMT
		Currency	1 CFA Franc (CFAFr/XOF) = 100 centimes
Capital	Dakar		
Chief towns	Thiès, Kaolack, St Louis, Ziguinchor	**Telephone**	+221
		Internet	.sn
Population	11 658 000 (2005e)	**Country code**	SEN

Location
A republic in West Africa, bounded to the north by Mauritania; to the east by Mali; to the south by Guinea and Guinea-Bissau; and to the west by the Atlantic Ocean; it surrounds The Gambia on three sides.

Physical description
Most westerly country in mainland Africa; coast is characterized by dunes, mangrove forests and mudbanks; extensive low-lying basin of savanna and semi-desert vegetation lies to the north; south rises to c.500m/1 640ft.

Climate
Tropical with a rainy season Jun–Sep; high humidity levels and high night-time temperatures, especially on the coast; rainfall decreases from the south to the north; average temperature at Dakar ranges from 22°C to 28°C.

National holidays
Jan 1, Feb 1 (Senegambia), Apr 4 (National), May 1, Aug 15, Nov 1, Dec 25; Ad, EM, ER, NY (Muslim), PB, WM.

Political leaders

President

1960–80	Léopold Sédar Senghor	2000–	Abdoulaye Wade
1981–2000	Abdou Diouf		

Prime Minister

1958–62	Mamadou Dia	1991–8	Habib Thiam
1962–70	*No Prime Minister*	1998–2000	Mamadou Lamine Loum
1970–80	Abdou Diouf	2000–1	Moustapha Niasse
1981–3	Habib Thiam	2001–2	Madior Boye
1983	Moustapha Niasse *Interim Prime Minister*	2002–4	Idrissa Seck
		2004–	Cherif Macky Sall
1983–91	*No Prime Minister*		

SERBIA AND MONTENEGRO

Official name	Serbia and Montenegro	**Nationality**	Serbian, Montenegrin
Local name	Srbija i Crna Gora	**Languages**	Serbo-Croat
Former name	Kingdom of Serbs, Croats and Slovenes (until 1929), Kingdom of Yugoslavia (1929–41), Federal People's Republic of Yugoslavia (1945–63), Socialist Federal Republic of Yugoslavia (1963–92), Federal Republic of Yugoslavia (until 2003)	**Ethnic groups**	Serb 62%, Albanian 17%, Montenegrin 5%, Magyar 3%, others 13%
		Religions	Christianity 70% (Orthodox 65%, RC 4%, Prot 1%), Islam 19%, others 11%
		Time zone	GMT +1
Area	256 409 sq km/98 974 sq mi	**Currency**	1 Serbian Dinar (D, Din/CSD) = 100 paras (Serbia); 1 Euro (€/EUR) = 100 cents (Montenegro)
Capital	Belgrade; Beograd		
Chief towns	Priština, Subotica	**Telephone**	+381
Population	10 503 000 (2005e)	**Internet**	.yu
		Country code	YUG

Location
A federal union in south-eastern Europe, bounded to the north by Hungary; to the north-east by Romania; to the east by Bulgaria; to the south by Macedonia and Albania; to the south-east by the Adriatic Sea; and to the west by Bosnia and Herzegovina and Croatia.

Physical description
Dominated in the north by the Danube and other rivers; fertile plains in the north-east; drained in the centre by the River Morava; southern ranges cut by deep river valleys; several great lakes in the south; highest point is Daravica (2 656m/8 714ft).

Climate
Mediterranean climate on the Adriatic coast; continental climate in the north and north-east; rain falls throughout the year; colder upland climate, with winter snow.

National holidays
Jan 1, 2, 7 (Orthodox Christmas), Feb 15 (National) (Serbia), Apr 27 (Constitution), May 1 (2), 9 (Victory), Jul 13 (Uprising) (Montenegro); Orthodox Easter (Apr/May) (4).

Political leaders

Kingdom of Yugoslavia

Monarch
1921–34   Aleksandar II
1934–45   Petar II (*in exile from* 1941)

Republic[1]

Chairman
1945–53   Ivan Ribar

President
1953–80   Josip Broz Tito

[1] *See Former names above for exact country names.*

Collective Presidency

1980	Lazar Koliševski	1987–8	Lazar Mojsov
1980–1	Cvijetin Mijatović	1988–9	Raif Dizdarević
1981–2	Serghei Kraigher	1989–90	Janez Drnovšek
1982–3	Petar Stambolić	1990–1	Borisav Jovic
1983–4	Mika Spiljak	1991	*vacant*
1984–5	Veselin Đuranović	1991	Stjepan Mesić
1985–6	Radovan Vlajković	1991–2	Branko Kostic *Acting President*
1986–7	Sinan Hasani		

Prime Minister

1929–32	Pear Živkovic	1934–5	Bogoljub Jevtić
1932	Vojislav Marinković	1935–9	Milan Stojadinović
1932–4	Milan Srškić	1939–41	Dragiša Cvetković
1934	Nikola Uzunović	1941–2	Dušan Simović

Prime Minister of government-in-exile

1942–3	Slobodan Jovanović	1944–5	Ivan Šubašić
1943	Miloš Irifunović	1945	Drago Marušić
1943–4	Božidar Purić		

Prime Minister/Premier

1941–4	Milan Nedić	1977–82	Veselin Đuranović
1943–63	Josip Broz Tito	1982–6	Milka Planinc
1963–7	Petar Stambolić	1986–9	Branko Mikulić
1967–9	Mika Špiljak	1989–91	Ante Marković
1969–71	Mitja Ribičič	1992	Aleksandar Mitrovic *Acting Prime*
1971–7	Džemal Bijedić		*Minister*

Communist Party

Secretary-General

1937–52	Josip Broz Tito

League of Communists

Secretary-General

1952–63	Josip Broz Tito

President of the Central Committee

1963–80	Josip Broz Tito	1984–5	Ali Sukrija
1979–80	Stevan Doronjski *Acting President*	1985–6	Vidoje Žarkovic
1980–1	Lazar Mojsov	1986–7	Milanko Renovica
1981–2	Dušan Dragosavac	1987–8	Boško Krunić
1982–3	Mitja Ribičič	1988–9	Stipe Suvar
1983–4	Dragoslav Marković	1989–90	Milan Pancevski

Federal Republic of Yugoslavia

President

1992–3	Dobrica Cosic	1997	Srdja Bozovic *Acting President*
1993	Milos Radulovic *Acting President*	1997–2000	Slobodan Milosevic
1993–7	Zoran Lilic	2000–3	Vojislav Kostunica

Prime Minister

1992–3	Milan Panic		2000–1	Zoran Zizic
1993–8	Radoje Kontic		2001–3	Dragisa Pesic
1998–2000	Momir Bulatovic			

Serbia and Montenegro

President
2003–   Svetozar Marović

Serbia

President

1992–7	Slobodan Milosevic		2004	Dragan Maršićanin *Acting President*
1997	Dragan Tomic *Acting President*		2004	Vojislav Mihailović *Acting President*
1997–2002	Milan Milutinovic		2004	Predrag Marković *Acting President*
2002–4	Nataša Mićić *Acting President*		2004–	Boris Tadić

Montenegro

President

1991–8	Momir Bulatovic		2002–	Filip Vujanović *Acting President until 2003*
1998–2002	Milo Djukanovic			

SEYCHELLES

Official name	Republic of Seychelles	**Ethnic groups**	mulatto 94%, Malagasy 3%, Chinese 2%, English 1%
Local name	Seychelles; République des Seychelles (French), Repiblik Sesel (Creole)	**Religions**	Christianity 98% (RC 90%, Prot 8%), others (including Hinduism) 2%
Independence	1976		
Area	453 sq km/175 sq mi	**Time zone**	GMT +4
Capital	Victoria	**Currency**	1 Seychelles Rupee (SR/SCR) = 100 cents
Population	81 000 (2005e)		
Nationality	Seychellois	**Telephone**	+248
Languages	Creole; French and English are spoken	**Internet**	.sc
		Country code	SYC

Location
An island group in the south-west Indian Ocean, north of Madagascar.

Physical description
Comprises 115 islands in two main groups; first, a compact group of 41 steep granitic islands, are mountainous, rising to 905m/2 969ft at Morne Seychellois on Mahé; steep forest-clad slopes; coastal lowlands of grass and dense scrub; second group are low-lying coralline islands and atolls situated to the south-west.

Climate
Tropical with a rainfall that varies with altitude and is higher on the southern sides of the islands; wettest months are Nov to Mar; rarely affected by tropical storms.

National holidays
Jan 1, 2, May 1, Jun 5 (Liberation), 18 (National), 29 (Independence), Aug 15, Nov 1, Dec 8, 25; CC, GF, HS.

Political leaders

President

1976–7	James R Mancham
1977–2004	France-Albert René
2004–	James Michel

SHARJAH *see* **UNITED ARAB EMIRATES**

SIERRA LEONE

Official name	Republic of Sierra Leone	**Ethnic groups**	Mende 35%, Temne 32%, Limba 8%, Kuranko 4%, others 21%
Local name	Sierra Leone		
Independence	1961	**Religions**	traditional beliefs 52%, Islam 39% (Sunni), Christianity 9%
Area	72 325 sq km/27 917 sq mi		
Capital	Freetown	**Time zone**	GMT
Chief towns	Bo, Sefadu, Makeni, Kenema, Lunsar	**Currency**	1 Leone (Le/SLL) = 100 cents
Population	5 525 000 (2005e)	**Telephone**	+232
Nationality	Sierra Leonean	**Internet**	.sl
Languages	English, Mende, Temnel; Krio (a Creole language) is also widely spoken	**Country code**	SLE

Location
A republic in West Africa, bounded to the north by Guinea; to the south-east by Liberia; and to the south and south-west by the Atlantic Ocean.

Physical description
A low, narrow coastal plain; western half rises to an average height of 500m/1 640ft in the Loma Mountains; highest point is Loma Mansa (also called Bintimani; 1 948m/6 391ft); Tingi Mountains in the south-east rise to 1 853m/6 079ft.

Climate
Equatorial, with a rainy season from May to Oct; highest rainfall is on the coast; temperatures are uniformly high throughout the year, c.27°C.

National holidays
Jan 1, Apr 19 (Republic), Apr 27 (Independence), Dec 25, 26; Ad, EM, ER, GF, PB.

Political leaders

President

1971	Christopher Okero Cole	1996–7	Ahmad Tejan Kabbah
1971–85	Siaka Stevens	1997	*Military coup*
1985–92	Joseph Saidu Momoh	1997	Johnny Paul Koroma
1992–6	Valentine Strasser	1998–	Ahmad Tejan Kabbah

Prime Minister

1961–4	Milton Margai	1967	Siaka Stevens
1964–7	Albert Michael Margai	1967	David Lansana

1967	Ambrose Genda	1968–71	Siaka Stevens
1967–8	*National Reformation Council*	1971–5	Sorie Ibrahim Koroma
	(Andrew Saxon-Smith)	1975–8	Christian Alusine Kamara Taylor
1968	John Bangura	1978–	*No Prime Minister*

SINGAPORE

Official name	Republic of Singapore		(Mandarin), Malay, Tamil; other Chinese dialects are also spoken
Local name	Singapore; Repablik Singapura (Malay), Singapur Kuṭiyara'su (Tamil), Xinjiapo Gongheguo (Chinese)	**Ethnic groups**	Chinese 76%, Malay 15%, Indian 7%, others 2%
Former name	part of Straits Settlement (until 1942), State of Singapore (1959–63), part of the Federation of Malaysia (1963–65)	**Religions**	Buddhism 28%, traditional beliefs 21%, none/unaffiliated 17%, Islam 16%, Taoism 13%, Hinduism 5%
Independence	1965	**Time zone**	GMT +8
Area	618 sq km/238 sq mi	**Currency**	1 Singapore Dollar (S$/SGD) = 1 Ringgit = 100 cents
Capital	Singapore; Singapura (Malay), Singapur (Tamil), Xinjiapo (Chinese)		
		Telephone	+65
Population	4 326 000 (2005e)	**Internet**	.sg
Nationality	Singaporean, Singapore	**Country code**	SGP
Languages	English, Chinese		

Location
A republic at the southern tip of the Malay Peninsula, south-east Asia, comprising the island of Singapore (linked to Malaysia in the north by a causeway) and about 50 adjacent islets.

Physical description
Singapore Island measures c.42km/26mi by 22km/14mi at its widest; low-lying; highest point is Bukit Timah (177m/581ft); important deep-water harbour lies to the south-east.

Climate
Equatorial, with high humidity, and a daily temperature range from 21°C to 34°C.

National holidays
Jan 1, May 1, Aug 9 (National), Dec 25; Ad, D, ER, GF, NY (Chinese) (Jan/Feb) (2), Vesak.

Political leaders

President (Yang di-Pertuan Negara)
1959–70	Yusof bin Ishak	1985–93	Wee Kim Wee
1970–81	Benjamin Henry Sheares	1993–9	Ong Teng Cheong
1981–5	Chengara Veetil Devan Nair	1999–	Sellapan Ramanathan Nathan

Prime Minister
1959–90	Lee Kuan Yew
1990–2004	Goh Chok Tong
2004–	Lee Hsien Loong

SLOVAKIA

Official name	Republic of Slovakia or the Slovak Republic	**Languages**	Slovak
Local name	Slovensko; Slovenská Republika	**Ethnic groups**	Slovak 86%, Magyar 11%, Romany 2%, others 1%
Former name	formerly part of Czechoslovakia (until 1993)	**Religions**	Christianity 69% (RC 59%, Prot 6%, Orthodox 4%), none/unaffiliated 31%
Independence	1993		
Area	49 035 sq km/18 927 sq mi	**Time zone**	GMT +1
		Currency	1 Slovak Koruna (Sk/SKK) = 100 halierov
Capital	Bratislava		
Chief towns	Košice, Banská Bystrica, Prešov	**Telephone**	+421
		Internet	.sk
Population	5 401 000 (2005e)	**Country code**	SVK
Nationality	Slovak		

Location
A republic in eastern Europe, bounded to the north by Poland; to the east by Ukraine; to the south by Hungary; to the south-west by Austria; and to the west by the Czech Republic.

Physical description
Lowlands in the south; Tatra Mountains in the north rise to 2 655m/8 710ft at Gerlachovsky Stit, Slovakia's highest point.

Climate
Continental; hot in summer, cold in winter.

National holidays
Jan 1 (New Year/Establishment of Republic), 6, May 1, 8 (Triumph over Fascism), Jul 5 (SS Cyril and Methodius), Aug 29 (Slovak National Uprising), Sep 1 (Constitution), 15 (Our Lady of the Seven Sorrows), Nov 1, Dec 24, 25, 26; GF, EM.

Political leaders

See entry for **Czech Republic** for political leaders prior to 1993.

President

1993–8	Michal Kovác	1999–2004	Rudolf Schuster
1998–9	*No President*	2004–	Ivan Gašparovič

Prime Minister

1993–4	Vladimír Mečiar	1994–8	Vladimír Mečiar
1994	Jozef Moravčik	1998–	Mikuláš Dzurinda

Thunder and Lightning

Slovakia's mighty Tatra mountains are commemorated in its national anthem, *Nad Tatrou sa blýska*, meaning 'Lightning over the Tatras'. It speaks of the lightning over the mountains and the roar of thunder reawakening the spirit of the Slovak people.

SLOVENIA

Official name	Republic of Slovenia		Koper
Local name	Slovenija; Republika Slovenija	**Population**	1 967 000 (2005e)
		Nationality	Slovene, Slovenian
Former name	formerly part of Kingdom of Serbs, Croats and Slovenes (until 1929), Kingdom of Yugoslavia (1929–41), Federal People's Republic of Yugoslavia (1945–63), Socialist Federal People's Republic of Yugoslavia (1963–91)	**Languages**	Slovene
		Ethnic groups	Slovene 91%, Croat 3%, Serb 2%, Bosniak 1%, others 3%
		Religions	Christianity 72% (RC, including Uniate, 71%, Prot 1%), none/unaffiliated 5%, Islam 1%, others 21%
Independence	1991	**Time zone**	GMT +1
Area	20 251 sq km/7 817 sq mi	**Currency**	1 Tolar (SIT) = 100 stotins
		Telephone	+386
Capital	Ljubljana	**Internet**	.si
Chief towns	Maribor, Kranj, Celje,	**Country code**	SVN

Location
A republic in central Europe, bounded to the north by Austria; to the east by Hungary; to the south by Croatia; and to the west by Italy.

Physical description
Forested and mountainous, linked to Austria by a number of pass roads; highest point is Mt Triglav (2 864m/9 396ft); drops down towards the Adriatic coast.

Climate
Hot summers and cold winters in the plateaux and valleys in the east; Mediterranean climate on the west coast.

National holidays
Jan 1, 2, Feb 8 (Culture), Apr 27 (National Resistance), May 1 (2), Jun 25 (National), Aug 15, Oct 31 (Reformation), Nov 1, Dec 25, 26 (Independence); EM.

Political leaders

See **Serbia and Montenegro** for political leaders of the former Yugoslavia.

President

1991–2002	Milan Kučan
2002–	Janez Drnovšek

Prime Minister

1990–2	Lojze Peterle	2000–2	Janez Drnovšek
1992–2000	Janez Drnovšek	2002–4	Anton Rop
2000	Andrej Bajuk	2004–	Janez Jansa

Slovenian Grammar

The Slovene language is unusual in that it has not only singular and plural forms but also an additional *dual* form. While most languages distinguish whether one person is doing something or many people are doing it, Slovene also has different words and grammar for two people.

SOLOMON ISLANDS

Official name	Solomon Islands		are also spoken
Local name	Solomon Islands	**Ethnic groups**	Melanesian 93%, Polynesian 4%, Micronesian 2%, others 1%
Former name	British Solomon Islands (until 1975)		
Independence	1978	**Religions**	Christianity 91% (Prot 62%, RC 19%, others 10%), others 9%
Area	27 556 sq km/10 637 sq mi		
Capital	Honiara	**Time zone**	GMT +11
Chief towns	Gizo, Auki, Kirakira	**Currency**	1 Solomon Islands Dollar (SI$/SBD) = 100 cents
Population	478 000 (2005e)		
Nationality	Solomon Islander (noun)	**Telephone**	+677
Languages	English; pidgin English and Melanesian dialects	**Internet**	.sb
		Country code	SLB

Location
An independent country consisting of an archipelago of several hundred islands in the south-west Pacific Ocean east of Papua New Guinea.

Physical description
Six main islands are Choiseul, Guadalcanal, Malaita, New Georgia, Makira and Santa Isabel; larger islands have forested mountain ranges of mainly volcanic origin, deep, narrow valleys, and coastal belts lined with coconut palms; ringed by reefs; highest point is Mt Makarakomburu (2 477m/8 127ft) on Guadalcanal, the largest island.

Climate
Equatorial; average temperature is 27°C; high humidity.

National holidays
Jan 1, Jul 7 (Independence), Dec 25, 26; EM, GF, HS, WM, Queen's Birthday (Jun).

Political leaders

Head of State: British monarch, represented by Governor General (Sir Nathaniel Waena since 2004).

Prime Minister

1978–82	Peter Kenilorea	1993–4	Francis Billy Hilly
1982–4	Solomon Mamaloni	1994–7	Solomon Mamaloni
1984–6	Peter Kenilorea	1997–2000	Bartholomew Ulufa'alu
1986–9	Ezekiel Alebua	2000–1	Manasseh Sogavare
1989–93	Solomon Mamaloni	2001–	Allan Kemakeza

War in the Pacific

The idyllic tropical islands, palm-fringed lagoons and sleepy islets of the Solomon Islands were the site of some of the fiercest fighting of World War II. Following the attacks on Pearl Harbor and Singapore (7–8 Dec 1941), Japan advanced into the South Pacific, reaching Guadalcanal in May 1942. US forces reinvaded and after six months of bitter fighting, in one of the crucial actions of the war, they halted the Japanese advance. Wreckage from the fighting can still be seen in the islands and surrounding waters.

SOMALIA

Official name	Somalia	**Chief towns**	Hargeysa, Berbera, Kismayu
Local name	Soomaaliya; Jamhuuriyadda Dimoqraadiya Soomaaliya	**Population**	8 228 000 (2005e)
		Nationality	Somali
Former name	British Somaliland (until 1960) and Italian Somalia (until 1936), Italian East Africa (1936–50), Somali Democratic Republic (1969–91)	**Languages**	Somali, Arabic; English and Italian are also spoken widely
		Ethnic groups	Somalian 98%, Arab 2%
		Religions	Islam 98% (Sunni), Christianity 2%
Independence	1960	**Time zone**	GMT +3
Area	686 803 sq km/265 106 sq mi	**Currency**	1 Somali Shilling (SoSh/SOS) = 100 cents
Capital	Mogadishu; Muqdisho (Somali), Muqdishu (Arabic)	**Telephone**	+252
		Internet	.so
		Country code	SOM

Location
A republic in north-east Africa, bounded to the north-west by Djibouti; to the north by the Gulf of Aden; to the east by the Indian Ocean; to the south-west by Kenya; and to the west by Ethiopia.

Physical description
Occupies the eastern Horn of Africa where a dry coastal plain broadens to the south and rises inland to a plateau at nearly 1 000m/3 280ft; forested mountains on the Gulf of Aden coast rise to 2 416m/7 926ft at Mt Shimbiris.

Climate
Considerable variation in climate; average maximum daily temperatures of 29–42°C (Berbera on the north coast) and 28–32°C (Mogadishu); higher rainfall on the east coast in Apr–Sep; serious and persistent threat of drought.

National holidays
Jan 1, May 1, Jun 26 (Independence), Jul 1 (Union), Oct 21 (Revolution) (2); Ad (2), ER (2), PB.

Political leaders

President

1961–7	Aden Abdallah Osman	1991–2000	*Civil War*
1967–9	Abdirashid Ali Shermarke	2000	Abdullahi Derow Isaq *Acting President*
1969–80	Mohammed Siad Barre *Supreme Revolutionary Council*	2000–4	Abd-al-Qassim Salat Hasan
1980–91	Mohammed Siad Barre	2004–	Abdullahi Yusuf Ahmed

Prime Minister

1960	Mohammed Haji Ibrahim Egal	1990–1	Mohammed Hawadie Madar
1960–4	Abdirashid Ali Shermarke	1991	Umar Arteh Ghalib
1964–7	Abdirizak Haji Hussein	1991–2000	*Civil War*
1967–9	Mohammed Haji Ibrahim Egal	2000–1	Ali Khalif Galaid
1969–70	Mohammed Siad Barre	2001–3	Hassan Abshir Farah
1970–87	*No Prime Minister*	2003–4	Abdi Yusuf Mohammed
1987–90	Mohammed Ali Samater	2004–	Ali Mohamed Gedi

SOUTH AFRICA

Official name	Republic of South Africa (RSA)		Afrikaans, English, IsiNdebele, IsiXosa,
Local name	South Africa; Republiek van Suid-Afrika		IsiZulu, Sepedi, Sosetho, SiSwati, Setswana,
Independence	1931 (within Commonwealth), 1961 (republic)	**Ethnic groups**	Tshivenda, Xitsonga
			black 75%, white 14%, mixed 9%, Asian 2%
Area	1 233 404 sq km/ 476 094 sq mi	**Religions**	Christianity 62% (Prot and others 54%, RC 8%),
Capital	Pretoria (administrative), Bloemfontein (judicial) and Cape Town (Kaapstad) (legislative)		traditional beliefs 35%, Hinduism 2%, Islam 1%
		Time zone	GMT +2
Chief towns	Durban, Johannesburg, Port Elizabeth	**Currency**	1 Rand (R/ZAR) = 100 cents
		Telephone	+27
Population	47 432 000 (2005e)	**Internet**	.za
Nationality	South African	**Country code**	ZAF
Languages	Eleven official languages:		

Location
A republic in southern Africa, bounded to the north-west by Namibia; to the north by Botswana; to the north-east by Zimbabwe, Mozambique and Swaziland; to the east and south-east by the Indian Ocean; and to the south-west and west by the southern Atlantic Ocean; it completely encloses Lesotho.

Physical description
Occupies the southern extremity of the African plateau, fringed by mountains and a lowland coastal margin; northern interior comprises the Kalahari Basin, scrub grassland and arid desert; highest point is Mafadi (3 451m/11 322ft).

Climate
Subtropical in the east, with lush vegetation; dry moistureless climate on the west coast; Cape Town has minimum daily temperatures of 7°C (Jul), to an average maximum of 26°C (Jan–Feb); desert region further north.

National holidays
Jan 1, Mar 21 (Human Rights), Apr 27 (Freedom Day), May 1, Jun 16 (Youth), Aug 9 (Women), Sep 24 (Heritage), Dec 16 (Reconciliation), 25, 26; GF, EM (Family).

Political leaders

Governor General

1910–14	Herbert, Viscount Gladstone	1943–5	Nicolaas Jacobus de Wet
1914–20	Sydney, Earl Buxton	1945–51	Gideon Brand Van Zyl
1920–4	Arthur, Duke of Connaught	1951–9	Ernest George Jansen
1924–31	Alexander, Earl of Athlone	1959	Lucas Cornelius Steyn
1931–7	George Herbert Hyde Villiers	1959–61	Charles Robberts Swart
1937–43	Patrick Duncan		

Republic

President

1961–7	Charles Robberts Swart	1967–8	Jozua François Nandé
1967	Theophilus Ebenhaezer Dönges	1968–75	Jacobus Johannes Fouché

1975–8	Nicolaas Diederichs	1989–94	Frederick Willem de Klerk
1978–9	Balthazar Johannes Vorster	1994–9	Nelson Rolihlahla Mandela
1979–84	Marais Viljoen	1999–	Thabo Mbeki
1984–89	Pieter Willem Botha		

Prime Minister

1910–19	Louis Botha *SAf*	1954–8	Johannes Gerardus Strijdom *Nat*
1919–24	Jan Christiaan Smuts *SAf*	1958–66	Hendrik Frensch Verwoerd *Nat*
1924–39	James Barry Munnick Hertzog *Nat*	1966–78	Balthazar Johannes Vorster *Nat*
1939–48	Jan Christiaan Smuts *Un*	1978–84	Pieter Willem Botha *Nat*
1948–54	Daniel François Malan *Nat*	1984	*post abolished*

Nat = National
SAf = South African Party
Un = United

Mineral Wealth

South Africa produces 20% of the world's gold, 62% of its vanadium and 48% of its chrome. It is the second largest producer of platinum, titanium and zirconium and is also famous for diamonds.

SOUTHERN AND ANTARCTIC TERRITORIES, FRENCH *see* **FRANCE**

SOUTH GEORGIA *see* **UNITED KINGDOM**

SOUTH KOREA *see* **KOREA, SOUTH**

SOUTH SANDWICH ISLANDS *see* **UNITED KINGDOM**

SPAIN

Official name	Kingdom of Spain		(Gallego) and Basque (Euskera) are also spoken in certain regions
Local name	España; Reino de España		
Former name	Spanish Republic (1931–9), Spanish State (1936–78)	**Ethnic groups**	Castilian Spanish 72%, Catalan 17%, Galician 6%, others 3%, Basque 2%
Area	492 431 sq km/190 078 sq mi		
Capital	Madrid	**Religions**	Christianity 97% (RC), others 3%
Chief towns	Barcelona, Valencia, Seville, Zaragoza, Málaga	**Time zone**	GMT +1
		Currency	1 Euro (€/EUR) = 100 cents
Population	43 064 000 (2005E)	**Telephone**	+34
Nationality	Spanish	**Internet**	.es
Languages	Spanish (Castilian); Catalan, Galician	**Country code**	ESP

Location
A kingdom in south-western Europe, bounded to the north by France, the Bay of Biscay and Andorra; to the east by the Mediterranean Sea; to the south by Gibraltar (UK) and the Strait of Gibraltar; to the west by Portugal; and to the north-west by the Atlantic Ocean.

Physical description
Consists mainly of a furrowed central plateau (the Meseta, average height 700m/2 297ft) crossed by mountains; Andalusian or Baetic Mountains in the south-east rise to 3 478m/ 11 410ft at Mulhacén; Pyrenees in the north rise to 3 404m/11 168ft at Pico de Aneto; highest point is Pico de Teide (3 718m/12 198ft) on the island of Tenerife in the Canary Islands.

Climate
Meseta has a continental climate, with hot summers, cold winters and low rainfall; high rainfall in the mountains, with deep winter snow; south Mediterranean coast has the warmest winter temperatures on the European mainland.

National holidays
Jan 1, 6, May 1, Aug 15, Nov 1, Dec 6 (Constitution), 8, 25; GF, HT (*most areas*); *much regional variation*.

Balearic Islands

Location	An archipelago of five major islands (Majorca, Minorca, Ibiza, Formentera and Cabrera) and eleven islets in the west Mediterranean Sea, situated near the east coast of Spain.
Area	5 014 sq km/1 935 sq mi **Capital** Palma de Mallorca

Canary Islands

Location	An island archipelago of eight major islands (Tenerife, Gran Canaria, Fuerteventura, Lanzarote, La Palma, Hierro and Gomera) in the Atlantic Ocean, lying 100km/62mi off the north-west coast of Africa.
Area	7 273 sq km/2 807 sq mi **Capital** Las Palmas

Political leaders

Monarch

1516–56	Charles I (Emperor Charles V)	1788–1808	Charles IV
1556–98	Philip II	1808	Ferdinand VII
1598–1621	Philip III	1808–14	Joseph Bonaparte
1621–65	Philip IV	1814–33	Ferdinand VII
1665–1700	Charles II	1833–68	Isabella II
1700–24	Philip V	1868–70	*No monarchy*
1724	Luis	1870–3	Amadeus of Savoy
1724–46	Philip V	1873–4	*Temporary republic*
1746–59	Ferdinand VI	1874–85	Alfonso XII
1759–88	Charles III	1886–1931	Alfonso XIII

President

1931	Niceto Alcalá Zamora y Torres	1936–9	Manuel Azaña y Díez *Civil War*
1931	Manuel Azaña y Díez	1936–9	Miguel Cabanellas Ferrer *Civil*
1931–6	Niceto Alcalá Zamora y Torres		*War*
1936	Diego Martínez Barrio *Acting President*		

Chief of State – Nationalist Government
1936–75   Francisco Franco Bahamonde

Monarch
1975–   Juan Carlos I

Prime Minister

1900–1	Marcelo de Azcárraga y Palmero	1919–20	Manuel Allendesalazar
1901–2	Práxedes Mateo Sagasta	1920–1	Eduardo Dato y Iradier
1902–3	Francisco Silvela y Le-Vielleuze	1921	Gabino Bugallal Araujo *Acting*
1903	Raimundo Fernández Villaverde		*Prime Minister*
1903–4	Antonio Maura y Montaner	1921	Manuel Allendesalazar
1904–5	Marcelo de Azcárraga y Palmero	1921–2	Antonio Maura y Montaner
1905	Raimundo Fernández Villaverde	1922	José Sánchez Guerra y Martínez
1905	Eugenio Montero Ríos	1922–3	Manuel García Prieto
1905–6	Segismundo Moret y Prendergast	1923–30	Miguel Primo de Rivera y Oranej
1906	José López Domínguez	1930–1	Dámaso Berenguer y Fusté
1906	Segismundo Moret y Prendergast	1931	Juan Bautista Aznar-Cabañas
1906–7	Antonio Aguilar y Correa	1931	Niceto Alcalá Zamora y Torres
1907–9	Antonio Maura y Montaner	1931–3	Manuel Azaña y Díez
1909–10	Segismundo Moret y Prendergast	1933	Alejandro Lerroux y García
1910–12	José Canalejas y Méndez	1933	Diego Martínez Barrio
1912	Álvaro Figueroa y Torres	1933–4	Alejandro Lerroux y García
1912–13	Manuel García Prieto	1934	Ricardo Samper Ibáñez
1913–15	Eduardo Dato y Iradier	1934–5	Alejandro Lerroux y García
1915–17	Álvaro Figueroa y Torres	1935	Joaquín Chapaprieta y Terragosa
1917	Manuel García Prieto	1935–6	Manuel Portela Valladares
1917	Eduardo Dato y Iradier	1936	Manuel Azaña y Díez
1917–18	Manuel García Prieto	1936	Santiago Casares Quiroga
1918	Antonio Maura y Montaner	1936	Diego Martínez Barrio
1918	Manuel García Prieto	1936	José Giral y Pereyra
1918–19	Álvaro Figueroa y Torres	1936–7	Francisco Largo Caballero
1919	Antonio Maura y Montaner	1937–9	Juan Negrín
1919	Joaquín Sánchez de Toca		

Chairman of the Council of Ministers
1939–73   Francisco Franco Bahamonde

Prime Minister

1973	Torcuato Fernández Miranda	1981–2	Calvo Sotelo
	y Hevía *Acting Prime Minister*	1982–96	Felipe González
1973–6	Carlos Arias Navarro	1996–2004	José María Aznar
1976–81	Adolfo Suárez	2004–	José Luis Rodríguez Zapatero

Talking Castles

The main language of Spain that most people consider to be 'Spanish' is actually Castilian Spanish – other regions also speak Galician, Basque, Catalan and Valencian. In Spain Castilian Spanish is often simply referred to as *castellano*, Castilian, rather than 'Spanish'. The word *castellano* comes from *Castilla*, the central area of Spain that started the 'reconquest' of the peninsula from eight centuries of dominance by the Moors. To defend themselves they built large numbers of castles, leading to the name.

SRI LANKA

Official name	Democratic Socialist Republic of Sri Lanka	**Nationality**	Sri Lankan
		Languages	Sinhala, Tamil
Local name	Sri Lanka; Sri Lanka Prajatantrika Samajavadi Janarajaya	**Ethnic groups**	Sinhalese 74%, Tamil 18%, Sri Lankan Moor 7%, others 1%
Former name	Ceylon (until 1972)	**Religions**	Buddhism 69%, Hinduism 15%, Christianity 8%, Islam 8%
Independence	1948 (from Britain), 1972 (republic)		
Area	65 610 sq km/25 325 sq mi	**Time zone**	GMT +5.5
Capital	Colombo (commercial) and Sri Jayawardenepura Kotte (administrative)	**Currency**	1 Sri Lanka Rupee (SLR, SLRs/LKR) = 100 cents
		Telephone	+94
Chief towns	Jaffna, Kandy, Galle, Trincomalee	**Internet**	.lk
		Country code	LKA
Population	20 743 000 (2005e)		

Location
An island republic in the Indian Ocean off the south-east coast of India.

Physical description
Pear-shaped; low-lying areas in the north and south, surrounding the south-central uplands; highest peak is Pidurutalagala (2 524m/8 281ft); coastal plain is fringed by sandy beaches and lagoons; nearly half is tropical monsoon forest or open woodland.

Climate
High temperatures and humidity in the northern plains; average daily temperatures at Trincomalee are 24–33°C; temperatures in the interior are reduced by altitude; greatest rainfall on the south-west coast and in the mountains.

National holidays
Jan 15 (Tamil Thai Pongal), Feb 4 (National), May 1, Dec 25; Ad, D, ER, GF, NY (Sinhala/Tamil) (Apr) (2), PB, Mahasivarathri (Feb/Mar), Full Moon (*monthly*), day following Vesak Full Moon (May).

Political leaders

President

1972–8	William Gopallawa	1989–93	Ranasinghe Premadasa
1978–89	Junius Richard Jayawardene	1994–	Chandrika Bandaranaike Kumaratunga

Prime Minister

Ceylon

1947–52	Don Stephen Senanayake	1959–60	Vijayananda Dahanayake
1952–3	Dudley Shelton Senanayake	1960	Dudley Shelton Senanayake
1953–6	John Lionel Kotelawala	1960–5	Sirimavo Ratwatte Dias Bandaranaike
1956–9	Solomon West Ridgeway Dias Bandaranaike	1965–70	Dudley Shelton Senanayake

Sri Lanka

1970–7	Sirimavo Ratwatte Dias Bandaranaike	1994–2000	Sirimavo Ratwatte Dias Bandaranaike
1977–89	Ranasinghe Premadasa	2000–1	Ratnasiri Wickremanayake
1989–93	Dingiri Banda Wijetunge	2001–4	Ranil Wickremasinghe
1993–4	Ranil Wickremasinghe	2004–	Mahinda Rajapakse
1994	Chandrika Bandaranaike Kumaratunga		

Serendipity

Serendipity, meaning the state of frequently making lucky discoveries by accident, comes from an ancient name for Sri Lanka, Serendip. It arrived in English via a Persian fairytale, 'The Three Princes of Serendip', whose heroes made many lucky discoveries by chance; the writer Horace Walpole coined serendipity in reference to the tale.

SUDAN

Official name	Republic of Sudan	**Nationality**	Sudanese
Local name	As-Sūdān; Al-Jumhūriyya as-Sūdān	**Languages**	Arabic
		Ethnic groups	Arab 50%, Dinka 13%, Nuba 8%, Beja 6%, Nuer 5%, Azande 3%, others 15%
Former name	Anglo-Egyptian Sudan (until 1956), Democratic Republic of The Sudan (1969–85)		
		Religions	Islam 70% (mostly Sunni), traditional beliefs 23%, Christianity 7%
Independence	1956		
Area	2 504 530 sq km/ 966 749 sq mi	**Time zone**	GMT +2
Capital	Khartoum; Al Khartūm, Al Khurtūm	**Currency**	1 Sudanese Dinar (SD/SDD) = 10 pounds
Chief towns	Port Sudan, Wad Medani, Omdurman	**Telephone**	+249
		Internet	.sd
Population	36 233 000 (2005e)	**Country code**	SDN

Location
A republic in north-east Africa, bounded to the north-west by Libya; to the north by Egypt; to the north-east by the Red Sea; to the east by Ethiopia and Eritrea; to the south-east by Uganda and Kenya; to the south by Democratic Republic of the Congo; to the south-west by the Central African Republic; and to the west by Chad.

Physical description
Largest country on the African continent, astride the middle reaches of the River Nile; eastern edge formed by the Nubian Highlands and an escarpment rising to over 2 000m/6 562ft on the Red Sea; Imatong Mountains in the south rise to 3 187m/10 456ft at Kinyeti (the highest point); White Nile flows north to meet the Blue Nile at Khartoum.

Climate
Desert conditions in the north; in the hottest months (Jul–Aug), the temperature rarely falls below 24°C in the north.

National holidays
Jan 1 (Independence), Mar 3 (Unity), Apr 6 (Revolution), Dec 25; Ad (5), ER (5), NY (Muslim), PB, Sham al-Naseem (Apr/May).

Political leaders

Chief of State
1956–8	*Council of State*	1969–85	Jaafar Mohammed Nimeiri
1958–64	Ibrahim Abboud		*President from 1971*
1964–5	*Council of Sovereignty*	1993–	Omar Hassan Ahmed Al-Bashir
1965–9	Ismail Al-Azhari		*President*

Chairman of Transitional Military Council
1985–6   Abd Al-Rahman Siwar Al-Dahab

Chairman of Supreme Council
1986–9   Ahmad Al-Mirghani

Chairman of Revolutionary Command Council
1989–93   Omar Hassan Ahmed Al-Bashir

Prime Minister
1955–6	Ismail Al-Azhari	1969–76	*As President*
1956–8	Abdullah Khalil	1976–7	Rashid Al-Tahir Bakr
1958–64	*As President*	1977–85	*As Chief of State*
1964–5	Serr Al-Khatim Al-Khalifa	1985–6	*Transitional Military Council* (Al-
1965–6	Mohammed Ahmed Mahjoub		Jazuli Dafallah)
1966–7	Sadiq Al-Mahdi	1986–9	Sadiq Al-Mahdi *Military Council,*
1967–9	Mohammed Ahmed Mahjoub		*Prime Minister*
1969	Babiker Awadalla	1989–	*No Prime Minister*

White and Blue Nile

Although Egypt is linked in the popular imagination to the River Nile, the mighty river actually crosses several countries, notably Sudan. The principal tributaries of the River Nile itself are the White Nile, from Uganda, and the Blue Nile, from Ethiopia, which meet near Khartoum and flow north.

SURINAME

Official name	Republic of Suriname	**Ethnic groups**	Hindustani 37%, Creole 31%, Javanese 15%, black 9%, Amerindian 3%, Chinese 3%, others 2%
Local name	Suriname; Republiek Suriname		
Former name	Netherlands Guiana, Dutch Guiana (until 1948)		
Independence	1975	**Religions**	Christianity 48% (Prot 25%, RC 23%), Hinduism 27%, Islam 21%, traditional beliefs 4%
Area	163 265 sq km/63 020 sq mi		
Capital	Paramaribo	**Time zone**	GMT –3
Chief towns	Brokopondo, Nieuw Amsterdam	**Currency**	1 Suriname Dollar ($/SRD) = 100 cents
Population	449 000 (2005e)	**Telephone**	+597
Nationality	Surinamese	**Internet**	.sr
Languages	Dutch; English, Hindi, Javanese and Sranang Tongo are also spoken	**Country code**	SUR

Location
A republic in north-eastern South America, bounded to the north by the Atlantic Ocean; to the east by French Guiana; to the south by Brazil; and to the west by Guyana.

Physical description
Diverse natural regions, ranging from coastal lowland through savanna to mountainous upland; coastal strip is mostly covered by swamp; highland interior in the south is overgrown with dense tropical forest; highest point is Julianatop (1 230m/4 035ft).

Climate
Tropically hot and humid, with two rainy seasons in May–Jul and Nov–Jan; Paramaribo temperatures range from 22–33°C.

National holidays
Jan 1, May 1, Jul 1 (Freedom), Nov 25 (Independence), Dec 25, 26; EM, ER, GF, Holi Phagwa (Mar).

Political leaders

President

1975–80	J H E Ferrier		1990–1	Johan Kraag
1980–2	Henk Chin-a-Sen		1991–6	Ronald Venetiaan
1982–8	L F Ramdat-Musier *Acting President*		1996–2000	Jules Wijdenbosch
			2000–	Ronald Venetiaan
1988–90	Ramsewak Shankar			

Chairman of National Military Council
1980–7	Desi Bouterse
1987	Iwan Granoogst *Acting Prime Minister*

Prime Minister

1975–80	Henk Arron		1986–7	Pretaapnarain Radhakishun
1980	Henk Chin-a-Sen		1987–8	Jules Wijdenbosch
1980–2	*No Prime Minister*		1988–90	Henk Arron
1982–3	Henry Weyhorst		1990–1	Jules Wijdenbosch
1983–4	Errol Alibux		1991–6	Jules Ajodhia
1984–6	Wim Udenhout			

Vice President/Chairman of the Council of Ministers
1996–2000	Pretaapnarain Radhakishun
2000–5	Jules Ajodhia
2005–	Ram Sardjoe

New Amsterdam, New York

Suriname was first settled by the British in 1651. However, in 1667 it was taken by a Dutch fleet. The British and the Dutch were also rivals in North America, and later in 1667 an agreement was reached by which the Dutch were allowed to keep Suriname in exchange for British possession of Nieuw Amsterdam – later to become New York City.

SVALBARD ISLANDS *see* **NORWAY**

SWAZILAND

Official name	Kingdom of Swaziland		European 4%, Tsonga 2%
Local name	Umbuso we Swatini	**Religions**	Christianity 60%, traditional beliefs 40%
Independence	1968		
Area	17 363 sq km/6 702 sq mi	**Time zone**	GMT +2
Capital	Mbabane (administrative) and Lobamba (legislative)	**Currency**	1 Lilangeni (plural Emalangeni) (Li, E/SZL) = 100 cents
Population	1 032 000 (2005e)	**Telephone**	+268
Nationality	Swazi	**Internet**	.sz
Languages	English, Siswati	**Country code**	SWZ
Ethnic groups	Swazi 84%, Zulu 10%,		

Location
A kingdom in south-east Africa, bounded to the north, west, south and south-east by South Africa, and to the north-east by Mozambique.

Physical description
Mountainous Highveld in the west; highest point is Emblembe (1 862m/6 109ft); more populated Middleveld in the centre descends to 600–700m/1 970–2 300ft; rolling, bush-covered Lowveld in the east is irrigated by river systems.

Climate
Humid, near-temperate climate in the west; subtropical and drier in the centre; tropical in the east, with relatively little rain (susceptible to drought); average annual temperature is 16°C in the west and 22°C in the east.

National holidays
Jan 1, Apr 19 (King's Birthday), 25 (National Flag), May 1, Sep 6 (Somhlolo), Dec 25, 26; A, EM, GF, Incwala (Dec/Jan), Umhlanga/Reed Dance (Aug/Sep), Jul public holiday.

Political leaders

Monarch
1967–82	Sobhuza II *Chief since 1921*	1983–6	Ntombi *Queen Regent*
1982–3	Dzeliwe *Queen Regent*	1986–	Mswati III
1983	Sozisa Dlamini *Regent*		

Prime Minister
1967–78	Prince Makhosini	1993–6	Jameson Mbilini Dlamini
1978–9	Prince Maphevu Dlamini	1996–2003	Barnabas Sibusiso Dlamini
1979–83	Prince Mbandla Dlamini	2003	Paul Shabangu
1983–6	Prince Bhekimpi Dlamini	2003–	Themba Dlamini
1986–9	Sotsha Dlamini		
1989–93	Obed Dlamini *Acting Prime Minister*		

Power Behind the Throne

Kings of Swaziland are permitted to have many wives, and King Sobhuza II is thought to have had more than 60. Upon the death of a king, the Royal Council chooses one of his favourite senior wives to be the new Queen Mother, an important position that makes her the most influential woman in the country. One of her unmarried sons is then chosen to be the new king.

SWEDEN

Official name	Kingdom of Sweden	Ethnic groups	Swedish 91%, Finnish and Lapp 3%, others 6%
Local name	Sverige; Konungariket Sverige	Religions	Christianity 93% (Prot 90%, RC 2%, others 1%), Islam 1%, others and none/unaffiliated 6%
Area	411 479 sq km/158 830 sq mi		
Capital	Stockholm	Time zone	GMT +1
Chief towns	Gothenburg, Malmö, Uppsala, Norrköping, Västerås, Örebro, Linköping	Currency	1 Swedish Krona (Skr/SEK) = 100 øre
		Telephone	+46
Population	9 041 000 (2005e)	Internet	.se
Nationality	Swedish	Country code	SWE
Languages	Swedish		

Location

A kingdom in northern Europe, occupying the eastern side of the Scandinavian Peninsula, bounded to the north-east by Finland; to the east by the Gulf of Bothnia and the Baltic Sea; to the south-west by the Skagerrak and Kattegat; and to the west and north-west by Norway.

Physical description

A large amount of inland water; many coastal islands; c.57% of the country is forested; Kjölen Mountains in the west form much of the boundary with Norway; highest peak is Kebnekaise (2 111m/6 926ft); many waterfalls.

Climate

Typically continental, with a considerable temperature range between summer and winter, except in the south-west where winters are warmer; average number of days with a mean temperature below freezing increases from 71 in Malmö to 184 near the Arctic Circle.

National holidays

Jan 1, 6, May 1, Nov 1, Dec 25, 26; A, EM, GF, WM, Midsummer (Jun).

Political leaders

Monarch

Vasa

1523–60	Gustav I	1599–1611	Karl IX
1560–8	Erik XIV	1611–32	Gustav II Adolf
1568–92	Johan III	1632–54	Kristina
1592–9	Sigismund		

Zweibrucken

| 1654–60 | Karl X Gustav | 1697–1718 | Karl XII |
| 1660–97 | Karl XI | 1718–20 | Ulrika Eleonora |

Hesse

| 1720–51 | Fredrik |

Oldenburg-Holstein-Gottorp

1751–71	Adolf Fredrik		1792–1809	Gustav IV Adolf
1771–92	Gustav III		1809–18	Karl XIII

Bernadotte

1818–44	Karl XIV Johan		1907–50	Gustav V
1844–59	Oskar I		1950–73	Gustav VI Adolf
1859–72	Karl XV		1973–	Karl XVI Gustav
1872–1907	Oskar II			

Prime Minister

1900–2	Fredrik von Otter		1926–8	Carl Gustaf Ekman
1902–5	Erik Gustaf Boström		1928–30	Arvid Lindman
1905	Johan Ramstedt		1930–2	Carl Gustaf Ekman
1905	Christian Lundeberg		1932	Felix Hamrin
1905–6	Karl Staaf		1932–6	Per Albin Hansson
1906–11	Arvid Lindman		1936	Axel Pehrsson-Branstorp
1911–14	Karl Staaf		1936–46	Per Albin Hansson
1914–17	Hjalmar Hammarskjöld		1946–69	Tage Erlander
1917	Carl Swartz		1969–76	Olof Palme
1917–20	Nils Edén		1976–8	Thorbjörn Fälldin
1920	Hjalmar Branting		1978–9	Ola Ullsten
1920–1	Louis de Geer		1979–82	Thorbjörn Fälldin
1921	Oscar von Sydow		1982–6	Olof Palme
1921–3	Hjalmar Branting		1986–91	Ingvar Carlsson
1923–4	Ernst Trygger		1991–4	Carl Bildt
1924–5	Hjalmar Branting		1994–6	Ingvar Carlsson
1925–6	Rickard Sandler		1996–	Göran Persson

Crayfish Parties

Every Aug, Swedes get together for big parties in celebration of crayfish. The crayfish party tradition began in the early 20c, when stocks of Swedish crayfish were threatened and fishing was restricted to Aug; the weeks when crayfish could be caught were celebrated with a big party at which crayfish were eaten. Today, silly hats, colourful decorations, songs in the honour of the crayfish and copious quantities of schnapps to wash the crustaceans down are all part of the raucous festivities.

SWITZERLAND

Official name	Swiss Confederation		Romansch (1%); many of the Swiss speak more than one of these
Local name	Schweiz; Schweizerische Eidgenossenschaft (German), Suisse; Confédération Suisse (French), Svizzera; Confederazione Svizzera (Italian), Svizra; Confederaziun Svizra (Romansch)	**Ethnic groups**	German 65%, French 18%, Italian 10%, Romansch 1%, others 6%
		Religions	Christianity 86% (RC 46%, Prot 40%), none/unaffiliated 9%, Islam 2%, others 3%
Area	41 228 sq km/15 914 sq mi	**Time zone**	GMT +1
Capital	Berne; Bern, Berna	**Currency**	1 Swiss Franc (SFr, SwF/CHF) = 100 centimes = 100 rappen
Chief towns	Zurich, Lucerne, St Gallen, Lausanne, Basle, Geneva		
		Telephone	+41
Population	7 252 000 (2005e)	**Internet**	.ch
Nationality	Swiss	**Country code**	CHE
Languages	German (65%), French (18%), Italian (12%) and		

Location
A republic in central Europe, bounded to the north by Germany; to the east by Liechtenstein and Austria; to the south by Italy; and to the west by France.

Physical description
Mountainous; the Alps run roughly east to west in the south; highest peak is Dufourspitze (4 634m/15 203ft); average height of the Pre-Alps in the north-west is 2 000m/6 562ft; central plateau, at an average altitude of 580m/1 903ft, is fringed by large lakes; c.3 000 sq km/1 160 sq mi of glaciers.

Climate
Temperate, varying greatly with relief and altitude; warm summers, with considerable rainfall; winter temperatures average 0°C; average annual temperature is 7–9°C; the *Föhn*, a warm wind, is noticeable in the Alps during late winter and spring.

National holidays
Jan 1, Aug 1 (National), Dec 25, 26; A, EM, GF, WM; *other canton and local holidays*.

Political leaders

President

1900	Walter Hauser	1910	Robert Comtesse
1901	Ernst Brenner	1911	Marc-Emile Ruchet
1902	Joseph Zemp	1912	Ludwig Forrer
1903	Adolf Deucher	1913	Eduard Müller
1904	Robert Comtesse	1914	Arthur Hoffmann
1905	Marc-Emile Ruchet	1915	Giuseppe Motta
1906	Ludwig Forrer	1916	Camille Decoppet
1907	Eduard Müller	1917	Edmund Schulthess
1908	Ernst Brenner	1918	Felix Calonder
1909	Adolf Deucher	1919	Gustave Ador

1920	Giuseppe Motta	1963	Willy Spühler
1921	Edmund Schulthess	1964	Ludwig von Moos
1922	Robert Haab	1965	Hans Peter Tschudi
1923	Karl Scheurer	1966	Hans Schaffner
1924	Ernest Chuard	1967	Roger Bonvin
1925	Jean-Marie Musy	1968	Willy Spühler
1926	Heinrich Häberlin	1969	Ludwig von Moos
1927	Giuseppe Motta	1970	Hans Peter Tschudi
1928	Edmund Schulthess	1971	Rudolf Gnägi
1929	Robert Haab	1972	Nello Celio
1930	Jean-Marie Musy	1973	Roger Bonvin
1931	Heinrich Häberlin	1974	Ernst Brugger
1932	Giuseppe Motta	1975	Pierre Graber
1933	Edmund Schulthess	1976	Rudolf Gnägi
1934	Marcel Pilet-Golaz	1977	Kurt Furgler
1935	Rudolf Minger	1978	Willi Ritschard
1936	Albert Meyer	1979	Hans Hürlimann
1937	Giuseppe Motta	1980	Georges-André Chevallaz
1938	Johannes Baumann	1981	Kurt Furgler
1939	Philipp Etter	1982	Fritz Honegger
1940	Marcel Pilet-Golaz	1983	Pierre Aubert
1941	Ernst Wetter	1984	Leon Schlumpf
1942	Philipp Etter	1985	Kurt Furgler
1943	Enrico Celio	1986	Alphons Egli
1944	Walter Stampfli	1987	Pierre Aubert
1945	Eduard von Steiger	1988	Otto Stich
1946	Karl Kobelt	1989	Jean-Pascal Delamuraz
1947	Philipp Etter	1990	Arnold Koller
1948	Enrico Celio	1991	Flavio Cotti
1949	Ernst Nobs	1992	René Felber
1950	Max Petitpierre	1993	Adolf Ogi
1951	Eduard von Steiger	1994	Otto Stich
1952	Karl Kobelt	1995	Kaspar Villiger
1953	Philipp Etter	1996	Jean-Pascal Delamuraz
1954	Rodolphe Rubattel	1997	Arnold Koller
1955	Max Petitpierre	1998	Flavio Cotti
1956	Markus Feldmann	1999	Ruth Dreifuss
1957	Hans Streuli	2000	Adolf Ogi
1958	Thomas Holenstein	2001	Moritz Leuenberger
1959	Paul Chaudet	2002	Kaspar Villinger
1960	Max Petitpierre	2003	Pascal Couchepin
1961	Friedrich Wahlen	2004	Joseph Deiss
1962	Paul Chaudet	2005	Samuel Schmid

Orson Welles on Switzerland

'In Italy for thirty years under the Borgias they had warfare, terror, murder, bloodshed – they produced Michelangelo, Leonardo da Vinci and the Renaissance. In Switzerland they had brotherly love, five hundred years of democracy and peace, and what did they produce? The cuckoo clock.'
**1949 Orson Welles (1915–85) US director and actor
(from the film *The Third Man*).**

SYRIA

Official name	Syrian Arab Republic	**Nationality**	Syrian
Local name	As-Sūriyya; Al-Jumhūriyya Al-'Arabiyya as-Sūriyya	**Languages**	Arabic
		Ethnic groups	Arab 90%, Kurdish 6%, Armenian and others 4%
Former name	formerly part of the United Arab Republic, with Egypt (1958–61)	**Religions**	Islam 90% (Sunni 74%, others 16%), Christianity 10%
Independence	1946	**Time zone**	GMT +2
Area	185 180 sq km/71 479 sq mi	**Currency**	1 Syrian Pound (LS, S$/SYP) = 100 piastres
Capital	Damascus; Dimashq	**Telephone**	+963
Chief towns	Halab (Aleppo), Homs, Hama, Latakia	**Internet**	.sy
		Country code	SYR
Population	19 043 000 (2005e)		

Location
A republic in the Middle East, bounded to the north by Turkey; to the east by Iraq; to the south-west by Israel and Jordan; and to the west by the Mediterranean Sea and Lebanon.

Physical description
Behind a narrow coastal plain, the Jabal al Nusayriyah Mountains rise to c.1 500m/4 921ft; steep drop in the east to the Orontes River valley; Anti-Lebanon range in the south-west rises to 2 814m/9 232ft at Mt Hermon; open steppe and desert to the east.

Climate
Coastal Mediterranean climate, with hot, dry summers and mild, wet winters; 60% has a desert or semi-desert climate; the *khamsin* wind causes temperatures to rise to 43–49°C; in Damascus average temperatures from 7°C (Jan) to 27°C (Jul).

National holidays
Jan 1, Mar 8 (Revolution), Apr 17 (Evacuation), May 1, 6 (Martyrs), Jul 23 (Egyptian Revolution), Sep 1 (Libyan Unity), Oct 6 (Liberation), Dec 25; Ad (3), ER (4), ES, NY (Muslim), PB.

Political leaders

President

1943–9	Shukri Al-Quwwatli	1961–3	Nazim Al-Qudsi
1949	Husni Az-Zaim	1963	Luai Al-Atassi
1949–51	Hashim Al-Atassi	1963–6	Amin Al-Hafiz
1951–4	Adib Shishaqli	1966–70	Nureddin Al-Atassi
1954–5	Hashim Al-Atassi	1970–1	Ahmad Al-Khatib
1955–8	Shukri Al-Quwwatli	1971–2000	Hafez Al-Assad
1958–61	*Part of United Arab Republic*	2000–	Bashar Al-Assad

Prime Minister

1946–8	Jamil Mardam Bey	1949–50	Khalid Al-Azm
1948–9	Khalid Al-Azm	1950–1	Nazim Al-Qudsi
1949	Husni Az-Zaim	1951	Khalid Al-Azm
1949	Muhsi Al-Barazi	1951	Hassan Al-Hakim
1949	Hashim Al-Atassi	1951	Maruf Ad-Dawalibi
1949	Nazim Al-Qudsi	1951–3	Fauzi As-Salu

1953–4	Adib Shishaqli	1963–4	Amin Al-Hafez
1954	Shewqet Shuqair	1964	Salah Ad-Din Al-Bitaar
1954	Sabri Al-Asali	1964–5	Amin Al-Hafez
1954	Said Al-Ghazzi	1965	Yousif Zeayen
1954–5	Faris Al-Khuri	1966	Salah Ad-Din Al-Bitaar
1955	Sabri Al-Asali	1966–8	Yousif Zeayen
1955–6	Said Al-Ghazzi	1968–70	Nureddin Al-Atassi *Acting Prime*
1956–8	Sabri Al-Asali		*Minister*
1958–61	*Part of United Arab Republic*	1970–1	Hafez Al-Assad
1961	Abd Al-Hamid As-Sarraj	1971–2	Abdel Rahman Khleifawi
1961	Mamun Kuzbari	1972–6	Mahmoud Bin Saleh Al-Ayoubi
1961	Izzat An-Nuss	1976–8	Abdul Rahman Khleifawi
1961–2	Maruf Ad-Dawalibi	1978–80	Mohammed Ali Al-Halabi
1962	Bashir Azmah	1980–7	Abdel Rauof Al-Kasm
1962–3	Khalid Al-Azm	1987–2000	Mahmoud Al-Zubi
1963	Salah Ad-Din Al-Bitaar	2000–3	Muhammad Mustafa Mero
1963	Sami Al-Jundi	2003–	Muhammad Naji al-Otari
1963	Salah Ad-Din Al-Bitaar		

Ancient City

Damascus claims to be the world's oldest continuously inhabited city. It dates back to at least the third millennium BC, or perhaps even to the seventh. Documented history shows that Damascus was an important regional centre by the second millennium BC. It has been suggested that the name Damascus may come from old Arabic *Dar Meshq*, meaning 'well-watered place'. In ancient times it was a great trade and commercial centre.

TAIWAN

Official name	Republic of China; also sometimes known as Chinese Taipei	**Languages**	Mandarin Chinese
		Ethnic groups	Taiwanese Chinese (including Hakka) 84%, mainland Chinese 14%, Ainu 2%
Local name	T'ai-wan; Chung-hua Min-kuo		
Former name	Formosa (until 1949)	**Religions**	Chinese folk religion 45%, Buddhism 42%, Christianity 5%, Islam 1%, others 7%
Independence	1949 (creation of republic)		
Area	36 000 sq km/13 896 sq mi		
		Time zone	GMT +8
Capital	T'aipei	**Currency**	1 New Taiwan Dollar (NT$/TWD) = 100 cents
Chief towns	Chilung, Kaohsiung, Taichung		
		Telephone	+886
Population	22 894 000 (2005e)	**Internet**	.tw
Nationality	Taiwanese, Chinese	**Country code**	TWN

Location
An island republic, lying c.80mi/130km off the south-east coast of China between the East China Sea and the South China Sea.

Physical description
Mountain range runs north to south, covering two thirds of Taiwan Island; highest peak is Yu Shan (3 997m/13 113ft); low-lying land is mainly on the west; crossed by the Tropic of Cancer.

Climate
Tropical monsoon-type climate; wettest period is May–Sep, when it is hot and humid; typhoons bring heavy rains in Jul–Sep; short mild winters; average daily temperature at T'aipei is 12–19°C (Jan), 24–33°C (Jul–Aug).

National holidays
Jan 1 (Foundation of the Republic of China), Feb 28 (Peace Memorial), Apr 5 (National Tomb Sweeping), May 1, Oct 10 (National); NY (Chinese) (Jan/Feb) (3), Dragon Boat Festival (Jun), Mid-Autumn Festival (Sep/Oct).

Political leaders

President

1950–75	Chiang Kai-shek	1987–2000	Lee Teng-hui
1975–8	Yen Chia-kan	2000–	Chen Shui-bian
1978–87	Chiang Ching-kuo		

President of Executive Council

1950–4	Ch'eng Ch'eng	1978–84	Sun Yun-suan
1954–8	O K Yui	1984–9	Yu Kuo-hwa
1958–63	Ch'eng Ch'eng	1989–90	Lee Huan
1963–72	Yen Chia-ken	1990–3	Hau Pei-tsun
1972–8	Chiang Ching-kuo	1993–6	Lien Chan

Prime Minister

1996–7	Lien Chan	2000–2	Chang Chun-hsiung
1997–2000	Vincent Siew	2002–5	Yu Shyi-kun
2000	Tang Fei	2005–	Frank Hsieh

What's in a Name?

'Taiwan' is perhaps the most controversial country name in the world, for complex historical reasons. When the Communists took control of China in 1949, renaming it the People's Republic of China, the defeated Nationalist government fled to the island of Formosa and set up a 'Chinese government-in-exile'. They kept China's old name and so renamed the island Republic of China, which is still Taiwan's official name. Today there is a movement to rename the country simply as Taiwan and move on as an independent country. But China claims that Taiwan is a Chinese province that should be under mainland Chinese control, and many people fear that renaming the country would be viewed by the Chinese authorities as an act of wilful independence that would provoke violent retaliation.

TAJIKISTAN

Official name	Republic of Tajikistan	**Nationality**	Tajik or Tadzhik, Tajikistani
Local name	Cumhurii Tocikiston		
Former name	Tajik Soviet Socialist Republic (until 1991), within the Union of Soviet Socialist Republics (USSR; 1929–91)	**Languages**	Tajik, Uzbek, Russian
		Ethnic groups	Tajik 66%, Uzbek 26%, Russian 3%, others 5%
		Religions	Islam 85% (Sunni 80%, Shia 5%), others 15%
Independence	1991	**Time zone**	GMT +5
Area	143 100 sq km/55 200 sq mi	**Currency**	1 Somoni (S/TJS) = 100 dirams
Capital	Dushanbe; Dušanbe	**Telephone**	+992
Chief towns	Khudzand, Kulyab, Kurgan-Tyube	**Internet**	.tj
		Country code	TJK
Population	6 507 000 (2005e)		

Location
A republic in central Asia, bounded to the north by Kyrgyzstan; to the east by China; to the south by Afghanistan; and to the west and north by Uzbekistan.

Physical description
Tien Shan, Gissar-Alai and Pamir mountain ranges cover over 90% of the area; highest peak is Peak Ismoili Somoni (formerly Communism Peak; 7 495m/24 590ft); River Amudarya flows east to west along the southern border; largest lake is Lake Kara-Kul.

Climate
Predominantly continental; hot summers and mild winters.

National holidays
Jan 1, Mar 8 (Women), 21, May 9 (Victory), Sep 9 (Independence), Oct 14 (Formation of the Tajik Republic); ER.

Political leaders

President
1991–2	Rakhman Nabiev
1992	Akbarsho Iskandrov *Acting President*
1992–	Emomali Sharipovich Rakhmonov

Prime Minister
1991–2	Akbar Mirzoyev	1994–6	Jamshed Karimov
1992–3	Abdumalik Abdullojanov	1996–9	Yahya Azimov
1993–4	Abduljalil Samadov *Acting Prime Minister*	1999–	Akil Akilov

Ice White

The flag of Tajikistan has three horizontal stripes of green, white and red, with a gold crown and seven stars above it. The green is said to represent the country's valleys and the white to symbolize not only the snow and ice of Tajikistan's many mountains but also cotton, a major export. The red stripe suggests the unified republic and sympathy with other countries.

TANZANIA

Official name	United Republic of Tanzania	**Languages**	Kiswahili, English; local languages are also spoken
Local name	Tanzania		
Former name	Republic of Tanganyika (1962–4), United Republic of Tanganyika and Zanzibar (1964)	**Ethnic groups**	Nyamwezi and Sukuma 22%, Swahili 9%, Hehet and Bena 7%, Makonde 6%, Haya 6%, other tribes 50%
Independence	1961		
Area	939 652 sq km/362 706 sq mi	**Religions**	Christianity 35%, Islam 33%, traditional beliefs 30%, others 2%
Capital	Dodoma (political) and Dar es Salaam (commercial)	**Time zone**	GMT +3
		Currency	1 Tanzanian Shilling (Tsh/TZS) = 100 cents
Chief towns	Dar es Salaam, Zanzibar, Mwanza, Tanga, Arusha	**Telephone**	+255
Population	38 329 000 (2005e)	**Internet**	.tz
Nationality	Tanzanian	**Country code**	TZA

Location
An republic in eastern Africa, bounded to the north-west by Burundi and Rwanda; to the north by Uganda and Kenya; to the east by the Indian Ocean; to the south by Mozambique and Malawi; to the south-west by Zambia; and to the west by Democratic Republic of the Congo.

Physical description
Largest East African country, just south of the Equator; central plateau at average elevation of 1 000m/3 281ft; high grasslands and mountain ranges to the centre and south; Rift Valley branches around Lake Victoria in the north; several high volcanic peaks, notably Mt Kilimanjaro, the highest point (5 895m/19 340ft); extensive Serengeti plain to the west; island of Zanaibar lies off the coast.

Climate
Hot, humid and tropical on the coast and offshore islands; average temperature is c.23°C (Jun–Sept) and 27°C (Dec–Mar); hot and dry on the central plateau; semi-temperate at altitudes above 1 500m/4 921ft; permanent snow on high peaks.

National holidays
Jan 1, 12 (Zanzibar Revolution), Apr 26 (Union), May 1, Jul 7 (Industrial), Aug 8 (Farmers), Dec 9 (Independence/Republic), 25, 26; Ad, EM, ER (2), GF, PB.

Political leaders

President
1964–85	Julius Kambarage Nyerere
1985–95	Ali Hassan Mwinyi
1995–	Benjamin William Mkapa

That Sinking Feeling
The name 'Dodoma' comes from a local word meaning 'it has sunk', supposedly referring to an elephant that became stuck in a swamp in the area.

Prime Minister
1964–72	Rashid M Kawawa *Vice President*		1984–5	Salim A Salim
1972–7	Rashid M Kawawa		1985–90	Joseph S Warioba
1977–80	Edward M Sokoine		1990–4	John Malecela
1980–3	Cleopa D Msuya		1994–5	Cleopa Msuya
1983–4	Edward M Sokoine		1995–	Frederick Tluway Sumaye

THAILAND

Official name	Kingdom of Thailand	Languages	Thai
Local name	Prathet Thai	Ethnic groups	Thai 75%, Chinese 14%, others 11%
Former name	Siam (until 1939 and 1945–49)	Religions	Buddhism 95%, Islam 4%, others 1%
Area	513 115 sq km/198 062 sq mi	Time zone	GMT +7
Capital	Bangkok; Krung Thep	Currency	1 Baht (B/THB) = 100 satang
Chief towns	Chiang Mai, Nakhon Ratchasima	Telephone	+66
Population	64 233 000 (2005e)	Internet	.th
Nationality	Thai	Country code	THA

Location
A kingdom in south-east Asia, bounded to the north-east and east by Laos; to the south-east by Cambodia; to the south by Malaysia and the Gulf of Thailand; to the west by the Andaman Sea; and to the west and north-west by Myanmar.

Physical description
Central agricultural region dominated by the Chao Phraya River floodplain; large north-eastern plateau; mountainous north rises to 2 595m/8 514ft at Doi Inthanon; low-lying south covered in tropical rainforest; mangrove-forested coastal islands.

Climate
Equatorial climate in the south; tropical monsoon climate in the north and centre.

National holidays
Jan 1, Apr 6 (Chakri), 13 (Songkran) (3), May 1, 5 (Coronation), Aug 12 (Queen's Birthday), Oct 23 (Chulalongkorn Memorial), Dec 5 (King's Birthday), 10 (Constitution), 31; Buddhist Lent (Jul), Makha Bucha (Feb), Visakha Bucha (May).

Political leaders

Monarch

1868–1910	Chulalongkorn, Rama V	1939–46	Nai Pridi Phanomyong *Regent*
1910–25	Rama VI	1946	Rama IX
1925–35	Rama VII	1946–50	Rangsit of Chainat *Regent*
1935–9	Rama VIII (Ananda Mahidol)	1950–	Bhumibol Adulyadej

Prime Minister

1932–3	Phraya Manopakom	1957–8	Thanom Kittikatchorn
1933–8	Phraya Phahon Phonphahuyasena	1958–63	Sarit Thanarat
1938–44	Luang Phibun Songgram	1963–73	Thanom Kittikatchorn
1944–5	Nai Khuang Aphaiwong	1973–5	Sanya Dharmasakti
1945	Thawi Bunyaket	1975–6	Mom Rachawongse Kukrit Pramoj
1945–6	Mom Rachawongse Seni Pramoj	1976	Seni Pramoj
1946	Nai Khuang Aphaiwong	1976–7	Thanin Kraivichien
1946	Nai Pridi Phanomyong	1977–80	Kriangsak Chammanard
1946–7	Luang Thamrong Nawasawat	1980–7	Prem Tinsulanonda
1947–8	Nai Khuang Aphaiwong	1987–91	Chatichai Choonhaven
1948–57	Luang Phibun Songgram	1991–2	Anand Panyarachun
1957	Sarit Thanarat	1992	Suchinda Kraprayoon
1957	Nai Pote Sarasin	1992	Anand Panyarachun

1992–5	Chuan Leekpai	1997–2001	Chuan Leekpai
1995–6	Banharn Silpa-Archa	2001–	Thaksin Shinawatra
1996–7	Chavalit Yongchaiyudh		

TOBAGO see **TRINIDAD AND TOBAGO**

TOGO

Official name	Republic of Togo (also Togolese Republic)		languages are also spoken
Local name	Togo; République Togolaise	**Ethnic groups**	Ewe-Adja 41%, TemKabre 25%, Gurma 16%, others 18%
Former name	French Togoland (until 1956)	**Religions**	traditional beliefs 55%, Christianity 30% (RC 23%, Prot 7%), Islam 15%
Independence	1960		
Area	56 600 sq km/21 848 sq mi		
Capital	Lomé	**Time zone**	GMT
Chief towns	Sokodé, Kpalimé, Atakpamé	**Currency**	1 CFA Franc (CFAFr/XOF) = 100 centimes
Population	6 145 000 (2005e)	**Telephone**	+228
Nationality	Togolese	**Internet**	.tg
Languages	French; many local	**Country code**	TGO

Location
A republic in West Africa, bounded to the north by Burkina Faso; to the east by Benin; to the south by the Bight of Benin in the Gulf of Guinea; and to the west by Ghana.

Physical description
Rises from the lagoon coast of the Gulf of Guinea, past low-lying plains to the Atakora Mountains, which run north-east to south-west across the north of the country; highest peak is Pic Baumann (Mt Agou; 986m/3 235ft); flat plains lie to the north-west.

Climate
Tropical; rain throughout the year in the south; one rainy season in the north Jul–Sep.

National holidays
Jan 1, 13 (National Liberation), 24 (Economic Liberation), Feb 2 (Triumphant Return), Apr 24 (Victory), 27 (Independence), May 1, Jun 1 (Trees), 21 (Pya Martyrs), Aug 15, 30 (Historical Address of Kpalimé), Sep 23 (Anniversary of Terrorist Aggression), Nov 1, 30 (Creation of the RPT), Dec 25; A, Ad, EM, WM.

Political leaders

President

1960–3	Sylvanus Olympio	2005	Faure Gnassingbé *Acting President*
1963–7	Nicolas Grunitzky	2005	Abass Bonfoh *Acting President*
1967–2005	Gnassingbé Eyadéma	2005–	Faure Gnassingbé

Prime Minister

1991–4	Joseph Koukou Koffigoh	2000–2	Messan Agbeyome Kodjo
1994–6	Edem Kodjo	2002–5	Koffi Sama
1996–9	Kwassi Klutse	2005–	Edem Kodjo
1999–2000	Eugene Koffi Adoboli		

TOKELAU *see* **NEW ZEALAND**

TONGA

Official name	Kingdom of Tonga; also sometimes known as the Friendly Islands	**Languages**	English, Tongan
		Ethnic groups	Tongan 98%, others 2%
Local name	Tonga; Pule'anga Fakatu'I 'O Tonga	**Religions**	Christianity 79% (Prot 63%, RC 16%), others 21%
Independence	1970	**Time zone**	GMT +13
Area	646 sq km/249 sq mi	**Currency**	1 Pa'anga (T$/TOP) = 100 seniti
Capital	Nuku'alofa	**Telephone**	+676
Population	102 000 (2005e)	**Internet**	.to
Nationality	Tongan	**Country code**	TON

Location
An independent island kingdom in the south-west Pacific Ocean north-east of New Zealand.

Physical description
Comprises 171 islands, 45 of which are inhabited, divided into three main groups (coral formations of Ha'apai and Tongatapu-Eua, mountainous Vava'u); largest island is Tongatapu; western islands are mainly volcanic (some still active); highest point is the extinct volcano Kao (1 046m/3 432ft).

Climate
Semi-tropical; average annual temperature on Tongatapu is 23°C; occasional hurricanes in the summer months.

National holidays
Jan 1, Apr 25 (Anzac), May 4 (Birthday of Crown Prince Tupouto'a), Jun 4 (Emancipation), Jul 4 (King's Birthday), Nov 4 (Constitution), Dec 4 (King Tupou I), 25, 26; EM, GF.

Political leaders

Monarch
1893–1918	George Tupou II
1918–65	Salote Tupou III
1965–	Taufa'ahau Tupou IV

Prime Minister
1970–91	Fatafehi Tu'ipelehake
1991–2000	Baron Vaea
2000–	Prince 'Ulukalala Lavaka Ata

Catching a Kingdom

According to legend, Tonga was formed in ancient times by the Polynesian sun god Maui Fusi-Fonua, who was out fishing. The sun god's special tortoiseshell and whalebone fishhook became caught in the seabed, and as he pulled impatiently on the line to free it, he dragged a clump of land up from the ocean floor. Suddenly his hook snapped, and the land entangled on the hook broke up, scattering in pieces across the sea to create the islands of Tonga.

TRINIDAD AND TOBAGO

Official name	Republic of Trinidad and Tobago		40%, mixed 14%, others 6%
Local name	Trinidad and Tobago	**Religions**	Christianity 60% (RC 32%, Prot 28%), Hinduism 24%, Islam 6%, none/unaffiliated 5%, others 5%
Independence	1962		
Area	5 128 sq km/1 979 sq mi		
Capital	Port of Spain	**Time zone**	GMT –4
Chief towns	San Fernando, Arima, Scarborough	**Currency**	1 Trinidad and Tobago Dollar (TT$/TTD) = 100 cents
Population	1 305 000 (2005e)		
Nationality	Trinidadian, Tobagonian	**Telephone**	+1 868
Languages	English	**Internet**	.tt
Ethnic groups	black 40%, East Indian	**Country code**	TTO

Location
A republic in the Lesser Antilles in the south-east Caribbean Sea, just north of South America; Trinidad is separated from Venezuela in the south by the 11km/7mi wide Gulf of Paria; Tobago lies 30km/19mi north-east of Trinidad.

Physical description
Trinidad is roughly rectangular; crossed by three mountain ranges; highest point is El Cerro del Aripo (940m/3 084ft); rest is low-lying, with large coastal mangrove swamps; Pitch Lake is the world's largest reservoir of natural asphalt; Tobago's Main Ridge extends along most of the island, rising to 576m/1 890ft.

Climate
Tropical, with an annual average temperature of 29°C.

National holidays
Jan 1, Mar 30 (Spiritual Baptist Liberation Shouter), May 30 (Indian Arrival), Jun 19 (Labour), Aug 1 (Emancipation), 31 (Independence), Dec 25, 26; CC, D, EM, ER, GF.

Political leaders

President

1976–87	Ellis Emmanuel Clarke	1997–2003	Arthur Ray Robinson
1987–97	Noor Mohammed Hassanali	2003–	George Maxwell Richards

Premier

1956–62	Eric Williams

Prime Minister

1962–81	Eric Williams	1991–5	Patrick Manning
1981–6	George Chambers	1995–2001	Basdeo Panday
1986–91	Raymond Robinson	2001–	Patrick Manning

Steel Band Music

The music of steel bands plays a central part in the culture of Trinidad and Tobago, and the government lists the steel pan as one of the national symbols alongside the national bird, the national flower, the state flag and the coat of arms.

TUNISIA

Official name	Republic of Tunisia	**Ethnic groups**	Arab and Berber 98%, European 1%, Jewish and others 1%
Local name	Tūnisiya; Al-Jumhūriyya at-Tūnisiyya		
Independence	1956	**Religions**	Islam 98%, Christianity 1%, others 1%
Area	164 150 sq km/63 362 sq mi	**Time zone**	GMT +1
Capital	Tunis; Toûnis, Tunus	**Currency**	1 Tunisian Dinar (TD, D/TND) = 1 000 millimes
Chief towns	Bizerta, Sousse, Sfax, Gabes	**Telephone**	+216
Population	10 102 000 (2005e)	**Internet**	.tn
Nationality	Tunisian	**Country code**	TUN
Languages	Arabic; French is also spoken		

Location
A republic in North Africa, bounded to the north-east and north by the Mediterranean Sea; to the south-east by Libya; and to the west by Algeria.

Physical description
Atlas Mountains in the north-west rise to 1 544m/5 066ft at Djebel Chambi; central depression runs west to east, containing several salty lakes; dry, sandy upland lies to the south.

Climate
Mediterranean climate on the coast, with hot, dry summers and wet winters; daily maximum temperature is 14–33°C; higher rainfall in the Atlas Mountains; further south, rainfall decreases and temperatures can be extreme.

National holidays
Jan 1, 18 (Revolution), Mar 20 (Independence), Apr 9 (Martyrs), May 1, Jun 1 (Victory), 2 (Youth), Jul 25 (Republic), Aug 13 (Women), Sep 3 (3 Sep 1934), Oct 15 (Evacuation), Nov 7 (Election of President); Ad (2), ER (2), NY (Muslim), PB.

Political leaders

Bey
1943–57   Muhammad VIII

President
1957–87   Habib Bourguiba
1987–   Zine Al-Abidine Bin Ali

Prime Minister

1956–7	Habib Bourguiba	1986–7	Rashid Sfar
1957–69	*No Prime Minister*	1987	Zine Al-Abidine Bin Ali
1969–70	Bahi Ladgham	1987–9	Hadi Baccouche
1970–80	Hadi Nouira	1989–99	Hamed Karoui
1980–6	Mohammed Mezali	1999–	Mohammed Ghannouchi

TURKEY

Official name	Republic of Turkey		16%, Arab 2%, others 2%
Local name	Türkiye; Türkiye Çumhuriyeti	**Religions**	Islam 99% (mostly Sunni), others 1%
Area	779 452 sq km/300 868 sq mi	**Time zone**	GMT +2
Capital	Ankara; Angora	**Currency**	1 new Turkish Lira (TL/TRY) = 100 new kurus
Chief towns	Istanbul, Izmir, Adana, Bursa, Gaziantep		
Population	73 193 000 (2005e)	**Telephone**	+90
Nationality	Turkish	**Internet**	.tr
Languages	Turkish	**Country code**	TUR
Ethnic groups	Turkish 80%, Kurdish		

Location
A republic lying between Europe and Asia, bounded to the north by Bulgaria and the Black Sea; to the north-east by Georgia, Armenia, Azerbaijan and Iran; and to the south by Iraq, Syria and the Mediterranean Sea.

Physical description
Mountainous (average height 1 100m/3 609ft); average altitude of the central plateau is 1 000–2 000m/3 281–6 562ft; Taurus Mountains cover the entire southern part of Anatolia; highest peak is Mt Ararat (5 165m/16 945ft); alluvial coastal plains; the Turkish Straits (the Dardanelles, Sea of Marmara and Bosporus) connect the Black Sea in the north-east and the Mediterranean Sea in the south-west.

Climate
Typically Mediterranean climate on the Aegean and Mediterranean coasts, with hot, dry summers and warm, wet winters; further east along the Black Sea coast, rainfall becomes heavy in summer and autumn; low rainfall on the interior plateau, with cold winters and warm or hot summers.

National holidays
Jan 1, Apr 23 (National Sovereignty and Children), May 19 (Atatürk Commemoration/Youth and Sports), Aug 30 (Victory), Oct 29 (Republic); Ad (4), ER (3).

Political leaders

Sultan of the Ottoman Empire
1876–1909	Abdülhamit
1909–18	Mehmet Reşat
1918–22	Mehmet Vahideddin

President
1923–38	Mustafa Kemal Atatürk	1980–9	Kenan Evren *Chairman of National Security Council until 1982*
1938–50	İsmet İnönü		
1950–60	Celal Bayar		
1960–6	Cemal Gürsel	1989–93	Turgut Özal
1966–73	Cevdet Sunay	1993–2000	Süleyman Demirel
1973–80	Fahri S Korutürk	2000–	Ahmet Necdet Sezer
1980	Ihsan Çaglayangil *Acting President*		

Prime Minister

1923–4	İsmet İnönü	1974–5	Sadi Irmak
1924–5	Ali Fethi Okyar	1975–7	Süleyman Demirel
1925–37	İsmet İnönü	1977	Bülent Ecevit
1937–9	Celal Bayar	1977–8	Süleyman Demirel
1939–42	Dr Refik Saydam	1978–9	Bülent Ecevit
1942–6	Şükrü Saracoğlu	1979–80	Süleyman Demirel
1946–7	Recep Peker	1980–3	Bülent Ülüsü
1947–9	Hasan Saka	1983–9	Turgut Özal
1949–50	Şemşettin Günaltay	1989–91	Yildrim Akbulut
1950–60	Adnan Menderes	1991	Mesut Yilmaz
1960–1	Cemal Gürsel	1991–3	Süleyman Demirel
1961–5	İsmet İnönü	1993–6	Tansu Çiller
1965	S Hayri Ürgüplü	1996	Mesut Yilmaz
1965–71	Süleyman Demirel	1996–7	Necmettin Erbakan
1971–2	Nihat Erim	1997–8	Mesut Yilmaz
1972–3	Ferit Melen	1999–2002	Bülent Ecevit
1973–4	Naim Talu	2002–3	Abdullah Gül
1974	Bülent Ecevit	2003–	Recep Tayyip Erdoğan

TURKMENISTAN

Official name	Republic of Turkmenistan	**Population**	4 833 000 (2005e)
Local name	Turkmenostan; Turkmenostan Respublikasy	**Nationality**	Turkmen
		Languages	Turkmen, Russian, Uzbek
Former name	Turkmen Soviet Socialist Republic (1924–91), within the Union of Soviet Socialist Republics (USSR; 1925–91)	**Ethnic groups**	Turkmen 77%, Uzbek 9%, Russian 7%, Kazakh 2%, others 5%
		Religions	Islam 89% (mostly Sunni), Christianity 9% (Orthodox), others 2%
Independence	1991		
Area	488 100 sq km/188 400 sq mi	**Time zone**	GMT +5
		Currency	1 Manat (TMM) = 100 tenesi
Capital	Ashgabat; Ašgabat, Ašhabad	**Telephone**	+993
Chief towns	Chardzhou, Mary, Türkmenbashi, Nebit-Dag	**Internet**	.tm
		Country code	TKM

Location
A republic in central Asia, bounded to the north by Kazakhstan and Uzbekistan; to the south by Afghanistan and Iran; and to the west by the Caspian Sea.

Physical description
Low-lying with hills in the south; mainly desert; highest point is Ayrybaba (3 139m/10 298ft).

Climate
Continental, hot and arid in the large desert areas.

National holidays
Jan 1, 12 (Remembrance/Anniversary of the Battle of Geok-Tepe), Feb 19 (President's Birthday), Mar 8 (Women), 21, May 9 (Victory); Ad, Day of Revival and Unity (May), Independence (Oct).

Political leaders

President
1991–   Saparmurad Niyazov

Prime Minister
1991–2   Khan Akhmedov
1992–   *As President*

Beard Ban

President Niyazov of Turkmenistan has renamed January after himself, April after his late mother and built a 12m/39ft gold statue of himself which revolves to face the sun. He has also banned opera, ballet, beards and gold teeth.

TURKS AND CAICOS ISLANDS *see* **UNITED KINGDOM**

TUVALU

Official name	Tuvalu	**Languages**	Tuvaluan, English
Local name	Tuvalu; Fakavae Aliki-Malo I Tuvalu	**Ethnic groups**	Polynesia 95%, others 5%
Former name	Ellice Islands, as part of the Gilbert and Ellice Islands (until 1975)	**Religions**	Christianity 98%, Baha'i 1%, others 1%
		Time zone	GMT +12
Independence	1978	**Currency**	1 Australian Dollar (A$/AUD) = 100 cents
Area	26 sq km/10 sq mi		
Capital	Fongafale (on Funafuti)	**Telephone**	+688
Population	10 000 (2005e)	**Internet**	.tv
Nationality	Tuvaluan	**Country code**	TUV

Location
An island state in the south-west Pacific, 1 050km/650mi north of Fiji.

Physical description
Comprises nine low-lying coral atolls, rising no higher than 5m/16ft, running north-west to south-east in a chain 580km/360mi long.

Climate
Hot and humid; average annual temperature is 30°C.

National holidays
Jan 1, May 13 (Gospel), Jun 14 (Queen's Birthday), Aug 5 (Children), Oct 1 (Independence), Dec 25, 26; EM, GF; Commonwealth Day (2nd Mon in Mar).

Political leaders

Head of State: British monarch, represented by Governor General (Filoimea Telito since 2005).

Prime Minister

1978–81	Toalipi Lauti	2000–1	Lagitupu Tuilimu *Acting Prime Minister*
1981–9	Tomasi Puapua		
1989–93	Bikenibeu Paeniu	2001	Faimalaga Luka
1993–6	Kamuta Lataasi	2001–2	Koloa Talake
1996–9	Bikenibeu Paeniu	2002–4	Saufatu Sopoanga
1999–2000	Ionatana Ionatana	2004–	Maatia Toafa

UGANDA

Official name	Republic of Uganda	**Ethnic groups**	Ganda 19%, Banyoro 15%, Teso 9%, Banyan 8%, Basogo 8%, Bagisu 7%, Bachiga 7%, others 27%
Local name	Uganda		
Independence	1962		
Area	238 461 sq km/92 029 sq mi		
		Religions	Christianity 66% (RC 33%, Prot 33%), traditional beliefs 18%, Islam 16%
Capital	Kampala		
Chief towns	Jinja, Mbale, Tororo, Soroti, Entebbe		
Population	28 816 000 (2005e)	**Time zone**	GMT +3
Nationality	Ugandan	**Currency**	1 Uganda Shilling (USh/UGX) = 100 cents
Languages	English; Swahili and other languages are also spoken		
		Telephone	+256
		Internet	.ug
		Country code	UGA

Location
A republic in East Africa, bounded to the north by Sudan; to the east by Kenya; to the south by Tanzania and Rwanda; and to the west by Democratic Republic of the Congo.

Physical description
Mainly on a plateau with an elevation of 900–1 000m/2 950ft–3 280ft; population is concentrated in the fertile Lake Victoria basin; highest point is Margherita Peak (5 110m/16 765ft) in the Mt Stanley massif; main rivers are the upper reaches of the River Nile.

Climate
Highest rainfall is in the mountains to the west and south-west and along the shores of Lake Victoria; daily temperatures at Entebbe on the north shore of the lake are 24–28°C; central and north-eastern areas receive less rain.

National holidays
Jan 1, 26 (NRM Anniversary), Mar 8 (Women), May 1, Jun 3 (Martyrs), 9 (Heroes), Oct 9 (Independence), Dec 25, 26; Ad, EM, ER, GF.

Political leaders

Antelope Hill
The name of Uganda's capital city, Kampala, comes from *Kasozi Kampala*, meaning 'the hill of antelopes'.

Governor-General

1962–3	Walter Fleming Coutts

President

1963–6	Edward Muteesa II	1979–80	Godfrey Lukongwa Binaisa
1966–71	Apollo Milton Obote	1981–5	Apollo Milton Obote
1971–9	Idi Amin	1985–6	*Military Council* (Tito Okello Lutwa)
1979	Yusuf Kironde Lule	1986–	Yoweri Kaguta Museveni

Prime Minister

1962–71	Apollo Milton Obote	1986–91	Samson B Kisekka
1971–81	*No Prime Minister*	1991–4	George Cosmas Adyebo
1981–5	Eric Otema Alimadi	1994–9	Kintu Musoke
1985	Paulo Muwanga	1999–	Apolo Nsibambi
1985–6	Abraham N Waliggo		

UKRAINE

Official name	Ukraine	**Nationality**	Ukrainian
Local name	Ukraïna	**Languages**	Ukrainian, Russian
Former name	Ukrainian Soviet Socialist Republic (1919–91), within the Union of Soviet Socialist Republics (USSR; 1922–91)	**Ethnic groups**	Ukrainian 73%, Russian 22%, Jewish 1%, others 4%
		Religions	Christianity 93% (Orthodox 76%, RC 14%, Prot 3%), Judaism 2%, others 5%
Independence	1991		
Area	603 700 sq km/233 028 sq mi	**Time zone**	GMT +2
Capital	Kiev; Kyïv	**Currency**	1 Hryvnia (UAH) = 100 kopiykas
Chief towns	Kharkov, Donetsk, Odessa, Dnepropetrovsk, Lvov, Zaporozhye, Krivoy Rog	**Telephone**	+380
		Internet	.ua
		Country code	UKR
Population	46 481 000 (2005e)		

Location
A republic in eastern Europe, bounded to the north by Belarus; to the east by Russia; to the south by the Black Sea; to the south-west by Moldova and Romania; and to the west by Hungary, Slovakia and Poland.

Physical description
Generally a plain with high elevations in the west, south and south-east; Ukrainian Carpathian Mountains in the west rise to 2 061m/6 762ft at Hora Hoverla; Crimean Peninsula separates the Black Sea from the Sea of Azov; Crimean Mountains lie along the south coast of the peninsula; many reservoirs and lakes.

Climate
Temperate, continental; cold winters and warm summers.

National holidays
Jan 1, 7 (Eastern Orthodox Christmas), Mar 8 (Women), May 1 (2), 9 (Victory), Jun 28 (Constitution), Aug 24 (Independence); Orthodox Easter (Apr/May) (2).

Political leaders

President

1991–4	Leonid Kravchuk	2005–	Viktor Yushchenko
1994–2005	Leonid Kuchma		

Prime Minister

1990–2	Vitold Fokin	1997–9	Valery Pustovoytenko
1992	Valentin Symonenko	1999–2001	Viktor Yushchenko
1992–3	Leonid Kuchma	2001–2	Anatoli Kinakh
1993–4	Yukhim Zvyahilski *Acting Prime Minister*	2002–5	Viktor Yanukovich
		2005	Mykola Azarov *Acting Prime Minister*
1994–5	Vitalii Masol		
1995–6	Yevhenii Maruk	2005–	Yuliya Tymoshenko
1996–7	Pavlo Lazarenko		
1997	Vasyl Durdynets *Acting Prime Minister*		

UMM AL-QAIWAIN *see* **UNITED ARAB EMIRATES**

UNITED ARAB EMIRATES

Official name	United Arab Emirates (UAE)	**Nationality**	Emirati
		Languages	Arabic, English
Local name	Ittihād al-imārāt al-'Arabīyah	**Ethnic groups**	Asian 52%, Emirian 18%, other Arab 24%, others 6%
Former name	Trucial States (until 1971)		
		Religions	Islam 96%, others 4%
Independence	1971	**Time zone**	GMT +4
Area	83 600 sq km/32 300 sq mi	**Currency**	1 UAE Dirham (DH/AED) = 100 fils
Capital	Abu Dhabi; Abū Zhaby		
Chief towns	Dubai, Sharjah, Ras al-Khaimah	**Telephone**	+971
		Internet	.ae
		Country code	ARE
Population	4 496 000 (2005e)		

Location
A federation in the eastern central Arabian Peninsula comprising seven internally self-governing emirates (Abu Dhabi, Ajman, Dubai, Fujairah, Ras al-Khaimah, Sharjah and Umm al-Qaiwain), bounded to the north by the Arabian Gulf; to the east by Oman; and to the south and west by Saudi Arabia.

Physical description
Located along the southern shore of the Arabian Gulf; Fujairah has a coastline along the Gulf of Oman; salt marshes predominate on the coast; barren desert and gravel plain inland; Hajar Mountains in Fujairah rise to over 1 000m/3 280ft; highest point is Jabal Yibir (1 527m/5 010ft).

Climate
Hot with limited rainfall; winter temperatures average 21°C, with high humidity (in excess of 70%); less humid in summer, with maximum temperatures rising to 45°C; sandstorms are common.

National holidays
Jan 1, Aug 6 (Accession of Ruler), Dec 2 (National); Ad (4), Ascension of the Prophet, ER (3), NY (Muslim), PB, R.

Political leaders

President
1971–2004	Zayed Bin Sultan al-Nahayan
2004–	Khalifa Bin Zayed al-Nahayan

Prime Minister
1971–9	Maktoum Bin Rashid al-Maktoum
1979–91	Rashid Bin Said al-Maktoum
1991–	Maktoum Bin Rashid al-Maktoum

Abu Dhabi

Tribe: al Bu Falah or al Nahyan (Bani Yas)
Family name: al-Nahyan

Sheikh
1855–1909	Zayed	1926–8	Saqr
1909–12	Tahnoun	1928–66	Shakhbout
1912–22	Hamdan	1966–2004	Zayed
1922–6	Sultan	2004–	Khalifa

Ajman

Tribe: al Bu Kharayban (Naim)
Family name: al-Nuaimi

Sheikh

1900–10	Abdel-Aziz		1928–81	Rashid
1910–28	Humaid		1981–	Humaid

Dubai

Tribe: al Bu Flasah (Bani Yas)
Family name: al-Maktoum

Sheikh

1894–1906	Maktoum		1958–90	Rashid
1906–12	Butti		1990–	Maktoum
1912–58	Said			

Fujairah

Tribe: Sharqiyyin
Family name: al-Sharqi

Sheikh

1952–75	Mohammed
1975–	Hamad

Ras al-Khaimah

Tribe: Huwalah
Family name: al-Qasimi

Sheikh

1921–48	Sultan
1948–	Saqr

Sharjah

Tribe: Huwalah
Family name: al-Qasimi

Sheikh

1883–1914	Saqr		1965–72	Khaled
1914–24	Khaled		1972–87	Sultan
1924–51	Sultan		1987	Abdel-Aziz
1951–65	Saqr		1987–	Sultan

Umm al-Qaiwain

Tribe: al-Ali
Family name: al-Mualla

Sheikh

1873–1904	Ahmad		1923–9	Hamad
1904–22	Rashid		1929–81	Ahmad
1922–3	Abdullah		1981–	Rashid

UNITED KINGDOM

Official name	United Kingdom of Great Britain and Northern Ireland (UK)	**Ethnic groups**	white 94%, Asian 1%, West Indian 1%, Indian 1%, others 3%
Local name	United Kingdom	**Religions**	Christianity[1] 71.6%, none/unaffiliated 15.5%, unknown 7.3%, Islam 2.7%, Hinduism 1%, Sikhism 0.6%, Judaism 0.5%, Buddhism 0.3%, others 0.3%
Area	244 755 sq km/94 475 sq mi		
Capital	London		
Chief towns	Birmingham, Leeds, Glasgow, Sheffield, Bradford, Edinburgh, Liverpool, Manchester, Cardiff, Belfast, Newcastle upon Tyne	**Time zone**	GMT
		Currency	1 Pound Sterling (£/GBP) = 100 pence
Population	59 668 000 (2005e)	**Telephone**	+44
Nationality	British	**Internet**	.uk
Languages	English; Welsh and Gaelic are also spoken	**Country code**	GBR

Location
An island kingdom in western Europe, comprising England, Scotland, Wales and Northern Ireland; separated from France to the south by the English Channel, and from Ireland to the west by the Irish Sea; Northern Ireland borders Ireland to the south.

Climate
Temperate maritime climate, moderated by prevailing south-west winds; generally wetter and warmer in the west.

[1] 2001 Census data; did not distinguish different Christian denominations.

Political leaders

Monarch

House of Stuart

1603–25	James I (VI of Scotland)
1625–49	Charles I

Commonwealth and Protectorate

1649–53	*Council of State*
1653–8	Oliver Cromwell *Lord Protector*
1658–9	Richard Cromwell *Lord Protector*

House of Stuart (restored)

1660–85	Charles II	1694–1702	William III (*alone*)
1685–8	James II	1702–14	Anne
1689–94	Mary II and William III (*jointly*)		

House of Hanover

1714–27	George I	1820–30	George IV
1727–60	George II	1830–7	William IV
1760–1820	George III	1837–1901	Victoria

House of Saxe-Coburg

1901–10	Edward VII

House of Windsor

1910–36	George V	1936–52	George VI
1936	Edward VIII	1952–	Elizabeth II

Prime Minister

1721–42	Robert Walpole *Whig*	1852–5	Lord Aberdeen (George Hamilton Gordon) *Peelite*
1742–3	Earl of Wilmington (Spencer Compton) *Whig*	1855–8	Viscount Palmerston (Henry John Temple) *Lib*
1743–54	Henry Pelham *Whig*	1858–9	Earl of Derby *Con*
1754–6	Duke of Newcastle (Thomas Pelham-Holles) *Whig*	1859–65	Viscount Palmerston *Lib*
1756–7	Duke of Devonshire (William Cavendish) *Whig*	1865–6	Lord John Russell *Lib*
		1866–8	Earl of Derby *Con*
1757–62	Duke of Newcastle *Whig*	1868	Benjamin Disraeli *Con*
1762–3	Earl of Bute (John Stuart) *Tory*	1868–74	William Ewart Gladstone *Lib*
1763–5	George Grenville *Whig*	1874–80	Benjamin Disraeli *Con*
1765–6	Marquess of Rockingham (Charles Watson Wentworth) *Whig*	1880–5	William Ewart Gladstone *Lib*
		1885–6	Marquess of Salisbury (Robert Gascoyne-Cecil) *Con*
1766–70	Duke of Grafton (Augustus Henry Fitzroy) *Whig*	1886	William Ewart Gladstone *Lib*
		1886–92	Marquess of Salisbury *Con*
1770–82	Lord North (Frederick North) *Tory*	1892–4	William Ewart Gladstone *Lib*
1782	Marquess of Rockingham *Whig*	1894–5	Earl of Rosebery (Archibald Philip Primrose) *Lib*
1782–3	Earl of Shelburne (William Petty-Fitzmaurice) *Whig*	1895–1902	Marquess of Salisbury *Con*
1783	Duke of Portland (William Henry Cavendish Bentinck) *Coal*	1902–5	Arthur James Balfour *Con*
		1905–8	Henry Campbell-Bannerman *Lib*
1783–1801	William Pitt *Tory*	1908–15	Herbert Henry Asquith *Lib*
1801–4	Henry Addington *Tory*	1915–16	Herbert Henry Asquith *Coal*
1804–6	William Pitt *Tory*	1916–22	David Lloyd George *Coal*
1806–7	Lord Grenville (William Wyndham) *Whig*	1922–3	Andrew Bonar Law *Con*
		1923–4	Stanley Baldwin *Con*
1807–9	Duke of Portland (William Henry Cavendish Bentinck) *Tory*	1924	James Ramsay MacDonald *Lab*
		1924–9	Stanley Baldwin *Con*
1809–12	Spencer Perceval *Tory*	1929–31	James Ramsay MacDonald *Lab*
1812–27	Earl of Liverpool (Robert Banks Jenkinson) *Tory*	1931–5	James Ramsay MacDonald *Nat*
		1935–7	Stanley Baldwin *Nat*
1827	George Canning *Tory*	1937–40	Arthur Neville Chamberlain *Nat*
1827–8	Viscount Goderich (Frederick John Robinson) *Tory*	1940–5	Winston Churchill *Coal*
		1945–51	Clement Attlee *Lab*
1828–30	Duke of Wellington (Arthur Wellesley) *Tory*	1951–5	Winston Churchill *Con*
		1955–7	Anthony Eden *Con*
1830–4	Earl Grey (Charles Grey) *Whig*	1957–63	Harold Macmillan *Con*
1834	Viscount Melbourne (William Lamb) *Whig*	1963–4	Alec Douglas-Home *Con*
		1964–70	Harold Wilson *Lab*
1834–5	Robert Peel *Con*	1970–4	Edward Heath *Con*
1835–41	Viscount Melbourne *Whig*	1974–6	Harold Wilson *Lab*
1841–6	Robert Peel *Con*	1976–9	James Callaghan *Lab*
1846–52	Lord John Russell *Lib*	1979–90	Margaret Thatcher *Con*
1852	Earl of Derby (Edward George Smith Stanley) *Con*	1990–7	John Major *Con*
		1997–	Tony Blair *Lab*

Coal = Coalition *Lib* = Liberal *Lab* = Labour *Con* = Conservative *Nat* = Nationalist

England

Area	130 357 sq km/50 318 sq mi	Population	50 093 800 (2004e)
Chief towns	Birmingham, Bradford, Liverpool, Leeds, Manchester, Newcastle upon Tyne, Sheffield	Capital	London
		Nationality	English
Physical description	Largely undulating lowland, rising in the south to the Mendips, Cotswolds, Chilterns and North Downs, in the north to the north–south ridge of the Pennines and in the north-west to the Cumbria Mountains; drained in the east by the Tyne, Tees, Humber, Ouse and Thames rivers, and in the west by the Eden, Ribble, Mersey and Severn rivers; Lake District in the north-west includes Derwent Water, Ullswater, Windermere and Bassenthwaite; highest point is Scafell Pike at 978m/3 209ft.		
National holidays	Jan 1, Dec 25, 26; EM, GF, Early May, Spring (May) and Summer (Aug) Bank Holidays.		

Monarch

West Saxon Kings

802–39	Egbert	939–46	Edmund
839–58	Æthelwulf	946–55	Edred
858–60	Æthelbald	955–9	Edwy
860–5	Æthelbert	959–75	Edgar
866–71	Æthelred	975–8	Edward (the Martyr)
871–99	Alfred	978–1016	Æthelred (the Unready)
899–924	Edward (the Elder)	1016	Edmund (Ironside)
924–39	Athelstan		

Danish Kings

1016–35	Knut (Canute)	1040–2	Hardaknut
1035–7	Harold Regent	1042–66	Edward (the Confessor)
1037–40	Harold I (Harefoot)	1066	Harold II

House of Normandy

1066–87	William I (the Conqueror)
1087–1100	William II (Rufus)
1100–35	Henry I

House of Blois

1135–54	Stephen

House of Plantagenet

1154–89	Henry II	1272–1307	Edward I
1189–99	Richard I (the Lionheart)	1307–27	Edward II
1199–1216	John	1327–77	Edward III
1216–72	Henry III	1377–99	Richard II

House of Lancaster

1399–1413	Henry IV
1413–22	Henry V
1422–61	Henry VI

House of York

1461–70   Edward IV

House of Lancaster

1470–1   Henry VI

House of York

1471–83   Edward IV
1483   Edward V
1483–5   Richard III

House of Tudor

1485–1509   Henry VII
1509–47   Henry VIII
1547–53   Edward VI

1553–8   Mary I
1558–1603   Elizabeth I

Divorced, Beheaded, Died

King Henry VIII (1491–1547) is famous for his six wives who, as the schoolchildren's rhyme goes, were sequentially divorced, beheaded, died, divorced, beheaded and survived:

Catherine of Aragon (1485–1536) First married to Henry's brother Arthur, she was betrothed following his early death to her brother-in-law, Henry, who was then aged just 11. She married him in 1509. In 1527 Henry began a procedure for divorce, which he obtained in 1533. Catherine retired to lead an austere religious life until her death.

Anne Boleyn (c.1504–36) Secretly married to Henry in 1533, she was soon declared his legal wife but within months his passion for her had cooled. It was not revived by the birth of a daughter (later Elizabeth I), still less by that of a stillborn son. She was arrested and brought to the Tower, convicted of treason on fragile evidence and beheaded in 1536.

Jane Seymour (c.1509–37) A lady-in-waiting to Henry's first two wives, she married him 11 days after the execution of Anne Boleyn. She died soon after the birth of her son, the future Edward VI.

Anne of Cleves (1515–57) A Lutheran princess who became Henry's fourth queen in 1540, as part of a strategy to develop an alliance with German Protestant rulers. The marriage was declared null and void on grounds of non-consummation six months afterwards. On agreeing to the divorce, Anne was given a large income and she remained in England until her death.

Catherine Howard (c.1520–42) Became Queen in the same month as Anne of Cleves was divorced (Jul 1540). A year later she was charged with having had an affair before her marriage with a musician and a relation, and she was beheaded for treason.

Catherine Parr (1512–48) Married Henry in 1543. A learned, tolerant and tactful woman, she persuaded Henry to restore the succession to his daughters, and showed her stepchildren much kindness. Very soon after Henry's death in 1547 she married a former suitor and died in childbirth the following year.

Northern Ireland

Area	14 120 sq km/5 450 sq mi	**Capital**	Belfast
Chief towns	Armagh, Londonderry	**Population**	1 710 300 (2004e)
Nationality	Northern Irish		
Physical description	Northern Ireland occupies the north-eastern part of Ireland, and is centred on Lough Neagh; to the north and east are the Antrim Mountains; Mourne Mountains are in the south-east; highest point is Slieve Donard at 852m/2 795ft.		
National holidays	Jan 1, Mar 17 (St Patrick), Dec 25, 26; GF, EM, Early May, Spring (May) Bank Holiday, Battle of the Boyne/Orangemen (Jul), Summer Bank Holiday (Aug).		

Political leaders

Devolved power was transferred to the Northern Ireland Assembly in Dec 1999. Devolution was suspended Feb–May 2000, Aug 2001, Sep 2001 and from Oct 2002.

First Minister

1999–2001	David Trimble *(First Minister designate from 1998)*
2001	Reg Empey *Acting First Minister*
2001–2	David Trimble

Scotland

Area	78 742 sq km/30 394 sq mi	**Capital**	Edinburgh
Chief towns	Aberdeen, Dundee, Glasgow, Inverness, Perth	**Population**	5 078 400 (2004e)
Nationality	Scottish		
Physical description	Divided into the Southern Uplands (rising to 843m/2 766ft at Merrick), the Central Lowlands (the most densely populated area) and the Northern Highlands (divided by the fault line following the Great Glen); highest point is Ben Nevis (1 343m/4 406ft); 787 islands, most of which lie off the heavily-indented west coast and only c.60 exceed 8 sq km/3 sq mi; several wide estuaries on the east coast, primarily the firths of Forth, Tay and Moray; interior has many freshwater lochs, the largest being Loch Lomond (70 sq km/27 sq mi) and the deepest Loch Morar (310m/1 017ft); longest river is the River Tay (192km/119mi).		
National holidays	Jan 1, 2, Dec 25, 26; GF, Early May, Spring (May) and Summer (Aug) Bank Holidays; *local holidays may also be observed, in addition to or instead of the statutory days.*		

Monarch

1005–34	Malcolm II	1153–65	Malcolm IV
1034–40	Duncan I	1165–1214	William I
1040–57	Macbeth	1214–49	Alexander II
1057–8	Lulach	1249–86	Alexander III
1058–93	Malcolm III	1286–90	Margaret
1093–4	Donald Bane	1290–2	*Interregnum*
1094	Duncan II	1292–96	John Balliol
1094–7	Donald Bane	1296–1306	*Interregnum*
1097–1107	Edgar	1306–29	Robert I (the Bruce)
1107–24	Alexander I	1329–71	David II
1124–53	David I	1371–90	Robert II

1390–1406	Robert III	1488–1513	James IV
1406–37	James I	1513–42	James V
1437–60	James II	1542–67	Mary Queen of Scots
1460–88	James III	1567–1625	James VI[1]

[1] *In 1603, James VI succeeded Elizabeth I to the English throne and united the thrones of Scotland and England (Union of the Crowns).*

Political leaders

The Scottish parliament was officially opened on 1 Jul 1999.

First Minister

1999–2000	Donald Dewar	2001	Jim Wallace *Acting First Minister*
2000	Jim Wallace *Acting First Minister*	2001–	Jack McConnell
2000–1	Henry McLeish		

Wales

Area	20 761 sq km/8 014 sq mi	**Capital**	Cardiff
Chief towns	Swansea, Wrexham	**Population**	2 952 500 (2004e)
Nationality	Welsh		
Physical description	Rises in the north-west to 1 085m/3 560ft at Snowdon in the Snowdonia range (the highest point); the Cambrian Mountains rise in the centre, and the Brecon Beacons in the south; drained by the Severn, Clwyd, Conwy, Dee, Dovey, Taff, Tawe, Teifi, Towy, Usk and Wye rivers.		
National holidays	Jan 1, Dec 25, 26; EM, GF, Early May, Spring (May) and Summer (Aug) Bank Holidays.		

Political leaders

The opening session of the Welsh Assembly was held in June 1999. The post of First Minister was called First Secretary until Oct 2000.

First Minister

1999–2000	Alun Michael
2000–	Rhodri Morgan

British islands[1]

Channel Islands

Location	An island group of the British Isles in the English Channel, west of the Cotentin Peninsula of Normandy. A dependent territory of the British Crown, it has individual legislative assemblies and legal system and is divided into the Bailiwicks of Jersey and of Guernsey. Main islands: Guernsey, Jersey, Alderney, Sark; other islands include Herm, Jethou, Brechou, the Caskets, the Minquiers and the Chauseys.		
Area	194 sq km/75 sq mi	**Language**	Both English and Norman-French are spoken
Capital	St Helier (Jersey); St Peter Port (Guernsey)		
Population	149 000 (2005e)	**Internet**	.gg (Guernsey), .je (Jersey)

Isle of Man

Location	A British Crown Dependency in the Irish Sea, west of England and east of Northern Ireland.		
Area	572 sq km/221 sq mi	**Languages**	English; Manx is also spoken
Capital	Douglas		
Population	77 000 (2005e)	**Internet**	.im
Nationality	Manx	**Country code**	XIM

[1] *Part of the British Isles but not included in the United Kingdom.*

UK dependent territories

Anguilla

Location	The most northerly of the Leeward Islands, in the east Caribbean Sea.		
Area	155 sq km/60 sq mi	**Nationality**	Anguillan
Capital	The Valley	**Internet**	.ai
Population	12 000 (2005e)	**Country code**	AIA

Bermuda

Location	A group of c.150 low-lying, coral islands and islets situated in the west Atlantic Ocean c.900km/560mi east of Cape Hatteras, North Carolina (USA).		
Area	53 sq km/20 sq mi	**Nationality**	Bermudian
Capital	Hamilton	**Internet**	.bm
Population	64 000 (2005e)	**Country code**	BMU

Bermuda Triangle

The *Bermuda Triangle* is an area in the Atlantic Ocean off the south-eastern USA where ships and aeroplanes have mysteriously disappeared. The points of the triangle are thought to be the city of Miami in Florida, the island of Bermuda and the city of San Juan, Puerto Rico. The US Coast Guard reports rather sniffily that it 'is not impressed with supernatural explanations of disasters at sea'. It suggests that unpredictable weather, dangerous currents and seabed hazards are the more likely culprits. However, it does point out that the Bermuda Triangle area is one of only two places on Earth where a compass needle points to true north, rather than magnetic north. Inexperienced navigators who forget this may end up lost and miles off course.

British Antarctic Territory

Location	Includes the South Orkney Islands, the South Shetland Islands, the Antarctic Graham Land Peninsula, and the land mass extending to the South Pole.
Area	1 709 400 sq km/666 000 sq mi
Population	Populated solely by scientists of the British Antarctic Survey.

British Indian Ocean Territory

Location	Consists of 2 300 islands in the Chagos Archipelago in the Indian Ocean, 1 900km/1 180mi north-east of Mauritius; the largest island is Diego Garcia.		
Area	60 sq km/23 sq mi	**Internet**	.io
Population	Indigenous population relocated; military personnel and civilian support staff only.	**Country code**	IOT

British Virgin Islands

Location	An island group at the north-western end of the Lesser Antilles chain in the east Caribbean Sea.		
Area	153 sq km/59 sq mi	**Nationality**	British Virgin Islander
Capital	Road Town	**Internet**	.vg
Population	22 000 (2005e)	**Country code**	VGB

Cayman Islands

Location	An island group in the west Caribbean Sea, comprising the islands of Grand Cayman, Cayman Brac and Little Cayman, c.240km/150mi south of Cuba.		
Area	260 sq km/100 sq mi	**Nationality**	Caymanian
Capital	George Town	**Internet**	.ky
Population	45 000 (2005e)	**Country code**	CYM

Falkland Islands

Location	Situated in the South Atlantic Ocean, c.650km/400mi north-east of the Magellan Strait. Also known as the Malvinas.		
Area	12 200 sq km/4 700 sq mi	**Nationality**	Falkland Islander
Capital	Stanley	**Internet**	.fk
Population	3 000 (2005e)	**Country code**	FLK

Gibraltar

Location	The narrow peninsula rising steeply from the low-lying coast of south-west Spain at the eastern end of the Strait of Gibraltar, which is an important strategic point of control for the western Mediterranean.		
Area	5.9 sq km/2.3 sq mi	**Nationality**	Gibraltarian
Capital	Gibraltar	**Internet**	.gi
Population	28 000 (2005e)	**Country code**	GIB

Montserrat

Location	A volcanic island in the Leeward Islands, Lesser Antilles, in the east Caribbean Sea.		
Area	106 sq km/41 sq mi	**Population**	4 000 (2005e) *Note: The population has dropped from 10 639 in 1991 as a result of an exodus after the 1997 eruption.*
Capital	Brades *Note: The original capital, Plymouth, lies within the Exclusion Zone – an area abandoned after a devastating volcanic eruption from the Soufrière Hills volcano in 1997 into which entry is prohibited.*		
		Nationality	Montserratian
		Internet	.ms
		Country code	MSR

Pitcairn Islands

Location	An island group in the south-east Pacific Ocean, east of French Polynesia, comprising Pitcairn Island and the uninhabited islands of Ducie, Henderson and Oeno.		
Area	27 sq km/10 sq mi	**Nationality**	Pitcairn Islander
Capital	Adamstown	**Internet**	.pn
Population	67 (2005e)	**Country code**	PCN

St Helena

Location	A volcanic island in the South Atlantic Ocean, lying 1 920km/1 200mi from the south-west coast of Africa.		
Area	122 sq km/47 sq mi	**Nationality**	St Helenian
Capital	Jamestown	**Internet**	.sh
Population	5 000 (2005e)	**Country code**	SHN
Note: The territories of Ascension and Tristan da Cunha are dependencies of St Helena.			

South Georgia

Location	A barren, mountainous snow-covered uninhabited island in the South Atlantic Ocean, about 500km/300mi east of the Falkland Islands.		
Area	c.3 750 sq km/1 450 sq mi	**Internet**	.gs

South Sandwich Islands

Location	A group of small, uninhabited islands in the South Atlantic Ocean, lying c.720km/450mi south-east of South Georgia.		
Area	1 152 sq km/445 sq mi	**Internet**	.gs

Turks and Caicos Islands

Location	A pair of island groups which form the south-eastern archipelago of the Bahamas; they lie 920km/570mi south-east of Miami (USA).		
Area	500 sq km/200 sq mi	**Internet**	.tc
Capital	Cockburn Town	**Country code**	TCA
Population	26 000 (2005e)		

UNITED STATES OF AMERICA

Official name	United States of America (USA)		sizeable Spanish-speaking minority
Local name	United States of America	**Ethnic groups**	white (including Hispanic) 84%, black 12%, Asian 3%, Amerindian 1%
Independence	1776		
Area	9 160 454 sq km/ 3 535 935 sq mi		
Capital	Washington, DC (District of Columbia)	**Religions**	Christianity 84% (Prot 56%, RC 28%), none 10%, Judaism 2%, Islam 2%, others 2%
Chief towns	New York City, Los Angeles, Chicago, Houston, Philadelphia, Phoenix, San Diego, Dallas, San Antonio, Detroit	**Time zone**	GMT −5/10
		Currency	1 US Dollar ($, US$/USD) = 100 cents
		Telephone	+1
Population	298 213 000 (2005e)	**Internet**	.us
Nationality	American	**Country code**	USA
Languages	English; there is a		

Location
A republic in North America, bounded to the north by Canada; to the east by the northern Atlantic Ocean; to the south by Mexico and the Gulf of Mexico; and to the west by the Pacific Ocean.

Physical description
Fourth-largest country in the world; East Atlantic coastal plain is backed by the Appalachian Mountains from the Great Lakes in the north to Alabama in the south; this series of parallel ranges includes the Allegheny, Blue Ridge and Catskill mountains; to the south the plain broadens out towards the Gulf of Mexico and into the Florida Peninsula; to the west, the Gulf Plains stretch north to meet the higher Great Plains from which they are separated by the Ozark Mountains; further west, the Rocky Mountains rise to over 4 500m/14 760ft; highest point is Mt McKinley, Alaska, at 6 194m/20 322ft; lowest point is in Death Valley (−86m/−282ft); major rivers include the Hudson, Delaware, Potomac, Columbia, Colorado and the great Red River–Missouri–Mississippi River System.

Climate
Varies from conditions in hot tropical deserts (in the south-west) to those typical of Arctic continental regions; most regions are affected by westerly depressions that can bring changeable weather; rainfall is heaviest in the Pacific north-west, lightest in the south-west; in the Great Plains, wide temperature variation is the result of cold air from the Arctic as well as warm tropical air from the Gulf of Mexico; on the west coast the influence of the Pacific Ocean results in a smaller range of temperatures between summer and winter; on the east coast there is a gradual increase in winter temperatures southwards; the states bordering the Gulf of Mexico are subject to hurricanes and tornadoes moving north-east from the Caribbean Sea.

National holidays
Jan 1, Jul 4 (Independence), Nov 11 (Veterans), Dec 25; Martin Luther King's Birthday (3rd Mon in Jan), Washington's Birthday (3rd Mon in Feb), Memorial (last Mon in May), Labor (1st Mon in Sep), Columbus (2nd Mon in Oct), Thanksgiving (4th Thurs in Nov); *additional days vary between states*.

States of the USA

State (abbrev.; ZIP)	Entry to Union	Population (2004e)	Area	Capital	Inhabitant	Nickname
Alabama (Ala; AL)	1819 (22nd)	4 530 182	131 443 sq km/50 750 sq mi	Montgomery	Alabamian	Camellia State, Heart of Dixie
Alaska (Alaska; AK)	1959 (49th)	655 435	1 477 268 sq km/570 373 sq mi	Juneau	Alaskan	Mainland State, The Last Frontier
Arizona (Ariz; AZ)	1912 (48th)	5 743 834	295 276 sq km/114 006 sq mi	Phoenix	Arizonan	Apache State, Grand Canyon State
Arkansas (Ark; AR)	1836 (25th)	2 752 629	137 754 sq km/53 187 sq mi	Little Rock	Arkansan	Bear State, Land of Opportunity
California (Calif; CA)	1850 (31st)	35 893 799	403 971 sq km/156 973 sq mi	Sacramento	Californian	Golden State
Colorado (Colo; CO)	1876 (38th)	4 601 403	268 658 sq km/103 729 sq mi	Denver	Coloradan	Centennial State
Connecticut (Conn; CT)	1788 (5th)	3 503 604	12 547 sq km/4 844 sq mi	Hartford	Nutmegger	Nutmeg State, Constitution State
Delaware (Del; DE)	1787 (1st)	830 364	5 133 sq km/1 985 sq mi	Dover	Delawarean	Diamond State, First State
District of Columbia¹ (DC; DC)	*Established* 1791	553 523	159 sq km/61 sq mi	Washington	Washingtonian	—
Florida (Fla; FL)	1845 (27th)	17 397 161	139 697 sq km/53 937 sq mi	Tallahassee	Floridian	Everglade State, Sunshine State
Georgia (Ga; GA)	1788 (4th)	8 829 383	152 571 sq km/58 908 sq mi	Atlanta	Georgian	Empire State of the South, Peach State
Hawaii (Hawaii; HI)	1959 (50th)	1 262 840	16 636 sq km/6 423 sq mi	Honolulu	Hawaiian	Aloha State
Idaho (Idaho; ID)	1890 (43rd)	1 393 262	214 325 sq km/82 751 sq mi	Boise	Idahoan	Gem State
Illinois (Ill; IL)	1818 (21st)	12 713 634	144 123 sq km/55 646 sq mi	Springfield	Illinoisan	Prairie State, Land of Lincoln
Indiana (Ind; IN)	1816 (19th)	6 237 569	92 903 sq km/35 870 sq mi	Indianapolis	Hoosier	Hoosier State
Iowa (Iowa; IA)	1846 (29th)	2 954 451	144 716 sq km/55 875 sq mi	Des Moines	Iowan	Hawkeye State, Corn State

¹ Not counted as one of the 50 states but included for reference.

State (abbrev.; ZIP)	Entry to Union	Population (2004e)	Area	Capital	Inhabitant	Nickname
Kansas (Kans; KS)	1861 (34th)	2 735 502	211 922 sq km/81 823 sq mi	Topeka	Kansan	Sunflower State, Jayhawker State
Kentucky (Ky; KY)	1792 (15th)	4 145 922	102 907 sq km/39 732 sq mi	Frankfort	Kentuckian	Bluegrass State
Louisiana (La; LA)	1812 (18th)	4 515 770	112 836 sq km/43 566 sq mi	Baton Rouge	Louisianian	Pelican State, Sugar State, Creole State
Maine (Maine; ME)	1820 (23rd)	1 317 253	79 931 sq km/30 861 sq mi	Augusta	Downeaster	Pine Tree State
Maryland (Md; MD)	1788 (7th)	5 558 058	25 316 sq km/9 775 sq mi	Annapolis	Marylander	Old Line State, Free State
Massachusetts (Mass; MA)	1788 (6th)	6 416 505	20 300 sq km/7 838 sq mi	Boston	Bay Stater	Bay State, Old Colony
Michigan (Mich; MI)	1837 (26th)	10 112 620	150 544 sq km/58 125 sq mi	Lansing	Michigander	Wolverine State, Great Lake State
Minnesota (Minn; MN)	1858 (32nd)	5 100 958	206 207 sq km/79 617 sq mi	St Paul	Minnesotan	Gopher State, North Star State
Mississippi (Miss; MS)	1817 (20th)	2 902 966	123 510 sq km/47 687 sq mi	Jackson	Mississippian	Magnolia State
Missouri (Mo; MO)	1821 (24th)	5 754 618	178 446 sq km/68 898 sq mi	Jefferson City	Missourian	Bullion State, Show Me State
Montana (Mont; MT)	1889 (41st)	926 865	376 991 sq km/145 556 sq mi	Helena	Montanan	Treasure State, Big Sky Country
Nebraska (Nebr; NE)	1867 (37th)	1 747 214	199 113 sq km/76 878 sq mi	Lincoln	Nebraskan	Cornhusker State, Beef State
Nevada (Nev; NV)	1864 (36th)	2 334 771	273 349 sq km/105 540 sq mi	Carson City	Nevadan	Silver State, Sagebrush State
New Hampshire (NH; NH)	1788 (9th)	1 299 500	23 292 sq km/8 993 sq mi	Concord	New Hampshirite	Granite State
New Jersey (NJ; NJ)	1787 (3rd)	8 698 879	19 210 sq km/7 417 sq mi	Trenton	New Jerseyite	Garden State
New Mexico (N Mex; NM)	1912 (47th)	1 903 289	314 334 sq km/121 364 sq mi	Santa Fe	New Mexican	Sunshine State, Land of Enchantment
New York (NY; NY)	1788 (11th)	19 227 088	122 310 sq km/47 224 sq mi	Albany	New Yorker	Empire State
North Carolina (NC; NC)	1789 (12th)	8 541 221	126 180 sq km/48 718 sq mi	Raleigh	North Carolinian	Old North State, Tar Heel State

State (abbrev.; ZIP)	Entry to Union	Population (2004e)	Area	Capital	Inhabitant	Nickname
North Dakota (N Dak; ND)	1889 (39th)	634 366	178 695 sq km/68 994 sq mi	Bismarck	North Dakotan	Flickertail State, Sioux State, Peace Garden State
Ohio (Ohio; OH)	1803 (17th)	11 459 011	106 067 sq km/40 952 sq mi	Columbus	Ohioan	Buckeye State
Oklahoma (Okla; OK)	1907 (46th)	3 523 553	177 877 sq km/68 678 sq mi	Oklahoma City	Oklahoman	Sooner State
Oregon (Oreg; OR)	1859 (33rd)	3 594 586	251 385 sq km/97 060 sq mi	Salem	Oregonian	Sunset State, Beaver State
Pennsylvania (Pa; PA)	1787 (2nd)	12 406 292	116 083 sq km/44 820 sq mi	Harrisburg	Pennsylvanian	Keystone State
Rhode Island (RI; RI)	1790 (13th)	1 080 632	2 707 sq km/1 045 sq mi	Providence	Rhode Islander	Little Rhody, Plantation State
South Carolina (SC; SC)	1788 (8th)	4 198 068	77 988 sq km/30 111 sq mi	Columbia	South Carolinian	Palmetto State
South Dakota (S Dak; SD)	1889 (40th)	770 883	196 576 sq km/75 898 sq mi	Pierre	South Dakotan	Sunshine State, Coyote State
Tennessee (Tenn; TN)	1796 (16th)	5 900 962	106 759 sq km/41 220 sq mi	Nashville	Tennessean	Volunteer State
Texas (Tex; TX)	1845 (28th)	22 490 022	678 358 sq km/261 914 sq mi	Austin	Texan	Lone Star State
Utah (Utah; UT)	1896 (45th)	2 389 039	212 816 sq km/82 168 sq mi	Salt Lake City	Utahn	Mormon State, Beehive State
Vermont (Vt; VT)	1791 (14th)	621 394	23 955 sq km/9 249 sq mi	Montpelier	Vermonter	Green Mountain State
Virginia (Va; VA)	1788 (10th)	7 459 827	102 558 sq km/39 598 sq mi	Richmond	Virginian	Old Dominion State, Mother of Presidents
Washington (Wash; WA)	1889 (42nd)	6 203 788	172 447 sq km/66 582 sq mi	Olympia	Washingtonian	Evergreen State, Chinook State
West Virginia (W Va; WV)	1863 (35th)	1 815 354	62 758 sq km/24 231 sq mi	Charleston	West Virginian	Panhandle State, Mountain State
Wisconsin (Wis; WI)	1848 (30th)	5 509 026	145 431 sq km/56 151 sq mi	Madison	Wisconsinite	Badger State, America's Dairyland
Wyoming (Wyo; WY)	1890 (44th)	506 529	251 501 sq km/97 105 sq mi	Cheyenne	Wyomingite	Equality State

US non-self-governing territories

American Samoa (AS)

Location	A group of islands in the South Pacific Ocean, some 3 500km/2 175mi north-east of New Zealand.		
Area	197 sq km/76 sq mi	**Nationality**	American Samoan
Capital	Pago Pago	**Internet**	.as
Population	65 000 (2005e)	**Country code**	ASM

Guam

Location	The largest and southernmost island of the Mariana Islands, west Pacific Ocean.		
Area	541 sq km/209 sq mi	**Nationality**	Guamanian
Capital	Agaña	**Internet**	.gu
Population	170 000 (2005e)	**Country code**	GUM

Northern Mariana Islands

Location	A group of 14 islands in the north-west Pacific Ocean, c.2 400km/1 500mi to the east of the Philippines.		
Area	471 sq km/182 sq mi	**Internet**	.mp
Capital	Saipan	**Country code**	MNP
Population	81 000 (2005e)		

US Virgin Islands

Location	A group of more than 50 islands in the south and west of the Virgin Islands group, Lesser Antilles, Caribbean Sea, 64km/40mi east of Puerto Rico (USA). There are three main islands: St Croix, St Thomas and St John.		
Area	342 sq km/132 sq mi	**Nationality**	Virgin Islander
Capital	Charlotte Amalie	**Internet**	.vi
Population	112 000 (2005e)	**Country code**	VIR

US associated commonwealths

Puerto Rico

Location	The easternmost island of the Greater Antilles, situated between the Dominican Republic in the west and the US Virgin Islands in the east, c.1 600km/1 000mi south-east of Miami (USA).		
Area	8 897 sq km/3 434 sq mi	**Nationality**	Puerto Rican, American
Capital	San Juan	**Internet**	.pr
Population	3 955 000 (2005e)	**Country code**	PRI

Note: The USA also possesses Baker Island, Howland Island, Johnston Atoll, Kingman Reef, Midway Island, Palmyra Atoll and Wake Island in the North Pacific Ocean, Jarvis Island in the South Pacific Ocean and Navassa Island in the Caribbean Sea, all largely uninhabited.

Political leaders

President *(Vice President in parentheses)*

1789–97	George Washington (1st) (John Adams)
1797–1801	John Adams (2nd) *Fed* (Thomas Jefferson)
1801–9	Thomas Jefferson (3rd) *Dem-Rep* (Aaron Burr, 1801–5) (George Clinton, 1805–9)
1809–17	James Madison (4th) *Dem-Rep* (George Clinton, 1809–12) *no Vice President* 1812–13 (Elbridge Gerry, 1813–14) *no Vice President* 1814–17
1817–25	James Monroe (5th) *Dem-Rep* (Daniel D Tompkins)
1825–9	John Quincy Adams (6th) *Dem-Rep* (John C Calhoun)
1829–37	Andrew Jackson (7th) *Dem* (John C Calhoun, 1829–32) *no Vice President* 1832–3 (Martin van Buren, 1833–7)
1837–41	Martin van Buren (8th) *Dem* (Richard M Johnson)
1841	William Henry Harrison (9th) *Whig* (John Tyler)
1841–5	John Tyler (10th) *Whig no Vice President*
1845–9	James Knox Polk (11th) *Dem* (George M Dallas)
1849–50	Zachary Taylor (12th) *Whig* (Millard Fillmore)
1850–3	Millard Fillmore (13th) *Whig no Vice President*
1853–7	Franklin Pierce (14th) *Dem* (William R King, 1853) *no Vice President* 1853–7
1857–61	James Buchanan (15th) *Dem* (John C Breckinridge)
1861–5	Abraham Lincoln (16th) *Rep* (Hannibal Hamlin, 1861–5) (Andrew Johnson, 1865)
1865–9	Andrew Johnson (17th) *Dem-Nat no Vice President*
1869–77	Ulysses Simpson Grant (18th) *Rep* (Schuyler Colfax, 1869–73) (Henry Wilson, 1873–5) *no Vice President* 1875–7
1877–81	Rutherford Birchard Hayes (19th) *Rep* (William A Wheeler)
1881	James Abram Garfield (20th) *Rep* (Chester A Arthur)
1881–5	Chester Alan Arthur (21st) *Rep no Vice President*
1885–9	Grover Cleveland (22nd) *Dem* (Thomas A Hendricks, 1885) *no Vice President* 1885–9
1889–93	Benjamin Harrison (23rd) *Rep* (Levi P Morton)
1893–7	Grover Cleveland (24th) *Dem* (Adlai E Stevenson)
1897–1901	William McKinley (25th) *Rep* (Garrat A Hobart, 1897–9) *no Vice President* 1899–1901 (Theodore Roosevelt, 1901)
1901–9	Theodore Roosevelt (26th) *Rep no Vice President* 1901–5 (Charles W Fairbanks, 1905–9)
1909–13	William Howard Taft (27th) *Rep* (James S Sherman, 1909–12) *no Vice President* 1912–13
1913–21	Woodrow Wilson (28th) *Dem* (Thomas R Marshall)
1921–3	Warren Gamaliel Harding (29th) *Rep* (Calvin Coolidge)

Dead Presidents

John Adams, the 2nd President, and Thomas Jefferson, the 3rd President, both died on 4 Jul 1826 – the 50th anniversary of the Declaration of Independence.

1923–9	Calvin Coolidge (30th) *Rep no Vice President* 1923–5 (Charles G Dawes,1925–9)
1929–33	Herbert Clark Hoover (31st) *Rep* (Charles Curtis)
1933–45	Franklin Delano Roosevelt (32nd) *Dem* (John N Garner, 1933–41) (Henry A Wallace, 1941–5) (Harry S Truman, 1945)
1945–53	Harry S Truman (33rd) *Dem no Vice President* 1945-9 (Alben W Barkley, 1949–53)
1953–61	Dwight David Eisenhower (34th) *Rep* (Richard M Nixon)
1961–3	John Fitzgerald Kennedy (35th) *Dem* (Lyndon B Johnson)
1963–9	Lyndon Baines Johnson (36th) *Dem no Vice President* 1963–5 (Hubert H Humphrey, 1965–9)

1969–74	Richard Milhous Nixon (37th) *Rep* (Spiro T Agnew, 1969–73) *no Vice President* 1973,Oct–Dec (Gerald R Ford,1973–4)	1981–9	Ronald Wilson Reagan (40th) *Rep* (George H W Bush)
1974–7	Gerald Rudolph Ford (38th) *Rep no Vice President* 1974, Aug–Dec (Nelson A Rockefeller, 1974–7)	1989–93	George Herbert Walker Bush (41st) *Rep* (J Danforth Quayle)
		1993–2001	William Jefferson Blythe IV Clinton (42nd) *Dem* (Albert Gore)
1977–81	Jimmy Carter (39th) *Dem* (Walter F Mondale)	2001–	George Walker Bush (43rd) *Rep* (Richard B Cheney)

Dem = Democrat   *Nat* = National Union
Fed = Federalist   *Rep* = Republican

Keeping It in the Family

John Quincy Adams, the 6th President, was the son of John Adams, the 2nd President; Benjamin Harrison, the 23rd President, was the grandson of William Henry Harrison, the 9th President; Theodore Roosevelt, the 26th President, and Franklin D Roosevelt, the 32nd, were distant cousins; and George Bush, the 41st President, saw his son George W Bush become the 43rd President.

URUGUAY

Official name	Eastern Republic of Uruguay		Portuguese and Spanish, is also spoken on the Brazilian border
Local name	Uruguay; República Oriental del Uruguay	**Ethnic groups**	white 90%, mestizo 6%, black 4%
Independence	1828		
Area	176 215 sq km/68 018 sq mi	**Religions**	Christianity 63% (RC 60%, Prot 3%), Judaism 2%, others/unaffiliated 35%
Capital	Montevideo		
Chief towns	Salto, Paysandú, Mercedes, Las Piedras	**Time zone**	GMT –3
		Currency	1 Uruguayan Peso (Ur$, Urug$/UYU) = 100 centésimos
Population	3 463 000 (2005e)		
Nationality	Uruguayan		
Languages	Spanish; Portunol or Brazilero, a mix of	**Telephone**	+598
		Internet	.uy
		Country code	URY

Location
A republic in eastern South America, bounded to the north by Brazil; to the east by the Atlantic Ocean; and to the west by Argentina.

Physical description
Grass-covered plains of the south rise north to a high sandy plateau; River Negro flows south to west to meet the River Uruguay on the Argentine frontier; highest point is Cerro Catedral (514m/1 686ft).

Climate
Temperate with warm summers and mild winters; the average temperature at Montevideo is 16°C.

National holidays
Jan 6 (Children), May 1, Jun 19 (Artigas's Birthday), Jul 18 (Constitution), Oct 12 (Americas), Dec 25; C (2), GF, HT.

Political leaders

President

1899–1903	Juan Lindolfo Cuestas	1927–31	Juan Capisteguy
1903–7	José Batlle y Ordóñez	1931–8	Gabriel Terra
1907–11	Claudio Williman	1938–43	Alfredo Baldomir
1911–15	José Batlle y Ordóñez	1943–7	Juan José de Amézaga
1915–19	Feliciano Viera	1947	Tomás Berreta
1919–23	Baltasar Brum	1947–51	Luis Batlle Berres
1923–7	José Serrato	1951–5	Andrés Martínez Trueba

President of the National Government Council

1955–6	Luis Batlle Berres	1961–2	Eduardo Victor Haedo
1956–7	Alberto F Zubiría	1962–3	Faustino Harrison
1957–8	Alberto Lezama	1963–4	Daniel Fernández Crespo
1958–9	Carlos L Fischer	1964–5	Luis Giannattasio
1959–60	Martín R Etchegoyen	1965–6	Washington Beltrán
1960–1	Benito Nardone	1966–7	Alberto Heber Usher

President

1967	Oscar Daniel Gestido	1985–90	Julio María Sanguinetti Cairolo
1967–72	Jorge Pacheco Areco	1990–5	Luis Alberto Lacalle Herrera
1972–6	Juan María Bordaberry Arocena	1995–2000	Julio María Sanguinetti
1976–81	Aparicio Méndez	2000–5	Jorge Batlle Ibáñez
1981–5	Gregorio Conrado Álvarez Armelino	2005–	Tabaré Vázquez
1985	Rafael Addiego Bruno *Acting President*		

USSR (UNION OF SOVIET SOCIALIST REPUBLICS)

Political leaders

No longer in existence, but included for reference. See separate entries for former constituent states of the USSR since 1990–91 (Armenia, Azerbaijan, Belarus, Estonia, Georgia, Kazakhstan, Kyrgyzstan, Latvia, Lithuania, Moldova, Russia, Tajikistan, Turkmenistan, Ukraine, Uzbekistan).

President

1917	Leo Borisovich Kamenev	1977–82	Leonid Brezhnev
1917–19	Yakov Mikhailovich Sverlov	1982–3	Vasily Kuznetsov *Acting President*
1919–46	Mikhail Ivanovich Kalinin	1983–4	Yuri Andropov
1946–53	Nikolai Shvernik	1984	Vasily Kuznetsov *Acting President*
1953–60	Klimentiy Voroshilov	1984–5	Konstantin Chernenko
1960–4	Leonid Brezhnev	1985	Vasily Kuznetsov *Acting President*
1964–5	Anastas Mikoyan	1985–8	Andrei Gromyko
1965–77	Nikolai Podgorny	1988–90	Mikhail Gorbachev

Executive President

1990–91	Mikhail Gorbachev	1991	Mikhail Gorbachev
1991	Gennady Yanayev *Acting President*		

Chairman of the Council of Ministers

1917	Georgy Evgenyevich Lvov
1917	Aleksandr Fyodorovich Kerensky

Chairman of the Council of People's Commissars

1917–24	Vladimir Ilyich Lenin	1930–41	Vyacheslav Mikhailovich Molotov
1924–30	Aleksei Ivanovich Rykov	1941–53	Josef Stalin

Chairman of the Council of Ministers

1953–5	Georgiy Malenkov	1985–90	Nikolai Ryzhkov
1955–8	Nikolai Bulganin	1990–1	Yuri Maslyukov *Acting Chairman*
1958–64	Nikita Khrushchev	1991	Valentin Pavlov
1964–80	Alexei Kosygin	1991	Ivan Silayev *Acting Chairman*
1980–5	Nikolai Tikhonov		

General Secretary of the Communist Party

1922–53	Josef Stalin	1982–4	Yuri Andropov
1953	Georgiy Malenkov	1984–5	Konstantin Chernenko
1953–64	Nikita Khrushchev	1985–91	Mikhail Gorbachev
1964–82	Leonid Brezhnev		

US VIRGIN ISLANDS *see* **UNITED STATES OF AMERICA**

UZBEKISTAN

Official name	Republic of Uzbekistan	**Nationality**	Uzbek
Local name	Özbekiston; Özbekiston Respublikasia	**Languages**	Uzbek; Russian, Tajik and Kazakh are also spoken
Former name	Uzbek Soviet Socialist Republic (1924–91), within the Union of Soviet Socialist Republics (USSR; 1924–91)	**Ethnic groups**	Uzbek 71%, Russian 8%, Tajik 5%, Kazakh 4%, others 12%
Independence	1991	**Religions**	Islam 88% (Sunni), Christianity 9% (Orthodox), others/unaffiliated 3%
Area	447 400 sq km/172 696 sq mi	**Time zone**	GMT +5
Capital	Tashkent; Toškent, Taškent	**Currency**	1 Uzbekistan Sum (UZS) = 100 tiyin
Chief towns	Samarkand, Andizhan, Namangan	**Telephone**	+998
		Internet	.uz
Population	26 593 000 (2005e)	**Country code**	UZB

Location
A republic in central Asia, bounded to the north and west by Kazakhstan; to the east by Kyrgyzstan and Tajikistan; to the south by Afghanistan; and to the south-west by Turkmenistan.

Physical description
Large area occupied by the Kyzyl-Kum desert; highest point is Beshtor Peak (4 299m/14 104ft); the Aral Sea lies to the north on the border with Kazakhstan.

Climate
Long, hot summers, mild winters.

National holidays
Jan 1, Mar 8 (Women), 21, May 9 (Memory and Respect), Sep 1 (Independence), Oct 1 (Teachers), Dec 8 (Constitution); Ad, ER.

Political leaders

President

1991–	Islam Karimov

Prime Minister

1991–5	Abdulhashim Mutalov
1995–2003	Otkir Sultonov
2003–	Shavkat Mirziyayev

VANUATU

Official name	Republic of Vanuatu	**Ethnic groups**	Melanesian 95%, others 5%
Local name	Vanuatu; Ripablik Blong Vanuatu, République de Vanuatu	**Religions**	Christianity 77% (Prot 52%, RC 15%, others 10%), traditional beliefs 8%, others 15%
Former name	New Hebrides (until 1980)		
Independence	1980		
Area	14 763 sq km/5 698 sq mi	**Time zone**	GMT +11
		Currency	1 Vatu (V, VT/VUV) = 100 centimes
Capital	Port-Vila	**Telephone**	+678
Population	211 000 (2005e)	**Internet**	.vu
Nationality	Ni-Vanuatu	**Country code**	VUT
Languages	Bislama, English, French		

Location
An independent island republic in the south-west Pacific Ocean, 400km/250mi north-east of the French islands of New Caledonia.

Physical description
Comprises an irregular Y-shaped island chain; actively volcanic and rugged, with raised coral beaches fringed by reefs; highest peak, Tabwemasana, rises to 1 888m/6 194ft; densely forested, narrow strips of cultivated coastal land.

Climate
Tropical, with a hot and rainy season in Nov–Apr when cyclones may occur; annual temperatures at Port-Vila are 16–33°C.

National holidays
Jan 1, Feb 21 (Memory of the Father of Independence), Mar 5 (Custom Chiefs), May 1, Jul 24 (Children), 30 (Independence), Aug 15, Oct 5 (Constitution), Nov 29 (Unity), Dec 25, 26; A, EM, ES, GF.

Political leaders

President

1980–4	George Sokomanu *(formerly Kalkoa)*	1999	Edward Natapei *Acting President*
		1999–2004	John Bani
1984	Fred Timakata *Acting President*	2004	Roger Abiut *Interim President*
1984–9	George Sokomanu	2004	Alfred Maseng
1989	Onneyn Tahi *Acting President*	2004	Roger Abiut *Interim President*
1989–94	Fred Timakata	2004	Josias Moli *Interim President*
1994	Alfred Maseng *Acting President*	2004–	Kalkot Mataskelekele
1994–9	Jean-Marie Léyé		

Prime Minister

1980–91	Walter Lini	1991–5	Maxime Carlot Korman
1991	Donald Kalpokas	1995–6	Serge Vohor

1996	Maxime Carlot Korman	2001–4	Edward Natapei
1996–8	Serge Vohor	2004	Serge Vohor
1998–9	Donald Kalpokas	2004–	Ham Lini
1999–2001	Barak Sopé		

VATICAN

Official name	Vatican City State; the Holy See	**Ethnic groups**	predominantly European, especially Italian
Local name	Città del Vaticano; Stato della Citta del Vaticano; Santa Sede	**Religions**	Christianity 100% (RC)
		Time zone	GMT +1
Independence	1929 (formally)	**Currency**	1 Euro (€/EUR) = 100 cents
Area	0.4 sq km/0.2 sq mi	**Telephone**	+39
Capital	Vatican City	**Internet**	.va
Population	1 000 (2005e)	**Country code**	VAT
Languages	Latin; Italian is widely spoken		

Location
A papal sovereign state, the smallest independent state in the world, surrounded by Rome, Italy.

Physical description
Landlocked, urban and entirely enclosed within the Italian city of Rome; reaches 75m/246ft at its highest point.

Climate
Mediterranean; hot summers and mild winters.

National holidays
Jan 1, 6, Feb 11 (Lateran Treaty), Mar 19 (St Joseph), May 1, Jun 29 (SS Peter and Paul), Aug 15, Oct 16 (Holy Father's Elevation), Oct 22 (Coronation of Pope John Paul II), Nov 1, 2, Dec 8, 25, 26; CC, EM, WM.

Political leaders

The head of state is the Supreme Pontiff of the Roman Catholic Church, the pope, who is elected for life by the Sacred College of Cardinals and has full legislative, judicial and executive powers (see **Religions, Beliefs and Folklore** for lists of **popes**). The head of government is a Secretary of State appointed by the pope (since 1990, Cardinal Angelo Sodano).

Swiss Guards

The Vatican and the pope himself are protected by the distinctive Swiss Guards, with their blue- and yellow-striped dress uniform and red-tufted helmets. The Swiss Guards were instituted as the papal police corps by Pope Julius II, pope from 1503 to 1513. Their distinctive uniform was designed by Michelangelo. To be admitted to the Swiss Guards, one must be Roman Catholic, of good moral and ethical background, have attended military school in Switzerland, be 19–30 years old, at least 1.74m/5.7ft tall, unmarried, hold a professional diploma or high school degree, and, of course, be Swiss.

VENEZUELA

Official name	Bolivarian Republic of Venezuela
Local name	Venezuela; República Bolivariana de Venezuela
Independence	1830
Area	912 050 sq km/352 051 sq mi
Capital	Caracas
Chief towns	Maracaibo, Ciudad Guayana, Valencia, Barquisimeto
Population	26 749 000 (2005e)
Nationality	Venezuelan
Languages	Spanish; indigenous languages are also spoken
Ethnic groups	mestizo 69%, white 21%, black 9%, Amerindian 1%
Religions	Christianity 94% (RC 92%, Prot 2%), others/unaffiliated 6%
Time zone	GMT −4
Currency	1 Bolívar (Bs/VEB) = 100 céntimos
Telephone	+58
Internet	.ve
Country code	VEN

Location
A republic in northern South America, bounded to the north by the Caribbean Sea; to the east by Guyana; to the south by Brazil; and to the south-west and west by Colombia.

Physical description
Guiana Highlands in the south-east cover over half the country; Venezuelan Highlands in the west and along the coast reach heights of around 5 000m/16 400ft; highest point is Pico Bolívar (5 007m/16 427ft); lowlands around Lake Maracaibo and in the Orinoco River valley, which runs south to north-east.

Climate
Generally hot and humid; one rainy season from Apr to Oct; annual temperatures at Caracas are 13–27°C; very little rainfall on the coast around Lake Maracaibo, increasing in the east.

National holidays
Jan 1, Apr 19 (Independence), May 1, Jun 24 (Battle of Carabobo), Jul 5 (National), 24 (Bolívar's Birthday), Oct 12 (Discovery), Dec 17 (Liberator's Death), 25; C (2), GF, HT.

Political leaders

President
1899–1908	Cipriano Castro
1908–36	Juan Vicente Gomez
1936–41	Eleazar Lopez Contreras
1941–5	Isaias Medina Angarita
1945–7	*Military Junta* (Rómulo Betancourt)
1947–8	Romulo Gallegos
1948–50	*Military Junta* (Carlos Delgado Chalbaud)
1950–9	*Military Junta* (Marcos Pérez Jiménez)
1959–64	Rómulo Betancourt
1964–9	Raul Leoni
1969–74	Rafael Caldera Rodriguez
1974–9	Carlos Andres Pérez
1979–84	Luis Herrera Campins
1984–9	Jaime Lusinchi
1989–93	Carlos Andres Pérez
1994–8	Rafael Caldera Rodríguez
1998–2002	Hugo Chávez Frías
2002	Pedro Carmona *Head of Transitional Government*
2002–	Hugo Chávez Frías

VIETNAM

Official name	Socialist Republic of Vietnam (SRV)	**Population**	84 238 000 (2005e)
		Nationality	Vietnamese
Local name	Viêt Nam; Công-Hòa Xã-Hôi Chu-Ngh Viêt Nam	**Languages**	Vietnamese
		Ethnic groups	Vietnamese 86%, Chinese 3%, Thai 2%, others 9%
Former name	formerly part of Indochina (until 1945), *post-1945 as listed below under Political leaders*		
		Religions	Buddhism 55%, none/unaffiliated 15%, Christianity 7%, others 23%
Independence	1945 (declared), 1976 (republic)		
		Time zone	GMT +7
Area	329 566 sq km/127 213 sq mi	**Currency**	1 Dông (D/VND) = 10 hào = 100 xu
Capital	Hanoi; Hà Nôi		
		Telephone	+84
Chief towns	Ho Chi Minh City (formerly Saigon), Haiphong, Da Nang, Nha Trang	**Internet**	.vn
		Country code	VNM

Location
An independent republic in south-east Asia, bounded to the north by China; to the east by the South China Sea and the Gulf of Tongking; to the south-west by the Gulf of Thailand; and to the west by Laos and Cambodia.

Physical description
Occupies a narrow strip along the coast of the Gulf of Tongking and the South China Sea; broader at the Mekong River Delta, in the south, and along the Red River Valley to the north; highest peak is Fan si Pan (3 143m/10 312ft).

Climate
Tropical monsoon-type, dominated by south to south-east winds during May–Sep and north to north-east winds during Oct–Apr; high humidity in the rainy season; temperatures are high in the south during Oct–Apr.

National holidays
Jan 1, Apr 30 (Saigon Liberation), May 1, Sep 2 (National); NY (Vietnamese) (4).

Political leaders

Democratic Republic of Vietnam (North Vietnam)

President

1945–69	Ho Chi Minh
1969–76	Ton Duc Thang

Prime Minister

1945–55	*As President*
1955–76	Pham Van Dong

State of Vietnam (South Vietnam)

Chief of State

1949–55	Bao Dai

Prime Minister

1949–50	Nguyen Van Xuan	1952–3	Nguyen Van Tam
1950	Nguyen Phan Long	1953–4	Buu Loc
1950–2	Tran Van Huu	1954–5	Ngo Dinh Diem
1952	Tran Van Huong		

Republic of Vietnam (South Vietnam)

President

1955–63	Ngo Dinh Diem	1964–5	Phan Khac Suu
1963–4	Duong Van Minh	1965–75	Nguyen Van Thieu
1964	Nguyen Khanh	1975	Tran Van Huong
1964	Duong Van Minh	1975	Duong Van Minh
1964	Nguyen Khanh	1975–6	*Provisional Revolutionary*
1964	Duong Van Minh		*Government* (Huynh Tan Phat)

Prime Minister

1955–63	Ngo Dinh Diem	1967–8	Nguyen Van Loc
1963–4	Nguyen Ngoc Tho	1968–9	Iran Van Huong
1964	Nguyen Khanh	1969–75	Tran Thien Khiem
1964–5	Tran Van Huong	1975	Nguyen Ba Can
1965	Phan Huy Quat	1975–6	Vu Van Mau
1965–7	Nguyen Cao Ky		

Socialist Republic of Vietnam

President

1976–80	Ton Duc Thang	1987–92	Vo Chi Cong
1980–1	Nguyen Hun Tho *Acting President*	1992–7	Le Duc Anh
1981–7	Truong Chinh	1997–	Tran Duc Luong

Premier

1976–87	Pham Van Dong	1988–91	Do Muoi
1987–8	Pham Hung	1991–7	Vo Van Kiet
1988	Vo Van Kiet *Acting Premier*	1997–	Phan Van Khai

General Secretary

1976–86	Le Duan	1991–7	Do Muoi
1986	Truong Chinh	1997–2001	Le Kha Phieu
1986–91	Nguyen Van Linh	2001–	Nong Duc Manh

Vietnamese Customs

Chewing betel and areca is an old Vietnamese custom. Betel and areca nuts are shared for enjoyment at weddings, are a source of comfort at funerals, are used during ancestor worship, and as a symbol of friendship during festivals. Betel is a relaxant and intoxicant; the chewed quid often comprises a mixture of betel bark, areca leaf, chay root and hydrated lime, giving a mixture of hot, sweet, bitter and pungent tastes.

VIRGIN ISLANDS, BRITISH *see* **UNITED KINGDOM**

VIRGIN ISLANDS, US *see* **UNITED STATES OF AMERICA**

WALES *see* **UNITED KINGDOM**

WALLIS AND FUTUNA ISLANDS *see* **FRANCE**

WEST BANK *see* **PALESTINIAN AUTONOMOUS AREAS** *under* **ISRAEL**

WESTERN SAHARA

Official name	Saharawi Arab Democratic Republic; Saharan Arab Democratic Republic; claimed by Morocco	**Nationality**	Sahrawi, Sahraoui; Sahrawian, Sahraouian
		Languages	Arabic; French, Berber and Spanish are also spoken
Local name	Sahara Occidental; République Arabe Saharouie Démocratique	**Ethnic groups**	Arab, Berber
		Religions	Islam (Sunni) 100%
Former name	Spanish Sahara (until 1976)	**Time zone**	GMT
		Currency	1 Moroccan Dirham (DH/MAD) = 100 centimes
Area	252 126 sq km/97 321 sq mi		
Capital	El Aaiún; Laâyoune, La 'Youn	**Telephone**	+212
		Internet	.eh
Chief towns	Smara, Bu Craa, Dakhla	**Country code**	ESH
Population	341 000 (2005e)		

Location
A disputed non-self-governing territory in north-west Africa, administered by Morocco, and bounded to the north by Morocco; to the north-east by Algeria; to the east and south by Mauritania; and to the west by the Atlantic Ocean.

Physical description
Low, flat desert terrain, composed principally of plains and low plateaus; rises in the south to hills; rocky desert in the north-east, rising to steep hills; highest point reaches 463m/1 519ft; ergs and sand dunes inland, with sparse desert vegetation.

Climate
Hot, dry climate, with little rainfall; coastal fog, mists and dew; subject to the hot, dry *sirocco* wind in winter and spring.

Political leaders

Disputed; Morocco claims sovereignty and views Western Sahara as Moroccan provinces administered by the Moroccan government (see Morocco). The Western Saharan independence movement, the Polisario Front, proclaimed a government-in-exile in 1976 (see below).

Saharawi Arab Democratic Republic

Chairman of Revolutionary Council
1976	El Wali Mustafa Sayed
1976	Mahfoud Ali Beiba *Acting Chairman*

Chairman of Revolutionary Command Council
1976–82   Mohamed Abdelaziz

President
1982–   Mohamed Abdelaziz

Prime Minister

1976–82	Mohamed Lamine Ould Ahmed	1993–5	Bouchraya Hammoudi Bayoune
1982–5	Mahfoud Ali Beiba	1995–9	Mahfoud Ali Beiba
1985–8	Mohamed Lamine Ould Ahmed	1999–2003	Bouchraya Hamoudi Bayoune
1988–93	Mahfoud Ali Beiba	2003–	Abdelkader Taleb Oumar

Coming of the Camel

It is thought that the camel first arrived in
Western Sahara in the 1c AD.

WESTERN SAMOA *see* **SAMOA**

YEMEN

Official name	Republic of Yemen	**Nationality**	Yemeni
Local name	Al-Yamaniyya; Al-Jumhūriyya Al-Yamaniyya	**Languages**	Arabic
		Ethnic groups	Arab 96%, others 4%
Former name	*as listed below under Political leaders*	**Religions**	Islam 97% (Shia 56%, Sunni 41%), others 3%
Independence	1990 (united republic)	**Time zone**	GMT +3
Area	531 570 sq km/205 186 sq mi	**Currency**	1 Yemeni Rial (YR, YRI/YER) = 100 fils
Capital	Sana'a; San'ā', Sanaa	**Telephone**	+967
Chief towns	Ta'iz	**Internet**	.ye
Population	20 975 000 (2005e)	**Country code**	YEM

Location
A republic in the south of the Arabian Peninsula, bounded to the north by Saudi Arabia; to the east by Oman; to the south by the Gulf of Aden; and to the west by the Red Sea.

Physical description
Narrow desert plain bordering the Red Sea rises abruptly to mountains at 3 000–3 700m/ 9 840–12 140ft; highest point is Jabal an Nabi Shu'ayb (3 760m/12 336ft); to the north, a plateau merges with the gravel plains and sand of the Rub al Khali Basin.

Climate
Hot and humid on the western coastal strip, with an annual temperature of 29°C; milder in the highlands; rainfall is highest in the north and west; hot all year round in the south, with maximum temperatures over 40°C (Jul–Aug) and very high humidity.

National holidays
May 1, 22 (National), Sep 26 (Revolution), Oct 14 (Revolution), Nov 30 (Independence); Ad (5), ER (5), NY (Muslim).

Political leaders

Yemen Arab Republic (North Yemen)

Monarch (Imam)

1918–48	Yahya Mohammed Bin Mohammed
1948–62	Ahmed Bin Yahya
1962–70	Mohammed Bin Ahmed
1962	*Civil War*

President

1962–7	Abdullah Al-Sallal	1977–8	Ahmed Bin Hussein Al-Ghashmi
1967–74	Abdur Rahman Al-Iriani		
1974–7	*Military Command Council* (Ibrahim Al-Hamadi)	1978–90	Ali Abdullah Saleh

Prime Minister

1964	Hamud Al-Jaifi	1971	Ahmed Mohammed Numan
1965	Hassan Al-Amri	1971	Hassan Al-Amri
1965	Ahmed Mohammed Numan	1971–2	Muhsin Al-Aini
1965	*As President*	1972–4	Qadi Abdullah Al-Hijri
1965–6	Hassan Al-Amri	1974	Hassan Makki
1966–7	*As President*	1974–5	Muhsin Al-Aini
1967	Muhsin Al-Aini	1975	Abdel Latif Deifallah *Acting Prime Minister*
1967–9	Hassan Al-Amri		
1969–70	Abd Allah Kurshumi	1975–90	Abdel-Aziz Abdel-Ghani
1970–1	Muhsin Al-Aini		
1971	Abdel Salam Sabra *Acting Prime Minister*		

People's Democratic Republic of Yemen (South Yemen)

President

1967–9	Qahtan Mohammed Al-Shaabi	1978–80	Abdel Fattah Ismail
1969–78	Salim Ali Rubai	1980–6	Ali Nasir Mohammed Husani
1978	Ali Nasir Mohammed Husani	1986–90	Haidar Abu Bakr Al-Attas

Prime Minister

1969	Faisal Abd Al-Latif Al-Shaabi	1985–6	Haidar Abu Bakr Al-Attas
1969–71	Mohammed Ali Haithem	1986–90	Yasin Said Numan
1971–85	Ali Nasir Mohammed Husani		

Republic of Yemen

President

1990–	Ali Abdullah Saleh

Prime Minister

1990–3	Haidar Abu Bakr Al-Attas	1998–2001	Abdul Ali Al-Karim Al-Iryani
1993–7	Abdel-Aziz Abdel-Ghani	2001–	Abd al-Qadir Abd al-Rahman Bajammal
1997	Farag Said Ben Ghanem		

YUGOSLAVIA *see* **SERBIA AND MONTENEGRO**

ZAÏRE *see* **CONGO, DEMOCRATIC REPUBLIC OF THE**

ZAMBIA

Official name	Republic of Zambia	**Languages**	English; local languages are also spoken
Local name	Zambia	**Ethnic groups**	Bemba 35%, Maravi 19%, Tonga 14%, others 32%
Former name	Northern Rhodesia (until 1964), part of the Federation of Rhodesia and Nyasaland (1953–63)	**Religions**	Christianity 68% (Prot 35%, RC 27%, African Christian 6%), traditional beliefs 31%, Islam and Hinduism 1%
Independence	1964		
Area	752 613 sq km/290 509 sq mi	**Time zone**	GMT +2
Capital	Lusaka	**Currency**	1 Kwacha (K/ZMK) = 100 ngwee
Chief towns	Ndola, Kitwe, Kabwe, Livingstone	**Telephone**	+260
Population	11 668 000 (2005e)	**Internet**	.zm
Nationality	Zambian	**Country code**	ZMB

Location
A republic in southern Africa, bounded to the north by Democratic Republic of the Congo; to the north-east by Tanzania; to the east by Malawi; to the south-east by Zimbabwe and Mozambique; to the south by Botswana and Namibia; and to the west by Angola.

Physical description
Occupies a high plateau at an altitude of 1 000–1 400m/3 280–4 590ft; highest point is 2 067m/6 781ft south-east of Mbala; Zambezi River rises in the north extremity of North-West Province.

Climate
Temperate climate on upland plateau; rainy season is Oct–Mar; at Lusaka the maximum average daily temperatures range between 23°C and 35°C; tropical climate in the lower river valleys.

National holidays
Jan 1, May 1, 25 (Africa Freedom), Oct 24 (Independence), Dec 25; EM, GF, HS, Youth (2nd Mon in Mar), Heroes (1st Mon in Jul), Unity (1st Tues in Jul), Farmers (1st Mon in Aug).

Political leaders

President

1964–91	Kenneth Kaunda
1991–2002	Frederick Chiluba
2002–	Levy Mwanawasa

Prime Minister

1964–73	Kenneth Kaunda
1973–5	Mainza Chona
1975–7	Elijah Mudenda
1977–8	Mainza Chona
1978–81	Daniel Lisulu
1981–5	Nalumino Mundia
1985–9	Kebby Musokotwane
1989–91	Malimba Masheke
1991–	*No Prime Minister*

Smoke that Thunders

Zambia is renowned for the Victoria Falls, the waterfalls on the Zambezi River which lie on the border with Zimbabwe. The falls are 61–108m/200–350ft high and 1 688m/5 538ft wide. In 1855 the explorer David Livingstone became the first European to see the falls, which he named after Queen Victoria. However, the indigenous Kololo people knew the falls as *Mosi oa Tunya*, 'the smoke that thunders', while the Leya people called the falls *Shongwe*, meaning 'rainbow'.

ZIMBABWE

Official name	Republic of Zimbabwe		and other local languages are also spoken
Local name	Zimbabwe		
Former name	Southern Rhodesia (until 1965), part of the Federation of Rhodesia and Nyasaland (1953–63), Rhodesia (1965–80)	**Ethnic groups**	Shona 71%, Ndebele 16%, other Bantu-speaking peoples 11%, white 1%, mixed and Asian 1%
Independence	1980	**Religions**	Christianity 45% (Prot 33%, RC 12%), traditional beliefs 40%, Islam 1%, others 14%
Area	391 090 sq km/150 961 sq mi		
Capital	Harare	**Time zone**	GMT +2
Chief towns	Bulawayo, Gweru, Mutare	**Currency**	1 Zimbabwe Dollar (Z$/ZWD) = 100 cents
Population	13 010 000 (2005e)	**Telephone**	+263
Nationality	Zimbabwean	**Internet**	.zw
Languages	English; Shona, Sindebele	**Country code**	ZWE

Location
A republic in southern Africa, bounded to the north-west by Zambia; to the north-east, east and south-east by Mozambique; to the south by South Africa; and to the south-west by Botswana.

Physical description
High plateau country, with the Middleveld at 900–1 200m/2 950–3 940ft and the Highveld at 1 200–1 500m/3 940–4 920ft; lower towards the Zambezi River in the north and the Limpopo River in the south; mountains in the east rise to 2 592m/8 504ft at Mt Inyangani.

Climate
Generally subtropical, strongly influenced by altitude; warm and dry in the lowlands; average maximum daily temperatures at Harare, in the Highveld, range between 21°C and 29°C.

National holidays
Jan 1, Apr 18 (Independence), May 1, 25 (Africa), Aug 11 (Heroes), 12 (Defence Forces), Dec 22 (Unity), 25, 26; EM, ES, GF, HS.

Political leaders

President
1980–7	Canaan Sodindo Banana
1987–	Robert Gabriel Mugabe

Prime Minister
1980–7	Robert Gabriel Mugabe

Politicians and Chiefs

Zimbabwe's capital was founded in 1890 and was named Salisbury after the British prime minister of the time, Lord Salisbury. After Zimbabwe gained its independence the capital was renamed Harare in 1982, this time after Chief Neharawa, a former indigenous ruler of the area.

HISTORICAL EMPIRES

For the Roman Empire see **Ancient Greece and Rome**, for ancient Chinese dynasties see **China** in **Countries A–Z**, for ancient Egyptian dynasties see **Egypt** in **Countries A–Z** and for ancient Japanese emperors see **Japan** in **Countries A–Z**.

Holy Roman Empire

The establishment of the Holy Roman Empire (HRE) is usually dated to the coronation of Charlemagne in 800 as emperor over most of Christian Western Europe. It was known as the Roman Empire and the Holy Empire before its full title was adopted in 1254. It was always based principally in the territory of modern-day Germany, though its full extent fluctuated considerably. It was at its zenith in the early Middle Ages, but remained officially in existence until 1806, when it was abolished by Francis II.

800–814	Charlemagne (Charles I)		1247–56	William of Holland[2, 4]
814–840	Louis I (the Pious)		1250–4	Conrad IV[4]
840–843	*Civil War*		1254–73	*Great Interregnum*
843–855	Lothair I		1257–72	Richard[2, 4]
855–875	Louis II		1257–75	Alfonso (Alfonso X of Castile)[2, 4]
875–877	Charles II (the Bald)		1273–91	Rudolf I[4]
877–881	*Interregnum*		1292–8	Adolf[4]
881–887	Charles III (the Fat)		1298–1308	Albert[4]
887–891	*Interregnum*		1308–13	Henry VII
891–894	Guido of Spoleto		1314–26	Frederick (III)[3, 4]
892–898	Lambert of Spoleto[1]		1314–46	Louis IV
896–899	Arnulf[2]		1346–78	Charles IV
901–905	Louis III		1378–1400	Wenceslas[4]
905–924	Berengar		1400–10	Rupert[4]
911–918	Conrad I[2, 4]		1410–37	Sigismund
919–936	Henry I, the Fowler[4]		1438–9	Albert II[4]
936–973	Otto I (the Great)		1440–93	Frederick III
973–983	Otto II		1493–1519	Maximilian I[4]
983–1002	Otto III		1519–56	Charles V[4]
1002–24	Henry II (the Saint)		1556–64	Ferdinand I[4]
1024–39	Conrad II		1564–76	Maximilian II[4]
1039–56	Henry III (the Black)		1576–1612	Rudolf II[4]
1056–1106	Henry IV		1612–19	Matthias[4]
1077–80	Rudolf of Rheinfelden[2, 4]		1619–37	Ferdinand II[4]
1081–93	Hermann[2, 4]		1637–57	Ferdinand III[4]
1093–1101	Conrad[2, 4]		1658–1705	Leopold I[4]
1106–25	Henry V		1705–11	Joseph I[4]
1125–37	Lothair II		1711–40	Charles VI[4]
1138–52	Conrad III[4]		1740–42	*Interregnum*
1152–90	Frederick I (Barbarossa)		1742–5	Charles VII[4]
1190–7	Henry VI		1745–65	Francis I[4]
1198–1214	Otto IV		1765–90	Joseph II[4]
1198–1208	Philip[2, 4]		1790–2	Leopold II[4]
1215–50	Frederick II		1792–1806	Francis II[4, 5]
1246–7	Henry Raspe[2, 4]			

[1] *Co-emperor.*
[2] *Rival.*
[3] *Co-regent.*
[4] *Ruler not crowned at Rome; therefore, strictly speaking, only King of Germany.*

[5] *The threat that Napoleon I might endeavour to appropriate the Holy Roman title in an attempt to establish a European hegemony led Francis II to abolish the HRE and restyle himself Emperor of Austria.*

Inca Empire

The Incas were originally a small group of Quechua-speaking Indians living in the Cuzco Basin of the central Andean highlands. In the 11c the Inca established their capital at Cuzco, the Sacred City of the Sun, where they built huge stone temples and fortresses, and occasionally covered important buildings in sheets of gold. During the 15c they brought together much of the Andean area, stretching along the entire western length of South America, from near the present Ecuador–Columbia border to south central Chile, and occupied much of the Andean region of Bolivia as well. They ruled more than 12 million people. The Inca emperor was a despotic ruler of a highly stratified society, and a quasi-religious figure thought to be a direct descendant of the sun god, Inti. In 1532 Spanish invaders under Pizarro encountered the Incas. They captured the emperor, Atahualpa, whom they later murdered, and seized control of the empire. By the 1570s Inca power was totally destroyed.

Note: The earliest Inca emperors are considered to be mythical, rather than historical figures. Dates are not known for the early emperors. The Spanish names, rather than the Inca names, of the emperors are given.

dates unknown	Manco Capac	1471–93	Topa Inca Yupanqui
dates unknown	Sinchi Roca	1493–1525	Huayna Capac
dates unknown	Lloque Yupanqui	1525–32	Huascar
dates unknown	Mayta Capac	1532–3	Atahualpa
dates unknown	Capac Yupanqui	1533	Topa Huallpa
dates unknown	Inca Roca	1533–45	Manco Inca Yupanqui
dates unknown	Yahuar Huacac	1545–60	Sayri Tupac
dates unknown	Viracocha Inca	1560–71	Titu Cusi Yupanqui
dates unknown	Inca Urcon	1571–2	Tupac Amaru
1438–71	Pachacuti Inca Yupanqui		

Mughal Empire

The Mughal Empire was an important Indian Muslim state, founded in 1526 by Babur. The empire was extended during the 16c and 17c, but its last great emperor was Aurangzeb and by the mid-18c it ruled only a small area around Delhi, although its administrative forms and culture continued to have great influence.

1526–30	Babur	1719	Rafi-ud-Daulat
1530–56	Humayun[1]	1719	Nekusiyar
1556–1605	Akbar	1719	Ibrahim
1605–27	Jahangir	1719–48	Muhammad Shah
1627–58	Shah Jahan	1748–54	Ahmad Shah
1658–1707	Aurangzeb (Alamgir)	1754–9	Alamgir II
1707–12	Bahadur Shah I (or Shah Alam I)	1759–1806	Shah Alam II
1712–13	Jahandar Shah	1806–37	Akbar II
1713–19	Farruksiyar	1837–57	Bahadur Shah II[2]
1719	Rafid-ud-Darajat		

[1] *Humayun lost his throne to the Afghan chieftain Sher Shah in 1540, became a fugitive, and did not regain his title until 1555.*
[2] *Bahadur Shah II was exiled by the British to Rangoon after the Indian Uprising of 1857–8.*

WORLD POLITICAL MAPS

Europe
Countries and capital cities

ATLANTIC
OCEAN

ICELAND
★ Reykjavik

SWEDEN

FINLAND

NORWAY

Oslo

Helsinki

Stockholm

Tallinn

NORTHERN
IRELAND

North Sea

Baltic
Sea

ESTONIA

RUSSIA

SCOTLAND

★ Edinburgh

DENMARK

Riga

LATVIA

★
Moscow

Copenhagen

LITHUANIA

Vilnius

★ Belfast

ENGLAND

Amsterdam

Berlin

POLAND

Minsk
★

Dublin

IRELAND

WALES

London

Warsaw

BELARUS

Cardiff

Brussels

GERMANY

Prague

Kiev

2

3

Luxembourg

4

Bratislava

UKRAINE

★ Paris

LIECHTENSTEIN
Vaduz

Vienna★

5

Budapest

16

Chisinau

Berne ★

7

8

FRANCE

6

Ljubljana

Zagreb

ROMANIA

ANDORRA
Andorra
la Vella

MONACO
Monaco

ITALY

9

10

Belgrade

Bucharest

11

Sarajevo ★

12

Black Sea

SAN MARINO
San Marino

15

Corsica

Rome

Tirana

13

Sofia

Skopje

PORTUGAL

Madrid

★

Sardinia

14

Ankara

SPAIN

GREECE

TURKEY

Lisbon

Mediterranean Sea

Sicily

Athens

Gibraltar

★ MALTA
Valletta

Nicosia

CYPRUS

1 THE NETHERLANDS	7 AUSTRIA	12 SERBIA AND
2 BELGIUM	8 HUNGARY	MONTENEGRO
3 LUXEMBOURG	9 SLOVENIA	13 MACEDONIA
4 CZECH REPUBLIC	10 CROATIA	14 ALBANIA
5 SLOVAKIA	11 BOSNIA AND	15 BULGARIA
6 SWITZERLAND	HERZEGOVINA	16 MOLDOVA

North America

Countries, capital cities and states

GREENLAND
(DENMARK)

ARCTIC
OCEAN

AK

Yukon

Nunavut

North West Territories

Saskatchewan

Newfoundland
and
Labrador

Key to US states

AK	Alaska
AL	Alabama
AR	Arkansas
AZ	Arizona
CA	California
CO	Colorado
CT	Connecticut
DC	District of Columbia
DE	Delaware
FL	Florida
GA	Georgia
HI	Hawaii
IA	Iowa
ID	Idaho
IL	Illinois
IN	Indiana
KS	Kansas
KY	Kentucky
LA	Louisiana
MA	Massachusetts
MD	Maryland
ME	Maine
MI	Michigan
MN	Minnesota
MO	Missouri
MS	Mississippi
MT	Montana
NC	North Carolina
ND	North Dakota
NE	Nebraska
NH	New Hampshire
NJ	New Jersey
NM	New Mexico
NV	Nevada
NY	New York
OH	Ohio
OK	Oklahoma
OR	Oregon
PA	Pennsylvania
RI	Rhode Island
SC	South Carolina
SD	South Dakota
TN	Tennessee
TX	Texas
UT	Utah
VA	Virginia
VT	Vermont
WA	Washington
WI	Wisconsin
WV	West Virginia
WY	Wyoming

Manitoba

Québec

Alberta

British
Columbia

Ontario

Prince
Edward
Island

CANADA

New
Brunswick

Ottawa

ME

Nova Scotia

WA   MT   ND   MN   WI   MI   NY   VT
OR   ID   WY   SD   IA   IL IN OH PA   NH
         NE   WV VA   MA
USA   NV UT CO KS   MO KY   NC   RI
CA   OK   AR TN   SC   NJ
    AZ   NM   LA MS AL GA   MD
                TX   Washington DC   DE

FL

MEXICO

ATLANTIC
OCEAN

Mexico City
★

Caribbean Sea

PACIFIC
OCEAN

EQUATOR

Central & South America
Countries and capital cities

Havana
THE BAHAMAS
Nassau
Port-au-Prince
ST KITTS AND NEVIS
Basseterre
CUBA
DOMINICAN
REPUBLIC
San Juan
ANTIGUA AND BARBUDA
St John's
JAMAICA
Belmopan
HAITI
PUERTO
RICO
DOMINICA
Roseau
ST LUCIA
Castries
BELIZE
Tegucigalpa
Kingston
Santo
Domingo
GUATEMALA
HONDURAS
BARBADOS
Bridgetown
Managua
Caribbean Sea
ST VINCENT AND
THE GRENADINES
Kingstown
NICARAGUA
San
Salvador
Panama City
Caracas
GRENADA
St George's
TRINIDAD AND TOBAGO
Port of Spain
Guatemala
City
PANAMA
VENEZUELA
Georgetown
Paramaribo
EL
SALVADOR
Bogotá
GUYANA
Cayenne
COSTA
RICA
SURINAME
FRENCH GUIANA
San José
COLOMBIA
EQUATOR
Quito
ECUADOR
PERU
Lima
BRAZIL
BOLIVIA
Brasília
La Paz
Sucre
PARAGUAY
CHILE
Asunción
PACIFIC
OCEAN
ARGENTINA
URUGUAY
Santiago
Buenos Aires
Montevideo
ATLANTIC
OCEAN
FALKLANDS
Port Stanley

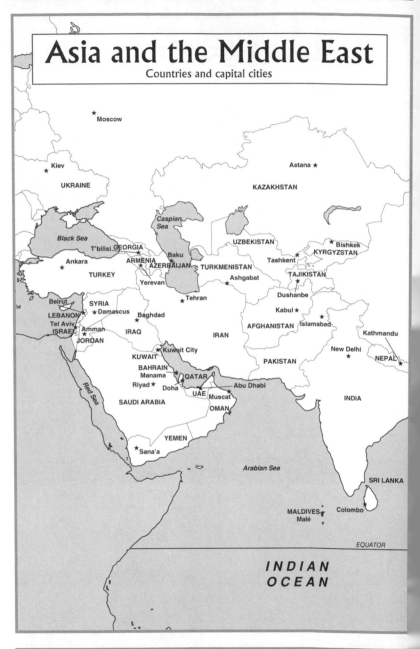

Asia and the Middle East
Countries and capital cities

★ Moscow

★ Kiev

UKRAINE

Astana ★

KAZAKHSTAN

Caspian Sea

Black Sea

T'bilisi ★ GEORGIA

★ Baku

UZBEKISTAN

★ Bishkek
KYRGYZSTAN

Ankara ★

ARMENIA
★ AZERBAIJAN

TURKMENISTAN

Tashkent ★

TAJIKISTAN

TURKEY

Yerevan ★

Ashgabat ★

Dushanbe ★

Beirut ★

SYRIA
★ Damascus

★ Tehran

Kabul ★

AFGHANISTAN

Islamabad ★

Kathmandu ★

LEBANON
Tel Aviv ★
ISRAEL ★ Amman

Baghdad ★

IRAQ

IRAN

New Delhi
★

NEPAL ★

JORDAN

★ Kuwait City

KUWAIT

PAKISTAN

BAHRAIN
Manama

★ QATAR

Abu Dhabi

INDIA

Riyad ★

Doha ★

UAE Muscat ★

SAUDI ARABIA

OMAN

YEMEN

★ Sana'a

Arabian Sea

SRI LANKA

MALDIVES ★
Malé

Colombo ★

EQUATOR

INDIAN
OCEAN

Far East
Countries and capital cities

RUSSIA

Ulan Bator ★

MONGOLIA

Beijing ★

KOREA, NORTH
Pyongyang ★

KOREA, SOUTH
Seoul ★

Tokyo ★

JAPAN

CHINA

Thimphu ★
BHUTAN

Dhaka ★

T'aipei ★

TAIWAN

PACIFIC
OCEAN

Hanoi ★

MYANMAR
(Burma)
LAOS

BANGLADESH

Rangoon ★

Vientiane ★
THAILAND
Bangkok ★

CAMBODIA
Phnom Penh ★

VIETNAM

South China
Sea

Manila ★

PHILIPPINES

Bandar Seri Begawan ★
BRUNEI
DARUSSALAM

Kuala Lumpur ★
MALAYSIA

Singapore ★

EQUATOR

SINGAPORE

INDIAN
OCEAN

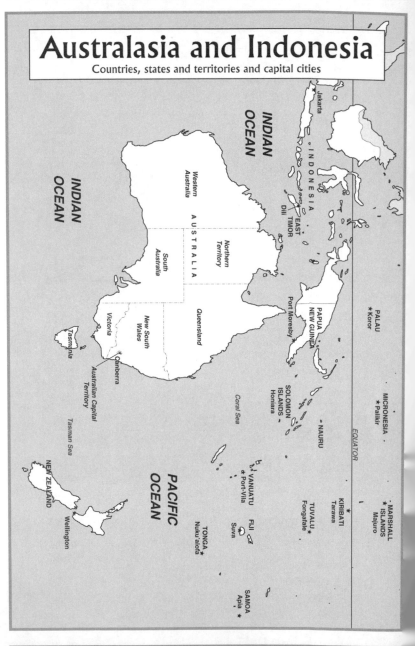

Australasia and Indonesia
Countries, states and territories and capital cities

INDIAN OCEAN

INDIAN OCEAN

Jakarta

INDONESIA

EAST TIMOR
Dili

Western Australia

Northern Territory

AUSTRALIA

South Australia

Queensland

New South Wales

Victoria

Tasmania

★ Canberra
Australian Capital Territory

Tasman Sea

NEW ZEALAND

★ Wellington

Coral Sea

PACIFIC OCEAN

PAPUA NEW GUINEA
Port Moresby ★

SOLOMON ISLANDS
Honiara

NAURU

VANUATU
★ Port-Vila

TONGA
Nuku'alofa ★

PALAU
★ Koror

MICRONESIA
★ Palikir

EQUATOR

KIRIBATI
Tarawa

FIJI
Suva

TUVALU ★
Fongafale

SAMOA
Apia ★

MARSHALL ISLANDS
Majuro

Africa
Countries and capital cities

Tunis

Algiers ★ TUNISIA

★ Rabat
MOROCCO
Tripoli ★   *Mediterranean Sea*

ALGERIA
Cairo ★

WESTERN
SAHARA
LIBYA   EGYPT

El Aaiún

MAURITANIA
Nouakchott ★

MALI
Ouagadougou
Bamako ★ Niamey ★   NIGER   CHAD   Khartoum ★   ERITREA   Djibouti

See below
for area
enlargement
BURKINA FASO
BENIN
CÔTE   TOGO   NIGERIA   N'Djamena ★   Asmara ★   ★ DJIBOUTI
D'IVOIRE   Abuja ★   SUDAN   Addis Ababa ★   SOMALIA
GHANA   Porto Novo   CENTRAL AFRICAN   ETHIOPIA
Accra   Lomé   CAMEROON   REPUBLIC
Yamoussoukro   EQUATORIAL GUINEA ★ Yaoundé   ★ Bangui
EQUATOR   Malabo ★   UGANDA   KENYA
SÃO TOMÉ & PRÍNCIPE   Libreville   CONGO   Kigali ★ Kampala ★   Nairobi   Mogadishu ★
São Tomé   GABON   RWANDA   ★
Brazzaville ★   Bujumbura ★
Kinshasa ★   CONGO,   BURUNDI   SEYCHELLES
DEMOCRATIC   TANZANIA   Victoria ★
Luanda ★   REPUBLIC OF   Dodoma ★
THE   ★
Lilongwe ★   MOZAMBIQUE   COMOROS
ANGOLA   ZAMBIA   Moroni ★
Lusaka ★   MALAWI   Antananarivo ★
Harare ★
NAMIBIA   ZIMBABWE
Windhoek   BOTSWANA   MADAGASCAR
★   Gaborone
Pretoria ★   MAURITIUS
Mbabane ★ ★ Maputo   Port Louis
Maseru ★   SWAZILAND
SOUTH AFRICA   LESOTHO

Cape Town

Area enlargement (inset)

CAPE
VERDE   THE
★ Praia   GAMBIA
SENEGAL
★ Dakar
MALI
Banjul ★
Bissau ★   Bamako ★
GUINEA
BISSAU   GUINEA

Conakry ★
Freetown ★
SIERRA LEONE

Monrovia ★
LIBERIA

*INDIAN
OCEAN*

*ATLANTIC
OCEAN*

Red Sea

LARGEST COUNTRIES

The ten largest countries in the world by area.

Country	Area
Russia	17 075 400 sq km/6 591 104 sq mi
Canada	9 970 610 sq km/3 848 655 sq mi
China	9 597 000 sq km/3 704 000 sq mi
United States of America	9 160 454 sq km/3 535 935 sq mi
Brazil	8 511 965 sq km/3 285 618 sq mi
Australia	7 692 300 sq km/2 969 228 sq mi
Argentina	3 761 274 sq km/1 451 852 sq mi
India	3 166 829 sq km/1 222 396 sq mi
Kazakhstan	2 717 300 sq km/1 048 878 sq mi
Sudan	2 504 530 sq km/966 749 sq mi

SMALLEST COUNTRIES

The ten smallest countries in the world by area.

Country	Area
Vatican	0.4 sq km/0.2 sq mi
Monaco	1.9 sq km/0.75 sq mi
Nauru	21 sq km/8 sq mi
Tuvalu	26 sq km/10 sq mi
San Marino	61 sq km/24 sq mi
Liechtenstein	160 sq km/62 sq mi
Marshall Islands	180 sq km/70 sq mi
St Kitts and Nevis	269 sq km/104 sq mi
Maldives	300 sq km/120 sq mi
Malta	316 sq km/122 sq mi

MOST POPULOUS COUNTRIES

The ten most populous countries in the world.

Country	Population estimate[1]
China	1 315 844 000
India	1 103 371 000
United States of America	298 213 000
Indonesia	222 781 000
Brazil	186 405 000
Pakistan	157 935 000
Russia	143 202 000
Bangladesh	141 822 000
Nigeria	131 530 000
Japan	128 085 000

[1] Population figures are 2005 estimates rounded to the nearest 1 000. Data source: United Nations Population Division, 'World Population Prospects: The 2004 Revision'.

LEAST POPULOUS COUNTRIES

The ten least populous countries in the world.

Country	Population estimate[1]
Vatican	1 000
Tuvalu	10 000
Nauru	14 000
Palau	20 000
San Marino	28 000
Liechtenstein	35 000
Monaco	35 000
St Kitts and Nevis	43 000
Marshall Islands	62 000
Andorra	67 000

[1] *Population figures are 2005 estimates rounded to the nearest 1 000. Data source: United Nations Population Division, 'World Population Prospects: The 2004 Revision'.*

COUNTRY POPULATION ESTIMATES

The six most populous countries in the world.

	1950		2000		2050	
	Country	Population estimate[1]	Country	Population estimate[1]	Country	Population estimate[1]
1	China	554 760 000	China	1 275 133 000	India	1 592 704 000
2	India	357 561 000	India	1 008 937 000	China	1 392 307 000
3	USA	157 813 000	USA	283 230 000	USA	394 976 000
4	Russia	102 702 000	Indonesia	212 092 000	Pakistan	304 700 000
5	Japan	83 625 000	Brazil	170 406 000	Indonesia	284 640 000
6	Indonesia	79 538 000	Russia	145 491 000	Nigeria	258 108 000

[1] *Population figures are rounded to the nearest 1 000. Data source: United Nations Population Division, 'World Population Prospects: The 2004 Revision'.*

WORLD POPULATION

World population estimates (medium variant predictions) published by the UN in 2002. In 2005 the estimated world population in 2050 was revised to 9 076 million.

Date (AD)	Millions[1]	Date (AD)	Millions[1]	Date (AD)	Millions[1]
1	300	1900	1 650	2000	6 071
1000	310	1950	2 519	2010	6 830
1250	400	1960	3 021	2020	7 540
1500	500	1970	3 692	2030	8 130
1750	790	1980	4 435	2040	8 594
1800	980	1990	5 264	2050	8 919
1850	1 260				

[1] *Population figures are rounded to the nearest 1 000 000. Data source: United Nations Population Division.*

LIFE EXPECTANCY

Highest life expectancy at birth		Lowest life expectancy at birth	
Country	Years[1]	Country	Years[1]
Japan	81.9	Swaziland	32.9
Hong Kong, China	81.5	Botswana	36.6
Iceland	80.6	Lesotho	36.7
Switzerland	80.4	Zimbabwe	37.2
Australia	80.2	Zambia	37.4
Sweden	80.1	Central African Republic	39.4
Italy	80.0	Malawi	39.6
Macao, China	80.0	Sierra Leone	40.6
Canada	79.9	Angola	40.7
Israel	79.6	Mozambique	41.9

[1] Figures are 2005 estimates. Data source: United Nations Population Division, 'World Population Prospects: The 2004 Revision'.

Oldest and Youngest

Japan has the oldest overall population in the world, with a median average age in 2005 estimated to be 42.9 years. The youngest population is that of Uganda, where the median average age in 2005 was estimated to be 14.8 years.

CAPITAL CITIES

The principal English names of capital cities are listed. For local names, names in other languages and alternative spellings, see the entry for the country in **Countries A–Z**. Capitals of states, provinces, dependencies, overseas possessions and other territories are not listed.

Capital city	Country	Capital city	Country
Abidjan	Côte d'Ivoire (administrative and economic capital)	Baghdad	Iraq
		Baku	Azerbaijan
Abu Dhabi	United Arab Emirates	Bamako	Mali
Abuja	Nigeria	Bandar Seri Begawan	Brunei Darussalam
Accra	Ghana		
Addis Ababa	Ethiopia	Bangkok	Thailand
Algiers	Algeria	Bangui	Central African Republic
Amman	Jordan	Banjul	The Gambia
Amsterdam	The Netherlands	Basseterre	St Kitts and Nevis
Andorra la Vella	Andorra	Beijing	China
Ankara	Turkey	Beirut	Lebanon
Antananarivo	Madagascar	Belgrade	Serbia and Montenegro
Apia	Samoa	Belmopan	Belize
Ashgabat	Turkmenistan	Berlin	Germany
Asmara	Eritrea	Berne	Switzerland
Astana	Kazakhstan	Bishkek	Kyrgyzstan
Asunción	Paraguay	Bissau	Guinea-Bissau
Athens	Greece	Bloemfontein	South Africa (judicial capital)

Capital city	Country
Bogotá	Colombia
Brasília	Brazil
Bratislava	Slovakia
Brazzaville	Congo
Bridgetown	Barbados
Brussels	Belgium
Bucharest	Romania
Budapest	Hungary
Buenos Aires	Argentina
Bujumbura	Burundi
Cairo	Egypt
Canberra	Australia
Cape Town	South Africa *(legislative capital)*
Caracas	Venezuela
Castries	St Lucia
Chisinau	Moldova
Colombo	Sri Lanka *(commercial capital)*
Conakry	Guinea
Copenhagen	Denmark
Cotonou	Benin *(seat of government and economic capital)*
Dakar	Senegal
Damascus	Syria
Dar es Salaam	Tanzania *(commercial capital)*
Dhaka	Bangladesh
Dili	East Timor
Djibouti	Djibouti
Dodoma	Tanzania *(political capital)*
Doha	Qatar
Dublin	Ireland
Dushanbe	Tajikistan
El Aaiún	Western Sahara
Fongafale	Tuvalu
Freetown	Sierra Leone
Gaborone	Botswana
Georgetown	Guyana
Guatemala City	Guatemala
Hanoi	Vietnam
Harare	Zimbabwe
Havana	Cuba
Helsinki	Finland
Honiara	Solomon Islands
Islamabad	Pakistan
Jakarta	Indonesia
Kabul	Afghanistan
Kampala	Uganda
Kathmandu	Nepal
Khartoum	Sudan
Kiev	Ukraine
Kigali	Rwanda
Kingston	Jamaica
Kingstown	St Vincent and the Grenadines
Kinshasa	Democratic Republic of the Congo

Capital city	Country
Koror	Palau
Kuala Lumpur	Malaysia *(official capital)*
Kuwait City	Kuwait
La Paz	Bolivia *(administrative capital)*
Libreville	Gabon
Lilongwe	Malawi
Lima	Peru
Lisbon	Portugal
Ljubljana	Slovenia
Lobamba	Swaziland *(legislative capital)*
Lomé	Togo
London	United Kingdom
Luanda	Angola
Lusaka	Zambia
Luxembourg	Luxembourg
Madrid	Spain
Majuro	Marshall Islands
Malabo	Equatorial Guinea
Malé	Maldives
Managua	Nicaragua
Manama	Bahrain
Manila	Philippines
Maputo	Mozambique
Maseru	Lesotho
Mbabane	Swaziland *(administrative capital)*
Mexico City	Mexico
Minsk	Belarus
Mogadishu	Somalia
Monaco	Monaco
Monrovia	Liberia
Montevideo	Uruguay
Moroni	Comoros
Moscow	Russia
Muscat	Oman
Nairobi	Kenya
Nassau	The Bahamas
N'Djamena	Chad
New Delhi	India
Niamey	Niger
Nicosia	Cyprus
Nouakchott	Mauritania
Nuku'alofa	Tonga
Oslo	Norway
Ottawa	Canada
Ouagadougou	Burkina Faso
Palikir	Micronesia
Panama City	Panama
Paramaribo	Suriname
Paris	France
Phnom Penh	Cambodia
Port-au-Prince	Haiti
Port Louis	Mauritius
Port Moresby	Papua New Guinea
Port of Spain	Trinidad and Tobago

Capital city	Country
Porto Novo	Benin *(administrative and constitutional capital)*
Port-Vila	Vanuatu
Prague	Czech Republic
Praia	Cape Verde
Pretoria	South Africa *(administrative capital)*
Putrajaya	Malaysia *(seat of government and administrative capital)*
Pyongyang	Korea, North
Quito	Ecuador
Rabat	Morocco
Rangoon[1]	Myanmar (Burma)
Reykjavík	Iceland
Riga	Latvia
Riyadh	Saudi Arabia
Rome	Italy
Roseau	Dominica
St George's	Grenada
St John's	Antigua and Barbuda
San José	Costa Rica
San Marino	San Marino
San Salvador	El Salvador
Sana'a	Yemen
Santiago	Chile
Santo Domingo	Dominican Republic
São Tomé	São Tomé and Príncipe
Sarajevo	Bosnia and Herzegovina
Seoul	Korea, South
Singapore	Singapore
Skopje	Macedonia
Sofia	Bulgaria
Sri Jayawardenepura Kotte	Sri Lanka *(administrative capital)*

Capital city	Country
Stockholm	Sweden
Sucre	Bolivia *(official and legislative capital)*
Suva	Fiji
T'aipei	Taiwan
Tallinn	Estonia
Tarawa	Kiribati
Tashkent	Uzbekistan
T'bilisi	Georgia
Tegucigalpa	Honduras
Tehran	Iran
Tel Aviv-Jaffa[2]	Israel
Thimphu	Bhutan
Tirana	Albania
Tokyo	Japan
Tripoli	Libya
Tunis	Tunisia
Ulan Bator	Mongolia
Vaduz	Liechtenstein
Valletta	Malta
Vatican City	Vatican
Victoria	Seychelles
Vienna	Austria
Vientiane	Laos
Vilnius	Lithuania
Warsaw	Poland
Washington, DC	United States of America
Wellington	New Zealand
Windhoek	Namibia
Yamoussoukro	Côte d'Ivoire *(official capital)*
Yaoundé	Cameroon
Yaren District[3]	Nauru
Yerevan	Armenia
Zagreb	Croatia

[1] Capital transferred in late 2005 to Pyinmana, renamed Yanlon.
[2] Israel claims Jerusalem as its capital, but this is not recognized internationally.
[3] There is no capital as such, but government offices are situated in this area.

City of the North

The Icelandic city of Reykjavík, founded in 874, is the most northerly capital city in the world.

CAPITAL CITIES ON RIVERS

Information for selected major capital cities is given. Capital cities that are sea ports or that lie on bays, estuaries, lakes or other water expanses are not included.

Capital city	Country	River
Amman	Jordan	Zarqa
Amsterdam	The Netherlands	Amstel (and the IJsselmeer)
Ankara	Turkey	a tributary of the Ova

Capital city	Country	River
Baghdad	Iraq	Tigris
Bangkok	Thailand	Chao Phraya
Belgrade	Serbia and Montenegro	Danube, Sava
Berlin	Germany	Spree, Havel (and others)
Bratislava	Slovakia	Danube
Brussels	Belgium	Senne
Bucharest	Romania	Dambovit
Budapest	Hungary	Danube
Buenos Aires	Argentina	Plate
Cairo	Egypt	Nile
Canberra	Australia	Molonglo
Damascus	Syria	Barada
Dhaka	Bangladesh	Meghna
Dublin	Ireland	Liffey
Hanoi	Vietnam	Red
Islamabad	Pakistan	Jhelum
Jakarta	Indonesia	Liwung
Kiev	Ukraine	Dnieper
Lima	Peru	Rimac
Lisbon	Portugal	Tagus
Ljubljana	Slovenia	Sava, Ljubljanica
London	United Kingdom	Thames
Luxembourg	Luxembourg	Alzette and Petrusse
Madrid	Spain	Manzanares
Manila	Philippines	Pasig
Minsk	Belarus	Svisloch
Moscow	Russia	Moskva
New Delhi	India	Yamuna (Old Delhi)
Ottawa	Canada	Ottawa, Rideau
Paris	France	Seine
Phnom Penh	Cambodia	Mekong (at confluence with the Tonlé Sap lake)
Prague	Czech Republic	Vltava
Pyongyang	Korea, North	Taedong
Rabat	Morocco	Bou Regreg
Riga	Latvia	Daugava
Rome	Italy	Tiber
Santiago	Chile	Mapocho
Sarajevo	Bosnia and Herzegovina	Miljacka
Seoul	Korea, South	Han
Skopje	Macedonia	Vardar
Tokyo	Japan	Sumida
Vienna	Austria	Danube
Vilnius	Lithuania	Vilnya
Warsaw	Poland	Vistula
Washington, DC	United States of America	Potomac, Anacostia
Zagreb	Croatia	Sava

Skinny-Dipping Presidents

Rivers in capital cities are liable to receive
unexpected visitors. John Quincy Adams
(1767–1848), the sixth president of the United States
of America, reportedly swam naked in the Potomac
every day.

CAPITAL CITY POPULATION

Capital city	Population[1]	Capital city	Population[1]
Abidjan	3 337 000	Dakar	2 167 000
Abu Dhabi	475 000	Damascus	2 278 000
Abuja	452 000	Dar es Salaam[2]	2 116 000
Accra	1 847 000	Dhaka	11 560 000
Addis Ababa	2 723 000	Dili	49 000
Algiers	3 060 000	Djibouti	502 000
Amman	1 237 000	Dodoma	155 000
Amsterdam	1 145 000	Doha	286 000
Andorra la Vella	21 000	Dublin	1 015 000
Ankara	3 428 000	Dushanbe	554 000
Antananarivo	1 678 000	El Aaiún	187 000
Apia	40 000	Fongafale	6 000
Ashgabat	574 000	Freetown	921 000
Asmara	556 000	Gaborone	199 000
Astana	332 000	Georgetown	231 000
Asunción	1 639 000	Guatemala City	951 000
Athens	3 215 000	Hanoi	3 977 000
Baghdad	5 620 000	Harare	1 469 000
Baku	1 816 000	Havana	2 189 000
Bamako	1 264 000	Helsinki	1 075 000
Bandar Seri Begawan	61 000	Honiara	56 000
Bangkok	6 486 000	Islamabad	698 000
Bangui	698 000	Jakarta	12 296 000
Banjul	372 000	Kabul	2 956 000
Basseterre	13 000	Kampala	1 246 000
Beijing	10 848 000	Kathmandu	741 000
Beirut	1 792 000	Khartoum	4 286 000
Belgrade	1 118 000	Kiev	2 618 000
Belmopan	9 000	Kigali	656 000
Berlin	3 327 000	Kingston	575 000
Berne	320 000	Kingstown	29 000
Bishkek	806 000	Kinshasa	5 277 000
Bissau	336 000	Koror	14 000
Bloemfontein	381 000	Kuala Lumpur[3]	1 352 000
Bogotá	7 290 000	Kuwait City	1 222 000
Brasília	3 099 000	La Paz	1 477 000
Bratislava	425 000	Libreville	611 000
Brazzaville	1 080 000	Lilongwe	587 000
Bridgetown	140 000	Lima	7 899 000
Brussels	998 000	Lisbon	1 962 000
Bucharest	1 853 000	Ljubljana	256 000
Budapest	1 708 000	Lomé	799 000
Buenos Aires	13 047 000	London	7 619 000
Bujumbura	378 000	Luanda	2 623 000
Cairo	10 834 000	Lusaka	1 394 000
Canberra	373 000	Luxembourg	77 000
Cape Town	2 967 000	Madrid	5 103 000
Caracas	3 226 000	Majuro	25 000
Castries	14 000	Malabo	95 000
Chisinau	662 000	Malé	83 000
Colombo	648 000	Managua	1 098 000
Conakry	1 366 000	Manama	139 000
Copenhagen	1 066 000	Manila (Metro)	10 352 000
Cotonou	828 000	Maputo	1 221 000

Capital city	Population[1]	Capital city	Population[1]
Maseru	170 000	St John's	28 000
Mbabane[4]	70 000	San José	1 085 000
Mexico City	18 660 000	San Marino	5 000
Minsk	1 705 000	San Salvador	1 424 000
Mogadishu	1 175 000	Sana'a	1 469 000
Monaco	34 000	Santiago	5 478 000
Monrovia	572 000	Santo Domingo	1 865 000
Montevideo	1 341 000	São Tomé	54 000
Moroni	53 000	Sarajevo	579 000
Moscow	10 469 000	Seoul	9 714 000
Muscat	638 000	Singapore	4 253 000
Nairobi	2 575 000	Skopje	447 000
Nassau	222 000	Sofia	1 076 000
Nauru[5]	13 000	Sri Jayewardenepura	
N'Djamena	797 000	Kotte	117 000
New Delhi	14 146 000	Stockholm	1 697 000
Niamey	890 000	Sucre	212 000
Nicosia	205 000	Suva (Greater)	210 000
Nouakchott	600 000	T'aipei	2 473 000
Nuku'alofa	35 000	Tallinn	391 000
Oslo	795 000	Tarawa	42 000
Ottawa	1 093 000	Tashkent	2 155 000
Ouagadougou	821 000	T'bilisi	1 064 000
Palikir	7 000	Tegucigalpa	1 007 000
Panama City	930 000	Tehran	7 190 000
Paramaribo	253 000	Tel Aviv-Jaffa[7]	3 025 000
Paris	9 794 000	Thimphu	35 000
Phnom Penh	1 157 000	Tirana	367 000
Port-au-Prince	1 961 000	Tokyo	34 997 000
Port Louis	143 000	Tripoli	2 006 000
Port Moresby	275 000	Tunis	1 996 000
Port of Spain	55 000	Ulan Bator	812 000
Porto Novo	238 000	Vaduz	5 000
Port-Vila	34 000	Valletta	83 000
Prague	1 170 000	Vatican City	1 000
Praia	107 000	Victoria	25 000
Pretoria	1 209 000	Vienna	2 179 000
Pyongyang	3 228 000	Vientiane	716 000
Quito	1 451 000	Vilnius	549 000
Rabat	1 759 000	Warsaw	2 200 000
Rangoon[6]	3 874 000	Washington, DC	4 098 000
Reykjavík	184 000	Wellington	343 000
Riga	733 000	Windhoek	237 000
Riyadh	5 126 000	Yamoussoukro	416 000
Rome	2 665 000	Yaoundé	1 616 000
Roseau	27 000	Yerevan	1 079 000
St George's	33 000	Zagreb	688 000

[1] Population figures are 2003 estimates and are rounded to the nearest 1 000.
[2] 2002 estimate.
[3] No accurate figure available for Putrajaya, Malaysia's administrative capital.
[4] No accurate figure available for Lobamba, Swaziland's legislative capital.
[5] No capital of Nauru, although government is located in Yaren District; figure given is for the entire island.
[6] No figure available for Yanlon, Myanmar's newly-announced capital.
[7] Israel claims Jerusalem as its capital, but this is not recognized internationally.

Data source: United Nations Population Division, 'World Population Prospects: The 2003 Revision'.

LARGEST CITIES

World

UN estimates for the world's ten largest urban agglomerations ranked by population size. The agglomeration includes not only the city itself but also the greater metropolitan area. This means that the figures vary from estimates for the city alone. Population estimates also vary according to the criteria used in their calculation.

City	Country	Population[1]
Tokyo	Japan	34 327 000
Mexico City	Mexico	19 013 000
New York	United States of America	18 498 000
Mumbai	India	18 336 000
São Paulo	Brazil	18 333 000
Delhi	India	15 334 000
Kolkata	India	14 299 000
Buenos Aires	Argentina	13 349 000
Jakarta	Indonesia	13 194 000
Shanghai	China	12 665 000

[1] Population figures are 2005 estimates rounded to the nearest 1 000. Data source: United Nations Population Division, 'World Urbanization Prospects: The 2003 Revision'.

UK

The ten largest cities in the United Kingdom ranked by population size.

City	Population[1]
London	7 429 200
Birmingham	992 400
Leeds	719 600
Glasgow	577 700
Sheffield	516 100
Bradford	481 100
Edinburgh	453 700
Liverpool	444 500
Manchester	437 000
Bristol	393 900

[1] Population figures are 2004 estimates. Data source: Office for National Statistics and General Register Office for Scotland.

Cities of the Future

People are increasingly living in cities in the modern world. The United Nations predicts that more than half of the world's population will live in urban areas by 2008 – compared to just 2% of people in 1800, 30% in 1950 and 47% in 2000.

USA

The ten largest cities in the United States of America ranked by population size.

City	State	Population (2004e)
New York	New York	8 104 079
Los Angeles	California	3 845 541
Chicago	Illinois	2 862 244
Houston	Texas	2 012 626
Philadelphia	Pennsylvania	1 470 151
Phoenix	Arizona	1 418 041
San Diego	California	1 263 756
San Antonio	Texas	1 236 249
Dallas	Texas	1 210 393
San José	California	904 522

Data source: Population Division, US Census Bureau.

World's Best City

According to a study by the Economist Intelligence Unit in 2005, Vancouver is the best city in the world in which to live. Based on five criteria – stability, healthcare, culture and environment, education and infratructure – the study put the Canadian west coast city ahead of runners-up Melbourne, Vienna, Geneva, Perth, Adelaide, Sydney, Zurich, Toronto and Calgary.

POLITICS, LAW AND ORDER

UNITED NATIONS (UN)

An organization formed to maintain world peace and foster international co-operation, formally established on 24 Oct 1945 with 51 member states. It has six 'principal organs': the General Assembly, the Security Council, the Secretariat, the International Court of Justice, the Economic and Social Council and the Trusteeship Council.

United Nations membership

The United Nations has 191 member states. Countries are grouped according to year of entry; only the country's current name is given, although its name may have changed during its membership (for example Belarus joined the UN in 1945 as Byelorussia). For information on former names see each country's entry in **Countries A–Z** under **Human Geography**.

1945	Argentina, Australia, Belarus, Belgium, Bolivia, Brazil, Canada, Chile, China[1], Colombia, Costa Rica, Cuba, Czechoslovakia (until 1992), Denmark, Dominican Republic, Ecuador, Egypt, El Salvador, Ethiopia, France, Greece, Guatemala, Haiti, Honduras, India, Iran, Iraq, Lebanon, Liberia, Luxembourg, Mexico, The Netherlands, New Zealand, Nicaragua, Norway, Panama, Paraguay, Peru, Philippines, Poland, Russia, Saudi Arabia, South Africa, Syria, Turkey, Ukraine, United Kingdom, United States of America, Uruguay, Venezuela, Yugoslavia (until 1992)
1946	Afghanistan, Iceland, Sweden, Thailand
1947	Pakistan, Yemen[2]
1948	Myanmar (Burma)
1949	Israel
1950	Indonesia
1955	Albania, Austria, Bulgaria, Cambodia, Finland, Hungary, Ireland, Italy, Jordan, Laos, Libya, Nepal, Portugal, Romania, Spain, Sri Lanka
1956	Japan, Morocco, Sudan, Tunisia
1957	Ghana, Malaysia
1958	Guinea
1960	Benin, Burkina Faso, Cameroon, Central African Republic, Chad, Congo, Congo (Democratic Republic of the), Côte d'Ivoire, Cyprus, Gabon, Madagascar, Mali, Niger, Nigeria, Senegal, Somalia, Togo
1961	Mauritania, Mongolia, Sierra Leone, Tanzania[3]
1962	Algeria, Burundi, Jamaica, Rwanda, Trinidad and Tobago, Uganda
1963	Kenya, Kuwait
1964	Malawi, Malta, Zambia
1965	The Gambia, Maldives, Singapore
1966	Barbados, Botswana, Guyana, Lesotho
1968	Equatorial Guinea, Mauritius, Swaziland
1970	Fiji
1971	Bahrain, Bhutan, Oman, Qatar, United Arab Emirates

1973	The Bahamas, East Germany (until 1990), Germany
1974	Bangladesh, Grenada, Guinea-Bissau
1975	Cape Verde, Comoros, Mozambique, Papua New Guinea, São Tomé and Príncipe, Suriname
1976	Angola, Samoa, Seychelles
1977	Djibouti, Vietnam
1978	Dominica, Solomon Islands
1979	St Lucia
1980	St Vincent and the Grenadines, Zimbabwe
1981	Antigua and Barbuda, Belize, Vanuatu
1983	St Kitts and Nevis
1984	Brunei Darussalam
1990	Liechtenstein, Namibia
1991	Estonia, Korea (North), Korea (South), Latvia, Lithuania, Marshall Islands, Micronesia
1992	Armenia, Azerbaijan, Bosnia and Herzegovina, Croatia, Georgia, Kazakhstan, Kyrgyzstan, Moldova, San Marino, Slovenia, Tajikistan, Turkmenistan, Uzbekistan
1993	Andorra, Czech Republic, Eritrea, Macedonia, Monaco, Slovakia
1994	Palau
1999	Kiribati, Nauru, Tonga
2000	Tuvalu, Serbia and Montenegro
2002	East Timor, Switzerland

[1] *Taiwan, as the Republic of China, represented China at the UN until 25 Oct 1971, when the People's Republic of China was recognized instead; Taiwan has not since been a member of the UN.*
[2] *North Yemen joined the UN in 1947 and South Yemen joined in 1967; since unification in 1990 as Yemen the UN has considered 1947 to be the state's date of joining.*
[3] *Tanganyika joined the UN in 1961 and Zanzibar joined in 1963; since unification in 1964 as Tanzania the UN has considered 1961 to be the state's date of joining.*

Blue Berets for Peace

Between 1948 and Jun 2005, UN peacekeepers took part in 60 operations. They are currently deployed in 16 ongoing missions. The UN calculates that peacekeeping since 1948 has cost $36 billion.

United Nations Secretaries-General

The United Nations Secretariat, under the Secretary-General, employs around 8 900 people worldwide. The Secretary-General is often a significant figure in international diplomacy.

Secretary-General

1946–53	Trygve Lie *Norway*	1982–91	Javier Pérez de Cuéllar *Peru*
1953–61	Dag Hammarskjöld *Sweden*	1992–6	Boutros Boutros-Ghali *Egypt*
1962–71	U Thant *Burma*	1997–	Kofi Annan *Ghana*
1972–81	Kurt Waldheim *Austria*		

United Nations Security Council

The United Nations Security Council has 15 members: five permanent members, which each have the power of veto over any resolutions, and ten that are elected for two-year periods. The primary role of the Council is to maintain international peace and security; its decisions are binding on all other members. Only the permanent members are listed.

China
France
Russia

United Kingdom
United States of America

United Nations organizations

In addition to the bodies established under the UN Charter there is a range of subsidiary agencies, many with their own constitutions and membership. There are also a number of functional and regional commissions and research and training institutes.

UN specialized agencies

Food and Agriculture Organization of the United Nations (FAO)
International Civil Aviation Organization (ICAO)
International Fund for Agricultural Development (IFAD)
International Labour Organization (ILO)
International Maritime Organization (IMO)
International Monetary Fund (IMF)
International Telecommunication Union (ITU)
United Nations Educational, Scientific and Cultural Organization (UNESCO)
United Nations Industrial Development Organization (UNIDO)
Universal Postal Union (UPU)
World Bank Group[1]
World Health Organization (WHO)
World Intellectual Property Organization (WIPO)
World Meteorological Organization (WMO)
World Tourism Organization (WTO)

[1] *Includes the International Bank for Reconstruction and Development (IBRD), the International Development Association (IDA), the International Finance Corporation (IFC), the Multilateral Investment Guarantee Agency (MIGA) and the International Centre for Settlement of Investment Disputes (ICSID).*

UN programmes and funds

International Trade Centre (ITC)
Office of the United Nations High Commissioner for Refugees (UNHCR)
United Nations Capital Development Fund (UNCDF)
United Nations Children's Fund (UNICEF)
United Nations Conference on Trade and Development (UNCTAD)
United Nations Development Fund for Women (UNIFEM)
United Nations Development Programme (UNDP)
United Nations Drug Control Programme (UNDCP)
United Nations Environment Programme (UNEP)
United Nations Human Settlements Programme (UNHSP/UN-Habitat)
United Nations Population Fund (UNFPA)
United Nations Relief and Works Agency for Palestine Refugees in the Near East (UNRWA)
United Nations Volunteers (UNV)
World Food Programme (WFP)

Other UN entities

Joint United Nations Programme on HIV/AIDS (UNAIDS)
Office of the United Nations High Commissioner for Human Rights (OHCHR)
United Nations Office for Project Services (UNOPS)
United Nations System Staff College (UNSSC)
United Nations University (UNU)

UN related organizations

International Atomic Energy Agency (IAEA)
Organization for the Prohibition of Chemical Weapons (OPCW)
PrepCom for the Nuclear-Test-Ban-Treaty Organization (CTBTO Prep.com)
World Trade Organization (WTO)

International HQ

Deep in the heart of New York City in the United States of America lie 7.3 hectares/18 acres of foreign land. The United Nations headquarters on Manhattan Island is an 'international territory', owned by the UN and beyond US jurisdiction.

COMMONWEALTH

The Commonwealth is a voluntary organization of autonomous states which have in the past been imperial possessions of Britain. Its head is the reigning British monarch. It was formally established by the Statute of Westminster (1931) and meets frequently to discuss matters of mutual interest and concern. There are 53 member states, encompassing 1.8 billion people, or 30% of the world's population.

Commonwealth membership

Member countries are listed by year of entry.

1931	Australia, Canada, Irish Free State (left 1949), Newfoundland (joined Canada 1949), New Zealand, United Kingdom, South Africa (left 1961, rejoined 1994)
1947	India, Pakistan (left 1972, rejoined 1989; suspended 1999, readmitted 2004)
1948	Sri Lanka
1957	Ghana, Malaysia
1960	Nigeria (suspended 1995, readmitted 1999)
1961	Cyprus, Sierra Leone, Tanzania
1962	Jamaica, Trinidad and Tobago, Uganda
1963	Kenya
1964	Malawi, Malta, Zambia
1965	The Gambia, Singapore
1966	Barbados, Botswana, Guyana, Lesotho
1968	Mauritius, Nauru, Swaziland
1970	Tonga, Samoa, Fiji (left 1987, rejoined 1997; suspended 2000, readmitted 2001)
1972	Bangladesh
1973	The Bahamas
1974	Grenada
1975	Papua New Guinea
1976	Seychelles
1978	Dominica, Solomon Islands, Tuvalu
1979	Kiribati, St Lucia, St Vincent and the Grenadines
1980	Vanuatu, Zimbabwe (suspended 2002; left 2003)

1981	Antigua and Barbuda, Belize
1982	Maldives
1983	St Kitts and Nevis
1984	Brunei Darussalam
1990	Namibia
1995	Cameroon, Mozambique[1]

[1] *Although Mozambique is a former Portuguese colony it was allowed to join the Commonwealth because of its close relationship with the Commonwealth since its independence.*

Commonwealth Secretaries-General

Secretary-General

| 1965–75 | Arnold Smith *Canada* | 1990–2000 | Emeka Anyaoku *Nigeria* |
| 1975–90 | Shridath Ramphal *Guyana* | 2000– | Donald C McKinnon *New Zealand* |

EUROPEAN UNION (EU)

European Union membership

Member countries are listed by year of entry.

1958	Belgium, France, Germany, Italy, Luxembourg, The Netherlands
1973	Denmark, Republic of Ireland, United Kingdom
1981	Greece
1986	Portugal, Spain
1995	Austria, Finland, Sweden
2004	Cyprus, Czech Republic, Estonia, Hungary, Latvia, Lithuania, Malta, Poland, Slovakia, Slovenia

Bulgaria and Romania are 'acceding' countries expected to join the EU in 2007; Croatia and Turkey are 'candidate' countries for subsequent entry.

European Union Commission presidents

The European Commission is an executive body composed of 25 Commissioners from EU member countries led by a president.

President

1958–67	Walter Hallstein *West Germany*	1981–5	Gaston Thorn *Luxembourg*
1967–70	Jean Rey *Belgium*	1985–95	Jacques Delors *France*
1970–2	Franco Maria Malfatti *Italy*	1995–9	Jacques Santer *Luxembourg*
1972–3	Sicco L Mansholt *The Netherlands*	1999–2004	Romano Prodi *Italy*
1973–7	François-Xavier Ortoli *France*	2004–	José Manuel Barroso *Portugal*
1977–81	Roy Jenkins *United Kingdom*		

Note: The current Commission's term of office will end in 2009.

United in Diversity

'United in Diversity' is the official motto of the EU. There is also an official European anthem, Beethoven's Ninth Symphony, but this is always played without words. The EU celebrates its birthday on 9 May, 'Europe Day', as this was the day on which the idea of a European Union was first proposed in 1950.

AFRICAN UNION (AU)

The Organization of African Unity (OAU) was established in 1963 and changed its name to the African Union (AU) in 2002. Its stated aim is to promote accelerated socio-economic integration of the continent, leading to greater unity and solidarity between African countries and peoples. It has 53 member states.

Algeria	Eritrea	Niger
Angola	Ethiopia	Nigeria
Benin	Gabon	Rwanda
Botswana	The Gambia	São Tomé and Príncipe
Burkina Faso	Ghana	Senegal
Burundi	Guinea	Seychelles
Cameroon	Guinea-Bissau	Sierra Leone
Cape Verde	Kenya	Somalia
Central African Republic	Lesotho	South Africa
Chad	Liberia	Sudan
Comoros	Libya	Swaziland
Congo	Madagascar	Tanzania
Congo, Democratic Republic of the	Malawi	Togo
	Mali	Tunisia
Côte d'Ivoire	Mauritania	Uganda
Djibouti	Mauritius	Western Sahara
Egypt	Mozambique	Zambia
Equatorial Guinea	Namibia	Zimbabwe

ARAB LEAGUE

The League of Arab States, known as the Arab League, was established in 1945 and has 22 members from the Middle East and Africa. It exists primarily to promote political and economic co-operation, and its charter forbids its members from resorting to force against each other. Seven countries originally signed the treaty. Member countries are listed by year of entry.

1945	Egypt, Iraq, Jordan, Lebanon, Saudi Arabia, Syria, Yemen
1953	Libya
1956	Sudan
1958	Morocco, Tunisia
1961	Kuwait
1962	Algeria
1971	Bahrain, Oman, Qatar, United Arab Emirates
1973	Mauritania
1974	Somalia
1976	Palestine
1977	Djibouti
1993	Comoros

Atlantic Ocean, Arabian Sea

The Arab League estimates that the Arabic world covers approximately 14.2 million sq km/ 5.5 million sq mi, stretching across two continents from northern Africa's Atlantic coast to the Middle East and Asia, and encompassing a population of approximately 273 million people.

ASSOCIATION OF SOUTH EAST ASIAN NATIONS (ASEAN)

The Association of South East Asian Nations (ASEAN) was established in 1967 and has ten member states. Its aims are 'to accelerate economic growth, social progress and cultural development in the region' and 'to promote regional peace and stability'. Member countries are listed by year of entry.

1967	Indonesia, Malaysia, Philippines, Singapore, Thailand
1984	Brunei Darussalam
1995	Vietnam
1997	Laos, Myanmar (Burma)
1999	Cambodia

COMMONWEALTH OF INDEPENDENT STATES (CIS)

The Commonwealth of Independent States (CIS) is a grouping of twelve independent states formed in 1991 from the 15 republics which previously made up the USSR. Each member state has sovereign equality, and in 1993 all states signed an agreement to co-ordinate policies on taxation, customs, labour movement and other aspects of economic activity. Eleven countries originally joined the CIS in 1991; Georgia joined in 1993.

Armenia	Kazakhstan	Tajikistan
Azerbaijan	Kyrgyzstan	Turkmenistan
Belarus	Moldova	Ukraine
Georgia	Russia	Uzbekistan

GROUP OF EIGHT (G8)

The Group of Eight (G8) comprises the world's leading industrialized democracies. The first G8 summit was held in 1975; the annual summit meetings have a wide remit, dealing with economic, political and social issues on a global level. At other times these and other economically powerful countries have met to discuss matters of mutual interest as the Group of Five (G5), Seven (G7), Ten (G10), etc. Current member countries are listed by year of entry.

1975	France, Germany, Italy, Japan, United Kingdom, United States of America
1976	Canada
1998	Russia

G8 presidency and summits

The presidency of the G8 is held by each country in rotation for one year; that country hosts the annual summit meeting, at which the European Union is also represented.

2000	Japan (Okinawa)	2005	United Kingdom (Gleneagles)
2001	Italy (Genoa)	2006	Russia (St Petersburg)
2002	Canada (Kananaskis)	2007	Germany (Heiligendamm)
2003	France (Evian)	2008	Japan
2004	United States of America (Sea Island)	2009	Italy
		2010	Canada

NORTH ATLANTIC TREATY ORGANIZATION (NATO)

The North Atlantic Treaty Organization (NATO) comprises 26 countries from Europe and North America. It was created from the signatories to the North Atlantic Treaty in 1949. Its stated aim is to 'safeguard the freedom and security of its member countries by political and military means'. Member countries are listed by year of entry.

1949	Belgium, Canada, Denmark, France, Iceland, Italy, Luxembourg, The Netherlands, Norway, Portugal, United Kingdom, United States of America
1952	Greece, Turkey
1955	Germany
1982	Spain
1999	Czech Republic, Hungary, Poland
2004	Bulgaria, Estonia, Latvia, Lithuania, Romania, Slovakia, Slovenia

ORGANIZATION OF AMERICAN STATES (OAS)

The Organization of American States (OAS) comprises 35 countries from North and South America and the Caribbean. It seeks to promote unity and co-operation on economic, social and political issues. Member countries are listed by year of entry.

1948	Argentina, Bolivia, Brazil, Chile, Colombia, Costa Rica, Cuba[1], Dominican Republic, Ecuador, El Salvador, Guatemala, Haiti, Honduras, Mexico, Nicaragua, Panama, Paraguay, Peru, United States of America, Uruguay, Venezuela
1967	Barbados, Trinidad and Tobago
1969	Jamaica
1975	Grenada
1977	Suriname
1979	Dominica, St Lucia
1981	Antigua and Barbuda, St Vincent and the Grenadines
1982	The Bahamas
1984	St Kitts and Nevis
1990	Canada
1991	Belize, Guyana

[1] *Since 1962 the current government of Cuba, while remaining a member, has been excluded from participation in the OAS.*

ORGANIZATION OF PETROLEUM EXPORTING COUNTRIES (OPEC)

The Organization of Petroleum Exporting Countries (OPEC) comprises eleven countries from Africa, Asia, the Middle East and Latin America which are reliant on oil exports as their main source of income. Member countries are listed by year of entry.

1960	Iran, Iraq, Kuwait, Saudi Arabia, Venezuela
1961	Qatar
1962	Indonesia, Libya
1967	United Arab Emirates
1969	Algeria
1971	Nigeria
1973	Ecuador (left 1992)
1975	Gabon (left 1994)

Black Gold

OPEC estimates that the total world demand for oil in 2000 was 76 million barrels per day, and that demand will rise to 90 million barrels per day by 2010. Saudi Arabia is the world's biggest crude oil producer, pumping out over 8.4 million barrels every day.

WARSAW PACT

The Warsaw Pact was a military alliance, formed in 1955, comprising the USSR and the Communist states of Eastern Europe (excluding Yugoslavia). It was intended as a counterbalance to NATO. The Warsaw Pact was dissolved in 1991 after the break-up of the USSR.

Albania (seceded 1968)	Hungary
Bulgaria	Poland
Czechoslovakia	Romania
East Germany (from 1990 part of united Germany)	USSR

GENEVA CONVENTIONS

The four Geneva Conventions and two additional Protocols are a series of international agreements regulating the treatment of victims of war. They deal with such matters as torture, deportation, treatment of women and children, hostage-taking and the use of chemical and biological weapons, and are signed by most states and some non-governmental bodies.

Convention/ Protocol	Date	Application
Convention I	12 Aug 1949	For the amelioration of the condition of the wounded and sick in armed forces in the field.
Convention II	12 Aug 1949	For the amelioration of the condition of wounded, sick and shipwrecked members of armed forces at sea.
Convention III	12 Aug 1949	Relative to the treatment of prisoners of war.
Convention IV	12 Aug 1949	Relative to the protection of civilian persons in time of war.
Protocol I	8 Jun 1977	Relative to the protection of victims of international armed conflicts.
Protocol II	8 Jun 1977	Relative to the protection of victims of non-international armed conflicts.

NOBEL PEACE PRIZE

Nobel Prizes were established by a bequest in the will of Alfred Nobel (1833–96) to honour 'those who, during the preceding year, shall have conferred the greatest benefit on mankind'. The Nobel Peace Prize is awarded annually to a person or organization judged to have 'done the most or the best work for fraternity between nations, for the abolition or reduction of standing armies and for the holding and promotion of peace congresses'; first awarded in 1901.

1901	Henri Dunant, Frédéric Passy	1908	Klas Pontus Arnoldson, Fredrik Bajer
1902	Élie Ducommun, Albert Gobat		
1903	Randal Cremer	1909	Auguste Beernaert, Paul Henri d'Estournelles de Constant
1904	Institute of International Law		
1905	Bertha von Suttner	1910	Permanent International Peace Bureau
1906	Theodore Roosevelt		
1907	Ernesto Teodoro Moneta, Louis Renault	1911	Tobias Asser, Alfred Fried
		1912	Elihu Root

1913	Henri La Fontaine
1914	*no award*
1915	*no award*
1916	*no award*
1917	International Committee of the Red Cross
1918	*no award*
1919	Woodrow Wilson
1920	Léon Bourgeois
1921	Hjalmar Branting, Christian Lange
1922	Fridtjof Nansen
1923	*no award*
1924	*no award*
1925	Sir Austen Chamberlain, Charles G Dawes
1926	Aristide Briand, Gustav Stresemann
1927	Ferdinand Buisson, Ludwig Quidde
1928	*no award*
1929	Frank B Kellogg
1930	Nathan Söderblom
1931	Jane Addams, Nicholas Murray Butler
1932	*no award*
1933	Sir Norman Angell
1934	Arthur Henderson
1935	Carl von Ossietzky
1936	Carlos Saavedra Lamas
1937	Robert Cecil
1938	Nansen International Office for Refugees
1939	*no award*
1940	*no award*
1941	*no award*
1942	*no award*
1943	*no award*
1944	International Committee of the Red Cross
1945	Cordell Hull
1946	Emily Greene Balch, John R Mott
1947	Friends Service Council, American Friends Service Committee
1948	*no award*
1949	Lord Boyd Orr
1950	Ralph Bunche
1951	Léon Jouhaux
1952	Albert Schweitzer
1953	George C Marshall
1954	Office of the United Nations High Commissioner for Refugees
1955	*no award*
1956	*no award*
1957	Lester Bowles Pearson
1958	Georges Pire
1959	Philip Noel-Baker

1960	Albert Lutuli
1961	Dag Hammarskjöld
1962	Linus Pauling
1963	International Committee of the Red Cross, League of Red Cross Societies
1964	Martin Luther King
1965	United Nations Children's Fund
1966	*no award*
1967	*no award*
1968	René Cassin
1969	International Labour Organization
1970	Norman Borlaug
1971	Willy Brandt
1972	*no award*
1973	Henry Kissinger, Le Duc Tho
1974	Seán MacBride, Eisaku Sato
1975	Andrei Sakharov
1976	Betty Williams, Mairead Corrigan
1977	Amnesty International
1978	Anwar al-Sadat, Menachem Begin
1979	Mother Teresa
1980	Adolfo Pérez Esquivel
1981	Office of the United Nations High Commissioner for Refugees
1982	Alva Myrdal, Alfonso García Robles
1983	Lech Walesa
1984	Desmond Tutu
1985	International Physicians for the Prevention of Nuclear War
1986	Elie Wiesel
1987	Oscar Arias Sánchez
1988	United Nations Peacekeeping Forces
1989	The 14th Dalai Lama
1990	Mikhail Gorbachev
1991	Aung San Suu Kyi
1992	Rigoberta Menchú Tum
1993	Nelson Mandela, F W de Klerk
1994	Yasser Arafat, Shimon Peres, Yitzhak Rabin
1995	Joseph Rotblat, Pugwash Conferences on Science and World Affairs
1996	Carlos Filipe Ximenes Belo, José Ramos-Horta
1997	International Campaign to Ban Landmines, Jody Williams
1998	John Hume, David Trimble
1999	Médecins Sans Frontières
2000	Kim Dae-jung
2001	United Nations, Kofi Annan
2002	Jimmy Carter

2003	Shirin Ebadi	2005	International Atomic Energy Agency, Mohamed ElBaradei
2004	Wangari Maathai		

RANKS OF THE POLICE

UK-wide police service
Chief Constable
Deputy Chief Constable
Assistant Chief Constable
Chief Superintendent
Superintendent
Chief Inspector
Inspector
Sergeant
Constable

Metropolitan Police
Commissioner
Deputy Commissioner
Assistant Commissioner
Deputy Assistant Commissioner
Commander
Chief Superintendent
Superintendent
Chief Inspector
Inspector
Sergeant
Constable

ASSASSINS

The list includes convicted, alleged and attempted assassins. Assassins working together, such as the three men who killed Malcolm X, have not been included.

Assassin	Victim	Date
Mehmet Ali Agca	Pope John Paul II	13 May 1981 (attempt)
Yigal Amir	Yitzhak Rabin	4 Nov 1995
John Wilkes Booth	Abraham Lincoln	14 Apr 1865
Marcus Junius Brutus and Cassius	Julius Caesar	15 May 44 BC
Mark Chapman	John Lennon	8 Dec 1980
Charlotte Corday	Jean Paul Marat	13 Jul 1793
Leon Czolgosz	William McKinley	6 Sep 1901
Nathuram Godse	Mahatma Gandhi	30 Jan 1948
Charles J Guiteau	James Garfield	2 Jul 1881
John Hinckley	Ronald Reagan	30 Mar 1981 (attempt)
Ramón Mercader	Leon Trotsky	20 Aug 1940
Lee Harvey Oswald	John F Kennedy	23 Nov 1963
Gavrilo Princip	Archduke Franz Ferdinand	28 Jun 1914
James Earl Ray	Martin Luther King, Jnr	4 Apr 1968
Sirhan Sirhan	Robert Kennedy	5 Jun 1968
Valerie Solanas	Andy Warhol	3 Jun 1968 (attempt)

Ra, Ra, Rasputin

One of history's most infamous assassinations was that of Russian mystic Rasputin in Dec 1916. The assassins, a clique of Russian aristocrats, first tried to poison him; when that failed they reportedly beat him and shot him three times. His body was then thrown into an icy river, and the post-mortem was reported to show that he had drowned.

PRECEDENCE OF LAW COURTS

Courts are listed from highest to lowest. The European Court of Justice is the recourse for cases concerning European Union law in the UK.

Criminal law

England and Wales
House of Lords
Court of Appeal
Crown Court
Magistrates' Court

Scotland
High Court of Justiciary
Sheriff's Court
District Court

Northern Ireland
House of Lords
Northern Ireland Court of Appeal
Crown Court
Magistrates' Court

Civil law

England and Wales
House of Lords
Court of Appeal
High Court of Justice
County Court
Magistrates' Court

Scotland
House of Lords
Court of Session
Sheriff's Principal Court
Sheriff's Court

Northern Ireland
House of Lords
Northern Ireland Court of Appeal
High Court Of Justice
County Court
Magistrates' Court

MILITARY RANKS

UK officer ranks

Army	Air Force	Navy
Field Marshal	Marshal of the Royal Air Force	Admiral of the Fleet
General	Air Chief Marshal	Admiral
Lieutenant-General	Air Marshal	Vice-Admiral
Major-General	Air Vice-Marshal	Rear-Admiral
Brigadier	Air Commodore	Commodore Admiral
Colonel	Group Captain	Captain RN
Lieutenant-Colonel	Wing Commander	Commander
Major	Squadron Leader	Lieutenant Commander
Captain	Flight Lieutenant	Lieutenant
Lieutenant	Flying Officer	Sub-Lieutenant
Second-Lieutenant	Pilot Officer	Midshipman

USA officer ranks

Army	Air Force	Navy
General of the Army	General of the Air Force	Fleet Admiral
General	General	Admiral
Lieutenant General	Lieutenant General	Vice Admiral
Major General	Major General	Rear Admiral (Upper Half)
Brigadier General	Brigadier General	Rear Admiral (Lower Half)
Colonel	Colonel	Captain
Lieutenant Colonel	Lieutenant Colonel	Commander
Major	Major	Lieutenant Commander
Captain	Captain	Lieutenant
First Lieutenant	First Lieutenant	Lieutenant Junior Grade
Second Lieutenant	Second Lieutenant	Ensign

PARLIAMENT (UK)

All information is for the year 2005–6 unless otherwise stated. For British prime ministers, monarchs and first ministers of devolved regional governments see **United Kingdom** in **Countries A–Z** under **Human Geography**.

Number of MPs (House of Commons)	646
Number of peers (House of Lords)	731 (1 Jul 2005)
MP's annual parliamentary salary	£59 095
Prime minister's annual salary	£183 932 (inclusive of MP's salary)
Days that the House of Commons sits	164 (annual average, 1979–2004)
Days that the House of Lords sits	123 (annual average, 1951–2005)
Father of the House	A traditional title given to the MP who has the 'longest unbroken service in the Commons'. Alan Williams MP became the Father of the House in May 2005; he entered Parliament in 1964.
Speaker	The person who presides over the debates in the House of Commons. Michael Martin MP became the 156th Speaker in Oct 2000.
Women MPs	127 (2005)
Maximum length of a Parliament	5 years, as decreed by the Parliament Act (1911); this term has only been extended twice, during World War I and World War II.
Palace of Westminster	The current Palace of Westminster dates to the mid-19c; it was built 1840–70 after the previous Palace was destroyed by a fire in 1834.
Big Ben	Big Ben weighs 13.8 tonnes/13.6 tons. It is believed that the bell was named after one Sir Benjamin Hall, the Commissioner of Works at the Houses of Parliament (1855–8), whose name is engraved on the bell. The famous clock tower that houses Big Ben is 96.3m/316ft tall.
Voting	Women aged 30 years and over were given the vote in 1918. In 1928 women aged 21 and over were allowed to vote, giving them equality with men. The voting age was reduced to 18 in 1969.

Boozy Budgets

According to an old House of Commons tradition, the Chancellor of the Exchequer is 'permitted to fortify himself with the liquid refreshment of his choice' (in the words of the House of Commons Information Office) while delivering the budget speech, although alcohol is not usually drunk in the House. Tipples of choice are reputed to have included brandy and water (Disraeli), sherry mixed with beaten egg (Gladstone), gin and tonic (Geoffrey Howe), neat whisky (Kenneth Clarke) and, simply, mineral water (Gordon Brown). Although the latter's speeches have hovered around the one hour mark, some of his predecessors must surely have required fortification: Gladstone holds the record for the longest continuous budget speech, having orated for 4 hours 45 minutes in Apr 1853.

US CONSTITUTIONAL AMENDMENTS

The US Constitution was framed in 1787 and came into effect in 1789. Amendments to the Constitution were later proposed, and the following is a list of those that have been ratified. The first ten Amendments collectively are known as the Bill of Rights.

Amendment	Date	Main areas of application
I	1791	Freedom of religion, speech, the press, assembly and petition
II	1791	Right to bear arms
III	1791	Restrictions on the quartering of troops
IV	1791	Restrictions on search and seizure
V	1791	Grand jury trial, double jeopardy, self-incrimination, due process
VI	1791	Criminal prosecutions, jury trial, right to confront and to counsel
VII	1791	Common law suits, jury trial
VIII	1791	Excess bail or fines, cruel and unusual punishment
IX	1791	Non-enumerated rights
X	1791	Rights reserved to states
XI	1795	Suits against a state
XII	1804	Election of the president and vice-president
XIII	1865	Abolition of slavery
XIV	1868	Privileges and immunities, due process, equal protection, apportionment of representatives, Civil War disqualification and debt
XV	1870	Rights not to be denied on account of race
XVI	1913	Income tax
XVII	1913	Election of senators
XVIII	1919	Prohibition
XIX	1920	Women's right to vote
XX	1933	Presidential term and succession
XXI	1933	Repeal of prohibition
XXII	1951	Two term limit on president
XXIII	1961	Presidential voting powers
XXIV	1964	Poll tax
XXV	1967	Presidential succession
XXVI	1971	Right to vote at age 18
XXVII	1992	Compensation of members of Congress

Constitutional Prohibition

The only constitutional amendment ever to have been repealed is the 18th, relating to Prohibition, which was ratified in Jan 1919. It stated that 'after one year ... the manufacture, sale, or transportation of intoxicating liquors within, the importation thereof into, or the exportation thereof from the United States ... for beverage purposes is hereby prohibited'. It was repealed by the 21st amendment, ratified in Dec 1933, but both remain in the Constitution.

ANCIENT GREECE AND ROME

GREEK GODS

Adonis	God of vegetation and rebirth	**Hebe**	Goddess of youth
Aeolus	God of the winds	**Hecate**	Goddess of the Moon
Alphito	Barley goddess of Argos	**Helios**	God of the Sun
Aphrodite	Goddess of love and beauty	**Hephaestus**	God of fire
Apollo	God of prophecy, music, youth, archery and healing	**Hera**	Goddess of marriage and childbirth; queen of heaven
Ares	God of war	**Hermes**	Messenger of the gods
Arethusa	Goddess of springs and fountains	**Hestia**	Goddess of the hearth
		Hypnos	God of sleep
Artemis	Goddess of fertility, chastity and hunting	**Iris**	Goddess of the rainbow
		Morpheus	God of dreams
Asclepius	God of healing	**Nemesis**	God of destiny
Athene	Goddess of prudence and wise counsel; protectress of Athens	**Nereus**	God of the sea
		Nike	Goddess of victory
Atlas	Titan who bears up the Earth	**Oceanus**	God of the river Oceanus
Attis	God of vegetation	**Pan**	God of male sexuality and of herds
Boreas	God of the north wind		
Cronus	Father of Zeus	**Persephone**	Goddess of the Underworld and of corn
Cybele	Goddess of the earth		
Demeter	Goddess of the harvest	**Poseidon**	God of the sea
Dionysus	God of wine, vegetation and ecstasy	**Rhea**	Original mother goddess; wife of Cronus
Eos	Goddess of the dawn	**Selene**	Goddess of the Moon
Eros	God of love	**Thanatos**	God of death
Gaia	Goddess of the earth	**Zeus**	Overlord of the Olympian gods and goddesses; god of the sky and all its properties
Ganymede	God of rain		
Hades	God of the Underworld		

Principal Greek gods

Rhea x Cronus
(Titans)

ZEUS[2] x 1. Metis[1]   2. Leto[1]   3. Maia[1]   4. Semele[1]   5. Dione[1]

Poseidon[2]   Demeter[2] (x Zeus)   Hera[2] (x Zeus)

Athene[2]   Hermes[2]   Dionysus[2]   Aphrodite[2]   Persephone   Ares[2]   Hebe   Eileithyia   Hephaestus[2]

Apollo[2]   Artemis[2]

[1] A consort of Zeus.
[2] One of the twelve Olympians in the 'central group' of gods on the Parthenon frieze.

Cruel Immortality

Eos, the Greek goddess of the dawn, abducted several mortal men to be her lovers. One of these handsome young men was Tithonus, who was granted immortality by Zeus at Eos's request. However, she forgot to ask for perpetual youth, so Tithonus became immensely old and decrepit, and Eos shut him away. Eventually the gods took pity on his plight and changed him into a cicada, a grasshopper-like insect. The myth inspired the poem *Tithonus* by Alfred, Lord Tennyson.

ROMAN GODS

Apollo	God of the Sun	**Libitina**	Goddess of funeral rites
Bacchus	God of wine and ecstasy	**Luna**	Goddess of the Moon
Bellona	Goddess of war	**Maia**	Goddess of fertility
Ceres	Goddess of corn	**Mars**	God of war
Consus	God of seed sowing	**Mercury**	Messenger of the gods; also god of merchants
Cupid	God of love		
Diana	Goddess of fertility and hunting	**Minerva**	Goddess of war, craftsmen, education and the arts
Egreria	Goddess of fountains and childbirth		
		Mithras	Sun god; also god of regeneration
Epona	Goddess of horses	**Neptune**	God of the sea
Fauna	Goddess of fertility	**Ops**	Goddess of the harvest
Faunus	God of crops and herbs	**Orcus**	God of death
Feronia	Goddess of spring flowers	**Pales**	Goddess of flocks
Fides	God of honesty	**Penates**	Gods of food and drink
Flora	Goddess of fruitfulness and flowers	**Picus**	God of woods
		Pluto	God of the Underworld
Fortuna	Goddess of chance and fate	**Pomona**	Goddess of fruit trees
Genius	Protective god of individuals, groups and the state	**Portunus**	God of husbands
		Proserpina	Goddess of the Underworld
Janus	God of entrances, travel and the dawn	**Rumina**	Goddess of nursing mothers
		Saturn	God of fertility and agriculture
Juno	Goddess of marriage, childbirth and light	**Silvanus**	God of trees and forests
		Venus	Goddess of spring, gardens and love
Jupiter	God of the sky and its attributes (Sun, Moon, thunder, rain, etc)		
		Vertumnus	God of fertility
Lares	Gods of the house	**Vesta**	Goddess of the hearth
Liber Pater	God of agricultural and human fertility	**Victoria**	Goddess of victory
		Vulcan	God of fire

Principal Roman gods

Saturn x Ops

Vesta¹ — Ceres — Juno — Pluto — **Neptune** — Jupiter

Proserpina — **Minerva** **Mercury** Bacchus **Venus** Apollo Diana

Vulcan Mars

The twelve major gods of Olympus are shown in **bold** type.
¹ In some accounts, Vesta is supplanted by Bacchus.

ROMAN EMPERORS

Dates overlap where there are periods of joint rule (eg Marcus Aurelius and Lucius Verus) and where the government of the empire divides between east and west. All dates are AD unless otherwise indicated.

Regnal dates	Name	Regnal dates	Name
27BC–AD14	Augustus (Caesar Augustus)	41–54	Claudius
14–37	Tiberius	54–68	Nero
37–41	Caligula (Gaius Caesar)	68–69	Galba

Regnal dates	Name	Regnal dates	Name
69	Otho	282–283	Carus
69	Vitellius	283–285	Carinus
69–79	Vespasian	283–284	Numerian
79–81	Titus	284–305	Diocletian (East)
81–96	Domitian	286–305	Maximian (West)
96–98	Nerva	305–311	Galerius (East)
98–117	Trajan	305–306	Constantius I
117–138	Hadrian	306–307	Severus (West)
138–161	Antoninus Pius	306–312	Maxentius (West)
161–180	Marcus Aurelius	306–337	Constantine I
161–169	Lucius Verus	308–324	Licinius (East)
176–192	Commodus	337–340	Constantine II
193	Pertinax	337–350	Constans I
193	Didius Julianus	337–361	Constantius II
193–211	Septimius Severus	350–351	Magnentius
198–217	Caracalla	360–363	Julian
209–212	Geta	364–375	Valentinian I (West)
217–218	Macrinus	364–378	Valens (East)
218–222	Elagabalus	365–366	Procopius (East)
222–235	Alexander Severus	375–383	Gratian (West)
235–238	Maximin	375–392	Valentinian II (West)
238	Gordian I	379–395	Theodosius I
238	Gordian II	395–408	Arcadius (East)
238	Maximus	395–423	Honorius (West)
238	Balbinus	408–450	Theodosius II (East)
238–244	Gordian III	421–423	Constantius III (West)
244–249	Philip	423–455	Valentinian III (West)
249–251	Decius	450–457	Marcian (East)
251	Hostilian	455	Petronius Maximus (West)
251–253	Gallus	455–456	Avitus (West)
253	Aemilian	457–474	Leo I (East)
253–260	Valerian	457–461	Majorian (West)
253–268	Gallienus	461–467	Libius Severus (West)
268–269	Claudius II (the Goth)	467–472	Anthemius (West)
269–270	Quintillus	472–473	Olybrius (West)
270–275	Aurelian	474–480	Julius Nepos (West)
275–276	Tacitus	474	Leo II (East)
276	Florian	474–491	Zeno (East)
276–282	Probus	475–476	Romulus Augustus (West)

Fiddling While Rome Burned

Nero, the Roman emperor from AD54–68, lived a wild and violent life. His reign was infamous for its debauchery, extravagance and tyranny. He caused his stepbrother to be poisoned, murdered his mother and his first wife and subsequently murdered his second wife in a fit of passion. He then proposed marriage to his murdered stepbrother's daughter, had her executed when she refused, and finally married a third wife after murdering her husband. Nero was also said to have been responsible for the fire which destroyed two-thirds of Rome in Jul AD64, but this is doubtful, as is the story that he admired the spectacle from a distance while reciting his poetry and playing his lyre. He finally met his end in AD68, when the army and guards rose against him; he fled Rome and committed suicide.

ROMAN KINGS

According to Roman literary tradition, Rome was founded by Romulus.

753–715BC	Romulus	616–578BC	Tarquinius Priscus
715–673BC	Numa Pompilius	578–534BC	Servius Tullius
673–642BC	Tullus Hostilius	534–509BC	Tarquinius Superbus
642–616BC	Ancus Marcius		

SEVEN WONDERS OF THE WORLD

Originally compiled by Antipater of Sidon, a Greek poet, c.100BC. Modern locations are shown in italics.

Pyramids of Egypt
Egypt

Oldest and only surviving 'wonder'. Built c.2000BC as royal tombs, about 80 are still standing. The largest, the Great Pyramid of Cheops, at el-Gizeh, is approximately 146m/482ft high, covering 5.3 hectares/13 acres at the base.

Hanging Gardens of Babylon
Iraq

Terraced gardens adjoining Nebuchadnezzar's palace, said to rise 23–91m/75–300ft. Supposedly built by the king c.600BC to please his wife, a princess from the mountains, they are also associated with the Assyrian Queen Semiramis.

Statue of Zeus at Olympia
Greece

Carved by Phidias, the 12m/40ft statue marked the site of the original Olympic Games c.400BC. It was constructed of ivory and gold, and showed Zeus (Jupiter) on his throne.

Temple of Artemis (Diana) at Ephesus *Turkey*

Constructed of Parian marble and more than 122m/400ft long with over 100 columns 18m/60ft high, it was begun c.350BC and took some 120 years to build. Destroyed by the Goths in AD262.

Mausoleum at Halicarnassus
Turkey

Erected by Queen Artemisia in memory of her husband King Mausolus of Caria (in Asia Minor), who died 353BC. It stood 43m/140ft high. All that remains are a few pieces in the British Museum.

Colossus of Rhodes
Greece

Gigantic bronze statue of sun god Helios (or Apollo); stood about 36m/117ft high, dominating the harbour entrance at Rhodes. The sculptor Chares supposedly laboured for twelve years before he completed it in 280BC. It was destroyed by an earthquake in 224BC.

Pharos of Alexandria
Egypt

Marble lighthouse and watchtower built c.270BC on the island of Pharos in Alexandria's harbour. Possibly standing 122m/400ft high, it was destroyed by an earthquake in 1375.

SEVEN HILLS OF ROME

The ancient city of Rome was built around seven hills.

Aventine	Quirinal
Esquiline	Viminal
Palatine	Capitoline
Cælian	

Language Legacy

The monument to King Mausolus at Halicarnassus was destroyed centuries ago, but his name still lives on in the English word *mausoleum*, a magnificent tomb or monument.

FURIES

Three Greek goddesses, inhabitants of hell who were responsible for punishing bloody crimes; represented as winged spirits with long hair entwined with snakes, carrying whips and torches; they tortured their victims and made them mad. Also known as *Erinyes*.

Alecto
Megara
Tisiphone

TWELVE LABOURS OF HERCULES

Hercules, also known as Heracles, was a Greek hero famous for his great strength. The son of Zeus and Alcmene, he demonstrated his strength from birth, choking the serpents sent by the jealous Hera, Zeus's wife. He undertook the twelve famous labours for Eurystheus of Tiryns.

To kill and flay the Nemean lion

To kill the monster Hydra

To capture the Arcadian stag

To destroy the Erymanthian boar

To clean the stables of Augeas, King of Elis, in a day

To destroy the man-eating birds of the Stymphalian marshes

To capture the Cretan bull

To catch the savage horses of the Thracian king Diomedes

To obtain the golden girdle of the Amazonian queen Hippolyta

To steal the oxen of the giant Geryon

To fetch the golden apples of the Hesperides

To capture Cerberus, the three-headed dog of Hades, the underworld

FATES

Three Greek goddesses, daughters of Zeus; the first spun a thread which signified birth, the second unravelled the thread, symbolizing the unravelling of life, and the third cut the thread, signifying death. Also known as *Moerae*.

Atropos
Clotho
Lachesis

THREE GRACES

Three daughters of Zeus and Hera; embodied beauty and social accomplishments.

Aglaia
Euphrosyne
Thalia

MUSES

Nine Greek goddesses, daughters of Zeus, each with the vocation to promote an area of the arts.

Calliope *epic poetry*	**Clio** *history and lyre-playing*
Erato *lyric poetry and hymns*	**Euterpe** *flute-playing*
Melpomene *tragedy*	**Polyhymnia** *dance, mime and acting*
Terpsichore *dance and lyric poetry*	**Thalia** *comedy and idyllic poetry*
	Urania *astronomy*

SEVEN AGAINST THEBES

Seven Greek champions; defeated by another seven champions at the seven gates of Thebes; all were killed in battle, except for Amphiarus, whom the earth swallowed alive, and Adrastus, who escaped.

Adrastus *or* Eteoklos	Amphiarus Capaneus
Hippomedon	Parthenopaeus
Polynices	Tydeus

RELIGIONS, BELIEFS AND FOLKLORE

For Greek and Roman gods see **Ancient Greece and Rome.**

NORSE GODS

Aegir	God of the sea	**Norns**	Goddesses of destiny
Aesir	Race of warlike gods	**Odin,**	Chief of the Aesir family of
Alcis	Twin gods of the sky	**Woden,**	gods, the 'father' god; the god
Balder	Odin's son; favourite of the gods	**Wotan**	of battle, death, inspiration
Bor	Father of Odin	**Otr**	Otter god
Bragi	God of poetry	**Ran**	Goddess of the sea
Fafnir	Dragon god	**Sif**	Goddess wife of Thor
Fjorgynn	Mother of Thor	**Sigyn**	Goddess wife of Loki
Frey	God of fertility	**Thor,**	God of thunder and sky; good
Freyja	Goddess of libido	**Donar**	crops
Frigg	Goddess of fertility; wife of Odin	**Tyr**	God of battle
Gefion	Goddess who received virgins	**Ull**	Stepson of Thor, an enchanter
	after death	**Valkyries**	Female helpers of the gods of war
Heimdall	Guardian of the bridge Bifrost	**Vanir**	Race of benevolent gods
Hel	Goddess of death; Queen of	**Vidar**	Slayer of the wolf, Fenrir
	Niflheim, the land of mists	**Weland,**	Craftsman god
Hermod	Son of Odin	**Volundr**	
Hoder	Blind god who killed Balder		
Hoenir	Companion to Odin and Loki		
Idunn	Guardian goddess of the golden		
	apples of youth		
Kvasir	God of wise utterances		
Logi	Fire god		
Loki	God of mischief		
Mimir	God of wisdom		
Nanna	Goddess wife of Balder		
Nehallenia	Goddess of plenty		
Nerthus	Goddess of earth		
Njord	God of ships and the sea		

World Tree

In Norse mythology the World Tree, a giant ash known as *Yggdrasil*, supported the sky, held the different realms of gods and men in its branches and had its roots in the Underworld. Odin created *Asgard*, the home of the gods, in the upper branches of the World Tree. Asgard was reached from earth by the rainbow bridge *Bifrost*, guarded by Heimdall, the watchman of the gods.

EGYPTIAN GODS

Amun-Re	Universal god	**Re, Ra**	Sun god (later Amun-Re)
Anubis	God of funerals	**Sekhmet**	Goddess of might
Apis	God of fertility	**Seth**	God of evil
Aten	Unique god	**Thoth**	Supreme scribe
Geb	God of the earth		
Hathor	Goddess of love		
Horus	God of light		
Isis	Goddess of magic		
Khnum	Goddess of creation		
Khonsou	Son of Amun-Re		
Maat	Goddess of order		
Nephthys	Goddess of funerals		
Nut	God of the sky		
Osiris	God of vegetation		
Ptah	God of creation		

Gods and Beasts

The gods of Ancient Egypt were often portrayed with human bodies but the heads of animals, for example Anubis (the head of a jackal), Hathor (cow), Horus (falcon), Sekhmet (lioness) and Thoth (ibis or baboon). Re was depicted as a falcon with the Sun's disc on his head during the day, while at night he appeared as a ram-headed god who sailed through the Underworld.

CELTIC GODS

Many Celtic gods and goddesses were known by different names by different Celtic peoples; where names differ, the British spelling is given.

Anna	Mother goddess of fecundity and plenty	**Lleu**	Hero god, deity of crafts, commerce and (in some traditions) youth and games
Arianrhod	Earth goddess		
Badhbh	Goddess of war	**Mabon**	God of youth, healing, music and hunting
Boann	River goddess		
Bel, Beli, Belinus	God of the Sun, light and fire	**Macha**	Goddess of horses
		Manawydan, Manawyddan	God of wisdom and patience
Blodeuwedd	Goddess of love and generosity		
Brigantia, Brighid	Goddess of livestock, agriculture, midwifery, poetry and crafts	**Matres, Matronae**	Trio of goddesses associated with earth, fecundity and motherhood
Cernunnos	Ruler of all the animals and lord of the Underworld	**Medhbh**	Warrior-goddess representing sexuality
Cerridwen	Goddess of the Underworld		
Cliodna	Goddess of peace and beauty	**Merlin**	Guardian god of the land
Dea Arduinna	Goddess of wild animals	**Modron**	Mother goddess
Don	Chief of the Irish gods; the lord of the Otherworld	**Morríghan**	Goddess of war
		Nemhain	Goddess of war
Dylan	God of the sea	**Ogmia**	God of strength and eloquence
Édain, Étain	Goddess of the Otherworld	**Rhiannon**	Goddess of horses, birds and the Moon, known as the Great Queen
Epona	Goddess of horses		
Flidhais	Goddess of wild animals		
Gofannon	God of smiths and of strength	**Silvanus, Sucellus**	God of the Underworld
Grannos	God of healing		
Llyr, Lir	God of the sea	**Taran**	God of thunder and war

Talking Heads

In Celtic mythology Bran was a gigantic god who featured in the Welsh tales *The Mabinogion* (14c) as King of Britain. He died in Ireland, and his severed head provided his followers with advice and entertainment for 80 years. It was finally buried at the site of the Tower of London, from where it protected Britain from invaders until it was eventually dug up.

BAHA'I

Founded	1863		inevitable unification of humankind, universal education and obedience to government.
Founder	Mirza Husayn Ali (1817–92)		
Sacred texts	Most Holy Book, The Seven Valleys, The Hidden Words, The Bayan.	**Organization**	There is a network of elected local and national level bodies, and an elected international governing body. There is little formal ritual.
Place of worship	Shrine, temple		
Beliefs	The oneness of God, the unity of all faiths, the		
		Divisions	No major divisions.

BUDDHISM

Founded	c.500BC		concerning suffering and freedom from it; the Eightfold Path leading to Nirvana; the law of Karma.
Founder	Prince Siddhartha Gautama (c.563–c.483BC)		
Sacred texts	The Pali Canon or Tripitaka. Other texts include the Mahayana Sutras, the Milindapanha (Questions of Milinda) and the Bardo Thodol (Tibetan Book of the Dead).	**Organization**	Monastic system; numerous festivals and ceremonies for the laity.
		Divisions	Two main historical divisions: Theravada and Mahayana. Other schools include Zen, Lamaism, Tendai, Nichiren and Soka Gakkai.
Place of worship	Temple		
Beliefs	The Four Noble Truths		

The Enlightened One

Buddha was born in c.563BC as Prince Siddhartha Gautama, the son of the rajah in a ruling tribe in Nepal. When he was about 30 he left the luxuries of the court, his beautiful wife and all earthly ambitions in exchange for the life of an ascetic; after six years of extreme self-mortification he saw in the contemplative life the perfect way to self-enlightenment. According to tradition, he achieved enlightenment when sitting beneath a banyan tree near Buddh Gaya in Bihar. For the next 40 years he taught, gaining many disciples and followers. He died aged about 80 in c.483BC.

DALAI LAMAS

Dalai Lama is the title given to the spiritual and political leader of Tibetan Buddhists. Each successive Dalai Lama is held to be a reincarnation of the previous one, and is also regarded as a manifestation of the Bodhisattva Avalokiteshavara, the Buddha of Compassion.

1391–1475	Gedun Truppa	1758–1804	Jampel Gyatso
1475–1542	Gedun Gyatso	1806–15	Luntok Gyatso
1543–88	Sonam Gyatso	1816–37	Tshultrim Gyatso
1589–17	Yonten Gyatso	1838–56	Khedrup Gyatso
1617–82	Ngawang Lobzang Gyatso	1856–75	Trinle Gyatso
1683–1706	Tsang-yang Gyatso	1876–1933	Thupten Gyatso
1708–57	Kezang Gyatso	1935–	Tenzin Gyatso

Ocean-like Guru

The name *Dalai Lama* comes from the Mongolian word *dalai*, meaning ocean, and the Tibetan word *lama*, high priest, and is sometimes translated as 'ocean-like guru' or 'ocean of wisdom'. The Panchen Lama, the Tibetan religious leader second in importance to the Dalai Lama, is named from the Tibetan *pandita chen-po*, meaning 'great scholar'.

FOUR NOBLE TRUTHS

The Four Noble Truths are a summary of the central teachings of Buddha.

Suffering is always present in life.
The origin of suffering is desire.
By ceasing to desire one ceases to suffer.
The Eightfold Path is the way of achieving release from desire and suffering.

EIGHTFOLD PATH

The fourth of Buddha's Four Noble Truths, prescribing the way to enlightenment.

Right views	Right livelihood
Right thoughts	Right effort
Right speech	Right mindfulness
Right action	Right concentration

CHRISTIANITY

Founded	1c AD	**Founder**	Jesus Christ, 'the Son of God' (c.4BC–c.30AD)
Sacred texts	The Bible consisting of the Old and New Testaments.		
Old Testament:	Genesis, Exodus, Leviticus, Numbers, Deuteronomy, Joshua, Judges, Ruth, 1 Samuel, 2 Samuel, 1 Kings, 2 Kings, 1 Chronicles, 2 Chronicles, Ezra, Nehemiah, Esther, Job, Psalms, Proverbs, Ecclesiastes, Song of Solomon, Isaiah, Jeremiah, Lamentations, Ezekiel, Daniel, Hosea, Joel, Amos, Obadiah, Jonah, Micah, Nahum, Habakkuk, Zephaniah, Haggai, Zechariah, Malachi.		
New Testament:	Matthew, Mark, Luke, John, Acts of the Apostles, Romans, 1 Corinthians, 2 Corinthians, Galatians, Ephesians, Philippians, Colossians, 1 Thessalonians, 2 Thessalonians, 1 Timothy, 2 Timothy, Titus, Philemon, Hebrews, James, 1 Peter, 2 Peter, 1 John, 2 John, 3 John, Jude, Revelation. Apocrypha (Revised standard version 1957): 1 Esdras, 2 Esdras, Tobit, Judith, Additions to Esther, Wisdom of Solomon, Ecclesiasticus, Epistle of Jeremiah, Baruch, Prayer of Azariah and the Song of the Three Young Men, (History of) Susanna, Bel and the Dragon, Prayer of Manasseh, 1 Maccabees, 2 Maccabees. (The Authorized version incorporates Jeremiah into Baruch; The prayer of Azariah is simply called the Song of the Three Holy Children. The Roman Catholic Church includes Tobit, Judith, all of Esther, Maccabees 1 and 2, Wisdom of Solomon, Ecclesiasticus and Baruch in its canon.)		
Place of worship	Cathedral, chapel, church		
Beliefs	Monotheistic: centred on the life and works of Jesus of Nazareth. Christians believe that Jesus was crucified and resurrected from the dead.		deriving from the traditions of the Apostles and their successors.
		Divisions	Major divisions are the Orthodox or Eastern church, the Roman Catholic church and the Protestant churches.
Organization	Various priestly hierarchies, often involving bishops and lesser clergy, ultimately		

POPES

Antipopes (who claimed to be pope in opposition to those canonically chosen) are given in square brackets. All dates listed are AD.

until c.64	Peter	440–61	Leo I
c.64–c.76	Linus	461–8	Hilarus
c.76–c.90	Anacletus	468–83	Simplicius
c.90–c.99	Clement I	483–92	Felix III (II)
c.99–c.105	Evaristus	492–6	Gelasius I
c.105–c.117	Alexander I	496–8	Anastasius II
c.117–c.127	Sixtus I	498–514	Symmachus
c.127–c.137	Telesphorus	[498, 501–5	Laurentius]
c.137–c.140	Hyginus	514–23	Hormisdas
c.140–c.154	Pius I	523–6	John I
c.154–c.166	Anicetus	526–30	Felix IV (III)
c.166–c.175	Soter	530–2	Boniface II
175–89	Eleutherius	[530	Dioscorus]
189–98	Victor I	533–5	John II
198–217	Zephyrinus	535–6	Agapetus I
217–22	Callistus I	536–7	Silverius
[217–c.235	Hippolytus]	537–55	Vigilius
222–30	Urban I	556–61	Pelagius I
230–5	Pontian	561–74	John III
235–6	Anterus	575–9	Benedict I
236–50	Fabian	579–90	Pelagius II
251–3	Cornelius	590–604	Gregory I
[251–c.258	Novatian]	604–6	Sabinianus
253–4	Lucius I	607	Boniface III
254–7	Stephen I	608–15	Boniface IV
257–8	Sixtus II	615–18	Deusdedit or Adeodatus I
259–68	Dionysius	619–25	Boniface V
269–74	Felix I	625–38	Honorius I
275–83	Eutychianus	640	Severinus
283–96	Caius	640–2	John IV
296–304	Marcellinus	642–9	Theodore I
304–8	*interregnum*	649–55	Martin I
308–9	Marcellus I	654–7	Eugenius I'
310	Eusebius	657–72	Vitalian
311–14	Miltiades	672–6	Adeodatus II
314–35	Sylvester I	676–8	Donus
336	Mark	678–81	Agatho
337–52	Julius I	682–3	Leo II
352–66	Liberius	684–5	Benedict II
[355–65	Felix II]	685–6	John V
366–84	Damasus I	686–7	Cono
[366–7	Ursinus]	[687	Theodore]
384–99	Siricius	[687–92	Paschal]
399–401	Anastasius I	687–701	Sergius I
402–17	Innocent I	701–5	John VI
417–18	Zosimus	705–7	John VII
418–22	Boniface I	708	Sisinnius
[418–19	Eulalius]	708–15	Constantine
422–32	Celestine I	715–31	Gregory II
432–40	Sixtus III	731–41	Gregory III

741–52	Zacharias	936–9	Leo VII
752	Stephen II (*not consecrated*)	939–42	Stephen IX
752–7	Stephen II (III)	942–6	Marinus II
757–67	Paul I	946–55	Agapetus II
[767–9	Constantine II]	955–64	John XII
[768	Philip]	[963–5	Leo VIII]
768–72	Stephen III (IV)	964	Benedict V
772–95	Hadrian I	965–72	John XIII
795–816	Leo III	973–4	Benedict VI
816–17	Stephen IV (V)	[974, 984–5	Boniface VII]
817–24	Paschal I	974–83	Benedict VII
824–7	Eugenius II	983–4	John XIV
827	Valentine	985–96	John XV
827–44	Gregory IV	996–9	Gregory V
[844	John]	[997–8	John XVI]
844–7	Sergius II	999–1003	Sylvester II
847–55	Leo IV	1003	John XVII
855–8	Benedict III	1004–9	John XVIII
[855	Anastasius Bibliothecarius]	1009–12	Sergius IV
858–67	Nicholas I	1012–24	Benedict VIII
867–72	Hadrian II	[1012	Gregory]
872–82	John VIII	1024–32	John XIX
882–4	Marinus I	1032–44	Benedict IX
884–5	Hadrian III	1045	Sylvester III
885–91	Stephen V (VI)	1045	Benedict IX (*second reign*)
891–6	Formosus	1045–6	Gregory VI
896	Boniface VI	1046–7	Clement II
896–7	Stephen VI (VII)	1047–8	Benedict IX (*third reign*)
897	Romanus	1048	Damasus II
897	Theodore II	1048–54	Leo IX
898–900	John IX	1055–7	Victor II
900–3	Benedict IV	1057–8	Stephen IX (X)
903	Leo V	[1058–9	Benedict X]
[903–4	Christopher]	1059–61	Nicholas II
904–11	Sergius III	1061–73	Alexander II
911–13	Anastasius III	[1061–72	Honorius II]
913–14	Lando	1073–85	Gregory VII
914–28	John X	[1080, 1084–1100	Clement VII]
928	Leo VI	1086–7	Victor III
928–31	Stephen VII (VIII)	1088–99	Urban II
931–5	John XI	1099–1118	Paschal II

Choosing the Pope

Upon the death of the pope a set of ancient ceremonies are held to choose a successor. Firstly, the *camerlengo* (papal treasurer) strikes the dead pope's forehead three times with a silver hammer and calls him by his real name to ensure he is truly dead. All the cardinals of the Roman Catholic church who are younger than 80 years then assemble in a *conclave*. The cardinals are locked into a specially prepared area of the Vatican palace, guarded and unable to leave or communicate with the outside world; the door will not be reopened until a successor has been elected, which may take days. The election itself is by secret ballot in the Sistine Chapel; the ballot papers are burned with chemicals after each inconclusive round of voting, sending black smoke into the air above the Vatican, while burning of the ballots alone after a successful vote sends up white smoke and signals to the waiting crowds outside that a new pope has been chosen.

[1100–2	Theodoric]	1352–62	Innocent VI
[1102	Albert]	1362–70	Urban V
[1105–11	Sylvester IV]	1370–8	Gregory XI
1118–19	Gelasius II	1378–89	Urban VI
[1118–21	Gregory VIII]	[1378–94	Clement VII]
1119–24	Callistus II	1389–1404	Boniface IX
1124–30	Honorius II	[1394–1423	Benedict XIII]
[1124	Celestine II]	1404–6	Innocent VII
1130–43	Innocent II	1406–15	Gregory XII
[1130–8	Anacletus II]	[1409–10	Alexander V]
[1138	Victor IV]²	[1410–15	John XXIII]
1143–4	Celestine II	1416	*interregnum*
1144–5	Lucius II	1417–31	Martin V
1145–53	Eugenius III	[1423–9	Clement VIII]
1153–4	Anastasius IV	[1425–30	Benedict XIV]
1154–9	Hadrian IV	1431–47	Eugenius IV
1159–81	Alexander III	[1439–49	Felix V]
[1159–64	Victor IV]²	1447–55	Nicholas V
[1164–8	Paschal III]	1455–8	Callistus III
[1168–78	Callistus III]	1458–64	Pius II
[1179–80	Innocent III]	1464–71	Paul II
1181–5	Lucius III	1471–84	Sixtus IV
1185–7	Urban III	1484–92	Innocent VIII
1187	Gregory VIII	1492–1503	Alexander VI
1187–91	Clement III	1503	Pius III
1191–8	Celestine III	1503–13	Julius II
1198–1216	Innocent III	1513–21	Leo X
1216–27	Honorius III	1522–3	Hadrian VI
1227–41	Gregory IX	1523–34	Clement VII
1241	Celestine IV	1534–49	Paul III
1241–3	*interregnum*	1550–5	Julius III
1243–54	Innocent IV	1555	Marcellus II
1254–61	Alexander IV	1555–9	Paul IV
1261–4	Urban IV	1559–65	Pius IV
1265–8	Clement IV	1566–72	Pius V
1268–71	*interregnum*	1572–85	Gregory XIII
1271–6	Gregory X	1585–90	Sixtus V
1276	Innocent V	1590	Urban VII
1276	Hadrian V	1590–1	Gregory XIV
1276–7	John XXI³	1591	Innocent IX
1277–80	Nicholas III	1592–1605	Clement VIII
1281–5	Martin IV	1605	Leo XI
1285–7	Honorius IV	1605–21	Paul V
1288–92	Nicholas IV	1621–3	Gregory XV
1292–4	*interregnum*	1623–44	Urban VIII
1294	Celestine V	1644–55	Innocent X
1294–1303	Boniface VIII	1655–67	Alexander VII
1303–4	Benedict XI	1667–9	Clement IX
1304–5	*interregnum*	1670–6	Clement X
1305–14	Clement V	1676–89	Innocent XI
1314–16	*interregnum*	1689–91	Alexander VIII
1316–34	John XXII	1691–1700	Innocent XII
[1328–30	Nicholas V]	1700–21	Clement XI
1334–42	Benedict XII	1721–4	Innocent XIII
1342–52	Clement VI	1724–30	Benedict XIII

1730–40	Clement XII	1878–1903	Leo XIII
1740–58	Benedict XIV	1903–14	Pius X
1758–69	Clement XIII	1914–22	Benedict XV
1769–74	Clement XIV	1922–39	Pius XI
1775–99	Pius VI	1939–58	Pius XII
1800–23	Pius VII	1958–63	John XXIII
1823–9	Leo XII	1963–78	Paul VI
1829–30	Pius VIII	1978	John Paul I
1831–46	Gregory XVI	1978–2005	John Paul II
1846–78	Pius IX	2005–	Benedict XVI

[1] *Elected during the banishment of Martin I.*
[2] *Different individuals.*
[3] *There was no John XX.*

ARCHBISHOPS OF YORK

The date of succession is given.

627	Paulinus[1]	1265	Walter Giffard
644	Chad (Ceadda)[1]	1279	William Wickwane
669	Wilfrid I (St Wilfrid)[1]	1286	John le Romeyn (Romanus)
678	Bosa[1]	1298	Henry of Newark
705	John (St John of Beverley)[1]	1300	Thomas of Corbridge
718	Wilfrid II[1]	1306	William Greenfield
735	Egbert	1317	William of Melton
767	Ethelbert	1342	William le Zouche
780	Eanbald I	1352	John of Thoresby
796	Eanbald II	1374	Alexander Neville
808	Wulfsige	1388	Thomas Arundel
837	Wigmund	1396	Robert Waldby
854	Wulfhere	1398	Richard le Scrope
900	Ethelbald	1407	Henry Bowet
904	Hrotheweard (or Lodeward)	1425	John Kempe
931	Wulfstan I	1452	William Booth
958	Oskytel	1465	George Neville
971	Edwald (or Ethelwold)	1476	Lawrence Booth
972	Oswald	1480	Thomas Rotheram (or Scott)
992	Ealdulf (Abbot of Peterborough)	1501	Thomas Savage
1003	Wulfstan II	1508	Christopher Bainbridge
1023	Aelfric Puttoc	1514	Thomas Wolsey
1051	Cynesige	1531	Edward Lee
1061	Ealdred	1545	Robert Holgate
1070	Thomas I	1555	Nicholas Heath
1101	Gerard	1561	Thomas Young
1109	Thomas II	1570	Edmund Grindal
1119	Thurstan	1577	Edwin Sandys
1143	William Fitzherbert	1589	John Piers
1147	Henry Fitzherbert/William Fitzherbert	1595	Matthew Hutton
		1606	Tobias Matthew
1154	William Fitzherbert	1628	George Monteigne
1154	Roger of Pont-L'Eveque	1628	Samuel Harsnett
1181	Geoffrey Plantagenet	1632	Richard Neile
1215	Walter de Grey	1641	John Williams
1256	Sewal de Bovill	1660	Accepted Frewen
1258	Godfrey of Ludham (or Kineton)	1664	Richard Sterne

1683	John Dolben	1860	Charles Thomas Longley
1688	Thomas Lamplugh	1862	William Thomson
1691	John Sharp	1890	William Connor Magee
1714	Sir William Dawes	1891	William Dalrymple
1724	Lancelot Blackburne	1908	Cosmo Gordon Lang
1743	Thomas Herring	1929	William Temple
1747	Matthew Hutton	1942	Cyril Forster Garbett
1757	John Gilbert	1956	Arthur Michael Ramsey
1761	Robert Hay Drummond	1961	Frederic Donald Coggan
1777	William Markham	1975	Stuart Yarworth Blanch
1807	Edward Venables Vernon	1983	John Stapylton Habgood
	(afterwards Harcourt)	1995	David Hope
1847	Thomas Musgrave	2005	John Sentamu

[1] *Bishop of York; the first Archbishop was Egbert in 735.*
Note: Gaps in the chronology indicate that the see was vacant or subject to conflict.

ARCHBISHOPS OF CANTERBURY

The date of succession is given.

597	Augustine	1093	Anselm
604	Laurentius	1114	Ralph d'Escures
619	Mellitus	1123	William de Corbeil
624	Justus	1139	Theobald
627	Honorius	1162	Thomas à Becket
655	Deusdedit	1174	Richard (of Dover)
668	Theodore	1184	Baldwin
693	Berhtwald	1193	Hubert Walter
731	Tatwine	1207	Stephen Langton
735	Nothelm	1229	Richard le Grant
740	Cuthbert	1234	Edmund of Abingdon
761	Bregowine	1245	Boniface of Savoy
765	Jaenbert	1273	Robert Kilwardby
793	Ethelhard	1279	John Peckham
805	Wulfred	1294	Robert Winchelsey
832	Feologeld	1313	Walter Reynolds
833	Ceolnoth	1328	Simon Meopham
870	Ethelred	1333	John de Stratford
890	Plegmund	1349	Simon Islip
914	Athelm	1349	Thomas Bradwardine
923	Wulfhelm	1366	Simon Langham
942	Oda	1368	William Whittlesey
959	Aelfsige	1375	Simon Sudbury
959	Brithelm	1381	William Courtenay
960	Dunstan	1396	Thomas Arundel
990	Sigeric	1398	Roger Walden
995	Aelfric	1399	Thomas Arundel (*restored*)
c.988	Ethelgar	1414	Henry Chichele
1005	Alphege	1443	John Stafford
1013	Lyfing	1452	John Kempe
1020	Ethelnoth	1454	Thomas Bourchier
1038	Eadsige	1486	John Morton
1051	Robert of Jumieges	1501	Henry Deane
1052	Stigand	1503	William Warham
1070	Lanfranc	1533	Thomas Cranmer

1556	Reginald Pole	1783	John Moore
1559	Matthew Parker	1805	Charles Manners-Sutton
1576	Edmund Grindal	1828	William Howley
1583	John Whitgift	1848	John Sumner
1604	Richard Bancroft	1862	Charles Longley
1611	George Abbot	1868	Archibald Tait
1633	William Laud	1883	Edward Benson
1660	William Juxon	1896	Frederick Temple
1663	Gilbert Sheldon	1903	Randall Davidson
1678	William Sancroft	1928	William Lang
1691	John Tillotson	1942	William Temple
1695	Thomas Tenison	1945	Geoffrey Fisher
1716	William Wake	1961	Arthur Ramsey
1737	John Potter	1974	Frederick Coggan
1747	Thomas Herring	1980	Robert Runcie
1757	Matthew Hutton	1991	George Carey
1758	Thomas Secker	2002	Rowan Williams
1768	Frederick Cornwallis		

Chair of St Augustine

The post of Archbishop of Canterbury is known as the 'Chair of St Augustine', after the first Archbishop. St Augustine was probably born in Rome, where he became the prior of a Benedictine monastery. In 596 he was sent by Pope Gregory I to convert the Anglo-Saxons to Christianity, and it is recorded that he baptized 1 000 people in the River Swale in a single day. Augustine became Bishop of the English in 597 and established his church at Canterbury, where he died in 604.

APOSTLES

In Christianity, the Apostles were Christ's twelve chosen followers. The apostles are generally taken to include the twelve original followers of Christ (excluding Judas Iscariot in some versions), who witnessed the resurrected Jesus and were charged with proclaiming his gospel.

Peter (brother of Andrew)	**Thomas**
Andrew (brother of Peter)	**Matthew**
James, son of Zebedee (brother of John)	**James of Alphaeus**
John (brother of James)	**Simon the Canaanite** (*in Matthew and Mark*) or **Simon the Zealot** (*in Luke and Acts*)
Philip	
Bartholomew	**Judas Iscariot**

The twelfth apostle is Thaddeus in the biblical gospels of Matthew and Mark; in Luke and Acts it is Judas or James. Matthias succeeded to Judas's place.

FATHERS OF THE CHURCH

'Father of the Church' is a title usually applied to the leaders of the early Christian Church. Recognized as eminent teachers of the faith, they were characterized by orthodoxy of doctrine and personal holiness, and were usually beatified.

Note: The title has also been subsequently awarded by the Roman Catholic church to later Christian writers.

Apostolic Fathers

The Apostolic Fathers were the immediate disciples and fellow labourers of the Apostles, more especially those who have left writings. Only the three major Fathers are listed.

St Clement of Rome

St Ignatius of Antioch

St Polycarp of Smyrna

Doctors of the Church

A small number of especially revered early ecclesiastical writers are known as Doctors of the Church. There were eight from medieval times, originally four from the Greek Church and four from the Latin Church.

St Basil the Great	**St Ambrose**
St Gregory Nazianzen	**St Jerome**
St John Chrysostom	**St Augustine**
St Gregory the Great	**St Athanasius**

TEN COMMANDMENTS

In the Bible, the ten commandments given by God to Moses on Mount Sinai, as described in the Old Testament Book of Exodus.

I	I am the Lord your God, who brought you out of the land of Egypt, out of the house of bondage. You shall have no other gods before me.
II	You shall not make for yourself a graven image. You shall not bow down to them or serve them.
III	You shall not take the name of the Lord your God in vain.
IV	Remember the sabbath day, to keep it holy.
V	Honour your father and your mother.
VI	You shall not kill.
VII	You shall not commit adultery.
VIII	You shall not steal.
IX	You shall not bear false witness against your neighbour.
X	You shall not covet.

The Ten Commandments appear in two different places in the Bible – Exodus 20.17 and Deuteronomy 5.6–21. Most Protestant, Anglican and Orthodox Christians enumerate the Commandments differently from Roman Catholics and Lutherans.

CHAMPIONS OF CHRISTENDOM

In medieval times the patron saints of seven nations were known as the Champions of Christendom. Their supposed exploits were celebrated in *The Famous History of the Seven Champions of Christendom*, published c.1597 by Richard Johnson (1573–c.1659).

St George of England	**St Denys of France**
St Andrew of Scotland	**St James of Spain**
St Patrick of Ireland	**St Anthony of Italy**
St David of Wales	

PATRON SAINTS

A patron saint is a saint regarded as the protector of a particular group.

Accountants	Matthew	Messengers	Gabriel
Actors	Genesius, Vitus	Metalworkers	Eligius
Advertisers	Bernardino of Siena	Midwives	Raymond Nonnatus
Architects	Thomas (Apostle)	Miners	Anne, Barbara
Artists	Luke, Angelico	Motorists	Christopher
Astronauts	Joseph (Cupertino)	Musicians	Cecilia, Gregory the Great
Astronomers	Dominic	Nurses	Camillus de Lellis, John of
Athletes	Sebastian		God
Authors	Francis de Sales	Philosophers	Thomas Aquinas, Catherine
Aviators	Our Lady of Loreto		of Alexandria
Bakers	Honoratus	Poets	Cecilia, David
Bankers	Bernardino (Feltre)	Police	Michael
Barbers	Cosmas and Damian	Politicians	Thomas More
Blacksmiths	Eligius	Postal Workers	Gabriel
Bookkeepers	Matthew	Priests	Jean-Baptiste Vianney
Book trade	John of God	Printers	John of God
Brewers	Amand, Wenceslaus	Prisoners	Leonard
Builders	Barbara, Thomas (Apostle)	Radio Workers	Gabriel
Butchers	Luke	Sailors	Christopher, Erasmus,
Carpenters	Joseph		Francis of Paola
Chemists	Cosmas and Damian	Scholars	Thomas Aquinas
Comedians	Vitus	Scientists	Albert the Great
Cooks	Lawrence, Martha	Sculptors	Luke, Louis
Dancers	Vitus	Secretaries	Genesius
Dentists	Apollonia	Servants	Martha, Zita
Doctors	Cosmas and Damian, Luke	Shoemakers	Crispin, Crispinian
Editors	Francis de Sales	Singers	Cecilia, Gregory
Farmers	Isidore	Soldiers	George, Joan of Arc, Martin
Firemen	Florian		of Tours, Sebastian
Fishermen	Andrew, Peter	Students	Thomas Aquinas
Florists	Dorothy, Thérèse of Lisieux	Surgeons	Luke, Cosmas and Damian
Gardeners	Adam, Fiacre	Tailors	Homobonus
Glassworkers	Luke, Lucy	Tax Collectors	Matthew
Gravediggers	Joseph of Arimathea	Taxi Drivers	Fiacre
Grocers	Michael	Teachers	Gregory the Great, John
Hotelkeepers	Amand, Julian the		Baptiste de la Salle
	Hospitaler	Television	Gabriel
Housewives	Martha	Workers	
Jewellers	Eligius	Theologians	Augustine, Alphonsus
Journalists	Francis de Sales		Liguori, Thomas Aquinas
Labourers	James, John Bosco	Undertakers	Dismas, Joseph of
Lawyers	Ivo, Thomas More		Arimathea
Librarians	Jerome, Catherine of	Waiters	Martha
	Alexandria	Writers	Lucy
Merchants	Francis of Assisi		

Politicians' Patron

In 2000 Pope John Paul II declared the martyr Sir Thomas More (1478–1535) to be the patron saint of politicians and statesmen. More was Speaker of the House of Commons and Lord Chancellor under King Henry VIII; he was beheaded in 1535.

SAINTS

Information on selected well-known saints is given below. The official recognition of saints, and the choice of a saint's day, varies greatly between different branches of Christianity, calendars and localities. Where there are major variations, the dates given refer to the dates in the Western church calendar.

Saint	Lived	Saint's Day
Alban	3c AD	22 Jun

The first Christian martyr in Britain, he was a pagan living in the town of Verulamium who was scourged and beheaded around AD300 for helping a fugitive Christian priest who had converted him. A monastery was founded on the site in 793, and the place was renamed St Albans.

Andrew	1c AD	30 Nov

One of the twelve Apostles of Jesus Christ, he was a fisherman who preached the Gospel in Asia Minor, and was crucified in Greece. The belief that his cross was X-shaped dates only from the 14c. He is a patron saint not only of Scotland but of Greece and Russia.

Bernard	923–1008	28 May or 15 Jun

Also known as the Apostle of the Alps, he founded hospices in Alpine passes which were named after him, as were St Bernard dogs, trained by the monks to go to the aid of travellers.

Catherine	died AD307	25 Nov

Born in Alexandria, she is said to have publicly confessed the Gospel at a sacrificial feast appointed by Emperor Maximinus, and was consequently beheaded, after being tortured on a spiked wheel (later known as a 'catherine wheel').

Christopher	3c AD	25 Jul

He was, according to tradition, a man some 3.5m/11.5ft tall. His name in Greek (*Christophoros*) means 'Christ-bearing', which gave rise to the legend that he had carried the Christ-child (and all the weight of the world's sin) across a river. He is the patron saint of travellers.

David	c.520–601	1 Mar

He presided over two Welsh synods and is believed to have died in 601 as Bishop of Moni Judeorum, or Menevia, afterwards St David's. He is the patron saint of Wales.

George	early 4c AD	23 Apr

Little is known about him, the date of his death is uncertain, and he has been confused with others; his name was soon obscured by fables and myth. The famous story of his fight with the dragon cannot be traced much earlier than the 13c. He is the patron saint of England and Portugal.

Nicholas	4c AD	6 Dec

In legend he gave gifts of gold to three poor girls for their dowries, which gave rise to the custom of giving gifts on his feast day. His identification with Father Christmas began in Europe and spread to the USA. He is a patron saint of Greece and Russia, and also of children, scholars, merchants, sailors, travellers and thieves.

Pancras   died AD304   12 May

He was killed in persecutions while still a child, and is one of the patron saints of children.

Patrick   5c   17 Mar

In AD432 it is thought he was sent by the Pope as a missionary to Ireland. He converted his old master Milchu and other chiefs, and after 20 years spent in missionary work fixed his see at Armagh (AD454). He is the patron saint of Ireland.

Stephen   1c AD   26 Dec

All that is known is from the Bible, Acts 6–7. He was appointed by the Apostles to manage the finances and alms of the early Church, was tried for blasphemy and stoned to death.

Swithin   died 862   15 Jul

An English ecclesiastic, he was made Bishop of Winchester in 852. When the monks exhumed his body in 971 to bury it in the rebuilt cathedral, the removal, which was to have taken place on 15 Jul, is said to have been delayed by violent rain. This led to the belief that if it rains on his feast day it will rain for a further 40 days.

Valentine   died AD269   14 Feb

He is said to have been executed during Roman persecutions, but claims have been made for another St Valentine who was martyred in Rome. Neither is associated with romance, hardly surprisingly; the custom of sending love letters on his feast day originated in the Middle Ages, when it was thought the birds' mating season started then.

Death of Saints

Many early saints met a premature end through martyrdom. Their gruesome fates include being rolled over burning coals (St Agatha, died AD251), tortured on a spiked wheel and beheaded (St Catherine, died AD307), pressed to death (St Margaret Clitherow, c.1556–86), tied to a tree and shot to death with arrows by the Danes (St Edmund, c.841–70), murdered by a heathen daughter-in-law (St Ludmilla, died 921), impaled or crucified head downward (St Peter, 1c AD), beaten to death with rods (St Sebastian, died AD288) and being killed, along with 11 000 virgin companions, by a horde of Huns (St Ursula, 4c AD).

DAYS OF CHRISTMAS

According to the old song, 'my true love' gave a present on each of the twelve days of Christmas.

Day	Gift	Day	Gift
1st	Partridge in a pear tree	7th	Swans a-swimming
2nd	Turtle doves	8th	Maids a-milking
3rd	French hens	9th	Ladies dancing
4th	Calling birds	10th	Lords a-leaping
5th	Gold rings	11th	Pipers piping
6th	Geese a-laying	12th	Drummers drumming

Christmas Birds

It is thought that 'calling birds' is a corruption of the older 'colly birds' – a dialect word for blackbirds. 'Gold rings' may be ring-necked birds, rather than jewellery, meaning that the first seven gifts are all birds.

TRIBES OF ISRAEL

In the Bible (Genesis 49), a confederacy of twelve tribes generally traced to Jacob's twelve sons – six by Leah (Reuben, Simeon, Levi, Judah, Issachar, Zebulun), two by Rachel (Joseph, Benjamin), two by Rachel's maid Bilhah (Dan, Naphtali), and two by Leah's maid Zilpah (Gad, Asher). Joseph's sons Ephraim and Manasseh gave rise to two tribes; the Tribe of Levi is not conventionally listed as they served in the Holy Temple rather than owning land. Jacob had received the name Israel (Genesis 32.28) when he wrestled with a divine being.

Reuben	Simeon	Gad
Judah	Issachar	Zebulun
Ephraim	Manasseh	Benjamin
Dan	Asher	Naphtali

PLAGUES OF EGYPT

Ten biblical plagues, described in the book of Exodus, that afflicted the Egyptians as a result of the Pharaoh's refusal to release the Israelites from captivity.

Water turns to blood	Boils
Frogs	Hail
Lice	Locusts
Flies	Darkness
Cattle disease	Death of first-born

SEVEN DEADLY SINS

Pride *or* vanity	Envy	Gluttony
Lust	Anger *or* wrath	Sloth
Avarice, greed *or* covetousness		

VIRTUES

Cardinal virtues

Also known as the natural virtues.

Justice	Prudence	Temperance
Fortitude		

Theological virtues

Also known as the supernatural or Christian virtues.

Faith	Hope	Charity

SEVEN SLEEPERS

The Seven Sleepers of Ephesus in medieval legend were seven persecuted Christians who fled into a cave at the time of the emperor Decius (AD250). They slept for 200 years, emerging in AD447 at the time of Theodosius II. The story was thought to confirm the resurrection of Christ.

Achillides	Diomedes	Diogenus
Probatus	Stephanus	Sambatus
Quiriacus		

HORSEMEN OF THE APOCALYPSE

The symbolic biblical characters described in Revelation 6 and Zechariah 6.1–7, who signal the beginning of the messianic age. Each comes on a steed of different colour, symbolizing devastations associated with the end of the world, except for the white horse's rider, who is given a crown and sent to conquer (Revelation 6.2).

Black horse	Famine
Red	Bloodshed and War
Pale	Pestilence and Death
White	various interpretations

WISE MEN

In the Bible, a group who came from 'the East' guided by a star (Matthew 2.1–12) to visit the infant Jesus in Bethlehem, bringing three gifts.

gold	frankincense	myrrh

We Three Kings

The three wise men are a Christian tradition. But the Bible doesn't specify how many wise men there were: the belief that there were three developed in later centuries. Tradition also suggests the three were called Balthasar, Gaspar and Melchior. The wise men are also sometimes known as the *Magi*. The word is the plural of *magus*, which comes from the Old Persian word for magician.

CONFUCIANISM

Founded	6c BC	**Organization**	Confucianism is not an institution and has no church or clergy. Weddings and funerals follow a tradition handed down by Confucian scholars.
Founder	K'ung-fu-tzu (Confucius) (c.551–479BC), a Chinese philosopher		
Sacred texts	Shih Ching, Li Ching, Shu Ching, Chu'un Ch'iu, I Ching.		
Place of worship	Temple	**Divisions**	Two major divisions: the first is associated with Confucius and Hsun Tzu (c.298–238BC), and the second with Mencius (c.371–289BC) and medieval neo-Confucians.
Beliefs	Confucius was concerned with the best way to live and behave in this world and was not concerned with the afterlife. He laid particular emphasis on the family.		

Act Wisely

'Man has three ways of acting wisely. First, on meditation; that is the noblest. Secondly, on imitation; that is the easiest. Thirdly, on experience; that is the bitterest.'
From *The Analects* (c.479BC), a collection of the sayings and doings of Confucius.

HINDUISM

Founded	c.1500BC		including dharma (right living), the law of karma and reincarnation; numerous gods.
Founder	No single founder		
Sacred texts	The Vedas ('knowledge') including the Upanishads, the Ramayana and the Mahabharata, the Bhagavad Gita, the Agamas.	**Organization**	A Brahmanic priesthood officiates at prayer and festivals.
		Divisions	The three major living traditions are those devoted to Vishnu, Shiva and the goddess Shakti. Many folk traditions exist.
Place of worship	Temple		
Beliefs	Many diverse religious beliefs and practices,		

HINDU GODS

Agni	God of fire	**Iswara**	God of nature and the soul
Brahma	God of creation	**Kali**	Goddess of destruction and wife of Shiva
Durga	Shiva's wife		
Ganesh	Elephant-headed son of Shiva	**Kama**	God of lust and desire
Garuda	Bird that carries Shiva	**Kartikeya**	Six-headed war god mounted on a peacock
Hanuman	Monkey god		
Indra	God of storms and war	**Krishna**	Incarnation of Vishnu

Kurma	Incarnation of Vishnu in the form of a tortoise	**Rudra**	Destructive aspect of Shiva	
Lakshmana	Half-brother of Rama	**Sarasvati**	Mother goddess representing art, learning and music	
Lakshmi	Goddess of wealth and good luck	**Shakti**	Female principle of power and energy	
Narada	Incarnation of Vishnu	**Shani**	Bringer of bad luck	
Narasimha	Incarnation of Vishnu as a lion-man	**Shiva**	God of creation and destruction	
Nataraja	Aspect of Shiva as the Lord of Dance	**Sita**	Rama's wife	
		Soma	God of speech and deity of the soma creeper	
Parvati	Shiva's wife	**Surya**	God of the Sun	
Pushan	God of enlightenment	**Varuna**	God of the sea	
Radha	Goddess of love and consort of Krishna	**Vishnu**	God of creation	
Rama	Incarnation of Vishnu	**Yama**	God of death	

HINDU CALENDAR

The Indian classical calendar was based on the Sun for purposes of astrology, but the lunar one was necessary for the sacred calendar. In the 6c AD the practice of dating years relative to the revolutions of the orbit of Jupiter was introduced, creating a 60-year cycle. In recent times the National Calendar of India was introduced in 1957, using Gregorian dates alongside the Saka era calendar (calculated from AD78, each year beginning on 22 Mar, or 21 Mar in a leap year). Other calendars in use include the Vikrama era calendar (calculated from 58BC) and the Kalacuri era calendar (calculated from AD248). Other important Hindu eras include the Gupta era (AD320) and Harsa era (AD606).

Months (solar days)

Basis: Moon

Chaitra (29 or 30)
Vaisakha (29 or 30)
Jyaistha (29 or 30)
Asadha (29 or 30)
Dvitiya Asadha (*certain leap years*)
Sravana (29 or 30)
Dvitiya Sravana (*certain leap years*)

Bhadrapada (29 or 30)
Asvina (29 or 30)
Karttika (29 or 30)
Margasirsa (29 or 30)
Pausa (29 or 30)
Magha (29 or 30)
Phalguna (29 or 30)

Saka era

Year	Gregorian equivalents (AD)	Year	Gregorian equivalents (AD)
1917	(22 Mar 1995–20 Mar 1996)	1930	(21 Mar 2008–21 Mar 2009)
1918	(21 Mar 1996–21 Mar 1997)	1931	(22 Mar 2009–21 Mar 2010)
1919	(22 Mar 1997–21 Mar 1998)	1932	(22 Mar 2010–21 Mar 2011)
1920	(22 Mar 1998–21 Mar 1999)	1933	(22 Mar 2011–20 Mar 2012)
1921	(22 Mar 1999–20 Mar 2000)	1934	(21 Mar 2012–21 Mar 2013)
1922	(21 Mar 2000–21 Mar 2001)	1935	(22 Mar 2013–21 Mar 2014)
1923	(22 Mar 2001–21 Mar 2002)	1936	(22 Mar 2014–21 Mar 2015)
1924	(22 Mar 2002–21 Mar 2003)	1937	(22 Mar 2015–20 Mar 2016)
1925	(22 Mar 2003–20 Mar 2004)	1938	(21 Mar 2016–21 Mar 2017)
1926	(21 Mar 2004–21 Mar 2005)	1939	(22 Mar 2017–21 Mar 2018)
1927	(22 Mar 2005–21 Mar 2006)	1940	(22 Mar 2018–21 Mar 2019)
1928	(22 Mar 2006–21 Mar 2007)	1941	(22 Mar 2019–20 Mar 2020)
1929	(22 Mar 2007–20 Mar 2008)		

Vikrama era

Year	Gregorian equivalents (AD)	Year	Gregorian equivalents (AD)
2052	(14 Mar 1995–13 Mar 1996)	2065	(14 Mar 2008–13 Mar 2009)
2053	(14 Mar 1996–13 Mar 1997)	2066	(14 Mar 2009–13 Mar 2010)
2054	(14 Mar 1997–13 Mar 1998)	2067	(14 Mar 2010–13 Mar 2011)
2055	(14 Mar 1998–13 Mar 1999)	2068	(14 Mar 2011–13 Mar 2012)
2056	(14 Mar 1999–13 Mar 2000)	2069	(14 Mar 2012–13 Mar 2013)
2057	(14 Mar 2000–13 Mar 2001)	2070	(14 Mar 2013–13 Mar 2014)
2058	(14 Mar 2001–13 Mar 2002)	2071	(14 Mar 2014–13 Mar 2015)
2059	(14 Mar 2002–13 Mar 2003)	2072	(14 Mar 2015–13 Mar 2016)
2060	(14 Mar 2003–13 Mar 2004)	2073	(14 Mar 2016–13 Mar 2017)
2061	(14 Mar 2004–13 Mar 2005)	2074	(14 Mar 2017–13 Mar 2018)
2062	(14 Mar 2005–13 Mar 2006)	2075	(14 Mar 2018–13 Mar 2019)
2063	(14 Mar 2006–13 Mar 2007)	2076	(14 Mar 2019–13 Mar 2020)
2064	(14 Mar 2007–13 Mar 2008)		

ISLAM

Founded	7c AD		Prophet Muhammad.
Founder	Muhammad (c.570–c.632)	**Organization**	No organized priesthood, but great respect is accorded to descendants of Muhammad and holy men, scholars and teachers such as mullahs and ayatollahs.
Sacred texts	The Koran (the word of God as revealed to Muhammad) and the Hadith (a collection of the Prophet's sayings).		
Place of worship	Mosque	**Divisions**	Two main groups: the Sunni (the majority and the more orthodox) and the Shiites. Other sub-sects include the Sufis, the Ismailis and the Wahhabis.
Beliefs	Monotheistic: God is the creator of all things and holds absolute power over man; the perfect word of God was revealed to the		

PILLARS OF ISLAM

Islam has five essential religious duties.

Shahada	Profession of faith, the sincere recitation of the two-fold creed, 'There is no god but God' and 'Muhammad is the Messenger of God'.
Salat	Formal prayer, to be performed at fixed hours five times a day while facing towards the holy city of Mecca.
Zakat	Almsgiving, through the payment of zakat, is the duty of sharing one's wealth out of gratitude for God's favour, according to the uses laid down in the Koran.
Saum	Fasting, during the hours of daylight of the month of Ramadan.
Hajj	Pilgrimage to Mecca, to be performed if at all possible at least once during one's lifetime.

ISLAMIC CALENDAR

The Islamic calendar is calculated from the Hegira (the year Muhammad migrated from Mecca to Medina, and the beginning of the Muslim era) in AD622. Still used by Muslims for religious purposes, it has twelve lunar months, with no intercalations.

Months (solar days)

Basis: Moon

Muharram (30)	Rajab (30)
Safar (29)	Shaban (29)
Rabi I (30)	Ramadan (30)
Rabi II (29)	Shawwal (29)
Jumada I (30)	Dhu al-Qadah (30)
Jumada II (29)	Dhu al-Hijjah (29 or 30)

Year	Gregorian equivalents (AD)	Year	Gregorian equivalents (AD)
1416	(31 May 1995–18 May 1996)	1429	(10 Jan 2008–28 Dec 2008)
1417	(19 May 1996–8 May 1997)	1430	(29 Dec 2008–17 Dec 2009)
1418	(9 May 1997–27 Apr 1998)	1431	(18 Dec 2009–6 Dec 2010)
1419	(28 Apr 1998–16 Apr 1999)	1432	(7 Dec 2010–26 Nov 2011)
1420	(17 Apr 1999–5 Apr 2000)	1433	(27 Nov 2011–14 Nov 2012)
1421	(6 Apr 2000–25 Mar 2001)	1434	(15 Nov 2012–4 Nov 2013)
1422	(26 Mar 2001–14 Mar 2002)	1435	(5 Nov 2013–24 Oct 2014)
1423	(15 Mar 2002–3 Mar 2003)	1436	(25 Oct 2014–13 Oct 2015)
1424	(4 Mar 2003–21 Feb 2004)	1437	(14 Oct 2015–1 Oct 2016)
1425	(22 Feb 2004–9 Feb 2005)	1438	(2 Oct 2016–21 Sep 2017)
1426	(10 Feb 2005–30 Jan 2006)	1439	(22 Sep 2017–10 Sep 2018)
1427	(31 Jan 2006–20 Jan 2007)	1440	(11 Sep 2018–31 Aug 2019)
1428	(21 Jan 2007–9 Jan 2008)	1441	(1 Sep 2019–19 Aug 2020)

One God

Allah is simply the Arabic name for 'God'. Muslims, Christians and Jews all worship this same God.

JAINISM

Founded	6c BC		karma can be acquired by ascetic practices. All living things are sacred and must not be harmed.
Founder	Vardhamana Mahavira (c.540–468BC)		
Sacred texts	The Svetambara canon of scripture and Digambara texts.	**Organization**	Jain monks and nuns have a strong relationship with lay people and officiate at temple rituals.
Place of worship	Temple		
Beliefs	Salvation and freedom from the working of	**Divisions**	Svetambara and Digambara.

JUDAISM

Founded	c.2000BC
Founder	Abraham (c.2000–1650BC) and Moses (c.1500–1300BC)
Sacred texts	The Hebrew Bible: Torah (Pentateuch): Genesis, Exodus, Leviticus, Numbers, Deuteronomy. Also the books of the Prophets, Psalms, Chronicles and Proverbs, as well as the Talmud (made up of the Mishna, the oral law, and the Gemara, an extensive commentary). The Zohar (Book of Splendour) is a famous cabbalistic book.
Place of worship	Synagogue
Beliefs	Monotheistic: God created the world, delivered the Israelites out of bondage in Egypt, and chose them to be a light to all humankind.
Organization	Hierarchy of chief rabbis, rabbis and congregations.
Divisions	Today most Jews are descendants of either the Ashkenazim or the Sephardim.

CHIEF RABBIS

The spiritual leader of the Jewish community in the UK is given the title of Chief Rabbi of the United Hebrew Congregations of the Commonwealth. The Chief Rabbinate consists of the Chief Rabbi and his Cabinet.

1704–56	Aaron Hart	1891–1911	Hermann Marcus Adler
1756–8	*post vacant*	1911–13	*post vacant*
1758–64	Hart Lyon	1913–46	Joseph Herman Hertz
1765–91	David Tevele Schiff	1946–8	*post vacant*
1791–1802	*post vacant*	1948–65	Israel Brodie
1802–42	Solomon Hirschell	1966–91	Lord Immanuel Jakobovits
1842–5	*post vacant*	1991–	Sir Jonathan Sacks
1845–91	Nathan Marcus Adler		

JEWISH CALENDAR

The Jewish religious calendar dates in its modern form from the Babylonian Exile in the 6c BC, when the Jews adopted the Babylonian calendar. This was lunar-solar, with a lunar year of 354 days and a solar year (important to agriculture) of 365 days. By the 4c BC an accurate system of intercalation had been devised. Each month starts with the new moon, but each day begins at sunset. These features were retained in the Jewish calendar. The year count of the Jewish era is calculated from 3761BC, said to be the year of the creation of the world.

Months (solar days)

Basis: Moon

Tishri (30)	Nisan (30)
Heshvan (29 or 30)	Iyar (29)
Kislev (29 or 30)	Sivan (30)
Tevet (29)	Tammuz (29)
Shevat (30)	Av (30)
Adar (29 or 30)	Elul (29)
Adar Sheni (*leap years only*)	

Year	Gregorian equivalents (AD)	Year	Gregorian equivalents (AD)
5756	(25 Sep 1995–13 Sep 1996)	5769	(30 Sep 2008–18 Sep 2009)
5757	(14 Sep 1996–1 Oct 1997)	5770	(19 Sep 2009–8 Sep 2010)
5758	(2 Oct 1997–20 Sep 1998)	5771	(9 Sep 2010–28 Sep 2011)
5759	(21 Sep 1998–10 Sep 1999)	5772	(29 Sep 2011–16 Sep 2012)
5760	(11 Sep 1999–29 Sep 2000)	5773	(17 Sep 2012–4 Sep 2013)
5761	(30 Sep 2000–17 Sep 2001)	5774	(5 Sep 2013–24 Sep 2014)
5762	(18 Sep 2001–6 Sep 2002)	5775	(25 Sep 2014–13 Sep 2015)
5763	(7 Sep 2002–26 Sep 2003)	5776	(14 Sep 2015–2 Oct 2016)
5764	(27 Sep 2003–15 Sep 2004)	5777	(3 Oct 2016–20 Sep 2017)
5765	(16 Sep 2004–3 Oct 2005)	5778	(21 Sep 2017–9 Sep 2018)
5766	(4 Oct 2005–22 Sep 2006)	5779	(10 Sep 2018–29 Sep 2019)
5767	(23 Sep 2006–12 Sep 2007)	5780	(30 Sep 2019–18 Sep 2020)
5768	(13 Sep 2007–29 Sep 2008)		

SHINTOISM

Founded	8c	**Organization**	Shamans originally performed the ceremonies; in the 8c the imperial family were ascribed divine origins and state Shintoism was established.
Founder	No single founder		
Sacred texts	Kojiki and Nihon Shoki		
Place of worship	Shrine		
Beliefs	Founded on Japanese folk religions, Shinto is made up of many elements, including animism, veneration of nature and ancestor worship.	**Divisions**	In the 19c Shinto was divided into Shrine (jinga) Shinto and Sectarian (kyoko) Shinto. Jinga was a state cult until 1945.

SIKHISM

Founded	15c	**Organization**	No priestly caste. All Sikhs are empowered to perform rituals connected with births, marriages and deaths.
Founder	Guru Nanak (1469–1539)		
Sacred texts	Adi Granth		
Place of worship	Temple		
Beliefs	Monotheistic; a fusion of Brahmanism and Islam, preaching tolerance and equality in the sight of God; initiates wear the Five Ks.	**Divisions**	There are several religious orders of Sikhs based either on disputes over the succession of gurus or points of ritual and tradition.

FIVE KS OF SIKHISM

The Five Ks are the symbols of a Sikh's spiritual and cultural allegiance to Sikhism, worn by baptized Sikhs.

Kesh (uncut hair)

Kanga (comb)

Kara (steel bangle symbolizing the one God)

Kirpan (ceremonial dagger to fight injustice)

Kaccha (short trousers signifying willingness to ride into battle)

TAOISM

Founded	c.600BC	**Organization**	Monastic orders and priests practise temple worship and divination, including the I Ching.
Founder	Lao-tzu (6c BC)		
Sacred texts	Chuang-tzu, Lao-tzu (Tao-te-ching)		
Place of worship	Temple	**Divisions**	Taoism emerged from many sects, each emphasizing different aspects such as worship of the Immortals, exorcism, faith healing, alchemy or meditative practice.
Beliefs	Tao ('the way') stresses harmony with nature, meditation, worship of a pantheon of gods and spirits and the theory of Yin-Yang.		

TEMPLETON PRIZE

Awarded annually for progress towards research or discoveries about spiritual realities; first awarded in 1973.

1973	Mother Teresa	1990	Baba Amte; L Charles Birch
1974	Brother Roger	1991	Lord Jakobovits
1975	Sir Sarvepalli Radhakrishnan	1992	Kyung-Chik Han
1976	Leon Joseph Suenens	1993	Charles W Colson
1977	Chiara Lubich	1994	Michael Novak
1978	Thomas F Torrance	1995	Paul Davies
1979	Nikkyo Niwano	1996	William R Bright
1980	Ralph Wendell Burhoe	1997	Pandurang Shastri Athavale
1981	Dame Cicely Saunders	1998	Sir Sigmund Sternberg
1982	Billy Graham	1999	Ian Graeme Barbour
1983	Aleksandr Solzhenitsyn	2000	Freeman J Dyson
1984	Michael Bourdeaux	2001	Arthur Peacocke
1985	Alister Hardy	2002	John C Polkinghorne
1986	James McCord	2003	Holmes Rolston III
1987	Stanley L Jaki	2004	George F R Ellis
1988	Inamullah Khan	2005	Charles H Townes
1989	Lord MacLeod; Carl Friedrich von Weizsäcker		

SIGNS OF THE ZODIAC

The zodiac is the band of sky, about 18° wide, through the centre of which the Sun appears to move. It forms the background for the motions of the Sun, Moon and major planets, and is divided into twelve equal parts of 30°, each of which once contained one of the zodiacal constellations. The passing of time means that the Sun no longer passes through each constellation on the accepted dates.

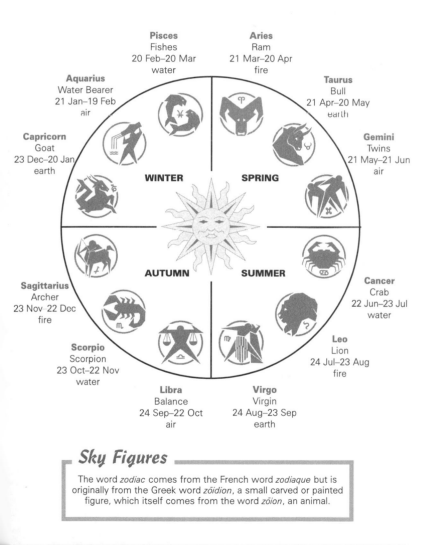

Pisces
Fishes
20 Feb–20 Mar
water

Aries
Ram
21 Mar–20 Apr
fire

Aquarius
Water Bearer
21 Jan–19 Feb
air

Taurus
Bull
21 Apr–20 May
earth

Capricorn
Goat
23 Dec–20 Jan
earth

Gemini
Twins
21 May–21 Jun
air

WINTER

SPRING

Sagittarius
Archer
23 Nov–22 Dec
fire

AUTUMN

SUMMER

Cancer
Crab
22 Jun–23 Jul
water

Scorpio
Scorpion
23 Oct–22 Nov
water

Leo
Lion
24 Jul–23 Aug
fire

Libra
Balance
24 Sep–22 Oct
air

Virgo
Virgin
24 Aug–23 Sep
earth

Sky Figures

The word *zodiac* comes from the French word *zodiaque* but is originally from the Greek word *zōidion*, a small carved or painted figure, which itself comes from the word *zōion*, an animal.

BIRTHSTONES

In many Western countries, the months are traditionally associated with gemstones. There is considerable variation between countries; the following combinations are widely recognized in North America and the UK.

Month	Gemstone	Month	Gemstone
Jan	garnet	Jul	ruby
Feb	amethyst	Aug	peridot, sardonyx
Mar	aquamarine, bloodstone	Sep	sapphire
Apr	diamond	Oct	opal, tourmaline
May	emerald	Nov	topaz
Jun	alexandrite, moonstone, pearl	Dec	turquoise, zircon

BIRTH FLOWERS

In many Western countries, the months are traditionally associated with flowers. There is considerable variation between countries; the following combinations are widely recognized in North America and the UK.

Month	Flower	Month	Flower
Jan	carnation, snowdrop	Jul	larkspur, water lily
Feb	primrose, violet	Aug	gladiolus, poppy
Mar	jonquil, violet	Sep	aster, morning glory
Apr	daisy, sweet pea	Oct	calendula, cosmos
May	hawthorn, lily of the valley	Nov	chrysanthemum
Jun	honeysuckle, rose	Dec	holly, narcissus, poinsettia

KNIGHTS OF THE ROUND TABLE

Tradition has it that King Arthur and his knights sat at the Round Table, a table shaped so that no individual knight should have precedence. Lists of the knights vary considerably; below are those recorded on the Winchester Round Table.

Sir Alymere
King Arthur
Sir Bedivere
Sir Bleoberis
Sir Bors de Ganis
Sir Brunor le Noir
La Cote Male Taile
Sir Dagonet
Sir Degore
Sir Ector de Maris
Sir Galahad
Sir Gareth
Sir Gawaine

Sir Kay
Sir Lamorak
Sir Lancelot (Launcelot) Du Lac
Sir Le Bel Desconneu
Sir Lionell
Sir Lucan
Sir Mordred
Sir Palomedes
Sir Pelleas
Sir Percivale
Sir Safer
Sir Tristan (Tristram)

SANTA'S REINDEER

Clement Clarke Moore (1779–1863) christened Santa's reindeer in his poem 'A Visit from St Nicholas' (1823), popularly known as "Twas the Night Before Christmas".

Blitzen	Dancer
Comet	Donder[1]
Cupid	Prancer
Dasher	Vixen

[1] *Donder is also known as Donner.*

Rudolph the Red-Nosed Reindeer

Shopping chains and promotional gimmicks might not seem to have anything to do with the spirit of Christmas. However, Rudolph, the famous reindeer with the 'very shiny nose', was originally devised as a character in a storybook to be given away as a Christmas freebie in 1939 to customers of Montgomery Ward department stores in Chicago, USA. His creator, Robert L May, supposedly went through a number of names before settling on Rudolph: Santa's red-nosed pal was nearly called Rollo, or even Reginald.

SEASONS

Northern hemisphere

Season	Duration
Spring	From vernal equinox (c.21 Mar) to summer solstice (c.21 Jun)
Summer	From summer solstice (c.21 Jun) to autumnal equinox (c.23 Sep)
Autumn	From autumnal equinox (c.23 Sep) to winter solstice (c.21 Dec)
Winter	From winter solstice (c.21 Dec) to vernal equinox (c.21 Mar)

Southern hemisphere

Season	Duration
Spring	From vernal equinox (c.23 Sep) to summer solstice (c.21 Dec)
Summer	From summer solstice (c.21 Dec) to autumnal equinox (c.21 Mar)
Autumn	From autumnal equinox (c.21 Mar) to winter solstice (c.21 Jun)
Winter	From winter solstice (c.21 Jun) to vernal equinox (c.23 Sep)

MONTHS

Month	Days	Name origin
January	31	From the Latin *Jānuārius* (*mēnsis*), the month dedicated to Janus, the god of gates, doorways, and beginnings, usually depicted with a two-faced head.
February	28 or 29	From the Latin *Februārius* (*mēnsis*) the month of expiation, and *februa* the feast of expiation.
March	31	From the Latin *Martius* (*mēnsis*) the month dedicated to Mars, the Roman god of war.
April	30	From the Latin *Aprīlis*, probably from Latin *aperire*, to open.
May	31	From the Old French *Mai*, from Latin *Māius* (*mēnsis*), probably meaning the month sacred to Māia, the Roman goddess of fertility.
June	30	From the Latin *Jūnius* (*mēnsis*) the month of Juno, the Roman goddess of marriage, childbirth and light.
July	31	From the Latin *Jūlius*, from the Roman emperor Julius Caesar, who was born in it.
August	31	From the first Roman emperor, Augustus, who amended the Roman calendar in 8BC.
September	30	From the Latin *September*, from *septem* seven; in the original Roman calendar, September was the seventh month of a ten-month year.
October	31	From the Latin *Octōber*, from *octō* eight; in the original Roman calendar, October was the eighth month of a ten-month year.
November	30	From the Latin *November*, from *novem* nine; in the original Roman calendar, November was the ninth month of a ten-month year.
December	31	From the Latin *December*, from *decem* ten; in the original Roman calendar, December was the tenth month of a ten-month year.

For the Hindu, Islamic and Jewish calendars and months see **Religions, Beliefs and Folklore**.

Gregorian Calendar

The calendar in general use throughout the world is the Gregorian New Style calendar. The calendar was reformed by Pope Gregory XIII in 1582.

The Julian calendar that was previously in use had a shortcoming in that the value of 365¼ days placed on the solar year was too long by 11 minutes and 14 seconds. By 1545 the vernal equinox, used by the Church to determine the date of Easter, had moved ten days. It took time for astronomers to work out a satisfactory method of correction, but finally the Pope instructed that ten days should be omitted from Oct 1582.

Britain didn't adopt the new calendar until 1752. At that time the difference between the two calendars was eleven days. The changeover meant that 2 Sep was immediately followed by 14 Sep. This led to popular protests; people who felt swindled out of the missing days chanted 'Give us back our eleven days!'

DAYS

Day	Name origin
Sunday	From the Old English _sunnan dæg_, a translation of the Latin _diēs sōlis_, meaning day of the Sun.
Monday	From the Old English _mōnandæg_, from _monan_, _mōna_ meaning Moon, and _dæg_ meaning day, a translation of the Latin _diēs lūnae_, Moon's day.
Tuesday	From the Old English _Tiwes dæg_, the day of Tiw, the god of war, corresponding to the Latin _diēs Martis_, the day of Mars.
Wednesday	From the Old English _Wōdnes dæg_, the day of Woden, or Odin, the chief god.
Thursday	From the Old English _Thunres dæg_, the day of Thunor, the thunder god, and the Old Norse _Thōrsdagr_, Thor's day.
Friday	From the Old English _Frīgedæg_, the day of _Frīg_, the goddess of married love, corresponding to the Latin _diēs Veneris_, the day of Venus.
Saturday	From the Old English _Sæterdæg_ or _Sætern(es)dæg_, a translation of the Latin _diēs Saturni_, the day of Saturn.

Hot Dogs

The hottest days of the year are known as the _dog days_, and are associated with the rising of the Dog Star (Sirius). The definition of this period varies, but it is generally reckoned to last from 3 Jul to 11 Aug. According to ancient superstition, disease and disaster were rife at this time and dogs were at their most susceptible to rabies: in some towns and cities all dogs had to wear muzzles in public places for the duration.

QUARTER DAYS

Traditionally, the quarter days were those days in each of the year's quarters on which rent or interest was due to be paid.

England, Wales and Ireland		Scotland[1]	
Lady Day	25 Mar	Candlemas	28 Feb
Midsummer Day	24 Jun	Whitsunday	28 May
Michaelmas Day	29 Sep	Lammas	28 Aug
Christmas Day	25 Dec	Martinmas	28 Nov

[1] _As defined in the Term and Quarter Days (Scotland) Act 1990._

FRENCH REVOLUTIONARY CALENDAR

The French Revolutionary Calendar, also known as the French Republican Calendar, was introduced in 1793 and attempted to move the organization of the calendar away from all religious connections. Instead, Year 1 dated from the declaration of the First Republic on 22 Sep 1792. Twelve 30-day months were introduced, named to be appropriate to the season, and were divided into three ten-day weeks called *decadi*. Five supplementary days (or six in leap years) were known as *sans-culottides*. The calendar worked well enough in France but caused problems for international communications, and Napoleon I replaced it with the Gregorian calendar in 1805.

Month	Derivation of name	Month	Derivation of name
Vendémiaire	vintage	Germinal	seed
Brumaire	mist	Floréal	blossom
Frimaire	frost	Prairial	meadow
Nivôse	snow	Messidor	harvest
Pluviôse	rain	Thermidor	heat
Ventôse	wind	Fructidor	fruits

CHINESE ANIMAL YEARS AND TIMES

Years

Rat	1924	1936	1948	1960	1972	1984	1996	2008	2020
Ox	1925	1937	1949	1961	1973	1985	1997	2009	2021
Tiger	1926	1938	1950	1962	1974	1986	1998	2010	2022
Hare	1927	1939	1951	1963	1975	1987	1999	2011	2023
Dragon	1928	1940	1952	1964	1976	1988	2000	2012	2024
Serpent	1929	1941	1953	1965	1977	1989	2001	2013	2025
Horse	1930	1942	1954	1966	1978	1990	2002	2014	2026
Sheep	1931	1943	1955	1967	1979	1991	2003	2015	2027
Monkey	1932	1944	1956	1968	1980	1992	2004	2016	2028
Cock	1933	1945	1957	1969	1981	1993	2005	2017	2029
Dog	1934	1946	1958	1970	1982	1994	2006	2018	2030
Boar	1935	1947	1959	1971	1983	1995	2007	2019	2031

Time of day (hours)

Rat	2300–0100	Horse	1100–1300
Ox	0100–0300	Sheep	1300–1500
Tiger	0300–0500	Monkey	1500–1700
Hare	0500–0700	Cock	1700–1900
Dragon	0700–0900	Dog	1900–2100
Serpent	0900–1100	Boar	2100–2300

WEDDING ANNIVERSARIES

In many Western countries, wedding anniversaries have become associated with gifts of different materials. There is some variation between countries.

Anniversary	Traditional gift	Modern gift
1st	paper	clocks
2nd	cotton	china
3rd	leather	crystal, glass
4th	fruit, flowers	appliances
5th	wood	silverware
6th	sugar, iron	wood
7th	copper, wool	desk sets
8th	bronze, pottery	linen, lace
9th	pottery, willow	leather
10th	tin, aluminium	diamond jewellery
11th	steel	fashion jewellery
12th	silk, linen	pearl
13th	lace	textiles, fur
14th	ivory	gold jewellery
15th	crystal	watches
20th	china	platinum
25th	silver	silver
30th	pearl	diamond
35th	coral	jade
40th	ruby	ruby
45th	sapphire	sapphire
50th	gold	gold
55th	emerald	emerald
60th	diamond	diamond
70th	platinum	platinum

A Call from the Queen

It is well known that the monarch will send congratulations to centenarians upon their 100th birthday, a tradition that dates back to 1917. But the sovereign will also send royal best wishes to couples reaching their diamond wedding anniversary, and also to husbands and wives celebrating 65 years of marriage, 70 years and every subsequent anniversary.

SCIENCE

CHEMICAL ELEMENTS

Chemical elements with atomic numbers between 1 and 112 are listed.

Symbol	Element	Derived from	Atomic no
Ac	actinium	Greek *aktis* = ray	89
Ag	silver	Old English *silfer, seolfor*	47
Al	aluminium	Latin *alumen* = alum	13
Am	americium	America	95
Ar	argon	Greek *argon* = inactive	18
As	arsenic	Greek *arsenikon* = yellow orpiment	33
At	astatine	Greek *astatos* = unstable	85
Au	gold	Old English *gold*	79
B	boron	Arabic *buraq* = borax	5
Ba	barium	Greek *barys* = heavy	56
Be	beryllium	Greek *beryllos* = beryl	4
Bh	bohrium	Niels Bohr, Danish physicist	107
Bi	bismuth	German (origin unknown)	83
Bk	berkelium	Berkeley, California	97
Br	bromine	Greek *bromos* = stink	35
C	carbon	Latin *carbo* = coal, charcoal	6
Ca	calcium	Latin *calx* = lime	20
Cd	cadmium	Greek *kadmeia* = calamine	48
Ce	cerium	asteroid Ceres	58
Cf	californium	California	98
Cl	chlorine	Greek *chloros* = pale green	17
Cm	curium	Marie and Pierre Curie, French physicists	96
Co	cobalt	German *Kobold* = demon	27
Cr	chromium	Greek *chroma* = colour	24
Cs	caesium	Latin *caesius* = bluish-grey	55
Cu	copper	Cyprus	29
Db	dubnium	Dubna, Russia	105
Ds	darmstadtium	Darmstadt, Germany	110
Dy	dysprosium	Greek *dysprositos* = difficult to reach	66
Er	erbium	Ytterby, Sweden	68
Es	einsteinium	Albert Einstein, US physicist	99
Eu	europium	Europe	63
F	fluorine	Latin *fluor* = flow	9
Fe	iron	Old English *iren*	26
Fm	fermium	Enrico Fermi, Italian physicist	100
Fr	francium	France	87
Ga	gallium	Latin *Gallia* = France, or *gallus* = cock	31

Symbol	Element	Derived from	Atomic no
Gd	gadolinium	Johan Gadolin, Finnish chemist	64
Ge	germanium	Germany	32
H	hydrogen	Greek *hydor* = water + *gennaein* = to produce	1
He	helium	Greek *helios* = sun	2
Hf	hafnium	Latin *Hafnia* = Copenhagen	72
Hg	mercury	Latin *Mercurius*	80
Ho	holmium	Latin *Holmia* = Stockholm	67
Hs	hassium	Latin *Hassias* = Hesse	108
I	iodine	Greek *ioeides* = violet-coloured	53
In	indium	indigo lines in the spectrum	49
Ir	iridium	Latin *iris* = rainbow goddess	77
K	potassium	potash	19
Kr	krypton	Greek *kryptein* = to hide	36
La	lanthanum	Greek *lanthanein* = to escape notice	57
Li	lithium	Greek *lithos* = stone	3
Lr	lawrencium	Ernest O Lawrence, US physicist	103
Lu	lutetium	Latin *Lutetia* = Paris	71
Md	mendelevium	Dmitri Mendeleev, Russian scientist	101
Mg	magnesium	Magnesia, Thessaly, Greece	12
Mn	manganese	Latin *magnesia*	25
Mo	molybdenum	Greek *molybdos* = lead	42
Mt	meitnerium	Lise Meitner, Austrian physicist	109
N	nitrogen	Greek *nitron* = sodium carbonate + *gennaein* = to produce	7
Na	sodium	soda	11
Nb	niobium	Niobe (Greek myth)	41
Nd	neodymium	Greek *neos* = new + *didymos* = twin	60
Ne	neon	Greek *neos* = new	10
Ni	nickel	German *Kupfernickel* = niccolite	28
No	nobelium	Nobel Institute	102
Np	neptunium	planet Neptune	93
O	oxygen	Greek *oxys* = acid + *gennaein* = to produce	8
Os	osmium	Greek *osme* = smell	76
P	phosphorus	Greek *phosphoros* = light-bearer	15
Pa	protactinium	Greek *protos* = first + *actinium* (see above)	91
Pb	lead	Old English *lead*	82
Pd	palladium	minor planet Pallas	46
Pm	promethium	Prometheus (Greek myth)	61
Po	polonium	Poland	84
Pr	praseodymium	Greek *prasios* = leek green + *didymos* = twin	59

Symbol	Element	Derived from	Atomic no
Pt	platinum	Spanish *plata* = silver	78
Pu	plutonium	planet Pluto	94
Ra	radium	Latin *radius* = ray	88
Rb	rubidium	Latin *rubidus* = red	37
Re	rhenium	Latin *Rhenus* = the Rhine	75
Rf	rutherfordium	Ernest Rutherford, British physicist	104
Rg	roentgenium	Wilhelm Roentgen, German physicist	111
Rh	rhodium	Greek *rhodon* = rose	45
Rn	radon	radium	86
Ru	ruthenium	Latin *Ruthenia* = Russia	44
S	sulphur	Latin *sulphur*	16
Sb	antimony	Latin *antimonium*	51
Sc	scandium	Scandinavian	21
Se	selenium	Greek *selene* = moon	34
Sg	seaborgium	Glenn Seaborg, US physicist	106
Si	silicon	Latin *silex* = flint	14
Sm	samarium	Colonel M S Samarski, Russian engineer	62
Sn	tin	Old English *tin*	50
Sr	strontium	Strontian, Scotland	38
Ta	tantalum	Tantalus (Greek myth)	73
Tb	terbium	Ytterby, Sweden	65
Tc	technetium	Greek *technetos* = artificial	43
Te	tellurium	Latin *tellus* = earth	52
Th	thorium	Scandinavian god Thor	90
Ti	titanium	Greek *Titan* = Titan	22
Tl	thallium	Greek *thallos* = a young shoot	81
Tm	thulium	Latin *Thule* = an island in the extreme north	69
U	uranium	planet Uranus	92
V	vanadium	Old Norse *Vanadis* = goddess Freya	23
W	tungsten	Swedish *tungsten* = heavy stone	74
Xe	xenon	Greek *xenos* = stranger	54
Y	yttrium	Ytterby, Sweden	39
Yb	ytterbium	Ytterby, Sweden	70
Zn	zinc	German *zink*	30
Zr	zirconium	Persian *zargun* = gold-coloured	40

Radioactive Family

Curium is named after the French physicists Pierre (1859–1906) and Marie Curie (1867–1934). They were jointly awarded the Nobel Prize for Physics in 1903; Marie later received the Nobel Prize for Chemistry (1911). Their daughter, Irène Joliot-Curie (1897–1956), and her husband, Frédéric (1900–58), also won the Nobel Prize for Chemistry in 1935.

PERIODIC TABLE

Key:
- element symbol — atomic number
- element name

Transition metals

1	2	3	4	5	6	7	8	9	10	11	12	13	14	15	16	17	18
H 1 hydrogen																	He 2 helium
Li 3 lithium	Be 4 beryllium											B 5 boron	C 6 carbon	N 7 nitrogen	O 8 oxygen	F 9 fluorine	Ne 10 neon
Na 11 sodium	Mg 12 magnesium											Al 13 aluminium	Si 14 silicon	P 15 phosphorus	S 16 sulphur	Cl 17 chlorine	Ar 18 argon
K 19 potassium	Ca 20 calcium	Sc 21 scandium	Ti 22 titanium	V 23 vanadium	Cr 24 chromium	Mn 25 manganese	Fe 26 iron	Co 27 cobalt	Ni 28 nickel	Cu 29 copper	Zn 30 zinc	Ga 31 gallium	Ge 32 germanium	As 33 arsenic	Se 34 selenium	Br 35 bromine	Kr 36 krypton
Rb 37 rubidium	Sr 38 strontium	Y 39 yttrium	Zr 40 zirconium	Nb 41 niobium	Mo 42 molybdenum	Tc 43 technetium	Ru 44 ruthenium	Rh 45 rhodium	Pd 46 palladium	Ag 47 silver	Cd 48 cadmium	In 49 indium	Sn 50 tin	Sb 51 antimony	Te 52 tellurium	I 53 iodine	Xe 54 xenon
Cs 55 caesium	Ba 56 barium	57–71 *	Hf 72 hafnium	Ta 73 tantalum	W 74 tungsten	Re 75 rhenium	Os 76 osmium	Ir 77 iridium	Pt 78 platinum	Au 79 gold	Hg 80 mercury	Tl 81 thallium	Pb 82 lead	Bi 83 bismuth	Po 84 polonium	At 85 astatine	Rn 86 radon
Fr 87 francium	Ra 88 radium	89–103 **	Rf 104 rutherfordium	Db 105 dubnium	Sg 106 seaborgium	Bh 107 bohrium	Hs 108 hassium	Mt 109 meitnerium	Ds 110 darmstadtium	Rg 111 röntgenium	Uub 112 ununbium						

*Lanthanide series

La 57 lanthanum	Ce 58 cerium	Pr 59 praseodymium	Nd 60 neodymium	Pm 61 promethium	Sm 62 samarium	Eu 63 europium	Gd 64 gadolinium	Tb 65 terbium	Dy 66 dysprosium	Ho 67 holmium	Er 68 erbium	Tm 69 thulium	Yb 70 ytterbium	Lu 71 lutetium

**Actinide series

Ac 89 actinium	Th 90 thorium	Pa 91 protactinium	U 92 uranium	Np 93 neptunium	Pu 94 plutonium	Am 95 americium	Cm 96 curium	Bk 97 berkelium	Cf 98 californium	Es 99 einsteinium	Fm 100 fermium	Md 101 mendelevium	No 102 nobelium	Lr 103 lawrencium

SUBATOMIC PARTICLES

Subatomic particles are those that constitute the atom.

hadrons	quarks	leptons	gauge bosons
baryons	up quark	electron	photon
proton	down quark	positron	W
neutron	charmed quark	muon	Z
	strange quark	tau lepton	gluon
mesons	bottom quark	neutrino (electron)	gravitron
pion	top quark	neutrino (muon)	
kaon		neutrino (tau)	
J/psi			
upsilon			

Flavours of Quark

The language of *quarks* is one of the quirkier areas of particle physics. It is thought that there are six types of quark, known as *flavours – up*, *down*, *top*, *bottom*, *strange* and *charmed*. *Bottom* is sometimes also known as *beauty*, and *top* as *truth*. Each flavour of quark is also believed to have an antiparticle known as an *antiquark*. Flavours of quark come in three *colours*: red, blue and green; and for antiquarks, three *anticolours*. The term *quark* was coined by the writer James Joyce (1882–1941) in *Finnegans Wake* (1939), and adopted for scientific use by the US physicist Murray Gell-Mann (born 1929).

DECIBEL SCALE

A decibel is a term used to express a level of sound. It is the tenth part of a bel, a measure for comparing the intensity of noises, which was named after Alexander Graham Bell (1847–1922), the inventor of the telephone.

Source	Decibel level (dB)	Source	Decibel level (dB)
Breathing	10	Traffic	60–90
Whisper	20	Pneumatic drill	110
Conversation	50–60	Jet aircraft	120
Vacuum cleaner	80	Space vehicle launch	140–170

WENTWORTH SCALE

The Wentworth scale is one of the main scales used in geology to describe the general dimensions of grains in a rock, especially sediment. It was devised by Chester K Wentworth (1891–1969), a US geologist.

Name	Dimension[1]	Name	Dimension[1]
boulder	greater than 256mm	sand	$1/16$–2mm
cobble	64–256mm	silt	$1/256$–$1/16$mm
pebble	4–64mm	clay	less than $1/256$mm
gravel	2–4mm		

[1] *To convert millimetres to inches, multiply by 0.0394.*

SCOVILLE SCALE *see* **FOOD AND DRINK**

MOHS HARDNESS SCALE

The relative hardness of solids can be expressed using a scale of numbers from 1 to 10, each relating to a mineral. The method was devised by Friedrich Mohs (1773–1839), a German mineralogist. Sets of hardness pencils are used to test specimens to see what will scratch them. Other useful instruments for testing include: fingernail (2.5), copper coin (3.5), steel knife (5.5), glass (6.0).

Talc	1	Fluorite	4	Quartz	7	Diamond	10
Gypsum	2	Apatite	5	Topaz	8		
Calcite	3	Orthoclase	6	Corundum	9		

pH SCALE

pH or pH value is a number used to express degrees of acidity or alkalinity in solutions. The term comes from the German word *Potenz* meaning power, and *H* the symbol for hydrogen. The scale ranges from 0 to 14; a pH below 7 indicates acidity, and one above 7 alkalinity. A solution with a pH of 7 is neutral.

ELECTROMAGNETIC SPECTRUM

The electromagnetic spectrum ranges from long to short wavelengths, with a length of between approximately 10^4m and 10^{-12}m. *To convert metres to feet multiply by 3.2808.*

Light Speed

The speed of light is 2.99792458×10^8m/sec, equivalent to 300 000km, or 186 000mi, per second. The speed of sound is a tardy 331.4m/sec, or 1 193kph/741mph.

SI PREFIXES

Factor	Prefix	Symbol	Factor	Prefix	Symbol
10^{24}	yotta	Y	10^{-1}	deci	d
10^{21}	zetta	Z	10^{-2}	centi	c
10^{18}	exa	E	10^{-3}	milli	m
10^{15}	peta	P	10^{-6}	micro	μ
10^{12}	tera	T	10^{-9}	nano	n
10^{9}	giga	G	10^{-12}	pico	p
10^{6}	mega	M	10^{-15}	femto	f
10^{3}	kilo	k	10^{-18}	atto	a
10^{2}	hecto	h	10^{-21}	zepto	z
10^{1}	deca	da	10^{-24}	yocto	y

GEMSTONES

Nearly all gemstones are minerals; the four non-mineral gems are amber, coral, jet and pearl. Their hardness is expressed on the Mohs scale.

Gem	Colour	Mohs of hardness
agate	brown, red, blue, green, yellow	7.0
alexandrite	green, red	8.5
amber	yellow, brown and other colours	2–2.5
amethyst	violet	7.0
aquamarine	sky blue, greenish blue	7.5
beryl	green, blue, pink	7.5
bloodstone	green with red spots	7.0
chalcedony	all colours	7.0
chrysoprase	apple green	7.0
citrine	yellow	7.0
coral	white, pink, red, orange, blue, violet and other colours	3.5–4
diamond	colourless, tints of various colours	10.0
emerald	green	7.5
garnet	red and other colours	6.5–7.25
jade	green, whitish, mauve, brown	7.0
jasper	dark red, multi-coloured	7.0
jet	black	2.5–4
lapis lazuli	deep blue	5.5
malachite	dark green banded	3.5
moonstone	whitish with blue shimmer	6.0
onyx	various colours with straight coloured bands	7.0
opal	black, white, orange-red, rainbow coloured	6.0
pearl	cream, white, pink and other colours	2.5–4.5
peridot	green	6.5
ruby	red	9.0
sapphire	blue and other colours	9.0
serpentine	red and green	3.0
soapstone	white, may be stained with impurities	2.0
sunstone	whitish red-brown flecked with golden particles	6.0
topaz	blue, green, pink, yellow, colourless	8.0
tourmaline	brown-black, blue, pink, red, violet-red, yellow, green	7.5
turquoise	greenish grey, sky blue	6.0
zircon	all colours	7.5

Diamonds are Forever

Until the 18c, all the world's diamonds came from India, where they were mined from c.2000BC. The largest diamond ever found is the Cullinan, a huge 3106 carat crystal mined in South Africa in 1903.

DRUGS DERIVED FROM PLANTS

Some commonly prescribed drugs of plant origin are listed.

Drug	Plant	Effect
aspirin	white willow	pain relief
cocaine	coca	local anaesthetic/central nervous system stimulant
codeine	opium poppy	pain relief
curare	various tropical American plants	muscle relaxant
digitalis	foxglove	heart stimulant
morphine	opium poppy	pain relief/narcotic
penicillin	*Penicillium notatum* fungus	antibiotic
quinine	yellow cinchona	antimalarial
strychnine	Nux vomica	central nervous system stimulant

MEASURING DEVICES

Device	Measures
accelerometer	acceleration
altimeter	height
ammeter	electric current
anemometer	wind
barometer	atmospheric pressure
calorimeter	heat capacities, etc
chronometer	time
cryometer	low temperatures
decelerometer	deceleration
dosimeter	radiation
dynamometer	force
evaporimeter, evaporometer	rate of evaporation
flowmeter	rate of flow of a fluid in a pipe
focimeter	focal length of a lens
galvanometer	electric currents
Geiger counter	radioactivity
geothermometer	subterranean temperatures
gravimeter	variations in the Earth's surface gravity
hyetometer, ombrometer, pluviometer	rain
hygrometer	humidity of the air or of other gases
inclinometer	slopes
interferometer	wavelengths, wave speeds, angles, etc
luxmeter	illumination
magnetometer	strength/direction of a magnetic field
mileometer, milometer	miles that a vehicle, etc has travelled
odometer, hodometer	distance travelled by a wheeled vehicle
ohmmeter	electrical resistance
optometer	vision
pedometer	paces (approximate distance walked)
photometer	luminous intensity
pulsimeter	strength or quickness of the pulse
pyrometer	high temperatures
respirometer	breathing
seismometer	intensity and duration of earthquakes
spectrometer	refractive indices
speedometer	speed at which a vehicle is travelling

Device	Measures
sphygmomanometer, sphygmometer	arterial blood pressure
tachometer	velocity
theodolite	horizontal and vertical angles
thermometer	temperature
vaporimeter	vapour pressure or vapour
velocimeter	velocity
vibrograph, vibrometer	vibrations
viscometer, viscosimeter	viscosity
voltmeter	electromotive force
volumeter	volumes of gases and liquids
wattmeter	circuit power
wavemeter	wavelengths

Unusual Measuring Devices

In the realm of science there are instruments to measure almost everything. Some of the less common are the *cyanometer* (measures the blueness of the sky or ocean), *diaphanometer* (the transparency of the air), *drosometer* (dew), *konimeter* (dust in the air), *oenometer* (the alcoholic strength of wines), *Nilometer* (the height of the River Nile), *weatherometer* (the weather-resisting properties of paints or other surfaces) and *xylometer* (the specific gravity of wood). The specific gravity, relative density and purity or richness of milk are measured by the *galactometer*, *lactometer* and *lactoscope* respectively, while the *plethysmograph* measures variations in the size of body parts, for example when varying amounts of blood flow through them.

NOBEL PRIZE FOR PHYSICS

Nobel Prizes were established by a bequest in the will of Alfred Nobel (1833–96) to honour 'those who, during the preceding year, shall have conferred the greatest benefit on mankind'. The Nobel Prize for Physics is awarded annually to a person who has 'made the most important discovery or invention within the field of physics'; first awarded in 1901.

1901	Wilhelm Conrad Röntgen	1918	Max Planck
1902	Hendrik A Lorentz, Pieter Zeeman	1919	Johannes Stark
1903	Henri Becquerel, Pierre Curie, Marie Curie	1920	Charles Edouard Guillaume
1904	Lord Rayleigh	1921	Albert Einstein
1905	Philipp Lenard	1922	Niels Bohr
1906	J J Thomson	1923	Robert A Millikan
1907	Albert A Michelson	1924	Manne Siegbahn
1908	Gabriel Lippmann	1925	James Franck, Gustav Hertz
1909	Guglielmo Marconi, Ferdinand Braun	1926	Jean Baptiste Perrin
1910	Johannes Diderik van der Waals	1927	Arthur H Compton, C T R Wilson
1911	Wilhelm Wien	1928	Owen Willans Richardson
1912	Gustaf Dalén	1929	Louis de Broglie
1913	Heike Kamerlingh Onnes	1930	Venkata Raman
1914	Max von Laue	1931	*no award*
1915	William Bragg, Lawrence Bragg	1932	Werner Heisenberg
1916	*no award*	1933	Erwin Schrödinger, Paul A M Dirac
1917	Charles Glover Barkla	1934	*no award*
		1935	James Chadwick
		1936	Victor F Hess, Carl D Anderson

1937	Clinton Davisson, George Paget Thomson	1977	Philip W Anderson, Sir Nevill F Mott, John H van Vleck
1938	Enrico Fermi	1978	Pyotr Kapitsa, Arno Penzias, Robert Woodrow Wilson
1939	Ernest Lawrence		
1940	*no award*	1979	Sheldon Glashow, Abdus Salam, Steven Weinberg
1941	*no award*		
1942	*no award*	1980	James Cronin, Val Fitch
1943	Otto Stern	1981	Nicolaas Bloembergen, Arthur L Schawlow, Kai M Siegbahn
1944	Isidor Isaac Rabi		
1945	Wolfgang Pauli	1982	Kenneth G Wilson
1946	Percy W Bridgman	1983	Subramanyan Chandrasekhar, William A Fowler
1947	Edward V Appleton		
1948	Patrick M S Blackett	1984	Carlo Rubbia, Simon van der Meer
1949	Hideki Yukawa	1985	Klaus von Klitzing
1950	Cecil Powell	1986	Ernst Ruska, Gerd Binnig, Heinrich Rohrer
1951	John Cockcroft, Ernest T S Walton		
1952	Felix Bloch, E M Purcell	1987	J Georg Bednorz, K Alex Müller
1953	Frits Zernike	1988	Leon M Lederman, Melvin Schwartz, Jack Steinberger
1954	Max Born, Walther Bothe		
1955	Willis E Lamb, Polykarp Kusch	1989	Norman F Ramsey, Hans G Dehmelt, Wolfgang Paul
1956	William B Shockley, John Bardeen, Walter H Brattain		
		1990	Jerome I Friedman, Henry W Kendall, Richard E Taylor
1957	Chen Ning Yang, Tsung-Dao Lee		
1958	Pavel A Cherenkov, Il´ja M Frank, Igor Y Tamm	1991	Pierre-Gilles de Gennes
		1992	Georges Charpak
1959	Emilio Segrè, Owen Chamberlain	1993	Russell A Hulse, Joseph H Taylor Jr
1960	Donald A Glaser	1994	Bertram N Brockhouse, Clifford G Shull
1961	Robert Hofstadter, Rudolf Mössbauer		
		1995	Martin L Perl, Frederick Reines
1962	Lev Landau	1996	David M Lee, Douglas D Osheroff, Robert C Richardson
1963	Eugene Wigner, Maria Goeppert-Mayer, J Hans D Jensen		
		1997	Steven Chu, Claude Cohen-Tannoudji, William D Phillips
1964	Charles H Townes, Nicolay G Basov, Aleksandr M Prokhorov		
		1998	Robert B Laughlin, Horst L Störmer, Daniel C Tsui
1965	Sin-Itiro Tomonaga, Julian Schwinger, Richard P Feynman		
		1999	Gerardus 't Hooft, Martinus JG Veltman
1966	Alfred Kastler		
1967	Hans Bethe	2000	Zhores I Alferov, Herbert Kroemer, Jack S Kilby
1968	Luis Alvarez		
1969	Murray Gell-Mann	2001	Eric A Cornell, Wolfgang Ketterle, Carl E Wieman
1970	Hannes Alfvén, Louis Néel		
1971	Dennis Gabor	2002	Raymond Davis Jr, Masatoshi Koshiba, Riccardo Giacconi
1972	John Bardeen, Leon N Cooper, Robert Schrieffer		
		2003	Alexei A Abrikosov, Vitaly L Ginzburg, Anthony J Leggett
1973	Leo Esaki, Ivar Giaever, Brian D Josephson		
		2004	David J Gross, H David Politzer, Frank Wilczek
1974	Martin Ryle, Antony Hewish		
1975	Aage N Bohr, Ben R Mottelson, James Rainwater	2005	Roy J Glauber, John L Hall, Theodor W Hänsch
1976	Burton Richter, Samuel C C Ting		

Bragging About Physics

Lawrence Bragg (1890–1971) was just 25 years old when he won the Nobel Prize for Physics, making him the youngest ever winner of a Nobel award.

NOBEL PRIZE FOR CHEMISTRY

Nobel Prizes were established by a bequest in the will of Alfred Nobel (1833–96) to honour 'those who, during the preceding year, shall have conferred the greatest benefit on mankind'. The Nobel Prize for Chemistry is awarded annually to a person who has 'made the most important chemical discovery or improvement'; first awarded in 1901.

1901	Jacobus H van't Hoff	1947	Sir Robert Robinson
1902	Emil Fischer	1948	Arne Tiselius
1903	Svante Arrhenius	1949	William F Giauque
1904	Sir William Ramsay	1950	Otto Diels, Kurt Alder
1905	Adolf von Baeyer	1951	Edwin M McMillan, Glenn T Seaborg
1906	Henri Moissan		
1907	Eduard Buchner	1952	Archer J P Martin, Richard L M Synge
1908	Ernest Rutherford		
1909	Wilhelm Ostwald	1953	Hermann Staudinger
1910	Otto Wallach	1954	Linus Pauling
1911	Marie Curie	1955	Vincent du Vigneaud
1912	Victor Grignard, Paul Sabatier	1956	Sir Cyril Hinshelwood, Nikolay Semenov
1913	Alfred Werner		
1914	Theodore W Richards	1957	Lord Todd
1915	Richard Willstätter	1958	Frederick Sanger
1916	no award	1959	Jaroslav Heyrovsky
1917	no award	1960	Willard F Libby
1918	Fritz Haber	1961	Melvin Calvin
1919	no award	1962	Max F Perutz, John C Kendrew
1920	Walther Nernst	1963	Karl Ziegler, Giulio Natta
1921	Frederick Soddy	1964	Dorothy Crowfoot Hodgkin
1922	Francis W Aston	1965	Robert B Woodward
1923	Fritz Pregl	1966	Robert S Mulliken
1924	no award	1967	Manfred Eigen, Ronald G W Norrish, George Porter
1925	Richard Zsigmondy		
1926	The Svedberg	1968	Lars Onsager
1927	Heinrich Wieland	1969	Derek Barton, Odd Hassel
1928	Adolf Windaus	1970	Luis Leloir
1929	Arthur Harden, Hans von Euler-Chelpin	1971	Gerhard Herzberg
		1972	Christian Anfinsen, Stanford Moore, William H Stein
1930	Hans Fischer		
1931	Carl Bosch, Friedrich Bergius	1973	Ernst Otto Fischer, Geoffrey Wilkinson
1932	Irving Langmuir		
1933	no award	1974	Paul J Flory
1934	Harold C Urey	1975	John Cornforth, Vladimir Prelog
1935	Frédéric Joliot, Irène Joliot-Curie	1976	William Lipscomb
1936	Peter Debye	1977	Ilya Prigogine
1937	Norman Haworth, Paul Karrer	1978	Peter Mitchell
1938	Richard Kuhn	1979	Herbert C Brown, Georg Wittig
1939	Adolf Butenandt, Leopold Ruzicka	1980	Paul Berg, Walter Gilbert, Frederick Sanger
1940	no award		
1941	no award	1981	Kenichi Fukui, Roald Hoffmann
1942	no award	1982	Aaron Klug
1943	George de Hevesy	1983	Henry Taube
1944	Otto Hahn	1984	Bruce Merrifield
1945	Artturi Virtanen	1985	Herbert A Hauptman, Jerome Karle
1946	James B Sumner, John H Northrop, Wendell M Stanley	1986	Dudley R Herschbach, Yuan T Lee, John C Polanyi

1987	Donald J Cram, Jean-Marie Lehn, Charles J Pedersen	1998	Walter Kohn, John Pople
1988	Johann Deisenhofer, Robert Huber, Hartmut Michel	1999	Ahmed Zewail
		2000	Alan Heeger, Alan G MacDiarmid, Hideki Shirakawa
1989	Sidney Altman, Thomas R Cech	2001	William S Knowles, Ryoji Noyori, K Barry Sharpless
1990	Elias James Corey		
1991	Richard R Ernst	2002	John B Fenn, Koichi Tanaka, Kurt Wüthrich
1992	Rudolph A Marcus		
1993	Kary B Mullis, Michael Smith	2003	Peter Agre, Roderick MacKinnon
1994	George A Olah	2004	Aaron Ciechanover, Avram Hershko, Irwin Rose
1995	Paul J Crutzen, Mario J Molina, F Sherwood Rowland		
		2005	Yves Chauvin, Robert H Grubbs, Richard R Schrock
1996	Robert F Curl Jr, Sir Harold Kroto, Richard E Smalley		
1997	Paul D Boyer, John E Walker, Jens C Skou		

Back to the Housework

When Professor Dorothy Hodgkin won the Nobel Prize for Chemistry in 1964, the *Daily Mail*'s headline ran 'Nobel Prize for British Wife'.

NOBEL PRIZE FOR PHYSIOLOGY OR MEDICINE

Nobel Prizes were established by a bequest in the will of Alfred Nobel (1833–96) to honour 'those who, during the preceding year, shall have conferred the greatest benefit on mankind'. The Nobel Prize for Physiology or Medicine is awarded annually to a person who has 'made the most important discovery within the domain of physiology or medicine'; first awarded in 1901.

1901	Emil von Behring	1922	Archibald V Hill, Otto Meyerhof
1902	Ronald Ross	1923	Frederick G Banting, John Macleod
1903	Niels Ryberg Finsen	1924	Willem Einthoven
1904	Ivan Pavlov	1925	*no award*
1905	Robert Koch	1926	Johannes Fibiger
1906	Camillo Golgi, Santiago Ramón y Cajal	1927	Julius Wagner-Jauregg
		1928	Charles Nicolle
1907	Alphonse Laveran	1929	Christiaan Eijkman, Sir Frederick Hopkins
1908	Ilya Mechnikov, Paul Ehrlich		
1909	Theodor Kocher	1930	Karl Landsteiner
1910	Albrecht Kossel	1931	Otto Warburg
1911	Allvar Gullstrand	1932	Sir Charles Sherrington, Edgar Adrian
1912	Alexis Carrel		
1913	Charles Richet	1933	Thomas H Morgan
1914	Robert Bárány	1934	George H Whipple, George R Minot, William P Murphy
1915	*no award*		
1916	*no award*	1935	Hans Spemann
1917	*no award*	1936	Sir Henry Dale, Otto Loewi
1918	*no award*	1937	Albert Szent-Györgyi
1919	Jules Bordet	1938	Corneille Heymans
1920	August Krogh	1939	Gerhard Domagk
1921	*no award*	1940	*no award*

1941	*no award*
1942	*no award*
1943	Henrik Dam, Edward A Doisy
1944	Joseph Erlanger, Herbert S Gasser
1945	Sir Alexander Fleming, Ernst B Chain, Sir Howard Florey
1946	Hermann J Muller
1947	Carl Cori, Gerty Cori, Bernardo Houssay
1948	Paul Müller
1949	Walter Hess, Egas Moniz
1950	Edward C Kendall, Tadeus Reichstein, Philip S Hench
1951	Max Theiler
1952	Selman A Waksman
1953	Hans Krebs, Fritz Lipmann
1954	John F Enders, Thomas H Weller, Frederick C Robbins
1955	Hugo Theorell
1956	André F Cournand, Werner Forssmann, Dickinson W Richards
1957	Daniel Bovet
1958	George Beadle, Edward Tatum, Joshua Lederberg
1959	Severo Ochoa, Arthur Kornberg
1960	Sir Frank Macfarlane Burnet, Peter Medawar
1961	Georg von Békésy
1962	Francis Crick, James Watson, Maurice Wilkins
1963	Sir John Eccles, Alan L Hodgkin, Andrew F Huxley
1964	Konrad Bloch, Feodor Lynen
1965	François Jacob, André Lwoff, Jacques Monod
1966	Peyton Rous, Charles B Huggins
1967	Ragnar Granit, Haldan K Hartline, George Wald
1968	Robert W Holley, H Gobind Khorana, Marshall W Nirenberg
1969	Max Delbrück, Alfred D Hershey, Salvador E Luria
1970	Sir Bernard Katz, Ulf von Euler, Julius Axelrod
1971	Earl W Sutherland, Jr
1972	Gerald M Edelman, Rodney R Porter
1973	Karl von Frisch, Konrad Lorenz, Nikolaas Tinbergen

1974	Albert Claude, Christian de Duve, George E Palade
1975	David Baltimore, Renato Dulbecco, Howard M Temin
1976	Baruch S Blumberg, D Carleton Gajdusek
1977	Roger Guillemin, Andrew V Schally, Rosalyn Yalow
1978	Werner Arber, Daniel Nathans, Hamilton O Smith
1979	Allan M Cormack, Godfrey N Hounsfield
1980	Baruj Benacerraf, Jean Dausset, George D Snell
1981	Roger W Sperry, David H Hubel, Torsten N Wiesel
1982	Sune K Bergström, Bengt I Samuelsson, John R Vane
1983	Barbara McClintock
1984	Niels K Jerne, Georges JF Köhler, César Milstein
1985	Michael S Brown, Joseph L Goldstein
1986	Stanley Cohen, Rita Levi-Montalcini
1987	Susumu Tonegawa
1988	Sir James W Black, Gertrude B Elion, George H Hitchings
1989	J Michael Bishop, Harold E Varmus
1990	Joseph E Murray, E Donnall Thomas
1991	Erwin Neher, Bert Sakmann
1992	Edmond H Fischer, Edwin G Krebs
1993	Richard J Roberts, Phillip A Sharp
1994	Alfred G Gilman, Martin Rodbell
1995	Edward B Lewis, Christiane Nüsslein-Volhard, Eric F Wieschaus
1996	Peter C Doherty, Rolf M Zinkernagel
1997	Stanley B Prusiner
1998	Robert F Furchgott, Louis J Ignarro, Ferid Murad
1999	Günter Blobel
2000	Arvid Carlsson, Paul Greengard, Eric R Kandel
2001	Leland H Hartwell, Tim Hunt, Sir Paul Nurse
2002	Sydney Brenner, H Robert Horvitz, John E Sulston
2003	Paul C Lauterbur, Sir Peter Mansfield
2004	Richard Axel, Linda B Buck
2005	Barry J Marshall, J Robin Warren

HUMAN BODY

SKELETON

Humans have an internal skeleton or endoskeleton made of bone or cartilage. It supports the tissues and organs of the body, and protects soft internal organs such as the lungs. The muscles are attached to the bones of the skeleton by means of tendons, and when they contract they pull against the bones, causing them to move. The point of articulation or contact between two or more bones of the skeleton is known as a joint, different types of joint allowing varying degrees of movement. In total, the adult human skeleton has 206 bones; some are illustrated below.

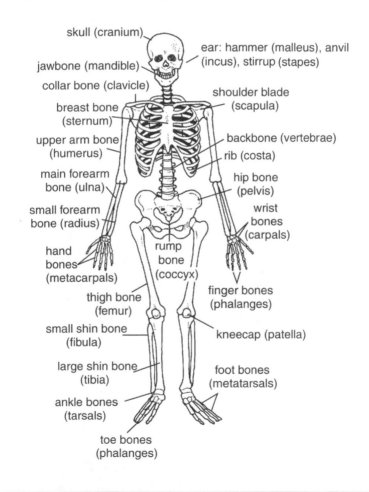

skull (cranium)

ear: hammer (malleus), anvil (incus), stirrup (stapes)

jawbone (mandible)

collar bone (clavicle)

shoulder blade (scapula)

breast bone (sternum)

upper arm bone (humerus)

backbone (vertebrae)

rib (costa)

main forearm bone (ulna)

hip bone (pelvis)

small forearm bone (radius)

wrist bones (carpals)

hand bones (metacarpals)

rump bone (coccyx)

finger bones (phalanges)

thigh bone (femur)

small shin bone (fibula)

kneecap (patella)

large shin bone (tibia)

foot bones (metatarsals)

ankle bones (tarsals)

toe bones (phalanges)

MUSCLES

Muscles consist of bundles of small fibres, each of which is in turn composed of many protein myofibrils, which lengthen or shorten as their filaments slide past each other. This movement, which occurs in response to a stimulus from the nervous system, or a hormonal signal, causes contraction of the whole muscle. *Voluntary muscle*, which is under conscious control, produces voluntary movements by pulling against the bones of the skeleton, to which it is attached by means of tendons, so that contractions of such muscles cause the bones to move. *Involuntary muscle* (also called *smooth muscle*) maintains the movements of the internal body systems, and forms part of many internal organs, such as the intestines and uterus. *Cardiac muscle*, found only in the heart, does not become fatigued, and continues to contract rhythmically even when it is disconnected from the nervous system. Some of the body's major superficial muscles are illustrated below.

masseter

sternocleidomastoid

pectoralis major

deltoid

abdominals (rectus abdominalis)

biceps

external oblique

extensor carpi radialis

sartorius

quadriceps femoris and rectus femoris

tibialis anterior

trapezius

deltoid

triceps

latissimus dorsi

flexor carpi ulnaris

gluteus maximus

hamstrings

calf muscles (gastrocnemius and soleus)

Achilles tendon

TEETH

In humans, the first set of teeth, consisting of 20 deciduous or milk teeth, is gradually replaced from about six years of age by 32 permanent teeth. These consist of chisel-shaped incisors for cutting, situated at the front of each jaw, and behind them the pointed canine teeth, for tearing food. Behind the canines are the molars and premolars, which have uneven surfaces for grinding and chewing food.

1 central incisors

2 lateral incisors

3 canines (cuspids)

4 first premolars (bicuspids)

5 second premolars (bicuspids)

6 first molars

7 second molars

8 third molars (wisdom teeth)

BLOOD

Blood performs many important functions as it circulates through the tissues of the body. It transports oxygen, nutrients and hormones, and carries waste products to the organs of excretion. It also helps to maintain a uniform temperature in humans and other warm-blooded organisms.

Blood composition

Component	Functions
Red blood cells	Carry oxygen, by means of haemoglobin
White blood cells	Defend the body against infection
Platelets	Needed for blood clotting
Plasma	Distribution of nutrients, salts, hormones, clotting factors and proteins needed for defence

ABO blood group system

Every person has a particular blood group, determined by genes inherited from their parents. The red blood cells of the A, B, AB and O groups carry, respectively, the A antigen, B antigen, both antigens and neither. The blood contains natural antibodies against the blood group antigens that are absent from the red blood cells. Before a transfusion, the blood of the recipient and donor is cross-matched to ensure that red blood cells from the donor are not given to a person possessing antibodies against them, as this could have fatal consequences.

Blood group	Can receive blood type	Blood group	Can receive blood type
A	A and O	AB	A, B, AB, O
B	B and O	O	O

SKIN

The skin consists of two main layers. The epidermis is a thin outer layer, which is continually being renewed as dead cells are shed from its surface. The thicker underlying layer is called the dermis and is composed of a network of collagen and elastic fibres. The dermis contains blood and lymph vessels, sensory nerve endings, hair follicles, sweat and sebaceous glands, and smooth muscle. In humans, as well as other warm-blooded animals, the skin has an important role in temperature regulation. Heat loss is achieved by sweating and by dilation of the skin capillaries. In order to conserve heat, the skin capillaries contract and the hairs on the surface are raised, trapping a layer of warm air next to the skin. The skin is an important sense organ, sensitive to touch, pressure, changes in temperature, and painful stimuli. It prevents fluid loss and dehydration, and protects the body from invasion by micro-organisms and parasites.

HUMAN BODY DATA

Number of bones	206
Number of muscles	approximately 650
Number of chromosomes	22 pairs and two sex chromosomes
Average body temperature	37°C/98.6°F
Average pulse rate	72 beats per minute (men), 80 beats per minute (women)
Average weight of brain	1 400g/3lb
Number of nerve cells in the brain	more than 10 billion
Total surface area of the skin of an adult	approximately 1.86 sq m/20 sq ft
Total dead skin cells shed per person per lifetime	approximately 18kg/40lb
Total surface area of the alveoli in the lungs	70 sq m/753 sq ft
Average total blood volume	5l/8pt

MATHEMATICS

FIELDS MEDAL

The Fields Medal is the world's highest award for achievement in mathematics. Named after a Canadian mathematician, Professor J C Fields (1863–1932), the medals are awarded at the International Congress of Mathematicians (ICM) every four years to 'recognize outstanding mathematical achievement' in a mathematician of no older than 40 years. Up to four medals may be awarded on each occasion.

1936	Lars Valerian Ahlfors, Jesse Douglas
1950	Laurent Schwartz, Atle Selberg
1954	Kunihiko Kodaira, Jean-Pierre Serre
1958	Klaus Friedrich Roth, René Thom
1962	Lars Hörmander, John Willard Milnor
1966	Michael Francis Atiyah, Paul Joseph Cohen, Alexander Grothendieck, Stephen Smale
1970	Alan Baker, Heisuke Hironaka, Serge Novikov, John Griggs Thompson
1974	Enrico Bombieri, David Bryant Mumford
1978	Pierre René Deligne, Charles Louis Fefferman, Gregori Alexandrovitch Margulis, Daniel G Quillen
1982	Alain Connes, William P Thurston, Shing-Tung Yau
1986	Simon K Donaldson, Gerd Faltings, Michael H Freedman
1990	Vladimir Drinfeld, Vaughan F R Jones, Shigefumi Mori, Edward Witten
1994	Jean Bourgain, Pierre-Louis Lions, Jean-Christophe Yoccoz, Efim Zelmanov
1998	Richard E Borcherds, W Timothy Gowers, Maxim Kontsevich, Curtis T McMullen
2002	Laurent Lafforgue, Vladimir Voevodsky

Fermat's Last Theorem

The most famous problem in mathematics was scrawled by the French mathematician Pierre de Fermat (1601–65) in the margin of a page of a book.

Fermat had studied law at Toulouse University, where he became a councillor of parliament, but his passion was mathematics. Most of his work was communicated in letters to friends, containing results without proof.

In what became known as his 'Last Theorem', Fermat stated that it is impossible to find a solution to the equation

$$x^n + y^n = z^n$$

if n is greater than 2. He added tantalizingly that 'I have a truly marvellous demonstration of this proposition which this margin is too narrow to contain'.

The puzzle to find Fermat's proof went on to baffle and outwit mathematicians for almost 350 years. The proof was finally announced in 1993 by the British mathematician Andrew Wiles, and revised by him in 1994. Wiles was just too old to qualify for the Fields Medal, so the International Mathematical Union instead honoured him with a silver plaque as a special tribute.

NUMERALS

Arabic	Roman	Greek	Binary numbers
1	I	α'	1
2	II	β'	10
3	III	γ'	11
4	IV	δ'	100
5	V	ε'	101
6	VI	ζ'	110
7	VII	ζ'	111
8	VIII	η'	1000
9	IX	θ'	1001
10	X	ι'	1010
11	XI	$\iota\alpha'$	1011
12	XII	$\iota\beta'$	1100
13	XIII	$\iota\gamma'$	1101
14	XIV	$\iota\delta'$	1110
15	XV	$\iota\varepsilon'$	1111
16	XVI	$\iota\zeta'$	10000
17	XVII	$\iota\zeta'$	10001
18	XVIII	$\iota\eta'$	10010
19	XIX	$\iota\theta'$	10011
20	XX	κ'	10100
30	XXX	λ'	11110
40	XL	μ'	101000
50	L	ν'	110010
60	LX	ξ'	111100
70	LXX	o'	1000110
80	LXXX	π'	1010000
90	XC	$,o'$	1011010
100	C	ρ'	1100100
200	CC	σ'	11001000
300	CCC	τ'	100101100
400	CD	υ'	110010000
500	D	φ'	111110100
1 000	M	$,\alpha$	1111101000
5 000	$\bar{V}$	$,\varepsilon$	1001110001000
10 000	$\bar{X}$	$,\iota$	10011100010000
100 000	$\bar{C}$	$,\rho$	11000011010100000

FRACTIONS AND DECIMALS

%	Decimal	Fraction	%	Decimal	Fraction
1	0.01	$1/100$	11	0.11	$11/100$
2	0.02	$1/50$	12	0.12	$3/25$
3	0.03	$3/100$	$12^1/_2$	0.125	$1/8$
4	0.04	$1/25$	13	0.13	$13/100$
5	0.05	$1/20$	14	0.14	$7/50$
6	0.06	$3/50$	15	0.15	$3/20$
7	0.07	$7/100$	16	0.16	$4/25$
8	0.08	$2/25$	$16^2/_3$	0.167	$1/6$
$8^1/_3$	0.083	$1/12$	17	0.17	$17/100$
9	0.09	$9/100$	18	0.18	$9/50$
10	0.10	$1/10$	19	0.19	$19/100$

%	Decimal	Fraction	%	Decimal	Fraction
20	0.20	$1/5$	40	0.40	$2/5$
21	0.21	$21/100$	41	0.41	$41/100$
22	0.22	$11/50$	42	0.42	$21/50$
23	0.23	$23/100$	43	0.43	$43/100$
24	0.24	$6/25$	44	0.44	$11/25$
25	0.25	$1/4$	45	0.45	$9/20$
26	0.26	$13/50$	46	0.46	$23/50$
27	0.27	$27/100$	47	0.47	$47/100$
28	0.28	$7/25$	48	0.48	$12/25$
29	0.29	$29/100$	49	0.49	$49/100$
30	0.30	$3/10$	50	0.50	$1/2$
31	0.31	$31/100$	55	0.55	$11/20$
32	0.32	$8/25$	60	0.60	$3/5$
33	0.33	$33/100$	65	0.65	$13/20$
$33^1/_3$	0.333	$1/3$	70	0.70	$7/10$
34	0.34	$17/50$	75	0.75	$3/4$
35	0.35	$7/20$	80	0.80	$4/5$
36	0.36	$9/25$	85	0.85	$17/20$
37	0.37	$37/100$	90	0.90	$9/10$
38	0.38	$19/50$	95	0.95	$19/20$
39	0.39	$39/100$	100	1.00	1

Fraction	Decimal	Fraction	Decimal	Fraction	Decimal
$1/2$	0.5000	$8/9$	0.8889	$15/16$	0.9375
$1/3$	0.3333	$1/10$	0.1000	$1/20$	0.0500
$2/3$	0.6667	$3/10$	0.3000	$3/20$	0.1500
$1/4$	0.2500	$7/10$	0.7000	$7/20$	0.3500
$3/4$	0.7500	$9/10$	0.9000	$9/20$	0.4500
$1/5$	0.2000	$1/11$	0.0909	$11/20$	0.5500
$2/5$	0.4000	$2/11$	0.1818	$13/20$	0.6500
$3/5$	0.6000	$3/11$	0.2727	$17/20$	0.8500
$4/5$	0.8000	$4/11$	0.3636	$19/20$	0.9500
$1/6$	0.1667	$5/11$	0.4545	$1/32$	0.0313
$5/6$	0.8333	$6/11$	0.5454	$3/32$	0.0938
$1/7$	0.1429	$7/11$	0.6363	$5/32$	0.1563
$2/7$	0.2857	$8/11$	0.7272	$7/32$	0.2188
$3/7$	0.4286	$9/11$	0.8181	$9/32$	0.2813
$4/7$	0.5714	$10/11$	0.9090	$11/32$	0.3438
$5/7$	0.7143	$1/12$	0.0833	$13/32$	0.4063
$6/7$	0.8571	$5/12$	0.4167	$15/32$	0.4688
$1/8$	0.1250	$7/12$	0.5833	$17/32$	0.5313
$3/8$	0.3750	$11/12$	0.9167	$19/32$	0.5938
$5/8$	0.6250	$1/16$	0.0625	$21/32$	0.6563
$7/8$	0.8750	$3/16$	0.1875	$23/32$	0.7188
$1/9$	0.1111	$5/16$	0.3125	$25/32$	0.7813
$2/9$	0.2222	$7/16$	0.4375	$27/32$	0.8438
$4/9$	0.4444	$9/16$	0.5625	$29/32$	0.9063
$5/9$	0.5556	$11/16$	0.6875	$31/32$	0.9688
$7/9$	0.7778	$13/16$	0.8125		

MULTIPLICATION TABLE

	2	3	4	5	6	7	8	9	10	11	12	13	14	15	16	17	18	19	20	21	22	23	24	25
2	4	6	8	10	12	14	16	18	20	22	24	26	28	30	32	34	36	38	40	42	44	46	48	50
3	6	9	12	15	18	21	24	27	30	33	36	39	42	45	48	51	54	57	60	63	66	69	72	75
4	8	12	16	20	24	28	32	36	40	44	48	52	56	60	64	68	72	76	80	84	88	92	96	100
5	10	15	20	25	30	35	40	45	50	55	60	65	70	75	80	85	90	95	100	105	110	115	120	125
6	12	18	24	30	36	42	48	54	60	66	72	78	84	90	96	102	108	114	120	126	132	138	144	150
7	14	21	28	35	42	49	56	63	70	77	84	91	98	105	112	119	126	133	140	147	154	161	168	175
8	16	24	32	40	48	56	64	72	80	88	96	104	112	120	128	136	144	152	160	168	176	184	192	200
9	18	27	36	45	54	63	72	81	90	99	108	117	126	135	144	153	162	171	180	189	198	207	216	225
10	20	30	40	50	60	70	80	90	100	110	120	130	140	150	160	170	180	190	200	210	220	230	240	250
11	22	33	44	55	66	77	88	99	110	121	132	143	154	165	176	187	198	209	220	231	242	253	264	275
12	24	36	48	60	72	84	96	108	120	132	144	156	168	180	192	204	216	228	240	252	264	276	288	300
13	26	39	52	65	78	91	104	117	130	143	156	169	182	195	208	221	234	247	260	273	286	299	312	325
14	28	42	56	70	84	98	112	126	140	154	168	182	196	210	224	238	252	266	280	294	308	322	336	350
15	30	45	60	75	90	105	120	135	150	165	180	195	210	225	240	255	270	285	300	315	330	345	360	375
16	32	48	64	80	96	112	128	144	160	176	192	208	224	240	256	272	288	304	320	336	352	368	384	400
17	34	51	68	85	102	119	136	153	170	187	204	221	238	255	272	289	306	323	340	357	374	391	408	425
18	36	54	72	90	108	126	144	162	180	198	216	234	252	270	288	306	324	342	360	378	396	414	432	450
19	38	57	76	95	114	133	152	171	190	209	228	247	266	285	304	323	342	361	380	399	418	437	456	475
20	40	60	80	100	120	140	160	180	200	220	240	260	280	300	320	340	360	380	400	420	440	460	480	500
21	42	63	84	105	126	147	168	189	210	231	252	273	294	315	336	357	378	399	420	441	462	483	504	525
22	44	66	88	110	132	154	176	198	220	242	264	286	308	330	352	374	396	418	440	462	484	506	528	550
23	46	69	92	115	138	161	184	207	230	253	276	299	322	345	368	391	414	437	460	483	506	529	552	575
24	48	72	96	120	144	168	192	216	240	264	288	312	336	360	384	408	432	456	480	501	528	552	576	600
25	50	75	100	125	150	175	200	225	250	275	300	325	350	375	400	425	450	475	500	525	550	575	600	625

SQUARES AND ROOTS

Number	Square	Cube	Square root	Cube root
1	1	1	1.000	1.000
2	4	8	1.414	1.260
3	9	27	1.732	1.442
4	16	64	2.000	1.587
5	25	125	2.236	1.710
6	36	216	2.449	1.817
7	49	343	2.646	1.913
8	64	512	2.828	2.000
9	81	729	3.000	2.080
10	100	1 000	3.162	2.154
11	121	1 331	3.317	2.224
12	144	1 728	3.464	2.289
13	169	2 197	3.606	2.351
14	196	2 744	3.742	2.410
15	225	3 375	3.873	2.466
16	256	4 096	4.000	2.520
17	289	4 913	4.123	2.571
18	324	5 832	4.243	2.621
19	361	6 859	4.359	2.668
20	400	8 000	4.472	2.714
25	625	15 625	5.000	2.924
30	900	27 000	5.477	3.107
40	1 600	64 000	6.325	3.420
50	2 500	125 000	7.071	3.684

POLYGONS

A polygon is a many-sided plane figure.

Sides	Polygon	Sides	Polygon
n	n-gon	12	dodecagon
3	trigon, triangle	13	tridecagon, triskaidecagon
4	tetragon, quadrilateral	14	tetradecagon, tetrakaidecagon
5	pentagon	15	pentadecagon, pentakaidecagon
6	hexagon	16	hexadecagon, hexakaidecagon
7	heptagon	17	heptadecagon, heptakaidecagon
8	octagon	18	octadecagon, octakaidecagon
9	enneagon, nonagon	19	enneadecagon, enneakaidecagon
10	decagon	1 000	chiliagon
11	hendecagon, undecagon		

Other names have been proposed for larger polygons using a system of prefixes but the form n-gon, eg 76-gon for a figure with 76 sides, is more common. The name myriagon *has been proposed for a polygon with 10 000 sides.*

LARGE NUMBERS

The names of large numbers formerly differed between the UK and the USA. In the UK, a billion was one million millions, rather than one thousand millions, as below. International economics has led to the US system becoming increasingly used worldwide. The US system is given below; to find the former British equivalents, increase the power by 6 each time (hence one billion becomes 10^{12}, one trillion becomes 10^{18} and one centillion 10^{600}).

thousand	10^3	1 000
million	10^6	1 000 000
billion	10^9	1 000 000 000
trillion	10^{12}	1 000 000 000 000
quadrillion	10^{15}	1 000 000 000 000 000
quintillion	10^{18}	1 000 000 000 000 000 000
sextillion	10^{21}	1 000 000 000 000 000 000 000
septillion	10^{24}	1 000 000 000 000 000 000 000 000
octillion	10^{27}	1 000 000 000 000 000 000 000 000 000
nonillion	10^{30}	1 000 000 000 000 000 000 000 000 000 000
decillion	10^{33}	1 000 000 000 000 000 000 000 000 000 000 000
googol	10^{100}	1 followed by 100 zeros
centillion	10^{303}	1 followed by 303 zeros
googolplex	10 to the power of a googol	1 followed by a googol of zeros

Googol, Google®

The popular internet search engine Google® is named after the *googol*, one followed by 100 zeros. The company's world headquarters in Mountain View, California, USA, is affectionately known as 'the Googleplex'.

ECONOMICS

NOBEL PRIZE FOR ECONOMICS

Nobel Prizes were established by a bequest in the will of Alfred Nobel (1833–96) to honour 'those who, during the preceding year, shall have conferred the greatest benefit on mankind'. However, the prize for economics was not among the original awards set up in this way. Instead, it was instituted by the Bank of Sweden and is officially called the 'Bank of Sweden Prize in Economic Sciences in Memory of Alfred Nobel'; first awarded in 1969.

1969	Ragnar Frisch, Jan Tinbergen
1970	Paul A Samuelson
1971	Simon Kuznets
1972	John R Hicks, Kenneth J Arrow
1973	Wassily Leontief
1974	Gunnar Myrdal, Friedrich August von Hayek
1975	Leonid Vitaliyevich Kantorovich, Tjalling C Koopmans
1976	Milton Friedman
1977	Bertil Ohlin, James E Meade
1978	Herbert A Simon
1979	Theodore W Schultz, Sir Arthur Lewis
1980	Lawrence R Klein
1981	James Tobin
1982	George J Stigler
1983	Gerard Debreu
1984	Richard Stone
1985	Franco Modigliani
1986	James M Buchanan Jr
1987	Robert M Solow
1988	Maurice Allais
1989	Trygve Haavelmo
1990	Harry M Markowitz, Merton H Miller, William F Sharpe
1991	Ronald H Coase
1992	Gary S Becker
1993	Robert W Fogel, Douglass C North
1994	John C Harsanyi, John F Nash Jr, Reinhard Selten
1995	Robert E Lucas Jr
1996	James A Mirrlees, William Vickrey
1997	Robert C Merton, Myron S Scholes
1998	Amartya Sen
1999	Robert A Mundell
2000	James J Heckman, Daniel L McFadden
2001	George A Akerlof, A Michael Spence, Joseph E Stiglitz
2002	Daniel Kahneman, Vernon L Smith
2003	Robert F Engle, Clive W J Granger
2004	Finn E Kydland, Edward C Prescott
2005	Robert J Aumann, Thomas C Schelling

STOCK EXCHANGE INDICES

Some of the world's major stock exchange indices are listed.

Index	Country
FTSE 100	United Kingdom
Dow Jones Industrial Average	United States of America
Nasdaq	United States of America
Nikkei 225	Japan
Hang Seng	Hong Kong
Dax	Germany
CAC 40	France

BANKNOTE DESIGNS

Bank of England

Banknotes featuring people were first issued by the Bank in 1970.

£50	Sir John Houblon (1632–1711, first Governor of the Bank of England)
£20	Sir Edward Elgar (1857–1934)
£10	Charles Darwin (1809–82)
£5	Elizabeth Fry (1780–1845)

Financial Faces

Famous people to have featured on now-withdrawn banknotes include Sir Christopher Wren (£50), William Shakespeare (£20), Michael Faraday (£20), Charles Dickens (£10), Florence Nightingale (£10), George Stephenson (£5), the Duke of Wellington (£5) and Sir Isaac Newton (£1).

Bank of Scotland

All banknotes feature Sir Walter Scott (1771–1832) on the front. On the back are illustrations of various aspects of Scottish industry, commerce and culture.

£100	Leisure and tourism
£50	Arts and culture
£20	Education and research
£10	Distilling and brewing
£5	Oil and energy

Royal Bank of Scotland

All banknotes feature Lord Ilay (1682–1761), first Governor of the Bank. On the back are illustrations of some of Scotland's famous castles.

£100	Balmoral Castle
£20	Brodick Castle
£10	Glamis Castle
£5	Culzean Castle
£1	Edinburgh Castle

Clydesdale Bank

Banknotes feature a notable figure on the front. On the back are relevant scenes from the person's life.

£100	Lord Kelvin (1824–1907)
£50	Adam Smith (1723–90)
£20	King Robert the Bruce (1274–1329)
£10	Mary Slessor (1848–1915)
£5	Robert Burns (1759–96)

First Trust Bank

All banknotes feature generic people of Northern Ireland on the front. On the back are coastal scenes or designs featuring the Spanish Armada.

£100   The Armada
£50   A commemorative medal
£20   The chimney at Lagada Point
£10   The ship *Girona*
£5   Dunluce Castle

Northern Bank

All banknotes except the £5 feature a notable figure on the front and a representation of Belfast City Hall on the back.

£100   Sir James Martin (1893–1981)
£50   Sir Samuel Davidson (1846–1921)
£20   Harry Ferguson (1884–1960)
£10   John Boyd Dunlop (1840–1921)
£5   US space shuttle

Ulster Bank

Banknotes are in £50, £20, £10 and £5 denominations. All notes feature a view of Belfast City Harbour, flanked by landscape views. On the back of each is the Bank's coat of arms.

Bank of Ireland

Banknotes are in £100, £50, £20, £10 and £5 denominations. All notes feature a seated woman representing Hibernia on the front. On the back of each is a view of Queen's University Belfast.

Million Pound Notes

The Bank of England is obliged to back notes issued by the Scottish and Northern Irish banks on a 'pound for pound' basis. The Bank calculates that over a billion pounds is needed to do so – far too much money to be stored in normal Bank of England notes. To get round the problem, they issue special £1 000 000 notes for the purpose. But it is unlikely that most people will ever see one: the Bank sternly declares that the notes 'are for internal use only and are never seen outside the Bank'.

POUND COIN INSCRIPTIONS

Scotland
nemo me impune lacessit
no one provokes me with impunity
(from the Motto of the Order of the Thistle)

Wales
pleidiol wyf i'm gwlad
true am I to my Country
(from the Welsh National Anthem)

England, Northern Ireland, United Kingdom
decus et tutamen
an ornament and a safeguard
(from Virgil's *Aeneid*)

Plastic Power

Consumers in the UK are spending less cash and are turning increasingly to plastic cards. APACS, the Association for Payment Clearing Services, estimates that 90% of UK adults own at least one plastic card, and that 189 million plastic cards are in use in the UK. In 2004, a total of £463.9 billion was spent on plastic cards.

BRITISH PRE-DECIMAL CURRENCY

Coins	Nickname	Value
Farthing	Jenny	$1/4$ penny
Half penny	Ha'penny	$1/2$ penny
Penny	Copper	$1/240$ pound, $1/12$ shilling
Three pence	Thruppence, throppence, threppence, thruppenny bit, joey	3 pence, $1/4$ shilling, $1/80$ pound
Six pence	Tanner	6 pence, $1/2$ shilling, $1/40$ pound
Shilling	Bob	12 pence, $1/20$ pound
Florin	Two bob	24 pence, 2 shillings, $1/10$ pound
Half crown	Half a crown, two and six	30 pence, 2 shillings and 6 pence, $1/8$ pound
Crown	Five bob	60 pence, 5 shillings, $1/4$ pound

Notes	Nickname	Value
Ten shilling note	Half a quid	120 pence, 10 shillings, ½ pound
Pound note	Quid	240 pence, 20 shillings

CURRENCY ABBREVIATIONS

International currency codes are regulated by the International Organization for Standardization's ISO 4217 standard. Countries which use the currency of another (for example Liechtenstein uses the Swiss Franc) do not have a separate currency code. For currency by country see **Human Geography**.

Abbrev	Country	Currency
AED	United Arab Emirates	UAE Dirham
AFN	Afghanistan	Afghani
ALL	Albania	Lek
AMD	Armenia	Armenian Dram
AOA	Angola	Kwanza
ARS	Argentina	Argentine Peso
AUD	Australia	Australian Dollar
AZM	Azerbaijan	Azerbaijani Manat
BAM	Bosnia and Herzegovina	Convertible Mark
BBD	Barbados	Barbados Dollar
BDT	Bangladesh	Taka
BGN	Bulgaria	Bulgarian Lev
BHD	Bahrain	Bahraini Dinar
BIF	Burundi	Burundi Franc
BND	Brunei Darussalam	Brunei Dollar

Abbrev	Country	Currency
BOB	Bolivia	Boliviano
BRL	Brazil	Brazilian Real
BSD	The Bahamas	Bahamian Dollar
BTN	Bhutan	Ngultrum
BWP	Botswana	Pula
BYR	Belarus	Belarussian Rouble
BZD	Belize	Belize Dollar
CAD	Canada	Canadian Dollar
CDF	Congo, Democratic Republic of the	Congolese Franc
CHF	Switzerland	Swiss Franc
CLP	Chile	Chilean Peso
CNY	China	Yuan[1]
COP	Colombia	Colombian Peso
CRC	Costa Rica	Costa Rican Colón
CSD	Serbia	Serbian Dinar
CUP	Cuba	Cuban Peso
CVE	Cape Verde	Cape Verde Escudo
CYP	Cyprus	Cyprus Pound
CZK	Czech Republic	Koruna
DJF	Djibouti	Djibouti Franc
DKK	Denmark	Danish Krone
DOP	Dominican Republic	Dominican Peso
DZD	Algeria	Algerian Dinar
EEK	Estonia	Kroon
EGP	Egypt	Egyptian Pound
ERN	Eritrea	Nakfa
ETB	Ethiopia	Ethiopian Birr
EUR	Euro member countries	Euro
FJD	Fiji	Fiji Dollar
GBP	United Kingdom	Pound Sterling
GEL	Georgia	Lari
GHC	Ghana	Cedi
GMD	The Gambia	Dalasi
GNF	Guinea	Guinea Franc
GTQ	Guatemala	Quetzal
GYD	Guyana	Guyana Dollar
HNL	Honduras	Lempira
HRK	Croatia	Kuna
HTG	Haiti	Gourde
HUF	Hungary	Forint
IDR	Indonesia	Rupiah
ILS	Israel	New Israeli Shekel
INR	India	Indian Rupee
IQD	Iraq	Iraqi Dinar
IRR	Iran	Iranian Rial
ISK	Iceland	Iceland Króna
JMD	Jamaica	Jamaican Dollar
JOD	Jordan	Jordanian Dinar
JPY	Japan	Yen
KES	Kenya	Kenyan Shilling
KGS	Kyrgyzstan	Som
KHR	Cambodia	Riel
KMF	Comoros	Comoran Franc
KPW	Korea (North)	North Korean Won

Abbrev	Country	Currency
KRW	Korea (South)	Won
KWD	Kuwait	Kuwaiti Dinar
KZT	Kazakhstan	Tenge
LAK	Laos	Kip
LBP	Lebanon	Lebanese Pound
LKR	Sri Lanka	Sir Lanka Rupee
LRD	Liberia	Liberian Dollar
LSL	Lesotho	Loti
LTL	Lithuania	Litas
LVL	Latvia	Lat
LYD	Libya	Libyan Dinar
MAD	Morocco	Moroccan Dirham
MDL	Moldova	Moldovan Leu
MGA	Madagascar ·	Ariary
MKD	Macedonia	Denar
MMK	Myanmar (Burma)	Kyat
MNT	Mongolia	Tugrik
MRO	Mauritania	Ouguiya
MTL	Malta	Maltese Lira
MUR	Mauritius	Mauritius Rupee
MVR	Maldives	Rufiyaa
MWK	Malawi	Kwacha
MXN	Mexico	Mexican Peso
MYR	Malaysia	Malaysian Ringgit
MZM	Mozambique	Metical
NAD	Namibia	Namibian Dollar
NGN	Nigeria	Naira
NIO	Nicaragua	Córdoba
NOK	Norway	Norwegian Krone
NPR	Nepal	Nepalese Rupee
NZD	New Zealand	New Zealand Dollar
OMR	Oman	Omani Rial
PAB	Panama	Balboa
PEN	Peru	Nuevo Sol
PGK	Papua New Guinea	Kína
PHP	Philippines	Philippine Peso
PKR	Pakistan	Pakistan Rupee
PLN	Poland	Zloty
PYG	Paraguay	Guaraní
QAR	Qatar	Qatari Riyal
RMB	China	Renminbi[1]
RON	Romania	Leu
RUB	Russia	Russian Rouble
RWF	Rwanda	Rwanda Franc
SAR	Saudi Arabia	Saudi Riyal
SBD	Solomon Islands	Solomon Islands Dollar
SCR	Seychelles	Seychelles Rupee
SDD	Sudan	Sudanese Dinar
SEK	Sweden	Swedish Krona
SGD	Singapore	Singapore Dollar
SIT	Slovenia	Tolar
SKK	Slovakia	Slovak Koruna
SLL	Sierra Leone	Leone
SOS	Somalia	Somali Shilling

Abbrev	Country	Currency
SRD	Suriname	Surinam Dollar
STD	São Tomé and Príncipe	Dobra
SVC	El Salvador	El Salvador Colón
SYP	Syria	Syrian Pound
SZL	Swaziland	Lilangeni
THB	Thailand	Baht
TJS	Tajikistan	Somoni
TMM	Turkmenistan	Manat
TND	Tunisia	Tunisian Dinar
TOP	Tonga	Pa'anga
TRY	Turkey	New Turkish Lira
TTD	Trinidad and Tobago	Trinidad and Tobago Dollar
TWD	Taiwan	New Taiwan Dollar
TZS	Tanzania	Tanzanian Shilling
UAH	Ukraine	Hryvnia
UGS	Uganda	Uganda Shilling
USD	United States of America	United States Dollar
UYU	Uruguay	Uruguayan Peso
UZS	Uzbekistan	Uzbekistan Sum
VEB	Venezuela	Bolívar
VND	Vietnam	Dông
VUV	Vanuatu	Vatu
WST	Samoa	Tala
XAF	African Financial Community, *Communauté Financière Africaine* (CFA); Bank of Central African States, *Banque des États de l'Afrique Centrale* (BEAC)	CFA Franc
XCD	East Caribbean states	East Caribbean Dollar
XOF	African Financial Community, *Communauté Financière Africaine* (CFA); Central Bank of West African States, *Banque Centrale des États de l'Afrique de l'Ouest* (BCEAO)	CFA Franc
XPF	Pacific Financial Community, *Comptoirs Français du Pacifique* (CFP)	CFP Franc
YER	Yemen	Yemeni Rial
ZAR	South Africa	Rand
ZMK	Zambia	Kwacha
ZWD	Zimbabwe	Zimbabwe Dollar

[1] *The Yuan is also known as the Renminbi; although the ISO code CNY covers both terms, RMB is also used.*

Colourful Currencies

Currency names can have surprisingly colourful origins. The Botswanan unit of currency, for example, is the pula, which means 'rain' in the Setswanan language. In such a dry country, rain has deep symbolic meaning. The smaller denomination is the thebe, which means 'shield'. In Croatia, the kuna means 'marten'. Historically, martens' pelts were used as payment in trading and bartering, and the kuna was first used on Croatian coins as far back as the 13c. Lipa, the name of the smaller currency unit, means 'lime tree'.

MEASUREMENT, CONVERSION AND SIZE

Figures in tables are rounded to two decimal places.

LENGTH

All miles are statute miles. See **Nautical Measurements** for nautical miles.

Metric units

1 millimetre (mm)
10 millimetres (mm) = 1 centimetre (cm)
10 centimetres (cm) = 1 decimetre (dm)
100 centimetres (cm) = 1 metre (m)
1 000 metres (m) = 1 kilometre (km)

Imperial units

1 inch (in)
12 inches (in) = 1 foot (ft)
3 feet (ft) = 1 yard (yd)
1 760 yards (yd) = 1 mile (mi)

Exact conversions

1 mm = 0.03937in	1 in = 25.4mm
1 cm = 0.3937in	1 in = 2.54cm
1 cm = 0.0328ft	1 in = 0.254dm
1 cm = 0.0109yd	1 in = 0.0254m
1 dm = 3.937in	1 ft = 30.48cm
1 m = 39.37in	1 ft = 0.3048m
1 m = 3.2808ft	1 ft = 0.0003km
1 m = 1.0936yd	1 yd = 91.44cm
1 m = 0.00062mi	1 yd = 0.9144m
1 km = 3 280.8ft	1 yd = 0.0009km
1 km = 1 093.6yd	1 mi = 1 609.3m
1 km = 0.6214mi	1 mi = 1.6093km

Inches to centimetres		Centimetres to inches		Inches to millimetres		Millimetres to inches	
in	*cm*	*cm*	*in*	*in*	*mm*	*mm*	*in*
1/8	0.32	1	0.39	1/8	3.18	1	0.04
1/4	0.64	2	0.79	1/4	6.35	2	0.08
3/8	0.95	3	1.18	3/8	9.53	3	0.12
1/2	1.27	4	1.57	1/2	12.70	4	0.16
5/8	1.59	5	1.97	5/8	15.88	5	0.20
3/4	1.91	6	2.36	3/4	19.05	6	0.24
7/8	2.22	7	2.76	7/8	22.23	7	0.28
1	2.54	8	3.15	1	25.40	8	0.31
2	5.08	9	3.54	2	50.80	9	0.35
3	7.62	10	3.94	3	76.20	10	0.39
4	10.16	20	7.87	4	101.60	20	0.79
5	12.70	30	11.81	5	127.00	30	1.18
6	15.24	40	15.75	6	152.40	40	1.58
7	17.78	50	19.69	7	177.80	50	1.97
8	20.32	60	23.62	8	203.20	60	2.36
9	22.86	70	27.56	9	228.60	70	2.76
10	25.40	80	31.50	10	254.00	80	3.15
11	27.94	90	35.43	11	279.40	90	3.54
12	30.48	100	39.37	12	304.80	100	3.94

AREA

Feet to metres		Metres to feet		Yards to metres		Metres to yards	
ft	*m*	*m*	*ft*	*yd*	*m*	*m*	*yd*
1	0.30	1	3.28	1	0.91	1	1.09
2	0.61	2	6.56	2	1.83	2	2.19
3	0.91	3	9.84	3	2.74	3	3.28
4	1.22	4	13.12	4	3.66	4	4.37
5	1.52	5	16.40	5	4.57	5	5.47
6	1.83	6	19.68	6	5.49	6	6.56
7	2.13	7	22.97	7	6.40	7	7.66
8	2.44	8	26.25	8	7.32	8	8.75
9	2.74	9	29.53	9	8.23	9	9.84
10	3.05	10	32.81	10	9.14	10	10.94
20	6.10	20	65.62	20	18.29	20	21.87
30	9.14	30	98.42	30	27.43	30	32.81
40	12.19	40	131.23	40	36.58	40	43.74
50	15.24	50	164.04	50	45.72	50	54.68
75	22.86	75	246.06	75	68.58	75	82.02
100	30.48	100	328.08	100	91.44	100	109.36
200	60.96	200	656.16	200	182.88	200	218.72
300	91.44	300	984.24	300	274.32	300	328.08
400	121.92	400	1 312.32	400	365.76	400	437.44
500	152.40	500	1 640.40	500	457.20	500	546.80
1 000	304.80	1 000	3 280.80	1 000	914.40	1 000	1 093.60
2 000	609.60	2 000	6 561.60	2 000	1 828.80	2 000	2 187.20
3 000	914.40	3 000	9 842.40	3 000	2 743.20	3 000	3 280.80
4 000	1 219.20	4 000	13 123.20	4 000	3 657.60	4 000	4 374.40
5 000	1 524.00	5 000	16 404.00	5 000	4 572.00	5 000	5 468.00

Miles to kilometres				Kilometres to miles			
mi	*km*	*mi*	*km*	*km*	*mi*	*km*	*mi*
1	1.61	50	80.47	1	0.62	50	31.07
2	3.22	75	120.70	2	1.24	75	46.61
3	4.83	100	160.93	3	1.86	100	62.14
4	6.44	200	321.86	4	2.49	200	124.28
5	8.05	300	482.79	5	3.11	300	186.42
6	9.66	400	643.72	6	3.73	400	248.56
7	11.27	500	804.65	7	4.35	500	310.70
8	12.87	1 000	1 609.30	8	4.97	1 000	621.40
9	14.48	2 000	3 218.60	9	5.59	2 000	1 242.80
10	16.09	3 000	4 827.90	10	6.21	3 000	1 864.20
20	32.19	4 000	6 437.20	20	12.43	4 000	2 485.60
30	48.28	5 000	8 046.50	30	18.64	5 000	3 107.00
40	64.37			40	24.86		

AREA

Metric units

1 square millimetre (sq mm)
100 square millimetres (sq mm) = 1 square centimetre (sq cm)
100 square centimetres (sq cm) = 1 square decimetre (sq dm)
100 square decimetres (sq dm) = 1 square metre (sq m)
10 000 square centimetres (sq cm) = 1 square metre (sq m)
10 000 square metres (sq m) = 1 hectare (ha)
100 hectares (ha) = 1 square kilometre (sq km)
1 000 000 square metres (sq m) = 1 square kilometre (sq km)

Imperial units

1 square inch (sq in)
144 square inches (sq in) = 1 square foot (sq ft)
9 square feet (sq ft) = 1 square yard (sq yd)
4 840 square yards (sq yd) = 1 acre (a)
640 acres (a) = 1 square mile (sq mi)

Exact conversions

1 sq mm = 0.0016 sq in	1 sq in = 645.16 sq mm
1 sq cm = 0.155 sq in	1 sq in = 6.4516 sq cm
1 sq cm = 0.0011 sq ft	1 sq in = 0.0645 sq dm
1 sq dm = 15.5 sq in	1 sq in = 0.0006 sq m
1 sq m = 1 550 sq in	1 sq ft = 929.03 sq cm
1 sq m = 10.7639 sq ft	1 sq ft = 0.0929 sq m
1 sq m = 1.196 sq yd	1 sq yd = 0.8361 sq m
1 sq m = 0.0002 a	1 sq yd = 0.00008 ha
1 ha = 2.471 a	1 a = 4 046.85 sq m
1 ha = 11 959.9 sq yd	1 a = 0.4047 ha
1 ha = 0.0039 sq mi	1 a = 0.0016 sq km
1 sq km = 0.3861 sq mi	1 sq mi = 258.9988 ha
1 sq km = 247.1 a	1 sq mi = 2.5899 sq km

Square inches to square centimetres		Square centimetres to square inches		Square feet to square metres		Square metres to square feet	
sq in	*sq cm*	*sq cm*	*sq in*	*sq ft*	*sq m*	*sq m*	*sq ft*
1	6.45	1	0.16	1	0.09	1	10.76
2	12.90	2	0.31	2	0.19	2	21.53
3	19.35	3	0.47	3	0.28	3	32.29
4	25.81	4	0.62	4	0.37	4	43.06
5	32.26	5	0.78	5	0.46	5	53.82
6	38.71	6	0.93	6	0.56	6	64.58
7	45.16	7	1.09	7	0.65	7	75.35
8	51.61	8	1.24	8	0.74	8	86.11
9	58.06	9	1.40	9	0.84	9	96.88
10	64.52	10	1.55	10	0.93	10	107.64
11	70.97	11	1.71	11	1.02	11	118.40
12	77.42	12	1.86	12	1.11	12	129.17
13	83.87	13	2.02	13	1.21	13	139.93
14	90.32	14	2.17	14	1.30	14	150.69
15	96.77	15	2.33	15	1.39	15	161.46
16	103.23	16	2.48	16	1.49	16	172.22
17	109.68	17	2.64	17	1.58	17	182.99
18	116.13	18	2.79	18	1.67	18	193.75
19	122.58	19	2.95	19	1.77	19	204.51
20	129.03	20	3.10	20	1.86	20	215.28
25	161.29	25	3.88	25	2.32	25	269.10
50	322.58	50	7.75	50	4.65	50	538.20
75	483.87	75	11.63	75	6.97	75	807.29
100	645.16	100	15.50	100	9.29	100	1 076.39
				250	23.23	250	2 690.98
				500	46.45	500	5 381.95
				750	69.68	750	8 072.93
				1 000	92.90	1 000	10 763.90

VOLUME

Acres to hectares		Hectares to acres		Square miles to square kilometres		Square kilometres to square miles	
a	*ha*	*ha*	*a*	*sq mi*	*sq km*	*sq km*	*sq mi*
1	0.40	1	2.47	1	2.59	1	0.39
2	0.81	2	4.94	2	5.18	2	0.77
3	1.21	3	7.41	3	7.77	3	1.16
4	1.62	4	9.88	4	10.36	4	1.54
5	2.02	5	12.36	5	12.95	5	1.93
6	2.43	6	14.83	6	15.54	6	2.32
7	2.83	7	17.30	7	18.13	7	2.70
8	3.24	8	19.77	8	20.72	8	3.09
9	3.64	9	22.24	9	23.31	9	3.47
10	4.05	10	24.71	10	25.90	10	3.86
11	4.45	11	27.18	20	51.80	20	7.72
12	4.86	12	29.65	30	77.70	30	11.58
13	5.26	13	32.12	40	103.60	40	15.44
14	5.67	14	34.59	50	129.50	50	19.31
15	6.07	15	37.07	100	258.99	100	38.61
16	6.48	16	39.54	200	517.98	200	77.22
17	6.88	17	42.01	300	776.97	300	115.83
18	7.28	18	44.48	400	1 035.96	400	154.44
19	7.69	19	46.95	500	1 294.95	500	193.05
20	8.09	20	49.42	1 000	2 589.90	1 000	386.10
25	10.12	25	61.78	1 500	3 884.85	1 500	579.15
50	20.23	50	123.55	2 000	5 179.80	2 000	772.20
75	30.35	75	185.33				
100	40.47	100	247.10				
250	101.17	250	617.75				
500	202.35	500	1 235.50				
750	303.52	750	1 853.25				
1 000	404.69	1 000	2 471.00				

VOLUME

Metric units

1 cubic centimetre (cu cm[1])
1 000 cubic centimetres (cu cm) = 1 cubic decimetre (cu dm)
1 000 cubic decimetres (cu dm) = 1 cubic metre (cu m)

[1] *Cubic centimetres sometimes abbreviated as cc.*

Imperial units

1 cubic inch (cu in)
1 728 cubic inches (cu in) = 1 cubic foot (cu ft)
27 cubic feet (cu ft) = 1 cubic yard (cu yd)

Exact conversions

1 cu cm = 0.0610 cu in
1 cu dm = 61.024 cu in
1 cu m = 61 023.74 cu in
1 cu m = 35.3147 cu ft
1 cu m = 1.308 cu yd

1 cu in = 16.3871 cu cm
1 cu in = 0.0164 cu dm
1 cu in = 0.000016 cu m
1 cu ft = 0.0283 cu m
1 cu yd = 0.7646 cu m

Cubic inches to cubic centimetres		Cubic centimetres to cubic inches		Cubic feet to cubic metres		Cubic metres to cubic feet	
cu in	cu cm	cu cm	cu in	cu ft	cu m	cu m	cu ft
1	16.39	1	0.06	1	0.03	1	35.31
2	32.77	2	0.12	2	0.06	2	70.63
3	49.16	3	0.18	3	0.08	3	105.94
4	65.55	4	0.24	4	0.11	4	141.26
5	81.93	5	0.31	5	0.14	5	176.57
6	98.32	6	0.37	6	0.17	6	211.89
7	114.71	7	0.43	7	0.20	7	247.20
8	131.10	8	0.49	8	0.23	8	282.52
9	147.48	9	0.55	9	0.25	9	317.83
10	163.87	10	0.61	10	0.28	10	353.15
15	245.81	15	0.92	15	0.42	15	529.72
20	327.74	20	1.22	20	0.57	20	706.29
50	819.36	50	3.05	50	1.41	50	1 765.74
100	1 638.71	100	6.10	100	2.83	100	3 531.47

Cubic yards to cubic metres				Cubic metres to cubic yards			
cu yd	cu m	cu yd	cu m	cu m	cu yd	cu m	cu yd
1	0.76	8	6.12	1	1.31	8	10.46
2	1.53	9	6.88	2	2.62	9	11.77
3	2.29	10	7.65	3	3.92	10	13.08
4	3.06	15	11.47	4	5.23	15	19.62
5	3.82	20	15.29	5	6.54	20	26.16
6	4.59	50	38.23	6	7.85	50	65.40
7	5.35	100	76.46	7	9.16	100	130.80

CAPACITY

Liquid capacity measures

Metric units

1 millilitre (ml)
10 millilitres (ml) = 1 centilitre (cl)
100 centilitres (cl) = 1 litre (l)
100 litres (l) = 1 hectolitre (hl)

Imperial units

1 fluid ounce (fl oz)
20 fluid ounces (fl oz) = 1 pint (pt)
2 pints (pt) = 1 quart (qt)
8 pints (pt) = 1 gallon (gal)
4 quarts (qt) = 1 gallon (gal)

Exact conversions

1 ml = 0.035 fl oz
1 cl = 0.352 fl oz
1 l = 35.196 fl oz
1 l = 1.7598pt
1 l = 0.220gal
1 hl = 22gal

1 fl oz = 28.41ml
1 fl oz = 2.84cl
1 fl oz = 0.0284 l
1 pt = 0.5682 l
1 qt = 1.14 l
1 gal = 4.546 l

US measures

8 fl oz = 1 cup

1 fl oz = 0.0296 l
1 pt = 0.4732 l
1 gal = 3.7854 l

1 l = 33.8140 fl oz
1 l = 2.1134pt
1 l = 0.2642gal

1 pt (UK) = 1.20pt (US)
1 pt (US) = 0.83pt (UK)

1 gal (UK) = 1.200929gal (US)
1 gal (US) = 0.832688gal (UK)

UK fluid ounces to litres

UK fl oz	l
1	0.03
2	0.06
3	0.09
4	0.11
5	0.14
6	0.17
7	0.20
8	0.23
9	0.26
10	0.28
11	0.31
12	0.34
13	0.37
14	0.40
15	0.43
20	0.57
50	1.42
100	2.84

US fluid ounces to litres

US fl oz	l
1	0.03
2	0.06
3	0.09
4	0.12
5	0.15
6	0.18
7	0.21
8	0.24
9	0.27
10	0.30
11	0.33
12	0.36
13	0.39
14	0.41
15	0.44
20	0.59
50	1.48
100	2.96

Litres to fluid ounces

l	UK fl oz	US fl oz
1	35.20	33.81
2	70.39	67.63
3	105.59	101.44
4	140.78	135.26
5	175.98	169.07
6	211.18	202.88
7	246.37	236.70
8	281.57	270.51
9	316.76	304.33
10	351.96	338.14
11	387.16	371.95
12	422.35	405.77
13	457.55	439.58
14	492.75	473.40
15	527.94	507.21
20	703.92	676.28
50	1 759.81	1 690.70
100	3 519.61	3 381.40

UK pints to litres

UK pt	l
1	0.57
2	1.14
3	1.70
4	2.27
5	2.84
6	3.41
7	3.98
8	4.55
9	5.11
10	5.68
11	6.25
12	6.82
13	7.38
14	7.95
15	8.52
20	11.36
50	28.41
100	56.82

US pints to litres

US pt	l
1	0.47
2	0.95
3	1.42
4	1.89
5	2.37
6	2.84
7	3.31
8	3.78
9	4.26
10	4.73
11	5.20
12	5.68
13	6.15
14	6.62
15	7.10
20	9.46
50	23.66
100	47.32

Litres to pints

l	UK pt	US pt
1	1.76	2.11
2	3.52	4.23
3	5.28	6.34
4	7.04	8.45
5	8.80	10.57
6	10.56	12.68
7	12.32	14.79
8	14.08	16.91
9	15.84	19.02
10	17.60	21.13
11	19.36	23.25
12	21.12	25.36
13	22.88	27.47
14	24.64	29.59
15	26.40	31.70
20	35.20	42.27
50	87.99	105.67
100	175.98	211.34

UK gallons to litres		US gallons to litres		Litres to gallons		
UK gal	*l*	*US gal*	*l*	*l*	*UK gal*	*US gal*
1	4.55	1	3.78	1	0.22	0.26
2	9.09	2	7.57	2	0.44	0.53
3	13.64	3	11.36	3	0.66	0.79
4	18.18	4	15.14	4	0.88	1.06
5	22.73	5	18.93	5	1.10	1.32
6	27.28	6	22.71	6	1.32	1.58
7	31.82	7	26.50	7	1.54	1.85
8	36.37	8	30.28	8	1.76	2.11
9	40.91	9	34.07	9	1.98	2.38
10	45.46	10	37.85	10	2.20	2.64
11	50.01	11	41.64	11	2.42	2.91
12	54.55	12	45.42	12	2.64	3.17
13	59.10	13	49.21	13	2.86	3.43
14	63.64	14	52.99	14	3.08	3.70
15	68.19	15	56.78	15	3.30	3.96
16	72.74	16	60.57	16	3.52	4.23
17	77.28	17	64.35	17	3.74	4.49
18	81.83	18	68.14	18	3.96	4.76
19	86.37	19	71.92	19	4.18	5.02
20	90.92	20	75.71	20	4.40	5.28
25	113.65	25	94.63	25	5.50	6.60
50	227.30	50	189.27	50	11.00	13.20
75	340.96	75	283.90	75	16.50	19.81
100	454.61	100	378.54	100	22.00	26.42

UK gallons to US gallons		US gallons to UK gallons	
UK gal	*US gal*	*US gal*	*UK gal*
1	1.20	1	0.83
2	2.40	2	1.67
3	3.60	3	2.50
4	4.80	4	3.33
5	6	5	4.16
6	7.21	6	5.00
7	8.41	7	5.83
8	9.61	8	6.66
9	10.81	9	7.49
10	12.01	10	8.33
11	13.21	11	9.16
12	14.41	12	9.99
13	15.61	13	10.82
14	16.81	14	11.66
15	18.01	15	12.49
20	24.02	20	16.65
25	30.02	25	20.82
50	60.05	50	41.63

Pottles and Kilderkins

The world of liquid capacity measures used not to be so regimented. Measures in use in past centuries included the *anker*, the *bath*, the *kilderkin*, the *pipe*, the *pottle*, the *puncheon* and the *rundlet*.

CAPACITY

Dry capacity measures

Metric units

Cubic metres (cu m) see **Volume** above.
Litres (l) see **Liquid capacity measures** above.

Imperial units

1 gallon (gal)
2 gallons (gal) = 1 peck (pk)

4 pecks (pk) = 1 bushel (bu)
8 gallons (gal) = 1 bushel (bu)

Exact conversions

1 cu m = 219.97gal	1 l = 0.1100pk	1 pk = 0.0091 cu m
1 cu m = 109.98pk	1 l = 0.0275bu	1 pk = 9.0919 l
1 cu m = 27.4962bu	1 gal = 0.0045 cu m	1 bu = 0.0369 cu m
1 l = 0.2200gal	1 gal = 4.546 l	1 bu = 36.3677 l

US measures

1 cu m = 227.02gal	1 pk = 0.0088 cu m	1 pt = 0.0006 cu m
1 cu m = 113.51pk	1 pk = 8.8095 l	1 pt = 0.5506 l
1 cu m = 28.3776bu	1 bu = 0.0353 cu m	1 cu cm = 0.0009qt
1 l = 0.227gal	1 bu = 35.2381 l	1 cu m = 908.08qt
1 l = 0.1135pk	1 qt = 1 101.22 cu cm	1 l = 0.908qt
1 l = 0.0284bu	1 qt = 0.0011012 cu m	1 cu cm = 0.0018pt
1 gal = 0.0044 cu m	1 qt = 1.1012 l	1 cu m = 1 816.17pt
1 gal = 4.4049 l	1 pt = 550.61 cu cm	1 l = 1.816pt

UK bushels to cubic metres and litres

UK bu	cu m	l
1	0.04	36.37
2	0.07	72.74
3	0.11	109.10
4	0.15	145.47
5	0.18	181.84
10	0.37	363.68

US bushels to cubic metres and litres

US bu	cu m	l
1	0.04	35.24
2	0.07	70.48
3	0.11	105.71
4	0.14	140.95
5	0.18	176.19
10	0.35	352.38

Cubic metres to bushels

cu m	UK bu	US bu
1	27.50	28.38
2	54.99	56.76
3	82.49	85.13
4	109.98	113.51
5	137.48	141.89
10	274.96	283.78

Litres to bushels

l	UK bu	US bu
1	0.03	0.03
2	0.06	0.06
3	0.08	0.09
4	0.11	0.11
5	0.14	0.14
10	0.28	0.28

UK pecks to litres

UK pk	l
1	9.09
2	18.18
3	27.28
4	36.37
5	45.46
10	90.92

US pecks to litres

US pk	l
1	8.81
2	17.62
3	26.43
4	35.24
5	44.05
10	88.10

Litres to pecks

l	UK pk	US pk
1	0.11	0.11
2	0.22	0.23
3	0.33	0.34
4	0.44	0.45
5	0.55	0.57
10	1.10	1.14

US dry quarts to cubic centimetres and litres

US qt	cu cm	l
1	1 101	1.1
2	2 202	2.2
3	3 304	3.3
4	4 405	4.4
5	5 506	5.5
10	11 012	11.0

US dry pints to cubic centimetres and litres

US pt	cu cm	l
1	551	0.55
2	1 101	1.10
3	1 652	1.65
4	2 202	2.20
5	2 753	2.75
10	5 506	5.51

WEIGHT

All ounces are avoirdupois.

Metric units

1 gram (g)
1 000 grams (g) = 1 kilogram (kg)
1 000 kilograms (kg) = 1 tonne[1]

[1] *The tonne is sometimes known as the metric ton.*

Imperial units

1 ounce (oz)
16 ounces (oz) = 1 pound (lb)
14 pounds (lb) = 1 stone (st)
8 stones (st) = 1 hundredweight[1] (cwt)
20 hundredweights (cwt) = 1 ton[2]

1 pound (lb) = 0.0714 stones (st)
1 hundredweight (cwt) = 112 pounds (lb)
1 ton = 2 240 pounds (lb)
1 ton = 160 stone (st)

[1] *The UK hundredweight of 112 lb is sometimes known as the long hundredweight.*
[2] *The UK ton of 2 240 lb is sometimes known as the long ton.*

Exact conversions

1 g = 0.0353oz
1 kg = 35.274oz
1 kg = 2.2046 lb
1 kg = 0.1575st
1 kg = 0.0197cwt
1 tonne = 157.5st
1 tonne = 19.684cwt
1 tonne = 0.9842 tons

1 oz = 28.3495g
1 lb = 0.4536kg
1 st = 6.350kg
1 cwt = 50.8023kg
1 cwt = 0.0508 tonnes
1 ton = 1 016.06kg
1 ton = 1.0160 tonnes

US measures

100 pounds (lb) = 1 hundredweight[1] (cwt)
2 000 pounds (lb) = 1 ton[2]
20 hundredweights (cwt) = 1 ton

1 kg = 0.0220 cwt
1 tonne = 1.1023 tons

1 cwt = 45.3592 kg
1 ton = 0.9072 tonnes

1 cwt (UK) = 1.1199 cwt (US)
1 cwt (US) = 0.8929 cwt (UK)
1 ton (UK) = 1.1199 tons (US)
1 ton (US) = 0.8929 ton (UK)

[1] *The US hundredweight of 100 lb is sometimes known as the short hundredweight.*
[2] *The US ton of 2 000 lb is sometimes known as the short ton.*

WEIGHT

Ounces to grams		Grams to ounces		Pounds to kilograms		Kilograms to pounds	
oz	*g*	*g*	*oz*	*lb*	*kg*	*kg*	*lb*
1	28.35	1	0.04	1	0.45	1	2.21
2	56.70	2	0.07	2	0.91	2	4.41
3	85.05	3	0.11	3	1.36	3	6.62
4	113.40	4	0.14	4	1.81	4	8.82
5	141.75	5	0.18	5	2.27	5	11.03
6	170.10	6	0.21	6	2.72	6	13.23
7	198.45	7	0.25	7	3.18	7	15.44
8	226.80	8	0.28	8	3.63	8	17.64
9	255.15	9	0.32	9	4.08	9	19.85
10	283.50	10	0.35	10	4.54	10	22.05
11	311.84	20	0.71	11	4.99	11	24.26
12	340.19	30	1.06	12	5.44	12	26.46
13	368.54	40	1.41	13	5.90	13	28.67
14	396.89	50	1.76	14	6.35	14	30.87
15	425.24	60	2.12	15	6.80	15	33.08
16	453.59	70	2.47	16	7.26	16	35.28
		80	2.82	17	7.71	17	37.49
		90	3.18	18	8.16	18	39.69
		100	3.53	19	8.62	19	41.90
				20	9.07	20	44.10
				30	13.61	30	66.15
				40	18.14	40	88.20
				50	22.68	50	110.25
				100	45.36	100	220.50
				200	90.72	200	441.00
				250	113.40	250	551.25
				500	226.80	500	1 102.50
				750	340.19	750	1 653.75
				1 000	453.59	1 000	2 205.00

Stones to kilograms		Kilograms to stones		Stones to pounds		Pounds to stones	
st	*kg*	*kg*	*st*	*st*	*lb*	*lb*	*st*
1	6.35	1	0.16	1	14	1	0.07
2	12.70	2	0.32	2	28	2	0.14
3	19.05	3	0.47	3	42	3	0.21
4	25.40	4	0.63	4	56	4	0.29
5	31.75	5	0.79	5	70	5	0.36
6	38.10	6	0.95	6	84	6	0.43
7	44.45	7	1.10	7	98	7	0.50
8	50.80	8	1.26	8	112	8	0.57
9	57.15	9	1.42	9	126	9	0.64
10	63.50	10	1.58	10	140	10	0.71
				11	154	11	0.79
				12	168	12	0.86
				13	182	13	0.93
				14	196	14	1.00
				15	210		
				16	224		
				17	238		
				18	252		
				19	266		
				20	280		

UK hundredweights to kilograms

UK cwt	kg
1	50.80
2	101.60
3	152.41
4	203.21
5	254.01
10	508.02
20	1 016.05
50	2 540.12
75	3 810.17
100	5 080.23

US hundredweights to kilograms

US cwt	kg
1	45.36
2	90.72
3	136.08
4	181.44
5	226.80
10	453.59
20	907.18
50	2 267.96
75	3 401.94
100	4 535.92

Kilograms to hundredweights

kg	UK cwt	US cwt
1	0.02	0.02
2	0.04	0.04
3	0.06	0.07
4	0.08	0.09
5	0.10	0.11
10	0.20	0.22
20	0.40	0.44
50	0.99	1.10
75	1.48	1.65
100	1.97	2.20

UK hundredweights to US hundredweights

UK cwt	US cwt
1	1.12
2	2.24
3	3.36
4	4.48
5	5.60
10	11.20
20	22.40
50	56.00
75	83.99
100	111.99

US hundredweights to UK hundredweights

US cwt	UK cwt
1	0.89
2	1.79
3	2.68
4	3.57
5	4.46
10	8.93
20	17.86
50	44.64
75	66.96
100	89.29

UK tons to tonnes

UK tons	tonnes
1	1.02
2	2.03
3	3.05
4	4.06
5	5.08
10	10.16
20	20.32
50	50.80
75	76.20
100	101.60

US tons to tonnes

US tons	tonnes
1	0.91
2	1.81
3	2.72
4	3.63
5	4.54
10	9.07
20	18.14
50	45.36
75	68.04
100	90.72

Tonnes to tons

tonnes	UK tons	US tons
1	0.98	1.10
2	1.97	2.20
3	2.95	3.30
4	3.94	4.40
5	4.92	5.50
10	9.84	11.02
20	19.68	22.05
50	49.21	55.11
75	73.82	82.67
100	98.42	110.23

UK tons to US tons

UK tons	US tons
1	1.12
2	2.24
3	3.36
4	4.48
5	5.60
10	11.20
20	22.40
50	56.00
75	83.99
100	111.99

US tons to UK tons

US tons	UK tons
1	0.89
2	1.79
3	2.68
4	3.57
5	4.46
10	8.93
20	17.86
50	44.64
75	66.96
100	89.29

TYRE PRESSURE

1 pound per square inch = 0.070307 kilogram per square centimetre.

lb per sq in	kg per sq cm	lb per sq in	kg per sq cm
10	0.70	26	1.83
15	1.05	28	1.97
20	1.41	30	2.11
24	1.69	40	2.81

TEMPERATURE

Temperature conversion

Carry out operations in sequence.

To convert	To	Equation
°Fahrenheit	°Celsius[1]	−32, ×5, ÷9
°Fahrenheit	°Rankine	+459.67
°Fahrenheit	°Réaumur	−32, ×4, ÷9
°Celsius[1]	°Fahrenheit	×9, ÷5, +32
°Celsius[1]	Kelvin	+273.15
°Celsius[1]	°Réaumur	×4, ÷5
Kelvin	°Celsius[1]	−273.15
°Rankine	°Fahrenheit	−459.67
°Réaumur	°Fahrenheit	×9, ÷ 4, +32
°Réaumur	°Celsius[1]	×5, ÷4

[1] *Celsius also known as Centigrade.*

Fahrenheit to Celsius (Centigrade)

°F	°C	°F	°C	°F	°C	°F	°C
1	−17.2	31	−0.5	61	16.1	91	32.8
2	−16.7	32	0.0	62	16.7	92	33.3
3	−16.1	33	0.6	63	17.2	93	33.9
4	−15.6	34	1.1	64	17.8	94	34.4
5	−15.0	35	1.7	65	18.3	95	35.0
6	−14.4	36	2.2	66	18.9	96	35.6
7	−13.9	37	2.8	67	19.4	97	36.1
8	−13.3	38	3.3	68	20.0	98	36.7
9	−12.8	39	3.9	69	20.6	99	37.2
10	−12.2	40	4.4	70	21.1	100	37.8
11	−11.6	41	5.0	71	21.7	101	38.3
12	−11.1	42	5.6	72	22.2	102	38.9
13	−10.6	43	6.1	73	22.8	103	39.4
14	−10.0	44	6.7	74	23.3	104	40.0
15	−9.4	45	7.2	75	23.9	105	40.6
16	−8.9	46	7.8	76	24.4	106	41.1
17	−8.3	47	8.3	77	25.0	107	41.7
18	−7.8	48	8.9	78	25.6	108	42.2
19	−7.2	49	9.4	79	26.1	109	42.8
20	−6.7	50	10.0	80	26.7	110	43.3
21	−6.1	51	10.6	81	27.2	111	43.9
22	−5.6	52	11.1	82	27.8	112	44.4
23	−5.0	53	11.7	83	28.3	113	45.0
24	−4.4	54	12.2	84	28.9	114	45.6
25	−3.9	55	12.8	85	29.4	115	46.1
26	−3.3	56	13.3	86	30.0	116	46.7
27	−2.8	57	13.9	87	30.6	117	47.2
28	−2.2	58	14.4	88	31.1	118	47.8
29	−1.7	59	15.0	89	31.7	119	48.3
30	−1.1	60	15.6	90	32.2	120	48.9

°F	°C	°F	°C	°F	°C	°F	°C
121	49.4	144	62.2	167	75.0	190	87.8
122	50.0	145	62.8	168	75.6	191	88.3
123	50.6	146	63.3	169	76.1	192	88.8
124	51.1	147	63.9	170	76.7	193	89.4
125	51.7	148	64.4	171	77.2	194	90.0
126	52.2	149	65.0	172	77.8	195	90.6
127	52.8	150	65.6	173	78.3	196	91.1
128	53.3	151	66.1	174	78.9	197	91.7
129	53.9	152	66.7	175	79.4	198	92.2
130	54.4	153	67.2	176	80.0	199	92.8
131	55.0	154	67.8	177	80.6	200	93.3
132	55.6	155	68.3	178	81.1	201	93.9
133	56.1	156	68.9	179	81.7	202	94.4
134	56.7	157	69.4	180	82.2	203	95.0
135	57.2	158	70.0	181	82.8	204	95.6
136	57.8	159	70.6	182	83.3	205	96.1
137	58.3	160	71.1	183	83.9	206	96.7
138	58.9	161	71.7	184	84.4	207	97.2
139	59.4	162	72.2	185	85.0	208	97.8
140	60.0	163	72.8	186	85.6	209	98.3
141	60.6	164	73.3	187	86.1	210	98.9
142	61.1	165	73.9	188	86.7	211	99.4
143	61.7	166	74.4	189	87.2	212	100.0

Celsius (Centigrade) to Fahrenheit

°C	°F	°C	°F	°C	°F	°C	°F
1	33.8	26	78.8	51	123.8	76	168.8
2	35.6	27	80.6	52	125.6	77	170.6
3	37.4	28	82.4	53	127.4	78	172.4
4	39.2	29	84.2	54	129.2	79	174.2
5	41.0	30	86.0	55	131.0	80	176.0
6	42.8	31	87.8	56	132.8	81	177.8
7	44.6	32	89.6	57	134.6	82	179.6
8	46.4	33	91.4	58	136.4	83	181.4
9	48.2	34	93.2	59	138.2	84	183.2
10	50.0	35	95.0	60	140.0	85	185.0
11	51.8	36	96.8	61	141.8	86	186.8
12	53.6	37	98.6	62	143.6	87	188.6
13	55.4	38	100.4	63	145.4	88	190.4
14	57.2	39	102.2	64	147.2	89	192.2
15	59.0	40	104.0	65	149.0	90	194.0
16	60.8	41	105.8	66	150.8	91	195.8
17	62.6	42	107.6	67	152.6	92	197.6
18	64.4	43	109.4	68	154.4	93	199.4
19	66.2	44	111.2	69	156.2	94	201.2
20	68.0	45	113.0	70	158.0	95	203.0
21	69.8	46	114.8	71	159.8	96	204.8
22	71.6	47	116.6	72	161.6	97	206.6
23	73.4	48	118.4	73	163.4	98	208.4
24	75.2	49	120.2	74	165.2	99	210.2
25	77.0	50	122.0	75	167.0	100	212.0

ASTRONOMICAL MEASUREMENTS

1 astronomical unit (AU) = 149 598 073 kilometres = 92 955 933 miles[1]
1 light year = 9 460 753 090 819 kilometres = 5 878 639 427 505 miles
1 parsec = 30 856 780 000 000 kilometres = 19 173 514 177 205 miles

[1] *The astronomical unit is equivalent to the mean distance between the Sun and the Earth.*

BREWING MEASUREMENTS

4.5 gallons = 1 pin
2 pins = 9 gallons = 1 firkin
4 firkins = 1 barrel = 36 gallons

6 firkins = 1 hogshead = 54 gallons
4 hogsheads = 1 tun

CLOTH MEASUREMENTS

1 ell = 45 inches

1 bolt = 120 feet = 32 ells

CRUDE OIL MEASUREMENTS (PETROLEUM)

1 barrel = 35 UK gallons = 42 US gallons

HORSES MEASUREMENTS

The height of horses is measured in hands.

1 hand = 4 inches = 10 centimetres

NAUTICAL MEASUREMENTS

1 span = 9 inches = 23 centimetres
8 spans = 1 fathom = 6 feet
1 cable's length = $^1/_{10}$ nautical mile
1 nautical mile (old) = 6 080 feet
1 nautical mile (international) = 6 076.1 feet = 1.151 statute mile = 1 852 metres[1]
60 nautical mile = 1 degree
3 nautical mile = 1 league (nautical)
1 knot = 1 nautical mile per hour
1 ton (shipping) = 42 cubic feet
1 ton (displacement) = 35 cubic feet
1 ton (register) = 100 cubic feet

[1] *1 kilometre = 0.54 nautical miles.*

PRINTING MEASUREMENTS

1 point = 0.3515 millimetres
1 pica = 4.2175 millimetres
1 pica = 12 points

TIMBER MEASUREMENTS

1 000 millisteres = 1 stere = 1 cubic metre
1 board foot = 144 cubic inches (12 ×12 ×1 inches)
1 cord foot = 16 cubic feet
1 cord = 8 cord feet
1 hoppus foot = 4/π cubic feet (round timber)
1 Petrograd standard = 165 cubic feet

COMPUTER MEMORY SIZES

1 byte = 8 bits
1 kilobyte (KB) = 1 024 bytes
1 megabyte (MB) = 1 024 kilobytes = 1 048 576 bytes
1 gigabyte (GB) = 1 024 megabytes = 1 048 576 kilobytes = 1 073 741 824 bytes

CLOTHING SIZES

Size equivalents are approximate, and may display some variation between manufacturers.

Women's suits/dresses

UK	USA	UK/continent	UK	USA	UK/continent
8	6	36	18	16	46
10	8	38	20	18	48
12	10	40	22	20	50
14	12	42	24	22	52
16	14	44			

Adults' shoes – women

UK	USA	UK/continent
3	4½	36
3½	5	37
4	5½	37
4½	6	38
5	6½	38
5½	7	39
6	7½	39
6½	8	40
7	8½	41
7½	9	42

Adults' shoes – men

UK	USA	UK/continent
6½	7	40
7	7½	41
7½	8	41
8	8½	42
8½	9	43
9	9½	43
9½	10	44
10	10½	44
10½	11	45
11	11½	45

Children's shoes

UK/USA	UK/continent	UK/USA	UK/continent
0	15	7	24
½	16	8	25
1	17	8½	26
2	18	9	27
3	19	10	28
4	20	11	29
4½	21	12	30
5	22	12½	31
6	23	13	32

Women's hosiery

UK/USA	continent	UK/USA	continent
8	0	9½	3
8½	1	10	4
9	2	10½	5

Men's suits and overcoats

UK/USA	continent	UK/USA	continent
36	46	42	52
38	48	44	54
40	50	46	56

Men's socks

UK/USA	continent	UK/USA	continent
9½	38–39	11	41–42
10	39–40	11½	42–43
10½	40–41		

Men's shirts

UK/USA	UK/continent	UK/USA	UK/continent
12	30–31	15	38
12½	32	15½	39–40
13	33	16	41
13½	34–35	16½	42
14	36	17	43
14½	37	17½	44–45

EGG SIZES

There are four weight grades for Class A eggs ('fresh eggs') as follows:

XL	Very large (73g and above)	M	Medium (53g–63g)
L	Large (63g–73g)	S	Small (under 53g)

Egg Science

Dr Charles Williams of the School of Physics at the University of Exeter has worked out a scientific formula to calculate the exact cooking time needed to produce a perfect soft-boiled egg. His investigation concluded that the equation is:

$$t = aM^{2/3}\log_e \left[2 \times \frac{(T_{egg} - T_{water})}{(T_{yolk} - T_{water})} \right]$$

where: t is the total cooking time in minutes;
a is a constant which depends on the egg's specific heat capacity and thermal conductivity (use $a = 16$ s g$^{-2/3}$ for eggs that are a week or two old – very fresh eggs will need a higher value, old eggs may need a lower value);
M is the mass of the egg in grams;
T_{egg} is the temperature in °C of the egg at the beginning;
T_{yolk} is the temperature in °C at which the egg is ready to be eaten (for soft-boiled eggs use 45°C);
T_{water} is the temperature in °C of the boiling water.

PAPER SIZES

All sizes in these series have sides in the proportion of $1:\sqrt{2}$.

A series Used for writing paper, books and magazines.

	mm	in		mm	in
A0	841×1 189	33.11×46.81	A6	105×148	4.13×5.83
A1	594×841	23.39×33.11	A7	74×105	2.91×4.13
A2	420×594	16.54×23.39	A8	52×74	2.05×2.91
A3	297×420	11.69×16.54	A9	37×52	1.46×2.05
A4	210×297	8.27×11.69	A10	26×37	1.02×1.46
A5	148×210	5.83×8.27			

B series Used for posters.

	mm	in		mm	in
B0	1 000×1 414	39.37×55.67	B6	125×176	4.92×6.93
B1	707×1 000	27.83×39.37	B7	88×125	3.46×4.02
B2	500×707	19.68×27.83	B8	62×88	2.44×3.46
B3	353×500	13.90×19.68	B9	44×62	1.73×2.44
B4	250×353	9.84×13.90	B10	31×44	1.22×1.73
B5	176×250	6.93×9.84			

C series Used for envelopes.

	mm	in		mm	in
C0	917×1 297	36.00×51.20	C6	114×162	4.50×6.40
C1	648×917	25.60×36.00	C7	81×114	3.19×4.50
C2	458×648	18.00×25.60	C8	57×81	2.24×3.19
C3	324×458	12.80×18.00	C9	40×57	1.57×2.24
C4	229×324	9.00×12.80	C10	28×40	1.10×1.57
C5	162×229	6.40×9.00			
DL	110×220	4.33×8.66			

Writing paper sizes

25 sheets = 1 quire
20 quires = 1 ream
500 sheets = 1 ream

PENCIL HARDNESS

Pencil lead classification uses *black*, abbreviated to B, to indicate softness in quality and darkness in use, and *hard*, abbreviated to H, to indicate durability in quality and faintness in use.

9H	HH or 2H	H	HB	B	BB or 2B	9B
extremely hard and faint	very hard	hard	hard black	black	very black	extremely soft and dark

INVENTIONS, DISCOVERIES AND FIRSTS

INVENTIONS, DISCOVERIES AND FIRSTS

Date	Invention, discovery or first
c.4000BC	**Lock** is invented in Mesopotamia.
c.3500BC	**Wheel** is invented in Mesopotamia.
c.3000BC	**Writing** (pictography) is invented in Egypt.
c.2500BC	**Soap** is invented in Sumer, Babylonia.
c.2250BC	**Maps** are invented in Mesopotamia.
245BC	**Gun** is invented by Ctesibius (fl.3c BC).
3c BC	**Cannon** is invented by Archimedes (c.287–212BC).
c.2c BC	**Parachute** is invented in China.
59BC	**Newspaper** is invented by Julius Caesar (100 or 102–44BC).
25BC	**Suspension bridge** is invented in China.
1c	**Discovery of magnetite** leads to the invention of the **compass** in China.
1c	**Concrete** is invented in Rome.
AD105	**Paper** is invented in China. **Parchment** had been invented by Eumenes II of Pergamon (died 159BC) in the 2c BC.
c.600	**Windmill** is invented in Syria.
725	**Mechanical clock** is invented in China.
c.10c	**Vaccination** is invented in Turkey and China.
c.980–1020	Coast of **America** is explored by first European, Leif Erikson (fl.1000).
1232	**Rocket** is invented by the Mongols in China.
c.1450	**Wooden printing press** is invented by Johannes Gutenberg (1400–68).
1513	**Pacific Ocean** is sighted by Vasco Nuñez de Balboa (1475–1519).
1519–22	First **circumnavigation of the world** by crew members of Ferdinand Magellan's (c.1480–1521) expedition.
1590	**Microscope** is invented by Zacharias Janssen (1580–1638).
1608	**Refractor telescope** is invented by Hans Lippershey (c.1570–c.1619).
1620	**Submarine** is invented by Cornelis Drebbel (c.1572–1633).
1628	**Blood circulation** is discovered by William Harvey (1578–1677).
1643	**Barometer** is invented by Evangelista Torricelli (1608–47).
1657	**Pendulum clock** is invented by Christiaan Huygens (1629–93).
1675	**Protozoa** are observed by Anton van Leeuwenhoek (1632–1723).
1675 or 1684	**Red corpuscles** are observed by Anton van Leeuwenhoek (1632–1723).
1677	**Spermatozoa** are observed by Anton van Leeuwenhoek (1632–1723).
1680	**Match** is invented by Robert Boyle (1627–91).
1698	**Steam engine** is invented by Thomas Savery (c.1650–1715); it is later refined by Thomas Newcomen (1663–1729) and James Watt (1736–1819).
1714	**Mercury thermometer** is invented by Daniel Fahrenheit (1686–1736). The **thermometer** itself had been invented by Ctesibius (fl.3c BC) in the 3c BC.
1718	**Machine gun** is invented by James Puckle (dates unknown).
1720	**Pianoforte** is invented by Bartolomeo Cristofori (1655–1731).
1735	**Chronometer** is invented by John Harrison (1693–1776).
1751	**Nickel** is discovered by Baron Axel Fredrik Cronstedt (1722–65).
1766	**Existence of carbon dioxide** and **hydrogen** in atmospheric air is demonstrated by Henry Cavendish (1731–1810).
1771	**Fluorine** is discovered by Carl Wilhelm Scheele (1742–86).
1772	**Nitrogen** is discovered by Daniel Rutherford (1749–1819).
1774	**Oxygen** is discovered by Joseph Priestley (1733–1804).
1774	**Chlorine** is discovered by Carl Wilhelm Scheele (1742–86).
1776	**Nitrous oxide** (laughing gas) is discovered by Joseph Priestley (1733–1804). Its analgesic and laughter-provoking effects are later discovered by Humphry Davy (1778–1829).

Date	Invention, discovery or first
1783	**Balloon** able to carry human passengers is invented by Jacques (1745–99) and Joseph (1740–1810) Montgolfier.
1789	**Uranium** is discovered by Martin Heinrich Klaproth (1743–1817).
1789	**Titanium** is discovered by William Gregor (1761–1817).
1795	**Pencil** is invented by Nicholas Jacques Conté (1755–1805).
1796	**Smallpox vaccination** is discovered by Edward Jenner (1749–1823).
1800	**Electric battery** is invented by Alessandro Volta (1745–1827).
1804	**Railed locomotive** is invented by Richard Trevithick (1771–1833).
1807	**Potassium** and **sodium** are discovered by Humphry Davy (1778–1829).
1808	**Barium** and **calcium** are discovered by Humphry Davy (1778–1829).
1811	**Iodine** is discovered by Bernard Courtois (1777–1838).
1816	**Photography** (on metal) is invented by Nicéphore Niepce (1765–1833). In 1838 William Henry Fox Talbot (1800–77) invents photography on paper. Colour photography is invented by James Clerk Maxwell (1831–79) in 1861.
1817	**Lithium** is discovered by Johan August Arfvedson (1792–1841).
1823	**Silicon** is discovered by Jöns Jacob Berzelius (1779–1848).
1828	**Aluminium** is discovered by Friedrich Wöhler (1800–82).
1829	**Magnesium** is discovered by Antoine Alexandre Brutus Bussy (1794–1882).
1829	A basic **typewriter**, called a typographer, is invented by William Burt (1792–1858). The first practical working typewriter was patented in 1868 by Christopher Sholes (1819–90). The electric typewriter was invented by Thomas Alva Edison (1847–1931) in 1872.
1835	**'Difference engine'**, considered to be the first computer, is invented by Charles Babbage (1791–1871).
1835	**Revolver** is invented by Samuel Colt (1814–62).
1837	**Telegraph code** is invented by Samuel Morse (1791–1872).
1839–40	**Bicycle** is invented by Kirkpatrick Macmillan (1813–78).
c.1840	**General anaesthetic** is invented; priority is claimed by Crawford Long (1815–78), Gardner Cotton (1814–98), Horace Wells (1815–48) and Charles Jackson (1805–80). **Local anaesthetic** had been described centuries before in *Natural History* by Pliny the Elder (AD23–79).
1844	**Ship with a metal hull and propeller** is built by Isambard Kingdom Brunel (1806–59).
1846	**Ether** is discovered by William Thomas Morton (1819–68).
1847	**Anaesthetic properties of chloroform** are discovered by James Young Simpson (1811–70).
1851	**Mechanical lift** is invented by Elisha G Otis (1811–61).
1855	**Cellular division** is discovered by Rudolph Virchow (1821–1902).
1858	**Theory of evolution** is presented by Charles Darwin (1809–82).
1859	Synthesization of **aspirin** by Hermann Kolbe (1818–84). Aspirin is introduced into medicine by Felix Hoffmann (1868–1946) in 1899.
1863	**Pasteurization** is invented by Louis Pasteur (1822–95).
1865	**Heredity** is discovered by Gregor Johann Mendel (1822–84).
1865	**Antisepsis** is developed by Joseph Lister (1827–1912).
1866	**Dynamite** is invented by Alfred Nobel (1833–96).
1868	**Plastics** are invented by John Wesley Hyatt (1837–1920).
1870	**DC electric motor** is invented by Zenobe Gramme (1826–1901).
1875	**Fertilization** is discovered by Oskar Hertwig (1849–1922).
1876	**Telephone** is invented by Alexander Graham Bell (1847–1922).
1877	**Phonograph** and the **gramophone** are invented by Thomas Alva Edison (1847–1931).
1879	**Electric light bulb** is invented by Thomas Alva Edison (1847–1931).
1884	First practical working **fountain pen** is patented by Lewis Waterman (1837–1901). It is not until 1938 that Laszlo Biró (1899–1985) invents the **ballpoint pen**.

Date	Invention, discovery or first
1885	**Car** is built using a high-speed internal combustion engine by Gottlieb Daimler (1834–1900).
1885	**Rabies vaccination** is pioneered by Louis Pasteur (1822–95).
1885	**Motorcycle** is invented by Gottlieb Daimler (1834–1900).
1886	**Petrol engine** is pioneered by Karl Benz (1844–1929).
1887	**Contact lenses** are invented by Adolph E Fick (1829–1901).
1888	**Chromosomes** are discovered by Thomas Hunt Morgan (1866–1945).
1888	**Radio telegraphy** is invented by Heinrich Hertz (1857–94).
1888	**AC electric motor** is invented by Nikola Tesla (1856–1943).
1889	**Photographic film** is invented by George Eastman (1854–1932).
1892	**Diesel engine** is invented by Rudolf Diesel (1858–1913).
1892	**X-rays** are discovered by Heinrich Hertz (1857–94). Their properties are discovered by Wilhelm Konrad von Röntgen (1845–1923) in 1895.
1895	**Helium** is discovered by William Ramsay (1852–1916).
1895	**Cinema** is pioneered by Auguste (1862–1954) and Louis (1865–1948) Lumière.
1895	**Safety razor** is invented by King Camp Gillette (1855–1932). The **electric razor** was invented by Jacob Schick (1878–1937) in 1928.
1898	**Radium** is discovered by Marie (1867–1934) and Pierre (1859–1906) Curie.
1898	**Neon** is discovered by William Ramsay (1852–1916) and Morris William Travers (1872–1961).
1900	**Rigid airship** is invented by Graf Ferdinand von Zeppelin (1838–1917).
1901	**Adrenaline** is discovered by Jokichi Takamine (1854–1922) based on work by Edward Sharpey-Schafer (1850–1935) and George Oliver (1841–1915).
1901	**Blood groups** A, O, B and AB are discovered by Karl Landsteiner (1868–1943).
1901	**Radio** (transatlantic) is invented by Guglielmo Marconi (1874–1937).
1903	**Aeroplane** is invented by Orville (1871–1948) and Wilbur (1867–1912) Wright.
1906	**Necessity of vitamins** in diet is demonstrated by Sir Frederick Gowland Hopkins (1861–1947).
1907	Electric **washing machine** is invented by Hurley Machine Co.
1909	**North Pole** is reached by Robert Edwin Peary (1856–1920).
1909	First **cross-Channel flight** is made by Louis Blériot (1872–1936).
1911	**South Pole** is reached by Roald Amundsen (1872–1928).
1919	First **nonstop transatlantic flight** is made by John Alcock (1892–1919) and Arthur Whitten Brown (1886–1948).
1921	**Insulin** is isolated by Frederick Grant Banting (1891–1941), Charles Herbert Best (1899–1978) and John James McLeod (1876–1935).
1926	**Television** is invented by John Logie Baird (1888–1946). Peter Goldmark (1906–77) went on to invent **colour television** in 1940.
1927	First **solo transatlantic flight** is made by Charles Lindbergh (1902–74). The first solo transatlantic flight by a woman was made by Amelia Earhart (1897–1937) in 1932.
1928	**Turbojet** is invented by Frank Whittle (1907–96).
1928	**Penicillin** is discovered by Alexander Fleming (1881–1955).
1933	First **solo circumnavigation of the globe by aeroplane** is made by Wiley Post (1900–35).
1935	**Sulphonamides** (the first **antibiotics**) are discovered by Gerhard (Johannes Paul) Domagk (1895–1964).
1937	**Nylon** is invented by Wallace H Carothers (1896–1937).
1938	**Xerography** is invented by Chester Carlson (1906–68).
1939–45	**Atomic bomb** is invented by Otto Frisch (1904–79).
1940	**Plutonium** is discovered by Glenn Theodore Seaborg (1912–99), Edwin Mattison McMillan (1907–91) and others.
1945	**Microwave oven** is invented by Percy L Spencer (1894–1970).
1947	**Polaroid camera** is invented by Edwin Land (1909–91).
1947	First **piloted supersonic flight** is made by Charles E Yeager (1923–).

Date	Invention, discovery or first
1948	Transistor is invented by John Bardeen (1908–91).
1949	First nonstop circumnavigation of the globe by aeroplane is made by a US B-50 Superfortress and crew of 15 in 94 hours.
1950	Contraceptive pill is invented by Gregor Pincus (1903–67) and others.
1952	Chemical regulation by genes is discovered by Jacques Monod (1910–76) and Edwin Joseph Cohn (1892–1953).
1953	Structure of DNA is unravelled by Francis Crick (1916–2004) and James D Watson (1928–).
1953	First people to reach the summit of Mt Everest are Edmund Hillary (1919–) and Tenzing Norgay (1914–86).
1955	Hovercraft is invented by Christopher Cockerell (1910–99).
1956	Video recorder is invented by Ampex Co.
1957	First satellite to orbit the Earth, Sputnik 1, is launched by the USSR.
1958	Microchip is invented by Jack Kilby (1923–2005).
1960	The first working laser is invented by Theodore Maiman (1927–); the laser was patented by Arthur L Schawlow (1921–99) and Charles H Townes (1915–).
1961	First human being in space as Yuri Gagarin (1934–68) makes one orbit of the Earth.
1961	Silicon chip is invented by Texas Instruments.
1969	First human beings to walk on the moon are Neil Armstrong (1930–) and Buzz Aldrin (1930–) of the Apollo 11 mission.
1971	Microprocessor is invented by Marcian E Hoff (1937–).
1979	Compact disc is invented by the Philips and Sony companies.
1981	AIDS (Acquired Immune Deficiency Syndrome) is identified by scientists in Los Angeles.
1981	Space shuttle flights are commenced by the USA.
1983	HIV (the Human Immuno-Deficiency Virus) is isolated by Luc Montagnier (1932–) and others.
1989	World Wide Web is invented by Tim Berners-Lee (1955–).
1990	Hubble Space Telescope (the first optical space-based telescope) is launched by NASA.
1999	First nonstop circumnavigation of the globe by balloon is made by Bertrand Piccard (1958–) and Brian Jones (1947–).
2001	First space tourist visits the International Space Station.
2003	Scientists sequencing the human genome announce its completion.
2004	Scientists in Korea announced the first successful, independently verified cloning of human embryos.
2005	First solo circumnavigation of the globe by aeroplane without refuelling is made by Steve Fossett (1944–) in the *Virgin Global Flyer*.

See also Space Firsts in **Astronomy and Space Exploration**.

Interesting Inventions

Other inventions that we now take for granted include the *aerosol* (Erik Rotheim, 1926), the *burglar alarm* (Edwin T Holmes, 1858), *chocolate* (François-Louis Cailler, 1819), the *credit card* (Ralph Scheider, 1950), the *crossword* (Arthur Wynne, 1913), the *automatic dishwasher* (Mrs W A Cockran, 1889), the *escalator* (Jesse W Reno, 1892), *instant coffee* (Nestlé, 1937), *jeans* (Levi-Strauss, 1872), the *lawnmower* (Edwin Beard Budding, 1830), the *paperclip* (Johann Vaaler, 1900), the *safety pin* (Walter Hunt, 1849), the *toaster* (Charles Strite, 1927), *automatic traffic lights* (Alfred Benesch, 1914) and the *zip* (Whitcomb L Judson, 1893).

ARCHITECTURE AND ENGINEERING

TALLEST BUILDINGS

The list includes only completed structures and buildings; proposed projects or those under construction have been excluded.

Tallest structures

Name	Location	Height	Date completed
KVLY-TV Mast	Blanchard, North Dakota, USA	629m/2 063ft	1963
CN Tower	Toronto, Canada	553m/1 815ft	1975

Tallest inhabited buildings

Name	Location	Height	Date completed
Taipei 101	Taipei, Taiwan	508m/1 667ft	2003
Petronas I	Kuala Lumpur, Malaysia	452m/1 483ft	1998
Petronas II	Kuala Lumpur, Malaysia	452m/1 483ft	1998
Sears Tower	Chicago, USA	442m/1 450ft	1974
Jin Mao Building	Shanghai, China	421m/1 381ft	1998
Two International Finance Centre	Hong Kong, China	415m/1 361ft	2003
CITIC Plaza	Guangzhou, China	391m/1 282ft	1997
Shun Hing Square	Shenzhen, China	384m/1 260ft	1996
Empire State Building	New York City, USA	381m/1 250ft	1931
Central Plaza	Hong Kong, China	374m/1 227ft	1992
Bank of China	Hong Kong, China	367m/1 204ft	1990
Emirates Office Tower	Dubai, United Arab Emirates	355m/1 164ft	2000
Tuntex Sky Tower	Kaohsiung, Taiwan	348m/1 141ft	1997
Aon Center	Chicago, USA	346m/1 135ft	1973

Towering Craziness

The CN Tower has had its fair share of wild and wacky climbers. Records have been set for carrying a piano, lugging a 91kg/200lb pumpkin, driving a motorbike and bouncing on a pogo stick up the Tower's many stairs. World records have also been set for the descent, notably in 1984 when a stuntman tumbled his way to the bottom, falling down the 1 760-odd steps in just under two hours.

LONGEST BRIDGES

Figures refer to main unsupported spans. All bridges are of the suspension type. The list includes only completed bridges; proposed projects or those under construction have been excluded.

Name	Location	Length	Date completed
Akashi-Kaikyo	Honshu–Shikoku, Japan	1 990m/6 527ft	1998
Great Belt East (Storebaelt)	Halsskov–Kudshoved, Denmark	1 624m/5 327ft	1998
Runyang South	Jiangsu Province, China	1 490m/4 888ft	2005
Humber Estuary	Hull–Grimsby, UK	1 410m/4 625ft	1981
Jiangyin	Jiangsu Province, China	1 385m/4 543ft	1999

Name	Location	Length	Date completed
Tsing Ma	Hong Kong, China	1 377m/4 516ft	1997
Verrazano Narrows	Brooklyn–Staten Island, New York Harbour, USA	1 298m/4 257ft	1964
Golden Gate	San Francisco, California, USA	1 280m/4 198ft	1937
Höga Kusten	Kramfors, Sweden	1 210m/3 969ft	1997
Mackinac	Mackinaw City–St Ignace, Michigan, USA	1 158m/3 799ft	1957
Minami Bisan-Seto	Honshu–Shikoku, Japan	1 100m/3 608ft	1988
Bosporus II	Istanbul, Turkey	1 090m/3 575ft	1988
Bosporus	Istanbul, Turkey	1 074m/3 523ft	1973
George Washington	Hudson River, New York City, USA	1 067m/3 500ft	1931
Kurushima-3	Onomichi–Imabari, Japan	1 030m/3 378ft	1999
Kurushima-2	Onomichi–Imabari, Japan	1 020m/3 346ft	1999
Ponte 25 de Abril	Lisbon, Portugal	1 013m/3 323ft	1966
Forth Road	Edinburgh, UK	1 006m/3 300ft	1964
Kita Bisan-seto	Kojima–Sakaide, Japan	990m/3 247ft	1988
Severn	Bristol, UK	988m/3 240ft	1966
Yichang	Hubei Province, China	960m/3 149ft	2001

Sky Bridge

In Dec 2004 the Millau Viaduct, the world's highest road bridge, was opened to traffic. Designed by British architect Lord Foster, the bridge spans the River Tarn in southern France. It is 2 460m/8 070ft long and the tallest pylon is 343m/1 125ft high; the road deck itself is at 270m/885ft.

LONGEST TUNNELS

The list includes only completed tunnels; proposed projects or those under construction have been excluded.

Name	Location	Length	Type	Date completed
Seikan	Honshu–Hokkaido, Japan	53.9km/33.4mi	rail	1985
Channel	Cheriton, England–Coquelles, France	50.4km/31.3mi	rail	1994
Moscow subway	Moscow, Russia	37.9km/23.5mi	rail	1990
Northern tube line	London, UK	27.8km/17.2mi	rail	1926
Iwate Ichinohe	Tanigawa Mountains, Japan	25.8km/16.0mi	rail	2002
Laerdal	Laerdal–Aurland, Norway	24.5km/15.2mi	road	2000
Dai-shimizu	Honshu, Japan	22.2km/13.8mi	rail	1979
Simplon I & II	Brigue, Switzerland–Iselle, Italy	19.8km/12.3mi	rail	1906, 1922
Vereina	Klosters–Sagliains, Switzerland	19.1km/11.8mi	rail	1999
Kanmon	Kanmon Strait, Japan	18.7km/11.6mi	rail	1975
Apennine	Vernio, Italy	18.5km/11.5mi	rail	1934
Qinling I-II	Qinling Mountains, China	18.5km/11.5mi	rail	2002
St Gotthard (road)	Göschenen, Switzerland–Airolo, Italy	16.3km/10.1mi	road	1980
Rokko	Osaka–Kōbe, Japan	16.1km/10.0mi	rail	1972
Furka Base	Andermatt–Brig, Switzerland	15.4km/9.5mi	rail	1982
Haruna	Gunma Prefecture, Japan	15.4km/9.5mi	rail	1982
Severomuyskiy	Baikal–Amur, Russia	15.3km/9.4mi	rail	2001
Gorigamine	Takasaki–Nagano, Japan	15.2km/9.4mi	rail	1997
Monte Santomarco	Paola–Cosenza, Italy	15.0km/9.3mi	rail	1987

St Gotthard (rail)	Göschenen, Switzerland–Airolo, Italy	14.9km/9.2mi	rail	1882
Nakayama	Nakayama Pass, Hokkaido, Japan	14.9km/9.2mi	rail	1982
Mount MacDonald	British Columbia, Canada	14.7km/9.1mi	rail	1989
Lotschberg	Thun–Brig, Switzerland	14.6km/9.0mi	rail	1913
Romeriksporten	Oslo–Gardermoen airport, Norway	14.6km/9.1mi	rail	1999
Dayaoshan	Nanling Mountains, China	14.3km/8.9mi	rail	1987
Arlberg	Austrian Alps	14.0km/8.7mi	road	1979
Hokuriku	Sea of Japan coast, Japan	13.8km/8.6mi	rail	1962
Frejus (Mont Cenis)	Modane, France–Bardonecchia, Italy	13.5km/8.4mi	rail	1871
Shin shimizu	Mikuni Mountains, Japan	13.5km/8.4mi	rail	1961

HIGHEST DAMS

The list includes only completed dams; proposed projects or those under construction have been excluded.

Name	River, country	Structural height	Date completed
Rogun	Vakhsh, Tajikistan	335m/1 099ft	1985
Nurek	Vakhsh, Tajikistan	300m/984ft	1980
Grande Dixence	Dixence, Switzerland	285m/935ft	1962
Inguri	Inguri, Georgia	272m/892ft	1984
Vaiont	Vaiont, Italy	262m/859ft	1961
Manuel M Torres	Grijalva, Mexico	261m/856ft	1981
Alvaro Obregon	Tenasco, Mexico	260m/853ft	1946
Mauvoisin	Drance de Bagnes, Switzerland	250m/820ft	1957
Alberto Lleras	Guavio, Colombia	243m/797ft	1989
Mica	Columbia, Canada	243m/797ft	1972
Sayano-Shushensk	Yenisei, Russia	242m/794ft	1980
Ertan	Yangtze/Yalong, China	240m/787ft	1999
La Esmeralda	Batá, Colombia	237m/777ft	1975

STIRLING PRIZE

The Stirling Prize of the Royal Institute of British Architects (RIBA) is awarded annually to the architects of the building which is judged to have made the greatest contribution to British architecture in the foregoing year. The building must be sited within the European Union and the architects must be RIBA members. The prize is named after the architect Sir James Stirling (1926–92).

Date	Building	Architects
1996	University of Salford Centenary Building, Salford, UK	Hodder Associates
1997	Stuttgart Music School, Stuttgart, Germany	James Stirling, Michael Wilford and Partners
1998	American Air Museum, Duxford, UK	Foster and Partners
1999	Natwest Media Centre, Lord's Cricket Ground, London, UK	Future Systems
2000	Peckham Library, London, UK	Alsop Architects
2001	Magna Centre, Rotherham, UK	Wilkinson Eyre Architects
2002	Millennium Bridge, Gateshead, UK	Wilkinson Eyre Architects
2003	Laban Centre, London, UK	Herzog and de Meuron
2004	30 St Mary Axe ('the Gherkin'), London, UK	Foster and Partners
2005	Scottish Parliament Building	EMBT/RMJM Ltd

SOCIETY AND LEARNING

LIBERAL ARTS

In the Middle Ages, the *trivium* and *quadrivium* were studied.

Trivium	Quadrivium
grammar	arithmetic
rhetoric	geometry
logic	astronomy
	music

OXFORD UNIVERSITY COLLEGES

Oxford University has 39 official colleges and seven permanent private halls.

College	Date founded	College	Date founded
All Souls College	1438	Oriel College	1326
Balliol College	1263	Pembroke College	1624
Blackfriars Hall[3]	1994	Queen's College, The	1341
Brasenose College	1509	Regent's Park College	1810
Campion Hall	1896	St Anne's College	1952
Christ Church	1546	St Antony's College[1]	1950
Corpus Christi College	1517	St Benet's Hall	1897
Exeter College	1314	St Catherine's College	1962
Green College[1]	1979	St Cross College[1]	1965
Greyfriars Hall[3]	1957	St Edmund Hall	c.1278
Harris Manchester College[3]	1889	St Hilda's College[2]	1893
Hertford College	1282	St Hugh's College	1886
Jesus College	1571	St John's College	1555
Keble College	1870	St Peter's College	1929
Kellogg College[3]	1994	St Stephen's House	1876
Lady Margaret Hall	1878	Somerville College	1879
Linacre College[1]	1962	Templeton College[1]	1965
Lincoln College	1427	Trinity College	1555
Magdalen College	1448	University College	1249
Mansfield College	1886	Wadham College	1609
Merton College	1264	Wolfson College[1]	1965
New College	1379	Worcester College	1714
Nuffield College[1]	1937	Wycliffe Hall	1877

[1] *Graduates only.*

[2] *Women only.*

[3] *Date that Private Hall status was granted, or that the College or Hall joined the University; may have been established previously.*

Old Oxford

Oxford University is the oldest university in Britain, having its origins in informal groups of masters and students that gathered in Oxford in the 12c. The closure of the University of Paris to the English in 1167 accelerated Oxford's development. Cambridge is the second oldest university; its first college, Peterhouse, was founded in 1284.

CAMBRIDGE UNIVERSITY COLLEGES

Cambridge University has 31 official colleges and halls.

College	Date founded	College	Date founded
Christ's College	1505	Magdalene College	1428
Churchill College	1960	New Hall[2]	1954
Clare College	1326	Newnham College[2]	1871
Clare Hall[1]	1965	Pembroke College	1347
Corpus Christi College	1352	Peterhouse	1284
Darwin College[1]	1964	Queens' College	1448
Downing College	1800	Robinson College	1979
Emmanuel College	1584	St Catharine's College	1473
Fitzwilliam College	1966	St Edmund's College	1896
Girton College	1869	St John's College	1511
Gonville & Caius College	1348	Selwyn College	1882
Homerton College	1976	Sidney Sussex College	1596
Hughes Hall	1885	Trinity College	1546
Jesus College	1497	Trinity Hall	1350
King's College	1441	Wolfson College	1965
Lucy Cavendish College[2]	1965		

[1] Graduates only.   [2] Women only.

IVY LEAGUE

The Ivy League is a group of eight long-established universities, of particular academic and social prestige, in the north-eastern USA . The league was formally established in 1956.

Brown University

Columbia University

Cornell University

Dartmouth College

Harvard University

Princeton University

University of Pennsylvania

Yale University

SEVEN SISTERS COLLEGES

The Seven Sisters Colleges are a group of long-established, prestigious women's colleges (some now co-educational) in the north-eastern USA. The group was formally established in 1927.

Barnard College

Bryn Mawr College

Mt Holyoke College

Radcliffe College

Smith College

Vassar College

Wellesley College

PRESIDENTS OF THE ROYAL SOCIETY

The Royal Society was founded in 1660 and is the UK's foremost body for the encouragement of research and development in science, engineering and technology. Since the late 19c the president has been appointed for a five-year term. Names are listed in their original form, regardless of later knighthoods, peerages, etc.

Dates	Names	Dates	Names
1662–77	William, Viscount Brouncker	1680–2	Sir Christopher Wren
1677–80	Sir Joseph Williamson	1682–3	Sir John Hoskins

Dates	Names
1683–4	Sir Cyril Wyche
1684–6	Samuel Pepys
1686–9	John, Earl of Carbery
1689–90	Thomas, Earl of Pembroke
1690–5	Sir Robert Southwell
1695–8	Charles Montagu
1698–1703	John, Lord Somers
1703–27	Sir Isaac Newton
1727–41	Sir Hans Sloane
1741–52	Martin Folkes
1752–64	George, Earl of Macclesfield
1764–8	James, Earl of Morton
1768	James Burrow
1768–72	James West
1772–8	Sir John Pringle
1778–1820	Sir Joseph Banks
1820	William Hyde Wollaston
1820–7	Sir Humphry Davy
1827–30	Davies Gilbert
1830–8	HRH The Duke of Sussex
1838–48	Joshua Alwyne Compton, Marquess of Northampton
1848–54	William Parsons, Earl of Rosse
1854–8	John, Lord Wrottesley
1858–61	Sir Benjamin Collins Brodie
1861–71	Sir Edward Sabine
1871–3	Sir George Biddell Airy
1873–8	Sir Joseph Dalton Hooker
1878–83	William Spottiswoode
1883–5	Thomas Henry Huxley

Dates	Names
1885–90	Sir George Gabriel Stokes
1890–5	Lord Kelvin
1895–1900	Lord Lister
1900–5	Sir William Huggins
1905–8	John William Strutt, Lord Rayleigh
1908–13	Sir Archibald Geikie
1913–15	Sir William Crookes
1915–20	Sir Joseph John Thomson
1920–5	Sir Charles Scott Sherrington
1925–30	Ernest, Lord Rutherford of Nelson
1930–5	Sir Frederick Gowland Hopkins
1935–40	Sir William Henry Bragg
1940–5	Sir Henry Dale
1945–50	Sir Robert Robinson
1950 5	Edgar Douglas Adrian
1955–60	Sir Cyril Hinshelwood
1960–5	Sir Howard Florey
1965–70	Patrick Maynard Stuart Blackett
1970–5	Sir Alan Hodgkin
1975–80	Alexander Robertus Todd
1980–5	Sir Andrew Huxley
1985–90	George Porter, Lord Porter of Luddenham
1990–5	Sir Michael Atiyah
1995–2000	Sir Aaron Klug
2000–2005	Lord May of Oxford
2005–	Sir Martin Rees

RANKS OF THE ARISTOCRACY (UK)

king

prince

duke

marquess

earl

viscount

baron

ROYAL SUCCESSION (UK)

The Prince of Wales

Prince William of Wales

Prince Henry of Wales

The Duke of York

Princess Beatrice of York

Princess Eugenie of York

The Earl of Wessex

The Lady Louise Windsor

The Princess Royal

Peter Phillips

LITERATURE

POETS LAUREATE

The Poet Laureate is a poet appointed to a lifetime post in the royal household. He or she is required to compose poems for state occasions, etc. The date of appointment is given.

1617	Ben Jonson	1813	Robert Southey
1638	Sir William D'Avenant	1843	William Wordsworth
1668	John Dryden	1850	Alfred, Lord Tennyson
1689	Thomas Shadwell	1896	Alfred Austin
1692	Nahum Tate	1913	Robert Bridges
1715	Nicholas Rowe	1930	John Masefield
1718	Laurence Eusden	1968	Cecil Day-Lewis
1730	Colley Cibber	1972	Sir John Betjeman
1757	William Whitehead	1984	Ted Hughes
1785	Thomas Warton	1999	Andrew Motion
1790	Henry Pye		

CHILDREN'S LAUREATE

The title of Children's Laureate is awarded once every two years to an eminent writer or illustrator of children's books.

1999	Quentin Blake	2003	Michael Morpurgo
2001	Anne Fine	2005	Jacqueline Wilson

PLAYS OF SHAKESPEARE

William Shakespeare (1564–1616) was an English playwright and poet, born in Stratford-upon-Avon. He is considered to be the greatest English dramatist.

Title	Date	Category
The Two Gentlemen of Verona	1590–1	comedy
Henry VI Part One	1592	history
Henry VI Part Two	1592	history
Henry VI Part Three	1592	history
Titus Andronicus	1592	tragedy
Richard III	1592–3	history
The Taming of the Shrew	1593	comedy
The Comedy of Errors	1594	comedy
Love's Labour's Lost	1594–5	comedy
Richard II	1595	history
Romeo and Juliet	1595	tragedy
A Midsummer Night's Dream	1595	comedy
King John	1596	history
The Merchant of Venice	1596–7	comedy
Henry IV Part One	1596–7	history
The Merry Wives of Windsor	1597–8	comedy
Henry IV Part Two	1597–8	history
Much Ado About Nothing	1598	dark comedy
Henry V	1598–9	history

Title	Date	Category
Julius Caesar	1599	tragedy
As You Like It	1599–1600	comedy
Hamlet, Prince of Denmark	1600–1	tragedy
Twelfth Night	1601	comedy
Troilus and Cressida	1602	tragedy
Measure for Measure	1603	dark comedy
Othello	1603–4	tragedy
All's Well That Ends Well	1604–5	dark comedy
Timon of Athens	1605	romantic drama
The Tragedy of King Lear	1605–6	tragedy
Macbeth	1606	tragedy
Antony and Cleopatra	1606	tragedy
Pericles	1607	romance
Coriolanus	1608	tragedy
The Winter's Tale	1609	romance
Cymbeline	1610	comedy
The Tempest	1611	comedy
Henry VIII	1613	history

Writers on Shakespeare

'The remarkable thing about Shakespeare is that he is really very good – in spite of all the people who say he is very good.'
Robert Graves, 1964 attributed.

'I have tried lately to read Shakespeare, and found it so intolerably dull that it nauseated me.'
Charles Darwin, 1860 autobiography.

'Shakespeare one gets acquainted with without knowing how. It is part of an Englishman's constitution. His thoughts and beauties are so spread abroad that one touches them everywhere, one is intimate with him by instinct.'
Jane Austen, 1814 *Mansfield Park*, chapter 34.

NOBEL PRIZE FOR LITERATURE

Nobel Prizes were established by a bequest in the will of Alfred Nobel (1833–96) to honour 'those who, during the preceding year, shall have conferred the greatest benefit on mankind'. The Nobel Prize for Literature is awarded annually to a person who has 'produced in the field of literature the most outstanding work in an ideal direction'; first awarded in 1901.

1901	Sully Prudhomme	1909	Selma Lagerlöf
1902	Theodor Mommsen	1910	Paul Heyse
1903	Bjørnstjerne Bjørnson	1911	Maurice Maeterlinck
1904	Frédéric Mistral, José Echegaray	1912	Gerhart Hauptmann
1905	Henryk Sienkiewicz	1913	Rabindranath Tagore
1906	Giosuè Carducci	1914	*no award*
1907	Rudyard Kipling	1915	Romain Rolland
1908	Rudolf Eucken	1916	Verner von Heidenstam

1917	Karl Gjellerup, Henrik Pontoppidan
1918	*no award*
1919	Carl Spitteler
1920	Knut Hamsun
1921	Anatole France
1922	Jacinto Benavente
1923	William Butler Yeats
1924	Wladyslaw Reymont
1925	George Bernard Shaw
1926	Grazia Deledda
1927	Henri Bergson
1928	Sigrid Undset
1929	Thomas Mann
1930	Sinclair Lewis
1931	Erik Axel Karlfeldt
1932	John Galsworthy
1933	Ivan Bunin
1934	Luigi Pirandello
1935	*no award*
1936	Eugene O'Neill
1937	Roger Martin du Gard
1938	Pearl S Buck
1939	Frans Eemil Sillanpää
1940	*no award*
1941	*no award*
1942	*no award*
1943	*no award*
1944	Johannes V Jensen
1945	Gabriela Mistral
1946	Hermann Hesse
1947	André Gide
1948	Thomas Stearns Eliot
1949	William Faulkner
1950	Bertrand Russell
1951	Pär Lagerkvist
1952	François Mauriac
1953	Winston Churchill
1954	Ernest Hemingway
1955	Halldór Kiljan Laxness
1956	Juan Ramón Jiménez
1957	Albert Camus
1958	Boris Pasternak
1959	Salvatore Quasimodo
1960	Saint-John Perse
1961	Ivo Andric
1962	John Steinbeck
1963	Giorgos Seferis
1964	Jean-Paul Sartre *declined*
1965	Michail Sholokhov
1966	Samuel Agnon, Nelly Sachs
1967	Miguel Angel Asturias
1968	Yasunari Kawabata
1969	Samuel Beckett
1970	Alexander Solzhenitsyn
1971	Pablo Neruda
1972	Heinrich Böll
1973	Patrick White
1974	Eyvind Johnson, Harry Martinson
1975	Eugenio Montale
1976	Saul Bellow
1977	Vicente Aleixandre
1978	Isaac Bashevis Singer
1979	Odysseus Elytis
1980	Czeslaw Milosz
1981	Elias Canetti
1982	Gabriel García Márquez
1983	William Golding
1984	Jaroslav Seifert
1985	Claude Simon
1986	Wole Soyinka
1987	Joseph Brodsky
1988	Naguib Mahfouz
1989	Camilo José Cela
1990	Octavio Paz
1991	Nadine Gordimer
1992	Derek Walcott
1993	Toni Morrison
1994	Kenzaburo Oe
1995	Seamus Heaney
1996	Wislawa Szymborska
1997	Dario Fo
1998	José Saramago
1999	Günter Grass
2000	Gao Xingjian
2001	V S Naipaul
2002	Imre Kertész
2003	J M Coetzee
2004	Elfriede Jelinek
2005	Harold Pinter

No Thanks!

The French existentialist philosopher, dramatist and novelist Jean-Paul Sartre declined the Nobel Prize for Literature in 1964 on the grounds that he had 'always declined official honours'; he said that 'a writer should not allow himself to be turned into an institution'.

BOOKER PRIZE

Awarded for the year's best novel, and open to all citizens of Commonwealth countries or the Republic of Ireland. It was established in 1968 in the UK.

1969	P H Newby *Something to Answer For*	1989	Kazuo Ishiguro *The Remains of the Day*
1970	Bernice Rubens *The Elected Member*	1990	A S Byatt *Possession*
1971	V S Naipaul *In a Free State*	1991	Ben Okri *The Famished Road*
1972	John Berger *G*	1992	Michael Ondaatje *The English Patient* and Barry Unsworth *Sacred Hunger*
1973	J G Farrell *The Siege of Krishnapur*	1993	Roddy Doyle *Paddy Clarke, Ha Ha Ha*
1974	Nadine Gordimer *The Conservationist* and Stanley Middleton *Holiday*	1994	James Kelman *How Late It Was, How Late*
1975	Ruth Prawer Jhabvala *Heat and Dust*	1995	Pat Barker *The Ghost Road*
1976	David Storey *Saville*	1996	Graham Swift *Last Orders*
1977	Paul Scott *Staying On*	1997	Arundhati Roy *The God of Small Things*
1978	Iris Murdoch *The Sea, the Sea*	1998	Ian McEwan *Amsterdam*
1979	Penelope Fitzgerald *Offshore*	1999	J M Coetzee *Disgrace*
1980	William Golding *Rites of Passage*	2000	Margaret Atwood *The Blind Assassin*
1981	Salman Rushdie *Midnight's Children*	2001	Peter Carey *True History of the Kelly Gang*
1982	Thomas Keneally *Schindler's Ark*	2002	Yann Martel *Life of Pi*
1983	J M Coetzee *Life and Times of Michael K*	2003	D B C Pierre *Vernon God Little*
1984	Anita Brookner *Hotel du Lac*	2004	Alan Hollinghurst *The Line of Beauty*
1985	Keri Hulme *The Bone People*	2005	John Banville *The Sea*
1986	Kingsley Amis *The Old Devils*		
1987	Penelope Lively *Moon Tiger*		
1988	Peter Carey *Oscar and Lucinda*		

Booze and Curtains

When Kingsley Amis was asked what he intended to spend his prize money on, his answer was 'Booze, of course, and then curtains'.

BOOKER INTERNATIONAL PRIZE

Awarded to a living author of any nationality whose work is available in English. Established in 2005; awarded every two years.

2005   Ismail Kadaré (Albania)

ORANGE PRIZE FOR FICTION

Awarded for the year's best English-language novel by a female author. It was established in 1996 in reaction to the perceived male domination of other literary awards.

1996	Helen Dunmore *A Spell of Winter*	2001	Kate Grenville *The Idea of Perfection*
1997	Anne Michaels *Fugitive Pieces*	2002	Ann Patchett *Bel Canto*
1998	Carol Shields *Larry's Party*	2003	Valerie Martin *Property*
1999	Suzanne Berne *A Crime in the Neighborhood*	2004	Andrea Levy *Small Island*
2000	Linda Grant *When I Lived in Modern Times*	2005	Lionel Shriver *We Need To Talk About Kevin*

WHITBREAD BOOK AWARDS

Since its establishment in 1971 in the UK, prizes have been awarded in several varying categories. Today there are five: Novel, First Novel, Biography, Poetry and Children's Book. Since 1985, one book has been chosen from these winners to be Whitbread Book of the Year.

1985	Douglas Dunn *Elegies* (Poetry)	1995	Kate Atkinson *Behind the Scenes at the Museum* (First Novel)
1986	Kazuo Ishiguro *An Artist of the Floating World* (Novel)	1996	Seamus Heaney *The Spirit Level* (Poetry)
1987	Christopher Nolan *Under the Eye of the Clock* (Biography)	1997	Ted Hughes *Tales from Ovid* (Poetry)
1988	Paul Sayer *The Comforts of Madness* (First Novel)	1998	Ted Hughes *Birthday Letters* (Poetry)
		1999	Seamus Heaney *Beowulf* (Poetry)
1989	Richard Holmes *Coleridge: Early Visions* (Biography)	2000	Matthew Kneale *English Passengers* (Novel)
1990	Nicholas Mosley *Hopeful Monsters* (Novel)	2001	Philip Pullman *The Amber Spyglass* (Children's Book)
1991	John Richardson *A Life of Picasso* (Biography)	2002	Claire Tomalin *Samuel Pepys: The Unequalled Self* (Biography)
1992	Jeff Torrington *Swing Hammer Swing!* (First Novel)	2003	Mark Haddon *The Curious Incident of the Dog in the Night-time* (Novel)
1993	Joan Brady *Theory of War* (Novel)	2004	Andrea Levy *Small Island* (Novel)
1994	William Trevor *Felicia's Journey* (Novel)		

Lengthy Literature

The French novelist Marcel Proust wrote what is widely considered to be the world's longest novel, *À la recherche du temps perdu* ('Remembrance of Things Past'; published between 1913 and 1927). Guinness World Records® estimate that the novel, originally published in 13 volumes, contains a whopping 9 609 000 letters.

PRIX GONCOURT

The Académie Goncourt was founded in the will of Edmond de Goncourt (1822–96), to further the aims of the 'Brothers Goncourt' – Goncourt and his brother Jules (1830–70). Its purpose is to foster fiction with the annual Prix Goncourt for 'the best imaginary prose work of the year'; first awarded in France in 1903.

1903	John-Antoine Nau *Force ennemie*	1914	Adrien Bertrand *L'appel du sol*
1904	Léon Frapié *La maternelle*	1915	René Benjamin *Gaspard*
1905	Claude Farrère *Les civilisés*	1916	Henri Barbusse *Le feu*
1906	Jérôme et Jean Tharaud *Dingley, l'illustre écrivain*	1917	Henri Malherbe *La flamme au poing*
1907	Émile Moselly *Terres lorraines*	1918	Georges Duhamel *Civilisation*
1908	Francis de Miomandre *Écrit sur de l'eau*	1919	Marcel Proust *A l'ombre des jeunes filles en fleurs*
1909	Marius et Ary Leblond *En France*	1920	Ernest Pérochon *Nêne*
1910	Louis Pergaud *De Goupil à Margot*	1921	René Maran *Batouala*
1911	Alphonse de Châteaubriant *Monsieur des Lourdines*	1922	Henri Béraud *Le vitriol de lune*
		1923	Lucien Fabre *Rabevel ou le mal des ardents*
1912	André Savignon *Filles de la pluie*	1924	Thierry Sandre *Le chèvrefeuille*
1913	Marc Elder *Le peuple de la mer*	1925	Maurice Genevoix *Raboliot*

1926	Henry Deberly *Le supplice de Phèdre*	1965	Jacques Borel *L'adoration*
1927	Maurice Bedel *Jérôme, 60° latitude Nord*	1966	Edmonde Charles-Roux *Oublier Palerme*
1928	Maurice Constantin-Weyer *Un homme se penche sur son passé*	1967	André Pieyre de Mandiargues *La marge*
1929	Marcel Arland *L'ordre*	1968	Bernard Clavel *Les fruits de l'hiver*
1930	Henri Fauconnier *Malaisie*	1969	Félicien Marceau *Creezy*
1931	Jean Fayard *Mal d'amour*	1970	Michel Tournier *Le roi des aulnes*
1932	Guy Mazeline *Les loups*	1971	Jacques Laurent *Les bétises*
1933	André Malraux *La condition humaine*	1972	Jean Carrière *L'épervier de Maheux*
1934	Roger Vercel *Capitaine Conan*	1973	Jacques Chessex *L'ogre*
1935	Joseph Peyré *Sang et lumières*	1974	Pascal Laîné *La dentellière*
1936	Maxence Van der Meersch *L'empreinte du Dieu*	1975	Émile Ajar *La vie devant soi*
1937	Charles Plisnier *Faux passeports*	1976	Patrick Grainville *Les flamboyants*
1938	Henri Troyat *L'araigne*	1977	Didier Decoin *John l'Enfer*
1939	Philippe Hériat *Les enfants gâtés*	1978	Patrick Modiano *Rue des boutiques obscures*
1940	Francis Ambrière *Les grandes vacances*	1979	Antonine Maillet *Pélagie-la-Charrette*
1941	Henri Pourrat *Vent de mars*	1980	Yves Navarre *Le jardin d'acclimatation*
1942	Marc Bernard *Pareils à des enfants*	1981	Lucien Bodard *Anne-Marie*
1943	Marius Grout *Passage de l'homme*	1982	Dominique Fernandez *Dans la main de l'ange*
1944	Elsa Triolet *Le premier accroc coûte deux cents francs*	1983	Frédérick Tristan *Les égarés*
1945	Jean-Louis Bory *Mon village à l'heure allemande*	1984	Marguerite Duras *L'amant*
		1985	Yann Queffélec *Les noces barbares*
1946	Jean-Jacques Gautier *Histoire d'un fait divers*	1986	Michel Host *Valet de nuit*
		1987	Tahar Ben Jelloun *La nuit sacrée*
1947	Jean-Louis Curtis *Les forêts de la nuit*	1988	Erik Orsenna *L'exposition coloniale*
1948	Maurice Druon *Les grandes familles*	1989	Jean Vautrin *Un grand pas vers le Bon Dieu*
1949	Robert Merle *Week-end à Zuydcoote*	1990	Jean Rouaud *Les champs d'honneur*
1950	Paul Colin *Les jeux sauvages*	1991	Pierre Combescot *Les filles du calvaire*
1951	Julien Gracq *Le rivage des Syrtes*		
1952	Béatrice Beck *Léon Morin, prêtre*	1992	Patrick Chamoiseau *Texaco*
1953	Pierre Gascar *Les bêtes, Le temps des morts*	1993	Amin Maalouf *Le rocher de Tanios*
		1994	Didier Van Cauwelaert *Un aller simple*
1954	Simone de Beauvoir *Les Mandarins*	1995	Andreï Makine *Le testament français*
1955	Roger Ikor *Les eaux mêlées* (volume two of *Les fils d'Avrom*)	1996	Pascale Roze *Le chasseur Zéro*
		1997	Patrick Rambaud *La bataille*
1956	Romain Gary *Les racines du ciel*	1998	Paule Constant *Confidence pour confidence*
1957	Roger Vailland *La loi*		
1958	Francis Walder *Saint-Germain ou la négociation*	1999	Jean Echenoz *Je m'en vais*
		2000	Jean-Jacques Schuhl *Ingrid Caven*
1959	André Schwartz-Bart *Le dernier des justes*	2001	Jean-Christophe Rufin *Rouge Brésil*
		2002	Pascal Quignard *Les ombres errantes*
1960	Vintila Horia *Dieu est né en exil* [2]	2003	Jacques-Pierre Amette *La maîtresse de Brecht*
1961	Jean Cau *La pitié de Dieu*		
1962	André Langfus *Les bagages de sable*	2004	Laurent Gaudé *Le soleil des Scorta*
1963	Armand Lanoux *Quand la mer se retire*	2005	François Weyergans *Trois jours chez ma mère*
1964	Georges Conchon *L'état sauvage*		

[1] *Prize awarded retrospectively in 1916 as a result of disruption caused by World War I.*
[2] *Horia refused the prize as a result of political pressure.*

PULITZER PRIZE IN LETTERS: FICTION

Pulitzer Prizes, first awarded in the United States of America in 1917, are given annually for literature, drama, music and journalism. Established in the will of Joseph Pulitzer (1847–1911); prize for fiction was first awarded in 1918; the prize was known as the prize for a novel, rather than fiction, until 1948.

1917	*no award*	1954	*no award*
1918	Ernest Poole *His Family*	1955	William Faulkner *A Fable*
1919	Booth Tarkington *The Magnificent Ambersons*	1956	MacKinlay Kantor *Andersonville*
		1957	*no award*
1920	*no award*	1958	James Agee *A Death in the Family*
1921	Edith Wharton *The Age of Innocence*	1959	Robert Lewis Taylor *The Travels of Jaimie McPheeters*
1922	Booth Tarkington *Alice Adams*		
1923	Willa Cather *One of Ours*	1960	Allen Drury *Advise and Consent*
1924	Margaret Wilson *The Able McLaughlins*	1961	Harper Lee *To Kill a Mockingbird*
		1962	Edwin O'Connor *The Edge of Sadness*
1925	Edna Ferber *So Big*		
1926	Sinclair Lewis *Arrowsmith*	1963	William Faulkner *The Reivers*
1927	Louis Bromfield *Early Autumn*	1964	*no award*
1928	Thornton Wilder *The Bridge of San Luis Rey*	1965	Shirley Ann Grau *The Keepers of the House*
1929	Julia Peterkin *Scarlet Sister Mary*	1966	Katherine Anne Porter *Collected Stories*
1930	Oliver Lafarge *Laughing Boy*		
1931	Margaret Ayer Barnes *Years of Grace*	1967	Bernard Malamud *The Fixer*
1932	Pearl S Buck *The Good Earth*	1968	William Styron *The Confessions of Nat Turner*
1933	T S Stribling *The Store*		
1934	Caroline Miller *Lamb in His Bosom*	1969	N Scott Momaday *House Made of Dawn*
1935	Josephine Winslow Johnson *Now in November*		
		1970	Jean Stafford *Collected Stories*
1936	Harold L Davis *Honey in the Horn*	1971	*no award*
1937	Margaret Mitchell *Gone With the Wind*	1972	Wallace Stegner *Angle of Repose*
		1973	Eudora Welty *The Optimist's Daughter*
1938	John Phillips Marquand *The Late George Apley*		
		1974	*no award*
1939	Marjorie Kinnan Rawlings *The Yearling*	1975	Michael Shaara *The Killer Angels*
		1976	Saul Bellow *Humboldt's Gift*
1940	John Steinbeck *The Grapes of Wrath*	1977	*no award*
1941	*no award*	1978	James Alan McPherson *Elbow Room*
1942	Ellen Glasgow *In This Our Life*	1979	John Cheever *The Stories of John Cheever*
1943	Upton Sinclair *Dragon's Teeth*		
1944	Martin Flavin *Journey in the Dark*	1980	Norman Mailer *The Executioner's Song*
1945	John Hersey *A Bell for Adano*		
1946	*no award*	1981	John Kennedy Toole *A Confederacy of Dunces*
1947	Robert Penn Warren *All the King's Men*		
		1982	John Updike *Rabbit is Rich*
1948	James A Michener *Tales of the South Pacific*	1983	Alice Walker *The Color Purple*
		1984	William Kennedy *Ironweed*
1949	James Gould Cozzens *Guard of Honor*	1985	Alison Lurie *Foreign Affairs*
		1986	Larry McMurtry *Lonesome Dove*
1950	A B Guthrie, Jnr *The Way West*	1987	Peter Taylor *A Summons to Memphis*
1951	Conrad Richter *The Town*	1988	Toni Morrison *Beloved*
1952	Herman Wouk *The Caine Mutiny*	1989	Anne Tyler *Breathing Lessons*
1953	Ernest Hemingway *The Old Man and the Sea*	1990	Oscar Hijuelos *The Mambo Kings Play Songs of Love*

1991	John Updike *Rabbit at Rest*	1999	Michael Cunningham *The Hours*
1992	Jane Smiley *A Thousand Acres*	2000	Jhumpa Lahiri *Interpreter of*
1993	Robert Olen Butler *A Good Scent*		*Maladies*
	From a Strange Mountain	2001	Michael Chabon *The Amazing*
1994	E Annie Proulx *The Shipping News*		*Adventures of Kavalier & Clay*
1995	Carol Shields *The Stone Diaries*	2002	Richard Russo *Empire Falls*
1996	Richard Ford *Independence Day*	2003	Jeffrey Eugenides *Middlesex*
1997	Steven Millhauser *Martin Dressler:*	2004	Edward P Jones *The Known World*
	The Tale of an American Dreamer	2005	Marilynne Robinson *Gilead*
1998	Philip Roth *American Pastoral*		

LIBRARY BOOKS

Most borrowed authors in the UK

Most Borrowed Adult Fiction Author: Danielle Steel
Most Borrowed Children's Author: Jacqueline Wilson
Most Borrowed Classic Author: J R R Tolkien

Top ten most borrowed authors in the UK

1. Jacqueline Wilson
2. Danielle Steel
3. Josephine Cox
4. Mick Inkpen
5. Catherine Cookson
6. James Patterson
7. Janet and Allan Ahlberg
8. Agatha Christie
9. Ian Rankin
10. Roald Dahl

Most borrowed books in the UK

Most Borrowed Adult Fiction Title: John Grisham *The King of Torts*
Most Borrowed Children's Fiction Title: J K Rowling *Harry Potter and the Order of the Phoenix*
Most Borrowed Non-Fiction Title: Bill Bryson *A Short History of Nearly Everything*

Top ten most borrowed books in the UK

1. *Harry Potter and the Order of the Phoenix* J K Rowling
2. *The King of Torts* John Grisham
3. *Quentin's* Maeve Binchy
4. *Beachcomber* Josephine Cox
5. *Jinnie* Josephine Cox
6. *Bad Boy Jack* Josephine Cox
7. *Blue Horizon* Wilbur Smith
8. *The Story of Tracy Beaker* Jacqueline Wilson
9. *The Summons* John Grisham
10. *Lost Light* Michael Connolly

Riveting Reads

Six authors had over 1 million loans in the UK in 2003–4:
Catherine Cookson, Josephine Cox, Mick Inkpen, James
Patterson, Danielle Steel and Jacqueline Wilson.

Data compiled and supplied by Public Lending Right, Stockton-on-Tees. Information is for Jul 2003–Jun 2004.

FICTIONAL LITERARY PLACES

Place	Author	Book
Airstrip One	George Orwell (1903–50)	*Nineteen Eighty-Four* (1949)
Ankh-Morpork	Terry Pratchett (1948–)	Discworld® books (since 1983)
Barchester	Anthony Trollope (1815–82)	Barsetshire Novels (1855–67)
Barset	Anthony Trollope (1815–82)	Barsetshire Novels (1855–67)
Barsetshire	Anthony Trollope (1815–82)	Barsetshire Novels (1855–67)
Brobdingnag	Jonathan Swift (1667–1745)	*Gulliver's Travels* (1726)
Celestial City	John Bunyan (1628–88)	*The Pilgrim's Progress* (1678–84)
Christminster	Thomas Hardy (1840–1928)	various novels (1871–95[1]), especially *Jude the Obscure* (1895)
Discworld®	Terry Pratchett (1948–)	Discworld® books (since 1983)
Earthsea	Ursula Le Guin (1929–)	Earthsea Tetralogy (1968–91)
Emerald City	L Frank Baum (1856–1919)	*The Wonderful Wizard of Oz* (1900)
Erewhon	Samuel Butler (1835–1902)	*Erewhon* (1872)
Eurasia	George Orwell (1903–50)	*Nineteen Eighty-Four* (1949)
Gormenghast	Mervyn Peake (1911–68)	Gormenghast Trilogy (1946–59)
Hogwarts	J K Rowling (1965–)	Harry Potter books (since 1997)
Lake Wobegon	Garrison Keillor (1942–)	various (since 1985)
Laputa	Jonathan Swift (1667–1745)	*Gulliver's Travels* (1726)
Lilliput	Jonathan Swift (1667–1745)	*Gulliver's Travels* (1726)
Llaregyb	Dylan Thomas (1914–53)	*Under Milk Wood* (1954)
Looking-Glass Land	Lewis Carroll (1832–98)	*Through the Looking-Glass* (1872)
Maple White Land	Arthur Conan Doyle (1859–1930)	*The Lost World* (1912)
Maycomb	Harper Lee (1926–)	*To Kill a Mockingbird* (1960)
Middle-Earth	J R R Tolkien (1892–1973)	*The Hobbit, The Lord of the Rings* (1937, 1954–5)
Narnia	C S Lewis (1898–1963)	*Chronicles of Narnia* (1950–6)
Never-Never Land	J M Barrie (1860–1937)	*Peter Pan* (1904 play; 1911 book)
Oceania	George Orwell (1903–50)	*Nineteen Eighty-Four* (1949)
Oz	L Frank Baum (1856–1919)	*The Wonderful Wizard of Oz* (1900)
Rivendell	J R R Tolkien (1892–1973)	*The Hobbit, The Lord of the Rings* (1937, 1954–5)
Shangri-la	James Hilton (1900–54)	*Lost Horizon* (1933)
The Shire	J R R Tolkien (1892–1973)	*The Hobbit, The Lord of the Rings* (1937, 1954–5)
Toyland	Enid Blyton (1897–1968)	*Noddy Goes to Toyland* (1949)
Treasure Island	Robert Louis Stevenson (1850–94)	*Treasure Island* (1883)
Utopia	Thomas More (1478–1535)	*Utopia* (1516)
Vanity Fair	John Bunyan (1628–88)	*The Pilgrim's Progress* (1678–84)
Wessex	Thomas Hardy (1840–1928)	various (1871–95[1])
Wonderland	Lewis Carroll (1832–98)	*Alice's Adventures in Wonderland* (1865)
Xanadu	Samuel Taylor Coleridge (1772–1834)	'Kubla Khan: A Vision in a Dream' (1816)
Yoknapatawpha County	William Faulkner (1897–1962)	various (1929–62[2])
Zenda	Anthony Hope (1863–1933)	*The Prisoner of Zenda* (1894)

[1] *Years between which he published novels, not those specifically set in Christminster or Wessex.*
[2] *Specifically covers period of works set in Yoknapatawpha County.*

AUTHORS' REAL NAMES

Pseudonym	Real name
Bachman, Richard	Stephen King
Bell, Acton	Anne Brontë
Bell, Currer	Charlotte Brontë
Bell, Ellis	Emily Brontë
Burgess, Anthony	John Anthony Burgess Wilson
Carroll, Lewis	Charles Lutwidge Dodgson
Charteris, Leslie	Leslie Charles Bowyer Yin
Conrad, Joseph	Józef Teodor Konrad Nalecz Korzeniowiski
Coolidge, Susan	Sarah Chauncy Woolsey
Dinesen, Isak	Karen Blixen
Eliot, George	Mary Ann *or* Marian Evans
Farrell, M J	Molly Keane, *originally* Mary Nesta Skrine
Ford, Ford Madox	Ford Hermann Hueffer
France, Anatole	Anatole François Thibault
Gibbon, Lewis Grassic	James Leslie Mitchell
Gorky, Maxim	Aleksei Maksimovich Peshkov
Henry, O	William Sydney Porter
Higgins, Jack	Harry Patterson
Hite, Shere	Shirley Diana Gregory
Kincaid, Jamaica	Elaine Potter Richardson
Le Carré, John	David John Moore Cornwell
London, Jack	John Griffith Chaney
McBain, Ed	Salvatore A Lambino
Molière	Jean Baptiste Poquelin
Morrison, Toni	Chloe Anthony Morrison, *née* Wofford
Orwell, George	Eric Arthur Blair
Peters, Ellis	Edith Mary Pargeter
Queen, Ellery	Frederick Dannay *and* Manfred B Lee
Rhys, Jean	Gwen Williams
Robbins, Harold	Francis Kane
Saki	Hector Hugh Munro
Salten, Felix	Siegmund Salzmann
Sand, George	Amandine Aurore Lucie Dupin, Baronne Dudevant
Sapper	Herman Cyril McNeile
Seuss, Dr	Theodor Seuss Geisel
Shute, Nevil	Nevil Shute Norway
Smith, Stevie	Florence Margaret Smith
Stern, Daniel	Marie de Flavigny, Comtesse d'Agoult
Stoppard, Tom	Thomas Straussler
Tey, Josephine	Elizabeth Mackintosh
Twain, Mark	Samuel Langhorne Clemens
Voltaire	François Marie Arouet
Weldon, Fay	Franklin Birkinshaw
Wesley, Mary	Mary Aline Siepmann, *née* Farmar
West, Dame Rebecca	Cecily Isabel Andrews, *née* Fairfield
West, Nathanael	Nathan Wallenstein Weinstein
Westmacott, Mary	Dame Agatha Christie, *née* Miller
Williams, Tennessee	Thomas Lanier
Wyndham, John	John Wyndham Parkes Lucas Beynon Harris

THREE MUSKETEERS

The Three Musketeers appear in the novel *The Three Musketeers* (1844) by Alexandre Dumas (1802–70). As the novel progresses, the three are joined by d'Artagnan.

Aramis
Athos
Porthos

SNOW WHITE'S DWARFS

In the fairy tale by the Brothers Grimm the seven dwarfs are not mentioned by name, but these names were used in the Walt Disney animated film of 1937.

Bashful
Doc
Dopey
Grumpy
Happy
Sleepy
Sneezy

Hi Ho, Hi Ho

When *Snow White and the Seven Dwarfs* (1937) won an honorary Oscar® at the 11th Academy Awards®, the award comprised one normal-sized statuette – and seven miniature Oscars, one for each of the dwarfs.

SUPERHEROES' REAL NAMES

Superhero	Real name
Batman	Bruce Wayne
Captain America	Steve Rogers
Captain Marvel	Billy Batson
Daredevil	Matt Murdock
The Incredible Hulk	Dr Robert Bruce Banner
Spiderman	Peter Parker
Superman	Kel-El (on Krypton); Clark Kent (on Earth)
Wonder Woman	Diana Prince

Speeding Bullets

'Faster than a speeding bullet! More powerful than a locomotive! Able to leap tall buildings in a single bound!'
Jerome Siegel; introduction for the Superman radio serial. Quoted in *Time*, 14 Mar 1988.

ART

TURNER PRIZE

The Turner Prize was founded in 1984 by the Patrons of New Art. It is awarded to a contemporary British artist under the age of 50 for an 'outstanding exhibition of work in the past twelve months'.

1984	Malcolm Morley, painter
1985	Sir Howard Hodgkin, painter
1986	Gilbert and George (Gilbert Proesch and George Passmore), performance and photopiece artists
1987	Richard Deacon, sculptor
1988	Tony Cragg, sculptor
1989	Richard Long, land artist
1990	*no award*
1991	Anish Kapoor, sculptor
1992	Grenville Davey, sculptor
1993	Rachel Whiteread, sculptor
1994	Antony Gormley, sculptor
1995	Damien Hirst, painter and conceptual and installation artist
1996	Douglas Gordon, video artist
1997	Gillian Wearing, photographer and video artist
1998	Chris Ofili, painter
1999	Steve McQueen, video artist
2000	Wolfgang Tillmans, photographer
2001	Martin Creed, conceptual and installation artist
2002	Keith Tyson, conceptual and installation artist
2003	Grayson Perry, potter
2004	Jeremy Deller, mixed media and video artist
2005	Simon Starling, conceptual and installation artist

Angel of the North

Antony Gormley, the Turner Prize winner in 1994, created the largest sculpture in the UK with his *Angel of the North* (1998) in Gateshead. Weighing 200 tonnes/197 tons, the *Angel* stands 20m/65ft high and has a wingspan of 54m/175ft. As a result of its prominent location by the A1 and the east coast railway line, it is estimated that the *Angel* is seen by 33 million people each year, or at least one person every second.

FAMOUS WORKS OF ART

Works are listed by the name by which they are popularly known.

Art work	Artist or sculptor	Location	Date
The Age of Bronze	Auguste Rodin	Leeds City Art Gallery, Leeds, UK	1877
The Ambassadors	Hans Holbein the Younger	National Gallery, London, UK	1533
Angel of the North	Antony Gormley	Gateshead, UK	1998
The Arnolfini Portrait	Jan Van Eyck	National Gallery, London, UK	1434
The Artist's Mother (also known as *Arrangement in Grey and Black: the Artist's Mother*)	James Abbott McNeill Whistler	Musée d'Orsay, Paris, France	1871–2

Art work	Artist or sculptor	Location	Date
At the Moulin Rouge	Henri de Toulouse-Lautrec	Art Institute of Chicago, USA	1895
The Baptism of Christ	Piero della Francesca	National Gallery, London, UK	c.1450
A Bar at the Folies-Bergère	Édouard Manet	Courtauld Institute of Art, London, UK	1882
The Birth of Venus	Sandro Botticelli	Uffizi Gallery, Florence, Italy	c.1485
Campbell's Soup Cans	Andy Warhol	Museum of Modern Art, New York City, USA	1962
Christ of St John of the Cross	Salvador Dalí	St Mungo Museum of Religious Life And Art, Glasgow, UK	1951
David	Michelangelo	Accademia Gallery, Florence, Italy	1504
Le Déjeuner sur l'herbe	Édouard Manet	Musée d'Orsay, Paris, France	1863
Les Demoiselles d'Avignon	Pablo Picasso	Museum of Modern Art, New York City, USA	1907
The Fighting Téméraire	J M W Turner	National Gallery, London, UK	1839
Girl with a Pearl Earring	Jan Vermeer	Mauritshuis, The Hague, The Netherlands	c.1665
Guernica	Pablo Picasso	Reina Sofia, Madrid, Spain	1937
Haystacks	Claude Monet	various collections worldwide	1890–1
The Hay Wain	John Constable	National Gallery, London, UK	1821
Impression: Rising Sun	Claude Monet	Marmottan Monet Museum, Paris, France	1872
The Kiss	Auguste Rodin	Rodin Museum, Paris, France	1888–9
The Kiss	Gustav Klimt	Österreichische Galerie Belvedere, Vienna, Austria	1907–08
The Last of England	Ford Madox Brown	Birmingham Museum and Art Gallery	1852–5
The Last Supper	Leonardo da Vinci	Santa Maria delle Grazie, Milan, Italy	completed c.1498
Mona Lisa	Leonardo da Vinci	Louvre, Paris, France	1503–6
Mr and Mrs Clark and Percy	David Hockney	Tate Britain, London, UK	1970–1
Night Café	Vincent van Gogh	Yale University Art Gallery, New Haven, USA	1888
The Night Watch	Rembrandt	Rijksmuseum, Amsterdam, The Netherlands	1642
The Persistence of Memory (Limp Watches)	Salvador Dalí	Museum of Modern Art, New York City, USA	1931
The Potato Eaters	Vincent van Gogh	Van Gogh Museum, Amsterdam, The Netherlands	1885
Rain, Steam and Speed	J M W Turner	National Gallery, London, UK	before 1844
A Rake's Progress	William Hogarth	Sir John Soane's Museum, London, UK	1733–5
Reverend Dr Robert Walker Skating on Duddingston Loch	Henry Raeburn	National Gallery of Scotland, Edinburgh, UK	1795
Rouen Cathedral	Claude Monet	various collections worldwide	1892–4
St George and the Dragon	Paolo Uccello	National Gallery, London, UK	c.1470
The Scream	Edvard Munch	National Gallery, Oslo, Norway	1893
The Starry Night	Vincent van Gogh	Museum of Modern Art, New York City, USA	1889

Art work	Artist or sculptor	Location	Date
Sunflowers	Vincent van Gogh	National Gallery, London, UK (and other versions elsewhere)	1888
The Thinker	Auguste Rodin	Rodin Museum, Paris, France (and other versions elsewhere)	1881
36 Views of Mount Fuji	Hokusai	various collections worldwide	c.1826–33
The Three Graces	Antonio Canova	shared between the Victoria & Albert Museum, London, UK and the National Gallery of Scotland, Edinburgh, UK	1814
The Toilet of Venus (also known as '*The Rokeby Venus*')	Diego Velázquez	National Gallery, London, UK	1647-51
Venus de Milo (also known as *Aphrodite of Melos*)	unknown	Louvre, Paris, France	c.100BC
Venus Rising from the Sea	Titian	National Gallery of Scotland, Edinburgh, UK	1520
Water Lilies	Claude Monet	various collections worldwide	1899–1906

Scissors, Paper, Stone

In April 2005 the auction houses Christie's and Sotheby's were rivals for the chance to sell a collection of paintings by Picasso, Cezanne and Van Gogh. Unable to decide between the two, the seller asked them to play the children's game of 'scissors, paper, stone'; Sotheby's chose paper but Christie's chose scissors, thus winning the right to sell the £11 million collection.

MUSEUMS AND ART GALLERIES

Museum/Gallery	City	Country
Acropolis Museum	Athens	Greece
Ashmolean Museum of Art and Archaeology	Oxford	United Kingdom
Guggenheim Museum	New York	United States of America
Louvre	Paris	France
Metropolitan Museum of Art	New York	United States of America
Musée d'Orsay	Paris	France
Museum of Modern Art (MoMA)	New York	United States of America
Museum of Modern Art at the Pompidou Centre	Paris	France
National Gallery	London	United Kingdom
Prado Museum	Madrid	Spain
Reina Sofia	Madrid	Spain
Rijksmuseum	Amsterdam	The Netherlands
Stedelijk Museum of Modern Art	Amsterdam	The Netherlands
Tate Gallery	London	United Kingdom
Tate Modern	London	United Kingdom
Uffizi Gallery	Florence	Italy
Van Gogh Museum	Amsterdam	The Netherlands
Victoria and Albert Museum	London	United Kingdom

ACADEMY AWARDS®

Awarded annually by the Academy of Motion Picture Arts and Sciences. Popularly known as Oscars®. Best Actor and Best Actress awards are for performance in a leading role.

Year	Best Picture (director)	Best Actor	Best Actress	Best Director
1927/8	Wings (William A Wellman)	Emil Jannings The Last Command, The Way of All Flesh	Janet Gaynor 7th Heaven, Street Angel, Sunrise	Lewis Milestone Two Arabian Knights; Frank Borzage 7th Heaven
1928/9	The Broadway Melody (Harry Beaumont)	Warner Baxter In Old Arizona	Mary Pickford Coquette	Frank Lloyd The Divine Lady
1929/30	All Quiet on the Western Front (Lewis Milestone)	George Arliss Disraeli	Norma Shearer The Divorcee	Lewis Milestone All Quiet on the Western Front
1930/1	Cimarron (Wesley Ruggles)	Lionel Barrymore A Free Soul	Marie Dressler Min and Bill	Norman Taurog Skippy
1931/2	Grand Hotel (Edmund Goulding)	Wallace Beery The Champ; Fredric March Dr Jekyll and Mr Hyde	Helen Hayes The Sin of Madame Claudet	Frank Borzage Bad Girl
1932/3	Cavalcade (Frank Lloyd)	Charles Laughton The Private Life of Henry VIII	Katharine Hepburn Morning Glory	Frank Lloyd Cavalcade
1934	It Happened One Night (Frank Capra)	Clark Gable It Happened One Night	Claudette Colbert It Happened One Night	Frank Capra It Happened One Night
1935	Mutiny on the Bounty (Frank Lloyd)	Victor Laglen The Informer	Bette Davis Dangerous	John Ford The Informer
1936	The Great Ziegfeld (Robert Z Leonard)	Paul Muni The Story of Louis Pasteur	Luise Rainer The Great Ziegfeld	Frank Capra Mr Deeds Goes to Town
1937	The Life of Emile Zola (William Dieterle)	Spencer Tracy Captains Courageous	Luise Rainer The Good Earth	Leo McCarey The Awful Truth
1938	You Can't Take It with You (Frank Capra)	Spencer Tracy Boys Town	Bette Davis Jezebel	Frank Capra You Can't Take It with You
1939	Gone with the Wind (Victor Fleming)	Robert Donat Goodbye, Mr Chips	Vivien Leigh Gone with the Wind	Victor Fleming Gone with the Wind
1940	Rebecca (Alfred Hitchcock)	James Stewart The Philadelphia Story	Ginger Rogers Kitty Foyle	John Ford The Grapes of Wrath

Year	Best Picture (director)	Best Actor	Best Actress	Best Director
1941	*How Green Was My Valley* (John Ford)	Gary Cooper *Sergeant York*	Joan Fontaine *Suspicion*	John Ford *How Green Was My Valley*
1942	*Mrs Miniver* (William Wyler)	James Cagney *Yankee Doodle Dandy*	Greer Garson *Mrs Miniver*	William Wyler *Mrs Miniver*
1943	*Casablanca* (Michael Curtiz)	Paul Lukas *Watch on the Rhine*	Jennifer Jones *The Song of Bernadette*	Michael Curtiz *Casablanca*
1944	*Going My Way* (Leo McCarey)	Bing Crosby *Going My Way*	Ingrid Bergman *Gaslight*	Leo McCarey *Going My Way*
1945	*The Lost Weekend* (Billy Wilder)	Ray Milland *The Lost Weekend*	Joan Crawford *Mildred Pierce*	Billy Wilder *The Lost Weekend*
1946	*The Best Years of Our Lives* (William Wyler)	Fredric March *The Best Years of Our Lives*	Olivia de Havilland *To Each His Own*	William Wyler *The Best Years of Our Lives*
1947	*Gentleman's Agreement* (Elia Kazan)	Ronald Colman *A Double Life*	Loretta Young *The Farmer's Daughter*	Elia Kazan *Gentleman's Agreement*
1948	*Hamlet* (Laurence Olivier)	Laurence Olivier *Hamlet*	Jane Wyman *Johnny Belinda*	John Huston *The Treasure of the Sierra Madre*
1949	*All the King's Men* (Robert Rossen)	Broderick Crawford *All the King's Men*	Olivia de Havilland *The Heiress*	Joseph L Mankiewicz *A Letter to Three Wives*
1950	*All About Eve* (Joseph L Mankiewicz)	José Ferrer *Cyrano de Bergerac*	Judy Holliday *Born Yesterday*	Joseph L Mankiewicz *All About Eve*
1951	*An American in Paris* (Vincente Minnelli)	Humphrey Bogart *The African Queen*	Vivien Leigh *A Streetcar Named Desire*	George Stevens *A Place in the Sun*
1952	*The Greatest Show on Earth* (Cecil B De Mille)	Gary Cooper *High Noon*	Shirley Booth *Come Back, Little Sheba*	John Ford *The Quiet Man*
1953	*From Here to Eternity* (Fred Zinnemann)	William Holden *Stalag 17*	Audrey Hepburn *Roman Holiday*	Fred Zinnemann *From Here to Eternity*
1954	*On the Waterfront* (Elia Kazan)	Marlon Brando *On the Waterfront*	Grace Kelly *The Country Girl*	Elia Kazan *On the Waterfront*
1955	*Marty* (Delbert Mann)	Ernest Borgnine *Marty*	Anna Magnani *The Rose Tattoo*	Delbert Mann *Marty*
1956	*Around the World in 80 Days* (Michael Anderson)	Yul Brynner *The King and I*	Ingrid Bergman *Anastasia*	George Stevens *Giant*

Year	Best Picture (director)	Best Actor	Best Actress	Best Director
1957	The Bridge on the River Kwai (David Lean)	Alec Guinness The Bridge on the River Kwai	Joanne Woodward The Three Faces of Eve	David Lean The Bridge on the River Kwai
1958	Gigi (Vincente Minnelli)	David Niven Separate Tables	Susan Hayward I Want To Live!	Vincente Minnelli Gigi
1959	Ben-Hur (William Wyler)	Charlton Heston Ben-Hur	Simone Signoret Room at the Top	William Wyler Ben-Hur
1960	The Apartment (Billy Wilder)	Burt Lancaster Elmer Gantry	Elizabeth Taylor Butterfield 8	Billy Wilder The Apartment
1961	West Side Story (Robert Wise, Jerome Robbins)	Maximilian Schell Judgment at Nuremberg	Sophia Loren Two Women	Robert Wise, Jerome Robbins West Side Story
1962	Lawrence of Arabia (David Lean)	Gregory Peck To Kill a Mockingbird	Anne Bancroft The Miracle Worker	David Lean Lawrence of Arabia
1963	Tom Jones (Tony Richardson)	Sidney Poitier Lilies of the Field	Patricia Neal Hud	Tony Richardson Tom Jones
1964	My Fair Lady (George Cukor)	Rex Harrison My Fair Lady	Julie Andrews Mary Poppins	George Cukor My Fair Lady
1965	The Sound of Music (Robert Wise)	Lee Marvin Cat Ballou	Julie Christie Darling	Robert Wise The Sound of Music
1966	A Man for All Seasons (Fred Zinnemann)	Paul Scofield A Man for All Seasons	Elizabeth Taylor Who's Afraid of Virginia Woolf?	Fred Zinnemann A Man for All Seasons
1967	In the Heat of the Night (Norman Jewison)	Rod Steiger In the Heat of the Night	Katharine Hepburn Guess Who's Coming to Dinner	Mike Nichols The Graduate
1968	Oliver! (Carol Reed)	Cliff Robertson Charly	Katharine Hepburn The Lion in Winter; Barbra Streisand Funny Girl	Carol Reed Oliver!
1969	Midnight Cowboy (John Schlesinger)	John Wayne True Grit	Maggie Smith The Prime of Miss Jean Brodie	John Schlesinger Midnight Cowboy
1970	Patton (Franklin J Schaffner)	George C Scott Patton	Glenda Jackson Women in Love	Franklin J Schaffner Patton
1971	The French Connection (William Friedkin)	Gene Hackman The French Connection	Jane Fonda Klute	William Friedkin The French Connection
1972	The Godfather (Francis Ford Coppola)	Marlon Brando The Godfather	Liza Minnelli Cabaret	Bob Fosse Cabaret

Year	Best Picture (director)	Best Actor	Best Actress	Best Director
1973	*The Sting* (George Roy Hill)	Jack Lemmon *Save the Tiger*	Glenda Jackson *A Touch of Class*	George Roy Hill *The Sting*
1974	*The Godfather Part II* (Francis Ford Coppola)	Art Carney *Harry and Tonto*	Ellen Burstyn *Alice Doesn't Live Here Anymore*	Francis Ford Coppola *The Godfather Part II*
1975	*One Flew Over the Cuckoo's Nest* (Milos Forman)	Jack Nicholson *One Flew Over the Cuckoo's Nest*	Louise Fletcher *One Flew Over the Cuckoo's Nest*	Milos Forman *One Flew Over the Cuckoo's Nest*
1976	*Rocky* (John G Avildsen)	Peter Finch *Network*	Faye Dunaway *Network*	John G Avildsen *Rocky*
1977	*Annie Hall* (Woody Allen)	Richard Dreyfuss *The Goodbye Girl*	Diane Keaton *Annie Hall*	Woody Allen *Annie Hall*
1978	*The Deer Hunter* (Michael Cimino)	Jon Voight *Coming Home*	Jane Fonda *Coming Home*	Michael Cimino *The Deer Hunter*
1979	*Kramer vs Kramer* (Robert Benton)	Dustin Hoffman *Kramer vs Kramer*	Sally Field *Norma Rae*	Robert Benton *Kramer vs Kramer*
1980	*Ordinary People* (Robert Redford)	Robert De Niro *Raging Bull*	Sissy Spacek *Coal Miner's Daughter*	Robert Redford *Ordinary People*
1981	*Chariots of Fire* (Hugh Hudson)	Henry Fonda *On Golden Pond*	Katharine Hepburn *On Golden Pond*	Warren Beatty *Reds*
1982	*Gandhi* (Richard Attenborough)	Ben Kingsley *Gandhi*	Meryl Streep *Sophie's Choice*	Richard Attenborough *Gandhi*
1983	*Terms of Endearment* (James L Brooks)	Robert Duvall *Tender Mercies*	Shirley MacLaine *Terms of Endearment*	James L Brooks *Terms of Endearment*
1984	*Amadeus* (Milos Forman)	F Murray Abraham *Amadeus*	Sally Field *Places in the Heart*	Milos Forman *Amadeus*
1985	*Out of Africa* (Sydney Pollack)	William Hurt *Kiss of the Spider Woman*	Geraldine Page *The Trip to Bountiful*	Sydney Pollack *Out of Africa*
1986	*Platoon* (Oliver Stone)	Paul Newman *The Color of Money*	Marlee Matlin *Children of a Lesser God*	Oliver Stone *Platoon*
1987	*The Last Emperor* (Bernardo Bertolucci)	Michael Douglas *Wall Street*	Cher *Moonstruck*	Bernardo Bertolucci *The Last Emperor*
1988	*Rain Man* (Barry Levinson)	Dustin Hoffman *Rain Man*	Jodie Foster *The Accused*	Barry Levinson *Rain Man*
1989	*Driving Miss Daisy* (Bruce Beresford)	Daniel Day-Lewis *My Left Foot*	Jessica Tandy *Driving Miss Daisy*	Oliver Stone *Born on the Fourth of July*

Year	Best Picture (director)	Best Actor	Best Actress	Best Director
1990	Dances With Wolves (Kevin Costner)	Jeremy Irons Reversal of Fortune	Kathy Bates Misery	Kevin Costner Dances With Wolves
1991	The Silence of the Lambs (Jonathan Demme)	Anthony Hopkins The Silence of the Lambs	Jodie Foster The Silence of the Lambs	Jonathan Demme The Silence of the Lambs
1992	Unforgiven (Clint Eastwood)	Al Pacino Scent of a Woman	Emma Thompson Howards End	Clint Eastwood Unforgiven
1993	Schindler's List (Steven Spielberg)	Tom Hanks Philadelphia	Holly Hunter The Piano	Steven Spielberg Schindler's List
1994	Forrest Gump (Robert Zemeckis)	Tom Hanks Forrest Gump	Jessica Lange Blue Sky	Robert Zemeckis Forrest Gump
1995	Braveheart (Mel Gibson)	Nicolas Cage Leaving Las Vegas	Susan Sarandon Dead Man Walking	Mel Gibson Braveheart
1996	The English Patient (Anthony Minghella)	Geoffrey Rush Shine	Frances McDormand Fargo	Anthony Minghella The English Patient
1997	Titanic (James Cameron)	Jack Nicholson As Good As It Gets	Helen Hunt As Good As It Gets	James Cameron Titanic
1998	Shakespeare in Love (Guy Madden)	Roberto Benigni Life Is Beautiful	Gwyneth Paltrow Shakespeare in Love	Steven Spielberg Saving Private Ryan
1999	American Beauty (Sam Mendes)	Kevin Spacey American Beauty	Hilary Swank Boys Don't Cry	Sam Mendes American Beauty
2000	Gladiator (Ridley Scott)	Russell Crowe Gladiator	Julia Roberts Erin Brockovich	Steven Soderbergh Traffic
2001	A Beautiful Mind (Ron Howard)	Denzel Washington Training Day	Halle Berry Monster's Ball	Ron Howard A Beautiful Mind
2002	Chicago (Rob Marshall)	Adrien Brody The Pianist	Nicole Kidman The Hours	Roman Polanski The Pianist
2003	The Lord of the Rings: The Return of the King (Peter Jackson)	Sean Penn Mystic River	Charlize Theron Monster	Peter Jackson The Lord of the Rings: The Return of the King
2004	Million Dollar Baby (Clint Eastwood)	Jamie Foxx Ray	Hilary Swank Million Dollar Baby	Clint Eastwood Million Dollar Baby

Most Successful

It Happened One Night (1934), One Flew Over the Cuckoo's Nest (1975) and The Silence of the Lambs (1991) are members of a very exclusive club: the only three films to have won all of the five most prestigious Oscars® (for Best Film, Actor, Actress, Director and Writing).

BRITISH ACADEMY FILM AWARDS

The British Film Academy was founded in 1947, and in 1975 changed its name to the British Academy of Film and Television Arts (BAFTA). Best Actor and Best Actress awards are for performance in a leading role.

Year	Best Film (director)	Best Actor	Best Actress	Best Direction
1947	The Best Years of our Lives (William Wyler)			
1948	Hamlet (Laurence Olivier)			
1949	The Bicycle Thief (Vittorio De Sica)			
1950	All About Eve (Joseph L Mankiewicz)			
1951	La Ronde (Max Ophuls)			
1952	The Sound Barrier (David Lean)	Ralph Richardson The Sound Barrier	Vivien Leigh A Streetcar Named Desire	
1953	Forbidden Games (René Clément)	John Gielgud Julius Caesar	Audrey Hepburn Roman Holiday	
1954	The Wages of Fear (Henri-Georges Clouzot)	Kenneth More Doctor in the House	Yvonne Mitchell The Divided Heart	
1955	Richard III (Laurence Olivier)	Laurence Olivier Richard III	Katie Johnson The Ladykillers	
1956	Gervaise (René Clément)	Peter Finch A Town Like Alice	Virginia McKenna A Town Like Alice	
1957	The Bridge on the River Kwai (David Lean)	Alec Guinness The Bridge on the River Kwai	Heather Sears The Story of Esther Costello	
1958	Room at the Top (Jack Clayton)	Trevor Howard The Key	Irene Worth Orders to Kill	
1959	Ben-Hur (William Wyler)	Peter Sellers I'm All Right Jack	Audrey Hepburn The Nun's Story	
1960	The Apartment (Billy Wilder)	Peter Finch The Trials of Oscar Wilde	Rachel Roberts Saturday Night and Sunday Morning	
1961	Ballad of a Soldier (Grigori Chukhraj); The Hustler (Robert Rossen)	Peter Finch No Love for Johnnie	Dora Bryan A Taste of Honey	
1962	Lawrence of Arabia (David Lean)	Peter O'Toole Lawrence of Arabia	Leslie Caron The L-shaped Room	

Year	Best Film (director)	Best Actor	Best Actress	Best Direction
1963	Tom Jones (Tony Richardson)	Dirk Bogarde The Servant	Rachel Roberts This Sporting Life	
1964	Dr Strangelove (Stanley Kubrick)	Richard Attenborough Séance on a Wet Afternoon, Guns at Batasi	Audrey Hepburn Charade	
1965	My Fair Lady (George Cukor)	Dirk Bogarde Darling	Julie Christie Darling	
1966	Who's Afraid of Virginia Woolf? (Mike Nichols)	Richard Burton The Spy Who Came in from the Cold	Elizabeth Taylor Who's Afraid of Virginia Woolf?	
1967	A Man for All Seasons (Fred Zinnemann)	Paul Scofield A Man for All Seasons	Edith Evans The Whisperers	
1968	The Graduate (Mike Nichols)	Spencer Tracy Guess Who's Coming to Dinner?	Katharine Hepburn Guess Who's Coming to Dinner?, The Lion in Winter	Mike Nichols The Graduate
1969	Midnight Cowboy (John Schlesinger)	Dustin Hoffman Midnight Cowboy, John and Mary	Maggie Smith The Prime of Miss Jean Brodie	John Schlesinger Midnight Cowboy
1970	Butch Cassidy and the Sundance Kid (George Roy Hill)	Robert Redford Butch Cassidy and the Sundance Kid, Tell Them Willie Boy is Here, Downhill Racer	Katharine Ross Butch Cassidy and the Sundance Kid, Tell Them Willie Boy is Here	George Roy Hill Butch Cassidy and the Sundance Kid
1971	Sunday, Bloody Sunday (John Schlesinger)	Peter Finch Sunday, Bloody Sunday	Glenda Jackson Sunday, Bloody Sunday	John Schlesinger Sunday, Bloody Sunday
1972	Cabaret (Bob Fosse)	Gene Hackman The French Connection, The Poseidon Adventure	Liza Minnelli Cabaret	Bob Fosse Cabaret
1973	Day for Night (François Truffaut)	Walter Matthau Pete 'n' Tillie, Charley Varrick	Stéphane Audran The Discreet Charm of the Bourgeoisie, Just Before Nightfall	François Truffaut Day for Night
1974	Lacombe Lucien (Louis Malle)	Jack Nicholson Chinatown, The Last Detail	Joanne Woodward Summer Wishes, Winter Dreams	Roman Polanski Chinatown
1975	Alice Doesn't Live Here Anymore (Martin Scorsese)	Al Pacino Dog Day Afternoon, The Godfather II	Ellen Burstyn Alice Doesn't Live Here Anymore	Stanley Kubrick Barry Lyndon
1976	One Flew Over the Cuckoo's Nest (Milos Forman)	Jack Nicholson One Flew Over the Cuckoo's Nest	Louise Fletcher One Flew Over the Cuckoo's Nest	Milos Forman One Flew Over the Cuckoo's Nest
1977	Annie Hall (Woody Allen)	Peter Finch Network	Diane Keaton Annie Hall	Woody Allen Annie Hall

Year	Best Film (director)	Best Actor	Best Actress	Best Direction
1978	*Julia* (Fred Zinnemann)	Richard Dreyfuss *The Goodbye Girl*	Jane Fonda *Julia*	Alan Parker *Midnight Express*
1979	*Manhattan* (Woody Allen)	Jack Lemmon *The China Syndrome*	Jane Fonda *The China Syndrome*	Francis Ford Coppola *Apocalypse Now*
1980	*The Elephant Man* (Jonathan Sanger)	John Hurt *The Elephant Man*	Judy Davis *My Brilliant Career*	Akira Kurosawa *Kagemusha*
1981	*Chariots of Fire* (Hugh Hudson)	Burt Lancaster *Atlantic City*	Meryl Streep *The French Lieutenant's Woman*	Louis Malle *Atlantic City*
1982	*Gandhi* (Richard Attenborough)	Ben Kingsley *Gandhi*	Katharine Hepburn *On Golden Pond*	Richard Attenborough *Gandhi*
1983	*Educating Rita* (Lewis Gilbert)	Michael Caine *Educating Rita*; Dustin Hoffman *Tootsie*	Julie Walters *Educating Rita*	Bill Forsyth *Local Hero*
1984	*The Killing Fields* (Roland Joffe)	Haing S Ngor *The Killing Fields*	Maggie Smith *A Private Function*	Wim Wenders *Paris, Texas*
1985	*The Purple Rose of Cairo* (Woody Allen)	William Hurt *Kiss of the Spider Woman*	Peggy Ashcroft *A Passage to India*	*no award*
1986	*A Room With a View* (James Ivory)	Bob Hoskins *Mona Lisa*	Maggie Smith *A Room With a View*	Woody Allen *Hannah and Her Sisters*
1987	*Jean de Florette* (Claude Berri)	Sean Connery *The Name of the Rose*	Anne Bancroft *84 Charing Cross Road*	Oliver Stone *Platoon*
1988	*The Last Emperor* (Bernardo Bertolucci)	John Cleese *A Fish Called Wanda*	Maggie Smith *The Lonely Passion of Judith Hearne*	Louis Malle *Au Revoir Les Enfants*
1989	*Dead Poets Society* (Peter Weir)	Daniel Day-Lewis *My Left Foot*	Pauline Collins *Shirley Valentine*	Kenneth Branagh *Henry V*
1990	*Goodfellas* (Martin Scorsese)	Philippe Noiret *Cinema Paradiso*	Jessica Tandy *Driving Miss Daisy*	Martin Scorsese *Goodfellas*
1991	*The Commitments* (Alan Parker)	Anthony Hopkins *The Silence of the Lambs*	Jodie Foster *The Silence of the Lambs*	Alan Parker *The Commitments*
1992	*Howards End* (James Ivory)	Robert Downey Jnr *Chaplin*	Emma Thompson *Howards End*	Robert Altman *The Player*
1993	*Schindler's List* (Steven Spielberg)	Anthony Hopkins *The Remains of the Day*	Holly Hunter *The Piano*	Steven Spielberg *Schindler's List*
1994	*Four Weddings and a Funeral* (Mike Newell)	Hugh Grant *Four Weddings and a Funeral*	Susan Sarandon *The Client*	Mike Newell *Four Weddings and a Funeral*
1995	*Sense and Sensibility* (Ang Lee)	Nigel Hawthorne *The Madness of King George*	Emma Thompson *Sense and Sensibility*	Michael Radford *Il Postino*

Year	Best Film (director)	Best Actor	Best Actress	Best Direction
1996	The English Patient (Anthony Minghella)	Geoffrey Rush Shine	Brenda Blethyn Secrets and Lies	Joel Coen Fargo
1997	The Full Monty (Peter Cattaneo)	Tom Wilkinson The Full Monty	Judi Dench Mrs Brown	Baz Luhrmann Romeo and Juliet
1998	Shakespeare in Love (John Madden)	Roberto Benigni Life is Beautiful	Cate Blanchett Elizabeth	Peter Weir The Truman Show
1999	American Beauty (Sam Mendes)	Kevin Spacey American Beauty	Annette Bening American Beauty	Pedro Almodovar All About My Mother
2000	Gladiator (Ridley Scott)	Jamie Bell Billy Elliot	Julia Roberts Erin Brockovich	Ang Lee Crouching Tiger, Hidden Dragon
2001	The Lord of the Rings: The Fellowship of the Ring (Peter Jackson)	Russell Crowe A Beautiful Mind	Judi Dench Iris	Peter Jackson The Lord of the Rings: The Fellowship of the Ring
2002	The Pianist (Roman Polanski)	Daniel Day-Lewis Gangs of New York	Nicole Kidman The Hours	Roman Polanski The Pianist
2003	The Lord of the Rings: The Return of the King (Peter Jackson)	Bill Murray Lost in Translation	Scarlett Johansson Lost in Translation	Peter Weir Master and Commander: The Far Side of the World
2004	The Aviator (Martin Scorsese)	Jamie Foxx Ray	Imelda Staunton Vera Drake	Mike Leigh Vera Drake

Continuity Chaos

Sharp-eyed movie buffs are constantly on the lookout for continuity errors, anachronisms and other mistakes in films. From camera crews reflected in plate-glass windows to Roman centurions wearing watches, some of the worst howlers have passed into film legend. These include the Von Trapp family fleeing over the mountains straight into enemy Germany at the end of *The Sound of Music* (1965), Dorothy's hair varying in length in *The Wizard of Oz* (1939) and a passenger in a lifeboat wearing a digital watch in *Titanic* (1997). Other classic gaffes include a distant aeroplane flying past in one scene in *Ben-Hur* (1959), a storm trooper banging his head in *Star Wars* (1977) and a building marked 'Est. 1953' in World War II film *Pearl Harbor* (2001). Scenes involving food, drink and cigars or cigarettes are also a continuity nightmare for filmmakers: watch the fluctuating levels of alcohol in the wine glasses in *The Godfather* (1972) and the half-eaten hamburgers in *Pulp Fiction* (1994). Fans can also spot an anachronism a mile off. One of the best known is in *The Rocky Horror Picture Show*, in which US President Richard Nixon's resignation speech can be heard on a car radio. Nixon resigned in August – but the narrator solemnly intones that the events of the film take place 'on a late November evening'.

PALME D'OR

The Cannes Film Festival began in 1946 and is the world's leading festival of its kind. The *Palme d'Or* (Golden Palm) for best film has been awarded every year since 1955. The director is given in brackets.

1955   *Marty* (Delbert Mann)
1956   *The Silent World* (*Le Monde du Silence*) (Jacques-Yves Cousteau)
1957   *Friendly Persuasion* (William Wyler)
1958   *The Cranes are Flying* (*Letiat Zhuravli*) (Mikhail Kalatozov)
1959   *Black Orpheus* (*Orfeu Negro*) (Marcel Camus)
1960   *La Dolce Vita* (Federico Fellini)
1961   *Viridiana* (Luis Buñuel); *Une Aussi Longue Absence* (Henri Colpi)
1962   *The Given Word* (*O Pagador de Promessas*) (Anselmo Duarte)
1963   *The Leopard* (*Il Gattopardi*) (Luchino Visconti)
1964   *The Umbrellas of Cherbourg* (*Les Parapluies de Cherbourg*) (Jacques Demy)
1965   *The Knack...And How to Get It* (Richard Lester)
1966   *A Man and a Woman* (*Un Homme et Une Femme*) (Claude Lelouch)
1967   *Blow-Up* (Michelangelo Antonioni)
1968   *festival cancelled*
1969   *If...* (Lindsay Anderson)
1970   *M*A*S*H* (Robert Altman)
1971   *The Go-Between* (Joseph Losey)
1972   *The Mattei Affair* (*Il Caso Mattei*) (Francesco Rossi); *The Working Class Go to Heaven* (*La Classe Operaia Va in Paradiso*) (Elio Petri)
1973   *Scarecrow* (Jerry Schatzberg); *The Hireling* (Alan Bridges)
1974   *The Conversation* (Francis Ford Coppola)
1975   *Chronicle of the Years of Embers* (*Ahdat Sanawouach Eldjamr*) (Mohammed Lakhdar Hamina)
1976   *Taxi Driver* (Martin Scorsese)
1977   *Padro Padrone* (Paolo and Vittorio Taviani)
1978   *The Tree of Wooden Clogs* (*L'Albero degli Zoccoli*) (Ermanno Olmi)
1979   *Apocalypse Now* (Francis Ford Coppola); *The Tin Drum* (*Die Blechtrommel*) (Volker Schlöndorff)
1980   *Kagemusha* (Akira Kurosawa); *All That Jazz* (Bob Fosse)
1981   *Man of Iron* (*Czolowieck z Zelaza*) (Andrzej Wajda)
1982   *Missing* (Costa-Gavras); *Yol* (Yilmaz Güney)
1983   *The Ballad of Narayama* (*Narayama Bushi Ko*) (Shohei Imamura)
1984   *Paris, Texas* (Wim Wenders)
1985   *When Father was Away on Business* (*Otak Na Sluzbenom Putu*) (Emir Kusturica)
1986   *The Mission* (Roland Joffe)
1987   *Under Satan's Sun* (*Sous le Soleil de Satan*) (Maurice Pialat)
1988   *Pelle the Conquerer* (*Pell Erobreren*) (Bille August)
1989   *sex, lies and videotape* (Steven Soderbergh)
1990   *Wild at Heart* (David Lynch)
1991   *Barton Fink* (Joel and Ethan Coen)
1992   *The Best Intentions* (*Den Goda Viljan*) (Bille August)
1993   *The Piano* (Jane Campion); *Farewell my Concubine* (Chen Kaige)
1994   *Pulp Fiction* (Quentin Tarantino)
1995   *Underground* (Emir Kusturica)
1996   *Secrets and Lies* (Mike Leigh)
1997   *The Eel* (*Unagi*) (Shohei Imamura); *A Taste of Cherry* (*Ta'me Guilass*) (Abbas Kiarostami)
1998   *Eternity and a Day* (*Mia Eoniotita Ke Mia Mera*) (Theo Angelopoulos)
1999   *Rosetta* (Luc and Jean-Pierre Dardenne)
2000   *Dancer in the Dark* (Lars von Trier)
2001   *The Son's Room* (*La Stanza del Figlio*) (Nanni Moretti)

2002	*The Pianist* (Roman Polanski)
2003	*Elephant* (Gus Van Sant)
2004	*Fahrenheit 9/11* (Michael Moore)
2005	*L'Enfant* (Jean-Pierre and Luc Dardenne)

Fear Factor

In 2004, researchers from King's College in London announced that they had calculated the formula for the perfect horror film:

$$(es+u+cs+t)^2 +s+ (tl+f)/2 + (a+dr+fs)/n + \sin x -1$$

In the equation es = escalating music, u = the unknown, cs = chase scenes, t = being trapped, s = shock, tl = true life, f = fantasy, a = being alone, dr = in the dark, fs = film setting, n = number of people, sin x = blood and guts and 1 = stereotypes. Using the equation, the researchers announced that *The Shining* was the best horror film of all time.

MAJOR FILM FESTIVALS

Festival	Location	Major Prize
Bangkok	Bangkok, Thailand	Golden Kinnaree
Berlin	Berlin, Germany	Golden Bear
Cairo	Cairo, Egypt	Golden Pyramid
Cannes	Cannes, France	Palme d'Or
Cartagena	Cartagena, Colombia	Golden India Catalina
Chicago	Chicago, Illinois, USA	Gold Hugo
Cleveland	Cleveland, Ohio, USA	Best Film
Copenhagen	Copenhagen, Denmark	Golden Swan
Edinburgh	Edinburgh, Scotland, UK	Audience Award
Havana	Havana, Cuba	Grand Coral
Istanbul	Istanbul, Turkey	Golden Tulip
Locarno	Locarno, Switzerland	Golden Leopard
London	London, England, UK	Sutherland Trophy
Melbourne	Melbourne, Australia	Best Film
Montreal	Montreal, Canada	Grand Prix des Amériques
Moscow	Moscow, Russia	Golden St George
Paris	Paris, France	Grand Prix
Rotterdam	Rotterdam, The Netherlands	Tiger Award
San Francisco	San Francisco, California, USA	Golden Gate
San Sebastian	San Sebastian, Spain	Golden Seashell
Seattle	Seattle, Washington, USA	Golden Space Needle
Stockholm	Stockholm, Sweden	Bronze Horse
Sundance	Park City, Utah, USA	Grand Jury Prize
Tokyo	Tokyo, Japan	Grand Prix
Toronto	Toronto, Canada	People's Choice Award
Venice	Venice, Italy	Golden Lion
Vevey	Vevey, Switzerland	Golden Cane

ACTORS' REAL NAMES

Pseudonym	Real name	Pseudonym	Real name
Alda, Alan	Alphonso Joseph d'Abruzzo	Andrews, Dame Julie	Julia Elizabeth Wells
Allen, Woody	Allen Stewart Konigsberg	Astaire, Fred	Frederick Austerlitz

Pseudonym	Real name	Pseudonym	Real name
Bacall, Lauren	Betty Perske	Jolson, Al	Asa Yoelson
Bancroft, Anne	Anna Maria Louisa Italiano	Karloff, Boris	William Henry Pratt
Bardot, Brigitte	Camille Javal	Keaton, Diane	Diane Hall
Bernhardt, Sarah	Sarah-Marie-Henriette Rosine Bernard	Keith, Penelope	Penelope Hatfield
		Kingsley, Ben	Krishna Bhanji
Bogarde, Sir Dirk	Derek Jules Ulric Niven van den Bogaerde	Lancaster, Burt	Stephen Burton Lancaster
		Laurel, Stan	Arthur Stanley Jefferson
Bronson, Charles	Charles Buchinsky	Leigh, Vivien	Vivian Mary Hartley
Brooks, Mel	Melvin Kaminsky	Lindsay, Robert	Robert Lindsay Stevenson
Burton, Richard	Richard Walter Jenkins	Lombard, Carole	Jane Alice Peters
Cage, Nicolas	Nicholas Coppola	Loren, Sophia	Sofia Scicolone
Caine, Sir Michael	Maurice Micklewhite	Lugosi, Bela	Bela Ferenc Denzso Blasko
Cher	Cheryl Sarkisian La Pier	MacLaine, Shirley	Shirley MacLean Beaty
Coltrane, Robbie	Robin McMillan	Matthau, Walter	Walter Matuschanskavasky
Crawford, Joan	Lucille Le Sueur		
Crosby, Bing	Harry Lillis Crosby	Mirren, Helen	Helen Lydia Mironoff
Cruise, Tom	Tom Cruise Mapother IV	Monroe, Marilyn	Norma Joan Mortenson
Curtis, Tony	Bernard Schwartz	Montand, Yves	Ivo Livi
Day, Doris	Doris Kappelhoff	Moore, Demi	Demi Guynes
Deneuve, Catherine	Catherine Dorléac	Moore, Julianne	Julie Anne Smith
		Neeson, Liam	William John Neeson
Dietrich, Marlene	Maria Magdalena Von Losch	Niven, David	James David Graham Nevins
Dors, Diana	Diana Fluck		
Douglas, Kirk	Issur Danielovich	Pickford, Mary	Gladys Mary Smith
Fairbanks, Douglas	Douglas Elton Ullman	Robinson, Edward G	Emanuel Goldenberg
Fields, W C	William Claude Dukenfield		
Flynn, Errol	Leslie Thomson Flynn	Rogers, Ginger	Virginia Katherine McMath
Foster, Jodie	Alicia Christian Foster	Russell, Lillian	Helen Louise Leonard
Garbo, Greta	Greta Lovisa Gustafsson	Ryder, Winona	Winona Horowitz
Gardner, Ava	Lucy Johnson	Scales, Prunella	Prunella Margaret Rumney Illingworth
Garland, Judy	Frances Ethel Gumm		
Gish, Lillian Diana	Lillian de Guiche	Shepard, Sam	Samuel Shepard Rogers
Goldberg, Whoopi	Caryn Johnson	Spacey, Kevin	Kevin Fowler
Grant, Cary	Archibald Leach	Stanwyck, Barbara	Ruby Stevens
Grant, Richard E	Richard Grant Esterhuysen	Streisand, Barbra	Barbara Joan Rosen
Hardy, Oliver	Norvell Hardy Junior	Swanson, Gloria	Gloria May Josephine Svensson
Harlow, Jean	Harlean Carpentier		
Hayworth, Rita	Margarita Carmen Cansino	Turner, Lana	Julia Jean Mildred Frances Turner
Hepburn, Audrey	Edda Van Heemstra Hepburn-Ruston	Valentino, Rudolph	Rodolpho Alphonso Guglielmi di Valentina d'Antonguolla
Heston, Charlton	Charles Carter		
Hill, Benny	Alfred Hawthorne Hill		
Holm, Sir Ian	Ian Holm Cuthbert	Wayne, John	Marion Michael Morrison
Irving, Sir Henry	John Henry Brodribb	Welch, Raquel	Raquel Tejada
Jacques, Hattie	Josephine Edwina Jacques	Wood, Natalie	Natasha Gurdin
		York, Susannah	Susannah Yolande-Fletcher
Jason, David	David John White		

Cameo Leach

Cary Grant used to enjoy sneaking his real name into his films. In *His Girl Friday* (1940) Grant refers in conversation to a man named Archie Leach, while the same name appears on a tombstone behind Grant in a graveyard scene in *Arsenic and Old Lace* (1944).

FILM RECORDS

First film	Thomas Edison and William Dickson pioneered the Kinetoscope in the early 1890s, showing short films such as 'The Sneeze' (1894); in 1895 Auguste and Louis Lumière patented the Cinematograph which they demonstrated in public with such short films as 'Arrival of Train at Station'.
First feature film with sound	*The Jazz Singer* (1927) featured short spoken clips and music, though other experiments with sound had been made with shorter films.
Oldest star	Jeanne Louise Calment appeared as herself in the film *Vincent And Me* (1990) at the age of 114. She lived to the age of 122.
Youngest star	Leroy Overacker appeared in the film *A Bedtime Story* (1933) at the age of 6 months, and received star billing.
Longest shot in a feature film	*Russian Ark* (2001) consists entirely of one long shot lasting 96 minutes.
Highest box office gross	*Titanic* (1997) is the most successful film of all time, and was the first to gross more than $1 billion internationally.
Film with most Academy Awards®	*Ben-Hur* (1959), *Titanic* (1997) and *The Lord of the Rings: The Return of the King* (2003) have won 11 Academy Awards®.
Most Academy Awards® for Best Actress	Katharine Hepburn won four Academy Awards®, all for Best Actress, in 1932, 1967, 1968 and 1981.
Most Academy Awards® for Best Actor	Seven actors have won two Academy Awards® for Best Actor: Spencer Tracy, Gary Cooper, Marlon Brando, Jack Nicholson, Fredric March, Dustin Hoffman and Tom Hanks.
Most Academy Awards® in total	Walt Disney won 26 Academy Awards®.
Most Academy Award® nominations	John Williams is the most nominated living person with 41 nominations; Metro-Goldwyn-Mayer holds the overall record with 62 nominations.

Play It Again, Sam

Perhaps the most famous line associated with *Casablanca* (1942), 'Play it again, Sam', was never actually spoken by either star. Rick, played by Humphrey Bogart, declares 'Play it!' while Ingrid Bergman's character Ilsa requests 'Play it, Sam. Play *As Time Goes By*' – but neither ever utters the famous line.

BRITISH ACADEMY TELEVISION AWARDS

The British Academy of Film and Television Arts (BAFTA) has awarded prizes for outstanding work in television entertainment since 1954. Programmes associated with the awards are given from 1968.

Year	Best Actress	Best Actor
1954	Googie Withers	Paul Rogers
1955	Virginia McKenna	Peter Cushing
1956	Rosalie Crutchley	Michael Gough
1957	*no award*	Michael Hordern
1958	Gwen Watford	Donald Pleasence

Year	Best Actress	Best Actor
1959	Catherine Lacey	Patrick McGoohan
1960	Billie Whitelaw	Lee Montague
1961	Ruth Dunning	Rupert Davies
1962	Brenda Bruce	Harry H Corbett
1963	Vivien Merchant	Alan Badel
1964	Katherine Blake	Patrick Wymark
1965	Gwen Watford	Alan Badel
1966	Vanessa Redgrave	Warren Mitchell
1967	Judi Dench	Eric Porter
1968	Wendy Craig *Not in Front of the Children*	Roy Dotrice *Brief Lives*
1969	Margaret Tyzack *The First Churchills*	Edward Woodward *Callan, A Dream Divided* (Omnibus), *A Bit of a Holiday*
1970	Annette Crosbie *The Six Wives of Henry VIII*	Keith Michell *The Six Wives of Henry VIII, An Ideal Husband*
1971	Patricia Hayes *Edna, the Inebriate Woman*	John Le Mesurier *Traitor*
1972	Billie Whitelaw *The Sextet* (eight plays)	Anthony Hopkins *War and Peace*
1973	Celia Johnson *Mrs Palfrey at the Claremont*	Frank Finlay *The Adventures of Don Quixote, Candide, The Death of Adolf Hitler*
1974	Lee Remick *Jennie*	Peter Barkworth *Crown Matrimonial*
1975	Annette Crosbie *Edward the Seventh*	John Hurt *The Naked Civil Servant, Nijinsky, God of the Dance*
1976	Siân Phillips *I, Claudius*	Derek Jacobi *I, Claudius*
1977	Penelope Keith *The Norman Conquests, Saving It for Albie*	Peter Barkworth *Professional Foul, The Country Party*
1978	Francesca Annis *Lillie, The Comedy of Errors*	Edward Fox *Edward and Mrs Simpson*
1979	Cheryl Campbell *Testament of Youth, The Duke of Wellington, Malice Aforethought*	Alec Guinness *Tinker Tailor Soldier Spy*
1980	Peggy Ashcroft *Caught on a Train, Cream in My Coffee*	Denholm Elliott *Gentle Folk/In Hiding/Blade on the Feather/The Stinker*
1981	Judi Dench *Going Gently, A Fine Romance, The Cherry Orchard*	Anthony Andrews *Brideshead Revisited*
1982	Beryl Reid *Smiley's People*	Alec Guinness *Smiley's People*
1983	Coral Browne *An Englishman Abroad*	Alan Bates *An Englishman Abroad*
1984	Peggy Ashcroft *The Jewel in the Crown*	Tim Pigott-Smith *The Jewel in the Crown*
1985	Claire Bloom *Shadowlands*	Bob Peck *Edge of Darkness*
1986	Anna Massey *Hotel Du Lac*	Michael Gambon *The Singing Detective*
1987	Emma Thompson *Fortunes of War, Tutti Frutti*	David Jason *Porterhouse Blue*
1988	Thora Hird *A Cream Cracker under the Settee*	Ray McAnally *A Very British Coup*
1989	Diana Rigg *Mother Love*	John Thaw *Inspector Morse*
1990	Geraldine McEwan *Oranges are not the Only Fruit*	Ian Richardson *House of Cards*
1991	Helen Mirren *Prime Suspect*	Robert Lindsay *G.B.H.*
1992	Helen Mirren *Prime Suspect 2*	John Thaw *Inspector Morse*
1993	Helen Mirren *Prime Suspect 3*	Robbie Coltrane *Cracker*
1994	Juliet Aubrey *Middlemarch*	Robbie Coltrane *Cracker*
1995	Jennifer Ehle *Pride and Prejudice*	Robbie Coltrane *Cracker*

SOAP OPERA PLACES

1996	Gina McKee *Our Friends in the North*	Nigel Hawthorne *The Fragile Heart*
1997	Daniela Nardini *This Life*	Simon Russell Beale *A Dance to the Music of Time*
1998	Thora Hird *Waiting for the Telegram*	Tom Courtenay *A Rather English Marriage*
1999	Thora Hird *Lost for Words*	Michael Gambon *Wives and Daughters*
2000	Judi Dench *Last of the Blonde Bombshells*	Michael Gambon *Longitude*
2001	Julie Walters *My Beautiful Son*	Michael Gambon *Perfect Strangers*
2002	Julie Walters *Murder*	Albert Finney *The Gathering Storm*
2003	Julie Walters *The Wife of Bath – Canterbury Tales*	Bill Nighy *State of Play*
2004	Anamarcia Marinca *Sex Traffic*	Rhys Ifans *Not Only But Always*

SOAP OPERA PLACES

Soap opera	Setting
The Archers	Ambridge, South Borsetshire, UK
The Bill	Sun Hill, Canley, London, UK
Brookside	Brookside Close, Liverpool, UK
Casualty	Holby City Hospital, Holby, UK
Coronation Street	Weatherfield, Manchester, UK
EastEnders	Albert Square, Walford, London, UK
Emmerdale	Emmerdale, Yorkshire, UK
Holby City	Holby City Hospital, Holby, UK
Hollyoaks	Hollyoaks, Chester, UK
Home and Away	Summer Bay, Australia
Neighbours	Ramsay Street, Erinsborough, Australia
River City	Montego Street, Shieldinch, Glasgow, UK

Soap and Beer

The pubs in television soaps are some of the best known in the country. From The Bull (*The Archers*) to The Rover's Return (*Coronation Street*) and The Woolpack (*Emmerdale*), the characters in soap operas are often found having a pint and mulling over their problems at their local. Perhaps the most famous imaginary pub is *EastEnders'* Queen Vic. The BBC says that the booze served in the Vic is real, albeit low-alcohol, beer.

Music

ORCHESTRAS

Orchestra layout

Empty Orchestra

The Japanese word *karaoke* literally means 'empty orchestra'.

Major orchestras

Name	Date founded	Location
Academy of Ancient Music	1973	UK (London)
Academy of St Martin-in-the-Fields	1959	UK (London)
Australian Chamber	1975	Sydney
BBC Philharmonic	1934	UK (Manchester)
BBC Scottish Symphony	1935	UK (Glasgow)
BBC Symphony	1930	UK (London)
BBC Welsh Symphony	1935	UK (Cardiff)
Berliner Philharmonic	1882	Germany
Boston Symphony	1881	USA
Bournemouth Symphony	1893	UK
Chicago Symphony	1891	USA
City of Birmingham Symphony	1920	UK
City of Glasgow Philharmonic	1990	UK
Cleveland Symphony	1918	USA
Concertgebouw	1888	The Netherlands (Amsterdam)
Detroit Symphony	1914	USA
English Chamber	1948	UK (London)
Hallé	1858	UK (Manchester)
Israel Philharmonic	1936	Israel (Tel Aviv)
London Philharmonic	1904	UK
London Symphony	1904	UK
Los Angeles Philharmonic	1904	USA
Melbourne Symphony	1906	Australia
Milan La Scala	1778	Italy
Minnesota	1903	USA (Minneapolis)
National Symphony	1931	USA (Washington DC)
NBC Symphony	1937–54	USA (New York)
New Orleans Philharmonic Symphony	1936	USA
New York Philharmonic	1842	USA
New York Symphony	1878	USA
Northern Sinfonia	1958	UK (Newcastle upon Tyne)
Orchestre Symphonique de Montréal	1842	Canada
Oslo Philharmonic	1919	Norway
Philadelphia	1900	USA
The Philharmonia	1945	UK (London)
Pittsburgh Symphony	1926	USA
Royal Liverpool Philharmonic	1840	UK
Royal Philharmonic	1946	UK (London)
Royal Scottish National	1891	UK (Glasgow)
St Petersburg Philharmonic	1921	Russia
San Francisco	1911	USA
Santa Cecelia Academy	1895	Italy (Rome)
Scottish Chamber	1974	UK (Edinburgh)
Seattle Symphony	1903	USA
Staatskapelle	1923	Germany (Dresden)
Sydney Symphony	1934	Australia
Toronto Symphony	1922	Canada
Ulster	1966	UK (Belfast)
Vienna Philharmonic	1842	Austria
Vienna Symphony	1900	Austria

OPERAS AND OPERETTAS

Name	Composer	Date	Name	Composer	Date
Aïda	Verdi	1871	Madame Butterfly	Puccini	1904
Andrea Chénier	Umberto Giordano	1896	The Magic Flute	Mozart	1791
			Manon	Massenet	1884
Ariadne auf Naxos	Richard Strauss	1916	Manon Lescaut	Puccini	1893
Un Ballo in Maschera	Verdi	1859	The Marriage of Figaro	Mozart	1786
The Barber of Seville	Rossini	1816	The Merry Wives of Windsor	Otto Nicolai	1849
The Bartered Bride	Smetana	1866	The Midsummer Marriage	Tippett	1955
La Bohème	Puccini	1896	The Mikado	Gilbert and Sullivan	1885
Boris Godunov	Mussorgsky	1874			
Carmen	Bizet	1875	Moses und Aron	Schönberg	1954
Cavalleria Rusticana	Mascagni	1890	Nabucco	Verdi	1842
Così Fan Tutte	Mozart	1790	Nixon in China	Peter Adams	1990
The Cunning Little Vixen	Janácek	1924	Norma	Bellini	1831
Dido and Aeneas	Purcell	1689	Orfeo ed Euridice	Gluck	1762
Don Carlos	Verdi	1867	Orpheus in the Underworld	Offenbach	1858
Don Giovanni	Mozart	1787	Otello	Verdi	1887
Don Pasquale	Donizetti	1843	Pagliacci	Leoncavallo	1892
Duke Bluebeard's Castle	Bartók	1918	Parsifal	Wagner	1882
Einstein on the Beach	Philip Glass	1976	Pelléas et Mélisande	Debussy	1902
Elektra	Richard Strauss	1909	Peter Grimes	Britten	1945
			Porgy and Bess	Gershwin	1935
Eugene Onegin	Tchaikovsky	1879	The Rake's Progress	Stravinsky	1951
Falstaff	Verdi	1893	Rigoletto	Verdi	1851
Faust	Gounod	1859	The Ring	Wagner	1876
Fidelio	Beethoven	1814	Salome	Richard Strauss	1911
La Fille du Régiment	Donizetti	1840			
Die Fledermaus	Johann Strauss	1874	Samson et Dalila	Saint-Saëns	1877
			Simon Boccanegra	Verdi	1857
The Flying Dutchman	Wagner	1843	La Sonnambula	Bellini	1831
			The Tales of Hoffman	Offenbach	1881
Hansel and Gretel	Humperdinck	1893			
HMS Pinafore	Gilbert and Sullivan	1878	Tannhäuser	Wagner	1845
			The Threepenny Opera	Weill	1928
Jenufa	Janácek	1904			
King Priam	Tippett	1962	Tosca	Puccini	1900
Lady Macbeth of Mtsensk	Shostakovich	1934	La Traviata	Verdi	1853
			Tristan und Isolde	Wagner	1865
Lohengrin	Wagner	1850	Il Trovatore	Verdi	1853
The Love for Three Oranges	Prokofiev	1920	Turandot	Puccini	1926
			The Turn of the Screw	Britten	1954
Lucia di Lammermoor	Donizetti	1835			
			Werther	Massenet	1892
Lulu	Berg	1937	William Tell	Rossini	1829
Macbeth	Verdi	1847	Wozzeck	Berg	1925

BALLETS

Ballet	Composer	Choreographer	First performance
Bolero	Ravel	Bejart	1961
Cinderella	Prokofiev	Ashton	1948
Coppélia	Delibes	St Léon	1870
La Fille mal gardée	Various (French popular songs and airs)	Dauberval	1789
The Firebird	Stravinsky	Fokine	1910
Giselle	Adam	Coralli and Perro (later revised by Petipa)	1841
Manon	Massenet	MacMillan	1974
The Nutcracker	Tchaikovsky	Ivanov	1892
Romeo and Juliet	Prokofiev	Lavrovsky	1940
Le Sacré du printemps (The Rite of Spring)	Stravinsky, Roerich	Nijinsky	1913
Schéhérazade	Rimsky-Korsakov	Fokine	1910
The Sleeping Beauty	Tchaikovsky	Petipa	1890
'Still Life' at the Penguin Café	Jeffes	Bintley	1988
Swan Lake	Tchaikovsky	Petipa and Ivanov	1895
La Sylphide	Løvenskjold	Bournonville	1836

Manuscript Millions

Original manuscripts of works by renowned composers are highly sought after by collectors and can fetch millions at auction. In May 2003 the working manuscript of Beethoven's 'Ninth Symphony' was sold for £2 133 600, setting a new record price both for a work by Beethoven and for a single musical manuscript. Described by Sotheby's as 'perhaps the single most important musical work ever to appear at auction', the pages, dating from 1826, have Beethoven's handwritten revisions scrawled throughout, including frustrated comments to his copyist such as *du verfluchter Kerl!* – 'you damned fool!' The record for the highest price ever paid for a manuscript was set in May 1987, when nine complete Mozart symphonies reached almost £2.6 million.

GRAMMY® AWARDS

Grammy® Awards are awarded annually, in a number of categories, by the US National Academy of Recording Arts and Sciences to 'to honor excellence in the recording arts and sciences'; first awarded in 1958.

Year	Best record	Best album
1958	Domenico Modugno 'Nel Blu Dipinto Di Blu (Volare)'	Henry Mancini *Peter Gunn*
1959	Bobby Darin 'Mack the Knife'	Frank Sinatra *Come Dance with Me*
1960	Percy Faith 'Theme from *A Summer Place*'	Bob Newhart *Button Down Mind*
1961	Henry Mancini 'Moon River'	Judy Garland *Judy at Carnegie Hall*
1962	Tony Bennett 'I Left My Heart in San Francisco'	Vaughn Meader *The First Family*
1963	Henry Mancini 'The Days of Wine and Roses'	Barbra Streisand *The Barbra Streisand Album*
1964	Stan Getz, Astrud Gilberto 'The Girl from Ipanema'	Stan Getz, João Gilberto *Getz/Gilberto*

Year	Best record	Best album
1965	Herb Alpert 'A Taste of Honey'	Frank Sinatra *September of My Years*
1966	Frank Sinatra 'Strangers in the Night'	Frank Sinatra *A Man and His Music*
1967	5th Dimension 'Up, Up and Away'	The Beatles *Sgt Pepper's Lonely Hearts Club Band*
1968	Simon and Garfunkel 'Mrs Robinson'	Glen Campbell *By the Time I Get to Phoenix*
1969	5th Dimension 'Aquarius/Let the Sunshine In'	Blood, Sweat and Tears *Blood, Sweat and Tears*
1970	Simon and Garfunkel 'Bridge Over Troubled Water'	Simon and Garfunkel *Bridge Over Troubled Water*
1971	Carole King 'It's Too Late'	Carole King *Tapestry*
1972	Roberta Flack 'The First Time Ever I Saw Your Face'	Various artists *The Concert for Bangladesh*
1973	Roberta Flack 'Killing Me Softly with His Song'	Stevie Wonder *Innervisions*
1974	Olivia Newton-John 'I Honestly Love You'	Stevie Wonder *Fulfillingness' First Finale*
1975	Captain and Tennille 'Love Will Keep Us Together'	Paul Simon *Still Crazy After All These Years*
1976	George Benson 'This Masquerade'	Stevie Wonder *Songs in the Key of Life*
1977	Eagles 'Hotel California'	Fleetwood Mac *Rumours*
1978	Billy Joel 'Just the Way You Are'	Bee Gees *Saturday Night Fever*
1979	The Doobie Brothers 'What a Fool Believes'	Billy Joel *52nd Street*
1980	Christopher Cross 'Sailing'	Christopher Cross *Christopher Cross*
1981	Kim Carnes 'Bette Davis Eyes'	John Lennon, Yoko Ono *Double Fantasy*
1982	Toto 'Rosanna'	Toto *Toto IV*
1983	Michael Jackson 'Beat It'	Michael Jackson *Thriller*
1984	Tina Turner 'What's Love Got to Do with It'	Lionel Richie *Can't Slow Down*
1985	USA for Africa 'We Are the World'	Phil Collins *No Jacket Required*
1986	Steve Winwood 'Higher Love'	Paul Simon *Graceland*
1987	Paul Simon 'Graceland'	U2 *The Joshua Tree*
1988	Bobby McFerrin 'Don't Worry, Be Happy'	George Michael *Faith*
1989	Bette Midler 'Wind Beneath My Wings'	Bonnie Raitt *Nick of Time*
1990	Phil Collins 'Another Day in Paradise'	Quincy Jones *Back on the Block*
1991	Natalie Cole with Nat 'King' Cole 'Unforgettable'	Natalie Cole with Nat 'King' Cole *Unforgettable*
1992	Eric Clapton 'Tears in Heaven'	Eric Clapton *Unplugged*
1993	Whitney Houston 'I Will Always Love You'	Whitney Houston *The Bodyguard*
1994	Sheryl Crow 'All I Wanna Do'	Tony Bennett *MTV Unplugged*
1995	Seal 'Kiss From a Rose'	Alanis Morissette *Jagged Little Pill*
1996	Eric Clapton 'Change the World'	Celine Dion *Falling into You*
1997	Shawn Colvin 'Sunny Came Home'	Bob Dylan *Time Out of Mind*
1998	Celine Dion 'My Heart Will Go On'	Lauryn Hill *The Miseducation of Lauryn Hill*
1999	Santana, featuring Rob Thomas 'Smooth'	Santana *Supernatural*
2000	U2 'Beautiful Day'	Steely Dan *Two Against Nature*
2001	U2 'Walk On'	Various artists *O Brother, Where Art Thou?*
2002	Norah Jones 'Don't Know Why'	Norah Jones *Come Away With Me*
2003	Coldplay 'Clocks'	Outkast *Speakerboxxx/The Love Below*
2004	Ray Charles and Norah Jones 'Here We Go Again'	Ray Charles and various artists *Genius Loves Company*

EUROVISION SONG CONTEST

The Eurovision Song Contest is held annually to choose a winning pop song from among those entered by the participating countries. Open to member countries of the European Broadcasting Union; first held in 1956.

1956	Switzerland	1981	UK
1957	The Netherlands	1982	Germany
1958	France	1983	Luxembourg
1959	The Netherlands	1984	Sweden
1960	France	1985	Norway
1961	Luxembourg	1986	Belgium
1962	France	1987	Ireland
1963	Denmark	1988	Switzerland
1964	Italy	1989	Yugoslavia
1965	Luxembourg	1990	Italy
1966	Austria	1991	Sweden
1967	UK	1992	Ireland
1968	Spain	1993	Ireland
1969	France, The Netherlands, Spain and UK[1]	1994	Ireland
		1995	Norway
1970	Ireland	1996	Ireland
1971	Monaco	1997	UK
1972	Luxembourg	1998	Israel
1973	Luxembourg	1999	Sweden
1974	Sweden	2000	Denmark
1975	The Netherlands	2001	Estonia
1976	UK	2002	Latvia
1977	France	2003	Turkey
1978	Israel	2004	Ukraine
1979	Israel	2005	Greece
1980	Ireland		

[1] Four-way tie.

La La Land

Eurovision entries are not usually noted for their lyrical brilliance. Silly Eurovision song titles have included 'Bana Bana' (Turkey, 1989), 'Boom Bang-a-Bang' (UK, 1969), 'Diggi-Loo-Diggi-Ley' (Sweden, 1984), 'A-Ba-Ni-Bi' (Israel, 1978) and 'Ding Dinge Dong' (The Netherlands, 1975), while Spain's 1968 entry 'La La La …' contained almost 140 instances of the word 'la'.

JAMES BOND FILM THEME SONGS

Year	Film	Song	Artist
1962	*Dr No*	'The James Bond Theme'	John Barry and orchestra
1963	*From Russia with Love*	'From Russia With Love'	Matt Munro
1964	*Goldfinger*	'Goldfinger'	Shirley Bassey
1965	*Thunderball*	'Thunderball'	Tom Jones
1967	*You Only Live Twice*	'You Only Live Twice'	Nancy Sinatra
1969	*On Her Majesty's Secret Service*	'We Have All the Time in the World'	Louis Armstrong

Year	Film	Song	Artist
1971	*Diamonds Are Forever*	'Diamonds Are Forever'	Shirley Bassey
1973	*Live and Let Die*	'Live and Let Die'	Paul McCartney and Wings
1974	*The Man With the Golden Gun*	'The Man with the Golden Gun'	Lulu
1977	*The Spy Who Loved Me*	'Nobody Does It Better'	Carly Simon
1979	*Moonraker*	'Moonraker'	Shirley Bassey
1981	*For Your Eyes Only*	'For Your Eyes Only'	Sheena Easton
1983	*Octopussy*	'All Time High'	Rita Coolidge
1985	*A View to a Kill*	'A View to a Kill'	Duran Duran
1987	*The Living Daylights*	'The Living Daylights'	A-Ha
1989	*Licence to Kill*	'Licence to Kill'	Gladys Knight
1995	*GoldenEye*	'GoldenEye'	Tina Turner
1997	*Tomorrow Never Dies*	'Tomorrow Never Dies'	Sheryl Crow
1999	*The World Is Not Enough*	'The World Is Not Enough'	Garbage
2002	*Die Another Day*	'Die Another Day'	Madonna

The Name's Norman

The famous signature tune of the James Bond movies, 'The James Bond Theme', was composed by Londoner Monty Norman. Norman, who insists that it was only the all-expenses paid trip to the *Dr No* set in Jamaica that convinced him to take on the project, based the theme on a song that he had written for a long-since abandoned musical. He reworked the song's simple melody into the now instantly recognizable riff that he describes as 'Dum de-de-dum-dum, dum dum dum, dum de-de dum dum, dum dum dum …'. The theme was then orchestrated by John Barry, who went on to have a lasting involvement in later Bond film scores. More than 25 million copies of the theme tune have since been sold worldwide.

MUSICAL REAL NAMES

Pseudonym	Real name	Pseudonym	Real name
Bennett, Tony	Anthony Dominick Benedetto	Cooper, Alice	Vincent Damon Furnier
Berlin, Irving	Israel Baline	Costello, Elvis	Declan Patrick McManus
Bizet, Georges	Alexandre Césare Léopold	Crosby, Bing	Harry Lillis Crosby
Black, Cilla	Priscilla Maria Veronica White	Dylan, Bob	Robert Allen Zimmerman
		The Edge	David Evans
Bo Diddley	Elias Bates, later McDaniel	Eminem	Marshall Mathers III
Bon Jovi, Jon	John Francis Bongiovi, Jnr	Fields, Dame Gracie	Grace Stansfield
Bono	Paul Hewson	Gershwin, George	Jacob Gershvin
Bowie, David	David Robert Jones		
Boy George	George O'Dowd	Gershwin, Ira	Israel Gershvin
Bygraves, Max	Walter William Bygraves	Holiday, Billie	Eleanora Fagan
Charles, Ray	Ray Charles Robinson	Holly, Buddy	Charles Hardin
Cher	Cheryl Sarkisian La Pier	Howlin' Wolf	Chester Arthur Burnett
Clark, Petula	Sally Owen	John, Sir Elton Hercules	Reginald Kenneth Dwight
Cline, Patsy	Virginia Petterson Hensley		
Cole, Nat 'King'	Nathaniel Adams Coles	Jones, Tom	Thomas Jones Woodward

Pseudonym	Real name	Pseudonym	Real name
King, B B	Riley B King	Pop, Iggy	James Newell Osterberg
Laine, Dame Cleo	Clementina Dinah Campbell	Prince	Prince Rogers Nelson
		Rainey, Ma	Gertrude Pridgett Rainey née Pridgett
Lanza, Mario	Alfredo Arnold Coccozza		
Leadbelly	Huddie William Ledbetter	Reed, Lou	Louis Firbank
Little Richard	Richard Wayne Penniman	Richard, Sir Cliff	Harry Rodger Webb
Lulu	Marie McDonald McLaughlin Lawrie	Ross, Diana	Diane Earle
Lynn, Dame Vera	Vera Margaret Welch	Rotten, Johnny	John Lydon
		Scott, Ronnie	Ronald Schatt
Madonna	Madonna Louise Veronica Ciccone	Simone, Nina	Eunice Kathleen Waymon
		Sly Stone	Sylvester Stewart
Manilow, Barry	Barry Allen Pincus	Solti, Sir Georg	György Stern
Manson, Marilyn	Brian Warner	Springfield, Dusty	Mary O'Brien
Meat Loaf	Marvin Lee Aday	Starr, Ringo	Richard Starkey
Mercury, Freddie	Farookh Bulsara	Steele, Tommy	Thomas Hicks
		Stevens, Cat	Stephen Demetre Georgiou
Michael, George	Georgios Kyriacos Panayiotou	Sting	Gordon Matthew Sumner
		Streisand, Barbra	Barbara Joan Rosen
Miranda, Carmen	Maria do Carmo Miranda Da Cunha	Twain, Shania	Eileen Regina Edwards
Morton, Jelly Roll	Ferdinand Joseph La Menthe or Lamothe	Turner, Tina	Annie Mae Bullock
		Vicious, Sid	John Simon Ritchie
Novello, Ivor	David Ivor Davies	Washington, Dinah	Ruth Jones
Offenbach, Jacques	Jakob Eberst	Waters, Muddy	McKinley Morganfield
Osbourne, Ozzy	John Osbourne	Wonder, Stevie	Steveland Judkins
		Wyman, Bill	William Perks
Piaf, Edith	Edith Giovanna Gassion	Wynette, Tammy	Virginia Wynette Pugh

Musical Monikers

Musicians, not content with renaming themselves, are also renowned for the intriguing and often unusual names with which they christen their offspring. In the 1960s, Keith Richards of the Rolling Stones named his daughter *Dandelion*, Sonny Bono and Cher christened their daughter *Chastity* and Frank Zappa famously called his daughter *Moon Unit*. From the 1970s came the euphonious *Zowie Bowie* (son of David) and *Rolan Bolan* (son of Marc). More recent additions to the pop world's second generation include children named after places (Victoria Beckham's son *Brooklyn*, Madonna's daughter *Lourdes* and Michael Jackson's daughter *Paris*), musical heroes (Liam Gallagher's son *Lennon*) and fruits (Chris Martin's daughter *Apple*). Other famous names include *Blue Angel* (U2's The Edge), *Fifi Trixibelle*, *Peaches Honeyblossom* and *Pixie* (Bob Geldof), *Heavenly Hiraani Tiger Lily* (Michael Hutchence), *Elijah Bob Patricius Guggi Q* (U2's Bono) and *Phoenix Chi* (the Spice Girls' Mel B).

FOOD AND DRINK

VITAMINS

Vitamins are any of numerous organic substances present in minute quantities in nutritive foods, and are essential for the health of animals.

Fat-soluble vitamins

Vitamin	Chemical name	Source
A	retinol (carotene)	milk, butter, cheese, egg yolk, liver, fatty fish, dark green vegetables, yellow/red fruits and vegetables, especially carrots
D	cholecalciferol	egg yolk, liver, fatty fish; made on skin in sunlight
E	tocopherols	vegetable oils
K	phytomenadione	green leafy vegetables, beef, liver

Water-soluble vitamins

Vitamin	Chemical name	Source
B_1	thiamin	germ and bran of seeds, grains, yeast
B_2	riboflavin	liver, milk, cheese, eggs, green leafy vegetables, pulses, yeast
B_6	pyridoxine	liver, meats, fruits, cereals, leafy vegetables
	pantothenic acid	widespread in plants and animals; destroyed in heavily-processed food
	biotin	liver, kidney, yeast extract; made by micro-organisms in large intestine
B_{12}	cyanocobalamin	liver, kidney, milk; none found in plants
	folic acid	liver, green leafy vegetables, peanuts; cooking and processing can cause serious losses in food
C	ascorbic acid	blackcurrants, citrus fruits, other fruits, green leafy vegetables, potatoes; losses occur during storage and cooking

MINERALS

Mineral	Source
calcium	milk, butter, cheese, sardines, green leafy vegetables, citrus fruits
chromium	brewer's yeast, black pepper, liver, wholemeal bread, beer
copper	green vegetables, fish, oysters, liver
fluorine	fluoridated drinking water, seafood, tea
iodine	seafood, saltwater fish, seaweed, iodized salt, table salt
iron	liver, kidney, green leafy vegetables, egg yolk, dried fruit, potatoes, molasses
magnesium	green leafy vegetables (eaten raw), nuts, whole grains
manganese	legumes, cereal grains, green leafy vegetables, tea
molybdenum	legumes, cereal grains, liver, kidney, some dark green vegetables
phosphorus	meat, poultry, fish, eggs, dried beans and peas, milk products
potassium	fresh vegetables, meat, orange juice, bananas, bran
selenium	seafood, cereals, meat, egg yolk, garlic
sodium	table salt, other naturally occurring salts (very rare)
zinc	meat, whole grains, legumes, oysters, milk

WINE BOTTLE SIZES

Name	Capacity[1]	Equivalent (standard bottles)
wine bottle	75cl	1
magnum	1.5 l	2
jeroboam	3 l	4
rehoboam	4.5 l	6
methuselah	6 l	8
salmanazar	9 l	12
balthazar	12 l	16
nebuchadnezzar	15 l	20

[1] To convert litres to pints, multiply by 0.56821.

Note: A flagon of wine contains 1.13 l/2pt.

Biblical Bottles

Many bottle sizes are named after biblical figures from the Old Testament. The *balthazar* and the *nebuchadnezzar* were both named after kings of Babylon, the *methuselah* after a patriarch said to have lived 969 years, the *salmanazar* by allusion to Shalmaneser, king of Assyria, and the *jeroboam* and *rehoboam* after figures in the Book of Kings. In contrast, the *magnum* simply comes from the Latin word for 'big'.

EUROPEAN CHEESES

Belgium
Limburger

Cyprus
halloumi

Denmark
Danish blue

England
Cheddar
Cheshire
Derby
double Gloucester
Ilchester
Lancashire
Red Leicester
Stilton®
Wensleydale

France
Boursin

Brie
Camembert
Cantal
Chaumes
Coulommiers
crottin
Munster
Pont l'Évêque
Port Salut
reblochon
Roquefort
St Paulin
vacherin

Germany
Cambozola®
Münster
Tilsit

Greece
feta

Italy
bel paese
dolcelatte
Fontina
Gorgonzola
mascarpone
mozzarella
Parmesan
pecorino
provolone
ricotta
Romano
stracchino
Taleggio

The Netherlands
Edam
Gouda
Leerdammer

Norway
Jarlsberg®

Scotland
crowdie
Dunlop

Spain
Manchego

Switzerland
Emmenthal
Gruyère
sapsago

Wales
Caerphilly

Red Hot Chilli Peppers

The heat of chilli peppers is measured by the Scoville scale, which was developed by pharmacologist Wilbur Scoville in 1912. Although originally a taste test, today it scientifically measures the amount of capsaicin – the substance that makes chillis taste hot – in each pepper. The higher the number of Scoville units, the hotter the pepper; pure capsaicin measures a sizzling 16 million Scoville units. A bell pepper measures 0 Scoville units, a jalapeño pepper measures 2 500–5 000 units and cayenne pepper measures 30 000–50 000 units. Guinness World Records® states that the world's hottest chilli pepper is the Red Savina habañero, which can contain up to an eye-watering 570 000 Scoville units; most habañero peppers peak at around 325 000 to 350 000 units.

COCKTAILS

There are many variations in cocktail ingredients; only the most common are listed.

Cocktail	Alcohol	Other common ingredients
Bellini	chilled champagne	peach nectar or peach schnapps
Between the Sheets	rum, brandy, Cointreau®	lemon juice
Black Russian	vodka, Kahlúa®	none
Bloody Mary	vodka	tomato juice and seasoning
Brandy Alexander	brandy, crème de cacao	cream
Bullshot	vodka	beef consommé
Caipirinha	cachaça	crushed lime and sugar
Champagne Cocktail	champagne, brandy	sugar and Angostura bitters
Collins	a spirit, for example vodka or whisky	lemon or lime juice, sugar and soda water
Cosmopolitan	vodka, orange liqueur	lime juice and cranberry juice
Daiquiri	rum	lime juice
Gimlet	gin or vodka	lime juice
Harvey Wallbanger	Galliano, vodka	orange juice
Horse's Neck	brandy	ginger ale and a twist of lemon
Mai tai	rum, triple sec, grenadine	lime juice
Manhattan	vermouth, whisky and sometimes curaçao or maraschino	Angostura bitters
Margarita	tequila, orange liqueur	lime or lemon juice
Martini	vermouth, gin, sometimes vodka	bitters etc and a twist of lemon
Moscow Mule	vodka	ginger ale and lemon juice
Old Fashioned	whisky	bitters, water and sugar
Pink Lady	gin, grenadine	cream, egg white and lemon juice
Planter's Punch	rum	lime or lemon juice and sugar
Rickey	gin or vodka	lime juice and soda water with ice
Rusty Nail	whisky and Drambuie®	
Sazerac®	Pernod and whisky	
Screwdriver	vodka	orange juice
Sea Breeze	vodka	cranberry juice and grapefruit juice
Sidecar	brandy, orange liqueur	lemon juice
Singapore Sling	brandy, gin, Cointreau®, Benedictine and grenadine	orange juice, lime juice
Slammer	tequila	
Sour	gin or whisky	lemon or lime juice
Stinger	brandy and white crème de menthe	
Tequila Sunrise	tequila, grenadine	orange juice
Tom Collins	gin	lime juice, soda and sugar or syrup
White Lady	gin, orange liqueur	lemon juice
White Russian	vodka, Kahlúa®	milk

Cocktail Salvation

'The greatest of all the contributions of the American way of life to the salvation of humanity.'
H L Mencken on the cocktail. Quoted by William Grimes in 'The American Cocktail', *Americana*, Dec 1992.

LIQUEURS

A liqueur is a potent alcoholic preparation that is flavoured or perfumed and sweetened.

Liqueur	Description
absinthe	bitter, green, aniseed-flavoured; containing (originally) extract of wormwood
advocaat	containing raw eggs and flavourings
amaretto	Italian; flavoured with almonds
anisette	prepared from anise seed (aromatic seeds, of a flavour similar to liquorice)
Benedictine	resembles Chartreuse; distilled at Fécamp in Normandy, formerly by Benedictine monks
Chartreuse	green or yellow; manufactured at La Grande Chartreuse monastery near Grenoble, France, by the monks; made from aromatic herbs, flowers and brandy
cherry brandy	made by steeping Morello cherries in brandy
Cointreau®	orange-flavoured
crème de cacao	chocolate-flavoured
crème de menthe	green, peppermint-flavoured
curaçao	flavoured with bitter orange peel
Drambuie®	Scotch whisky liqueur
eau des creoles	from Martinique; made by distilling the flowers of the mammee-apple with alcohol
Frangelico	Italian; flavoured with hazelnuts
Galliano	Italian; flavoured with anise
Grand Marnier®	orange-flavoured, with a cognac base
Kahlúa®	Mexican; made from coffee beans, cocoa beans and vanilla
kirsch	made from the wild cherry
kümmel	flavoured with cumin and caraway seeds
maraschino	distilled from a cherry grown in the Croatian region of Dalmatia
mirabelle	colourless; distilled from mirabelle plums
noyau	made from brandy flavoured with bitter almonds or peach kernels
ouzo	aniseed
ratafia	flavoured with fruit kernels
rum shrub	made from rum, sugar, lime or lemon juice, etc
sambuca	Italian; made from aniseed
Southern Comfort®	whisky liqueur originally produced in the southern US
Strega®	Italian; sweet, orange-flavoured
Tia Maria®	coffee-flavoured
Triple sec	clear, orange-flavoured
Van der Hum	South African; flavoured with tangerines

Monks and Sour Cherries

Liqueur names come from a variety of sources. Some reflect the liqueur's origin, for example *curaçao*, named after the island in the Caribbean where it was first made, or *Benedictine* after the Benedictine monks who first created it. Other names are derived from the taste of the liqueur, for example *amaretto*, which comes from the Italian word *amaro* meaning 'bitter'. And some are named after their ingredients, such as *maraschino* from the Italian *marasca*, 'sour cherry', and *absinthe*, from the Greek word *apsinthion* meaning 'wormwood'. *Advocaat*, however, comes from Dutch *advokaatenborrel* which means 'advocate's dram', as a clearer of the throat.

LANGUAGE

PROVERBS

Proverbs are arranged alphabetically by key words (which are shown in *italic*). In each case the proverb is followed by the century in which it first occurred in print in English in a recognizable form; in many cases related sentiments are attested earlier, often in Greek and Latin, or in medieval French sources. Some of the uses cited here in italics are not in the precise form given here.

Proverb / Date / Notable uses

absence makes the heart grow fonder 19c

actions speak louder than words 17c

all's well that ends well 14c

an *apple* a day keeps the doctor away 19c

don't throw the *baby* out with the bathwater 19c *Thomas Carlyle*

beauty is in the eye of the beholder 18c *David Hume*

beauty is only skin deep 17c

beggars can't be choosers 16c

the early *bird* catches the worm 17c

a *bird* in the hand is worth two in the bush 15c

birds of a feather flock together 16c *Bible, Ecclesiasticus 27*

once *bitten*, twice shy 19c

when the *blind* lead the blind, both shall fall into the ditch 9c *Bible, Matthew 15*

you can't get *blood* from a stone 17c

blood is thicker than water 19c

brevity is the soul of wit 17c *Shakespeare, Hamlet*

you can't make *bricks* without straw 17c *Bible, Exodus 5*

don't cross your *bridges* until you come to them 19c

a new *broom* sweeps clean 16c

you can't have your *cake* and eat it 16c

if the *cap* fits, wear it 18c

when the *cat's* away, the mice will play 17c

a *change* is as good as a rest 19c *Arthur Conan Doyle*

charity begins at home 14c *John Wycliffe*

don't count your *chickens* before they are hatched 16c

clothes make the man 15c

every *cloud* has a silver lining 19c

cut your *coat* according to your cloth 16c

too many *cooks* spoil the broth 16c

curiosity killed the cat 20c

there's none so *deaf* as those that will not hear 16c

needs must when the *devil* drives 15c *Shakespeare, All's Well that Ends Well*

the *devil* finds work for idle hands to do 14c *Geoffrey Chaucer*

the *devil* looks after his own 17c

better the *devil* you know than the devil you don't 16c

discretion is the better part of valour 16c *Shakespeare, Henry IV Part One*

give a *dog* a bad name and hang him 18c

Proverb / Date / Notable uses

you can't teach an old *dog* new tricks 16c
let sleeping *dogs* lie 14c *Geoffrey Chaucer*
barking *dogs* seldom bite 16c
to *err* is human, to forgive divine 16c
the *exception* proves the rule 17c
familiarity breeds contempt 14c
there are as good *fish* in the sea as ever came out of it 16c
a *fool* and his money are soon parted 16c
there's no *fool* like an old fool 16c
fools rush in where angels fear to tread 18c *Alexander Pope*
forewarned is forearmed 15c
a *friend* in need is a friend indeed 11c
those who live in *glass* houses shouldn't throw stones 14c *Geoffrey Chaucer*
all that *glitters* is not gold 13c *Shakespeare, Merchant of Venice, as 'all that glisters ...'*
don't teach your *grandmother* to suck eggs 18c
the *grass* is always greener on the other side of the fence 20c
old *habits* die hard 18c *Benjamin Franklin*
many *hands* make light work 14c
first you catch your *hare* 19c *William Makepeace Thackeray*
more *haste* less speed 14c
he who *hesitates* is lost 18c
there is *honour* among thieves 17c
never look a gift *horse* in the mouth 16c
you may take a *horse* to water but you can't make him drink 12c
hunger is the best sauce 16c
where *ignorance* is bliss, 'tis folly to be wise 18c *Thomas Gray*
strike while the *iron* is hot 14c *Geoffrey Chaucer*
a little *knowledge* is a dangerous thing 18c *Alexander Pope*
better *late* than never 14c
he who *laughs* last, laughs longest 20c
least said, soonest mended 15c
a *leopard* doesn't change its spots 16c *Bible, Jeremiah 13.23*
many a *little* makes a mickle 13c
half a *loaf* is better than no bread 16c
look before you leap 14c
one man's *meat* is another man's poison 16c
it's no use crying over spilt *milk* 17c
a *miss* is as good as a mile 17c
if the *mountain* won't come to Mahomet, Mahomet must go to the mountain 17c *Francis Bacon*
necessity is the mother of invention 16c
no *news* is good news 17c *James I*
don't cut off your *nose* to spite your face 16c
nothing ventured, nothing gained 17c
great *oaks* from little acorns grow 14c *Geoffrey Chaucer*
you can't make an *omelette* without breaking eggs 19c
out of sight, out of mind 13c

Proverb / Date / Notable uses

the *pen* is mightier than the sword 16c

take care of the *pence* and the pounds will take care of themselves 18c

in for a *penny*, in for a pound 17c

he that pays the *piper* calls the tune 19c

little *pitchers* have large ears 16c

there's no *place* like home 16c

a watched *pot* never boils 19c *Mrs Gaskell*

practice makes perfect 16c

prevention is better than cure 17c

pride goes before a fall 14c

procrastination is the thief of time 18c *Bible, Proverbs 16*

the *proof* of the pudding is in the eating 14c

you can't make a silk *purse* out of a sow's ear 16c

it never *rains* but it pours 18c

the *road* to hell is paved with good intentions 16c

spare the *rod* and spoil the child 11c *Bible, Proverbs 13*

Rome was not built in a day 16c

when in *Rome*, do as the Romans do 15c

better *safe* than sorry 19c

there is *safety* in numbers 17c *Bible, Proverbs 11*, and *John Bunyan*

what's *sauce* for the goose is sauce for the gander 17c

as well to be hanged for a *sheep* as a lamb 17c

there's no *smoke* without fire 14c

speech is silver, but silence is golden 19c *Thomas Carlyle*

it's no use shutting the *stable* door after the horse has bolted 14c

a *stitch* in time saves nine 18c

a rolling *stone* gathers no moss 14c

it's the last *straw* that breaks the camel's back 17c

little *strokes* fell great oaks 15c

one *swallow* doesn't make a summer 16c

what you lose on the *swings* you gain on the roundabouts 20c

you can have too much of a good *thing* 15c

little *things* please little minds 16c

time and tide wait for no man 14c *Geoffrey Chaucer, in Latin*

don't put off till *tomorrow* what you can do today 14c *Geoffrey Chaucer*

it's better to *travel* hopefully than to arrive 19c *Robert Louis Stevenson*

the *tree* is known by its fruit 16c *Bible, Matthew 12*

trouble shared is trouble halved 20c *Dorothy L Sayers*

there's many a good *tune* played on an old fiddle 20c *Samuel Butler*

one good *turn* deserves another 15c

variety is the spice of life 18c

all things come to those who *wait* 16c

waste not, want not 8c

Fat Ladies Singing

While some proverbs are thousands of years old, others are more recent arrivals in the language. One modern proverb, 'It ain't over 'til the fat lady sings', is thought to have been coined as recently as 1978 by Dan Cook, a Texan journalist, in the form 'the opera ain't over 'til the fat lady sings'. Although it has been suggested that the phrase was older and was simply popularized by Cook, it has certainly caught on in the public imagination and in collections it is found alongside proverbs coined many centuries before.

SIMILES

A simile is a figure of speech in which a person or thing is described by being explicitly likened to another.

as bald as a coot
as black as ink *or* pitch
as blind as a bat
as blue as the sky
as bold as brass
as bright as a button
as brown as a berry
as calm as a millpond
as clean as a whistle
as clear as a bell *or* as crystal *or* *(ironically)* as mud
as cold as charity *or* ice
as cool as a cucumber
as cross as two sticks
as daft as a brush
as dead as a dodo *or* a doornail *or* as mutton
as deaf as a post
as different as chalk and cheese
as drunk as a lord *or* a piper
as dry as a bone
as dull as ditchwater
as easy as falling off a log *or* as winking
as fair as a rose
as fit as a fiddle
as flat as a pancake
as free as a bird
as fresh as a daisy *or* as paint
as good as gold
as green as grass
as happy as a lark *or* as a sandboy *or* as Larry *or* as the day is long
as hard as nails
as high as a kite
as innocent as a lamb
as keen as mustard
as large as life
as light as a feather *or* as down
as like as two peas in a pod *or* *(ironically)* chalk and cheese
as lively as a cricket
as mad as a hatter *or* a March hare

as merry as a grig
as near as a touch
as neat as ninepence
as often as not
as old as Adam *or* Methuselah *or* the hills
as plain as a pikestaff
as pleased as Punch
as poor as a church mouse
as proud as a peacock
as pure as the driven snow
as quick as lightning
as quiet as a mouse
as red as a beetroot
as regular as clockwork
as rich as Croesus
as right as a trivet *or* as rain
as ripe as a cherry
as safe as houses
as sharp as a razor
as sick as a dog *or* a parrot
as silent as the grave
as slippery as an eel
as sober as a judge
as soft as a baby's bottom
as sound as a bell *or* a roach
as steady as a rock
as stiff as a poker
as straight as a die
as strong as a horse
as stubborn as a mule
as sure as a gun *or* as eggs is eggs
as thick *(= conspiratorial)* as thieves
as thick *(= stupid)* as a plank *or* as two short planks
as thin as a rake
as tough as leather *or* old boots
as ugly as sin
as warm as toast
as weak as a kitten
as white as a sheet *or* as snow
as wise as an owl

Common as a Simile

'One thing that literature would be greatly the better for
Would be a more restricted employment by authors of simile and metaphor.'
Ogden Nash, *Many Long Years Ago*, 'Very Like A Whale', 1945.

INTERESTING OLOGIES

An 'ology' is a science whose name ends in *-logy* or *-ology*. This ending comes from the Greek word *logos*, meaning 'word' or 'reason'.

Ology	Study of ...	Ology	Study of ...
acarology	mites	hippology	horses
agrostology	grasses	hoplology	weapons
aristology	dining	hymnology	hymns
astacology	crayfish	hypnology	sleep
autology	oneself	irenology	peace
balneology	bathing and mineral springs	koniology	dust in the air
		limacology	slugs
batology	brambles	malacology	molluscs
bryology	mosses	missiology	religious missions
caliology	birds' nests	myrmecology	ants
campanology	bells and bellringing	odonatology	dragonflies
carcinology	crustaceans	oenology	wines
chaology	chaos or chaos theory	oneirology	dreams
chirology	the language of gesture, and the hand	oology	birds' eggs
		ophiology	snakes
codicology	manuscript volumes	orchidology	orchids
conchology	molluscs and their shells	orology or oreology	mountains
coprology	the use of obscenity in speech, literature and art		
		paroemiology	proverbs
cryptology	codes	phycology	algae
cryptozoology	creatures, such as the Loch Ness monster, that are generally regarded as mythical	podology	feet
		pomology	fruit-growing
		pseudology	lying
		pteridology	ferns
dactyliology	rings or engraved gems	scatology	excrement
deltiology	picture postcards	sindonology	the Turin shroud
demonology	demons and their ways	spectrology	ghosts
garbology	a society's waste materials	speleology	caves
		sphygmology	the pulse
graphology	handwriting	storiology	folk tales
hagiology	saints' legends	thaumatology	miracles
helminthology	worms, especially parasitic ones	timbrology	stamp collecting
		ufology	UFOs
heortology	religious feasts	vexillology	flags
hepaticology	liverworts	xylology	the structure of wood
heresiology	heresies	zymology	the science of fermentation
hierology	sacred matters		

Mysterious Creatures

One of the more exciting 'ologies' is *cryptozoology*, the study and attempted discovery of creatures that are generally regarded as mythical. The Loch Ness monster, the Bigfoot or sasquatch, the Yeti and numerous other big cats, sea monsters and unexplained beasts – including the unlikely-sounding Mongolian Death Worm – are all the rather elusive targets of cryptozoologists.

ISMS

Most of the words included here denote beliefs and practices. Some, however, denote aspects of discrimination; these include **ageism** and **sexism**. Etymological information is given in parentheses.

ageism	discrimination on the grounds of age
agnosticism	belief in the impossibility of knowing God (Greek *agnostos* unknown, unknowable)
alcoholism	addiction to alcohol
altruism	unselfish concern for the welfare of others (Latin *alteri huic* to this other)
atavism	reversion to an earlier type (Latin *atavus* ancestor)
atheism	belief that God does not exist (Greek *atheos* without god)
barbarism	state of being coarse or uncivilized (Greek *barbaros* foreign, stammering)
behaviourism	basis of psychology in behaviour of people and animals
cannibalism	practice of eating human flesh (Spanish *Canibal* Carib)
capitalism	economic system based on the private ownership of wealth and resources
communism	political and economic system based on collective ownership of wealth and resources
conservatism	inclination to preserve the status quo
consumerism	economic policy of encouraging spending and consuming
cubism	artistic movement using geometrical shapes to represent objects
cynicism	belief in the worst in others (Greek *kynikos* dog-like)
defeatism	belief in the inevitability of defeat
dogmatism	tendency to present statements of opinion as if unquestionable (Greek *dogma* opinion)
dynamism	state of having limitless energy and enthusiasm
egoism	principle that self-interest is the basis of morality (Latin *ego* I)
elitism	belief in the natural superiority of some people (Latin *eligere* to elect)
empiricism	theory that knowledge can only be gained through experiment and observation (Greek *empeiria* experience)
environment-alism	concern to protect the natural environment
escapism	tendency to escape from unpleasant reality into fantasy
evangelism	practice of trying to persuade someone to adopt a particular belief or cause (Greek *evangelion* good news)
exhibitionism	tendency to behave so as to attract attention to oneself
existentialism	philosophy emphasizing freedom of choice and personal responsibility for one's actions
expressionism	artistic movement emphasizing expression of emotions over representation of external reality
extremism	adherence to fanatical or extreme opinions
fanaticism	excessive enthusiasm for something (Latin *fanaticus* filled with a god, frenzied)
favouritism	practice of giving unfair preference to a person or group
feminism	advocacy of equal rights and opportunities for women
feudalism	social system based on tenants' allegiance to a lord
functionalism	theory that the intended use of something should determine its design
hedonism	belief in the importance of pleasure above all else (Greek *hedone* pleasure)
heroism	quality of showing great courage in one's actions
holism	theory that any complex being or system is more than the sum of its parts (Greek *holos* whole)
humanism	philosophy emphasizing human responsibility for moral behaviour
hypnotism	practice of inducing a hypnotic state in others (Greek *hypnos* sleep)
idealism	practice of living according to ideals

imperialism	principle of extending control over other nations' territory (Latin *imperium* sovereignty)
Impressionism	artistic movement emphasizing artists' impressions of nature
individualism	belief in individual freedom and self-reliance
liberalism	belief in tolerance of different opinions or attitudes
magnetism	state of possessing magnetic attraction
mannerism	excessive use of an individual artistic style
Marxism	philosophy that political change is brought about by struggle between social classes
masochism	derivation of pleasure from one's own pain or suffering (named after the Austrian writer Sacher-Masoch)
materialism	excessive interest in material possessions and financial success
monarchism	support of the institution of monarchy
monetarism	economic theory emphasizing the control of a country's money supply
mysticism	practice of gaining direct communication with a deity through prayer and meditation (Greek *mystes* initiate)
narcissism	excessive admiration for oneself or one's appearance
nationalism	advocacy of national unity or independence
naturalism	realistic and non-idealistic representation of objects
nihilism	rejection of moral and religious principles (Latin *nihil* nothing)
objectivism	tendency to emphasize what is objective
opportunism	practice of taking advantage of opportunities regardless of principles
optimism	tendency to expect the best possible outcome (Latin *optimus* best)
pacifism	belief that violence and war are unjustified (Latin *pax* peace, and *facere* to make)
paganism	belief in a religion which worships many gods (Latin *paganus* peasant, civilian)
pantheism	doctrine that equates all natural forces and matter with god (Greek *pas* all, *theos* god)
parochialism	practice of being narrow or provincial in outlook (Latin *parochia* parish)
paternalism	practice of benevolent but over-protective management or government (Latin *pater* father)
patriotism	devotion to one's country (Greek *patriotes* compatriot)
pessimism	tendency to expect the worst possible outcome (Latin *pessimus* worst)
plagiarism	practice of stealing an idea from another's work and presenting it as one's own (Latin *plagiarius* kidnapper)
pluralism	co-existence of several ethnic and religious groups in a society (Latin *plus* more)
pointillism	artistic movement using small dabs of unmixed colour to suggest shapes (French *pointille* dot)
polytheism	belief in more than one god (Greek *polys* many, *theos* god)
pragmatism	a practical, matter-of-fact approach to dealing with problems (Greek *pragma* deed)
profession-alism	practice of showing professional competence and conduct
racism *or* **racialism**	discrimination on the grounds of ethnic origin
realism	tendency to present things as they really are
regionalism	devotion to or advocacy of one's own region
sadism	derivation of pleasure from inflicting pain on others (named after the French writer the Marquis de Sade)
Satanism	belief in and worship of the devil
scepticism	tendency to question widely-accepted beliefs (Greek *skeptikos* thoughtful)
sexism	discrimination on the grounds of sex
socialism	doctrine that a country's wealth belongs to the people as a whole

spiritualism	practice of communicating with the spirits of the dead through a medium
stoicism	tendency to accept misfortune or suffering without complaint (Greek *Stoa Poikile* Painted Porch, where Zeno taught)
surrealism	artistic movement emphasizing use of images from the unconscious
symbolism	use of symbols to express ideas or emotions
terrorism	practice of using violence to achieve political ends
Thatcherism	political system based on privatization and monetarism advocated by Margaret Thatcher
tokenism	practice of doing something once or with minimum effort to appear to comply with a law or principle
tourism	practice of travelling to and visiting places for pleasure and relaxation
vandalism	practice of inflicting indiscriminate damage on others' property
vegetarianism	practice of not eating meat or animal products
ventriloquism	practice of making one's voice appear to come from another source (Latin *ventri* belly, *loqui* to speak)
voyeurism	practice of watching private actions of others for pleasure or sexual gratification

PHOBIAS

A phobia is a fear, hatred or extreme dislike of something, especially an irrational one. The term comes from the Greek word *phobos* meaning 'fear'.

Technical term	Everyday term	Technical term	Everyday term
acerophobia	sourness	barophobia	gravity
achluophobia	darkness	basophobia	walking
acrophobia	heights	bathophobia	falling from a high place
aerophobia	draughts, air	batrachophobia	frogs, toads, newts
agoraphobia	open spaces	belonephobia	needles
aichmophobia	sharp or pointed objects	bibliophobia	books
aichurophobia	points	brontophobia	thunder
ailurophobia	cats	cancerphobia,	contracting or having
akousticophobia	sound	cancerophobia	cancer
algophobia	pain	canophobia	dogs
amakaphobia	carriages	cheimaphobia	cold
amathophobia	dust	chionophobia	snow
androphobia	men	chrometophobia	money
anemophobia	wind or draughts	chronophobia	duration
anginophobia	narrowness	chrystallophobia	crystals
anthropophobia	people or society	claustrophobia	closed spaces
antlophobia	flood	cnidophobia	stings
apeirophobia	infinity	cometophobia	comets
apiphobia	bees	cromophobia	colour
aquaphobia	water	cyberphobia	computers
arachnophobia	spiders	cynophobia	dogs
arithmophobia	numbers	demonophobia	demons
asthenophobia	weakness	demophobia	crowds
astraphobia,	lightning	dermatophobia	skin
astrapophobia		dikephobia	injustice
atephobia	ruin	doraphobia	fur
aulophobia	flutes	dromophobia	crossing streets
auroraphobia	Northern Lights	dysmorphophobia	personal physical
autophobia	being by oneself		deformity
bacilliphobia	microbes	ecophobia	one's home surroundings

Technical term	Everyday term	Technical term	Everyday term
eisoptrophobia	mirrors	misophobia	contamination
electrophobia	electricity	monophobia	one thing, or being alone
eleutherophobia	freedom	musicophobia	music
emetophobia	vomiting	musophobia	mice
entomophobia	insects	mysophobia	contamination
eosophobia	dawn	necrophobia	corpses
eremophobia	solitude	nelophobia	glass
eretephobia	pins	neophobia	newness, novelty
ereuthrophobia	blushing	nephophobia	clouds
ergasiophobia,	work	nosophobia	disease
ergophobia		nyctophobia	night or darkness
erotophobia	sexual involvement	ochlophobia	crowds
erythrophobia	blushing	ochophobia	vehicles
euphobia	good news	odontophobia	teeth
genophobia	sex	oikophobia	home
geumaphobia	taste	olfactophobia	smell
graphophobia	writing	ommatophobia	eyes
gymnophobia	nudity	oneirophobia	dreams
gynophobia	women	ophidiophobia,	snakes
hadephobia	hell	ophiophobia	
haematophobia	blood	ophthalmophobia	being stared at
hamartiophobia	sin	ornithophobia	birds
haphephobia	touch	ouranophobia	heaven
harpaxophobia	robbers	panphobia,	everything
hedonophobia	pleasure	pantophobia	
helminthophobia	worms	parthenophobia	girls
herpetophobia	reptiles	pathophobia	disease
hierophobia	sacred objects	patroiophobia	heredity
hippophobia	horses	peniaphobia	poverty
hodophobia	travel	phagophobia	eating
homichlophobia	fog	phasmophobia	ghosts
hormephobia	shock	phengophobia	daylight
hydrophobia	water	phobophobia	fears
hypegiaphobia	responsibility	phonophobia	noise or speaking
hypnophobia	sleep		aloud
ideophobia	ideas	photophobia	light
kakorraphiaphobia	failure	pnigerophobia	smothering
katagelophobia	ridicule	poinephobia	punishment
kenophobia	empty spaces, voids	polyphobia	many things
keraunophobia	thunder	potophobia	alcoholic drink
kinesophobia	motion	pteronophobia	feathers
kleptophobia	stealing	pyrophobia	fire
kopophobia	fatigue	rypophobia	soiling
kristallophobia	ice	satanophobia	the Devil
laliophobia	stuttering	scopophobia,	being looked at
linonophobia	string	scoptophobia	
logophobia	words	scotophobia	darkness
lyssophobia	insanity	selaphobia	flashes
maniaphobia	insanity	siderophobia	stars
mastigophobia	flogging	sitophobia,	food
mechanophobia	machinery	sitiophobia	
metallophobia	metals	spermaphobia,	germs
meteorophobia	meteors	spermatophobia	

Technical term	Everyday term	Technical term	Everyday term
stasiphobia	standing	theophobia	God
stygiophobia	hell	thermophobia	heat
symmetrophobia	symmetry	tonitrophobia	thunder
syphilophobia	syphilis	toxiphobia,	poison
tachophobia	speed	toxicophobia	
taphephobia,	being buried alive	tremophobia	trembling
taphophobia		triskaidekaphobia,	thirteen
technophobia	technology	triskaidecaphobia	
thaasophobia	sitting	xenophobia	strangers, foreigners
thalassophobia	sea	zelophobia	jealousy
thanatophobia	death	zoophobia	animals

Food Phobias

One infamous, if perhaps medically uncommon, phobia is *arachibutyrophobia* – the fear of peanut butter sticking to the roof of one's mouth. Other food phobias that may or may not have a scientific basis are *ostraconophobia*, fear of shellfish, *lachanophobia*, fear of vegetables and *ichthyophobia*, fear of fish. Fear of food itself is called *sitophobia* or *sitiophobia*.

Everyday term	Technical term	Everyday term	Technical term
alcoholic drink	potophobia	dawn	eosophobia
animals	zoophobia	daylight	phengophobia
bees	apiphobia	death	thanatophobia
being buried alive	taphephobia,	demons	demonophobia
	taphophobia	disease	nosophobia, pathophobia
being by oneself	autophobia	dogs	canophobia, cynophobia
being looked at	scopophobia,	draughts, air	aerophobia
	scoptophobia	dreams	oneirophobia
being stared at	ophthalmophobia	duration	chronophobia
birds	ornithophobia	dust	amathophobia
blood	haematophobia	eating	phagophobia
blushing	ereuthrophobia,	electricity	electrophobia
	erythrophobia	empty spaces,	kenophobia
books	bibliophobia	voids	
carriages	amakaphobia	everything	panphobia, pantophobia
cats	ailurophobia	eyes	ommatophobia
closed spaces	claustrophobia	failure	kakorraphiaphobia
clouds	nephophobia	falling from a high	bathophobia
cold	cheimaphobia	place	
colour	cromophobia	fatigue	kopophobia
comets	cometophobia	fears	phobophobia
computers	cyberphobia	feathers	pteronophobia
contamination	misophobia, mysophobia	fire	pyrophobia
contracting or	cancerphobia,	flashes	selaphobia
having cancer	cancerophobia	flogging	mastigophobia
corpses	necrophobia	flood	antlophobia
crossing streets	dromophobia	flutes	aulophobia
crowds	demophobia, ochlophobia	fog	homichlophobia
crystals	chrystallophobia	food	sitophobia, sitiophobia
darkness	achluophobia,	freedom	eleutherophobia
	scotophobia	frogs, toads, newts	batrachophobia

Everyday term	Technical term	Everyday term	Technical term
fur	doraphobia	personal physical	dysmorphophobia
germs	spermaphobia,	deformity	
	spermatophobia	pins	eretephobia
ghosts	phasmophobia	pleasure	hedonophobia
girls	parthenophobia	points	aichurophobia
glass	nelophobia	poison	toxiphobia, toxicophobia
God	theophobia	poverty	peniaphobia
good news	euphobia	punishment	poinephobia
gravity	barophobia	reptiles	herpetophobia
heat	thermophobia	responsibility	hypcgiaphobia
heaven	ouranophobia	ridicule	katagelophobia
heights	acrophobia	robbers	harpaxophobia
hell	stygiophobia, hadephobia	ruin	atephobia
heredity	patroiophobia	sacred objects	hierophobia
home	oikophobia	sea	thalassophobia
horses	hippophobia	sex	genophobia
ice	kristallophobia	sexual involvement	erotophobia
ideas	ideophobia	sharp or pointed	aichmophobia
infinity	apeirophobia	objects	
injustice	dikephobia	shock	hormephobia
insanity	lyssophobia,	sin	hamartiophobia
	maniaphobia	sitting	thaasophobia
insects	entomophobia	skin	dermatophobia
jealousy	zelophobia	sleep	hypnophobia
light	photophobia	smell	olfactophobia
lightning	astraphobia,	smothering	pnigerophobia
	astrapophobia	snakes	ophidiophobia,
machinery	mechanophobia		ophiophobia
many things	polyphobia	snow	chionophobia
men	androphobia	soiling	rypophobia
metals	metallophobia	solitude	eremophobia
meteors	meteorophobia	sound	akousticophobia
mice	musophobia	sourness	acerophobia
microbes	bacilliphobia	speed	tachophobia
mirrors	eisoptrophobia	spiders	arachnophobia
money	chrometophobia	standing	stasiphobia
motion	kinesophobia	stars	siderophobia
music	musicophobia	stealing	kleptophobia
narrowness	anginophobia	stings	cnidophobia
needles	belonephobia	strangers,	xenophobia
newness, novelty	neophobia	foreigners	
night or darkness	nyctophobia	string	linonophobia
noise or speaking	phonophobia	stuttering	laliophobia
aloud		symmetry	symmetrophobia
Northern Lights	auroraphobia	syphilis	syphilophobia
nudity	gymnophobia	taste	geumaphobia
numbers	arithmophobia	technology	technophobia
one thing, or being	monophobia	teeth	odontophobia
alone		the Devil	satanophobia
one's home	ecophobia	thirteen	triskaidekaphobia,
surroundings			triskaidecaphobia
open spaces	agoraphobia	thunder	brontophobia,
pain	algophobia		keraunophobia,
people or society	anthropophobia		tonitrophobia

Everyday term	Technical term	Everyday term	Technical term
touch	haphephobia	weakness	asthenophobia
travel	hodophobia	wind or draughts	anemophobia
trembling	tremophobia	women	gynophobia
vehicles	ochophobia	words	logophobia
vomiting	emetophobia	work	ergasiophobia,
walking	basophobia		ergophobia
water	aquaphobia,	worms	helminthophobia
	hydrophobia	writing	graphophobia

MANIAS

A mania is an abnormal and obsessive desire or inclination, or an extreme enthusiasm, for something. The term comes from the Greek word *mania* meaning 'madness'.

Technical term	Everyday term	Technical term	Everyday term
ablutomania	personal cleanliness	methomania	alcohol
acronymania	forming acronyms	metromania	writing verse
ailuromania	cats	monomania	single thought, idea or
anthomania	flowers		activity
arithmomania	numbers	morphinomania	morphine
balletomania	ballet	mythomania	lying or exaggerating
bibliomania	books	narcomania	drugs
cleptomania	stealing	necromania	dead bodies
cynomania	dogs	nostomania	returning to familiar places
demomania	crowds	nymphomania	sexual desire
demonomania	being possessed by devils	oenomania	alcohol
dipsomania	alcohol	opsomania	special kind of food
egomania	oneself	orchidomania	orchids
eleutheromania	freedom	potichomania	imitating Oriental porcelain
ergomania	work	pteridomania	ferns
erotomania	sexual passion	pyromania	fire-raising
etheromania	taking ether	technomania	technology
flagellomania	beating and flogging	thanatomania	death
graphomania	writing	theatromania	play-going
hedonomania	pleasure	theomania	God, religion
hippomania	horses	tomomania	surgery
hydromania	water	toxicomania	poison
infomania	gathering information	trichotillomania	pulling out tufts of one's
kleptomania	stealing		own hair
logomania	talking	tulipomania	tulip-growing
megalomania	power	xenomania	foreign things
melomania	music		

Everyday term	Technical term	Everyday term	Technical term
alcohol	dipsomania,	books	bibliomania
	methomania, oenomania	cats	ailuromania
ballet	balletomania	crowds	demomania
beating and	flagellomania	dead bodies	necromania
flogging		death	thanatomania
being possessed	demonomania	dogs	cynomania
by devils		drugs	narcomania

Everyday term	Technical term	Everyday term	Technical term
ferns	pteridomania	poison	toxicomania
fire-raising	pyromania	power	megalomania
flowers	anthomania	pulling out tufts of	trichotillomania
foreign things	xenomania	one's own hair	
forming acronyms	acronymania	religion	theomania
freedom	eleutheromania	returning to familiar	nostomania
gathering	infomania	places	
information		sexual desire	nymphomania
God	theomania	sexual passion	erotomania
horses	hippomania	single thought, idea	monomania
imitating Oriental	potichomania	or activity	
porcelain		special kind of food	opsomania
lying or	mythomania	stealing	kleptomania,
exaggerating			cleptomania
morphine	morphinomania	surgery	tomomania
music	melomania	taking ether	etheromania
numbers	arithmomania	talking	logomania
oneself	egomania	technology	technomania
orchids	orchidomania	tulip-growing	tulipomania
personal	ablutomania	water	hydromania
cleanliness		work	ergomania
play-going	theatromania	writing	graphomania
pleasure	hedonomania	writing verse	metromania

COLLECTIVE NAMES FOR ANIMALS

Collective name	Animal	Collective name	Animal
ambush	tigers	colony	ants, bees, penguins, rats
army	caterpillars, frogs	company	parrots
bale	turtles	congregation	plovers
band	gorillas	convocation	eagles
bask	crocodiles	covey	partridges, quail
bed	clams, oysters	crash	rhinoceros
bevy	larks, pheasants, quail,	cry	hounds
	swans	descent	woodpeckers
bloat	hippopotami	dole	doves, turtles
bouquet	pheasants	down	hares
brace	ducks	draught	fish
brood	chickens, hens	dray	squirrels
building	rooks	drift	hogs, swine
bury	rabbits	drove	cattle, horses, oxen,
busyness	ferrets, flies		sheep
cackle	hyenas	erst	bees
cast	hawks	exaltation	larks
cete	badgers	fall	woodcocks
charm	finches, goldfinches	family	otters
chirm	goldfinches	flight	birds
cloud	gnats	flock	birds, ducks, geese, sheep
clowder	cats	gaggle	geese
clutch	chickens	gam	whales

Collective name	Animal	Collective name	Animal
gang	buffalo, elk	rafter	turkeys
grist	bees	romp	otters
herd	buffalo, cattle, deer, elephants, goats, horses, kangaroos, oxen, seals, whales	rookery	rooks, seals
		rout	wolves
		route	wolves
		safe	ducks
hive	bees	school	dolphins, fish, porpoises, whales
horde	gnats		
host	sparrows	scurry	squirrels
hover	trout	sedge	cranes
husk	hares	shiver	sharks
intrusion	cockroaches	shoal	fish
kennel	dogs	shrewdness	apes
kindle	kittens	siege	cranes, herons
knot	toads	skein	geese
labour	moles	skulk	foxes
leap	leopards	sleuth	bears
leash	foxes	sloth	bears
litter	kittens, pigs	smack	jellyfish
mob	kangaroos	sounder	swine
murder	crows	span	mules
murmuration	starlings	spring	teal
muster	peacocks, penguins	stable	horses
mustering	storks	stand	flamingos
mute	hares, hounds	stare	owls
nest	ants, bees, pheasants, vipers	streak	tigers
		string	horses, ponies
nid	pheasants	swarm	ants, bees, flies, locusts
nide	pheasants	team	ducks, horses
nye	pheasants	tiding	magpies
obstinacy	buffalo	tittering	magpies
ostentation	peacocks	tower	giraffes
pace	asses	tribe	goats
pack	dogs, grouse, hounds, wolves	trip	goats, sheep
		troop	baboons, kangaroos, monkeys
paddling	ducks		
pandemonium	parrots	turmoil	porpoises
parade	elephants	turn	turtles
parcel	penguins	unkindness	ravens
parliament	owls, rooks	volery	birds
plague	locusts	watch	nightingales
pod	seals, whales	wedge	swans
pounce	cats	wing	plovers
prickle	porcupines	yoke	oxen
pride	lions	zeal	zebras

Collective Imagination

Some people enjoy inventing new and creative collective nouns for professions or other groups of people. Suggestions have included an *audit* of bookkeepers, a *complex* of psychologists, an *eloquence* of lawyers, a *flush* of plumbers, a *giggle* of girls, an *intrigue* of politicians, a *ponder* of philosophers, a *superfluity* of nuns and a *tedium* of golfers.

ANIMAL ADJECTIVES

Animal	Adjective	Animal	Adjective
ape	simian	hare	leporine
ass	asinine	hawk	accipitrine
badger	musteline	horse	equine, caballine, hippic
bear	ursine	lion	leonine
bee	apian	lizard	lacertian, saurian
bird	avian, avine, volucrine	monkey	simian
bull	taurine	mouse	murine
butterfly	papilionaceous	otter	musteline
calf	vituline	ox	bovine
camel	cameline	parrot	psittacine
cat	feline	pig	porcine, suilline
cattle	bovine	rattlesnake	crotaline
deer	cervine	red deer	elaphine
dog	canine	seal	phocine
donkey	asinine	sheep	ovine
dove	columbine	shrew	soricine
eagle	aquiline	slug	limacine
elephant	elephantine	snake	anguine, colubrine
falcon	falconine	swallow	hirundine
ferret	viverrine	thrush	turdine
finch	fringilline	tiger	tigrine
fish	piscine, ichthyic	viper	viperine
fowl	gallinaceous	vulture	vulturine
fox	vulpine	wasp	vespine
goat	caprine, hircine	weasel	musteline
goose	anserine	wolf	lupine
gull	larine		

EATING ADJECTIVES

Adjective	Feeds on ...	Adjective	Feeds on ...
anthropophagous	humans (cannibalism)	hippophagous	horses
apivorous	bees	hylophagous	wood
autophagous	itself	ichthyophagous	fish
baccivorous	berries	insectivorous	insects
carnivorous	flesh	lignivorous	wood
carpophagous	fruit	meliphagous	honey
coprophagous	dung	mellivorous	honey
creophagous	flesh	merdivorous	dung
entomophagous	insects	myristicivorous	nutmegs
fructivorous	fruit	myrmecophagous	ants
frugivorous	fruits or seeds	necrophagous	carrion
fucivorous	seaweed	nucivorous	nuts
geophagous	soil	omnivorous	both animal and vegetable food
graminivorous	grass, cereals, etc		
granivorous	seeds, grain	omophagous	raw flesh
haematophagous	blood	ophiophagous	snakes
herbivorous	grass or herbage	ossivorous	bones

Adjective	Feeds on ...	Adjective	Feeds on ...
ostreophagous	oysters	saprophagous	decaying organic matter
pantophagous	both animal and vegetable food	sarcophagous	flesh
phyllophagous	leaves	sarcosaprophagous	decaying flesh
phytophagous	plants	scatophagous	dung
piscivorous	fish	theophagous	gods
radicivorous	roots	toxicophagous	poison
ranivorous	frogs	vermivorous	worms
rhizophagous	roots	xylophagous	wood
sanguivorous, sanguinivorous	blood	zoophagous	animals

Wonderful Words

Often words like *myristicivorous*, meaning feeding on nutmegs, become people's favourite words simply because we don't expect such a word to exist. Other delightful oddities include *callipygous*, having beautiful buttocks, *genethliac*, relating to a birthday, *leiotrichy*, straight-hairedness, *mallemaroking*, the carousing of seamen in icebound ships, *paneity*, the state of being bread and *pogonotomy*, a wonderful word for shaving.

DIVINATION TECHNIQUES

Divination is seeking to know the future or hidden things by supernatural means, instinctive prevision and prediction.

Term	Divination by ...
aeromancy	atmospheric phenomena
axinomancy	the motions of an axe poised upon a stake, or of an agate placed upon a red-hot axe
belomancy	means of arrows
bibliomancy	opening the bible or other book at random
botanomancy	means of plants, especially the leaves of sage and fig
capnomancy	smoke
cartomancy	playing cards
ceromancy	dropping melted wax in water
chiromancy	reading the hand
cleromancy	lot
coscinomancy	a sieve and pair of shears
crithomancy	strewing meal over sacrificial animals
crystallomancy	transparent bodies
dactyliomancy	means of a ring
gastromancy	sounds from the belly, or by large-bellied glasses
geomancy	shapes formed, eg when earth is thrown down onto a surface
gyromancy	walking in a circle and falling from giddiness
hepatoscopy	inspection of the livers of animals
hieromancy	observing the objects offered in sacrifice
hydromancy	water
lampadomancy	flame
lithomancy	stones
myomancy	observing the way in which mice move when released from a cage
oenomancy	from the appearance of wine poured out in libations

Term	Divination by ...
omoplatoscopy, scapulomancy	observing the cracks appearing in a burning shoulder blade
omphalomancy	the knots in the umbilical cord, to tell the number of future children
oneiromancy	dreams
onychomancy	the fingernails
ornithomancy	means of birds, by observing their flight, etc
pyromancy	fire
rhabdomancy	rod, especially divining for water or ore
sortes	chance opening of the Bible, Homer, Virgil, etc
sortilege	drawing lots
spodomancy	means of ashes
taghairm	lying in a bullock's hide behind a waterfall
tephromancy	ashes, especially those left after a sacrifice
theomancy	means of oracles, or of persons directly inspired immediately by some divinity
tripudium	the hopping of birds feeding, or the dropping of scraps from their bills
zoomancy	observation of animals

COLLECTORS AND ENTHUSIASTS

Devotee	Item or activity
ailurophile, ailourophile	cats
antiquary	antiques
arachnologist	spiders/arachnids
arctophile	teddy bears
audiophile	broadcast sound
balletomane	ballet
bibliophile	books
campanologist	bell-ringing
canophilist, cynophilist	dogs
cartophile, cartophilist	cigarette cards
chirographist	handwriting
chrysophilite	gold
cinephile	cinema
conservationist	countryside
Dantophilist	Dante
deltiologist	postcards
discophile	gramophone records
entomologist	insects
environmentalist	the environment
ephemerist	ephemera
ex-librist	bookplates
gastronome	good living
gourmet	good food
hippophile	horses
incunabulist	early printed books
lepidopterist	butterflies
logophile	words
monarchist	the monarchy
neophile	novelty and new things
notaphilist	banknotes, cheques
numismatist	coins/medals

Curious Collections

People collect almost anything. Guinness World Records® includes people with the largest collections of airsickness bags, autographed drum sticks, beer bottles, belly button fluff, chamber pots, coloured vinyl records, 'do not disturb' signs, four-leaf clovers, garden gnomes, golf balls, hair from historical figures, handcuffs, nail clippers, piggy banks, spoon rests and weighing scales.

Devotee	Item or activity
oenophile, oenophilist	wine
ophiophilist	snakes
ornithologist	birds
paroemiographer	proverbs
philatelist, timbrophilist	stamps
phillumenist	matches/matchboxes
philomath	learning
pteridophilist	ferns
scripophile, scripophilist	bond and share certificates
stegophilist	climbing buildings for sport
stigmatophilist	tattooing or body piercing
technophile	technology
tegestologist	beer mats
toxophilite	archery
xenophile	foreigners
zoophile	animals

FAMOUS LAST WORDS

Prince Albert (1819–61)

'I have had wealth, rank and power, but, if these were all I had, how wretched I should be.'
Attributed.

Augustus (63BC–AD14)

'The play is over.'
Attributed.

Béla Bartók (1881–1945)

'The trouble is that I have to go with so much still to say.'
Quoted in David Pickering *Brewer's Twentieth Century Music* (1994).

Ludwig van Beethoven (1770–1827)

'I shall hear in heaven.'
Attributed. Quoted in Ian Crofton and Donald Fraser *A Dictionary of Musical Quotations* (1985).

Julius Caesar (100 or 102–44BC)

'*Et tu, Brute?*'
'You too, Brutus?'
Attributed, when struck by his murderers, Cassius and Brutus.

Sir Winston Churchill (1874–1965)

'I am so bored with it all.'
Attributed.

Dame Gladys Cooper (1888–1971)

'If this is what virus pneumonia does to one, I really don't think I shall bother to have it again.'

Bing Crosby (1904–77)

'That was a great game of golf.'
As he finished play at the 18th hole before suffering a heart attack.

Emily Dickinson (1830–86)

'Let us go in; the fog is rising.'
Attributed.

Johann Wolfgang von Goethe (1749–1832)

'More light!'

Henrik Ibsen (1828–1906)

'On the contrary!'
Refuting a nurse's suggestion that he was feeling better.

Lord Horatio Nelson (1758–1805)

'Kiss me, Hardy.'
Attributed, as he lay dying in the cockpit of the *Victory* during the Battle of Trafalgar.

Lawrence Oates (1880–1912)

'I am just going outside and may be some time.'

William Pitt (1759–1806)

'I think that I could eat one of Bellamy's veal pies.'
Attributed.

William Saroyan (1908–81)

'Now what?'

Tom Simpson (1938–67)

'Put me back on my bike.'
He died from heart failure during the Tour de France.

Lytton Strachey (1880–1932)

'If this is dying, then I don't think much of it.'
Attributed.

Dylan Thomas (1914–53)

'I've had 18 straight whiskies. I think that's the record.'
Attributed, before lapsing into his final coma.

Oscar Wilde (1854–1900)

'Either that wallpaper goes or I do.'
Attributed, as he lay dying in a Paris hotel bedroom.

COMMUNICATION

ARABIC ALPHABET

Letter	Name	Usual transliteration	Letter	Name	Usual transliteration
ا	'alif	'	ض	dad	d
ب	ba	b	ط	ta	t
ت	ta	t	ظ	za	z
ث	tha	th	ع	'ain	'
ج	jim	j	غ	ghain	gh
ح	ha	h	ف	fa	f
خ	kha	kh	ق	qaf	q
د	dal	d	ك	kaf	k
ذ	dhal	dh	ل	lam	l
ر	ra	r	م	mim	m
ز	za	a	ن	nun	n
س	sin	s	ه	ha	h
ش	shin	sh	و	waw	w
ص	sad	s	ي	ya	y

CYRILLIC ALPHABET

Letter	Usual transliteration	Letter	Usual transliteration
А а	a	С с	s
Б б	b	Т т	t
В в	v	У у	u
Г г	g	Ф ф	f
Д д	d	Х х	kh
Е е	e (ye)	Ц ц	ts
Ё ё	e (yö)	Ч ч	ch
Ж ж	zh	Ш ш	sh
З з	z	Щ щ	shch (often pronounced rather as *sh* followed by consonantal *y*)
И и	i (ē)		
Й й	(consonantal *y* sound; only used as the second letter of a diphthong)	Ъ ъ	(hard sign; used to separate in pronunciation a following palatalized vowel from a preceding consonant either palatalized or unpalatalized)
К к	k		
Л л	l	Ы ы	i (a sound similar to *i*)
М м	m	Ь ь	(soft sign; used after a consonant to indicate palatalization, a sound like consonantal *y*)
Н н	n		
О о	o	Э э	e (e)
П п	p	Ю ю	u (yoo)
Р р	r	Я я	ya (yä)

GREEK ALPHABET

Letter		Name	Usual transliteration	Letter		Name	Usual transliteration
A	α	alpha	a	N	ν	nū	n
B	β	bēta	b	Ξ	ξ	xī	x
Γ	γ	gamma	g	O	o	omicron	o
Δ	δ	delta	d	Π	π	pī	p
E	ε	epsīlon	e	P	ρ	rhō	r
Z	ζ	zēta	z	Σ	σ ς	sigma	s
H	η	ēta	ē	T	τ	tau	t
Θ	θ	thēta	th	Y	υ	upsīlon	u or y
I	ι	iōta	i	Φ	φ	phī	ph
K	κ	kappa	k	X	χ	chī	kh or ch
Λ	λ	lambda	l	Ψ	ψ	psī	ps
M	μ	mū	m	Ω	ω	ōmega	ō

HEBREW ALPHABET

Letter	Name	Usual transliteration	Letter	Name	Usual transliteration
א	aleph	ʼ	ל	lamed	l
ב	beth	b	מ ם	mem	m
ג	gimel	g	נ ן	nun	n
ד	daleth	d	ס	samekh	s
ה	heh	h	ע	ayin	ʻ
ו	vav	w	פ ף	peh	p, f
ז	zayin	z	צ ץ	sadhe	s
ח	cheth	h	ק	koph	q
ט	teth	t	ר	resh	r
י	yod	y, j	ש	sin	sh, s
כ ך	kaph	k	ת	tav	t

St Cyril's Alphabet

The Cyrillic alphabet is used for Russian, Ukrainian, Serbian and Bulgarian. It is so called because it is traditionally attributed to St Cyril (827–69), a Greek Christian missionary known as the Apostle of the Slavs, who made Slav translations of the Scriptures and whose feast day is still a national holiday in some Eastern European countries. Based on the Greek alphabet, the Cyrillic includes extra symbols to represent Slavic sounds not found in Greek.

RUNIC ALPHABET

The runic alphabet, known as *futhark*, was made up of 24 basic symbols, although there was considerable regional variation in the overall number of symbols and symbol shapes used. Around 4 000 runic inscriptions and a few manuscripts survive, principally made by the early Scandinavians and Anglo-Saxons.

ᚠ	f	ᚷ	g	ᛁ	ï	ᛖ	e
ᚢ	u	ᚹ	w	ᛈ	p	ᛗ	m
ᚦ	þ	ᚺ	h	ᛉ	x	ᛚ	l
ᛟ	o	ᚾ	n	ᛋ	s	ᛜ	ng
ᚱ	r	ᛁ	i	ᛏ	t	ᛟ	œ
ᚲ	k	ᛃ	j	ᛒ	b	ᛞ	d

Pictography

A *pictograph* is a picture used as a symbol for a word or phrase. Pictographs do not relate to the sounds of language, as in most modern writing systems, but represent an abstract idea related to a concrete object, and then the name for that object. In China pictographs developed into a complex system where the written symbol represents a complete word, or part of a word, meaning that in writing modern Chinese a knowledge of 2 000 characters is required, and in Japanese, where the writing system developed from the Chinese one, 1 850 characters are considered essential for everyday use. In contrast, most sound-based alphabets can manage with 30 or fewer symbols.

PHONETIC ALPHABET

The phonetic alphabet, also known as the NATO alphabet, is a system used in international radio communication in which letters of the alphabet are identified by means of code words.

A	Alpha	**F**	Foxtrot	**K**	Kilo	**P**	Papa	**U**	Uniform	**Z**	Zulu
B	Bravo	**G**	Golf	**L**	Lima	**Q**	Quebec	**V**	Victor		
C	Charlie	**H**	Hotel	**M**	Mike	**R**	Romeo	**W**	Whiskey		
D	Delta	**I**	India	**N**	November	**S**	Sierra	**X**	X-ray		
E	Echo	**J**	Juliet	**O**	Oscar	**T**	Tango	**Y**	Yankee		

BRAILLE

Braille is a system of printing for the blind, in which printed characters are represented by raised dots which can be read by touch. Each character is formed by a different combination taken from a basic six-dot matrix. It was invented in 1829 by the Frenchman Louis Braille (1809–52), who was blind from the age of three.

A	D	G	J	M	P	S	V	Y
B	E	H	K	N	Q	T	W	Z
C	F	I	L	O	R	U	X	

MORSE CODE

Morse is a method of signalling by a code in which each letter is represented by a combination of dashes and dots or long and short light flashes, sound signals, etc. In the spoken form of Morse code, the word *dah* represents the dash and the word *dit* represents the dot. It was invented by Samuel F B Morse (1791–1872), a US inventor. Morse created one of the first telegraph lines between Washington and Baltimore as an experiment, and developed 'Morse code' (originally called the 'Morse alphabet') for use with it.

A	•—	G	——•	M	——	S	•••	Y	—•——
B	—•••	H	••••	N	—•	T	—	Z	——••
C	—•—•	I	••	O	———	U	••—		
D	—••	J	•———	P	•——•	V	•••—		
E	•	K	—•—	Q	——•—	W	•——		
F	••—•	L	•—••	R	•—•	X	—••—		

SOS

SOS is an appeal for help or rescue, especially at sea. It is popularly believed to stand for 'Save Our Ship' or even 'Save Our Souls', but the truth is much simpler: it doesn't stand for anything. In fact, it was chosen for ease and clarity of transmission by Morse code (· · · – – – · · ·). The signal was adopted internationally in 1908; since 1999 the International Maritime Organization's new Global Maritime Distress and Safety System (GMDSS) for distress calls has led to SOS becoming almost obsolete, on larger ships at least.

SEMAPHORE

Semaphore was widely used in visual telegraphy, especially at sea, before the advent of electricity. Old-style railway signals are a simple form of semaphore, with a single arm having two positions to indicate 'stop' and 'go'.

SIGN LANGUAGE: FINGERSPELLING

Sign language is a means of communication using finger and hand movements, in which signs represent whole words or phrases. Fingerspelling uses the movements to represent letters of the alphabet, enabling words to be spelled letter by letter.

British

US

Silent Talking

Dactylology is the art of talking with the fingers using sign language. The word comes from an ancient Greek word, *daktylos*, which means 'finger'.

KEYBOARD LAYOUT

The standard arrangement of keys on an English-language computer keyboard is known as *qwerty*, from the letters at the top left-hand side of the keyboard.

Quirky Qwerty

It is widely believed that the arrangement of the letters on the qwerty keyboard was designed to slow typists down. But although it is true that the layout was designed to prevent jamming on the early typewriters, it wasn't achieved by slowing the fingers down. Instead the keys for common letter patterns, such as *sh*, are arranged so as to be far enough apart to prevent the typebars clashing when the keys were hit in rapid succession. An interesting side effect of the qwerty layout is that all the letters for the word *typewriter* are found on the keyboard's top row.

DEWEY DECIMAL CLASSIFICATION

Dewey decimal classification is a system of library classification, based on the division of books into numbered classes, with further subdivision shown by numbers following a decimal point. The system was invented by Melvil Dewey (1851–1931), a US librarian, who designed the system for the Amherst College Library between 1873 and 1876.

000	Generalities	500	Natural sciences and mathematics
100	Philosophy and psychology	600	Technology (applied sciences)
200	Religion	700	The arts
300	Social sciences	800	Literature and rhetoric
400	Language	900	Geography and history

Dewey Worldwide

The Dewey system is used in more than 35 countries. It has been modified and updated many times, has had 22 major editions published and is capable of being infinitely expanded to allow new subject areas to be included. Current topics of concern to librarians using the Dewey system include where to classify books about quidditch, the sport played in the Harry Potter novels by J K Rowling (under 823.914, apparently).

INTERNET SUFFIXES

General suffixes

.ac.uk	UK academic institution	.int	international organization
.aero	aviation industry	.mil	US military
.biz	business	.museum	museum
.com	commercial	.name	individual
.comp	newsgroup about computers	.net	major service provider
.coop	business co-operative	.org	non-profit organization
.co.uk	UK commercial	.pro	professional
.edu	US educational institution	.sci	newsgroup about science
.gov	US government	.soc	newsgroup about society
.info	general information		

Geographical suffixes

For suffixes listed by country see the individual entries in the **Countries A–Z** section of **Human Geography**.

.ac	Ascension Island	.bo	Bolivia	.dk	Denmark	.gs	Georgia and the South Sandwich Islands
.ad	Andorra	.br	Brazil	.dm	Dominica		
.ae	United Arab Emirates	.bs	The Bahamas	.do	Dominican Republic		
		.bt	Bhutan			.gt	Guatemala
.af	Afghanistan	.bv	Bouvet Island	.dz	Algeria	.gu	Guam
.ag	Antigua and Barbuda	.bw	Botswana	.ec	Ecuador	.gw	Guinea-Bissau
		.by	Belarus	.ee	Estonia	.gy	Guyana
.ai	Anguilla	.bz	Belize	.eg	Egypt	.hk	Hong Kong
.al	Albania	.ca	Canada	.eh	Western Sahara	.hm	Heard and McDonald Islands
.am	Armenia	.cc	Cocos (Keeling) Islands	.er	Eritrea		
.an	Netherlands Antilles			.es	Spain		
		.cd	Congo, Democratic Republic of the	.et	Ethiopia	.hn	Honduras
.ao	Angola			.eu	European Union (*proposed*)	.hr	Croatia
.aq	Antarctica			.fi	Finland	.ht	Haiti
.ar	Argentina	.cf	Central African Republic	.fj	Fiji	.hu	Hungary
.as	American Samoa			.fk	Falkland Islands	.id	Indonesia
		.cg	Congo, Republic of			.ie	Ireland
.at	Austria			.fm	Micronesia	.il	Israel
.au	Australia	.ch	Switzerland	.fo	Faroe Islands	.im	Isle of Man
.aw	Aruba	.ci	Côte d'Ivoire	.fr	France	.in	India
.az	Azerbaijan	.ck	Cook Islands	.ga	Gabon	.io	British Indian Ocean Territory
.ba	Bosnia and Herzegovina	.cl	Chile	.gd	Grenada		
		.cm	Cameroon	.ge	Georgia	.iq	Iraq
.bb	Barbados	.cn	China	.gf	French Guiana	.ir	Iran
.bd	Bangladesh	.co	Colombia	.gg	Guernsey	.is	Iceland
.be	Belgium	.cr	Costa Rica	.gh	Ghana	.it	Italy
.bf	Burkina Faso	.cu	Cuba	.gi	Gibraltar	.je	Jersey
.bg	Bulgaria	.cv	Cape Verde	.gl	Greenland	.jm	Jamaica
.bh	Bahrain	.cx	Christmas Island	.gm	The Gambia	.jo	Jordan
.bi	Burundi			.gn	Guinea	.jp	Japan
.bj	Benin	.cy	Cyprus	.gp	Guadeloupe	.ke	Kenya
.bm	Bermuda	.cz	Czech Republic	.gq	Equatorial Guinea	.kg	Kyrgyzstan
.bn	Brunei Darussalam	.de	Germany			.kh	Cambodia
		.dj	Djibouti	.gr	Greece	.ki	Kiribati

.km	Comoros	.ng	Nigeria	.sv	El Salvador
.kn	St Kitts and Nevis	.ni	Nicaragua	.sy	Syria
.kp	Korea, Democratic People's Republic	.nl	The Netherlands	.sz	Swaziland
		.no	Norway	.tc	Turks and Caicos Islands
.kr	Korea, Republic of	.np	Nepal	.td	Chad
.kw	Kuwait	.nr	Nauru	.tf	French Southern and Antarctic Territories
.ky	Cayman Islands	.nu	Niue		
.kz	Kazakhstan	.nz	New Zealand	.tg	Togo
.la	Laos	.om	Oman	.th	Thailand
.lb	Lebanon	.pa	Panama	.tj	Tajikistan
.lc	St Lucia	.pe	Peru	.tk	Tokelau
.li	Liechtenstein	.pf	French Polynesia	.tm	Turkmenistan
.lk	Sri Lanka	.pg	Papua New Guinea	.tn	Tunisia
.lr	Liberia	.ph	Philippines	.to	Tonga
.ls	Lesotho	.pk	Pakistan	.tp	East Timor
.lt	Lithuania	.pl	Poland	.tr	Turkey
.lu	Luxembourg	.pm	St Pierre and Miquelon	.tt	Trinidad and Tobago
.lv	Latvia	.pn	Pitcairn Islands	tv	Tuvalu
.ly	Libya	.pr	Puerto Rico	.tw	Taiwan
.ma	Morocco	.ps	Palestinian Territories	.tz	Tanzania
.mc	Monaco	.pt	Portugal	.ua	Ukraine
.md	Moldova	.pw	Palau	.ug	Uganda
.mg	Madagascar	.py	Paraguay	.uk	United Kingdom
.mh	Marshall Islands	.qa	Qatar	.um	US Minor Outlying Islands
.mk	Macedonia	.re	Réunion		
.ml	Mali	.ro	Romania	.us	United States
.mm	Myanmar (Burma)	.ru	Russia	.uy	Uruguay
.mn	Mongolia	.rw	Rwanda	.uz	Uzbekistan
.mo	Macau	.sa	Saudi Arabia	.va	Vatican
.mp	Northern Mariana Islands	.sb	Solomon Islands	.vc	St Vincent and the Grenadines
		.sc	Seychelles		
.mq	Martinique	.sd	Sudan	.ve	Venezuela
.mr	Mauritania	.se	Sweden	.vg	Virgin Islands (British)
.ms	Montserrat	.sg	Singapore	.vi	Virgin Islands (US)
.mt	Malta	.sh	St Helena	.vn	Vietnam
.mu	Mauritius	.si	Slovenia	.vu	Vanuatu
.mv	Maldives	.sj	Svalbard and Jan Meyen Islands	.wf	Wallis and Futuna Islands
.mw	Malawi				
.mx	Mexico	.sk	Slovakia	.ws	Samoa
.my	Malaysia	.sl	Sierra Leone	.ye	Yemen
.mz	Mozambique	.sm	San Marino	.yt	Mayotte
.na	Namibia	.sn	Senegal	.yu	Serbia and Montenegro
.nc	New Caledonia	.so	Somalia	.za	South Africa
.ne	Niger	.sr	Suriname	.zm	Zambia
.nf	Norfolk Island	.st	São Tomé and Príncipe	.zw	Zimbabwe

Tuvalu TV

The internet domain name .tv is highly desirable to television and media companies. Tuvalu, a small island group in the south-west Pacific Ocean approximately 1 050km/650mi north of Fiji, realized its good fortune and leased the rights to its domain name for $50 million in royalties over a ten-year period.

TRANSPORT

For road and rail bridges and tunnels see **Architecture and Engineering.**

INTERNATIONAL VEHICLE REGISTRATION (IVR) CODES

A	Austria	ETH	Ethiopia	MGL	Mongolia
AFG	Afghanistan	F	France	MK	Macedonia
AL	Albania	FIN	Finland	MOC	Mozambique[1]
AM	Armenia	FJI	Fiji[1]	MS	Mauritius[1]
AND	Andorra	FL	Liechtenstein	MW	Malawi[1]
AUS	Australia[1]	G	Gabon	N	Norway
AZ	Azerbaijan	GB	United Kingdom[1]	NAM	Namibia[1]
B	Belgium	GBA	Alderney[1]	NAU	Nauru[1]
BD	Bangladesh[1]	GBG	Guernsey[1]	NEP	Nepal[1]
BDS	Barbados[1]	GBJ	Jersey[1]	NGR	Nigeria
BF	Burkina Faso	GBM	Isle of Man[1]	NIC	Nicaragua
BG	Bulgaria	GBZ	Gibraltar	NL	The Netherlands
BIH	Bosnia and	GCA	Guatemala	NZ	New Zealand[1]
	Herzegovina	GE	Georgia	P	Portugal
BOL	Bolivia	GH	Ghana	PA	Panama
BR	Brazil	GR	Greece	PE	Peru
BRN	Bahrain	GUY	Guyana[1]	PK	Pakistan[1]
BRU	Brunei Darussalam[1]	H	Hungary	PL	Poland
BS	The Bahamas[1]	HKJ	Jordan	PNG	Papua New Guinea[1]
BUR	Myanmar (Burma)	HR	Croatia	PY	Paraguay
BW	Botswana[1]	I	Italy	Q	Qatar
BY	Belarus	IL	Israel	RA	Argentina
BZ	Belize	IND	India[1]	RC	Taiwan
C	Cuba	IR	Iran	RCA	Central African
CAM	Cameroon	IRL	Ireland[1]		Republic
CDN	Canada	IRQ	Iraq	RCB	Congo
CH	Switzerland	IS	Iceland	RCH	Chile
CI	Côte d'Ivoire	J	Japan[1]	RG	Guinea
CL	Sri Lanka[1]	JA	Jamaica[1]	RGB	Guinea-Bissau
CO	Colombia	K	Cambodia	RH	Haiti
CR	Costa Rica	KS	Kyrgyzstan	RI	Indonesia[1]
CY	Cyprus[1]	KWT	Kuwait	RIM	Mauritania
CZ	Czech Republic	KZ	Kazakhstan	RL	Lebanon
D	Germany	L	Luxembourg	RM	Madagascar
DK	Denmark	LAO	Laos	RMM	Mali
DOM	Dominican Republic	LAR	Libya	RN	Niger
DY	Benin	LB	Liberia	RO	Romania
DZ	Algeria	LS	Lesotho[1]	ROK	Korea (North)
E	Spain	LT	Lithuania	ROU	Uruguay
EAK	Kenya[1]	LV	Latvia	RP	Philippines
EAT	Tanzania[1]	M	Malta[1]	RSM	San Marino
EAU	Uganda[1]	MA	Morocco	RU	Burundi
EC	Ecuador	MAL	Malaysia[1]	RUS	Russia
ES	El Salvador	MC	Monaco	RWA	Rwanda
EST	Estonia	MD	Moldova	S	Sweden
ET	Egypt	MEX	Mexico	SA	Saudi Arabia

SCG	Serbia and Montenegro	TJ	Tajikistan	WG	Grenada[1]
SD	Swaziland[1]	TM	Turkmenistan	WL	St Lucia[1]
SGP	Singapore[1]	TN	Tunisia	WS	Samoa
SK	Slovakia	TR	Turkey	WV	St Vincent and the Grenadines[1]
SLO	Slovenia	TT	Trinidad and Tobago[1]	YAR	Yemen
SME	Suriname[1]	UA	Ukraine	YV	Venezuela
SN	Senegal	USA	United States of America	Z	Zambia[1]
SO	Somalia			ZA	South Africa[1]
SUD	Sudan	UZ	Uzbekistan	ZRE	Congo, Democratic Republic of the
SY	Seychelles[1]	V	Vatican		
SYR	Syria	VN	Vietnam		
T	Thailand[1]	WAG	The Gambia	ZW	Zimbabwe[1]
TCH	Chad	WAL	Sierra Leone		
TG	Togo	WD	Dominica[1]		

[1] *In countries so marked, the rule of the road is to drive on the left; in others, vehicles drive on the right.*

Rules of the Road

One theory suggests that driving on the left of the road arose in medieval times. As most people are right-handed, travelling on the left of the road meant that swords or other weapons would be nearest to other travellers. Some people believe that the rise in right-handed driving can be blamed on left-handed French ruler Napoleon I, who reversed the practice in France.

LONDON UNDERGROUND LINES

An underground railway system for London was first proposed in 1843, and construction work began on the Metropolitan Railway in 1860. The line opened between Farringdon and Paddington in 1863 using steam locomotives to pull trains. However, the first electrically-hauled underground line was the City and Southern which opened in 1890, the year in which London's new underground railway first became known as the Tube.

Line	Colour	Line	Colour
Bakerloo	brown	Jubilee	grey
Central	red	Metropolitan	maroon
Circle	yellow	Northern	black
District	green	Piccadilly	navy blue
East London	orange	Victoria	sky blue
Hammersmith and City	pink	Waterloo and City	sea green

Tracing the Tube

The standard London Underground map that we know today was designed by Harry Beck (1903–1974) back in the early 1930s. He abandoned the complicated geographic style of early Tube maps, instead creating a simple plan that was based on electrical circuit diagrams. It clearly showed the various lines (each a different colour) joining the stations. Beck's diagram – with some updates and modifications – is still in use today, more than 70 years after it was first published in 1933.

Rush Hour

The busiest station on the London Underground system is Victoria – London Underground estimate that 76.5 million passengers pass through it annually. Britain's busiest railway station is Clapham Junction, in the London borough of Wandsworth.

MOTORWAYS (UK)

The first British motorway was the M6 Preston Bypass, which opened in Dec 1958.

Motorway Madness

The busiest UK motorway is the M25, notably between junctions 14 and 15. The M61 in Greater Manchester has the most lanes, with 17, while 'Spaghetti Junction' on the M6 is officially the most complicated interchange. The highest motorway is the M62 across the Pennines.

ROAD DISTANCES (UK)

Road distances between British centres are given in statute miles, using routes recommended by the Automobile Association based on the quickest travelling time. *To convert to kilometres, multiply the number given by 1.6093.*

Roman Roads

The first people to construct surfaced roads on a large scale were the Romans. The total distance of the roads built by the Romans has been estimated at a lengthy 85 000km/53 000mi, and their road network covered the whole of the Roman Empire, circling the Mediterranean and extending deep into Asia and northwards across Europe. A traveller in late Roman times could make the entire journey from York to Jerusalem on good, safe roads – something that wasn't possible again until the 20c.

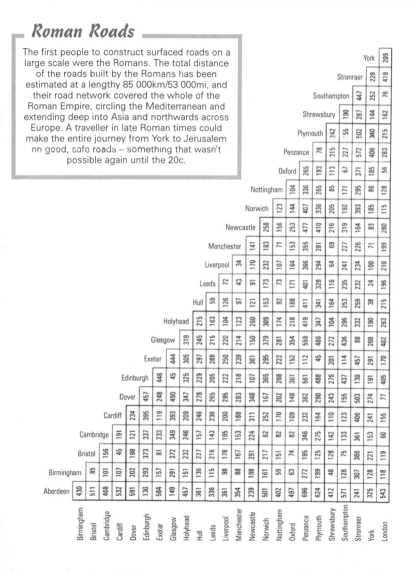

	Birmingham	Bristol	Cambridge	Cardiff	Dover	Edinburgh	Exeter	Glasgow	Holyhead	Hull	Leeds	Liverpool	Manchester	Newcastle	Norwich	Nottingham	Oxford	Penzance	Plymouth	Shrewsbury	Southampton	Stranraer	York	London
York																								209
Stranraer																						228	419	
Southampton																				447	252	76		
Shrewsbury																			190	287	144	162		
Plymouth																		242	55	502	340	215		
Penzance																	78	315	227	572	406	283		
Oxford																265	193	113	67	371	185	56		
Nottingham															104	336	265	85	171	295	86	128		
Norwich														123	144	407	336	205	192	393	185	115		
Newcastle													258	156	253	477	410	216	319	164	83	280		
Manchester												141	183	71	153	355	281	69	227	226	71	199		
Liverpool											34	170	232	107	164	366	294	64	241	234	100	210		
Leeds										72	43	91	173	73	171	401	328	116	235	232	24	196		
Hull									59	126	97	121	153	92	188	411	341	164	253	259	38	215		
Holyhead								215	163	104	123	260	309	174	218	419	347	104	296	332	190	263		
Glasgow							319	245	215	220	214	150	379	281	354	559	486	272	436	88	208	402		
Exeter						444	305	297	288	250	239	361	295	222	152	112	45	201	114	457	291	170		
Edinburgh					446	45	325	229	205	222	218	107	365	268	361	561	488	276	437	130	191	405		
Dover				457	248	490	347	278	265	295	283	348	167	202	148	362	164	503	274	77				
Cardiff			234	395	119	393	209	246	236	200	188	311	252	170	109	232	164	123	406	241	155			
Cambridge		191	121	337	233	349	246	157	143	195	153	224	62	82	82	346	275	142	133	361	153	60		
Bristol	156	45	198	373	81	372	232	227	216	178	167	291	217	151	74	195	125	128	75	386	221	119		
Birmingham	85	101	107	202	293	157	291	151	136	115	98	88	198	161	59	63	272	199	48	128	307	128	118	
Aberdeen	430	511	468	532	591	130	584	149	457	361	336	361	354	239	501	402	497	696	624	412	571	241	325	543

AIR DISTANCES

Air distances between some major cities, given in statute miles.
To convert to kilometres, multiply the number given by 1.6093.

[1] Shortest route.

	Washington	Tokyo	Sydney	Santiago	Rome	Perth	Paris	Nairobi	Moscow	Montreal	Mexico City	Los Angeles	London	Lagos	Johannesburg	Istanbul	Honolulu	Hong Kong	Delhi	Chicago	Cairo	Buenos Aires	Beijing
Amsterdam	3854	6006[1]	10391	7714	809	9118	261	4148	1338	3422	5724	5559	217	3161	5606	1373	8368	5926	3985	4109	2042	7153	6556
Beijing	7930	1313	5689	13622	5306	4987	5108	5888	3604	6495	7752	6250	5054	8030	8130	4763	5066	1235	2368	6573	4663	12000	
Buenos Aires	6097	13100	7330	710	6931	9734	6892	7427	8382	5632	4592	6140	6985	4959	5033	7783	7561	11471	9895	5587	7468		
Cairo	5859	6362	8790	8405	1320	7975	1994	2203	1795	5431	7688	7589	2181	2440	4472	767	8434	5061	2753	6135			
Chicago	590	6296	9246	5328	4828	11281	4140	8177	5500	737	1687	1746	3956	7066	8705	5502	4246	7827	8119				
Delhi	7841	3656	6446	11215	3690	4969	4089	3451	2698	7421	9806	8717	4169	5196	6765	2833	7888	2345					
Hong Kong	8385	1807	4589	11675	5773	3733	5986	5051	4437	8147	8794	7231	5979	7541	6728	4986	5543						
Honolulu	4822	3831	4943	6904	8022	7061	7438	10567	7037	4910	3779	2574	7220	7661	11534	8109							
Istanbul	5347	5757	9883	8089	852	7846	1394	2967	1089	4795	7235	6994	1552	3207	4776								
Johannesburg	8199	8535	7601	5738	4802	5564	5422	1809	6280	8322	10070	10443	5640	2854									
Lagos	5472	9130[1]	11700	6042	2497	10209	2922	2377	4462	5595	7343	7716	3115										
London	3672	6218	10565	7241	895	9008	214	4247	1555	3254	5558	5439											
Los Angeles	2294	5451	7498	5594	6340	9535	5633	8992	6068	2482	1563												
Mexico City	1871	7014	9061	4168	6601	11098	5714	9949	6700	2307													
Montreal	493	6913	9980	5551	5431	12402	3434	7498	4393														
Moscow	4884	4668	9425	10118	1478	8355	1540	3951															
Nairobi	7918	8565	9410	7547	3349	7373	4031																
Paris	3843	6208[1]	10150	7619	688	8990																	
Perth	11829	4925	2037	7830	8309																		
Rome	4495	6146	10149	7548																			
Santiago	5061	11049	13092																				
Sydney	9792	4640																					
Tokyo	6763																						

Long Haul

The world's longest non-stop commercial flight is operated by Singapore Airlines betwen Singapore and New Jersey, USA. The 15 500km/9 600mi route which was first flown in Jun 2004, takes an exhausting 18.5 hrs.

FAMOUS TRANSPORTATIONS

Argo	The ship that carried Jason and the Argonauts on the quest to bring back the Golden Fleece in Greek mythology.
Ark	The ship that saved Noah, his immediate family and a selection of animals from a widespread flood over the Earth (the Bible, Genesis 6–9).
HMS Beagle	The ship on which Charles Darwin (1809–82) sailed as naturalist (from 1831).
Black Bess	The horse that supposedly carried highwayman Dick Turpin (1705–39) on a famous ride to York (18c).
Bluebird	The hydroplane used in Donald Campbell's (1921–67) attempt to become the first man to break 300mph on water (1967).
HMS Bounty	The ship on board which there was a mutiny on 28 Apr 1789, led by Fletcher Christian, in which Captain William Bligh (1754–c.1817) and 18 men were cast adrift in an open boat without charts.
Chitty Chitty Bang Bang	The flying car in the film *Chitty Chitty Bang Bang* (1968), based on Ian Fleming's 1964 novel.
Copenhagen	The chestnut stallion that carried the Duke of Wellington (1769–1852) at the Battle of Waterloo (18 Jun 1815).
Discovery	The ship that carried Robert Scott (1868–1912) and his expedition exploring Antarctica (1901–04).
Endurance	The ship that carried Sir Ernest Henry Shackleton (1874–1922) in his Antarctic expeditions but was crushed in the ice on his 1914–16 expedition.
Enola Gay	The US Air Force B-29 Superfortress bomber, piloted by Paul Tibbets (born 1915), that dropped the world's first atomic bomb on Hiroshima, Japan, during World War II on 6 Aug 1945.
Fram	The purpose-built ship for Fridtjof Nansen's (1861–1930) scheme to reach the North Pole by getting frozen into the ice north of Siberia and drifting with currents towards Greenland (1893–5).
Golden Hind	Sir Francis Drake's (c.1540–96) ship in which he circumnavigated the globe (1577–80).
Marengo	The horse that carried Napoleon Bonaparte (1769–1821) at the Battle of Waterloo (18 Jun 1815).
Mayflower	The ship that carried the English religious dissenters the Pilgrim Fathers, who established Plymouth Colony in North America, across the Atlantic in 1620.
Rainbow Warrior	The direct action protest ship operated by enviromental charity Greenpeace (original ship 1978–85, current ship from 1989).
Spirit of St Louis	The monoplane in which Charles Lindbergh (1902–74) made the first solo transatlantic flight in 1927, flying from New York, USA, to Paris, France, in 33½ hours.
Victoria	The ship that completed the first circumnavigation of the world (10 Aug 1519–6 Sep 1522), captained by Ferdinand Magellan (c.1480–1521), although Magellan himself was killed in the Philippines.
HMS Victory	The ship from which Lord Horatio Nelson (1758–1805) directed the engagement with the French and Spanish fleets at Trafalgar (21 Oct 1805).
Wright Flyer	The first heavier-than-air flying machine that Orville (1871–1948) and Wilbur (1867–1912) Wright flew on 17 Dec 1903 at Kill Devil Hills, Kitty Hawk, North Carolina, USA.

OLYMPIC GAMES

The modern Olympic Games first took place in 1896, and were founded by the French educationist Baron Pierre de Coubertin (1863–1937). In 1894 he helped set up the International Olympic Committee (IOC), which still formulates policy and decides on venues. The Olympics are held every four years; women first competed in 1900; the first separate Winter Games were held in 1924.

Olympic venues

The host city of each Olympic Summer Games and Olympic Winter Games is chosen by the International Olympic Committee (IOC) seven years in advance.

Olympic Summer Games

1896	Athens, Greece	1956[2]	Melbourne, Australia
1900	Paris, France	1960	Rome, Italy
1904	St Louis, USA	1964	Tokyo, Japan
1906[1]	Athens, Greece	1968	Mexico City, Mexico
1908	London, UK	1972	Munich, West Germany
1912	Stockholm, Sweden	1976	Montréal, Canada
1916	*not held*	1980	Moscow, USSR
1920	Antwerp, Belgium	1984	Los Angeles, USA
1924	Paris, France	1988	Seoul, South Korea
1928	Amsterdam, The Netherlands	1992	Barcelona, Spain
1932	Los Angeles, USA	1996	Atlanta, USA
1936	Berlin, Germany	2000	Sydney, Australia
1940	*not held*	2004	Athens, Greece
1944	*not held*	2008	Beijing, China
1948	London, UK	2012	London, UK
1952	Helsinki, Finland		

[1] *Special Olympic Games held to commemorate the tenth anniversary of the birth of the modern Games.*
[2] *The 1956 equestrian events were held at Stockholm, Sweden, due to quarantine laws in Australia.*

Naked Olympics

According to tradition, the Olympics began in 776BC, when a festival of athletic competitions began to be held at Olympia, in western Greece, to honour the god Zeus. The festival was held at the end of each period of four years (known as an *Olympiad*), and at its peak attracted entrants from all over the Greek world. Many of the events are still familiar to us today, including boxing, wrestling, long jump, discus and javelin. Others were a little different – for example, a foot race run in full armour and a fiercely competitive chariot race of around 14km/8.7mi. There were separate events for boys and men, who competed naked. The winners were crowned simply with an olive wreath, but would be rewarded by their home city with privileges, money and free food and drink for life. The games were eventually ended by order of the Emperor Theodosius I in AD393.

Olympic Winter Games

1924	Chamonix, France[1]	1968	Grenoble, France
1928	St Moritz, Switzerland	1972	Sapporo, Japan
1932	Lake Placid, New York, USA	1976	Innsbruck, Austria
1936	Garmisch-Partenkirchen, Germany	1980	Lake Placid, New York, USA
		1984	Sarajevo, Yugoslavia
1940	*not held*	1988	Calgary, Canada
1944	*not held*	1992	Albertville, France
1948	St Moritz, Switzerland	1994[2]	Lillehammer, Norway
1952	Oslo, Norway	1998	Nagano, Japan
1956	Cortina, Italy	2002	Salt Lake City, USA
1960	Squaw Valley, USA	2006	Turin, Italy
1964	Innsbruck, Austria	2010	Vancouver, Canada

[1] *Held as the 'International Winter Sports Week'; recognized retrospectively as Olympic Winter Games by the IOC in 1926.*
[2] *In 1994, the Olympic Winter Games celebrations were re-adjusted to take place every four years between the Olympic Summer Games years.*

Note: The host city for the 2014 Olympic Winter Games will be announced in 2007.

A Long Wait

Anders Haugen was placed fourth in the skijumping event at the Winter Olympics of 1924. It was only 50 years later, in 1974, that officials realized that a scoring mistake had been made and that Haugen had actually won the bronze medal. The medal was then awarded at a special ceremony in Oslo, Norway, attended by the now-86-year-old skier.

Leading medal winners

Olympic Summer Games

Includes medals won in 2004.

		Gold	Silver	Bronze	Total
1	USA	897	691	605	2 193
2	Russia[1]	526	437	410	1 373
3	Germany[2]	231	274	304	809
4	Great Britain	189	242	234	665
5	France	183	191	213	587
6	Italy	182	147	164	493
7	Sweden	141	155	173	469
8	Hungary	156	136	156	448
9	East Germany	153	129	127	409
10	Australia	120	126	152	398

[1] *Includes medals won by the former USSR team, and by the Unified Team (Armenia, Azerbaijan, Belarus, Georgia, Kazakhstan, Kyrgyzstan, Moldova, Russia, Tajikistan, Turkmenistan, Ukraine and Uzbekistan) in 1992.*
[2] *Includes medals won as West Germany 1968–88.*
Data source: International Olympic Committee.

Olympic Winter Games

Includes medals won in 2002.

		Gold	Silver	Bronze	Total
1	Russia[1]	113	83	78	274
2	Norway	94	92	75	261
3	USA	69	72	51	192
4	Germany[2]	68	68	52	188
5	Austria	42	57	64	163
6	Finland	41	52	49	142
7	East Germany	39	36	35	110
8	Sweden	36	30	38	104
9	Switzerland	33	33	38	104
10	Canada	30	28	37	95

[1] *Includes medals won by the former USSR team, and by the Unified Team (Armenia, Azerbaijan, Belarus, Georgia, Kazakhstan, Kyrgyzstan, Moldova, Russia, Tajikistan, Turkmenistan, Ukraine and Uzbekistan) in 1992.*

[2] *Includes medals won as West Germany 1968–88.*

Data source: International Olympic Committee.

PARALYMPIC GAMES

An Olympic-style competition for elite athletes with a disability. Summer Games first held in 1952 (solely for competitors from the UK and the Netherlands), then once every four years from 1960; Winter Games first held in 1976, then once every four years until 1992, after which they were held once every four years from 1994, to coincide with the Winter Olympic Games.

Paralympic venues

Since 1988 (Summer Paralympic Games) and 1992 (Winter Paralympic Games) the Paralympics have taken place at the same venue as the Olympic Games; this is obligatory for Olympic host cities from 2012 onwards.

Paralympic Summer Games

1952	Stoke Mandeville, UK	1988	Seoul, South Korea
1960	Rome, Italy	1992	Barcelona, Spain
1964	Tokyo, Japan	1996	Atlanta, USA
1968	Tel Aviv, Israel	2000	Sydney, Australia
1972	Heidelberg, West Germany	2004	Athens, Greece
1976	Toronto, Canada	2008	Beijing, China
1980	Arnhem, The Netherlands	2012	London, UK
1984	Stoke Mandeville, UK and New York City, USA		

Deaflympics

Deaf athletes are not usually involved in the Paralympic Games. Instead, the International Committee of Sports for the Deaf (CISS) holds World Games for the Deaf (known as *Deaflympics*). More than 3 000 athletes from 75 countries took part in the most recent Deaflympic Summer Games in 2005.

Paralympic Winter Games

1976	Örnsköldsvik, Sweden	1994[1]	Lillehammer, Norway
1980	Geilo, Norway	1998	Nagano, Japan
1984	Innsbruck, Austria	2002	Salt Lake City, USA
1988	Innsbruck, Austria	2006	Turin, Italy
1992	Albertville, France	2010	Vancouver, Canada

[1] *In 1994, the Paralympic Winter Games celebrations were re-adjusted to take place every four years between the Paralympic Summer Games years.*

Leading medal winners

Totals are for the years 1984–2004.

Paralympic Summer Games

		Gold	Silver	Bronze	Total
1	USA	408	374	403	1 185
2	Great Britain	319	335	321	975
3	Germany	293	315	299	907
4	Canada	255	210	222	687
5	France	235	235	217	687
6	Australia	225	229	220	674
7	Spain	171	140	164	475
8	Sweden	153	130	86	369
9	Poland	115	129	101	345
10	China	143	117	83	343

Data source: International Paralympic Committee.

Paralympic Winter Games

		Gold	Silver	Bronze	Total
1	Germany	89	80	78	247
2	Austria	92	76	76	244
3	Norway	102	74	62	238
4	USA	85	91	61	237
5	Switzerland	35	53	47	135
6	Finland	54	31	39	124
7	France	36	39	37	112
8	Russia[1]	39	39	27	105
9	Canada	19	30	33	82
10	Sweden	13	22	22	57

[1] *Includes medals won by the former USSR team, and by the Unified Team (Armenia, Azerbaijan, Belarus, Georgia, Kazakhstan, Kyrgyzstan, Moldova, Russia, Tajikistan, Turkmenistan, Ukraine and Uzbekistan) in 1992.*

Data source: International Paralympic Committee.

COMMONWEALTH GAMES

Open to competitors from all Commonwealth countries, colonies and dependent or associated territories of a Commonwealth country. First held as the British Empire Games in 1930; take place every four years and between Summer Olympic celebrations; became the British Empire and Commonwealth Games in 1954; known as British Commonwealth Games from 1966 to 1974; current title adopted in 1978.

Commonwealth Games venues

The host city of each Commonwealth Games is chosen by the Commonwealth Games Federation (CGF) seven years in advance.

1930	Hamilton, Canada	1974	Christchurch, New Zealand
1934	London, England	1978	Edmonton, Canada
1938	Sydney, Australia	1982	Brisbane, Australia
1942	*not held*	1986	Edinburgh, Scotland
1946	*not held*	1990	Auckland, New Zealand
1950	Auckland, New Zealand	1994	Victoria, Canada
1954	Vancouver, Canada	1998	Kuala Lumpur, Malaysia
1958	Cardiff, Wales	2002	Manchester, England
1962	Perth, Australia	2006	Melbourne, Australia
1966	Kingston, Jamaica	2010	Delhi, India
1970	Edinburgh, Scotland		

Leading medal winners

Includes medals won in 2002.

		Gold	Silver	Bronze	Total
1	Australia	646	551	488	1 685
2	England	542	513	528	1 583
3	Canada	388	413	430	1 231
4	New Zealand	118	156	221	495
5	Scotland	71	87	142	300
6	South Africa	80	79	83	242
7	India	80	79	63	222
8	Wales	46	64	85	195
9	Kenya	53	42	49	144
10	Nigeria	35	41	50	126

Athletes' Villages

At the first Commonwealth Games in Hamilton in 1930 the facilities were somewhat spartan: the 400-odd competitors slept at a school near the stadium, with up to 24 athletes sharing each classroom. In contrast, the Athletes' Village at the 2002 Games in Manchester included a bar, cinema, entertainment marquee, games room, gym, internet cafe, medical centre, religious centre and restaurant. The organizers estimated beforehand that the beds would be made 120 500 times, 530km/331mi of toilet roll would be used and a stack of towels 4km/2.4mi high would be needed to cater for the thousands of athletes attending.

SPORTS INTRODUCTION

Sports results are listed for the last 25 years only. Where there are winners in a range of disciplines within one competition (for example Athletics), complete results are given for the last five competitions only. Exceptions exist (for example the FIFA World Cup) where all winners are listed.

Note: For 1992 Summer Olympic events the designation (UT) is given for members of the Unified Team (Armenia, Azerbaijan, Belarus, Georgia, Kazakhstan, Kyrgyzstan, Moldova, Russia, Tajikistan, Turkmenistan, Ukraine and Uzbekistan).

AMERICAN FOOTBALL

Players wear heavy padding and helmets, and passing of the ball by hand, including forward passing, is permitted; played on a rectangular field, divided gridiron-like into segments; object is to score *touchdowns* by moving the ball into the opposing team's *end zone*, but progress has to be made upfield by a series of *plays*: a team must make 9.1m/10yd of ground within four plays, otherwise they lose possession of the ball. Six points are awarded for a touchdown. An extra point can then be gained by kicking the ball between the posts and over the crossbar – the equivalent of a conversion in rugby – or two points can be gained by advancing the ball (through play rather than kicking) from the two-yard line into the end zone in a *two-point conversion*. A goal kicked from anywhere on the field (a *field goal*) is worth three points. Teams consist of more than 40 members, but only eleven are allowed on the field at any one time; special units of players have different roles so they change, eg when the team changes from attacking to defending. First intercollegiate game 1869.

Ruling body (USA): National Football League (NFL)

American football field

Vikings and Giants

NFL American football teams named after animals: Bears (Chicago), Colts (Indianapolis), Dolphins (Miami), Eagles (Philadelphia), Falcons (Atlanta), Jaguars (Jacksonville), Lions (Detroit), Panthers (Carolina), Rams (St Louis), Ravens (Baltimore) and Seahawks (Seattle).

Other NFL American football teams: Bengals (Cincinnati), Bills (Buffalo), Broncos (Denver), Browns (Cleveland), Buccaneers (Tampa Bay), Cardinals (Arizona), Chargers (San Diego), Chiefs (Kansas City), Cowboys (Dallas), 49ers (San Francisco), Giants (New York), Jets (New York), Packers (Green Bay), Patriots (New England), Raiders (Oakland), Redskins (Washington), Saints (New Orleans), Steelers (Pittsburgh), Texans (Houston), Titans (Tennessee) and Vikings (Minnesota).

Super Bowl

First held in 1967; takes place each Jan; an end-of-season meeting between the champions of the National Football Conference (NFC) and the American Football Conference (AFC).

1967	Green Bay Packers (NFC)	1987	New York Giants (NFC)
1968	Green Bay Packers (NFC)	1988	Washington Redskins (NFC)
1969	New York Jets (AFC)	1989	San Francisco 49ers (NFC)
1970	Kansas City Chiefs (AFC)	1990	San Francisco 49ers (NFC)
1971	Baltimore Colts (AFC)	1991	New York Giants (NFC)
1972	Dallas Cowboys (NFC)	1992	Washington Redskins (NFC)
1973	Miami Dolphins (AFC)	1993	Dallas Cowboys (NFC)
1974	Miami Dolphins (AFC)	1994	Dallas Cowboys (NFC)
1975	Pittsburgh Steelers (AFC)	1995	San Francisco 49ers (NFC)
1976	Pittsburgh Steelers (AFC)	1996	Dallas Cowboys (NFC)
1977	Oakland Raiders (AFC)	1997	Green Bay Packers (NFC)
1978	Dallas Cowboys (NFC)	1998	Denver Broncos (AFC)
1979	Pittsburgh Steelers (AFC)	1999	Denver Broncos (AFC)
1980	Pittsburgh Steelers (AFC)	2000	St Louis Rams (NFC)
1981	Oakland Raiders (AFC)	2001	Baltimore Ravens (AFC)
1982	San Francisco 49ers (NFC)	2002	New England Patriots (AFC)
1983	Washington Redskins (NFC)	2003	Tampa Bay Buccaneers (NFC)
1984	Los Angeles Raiders (AFC)	2004	New England Patriots (AFC)
1985	San Francisco 49ers (NFC)	2005	New England Patriots (AFC)
1986	Chicago Bears (NFC)		

Star-Spangled Super Bowl

The singing of the US National Anthem at the Super Bowl is a time-honoured tradition. While in the early years of the Super Bowl the anthem was often sung by bands or choirs (for example the US Air Force Academy Chorale in 1972 and the Little Angels of Holy Angels Church in 1973), in later years it has usually been the luminaries of US pop music who belt out the Banner. Thus, Super Bowl audiences have been treated to the patriotic warblings of Whitney Houston (1991) and Mariah Carey (2002), the country croonings of Garth Brooks (1993) and the Dixie Chicks (2003), plus the star-spangled likes of Barry Manilow (1984), Cher (1999), the Backstreet Boys (2001) and Beyoncé Knowles (2004). In 2005, however, the Super Bowl returned to its roots with the combined US forces choirs.

ATHLETICS

Tests of running, jumping, throwing and walking skills. The running or track events range from the 100m/328ft sprint to the 42km 195m/26mi 385yd marathon; jumping and throwing or field events consist of high jump, long jump, triple jump and pole vault, and the discus throw, shot put, javelin throw and hammer throw. Multi-event competitions are the decathlon (ten events) for men and the heptathlon (seven events) for women. Athletics dates to c.3800BC in Egypt; the International Amateur Athletic Federation was founded in 1912.

high jump
: Field event; competitors attempt to clear a bar without any aids; height increased gradually; three failed attempts means disqualification. The winner clears the greatest height, or has the fewest failures.

long jump
: Field event; contestant runs up to the take-off mark and leaps into a sandpit; length of the jump measured from front of take-off line to nearest break in the sand made by any part of the competitor's body; also called broad jump in North America.

triple jump
: Field event; takes place in the same part of the stadium as the long jump, governed by same rules. After the run-up, competitors must take off and hop on the same foot; second phase is a step onto the other foot, followed by a jump; previously called the hop, step and jump.

pole vault
: Field event; jumping contest for height using fibreglass pole for leverage to clear a bar, which is raised progressively; three attempts may be made to clear the height before attempting a new one.

discus throw
: Field event; uses a circular disc of wood with metal plates, weighing 2kg/4.4 lb for men and 1kg/2.2 lb for women. It is thrown with one hand from within the confines of a circle 2.5m/8ft 2in in diameter.

shot put
: Field event; the shot is a brass or iron sphere weighing 7.26kg/16 lb for men and 4kg/8 lb 13oz for women. It is propelled, using only one hand, from a starting position under the chin. The thrower must not leave the 2.1m/7ft diameter throwing circle. In competition six throws are allowed.

javelin throw
: Field event; throwing a spear-like javelin which consists of three parts: pointed metal head, shaft and grip; men's javelin is 2.6–2.7m/8ft 6in–8ft 10in in length and weighs 800g/1.8 lb; women's is 2.2–2.3m/7ft 2in–7ft 6in and weighs at least 600g/1.3 lb; the competitor runs to a specified mark with the javelin in one hand, and throws it; for throw to count, metal head must touch ground before any other part; first mark made by the head is the point used for measuring the distance achieved.

hammer throw
: Field event; hammer weighing 7.26kg/16 lb is thrown using one hand from within the confines of a circle 2.13m/7ft in diameter (protected by a wire cage). Six throws are allowed, the object being to attain the greatest distance.

decathlon
: Ten-event track-and-field competition held over two days, usually for men: 100m, long jump, shot put, high jump, 400m, 110m hurdles, discus, pole vault, javelin and 1 500m. Points are awarded in each event.

heptathlon
: Seven-event track-and-field competition held over two days, usually for women: 100m hurdles, shot put, high jump, 200m, long jump, javelin and 800m.

Ruling body: International Association of Athletics Federations (IAAF)

World Championships

First held in 1983; since 1995 every two years.

1997

Men		**Women**	
100m	Maurice Greene (USA)	100m	Marion Jones (USA)
200m	Ato Boldon (Trinidad)	200m	Zhanna Pintuşevich (Ukraine)
400m	Michael Johnson (USA)	400m	Cathy Freeman (Australia)
800m	Wilson Kipketer (Denmark)	800m	Ana Fidelia Quirot (Cuba)
1 500m	Hicham El Guerrouj (Morocco)	1 500m	Carla Sacramento (Portugal)
5 000m	Daniel Komen (Kenya)	5 000m	Gabriela Szabo (Romania)
10 000m	Haile Gebrselassie (Ethiopia)	10 000m	Sally Barsosio (Kenya)
marathon	Abel Antón (Spain)	marathon	Hiromi Suzuki (Japan)
3 000m steeplechase	Wilson Kipketer (Denmark)	100m hurdles	Ludmila Engquist (Sweden)
		400m hurdles	Nezha Bidouane (Morocco)
110m hurdles	Allen Johnson (USA)	10km walk	Annarita Sidoti (Italy)
400m hurdles	Stephane Diagana (France)	4×100m relay	USA
20km walk	Daniel Garcia (Mexico)	4×400m relay	Germany
50km walk	Robert Korzeniowski (Poland)	high jump	Hanne Haugland (Norway)
4×100m relay	Canada	long jump	Lyudmila Galkina (Russia)
4×400m relay	USA	triple jump	Sarka Kasparkova (Czech Republic)
high jump	Javier Sotomayor (Cuba)		
long jump	Iván Pedroso (Cuba)	shot	Astrid Kumbernuss (Germany)
triple jump	Yoelvis Quesada (Cuba)	discus	Beatrice Faumuina (New Zealand)
pole vault	Sergei Bubka (Ukraine)		
shot	John Godina[1] (USA)	javelin	Trine Hattestad (Norway)
discus	Lars Riedel (Germany)	heptathlon	Sabine Braun (Germany)
hammer	Heinz Weis (Germany)		
javelin	Marius Corbett (South Africa)		
decathlon	Tómas Dvorák (Czech Republic)		

[1] *Originally won by Aleksandr Bagach (Ukraine); Bagach was stripped of the medal following a positive drug test.*

1999

Men		**Women**	
100m	Maurice Greene (USA)	100m	Marion Jones (USA)
200m	Maurice Greene (USA)	200m	Inger Miller (USA)
400m	Michael Johnson (USA)	400m	Cathy Freeman (Australia)
800m	Wilson Kipketer (Denmark)	800m	Ludmilla Formanova (Czech Republic)
1 500m	Hicham El Guerrouj (Morocco)		
5 000m	Salah Hissou (Morocco)	1 500m	Svetlana Masterkova (Russia)
10 000m	Haile Gebrselassie (Ethiopia)	5 000m	Gabriela Szabo (Romania)
marathon	Abel Antón (Spain)	10 000m	Gete Wami (Ethiopia)
3 000m steeplechase	Christopher Koskei (Kenya)	marathon	Jong Song-Ok (North Korea)
		100m hurdles	Gail Devers (USA)
110m hurdles	Colin Jackson (Great Britain)	400m hurdles	Daimi Pernia (Cuba)
400m hurdles	Fabrizio Mori (Italy)	20km walk	Liu Hongyu (China)
20km walk	Ilya Markov (Russia)	4×100m relay	The Bahamas
50km walk	German Skurygin (Russia)	4×400m relay	Russia
4×100m relay	USA	high jump	Inga Babakova (Ukraine)
4×400m relay	USA	long jump	Niurka Montalvo (Spain)

Men		Women	
high jump	Vyacheslav Voronin (Russia)	triple jump	Paraskevi Tsiamita (Greece)
long jump	Iván Pedroso (Cuba)	pole vault	Stacy Dragila (USA)
triple jump	Charles Michael Friedek (Germany)	shot	Astrid Kumbernuss (Germany)
		discus	Franka Dietzsch (Germany)
pole vault	Maksim Tarasov (Russia)	hammer	Michaela Melinte (Romania)
shot	C J Hunter (USA)	javelin	Mirela Manjani-Tzelili (Greece)
discus	Anthony Washington (USA)	heptathlon	Eunice Barber (France)
hammer	Karsten Kobs (Germany)		
javelin	Aki Parviainen (Finland)		
decathlon	Tomás Dvořák (Czech Republic)		

2001

Men		Women	
100m	Maurice Greene (USA)	100m	Zhanna Pintusevich-Block (Ukraine)
200m	Konstantinos Kederis (Greece)		
400m	Avard Moncur (Bahamas)	200m	Marion Jones (USA)
800m	André Bucher (Switzerland)	400m	Amy Mbacke Thiam (Senegal)
1 500m	Hicham El Guerrouj (Morocco)	800m	Maria Mutola (Mozambique)
5 000m	Richard Limo (Kenya)	1 500m	Gabriela Szabo (Romania)
10 000m	Charles Kamathi (Kenya)	5 000m	Olga Yegorova (Russia)
marathon	Gezahegne Abera (Ethiopia)	10 000m	Derartu Tulu (Ethiopia)
3 000m steeplechase	Reuben Kosgei (Kenya)	marathon	Lidia Simon (Romania)
		100m hurdles	Anjanette Kirkland (USA)
110m hurdles	Allen Johnson (USA)	400m hurdles	Nezha Bidouane (Morocco)
400m hurdles	Felix Sánchez (Dominican Republic)	20km walk	Olimpiada Ivanova (Russia)
		4×100m relay	USA
20km walk	Roman Rasskazov (Russia)	4×400m relay	USA
50km walk	Robert Korzeniowski (Poland)	high jump	Hestrie Cloete (South Africa)
4×100m relay	USA	long jump	Fiona May (Italy)
4×400m relay	Jamaica	triple jump	Tatyana Lebedeva (Russia)
high jump	Buss Martin (Germany)	pole vault	Stacy Dragila (USA)
long jump	Iván Pedroso (Cuba)	shot	Yanina Korolchik (Belarus)
triple jump	Jonathan Edwards (Great Britain)	discus	Natalya Sadova (Russia)
		hammer	Yipsi Moreno (Cuba)
pole vault	Dmitry Markov (Russia)	javelin	Osleidys Menéndez (Cuba)
shot	John Godina (USA)	heptathlon	Yelena Prokhorova (Russia)
discus	Lars Riedel (Germany)		
hammer	Szymon Ziółkowski (Poland)		
javelin	Jan Železný (Czech Republic)		
decathlon	Tomás Dvořák (Czech Republic)		

Running Records

The world record for the fastest time for the 100m for men was set by the Jamaican athlete Asafa Powell in Athens in Jun 2005. Powell ran the distance – equivalent to 328ft – in just 9.77 seconds. This works out at 37kph, or 23mph. But even the fastest humans are slowcoaches compared with the fastest mammal, the cheetah, which can reach speeds of up to 100kph/62mph in short bursts.

2003

Men		**Women**	
100m	Kim Collins (St Kitts and Nevis)	100m	Torri Edwards[1] (USA)
200m	John Capel (USA)	200m	Anastasia Kapachinskaya[1]
400m	Jerome Young (USA)		(Russia)
800m	Djabir Saïd-Guerni (Algeria)	400m	Ana Guevara (Mexico)
1 500m	Hicham El Guerrouj (Morocco)	800m	Maria Mutola (Mozambique)
5 000m	Eliud Kipchoge (Kenya)	1 500m	Tatyana Tomashova (Russia)
10 000m	Kenenisa Bekele (Ethiopia)	5 000m	Tirunesh Dibaba (Ethiopia)
marathon	Jaoud Gharib (Morocco)	10 000m	Berhane Adere (Ethiopia)
3 000m	Saif Saaeed Shaheen (Qatar)	marathon	Catherine Ndereba (Kenya)
steeplechase		100m hurdles	Perdita Felicien (Canada)
110m hurdles	Allen Johnson (USA)	400m hurdles	Jana Pittman (Australia)
400m hurdles	Felix Sánchez (Dominican	20km walk	Yelena Nikolayeva (Russia)
	Republic)	4×100m relay	France
20km walk	Jefferson Pérez (Ecuador)	4×400m relay	USA
50km walk	Robert Korzeniowski (Poland)	high jump	Hestrie Cloete (South Africa)
4×100m relay	USA	long jump	Eunice Barber (France)
4×400m relay	USA	triple jump	Tatyana Lebedeva (Russia)
high jump	Jacques Freitag (South Africa)	pole vault	Svetlana Feofanova (Russia)
long jump	Dwight Phillips (USA)	shot	Svetlana Krivelyova (Russia)
triple jump	Christian Olsson (Sweden)	discus	Irina Yatchenko (Belarus)
pole vault	Giuseppe Gibilisco (Italy)	hammer	Yipsi Moreno (Cuba)
shot	Andrei Mikhnevich (Belarus)	javelin	Miréla Manjani (Greece)
discus	Virgilijus Alekna (Lithuania)	heptathlon	Carolina Kluft (Sweden)
hammer	Ivan Tikhon (Belarus)		
javelin	Sergey Makarov (Russia)		
decathlon	Tom Pappas (USA)		

[1] *Originally won by Kelli White (USA); White was stripped of the medal following a positive drug test.*

Changing Flags

Qatar won its first ever World Championships athletics medal in 2003 when Saif Saaeed Shaheen took the gold in the men's 3 000m steeplechase. But while Qatar celebrated, Kenya mourned: Shaheen, previously known as Stephen Cherono, was a Kenyan who had recently transferred his allegiance to run for Qatar for a reputed $1 000 a month for life plus large victory bonuses.

2005

Men		**Women**	
100m	Justin Gatlin (USA)	100m	Lauryn Williams (USA)
200m	Justin Gatlin (USA)	200m	Allyson Felix (USA)
400m	Jeremy Wariner (USA)	400m	Tonique Williams-Darling
800m	Rashid Ramzi (Bahrain)		(Bahamas)
1 500m	Rashid Ramzi (Bahrain)	800m	Zulia Calatayud (Cuba)
5 000m	Benjamin Limo (Kenya)	1 500m	Tatyana Tomashova (Russia)
10 000m	Kenenisa Bekele (Ethiopia)	5 000m	Tirunesh Dibaba (Ethiopia)
marathon	Jaouad Gharib (Morocco)	10 000m	Tirunesh Dibaba (Ethiopia)
3 000m		marathon	Paula Radcliffe (Great Britain)
steeplechase	Saif Saaeed Shaheen (Qatar)	3 000m	
110 m hurdles	Ladji Doucoure (France)	steeplechase	Docus Inzikuru (Uganda)

Men		**Women**	
400m hurdles	Bershawn Jackson (USA)	100 m hurdles	Michelle Perry (USA)
20km walk	Jefferson Pérez (Ecuador)	400m hurdles	Yuliya Pechonkina (Russia)
50km walk	Sergey Kirdyapkin (Russia)	20km walk	Olimpiada Ivanova (Russia)
4 x 100m relay	France	4 x 100m relay	USA
4 x 400m relay	USA	4 x 400m relay	Russia
high jump	Yuriy Kyrmarenko (Ukraine)	high jump	Kajsa Bergqvist (Sweden)
long jump	Dwight Phillips (USA)	long jump	Tianna Madison (USA)
triple jump	Walter Davis (USA)	triple jump	Trecia Smith (Jamaica)
pole vault	Rens Blom (Netherlands)	pole vault	Yelena Isinbayeva (Russia)
shot	Adam Nelson (USA)	shot	Nadezhda Ostapchuk(Belarus)
discus	Virgilijus Alekna (Lithuania)	discus	Franka Dietzsch (Germany)
hammer	Ivan Tikhon (Belarus)	hammer	Olga Kuzenkova (Russia)
javelin	Andrus Varnik (Estonia)	javelin	Osleidys Menéndez (Cuba)
decathlon	Bryan Clay (USA)	heptathlon	Carolina Kluft (Sweden)

AUSTRALIAN RULES FOOTBALL

A handling and kicking game with few rules, a cross between association football and rugby, with 18 players on an oval pitch. The object is to score by kicking the ball between the opponent's goal posts (six points). Smaller posts are positioned either side of the main goal: a ball kicked through that area scores one point; first recorded game played 1858.

Ruling body: Australian Football League (AFL)

Australian Rules football pitch

BADMINTON

Premiership Trophy

First held in 1897 as the Victorian Football League (1897–1989); inaugural winners were Essendon. The majority of Grand Finals have been played at the MCG in Melbourne.

1981	Carlton	1990	Collingwood	1999	North Melbourne
1982	Carlton	1991	Hawthorn		Kangaroos
1983	Hawthorn	1992	West Coast	2000	Essendon
1984	Essendon	1993	Essendon	2001	Brisbane Lions
1985	Essendon	1994	West Coast	2002	Brisbane Lions
1986	Hawthorn	1995	Carlton	2003	Brisbane Lions
1987	Carlton	1996	North Melbourne	2004	Port Adelaide
1988	Hawthorn	1997	Adelaide	2005	Sydney
1989	Hawthorn	1998	Adelaide		

Rugby and Rules

The game of Australian Rules football was concocted by Tom Wills, H C A Harrison, W J Hammersley and J B Thompson in the mid-1800s. Wills had been educated in the UK and was football captain at Rugby School. Upon his return to Australia he suggested that cricketers could keep fit during the winter by playing a version of rugby football. Wills worked out the rules for the new game, and the first ever Australian Rules match was held in 1858.

BADMINTON

Indoor game, with two or four players, played on a court using rackets, a shuttlecock (cork or plastic half sphere with 'feathers') and a raised central net; object is to volley the shuttlecock over the net so that the opponent is unable to return it.

Ruling body: International Badminton Federation (IBF)

Badminton court

World Championships

First held in 1977; initially took place every three years; since 1983 every two years.

Men		Women	
1983	Icuk Sugiarto (Indonesia)	1983	Li Lingwei (China)
1985	Han Jian (China)	1985	Han Aiping (China)
1987	Yang Yang (China)	1987	Han Aiping (China)
1989	Yang Yang (China)	1989	Li Lingwei (China)
1991	Zhao Jianhua (China)	1991	Tang Jiuhong (China)
1993	Joko Suprianto (Indonesia)	1993	Susi Susanti (Indonesia)
1995	Heryanto Arbi (Indonesia)	1995	Ye Zhaoying (China)
1997	Peter Rasmussen (Denmark)	1997	Ye Zhaoying (China)
1999	Sun Jun (China)	1999	Camilla Martin (Denmark)
2001	Hendra Wan (Indonesia)	2001	Gong Ruina (China)
2003	Xia Xuanze (China)	2003	Zhang Ning (China)
2005	Taufik Hidayat (Indonesia)	2005	Xie Xingfang (China)

Beaufort's Badminton

The name *badminton* derives from Badminton House in Gloucestershire, the seat of the Duke of Beaufort, where the game was played by house guests in the 19c. However, the game actually originated in China over 2 200 years ago.

Thomas Cup

An international team event for men's teams; inaugurated 1949; now held every two years.

1981–2	China	1990	China	1998	Indonesia
1984	Indonesia	1992	Malaysia	2000	Indonesia
1986	China	1994	Indonesia	2002	Indonesia
1988	China	1996	Indonesia	2004	China

Uber Cup

An international event for women's teams; first held in 1957; now held every two years.

1980–1	Japan	1990	China	1998	China
1984	China	1992	China	2000	China
1986	China	1994	Indonesia	2002	China
1988	China	1996	Indonesia	2004	China

All-England Championship

Badminton's premier event prior to the inauguration of the World Championships; first held in 1900.

Men		Women	
1981	Liem Swie King (Indonesia)	1981	Hwang Sun Ai (Korea)
1982	Morten Frost (Denmark)	1982	Zhang Ailing (China)
1983	Luan Jin (China)	1983	Zhang Ailing (China)
1984	Morten Frost (Denmark)	1984	Li Lingwei (China)
1985	Zhao Jianhua (China)	1985	Han Aiping (China)
1986	Morten Frost (Denmark)	1986	Yun-Ja Kim (Korea)
1987	Morten Frost (Denmark)	1987	Kirsten Larsen (Denmark)
1988	Ib Frederikson (Denmark)	1988	Gu Jiaming (China)
1989	Yang Yang (China)	1989	Li Lingwei (China)
1990	Zhao Jianhua (China)	1990	Susi Susanti (Indonesia)
1991	Ardi Wiranata (Indonesia)	1991	Susi Susanti (Indonesia)
1992	Liu Jun (China)	1992	Tang Jiuhong (China)
1993	Heryanto Arbi (Indonesia)	1993	Susi Susanti (Indonesia)
1994	Heryanto Arbi (Indonesia)	1994	Susi Susanti (Indonesia)
1995	Poul-Erik Hoyer-Larsen (Denmark)	1995	Lim Xiao Qing (Sweden)
1996	Poul-Erik Hoyer-Larsen (Denmark)	1996	Bang Soo Hyun (South Korea)
1997	Dong Jiong (China)	1997	Ye Zhaoying (China)
1998	Sun Jun (China)	1998	Ye Zhaoying (China)
1999	Peter Gade Christensen (Denmark)	1999	Ye Zhaoying (China)
2000	Xia Xuanze (China)	2000	Zichao Gong (China)
2001	Pulella Gopichand (India)	2001	Zichao Gong (China)
2002	Chen Hong (China)	2002	Camilla Martin (Denmark)
2003	Muhammad Hafiz Hashim (Malaysia)	2003	Mi Zhou (China)
2004	Lin Dan (China)	2004	Gong Ruina (China)
2005	Chen Hong (China)	2005	Xie Xingfang (China)

BASEBALL

Team game played by two sides of 25 possible players on a diamond-shaped field which has bases at the corners. Essential pieces of equipment are long solid bats, the solid ball *pitched* from the *mound*, and the glove worn by each fielder; team *at bat* tries to score most runs by having its players circle the three bases and touch home plate before being put out by the team *in the field*; players out if their hit is caught, if they are tagged with the ball when *off-base*, if the base is touched by the ball before they arrive at it, or if they *strike out*, ie fail to hit the ball after three pitches have been judged strikes by the umpire; *home run* scored when player hits ball, circles all three bases and crosses home plate; game consists of nine innings; popularly believed to have been invented by Abner Doubleday (1819–93), at Cooperstown, NY in 1839, but it is now known that a game similar to baseball was played in the USA and England long before Doubleday's time.

Ruling body: International Baseball Federation (IBAF)

Baseball field

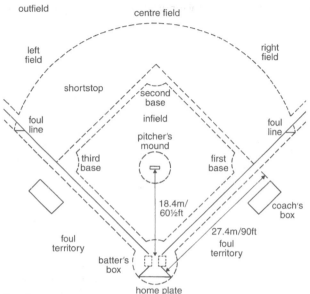

World Series

First held in 1903; takes place each Oct, the best of seven matches; professional baseball's leading event, the end-of-season meeting between the winners of the two major baseball leagues in the USA, the National League (NL) and American League (AL).

1981	Los Angeles Dodgers (NL)	1994	*not held*
1982	St Louis Cardinals (NL)	1995	Atlanta Braves (NL)
1983	Baltimore Orioles (AL)	1996	New York Yankees (AL)
1984	Detroit Tigers (AL)	1997	Florida Marlins (NL)
1985	Kansas City Royals (AL)	1998	New York Yankees (AL)
1986	New York Mets (NL)	1999	New York Yankees (AL)
1987	Minnesota Twins (AL)	2000	New York Yankees (AL)
1988	Los Angeles Dodgers (NL)	2001	Arizona Diamondbacks (NL)
1989	Oakland Athletics (AL)	2002	Anaheim Angels (AL)
1990	Cincinnati Reds (NL)	2003	Florida Marlins (NL)
1991	Minnesota Twins (AL)	2004	Boston Red Sox (AL)
1992	Toronto Blue Jays (AL)	2005	Chicago White Sox (AL)
1993	Toronto Blue Jays (AL)		

Where Have You Gone, Joe DiMaggio?

New York Yankees star Joe DiMaggio (1914–99) was a hit off the field as well as on, marrying actress Marilyn Monroe in 1954. He is also mentioned in the lyrics of Simon and Garfunkel's 1967 hit song *Mrs Robinson*.

World Cup

Instituted in 1938; since 2001 held approximately every two years.

1982	Korea	1990	Cuba	2003	Cuba
1984	Cuba	1994	Cuba	2005	Cuba
1986	Cuba	1998	Cuba		
1988	Cuba	2001	Cuba		

Peaches and Sultans

The Iron Horse, the Georgia Peach, Mr October and the Sultan of Swat are just some of the nicknames of major league baseball players (in reality Lou Gehrig (1903–41), Ty Cobb (1886–1961), Reggie Jackson (1946–) and Babe Ruth (1895–1948) respectively). Joe DiMaggio (1914–99) was known as Joltin' Joe and the Yankee Clipper, while Hank Aaron (1934–) was called Hammerin' Hank, Honus Wagner (1874–1955) was the Flying Dutchman and James Hunter (1946–99) was better known as Catfish.

BASKETBALL

Five-a-side team ball game played on a hard surface court with a bottomless basket at each end; object is to move the ball by a series of passing and bouncing moves and throw it through the opponent's basket.

Ruling body: International Basketball Federation (FIBA; Fédération Internationale de Basketball)

Basketball court

Note: The centre of the hoop is 1.58m/5.17ft from the endline; the backboard is 1.2m/3.9ft from the endline.

World Championship

First held 1950 for men, 1953 for women; takes place approximately every four years.

Men		Women	
1982	USSR	1983	USSR
1986	USA	1986	USA
1990	Yugoslavia	1990	USA
1994	USA	1994	Brazil
1998	Yugoslavia	1998	USA
2002	Yugoslavia	2002	USA

Basketball's Beginnings

A Canadian, James Naismith (1861–1939), is regarded as being the originator of basketball. He invented the game in 1891 at the YMCA college in Springfield, Massachusetts, USA, using peach baskets on a gym wall. The game was originally designed merely to bridge the gap between the baseball and American football seasons, but it soon became popular in its own right. A similar game is believed to have been played in Mexico in the 10c.

NBA Championship

First held in 1947; the major competition in professional basketball in the USA; an end-of-season play-off involving the champion teams from the Eastern Conference (EC) and Western Conference (WC).

1981	Boston Celtics (EC)	1994	Houston Rockets (WC)
1982	Los Angeles Lakers (WC)	1995	Houston Rockets (WC)
1983	Philadelphia 76ers (EC)	1996	Chicago Bulls (EC)
1984	Boston Celtics (EC)	1997	Chicago Bulls (EC)
1985	Los Angeles Lakers (WC)	1998	Chicago Bulls (EC)
1986	Boston Celtics (EC)	1999	San Antonio Spurs (WC)
1987	Los Angeles Lakers (WC)	2000	Los Angeles Lakers (WC)
1988	Los Angeles Lakers (WC)	2001	Los Angeles Lakers (WC)
1989	Detroit Pistons (EC)	2002	Los Angeles Lakers (WC)
1990	Detroit Pistons (EC)	2003	San Antonio Spurs (WC)
1991	Chicago Bulls (EC)	2004	Detroit Pistons (EC)
1992	Chicago Bulls (EC)	2005	San Antonio Spurs (WC)
1993	Chicago Bulls (EC)		

Magic and Mavericks

NBA basketball teams named after animals: Bobcats (Charlotte), Bucks (Milwaukee), Bulls (Chicago), Grizzlies (Memphis), Hawks (Atlanta), Hornets (New Orleans/Oklahoma City), Raptors (Toronto) and Timberwolves (Minnesota).

Other NBA basketball teams: Cavaliers (Cleveland), Celtics (Boston), Clippers (Los Angeles), Heat (Miami), Jazz (Utah), Kings (Sacramento), Knicks (New York), Lakers (Los Angeles), Magic (Orlando), Mavericks (Dallas), Nets (New Jersey), Nuggets (Denver), Pacers (Indiana), Pistons (Detroit), Rockets (Houston), 76ers (Philadelphia), Spurs (San Antonio), Suns (Phoenix), SuperSonics (Seattle), Trail Blazers (Portland), Warriors (Golden State) and Wizards (Washington).

BOXING

Fistfighting between two people, usually men, in a roped ring 4.3–6.1m/14–20ft square. Professional championship bouts comprise twelve three-minute rounds; amateur bouts three rounds, unless one fighter is knocked out or retires, the referee halts the fight, or a fighter is disqualified. There are 17 weight divisions (see below).

Ruling bodies: International Boxing Federation (IBF), World Boxing Association (WBA), World Boxing Council (WBC), World Boxing Organization (WBO)

Butlers and Butchers

Boxing dates from Greek and Roman times. The first known match in Britain was in 1681 when the Duke of Albemarle organized a bout between his butler and his butcher in New Hall, Essex. The first rules were drawn up in 1743, when each round lasted until one fighter was knocked down; gloves and three-minute rounds were introduced in 1867.

Boxing weight categories

Category	Weight
mini flyweight, minimum weight or strawweight	under 48kg/105 lb
light flyweight or junior flyweight	maximum 49kg/108 lb
flyweight	maximum 51kg/112 lb
super flyweight/junior bantamweight	maximum 52kg/115 lb
bantamweight	maximum 54kg/118 lb
super bantamweight/junior featherweight	maximum 55kg/122 lb
featherweight	maximum 57kg/126 lb
super featherweight/junior lightweight	maximum 59kg/130 lb
lightweight	maximum 61kg/135 lb
super lightweight/junior welterweight	maximum 63.5kg/140 lb
welterweight	maximum 67kg/147 lb
junior middleweight, light middleweight or super welterweight	maximum 70kg/154 lb
middleweight	maximum 73kg/160 lb
super middleweight	maximum 76kg/168 lb
light heavyweight	maximum 79kg/175 lb
cruiserweight	maximum 86kg/190 lb
heavyweight	above 86kg/190 lb

Wilde in the Ring

In 1867 the 8th Marquess of Queensberry, Sir John Douglas (1844–1900), supervised the formulation of new rules to govern boxing, since known as the 'Queensberry Rules'. The same Marquess was unsuccessfully sued for criminal libel by Oscar Wilde in 1895; Queensberry disapproved of Wilde's friendship with his son, Lord Alfred Douglas, and it was Queensberry's allegations of homosexuality that led in turn to Wilde's trial and imprisonment.

World heavyweight champions

The first world heavyweight champion under Queensberry Rules with gloves was James J Corbett in 1892.

1982	Michael Dokes (USA)	WBA	1995	Riddick Bowe (USA)	WBO
1983	Gerrie Coetzee (South	WBA	1995	Bruce Seldon (USA)	WBA
	Africa)	WBA	1995	Frank Bruno (UK)	WBC
1984	Tim Witherspoon (USA)	WBC	1995	Frans Botha (South	IBF
1984	Pinklon Thomas (USA)	WBC		Africa)[4]	
1984	Larry Holmes (USA)	IBF	1996	Mike Tyson (USA)[5]	WBA/WBC
1984	Greg Page (USA)	WBA	1996	Henry Akinwande (UK)	WBO
1985	Tony Tubbs (USA)	WBA	1996	Michael Moorer (USA)	IBF
1985	Pinklon Thomas (USA)	WBC	1996	Evander Holyfield (USA)	WBA
1985	Michael Spinks (USA)	IBF	1997	Evander Holyfield (USA)	WBA/IBF
1986	Tim Witherspoon (USA)	WBA	1997	Lennox Lewis (UK)	WBC
1986	Trevor Berbick (Canada)	WBC	1997	Herbie Hide (UK)	WBO
1986	Mike Tyson (USA)	WBC	1999	Vitali Klitschko (Ukraine)	WBO
1986	James Smith (USA)	WBA	1999	Lennox Lewis (UK)[6]	UND (WBA/
1987	Tony Tucker (USA)	IBF			WBC/IBF)
1987	Mike Tyson (USA)	WBA/WBC	2000	Chris Byrd (USA)	WBO
1987	Mike Tyson (USA)	UND	2000	Evander Holyfield (USA)	WBA
1989	Francesco Damiani (Italy)	WBO	2000	Lennox Lewis (UK)	WBC/IBF
1990	James (Buster) Douglas	WBA/WBC/	2001	John Ruiz (USA)	WBA
	(USA)	IBF	2000	Wladimir Klitschko	WBO
1990	Evander Holyfield (USA)	WBA/WBC/		(Ukraine)	
		IBF	2001	Hashim Rahman (USA)	WBC/IBF
1991	Ray Mercer (USA)	WBO	2001	Lennox Lewis (UK)	WBC/IBF
1992	Riddick Bowe (USA)[1]	WBA/WBC/	2002	Lennox Lewis (UK)[7]	IBF
		IBF	2002	Chris Byrd (USA)	IBF
1992	Michael Moorer (USA)	WBO	2003	Roy Jones Jr (USA)	WBA
1993	Evander Holyfield (USA)	WBA/IBF	2003	Corrie Sanders (South	WBO
1993	Lennox Lewis (UK)	WBC		Africa)[8]	
1993	Tommy Morrison (USA)	WBO	2004	John Ruiz (USA)	WBA
1993	Michael Bentt (USA)	WBO	2004	Lamon Brewster (USA)	WBO
1994	Herbie Hide (UK)	WBO	2004	Vitali Klitschko (Ukraine)	WBC
1994	Michael Moorer (USA)	WBA/IBF	2005	James Toney[9] (USA)	WBA
1994	Oliver McCall (USA)	WBC	2005	John Ruiz (USA)	WBA
1994	George Foreman (USA)[2,3]	WBA/IBF	2005	Hasim Rahman[10] (USA)	WBC

[1] *Stripped of WBC title in 1992.*
[2] *Gave up IBF title in 1995.*
[3] *Stripped of WBA title in 1995.*
[4] *Stripped of IBF title in 1996.*
[5] *Gave up WBC title in 1996.*
[6] *Stripped of WBA title in 2000.*
[7] *Gave up IBF title in 2002*
[8] *Gave up WBO title in 2003*
[9] *Failed drugs test; title returned to John Ruiz.*
[10] *Awarded WBC title upon retirement of Vitali Klitschko.*

IBF	*International Boxing Federation*
UND	*Undisputed Champion*
WBA	*World Boxing Association*
WBC	*World Boxing Council*
WBO	*World Boxing Organization*

CHESS

Game of strategy for two players using chequered board of 64 squares. Each player has 16 pieces: eight pawns, two rooks, two knights, two bishops, queen and king; object is to capture or *checkmate* opponent's king; all pieces have set moves, queen is most versatile.

Ruling body: World Chess Federation (FIDE; Fédération Internationale des Échecs)

World Champions

World Champions have been recognized since 1886; first women's champion recognized in 1927. In 1993 a new Professional Chess Association was created as a rival body to FIDE but it collapsed in 1996; replaced by the World Chess Council which also collapsed in 2000.

Men		Women	
1975–85	Anatoly Karpov (USSR)	1978–91	Maya Chiburdanidze (USSR)
1985–93	Garry Kasparov (USSR)[1]	1991–6	Xie Jun (China)
1993–9	Anatoly Karpov (Russia)	1996–9	Zsuza Polgar (Hungary)
1999	Alexander Khalifman (Russia)	1999–2001	Xie Jun (China)
2000–2	Vishwanathan Anand (India)	2001–04	Zhu Chen (China)
2002–4	Ruslan Ponomariov (Ukraine)	2004–	Antoaneta Stefanova (Bulgaria)
2004–5	Rustam Kasimdzhanov (Uzbekistan)		
2005–	Veselin Topalov (Bulgaria)		

[1] *Continued as PCA World Champion to 2000.*

Chaturanga and Chess

Chess was played in ancient India as *chaturanga*, and the earliest reference to it dates from c.600AD. The current pieces have existed in standard form for over 500 years.

CRICKET

Bat and ball eleven-a-side team game. A wicket consisting of three stumps (wooden sticks) surmounted by a pair of bails (smaller sticks) is placed at each end of a grassy pitch 20.1m/22yd in length. Each team takes it in turn to bat (with long flat-sided wooden bats) and bowl (with a solid ball), the object being to defend the two wickets while trying to score as many runs as possible. A bowler delivers an *over* of six balls to a batsman standing in front of one of the wickets before a different bowler attacks the other wicket. If the batsman hits a ball (and in certain other circumstances), he may exchange places with the other batsman, thus scoring at least one run. A ball reaching the boundary of the field scores four runs automatically, and six if it has not bounced on the way. A batsman can be got out by being *caught* (a fielder catches the ball before it reaches the ground), *bowled* (the ball from the bowler knocks the bails off the stumps), *stumped* (the wicketkeeper knocks the bails off the stumps with the ball while the defending batsman is standing outside his *safe ground* or *crease*), *run out* (the bails on the wicket towards which one of the batsmen is running are knocked off before the safe ground is reached), *leg before wicket* or *lbw* (when the lower part of the batsman's leg prevents the ball from the bowler reaching the wicket) and *hit wicket* (the batsman accidentally knocks the bails off the stumps). Once ten batsmen have been dismissed, the innings comes to a close, but a team can stop its innings or *declare* if it thinks it has made enough runs. In longer games each team has two innings, at the end of which the team with the greater number of runs at the end of the match wins. If both innings are not completed within the permitted time the match is declared a draw. Test matches usually last five days; county championship matches four, and limited-over competitions are normally concluded in one day, lasting for a specific number of overs per side.

Ruling bodies: International Cricket Council (ICC), England and Wales Cricket Board (ECB), Marylebone Cricket Club (MCC)

Cricket fielding positions

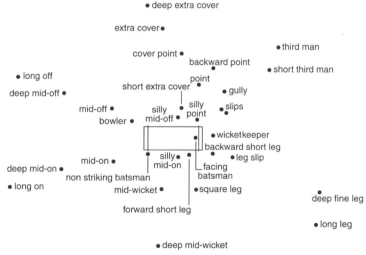

Ashes Series Winners

First played in 1882; held every two years; Australia and England take part.

1981	England	1990–1	Australia	2001	Australia
1982–3	Australia	1993	Australia	2002–3	Australia
1985	England	1994–5	Australia	2005	England
1986–7	England	1997	Australia		
1989	Australia	1998–9	Australia		

World Cup

First played in 1975; usually held every four years.

1975	West Indies	1987	Australia	1999	Australia
1979	West Indies	1992	Pakistan	2003	Australia
1983	India	1996	Sri Lanka		

Women's World Cup

First played in 1973.

1973	England	1988	Australia	2000	New Zealand
1977	Australia	1993	England	2005	Australia
1982	Australia	1997	Australia		

County Championship

The oldest cricket competition in the world; first won by Sussex in 1827; not officially recognized until 1890, when a proper points system was introduced; split into two divisions in 2000.

1981	Nottinghamshire	1993	Middlesex	2002	Surrey (Division 2 Essex)
1982	Middlesex	1994	Warwickshire		
1983	Essex	1995	Warwickshire	2003	Sussex (Division 2 Worcestershire)
1984	Essex	1996	Leicestershire		
1985	Middlesex	1997	Glamorgan	2004	Warwickshire (Division 2 Nottinghamshire)
1986	Essex	1998	Leicestershire		
1987	Nottinghamshire	1999	Surrey		
1988	Worcestershire	2000	Surrey (Division 2 Northamptonshire)	2005	Nottinghamshire (Division 2 Lancashire)
1989	Worcestershire				
1990	Middlesex	2001	Yorkshire (Division 2 Sussex)		
1991	Essex				
1992	Essex				

Totesport National Cricket League

First held in 1969; split into two divisions in 1999; known as the John Player League until 1987, the Refuge Assurance League until 1991, the Axa Equity and Law League until 1999, the CGU League until 2000 and the Norwich Union National Cricket League until 2003.

1981	Essex	1992	Middlesex	2001	Kent (Division 2 Glamorgan)
1982	Sussex	1993	Glamorgan		
1983	Yorkshire	1994	Warwickshire	2002	Glamorgan (Division 2 Gloucestershire)
1984	Essex	1995	Kent		
1985	Essex	1996	Surrey	2003	Surrey (Division 2 Lancashire)
1986	Hampshire	1997	Warwickshire		
1987	Worcestershire	1998	Lancashire	2004	Glamorgan (Division 2 Middlesex)
1988	Worcestershire	1999	Lancashire (Division 2 Sussex)		
1989	Lancashire			2005	Essex (Division 2 Sussex)
1990	Derbyshire	2000	Gloucestershire (Division 2 Surrey)		
1991	Nottinghamshire				

Cheltenham & Gloucester Trophy

First held in 1963; known as the Gillette Cup until 1981 and the NatWest Bank Trophy until 2000.

1981	Derbyshire	1990	Lancashire	1999	Gloucestershire
1982	Surrey	1991	Hampshire	2000	Gloucestershire
1983	Somerset	1992	Northamptonshire	2001	Somerset
1984	Middlesex	1993	Warwickshire	2002	Yorkshire
1985	Essex	1994	Worcestershire	2003	Gloucestershire
1986	Sussex	1995	Warwickshire	2004	Gloucestershire
1987	Nottinghamshire	1996	Lancashire	2005	Hampshire
1988	Middlesex	1997	Essex		
1989	Warwickshire	1998	Lancashire		

Twenty20 Cup

First held in 2003.

2003	Surrey
2004	Leicestershire
2005	Somerset

Benson and Hedges Cup

Competition ran from 1972 to 2002.

1981	Somerset	1989	Nottinghamshire	1997	Surrey
1982	Somerset	1990	Lancashire	1998	Essex
1983	Middlesex	1991	Worcestershire	1999	Gloucestershire
1984	Lancashire	1992	Hampshire	2000	Gloucestershire
1985	Leicestershire	1993	Derbyshire	2001	Surrey
1986	Middlesex	1994	Warwickshire	2002	Warwickshire
1987	Yorkshire	1995	Lancashire		
1988	Hampshire	1996	Lancashire		

Pura Cup

Australia's leading domestic competition; contested inter-state since 1892–3; known as the Sheffield Shield until 1999.

1981	Western Australia	1990	New South Wales	1999	Western Australia
1982	South Australia	1991	Victoria	2000	Queensland
1983	New South Wales	1992	Western Australia	2001	Queensland
1984	Western Australia	1993	New South Wales	2002	Queensland
1985	New South Wales	1994	New South Wales	2003	New South Wales
1986	New South Wales	1995	Queensland	2004	Victoria
1987	Western Australia	1996	South Australia	2005	New South Wales
1988	Western Australia	1997	Queensland		
1989	Western Australia	1998	Western Australia		

CROSS-COUNTRY RUNNING

An athletic running event using a predetermined course over natural terrain. The length of race varies; the current race distances are 12km/7.5mi for men's long course races, 8km/5mi for women's long course races and 4km/2.5mi for both short course races. The first recorded international race was in May 1898, and covered a 14.5km/9mi course at Ville D'Avray near Paris, France.

Ruling body: International Association of Athletics Federations (IAAF)

World Championships

First international championship held in 1903, but only included runners from England, Ireland, Scotland and Wales; recognized as an official world championship from 1973; first women's race in 1967.

Individual – Men's long course

1981	Craig Virgin (USA)
1982	Mohammed Kedir (Ethiopia)
1983	Bekele Debele (Ethiopia)
1984	Carlos Lopes (Portugal)
1985	Carlos Lopes (Portugal)
1986	John Ngugi (Kenya)
1987	John Ngugi (Kenya)
1988	John Ngugi (Kenya)
1989	John Ngugi (Kenya)
1990	Khalid Skah (Morocco)
1991	Khalid Skah (Morocco)
1992	John Ngugi (Kenya)
1993	William Sigei (Kenya)
1994	William Sigei (Kenya)
1995	Paul Tergat (Kenya)
1996	Paul Tergat (Kenya)
1997	Paul Tergat (Kenya)
1998	Paul Tergat (Kenya)
1999	Paul Tergat (Kenya)
2000	Mohammed Mourhit (Belgium)
2001	Mohammed Mourhit (Belgium)
2002	Kenenisa Bekele (Ethiopia)
2003	Kenenisa Bekele (Ethiopia)
2004	Kenenisa Bekele (Ethiopia)
2005	Kenenisa Bekele (Ethiopia)

Individual – Women's long course

1981	Grete Waitz (Norway)
1982	Maricica Puica (Romania)
1983	Grete Waitz (Norway)
1984	Maricica Puica (Romania)
1985	Zola Budd (England)
1986	Zola Budd (England)
1987	Annette Sergent (France)
1988	Ingrid Kristiansen (Norway)
1989	Annette Sergent (France)
1990	Lynn Jennings (USA)
1991	Lynn Jennings (USA)
1992	Lynn Jennings (USA)
1993	Albertina Dias (Portugal)
1994	Helen Chepngeno (Kenya)
1995	Derartu Tulu (Ethiopia)
1996	Gete Wami (Ethiopia)
1997	Derartu Tulu (Ethiopia)
1998	Sonia O'Sullivan (Ireland)
1999	Gete Wami (Ethiopia)
2000	Derartu Tulu (Ethiopia)
2001	Paula Radcliffe (England)
2002	Paula Radcliffe (England)
2003	Werknesh Kidane (Ethiopia)
2004	Benita Johnson (Australia)
2005	Tirunesh Dibaba (Ethiopia)

Team – Men's long course

1981	Ethiopia
1982	Ethiopia
1983	Ethiopia
1984	Ethiopia
1985	Ethiopia
1986	Kenya
1987	Kenya

Team – Women's long course

1981	USSR
1982	USSR
1983	USA
1984	USA
1985	USA
1986	England
1987	USA

Team – Men		Team – Women	
1988	Kenya	1988	USSR
1989	Kenya	1989	USSR
1990	Kenya	1990	USSR
1991	Kenya	1991	Ethiopia *and* Kenya *(shared)*
1992	Kenya	1992	Kenya
1993	Kenya	1993	Kenya
1994	Kenya	1994	Portugal
1995	Kenya	1995	Kenya
1996	Kenya	1996	Kenya
1997	Kenya	1997	Ethiopia
1998	Kenya	1998	Kenya
1999	Kenya	1999	Ethiopia
2000	Kenya	2000	Ethiopia
2001	Kenya	2001	Kenya
2002	Kenya	2002	Ethiopia
2003	Kenya	2003	Ethiopia
2004	Ethiopia	2004	Ethiopia
2005	Ethiopia	2005	Ethiopia

CYCLING

Bicycle riding as a sport can take several forms: *time trials* are raced against the clock; *cyclocross* is a mixture of cycling and cross-country running, carrying the bike; *track racing* takes place on purpose-built concrete or wooden velodromes; *criteriums* are races around town or city centres; *road races* are normally in excess of 150km/93mi in length, between two points or several circuits of a predetermined course; *stage races* involve many days' racing over more than 150km/93mi. First cycle race Paris 1868, won by James Moore of England.

Ruling body: International Cycling Union (UCI; Union Cycliste Internationale)

World Road Race Championships

Men's race first held in 1927; first women's race in 1958; takes place annually.

Men		Women	
1981	Freddy Maertens (Belgium)	1981	Ute Enzenauer (West Germany)
1982	Giuseppe Saronni (Italy)	1982	Mandy Jones (Great Britain)
1983	Greg LeMond (USA)	1983	Marianne Berglund (Switzerland)
1984	Claude Criquielion (Belgium)	1984	*not held*
1985	Joop Zoetemelk (The Netherlands)	1985	Jeannie Longo (France)
		1986	Jeannie Longo (France)
1986	Moreno Argentin (Italy)	1987	Jeannie Longo (France)
1987	Stephen Roche (Ireland)	1988	*not held*
1988	Maurizio Fondriest (Italy)	1989	Jeannie Longo (France)
1989	Greg LeMond (USA)	1990	Catherine Marsal (France)
1990	Rudy Dhaenens (Belgium)	1991	Leontien van Moorsel (The Netherlands)
1991	Gianni Bugno (Italy)		

Men		Women	
1992	Gianni Bugno (Italy)	1992	*not held*
1993	Lance Armstrong (USA)	1993	Leontien van Moorsel (The
1994	Luc Leblanc (France)		Netherlands)
1995	Abraham Olano (Spain)	1994	Monica Valvik (Norway)
1996	Johan Museeuw (Belgium)	1995	Jeannie Longo (France)
1997	Laurent Brochard (France)	1996	Barbara Heeb (Switzerland)
1998	Oskar Camenzind (Switzerland)	1997	Alessandra Cappellotto (Italy)
1999	Oscar Freire Gomez (Spain)	1998	Diana Ziliute (Lithuania)
2000	Romans Vainsteins (Latvia)	1999	Edita Pucinskaite (Lithuania)
2001	Oscar Freire Gomez (Spain)	2000	Zinaida Stahurskaia (Belarus)
2002	Mario Cipollini (Italy)	2001	Rosa Polikeviciute (Lithuania)
2003	Igor Astarloa (Spain)	2002	Susanne Ljungskog (Sweden)
2004	Oscar Freire Gomez (Spain)	2003	Susanne Ljungskog (Sweden)
2005	Tom Boonen (Belgium)	2004	Judith Arndt (Germany)
		2005	Regina Schleicher (Germany)

Tour de France

World's premier cycling event; first held in 1903.

1981	Bernard Hinault (France)	1994	Miguel Indurain (Spain)
1982	Bernard Hinault (France)	1995	Miguel Indurain (Spain)
1983	Laurent Fignon (France)	1996	Bjarne Riis (Denmark)
1984	Laurent Fignon (France)	1997	Jan Ullrich (Germany)
1985	Bernard Hinault (France)	1998	Marco Pantani (Italy)
1986	Greg LeMond (USA)	1999	Lance Armstrong (USA)
1987	Stephen Roche (Ireland)	2000	Lance Armstrong (USA)
1988	Pedro Delgado (Spain)	2001	Lance Armstrong (USA)
1989	Greg LeMond (USA)	2002	Lance Armstrong (USA)
1990	Greg LeMond (USA)	2003	Lance Armstrong (USA)
1991	Miguel Indurain (Spain)	2004	Lance Armstrong (USA)
1992	Miguel Indurain (Spain)	2005	Lance Armstrong (USA)
1993	Miguel Indurain (Spain)		

Yellow Jerseys

The famous *yellow jersey* (or *maillot jaune*) is worn each day of the Tour de France by the race's overall leader. The jersey, which was first worn in 1919, gained its distinctive colour from the yellow pages of *Auto*, the magazine which instituted the Tour in 1903. The Belgian Eddy Merckx holds the record for wearing the jersey, having been yellow-clad for an impressive 96 days. The Tour's cyclists also compete to wear the *green jersey*, since 1953 the reward for the best sprinter, the *red polka-dot jersey*, worn since 1975 by the best mountain climber, and the *white jersey*, first awarded in 1975 to the leading young cyclist under 25 years.

DARTS

Indoor game of throwing three 13cm/5in darts from a distance of 2.37m/7ft 9.25in at a circular board which has its centre 1.73m/5ft 8in from the floor. The standard board is divided into 20 segments numbered 1–20 (not in numerical order); each contains smaller segments which either double or treble that number's score if hit. The centre ring (the *bull*) is worth 50 points, and the area around it (the *outer*) is worth 25 points. Most popular game *501*: players start at that figure and deduct all scores from it, aiming to reduce the starting score exactly to zero; final shot must consist of a double.

Ruling body: British Darts Organization (BDO), World Darts Federation (WDF)

Dartboard

double

outer or 25 ring

bull (diameter 12.7mm/0.5in)

treble ring

170mm/6.7in

107mm/4.2in

8mm/0.32in

31.8mm/1.25in

45.3cm/17.8in

Embassy World Darts Championship

First held at Nottingham in 1978. Women's championship introduced in 2001.

Men		**Women**	
1981	Eric Bristow (England)	2001	Trina Gulliver (England)
1982	Jocky Wilson (Scotland)	2002	Trina Gulliver (England)
1983	Keith Deller (England)	2003	Trina Gulliver (England)
1984	Eric Bristow (England)	2004	Trina Gulliver (England)
1985	Eric Bristow (England)	2005	Trina Gulliver (England)
1986	Eric Bristow (England)		
1987	John Lowe (England)		
1988	Bob Anderson (England)		
1989	Jocky Wilson (Scotland)		
1990	Phil Taylor (England)		
1991	Dennis Priestley (England)		
1992	Phil Taylor (England)		

Men

1993	John Lowe (England)
1994	John Part (Canada)
1995	Richie Burnett (Wales)
1996	Steve Beaton (England)
1997	Les Wallace (Scotland)
1998	Raymond van Barneveld (The Netherlands)
1999	Raymond van Barneveld (The Netherlands)
2000	Ted Hankey (England)
2001	John Walton (England)
2002	Tony David (Australia)
2003	Raymond van Barneveld (The Netherlands)
2004	Andy Fordham (England)
2005	Raymond van Barneveld (The Netherlands)

Blowin' in the Wind

When Mervyn King lost 5–2 to Raymond van Barneveld in the semifinal of the Embassy World Darts Championship in 2003, the BBC reported that he blamed excessive air-conditioning for blowing his darts off course. Disgruntled King allegedly claimed that the air-conditioning 'was blowing [his] darts all over the shop', and reckoned that Barneveld was not affected because his darts were heavier. King reportedly threatened to boycott subsequent championships and was not swayed by organizers' protests that the air-conditioning had been switched off throughout.

EQUESTRIAN EVENTS

Events in which riders on horseback compete in various disciplines: *dressage*, performance of set manoeuvres signalled by the rider; *three-day event*, a competition in showjumping, cross-country riding and dressage; and *showjumping*, in which competitors take turns to jump a variety of obstacles, often against time; in most competitions, each pair of horse and rider has one attempt at clearing the fences; those that clear the fences and incur no penalty points are then involved in a *jump-off* against the clock, where speed as well as accuracy are important.

Ruling body: International Equestrian Federation (FEI; Fédération Équestre Internationale)

World Equestrian Games

Showjumping championships first held in 1953 (for men) and 1965 (for women); since 1978 men and women have competed together and on equal terms; team competition introduced in 1978; three-day event and dressage championships introduced in 1966; all three now held every four years. Formerly known as the World Championships.

Showjumping

Individual		Team	
1982	Norbert Koof (West Germany)	1982	France
1986	Gail Greenough (Canada)	1986	USA
1990	Eric Navet (France)	1990	France
1994	Franke Sloothaak (Germany)	1994	Germany
1998	Rodrigo Pessoa (Brazil)	1998	Germany
2002	Dermott Lennon (Ireland)	2002	France

Three-day event

Individual		**Team**	
1982	Lucinda Green (Great Britain)	1982	Great Britain
1986	Virginia Leng (Great Britain)	1986	Great Britain
1990	Blyth Tait (New Zealand)	1990	New Zealand
1994	Vaughn Jefferis (New Zealand)	1994	Great Britain
1998	Blyth Tait (New Zealand)	1998	New Zealand
2002	Jean Teulere (France)	2002	USA

Dressage

Individual		**Team**	
1982	Reiner Klimke (West Germany)	1982	West Germany
1986	Anne Grethe Jensen (Denmark)	1986	West Germany
1990	Nicole Uphoff (West Germany)	1990	West Germany
1994	Anky van Grunsven (Holland)	1994	Germany
1998	Isabell Werth (Germany)	1998	Germany
2002	Nadine Capellmann (Germany)	2002	Germany

FENCING

Sword fighting, using a light *foil*, heavier *épée*, or *sabre* (curved handle, narrow blade). Different target areas exist for each weapon, and protective clothing registers hits electronically.

Ruling body: International Fencing Federation (FIE; Fédération Internationale d'Escrime)

World Championships

Held annually since 1921 (1921–35, known as European Championships). Not held in Olympic years. Women's épée was introduced in 1989 and women's sabre in 1999.

1999

Men		**Women**	
foil individual	Sergei Golubitsky (Ukraine)	foil individual	Valentina Vezzali (Italy)
foil team	France	foil team	Germany
épée individual	Arnd Schmitt (Germany)	épée individual	Laura Flessel (France)
épée team	France	épée team	Hungary
sabre individual	Damien Touya (France)	sabre individual	Elena Jemayeva (Azerbaijan)
sabre team	France	sabre team	Italy

Note: A World Championships for women's sabre was held in 2000; the individual contest was won by Elena Jemayeva (Azerbaijan) and the team event by the USA.

2001

Men		Women	
foil individual	Salvatore Sanzo (Italy)	foil individual	Valentina Vezzali (Italy)
foil team	France	foil team	Italy
épée individual	Paulo Milanoli (Italy)	épée individual	Claudia Bokel (Germany)
épée team	Hungary	épée team	Russia
sabre individual	Stanislav Pozdniakov (Russia)	sabre individual	Anne Lise Touya (France)
sabre team	Russia	sabre team	Russia

2002

Men		Women	
foil individual	Simone Vanni (Italy)	foil individual	Svetlani Bojko (Russia)
foil team	Germany	foil team	Russia
épée individual	Pavel Kolobkov (Russia)	épée individual	Hee Hyun (Korea)
épée team	France	épée team	Hungary
sabre individual	Stanislav Pozdniakov (Russia)	sabre individual	Xue Tan (China)
sabre team	Russia	sabre team	Russia

2003

Men		Women	
foil individual	Peter Joppich (Germany)	foil individual	Valentina Vezzali (Italy)
foil team	Italy	foil team	Poland
épée individual	Fabrice Jeannet (France)	épée individual	Natalia Conrad (Ukraine)
épée team	Russia	épée team	Russia
sabre individual	Vladimir Lukashenko (Ukraine)	sabre individual	Dorina Mihai (Romania)
sabre team	Russia	sabre team	Italy

2005

Men		Women	
foil individual	Salvatore Sanzo (Italy)	foil individual	Valentina Vezzali (Italy)
foil team	France	foil team	South Korea
épée individual	Pavel Kolobkov (Russia)	épée individual	Danuta Dmowska (Poland)
épée team	France	épée team	France
sabre individual	Mihai Covaliu (Romania)	sabre individual	Anne Lise Touya (France)
sabre team	Russia	sabre team	USA

The Language of Fencing

Fencing can be traced back to Egypt in c.1300BC and was popular in the Middle Ages. It was first practised as a sport in Europe in the 14c–15c, and its many movements were originally named in 1570 by the Frenchman Henri Saint-Didier. Today fencing moves include the *appel*, the *botte*, the *flanconade*, the *imbroccata*, the *stoccado* or *stoccata* and the *tac-au-tac*. Fencing also provides the origin of the term *touché* (claiming or acknowledging a point scored in an argument) which originally referred to a fencing hit by an opponent.

FOOTBALL

A field team game using an inflated ball, formally known as *association football*, and sometimes called *soccer*. An 11-a-side team game played on a grass or synthetic pitch; object is to move the ball around using the foot or head until it can be put into the net, thus scoring a goal. Only the goalkeeper within a specific area is allowed to touch the ball with the hand while it is in play.

Ruling body: Fédération Internationale de Football Association (FIFA), Union of European Football Associations (UEFA), Confederación Sudamericana de Fútbol (CONMEBOL), Football Association (FA), Scottish Football Association (SFA)

Football pitch

FIFA World Cup

Football's premier event; first contested for the Jules Rimet Trophy in 1930; Brazil won it outright after winning for the third time in 1970; since then teams have competed for the FIFA World Cup; held every four years.

Host countries		**Winners**	
1930	Uruguay	1930	Uruguay
1934	Italy	1934	Italy
1938	France	1938	Italy
1942	*not held*	1942	*not held*
1946	*not held*	1946	*not held*
1950	Brazil	1950	Uruguay
1954	Switzerland	1954	West Germany
1958	Sweden	1958	Brazil
1962	Chile	1962	Brazil
1966	England	1966	England
1970	Mexico	1970	Brazil
1974	West Germany	1974	West Germany
1978	Argentina	1978	Argentina
1982	Spain	1982	Italy
1986	Mexico	1986	Argentina
1990	Italy	1990	West Germany
1994	USA	1994	Brazil
1998	France	1998	France
2002	South Korea/Japan	2002	Brazil
2006	Germany		
2010	South Africa		

European Championship

Held every four years since 1960; qualifying group matches held over the two years preceding the final.

1960	USSR	1976	Czechoslovakia	1992	Denmark
1964	Spain	1980	West Germany	1996	Germany
1968	Italy	1984	France	2000	France
1972	West Germany	1988	Netherlands	2004	Greece

Copa América

First held in 1916 for South American national sides; there were two tournaments in 1959, won by Argentina and Uruguay; discontinued in 1967, but revived eight years later; since 1987 played every two years; frequency may change to every four years.

1983	Uruguay	1993	Argentina	2001	Colombia
1987	Uruguay	1995	Uruguay	2004	Brazil
1989	Brazil	1997	Brazil		
1991	Argentina	1999	Brazil		

European Champions League

The leading club competition in Europe; open to the leading teams of countries affiliated to the Union of European Football Associations (UEFA), the Cup's ruling body, on a quota basis; commonly known as the 'European Cup'; inaugurated in the 1955–6 season; played annually.

1981	Liverpool (England)	1994	AC Milan (Italy)
1982	Aston Villa (England)	1995	Ajax (The Netherlands)
1983	Hamburg (West Germany)	1996	Juventus (Italy)
1984	Liverpool (England)	1997	Borussia Dortmund (Germany)
1985	Juventus (Italy)	1998	Real Madrid (Spain)
1986	Steaua Bucharest (Romania)	1999	Manchester United (England)
1987	FC Porto (Portugal)	2000	Real Madrid (Spain)
1988	PSV Eindhoven (The Netherlands)	2001	Bayern Munich (Germany)
1989	AC Milan (Italy)	2002	Real Madrid (Spain)
1990	AC Milan (Italy)	2003	AC Milan (Italy)
1991	Red Star Belgrade (Yugoslavia)	2004	FC Porto (Portugal)
1992	Barcelona (Spain)	2005	Liverpool (England)
1993	Olympique Marseille[1] (France)		

[1] Stripped of title because of match fixing.

--- Football Firsts ---

The Ancient Greeks, Chinese, Egyptians and Romans all played a form of football. It became an organized game in Britain in the 19c, and standard rules were drawn up in 1848. The Football Association (FA) was formed in 1863 and the first FA Cup final was played in 1872; the first World Cup was held in 1930.

UEFA Cup

Held since 1958; originally the Fairs Cup, renamed the UEFA Cup in 1971; open to the runners-up in domestic championships, as well as to the winners of certain other domestic competitions.

1981	Ipswich Town (England)	1993	Juventus (Italy)
1982	IFK Goteborg (Sweden)	1994	Inter Milan (Italy)
1983	Anderlecht (Belgium)	1995	Parma (Italy)
1984	Tottenham Hotspur (England)	1996	Bayern Munich (Germany)
1985	Real Madrid (Spain)	1997	Schalke 04 (Germany)
1986	Real Madrid (Spain)	1998	Inter Milan (Italy)
1987	IFK Goteborg (Sweden)	1999	Parma (Italy)
1988	Bayer 04 Leverkusen (West Germany)	2000	Galatasaray (Turkey)
		2001	Liverpool (England)
1989	Napoli (Italy)	2002	Feyenoord (The Netherlands)
1990	Juventus (Italy)	2003	FC Porto (Portugal)
1991	Inter Milan (Italy)	2004	Valencia (Spain)
1992	Ajax (The Netherlands)	2005	CSKA Moscow (Russia)

European Cup Winners Cup

Competititon ran from 1961 to 1999; for winners of European domestic cup competitions.

1981	Dynamo Tbilisi (USSR)	1992	Werder Bremen (Germany)
1982	Barcelona (Spain)	1993	Parma (Italy)
1983	Aberdeen (Scotland)	1994	Arsenal (England)
1984	Juventus (Italy)	1995	Real Zaragoza (Spain)
1985	Everton (England)	1996	Paris Saint-Germain (France)
1986	Dynamo Kiev (USSR)	1997	Barcelona (Spain)
1987	Ajax (The Netherlands)	1998	Chelsea (England)
1988	Mechelen (Belgium)	1999	Lazio (Italy)
1989	Barcelona (Spain)		
1990	Sampdoria (Italy)		
1991	Manchester United (England)		

The Other Final

While the World Cup Final was being contested by Germany and Brazil in Jun 2002 in front of more than 69 000 spectators and millions of television viewers worldwide, another final was taking place rather more quietly at the Chlanglimithang Stadium in Thimphu, Bhutan. FIFA's two lowest ranked teams – Bhutan and Montserrat, rated 202 and 203 in the world – had been brought together by a couple of Dutch filmmakers to contest what became known as 'The Other Final' for the sheer love of football. The altitude (2 250m/7 380ft above sea level), stray dogs rambling across the pitch, torrential Himalayan rain and repeated choruses of Montserrat's only worldwide hit song 'Hot Hot Hot' all combined to create a unique match in a nation where the national sport is archery. Despite Montserrat's initial optimism, the end result was 4–0 to Bhutan.

Football Association Challenge Cup (FA Cup)

The world's oldest club knockout competition held annually by the Football Association (FA); first contested in the 1871–2 season; first final at the Kennington Oval on 16 Mar 1872.

1981	Tottenham Hotspur	1990	Manchester United	1999	Manchester United
1982	Tottenham Hotspur	1991	Tottenham Hotspur	2000	Chelsea
1983	Manchester United	1992	Liverpool	2001	Chelsea
1984	Everton	1993	Arsenal	2002	Arsenal
1985	Manchester United	1994	Manchester United	2003	Arsenal
1986	Liverpool	1995	Everton	2004	Manchester United
1987	Coventry City	1996	Manchester United	2005	Arsenal
1988	Wimbledon	1997	Chelsea		
1989	Liverpool	1998	Arsenal		

Football League

The oldest league in the world, and regarded as the toughest; founded in 1888, it has four divisions, with the Premiership (founded in the 1992–3 season) as the top division.

1981	Aston Villa	1990	Liverpool	1999	Manchester United
1982	Liverpool	1991	Arsenal	2000	Manchester United
1983	Liverpool	1992	Leeds United	2001	Manchester United
1984	Liverpool	1993	Manchester United	2002	Arsenal
1985	Everton	1994	Manchester United	2003	Manchester United
1986	Liverpool	1995	Blackburn Rovers	2004	Arsenal
1987	Everton	1996	Manchester United	2005	Chelsea
1988	Liverpool	1997	Manchester United		
1989	Arsenal	1998	Arsenal		

Football League Cup (Carling Cup)

Founded 1961; open to the 92 members of the Football League and the Premiership; formerly known as the Milk Cup, Littlewoods Cup, Rumbelows Cup, Coca Cola Cup and Worthington Cup.

1981	Liverpool	1990	Nottingham Forest	1999	Tottenham Hotspur
1982	Liverpool	1991	Sheffield Wednesday	2000	Leicester City
1983	Liverpool	1992	Manchester United	2001	Liverpool
1984	Liverpool	1993	Arsenal	2002	Blackburn Rovers
1985	Norwich City	1994	Aston Villa	2003	Liverpool
1986	Oxford United	1995	Liverpool	2004	Middlesbrough
1987	Arsenal	1996	Aston Villa	2005	Chelsea
1988	Luton Town	1997	Leicester City		
1989	Nottingham Forest	1998	Chelsea		

Scottish Football League

Organized in various divisions since 1891; in 1998 the top ten teams broke away to form the new independent Scottish Premier League, which was expanded to twelve teams in 2000.

1981	Celtic	1990	Rangers	1999	Rangers
1982	Celtic	1991	Rangers	2000	Rangers
1983	Dundee United	1992	Rangers	2001	Celtic
1984	Aberdeen	1993	Rangers	2002	Celtic
1985	Aberdeen	1994	Rangers	2003	Rangers
1986	Celtic	1995	Rangers	2004	Celtic
1987	Rangers	1996	Rangers	2005	Rangers
1988	Celtic	1997	Rangers		
1989	Rangers	1998	Celtic		

Scottish FA Cup

Competition held by the Scottish Football Association (SFA); first contested in the 1873–4 season; first final held in 1874 at Hampden Park.

1981	Rangers	1990	Aberdeen	1999	Rangers
1982	Aberdeen	1991	Motherwell	2000	Rangers
1983	Aberdeen	1992	Rangers	2001	Celtic
1984	Aberdeen	1993	Rangers	2002	Rangers
1985	Celtic	1994	Dundee United	2003	Rangers
1986	Aberdeen	1995	Celtic	2004	Celtic
1987	St Mirren	1996	Rangers	2005	Celtic
1988	Celtic	1997	Kilmarnock		
1989	Celtic	1998	Heart of Midlothian		

Scottish League Cup (CIS Insurance Cup)

Founded 1947 and open to the 42 members of the Scottish Football League.

1981	Dundee United	1990	Aberdeen	1999	Rangers
1982	Rangers	1991	Rangers	2000	Celtic
1983	Celtic	1992	Hibernian	2001	Celtic
1984	Rangers	1993	Rangers	2002	Rangers
1985	Rangers	1994	Rangers	2003	Rangers
1986	Aberdeen	1995	Raith Rovers	2004	Livingston
1987	Rangers	1996	Aberdeen	2005	Rangers
1988	Rangers	1997	Rangers		
1989	Rangers	1998	Celtic		

English Premiership and Football League clubs

Club	Location	Stadium	Nickname
Arsenal	London	Highbury	The Gunners
Aston Villa	Birmingham	Villa Park	The Villans
Barnet	London	Underhill Stadium	The Bees
Barnsley	Barnsley	Oakwell	The Tykes
Birmingham City	Birmingham	St Andrews	The Blues
Blackburn Rovers	Blackburn	Ewood Park	The Rovers/ The Blue and Whites
Blackpool	Blackpool	Bloomfield Road	The Seasiders
Bolton Wanderers	Bolton	Reebok Stadium	The Trotters
Boston United	Boston	York Street	The Pilgrims
Bournemouth	Bournemouth	Fitness First Stadium	The Cherries
Bradford City	Bradford	Valley Parade[1]	The Bantams
Brentford	London	Griffin Park	The Bees
Brighton & Hove Albion	Brighton	Withdean Stadium	The Seagulls
Bristol City	Bristol	Ashton Gate	The Robins
Bristol Rovers	Bristol	Memorial Stadium	The Pirates
Burnley	Burnley	Turf Moor	The Clarets
Bury	Bury	Gigg Lane	The Shakers
Cardiff City	Cardiff	Ninian Park	The Bluebirds
Carlisle United	Carlisle	Brunton Park	The Cumbrians
Charlton Athletic	London	The Valley	The Addicks
Chelsea	London	Stamford Bridge	The Blues
Cheltenham Town	Cheltenham	Whaddon Road	The Robins
Chester City	Chester	Saunders Honda Stadium	The Blues
Chesterfield	Chesterfield	Saltergate[2]	The Spireites
Colchester United	Colchester	Layer Road	The U's
Coventry City	Coventry	Ricoh Arena	The Sky Blues
Crewe Alexandra	Crewe	Alexandra Stadium	The Railwaymen
Crystal Palace	London	Selhurst Park	The Eagles
Darlington	Darlington	Reynolds Arena	The Quakers
Derby County	Derby	Pride Park Stadium	The Rams
Doncaster Rovers	Doncaster	Belle Vue	The Rovers
Everton	Liverpool	Goodison Park	The Toffees
Fulham	London	Craven Cottage	The Cottagers
Gillingham	Gillingham	Priestfield Stadium	The Gills
Grimsby Town	Cleethorpes	Blundell Park	The Mariners
Hartlepool United	Hartlepool	Victoria Park	The Pool
Huddersfield Town	Huddersfield	The McAlpine Stadium	The Terriers
Hull City	Kingston upon Hull	Kingston Communications Stadium	The Tigers
Ipswich Town	Ipswich	Portman Road	The Tractor Boys
Leeds United	Leeds	Elland Road	The Whites
Leicester City	Leicester	The Walkers Stadium	The Foxes
Leyton Orient	London	The Matchroom Stadium	The O's
Lincoln City	Lincoln	Sincil Bank Stadium	The Red Imps
Liverpool	Liverpool	Anfield	The Reds
Luton Town	Luton	Kenilworth Stadium	The Hatters
Macclesfield Town	Macclesfield	The Moss Rose	The Silkmen
Manchester City	Manchester	City of Manchester Stadium	The Citizens
Manchester United	Manchester	Old Trafford	The Red Devils
Mansfield Town	Mansfield	Field Mill	The Stags

Club	Location	Stadium	Nickname
Middlesbrough	Middlesbrough	The Riverside Stadium	Boro
Millwall	London	The New Den	The Lions
Milton Keynes Dons	Milton Keynes	National Hockey Stadium	The Dons
Newcastle United	Newcastle upon Tyne	St James' Park	The Magpies
Northampton Town	Northampton	Sixfields Stadium	The Cobblers
Norwich City	Norwich	Carrow Road	The Canaries
Nottingham Forest	Nottingham	The City Ground	The Reds
Notts County	Nottingham	Meadow Lane	The Magpies
Oldham Athletic	Oldham	Boundary Park	The Latics
Oxford United	Oxford	The Kassam Stadium	The U's
Peterborough United	Peterborough	London Road	The Posh
Plymouth Argyle	Plymouth	Home Park	The Pilgrims
Portsmouth	Portsmouth	Fratton Park	Pompey
Port Vale	Stoke-on-Trent	Vale Park	The Valiants
Preston North End	Preston	Deepdale	The Lilywhites
Queen's Park Rangers	London	Loftus Road Stadium	The R's
Reading	Reading	Madejski Stadium	The Royals
Rochdale	Rochdale	Spotland Stadium	The Dale
Rotherham United	Rotherham	Millmoor	The Merry Millers
Rushden & Diamonds	Irthlingborough	Nene Park	The Diamonds
Scunthorpe United	Scunthorpe	Glanford Park	The Irons
Sheffield United	Sheffield	Bramall Lane	The Blades
Sheffield Wednesday	Sheffield	Hillsborough	The Owls
Shrewsbury Town	Shrewsbury	Gay Meadow	The Shrews
Southampton	Southampton	Friends Provident St Mary's Stadium[3]	The Saints
Southend United	Southend	Roots Hall	The Shrimpers
Stockport County	Stockport	Edgeley Park	The Hatters
Stoke City	Stoke-on-Trent	The Britannia Stadium	The Potters
Sunderland	Sunderland	Stadium of Light	The Black Cats
Swansea City	Swansea	Vetch Field	The Swans
Swindon Town	Swindon	County Ground	The Robins
Torquay United	Torquay	Plainmoor	The Gulls
Tottenham Hotspur	London	White Hart Lane	Spurs
Tranmere Rovers	Birkenhead	Prenton Park	The Rovers
Walsall	Walsall	Bescot Stadium	The Saddlers
Watford	Watford	Vicarage Road	The Hornets
West Bromwich Albion	West Bromwich	The Hawthorns	The Baggies/The Throstles
West Ham United	London	Upton Park[4]	The Hammers
Wigan Athletic	Wigan	JJB Stadium	The Latics
Wolverhampton Wanderers	Wolverhampton	Molineux Stadium	Wolves
Wrexham	Wrexham	The Racecourse Ground	The Robins
Wycombe Wanderers	High Wycombe	Causeway Stadium[5]	The Chairboys/The Blues
Yeovil Town	Yeovil	Huish Park	The Glovers

[1] *Officially now The Bradford & Bingley Stadium.*
[2] *Officially The Recreation Ground.*
[3] *Previous home ground was The Dell.*
[4] *Officially Boleyn Ground.*
[5] *Previously known as Adams Park.*

Scottish Premier League and Football League clubs

Club	Location	Stadium	Nickname
Aberdeen	Aberdeen	Pittodrie Stadium	The Dons
Airdrie United	Airdrie	Excelsior Stadium	The Diamonds
Albion Rovers	Coatbridge	Cliftonhill Stadium	The Wee Rovers
Alloa Athletic	Alloa	Recreation Park	The Wasps
Arbroath	Arbroath	Gayfield Park	The Red Lichties
Ayr United	Ayr	Somerset Park	The Honest Men
Berwick Rangers	Berwick	Shielfield Park	The Borderers
Brechin City	Brechin	Glebe Park	The City
Celtic	Glasgow	Celtic Park	The Bhoys
Clyde	Cumbernauld	Broadwood Stadium	The Bully Wee
Cowdenbeath	Cowdenbeath	Central Park	The Blue Brazil
Dumbarton	Dumbarton	Strathclyde Homes Stadium	The Sons
Dundee	Dundee	Dens Park	The Dark Blues
Dundee United	Dundee	Tannadice Park	The Arabs/The Terrors
Dunfermline Athletic	Dunfermline	East End Park	The Pars
East Fife	Methil	Bayview Stadium	The Fifers
East Stirlingshire	Falkirk	Firs Park	The Shire
Elgin City	Elgin	Borough Briggs	City/Black and Whites
Falkirk	Falkirk	Falkirk Stadium	The Bairns
Forfar Athletic	Forfar	Station Park	The Loons
Greenock Morton	Greenock	Cappielow Park	The Ton
Gretna	Gretna	Raydale Park	The Black and Whites
Hamilton Academical	Hamilton	New Douglas Park	The Accies
Heart of Midlothian	Edinburgh	Tynecastle Stadium	The Jam Tarts
Hibernian	Edinburgh	Easter Road Stadium	Hibees
Inverness Caledonian Thistle	Inverness	Caledonian Stadium	Caley Thistle
Kilmarnock	Kilmarnock	Rugby Park	Killie
Livingston	Livingston	Almondvale Stadium	The Livvy Lions
Montrose	Montrose	Links Park	The Gable Endies
Motherwell	Motherwell	Fir Park Stadium	The Well
Partick Thistle	Glasgow	Firhill Stadium	The Jags
Peterhead	Peterhead	Balmoor Stadium	The Blue Toon
Queen of the South	Dumfries	Palmerston Park	The Doonhamers
Queen's Park	Glasgow	Hampden Park	The Spiders
Raith Rovers	Kirkcaldy	Stark's Park	The Rovers
Rangers	Glasgow	Ibrox Stadium	'Gers/Teddy Bears
Ross County	Dingwall	Victoria Park	The County
St Johnstone	Perth	McDiarmid Park	Saints
St Mirren	Paisley	St Mirren Park	The Buddies
Stenhousemuir	Stenhousemuir	Ochilview Park	The Warriors
Stirling Albion	Stirling	Forthbank Stadium	The Albion/The Reds/The Binos
Stranraer	Stranraer	Stair Park	The Blues

Goals Galore

The record for the most goals scored in a season in the SPL is held by Celtic, who hit the back of the net 105 times in the 2003–4 season. Languishing at the other end of the table is St Johnstone; they scored just 24 times during 2002–3.

Major European football clubs

Club	City	Stadium
Belgium		
Anderlecht	Brussels	Constant van den Stock Stadium
France		
AS Monaco	Monaco	Stade Louis II
Paris Saint-Germain	Paris	Parc des Princes
Germany		
Bayer 04 Leverkusen	Leverkusen	Ulrich Haberland Stadion/BayArena
Bayern Munich	Munich	Olympiastadion
Borussia Dortmund	Dortmund	Westfalenstadion
Borussia Mönchengladbach	Mönchengladbach	Der Bökelberg
Eintracht Frankfurt	Frankfurt	Waldstadion
Hamburg	Hamburg	AOL Arena
Schalke 04	Gelsenkirchen	Parkstadion/Arena auf Schalke
Italy		
AC Milan	Milan	Stadio Giuseppe Meazza
AS Roma	Rome	Stadio Olimpico
Inter Milan	Milan	Stadio San Siro
Juventus	Turin	Stadio Delle Alpi
Lazio	Rome	Stadio Olimpico
Napoli	Naples	Stadio San Paolo
Parma	Parma	Stadio Ennio Tardini
The Netherlands		
Ajax	Amsterdam	Amsterdam ArenA
Feyenoord	Rotterdam	Stadion De Kuip
PSV Eindhoven	Eindhoven	Philips Stadion
Portugal		
Benfica	Lisbon	Estádio da Luz
FC Porto	Porto	Estádio das Antas
Sporting Lisbon	Lisbon	Estádio José Alvalade
Serbia and Montenegro		
Red Star Belgrade	Belgrade	Red Star Stadium ('Marakana')
Spain		
Atletico Madrid	Madrid	Vicente Calderon
Barcelona	Barcelona	Camp Nou
Deportivo la Coruña	La Coruña	Estadio Municipal de Riazor
Real Madrid	Madrid	Santiago Bernabeu
Valencia	Valencia	Mestalla
Turkey		
Fenerbahçe	Istanbul	Şükrü Saracoğlu
Galatasaray	Istanbul	Ali Sami Yen

GAELIC FOOTBALL

Mixture of rugby, soccer and Australian Rules football, played by teams of 15 on a rectangular pitch with goals resembling rugby posts with soccer-style nets attached; points scored by either putting the ball into the goal net (three), or over the crossbar and between the up-rights (one); first game resembling Gaelic football took place 1712 at Slane, Ireland.

Ruling body: Gaelic Athletic Association (GAA)

Gaelic football pitch

Note: Pitch size is approximate (length minimum 130m/426.5ft, maximum 145m/475.7ft; width minimum 80m/262.5ft, maximum 90m/295.3ft). The goalpost height of 7m/23ft is the minimum permitted.

All-Ireland Championship

First held in 1887; takes place in Dublin on the third Sunday in Sep each year.

1981	Kerry	1990	Cork	1999	Meath
1982	Offaly	1991	Down	2000	Kerry
1983	Dublin	1992	Donegal	2001	Galway
1984	Kerry	1993	Derry	2002	Armagh
1985	Kerry	1994	Down	2003	Tyrone
1986	Kerry	1995	Dublin	2004	Kerry
1987	Meath	1996	Meath	2005	Tyrone
1988	Meath	1997	Kerry		
1989	Cork	1998	Galway		

More Than Just Sport

The Gaelic Athletic Association (GAA) was founded to support traditional Irish national sports, including Gaelic football, hurling and camogie, but also to nurture and protect Irish cultural heritage, a role that the GAA is proud to continue today. The GAA's rules state that it 'shall actively support the Irish language, traditional Irish dancing, music, song and other aspects of Irish culture', and through its Scór programmes of cultural competitions it endeavours to 'enrich the culture of the nation and further Gaelic ideals'.

GOLF

Outdoor sport played on a course normally 5 500–7 000m/6 000–7 500yd long, usually with 18 but sometimes nine holes; object is to hit a small ball using a long-handled club from a flat starting point or *tee* along a *fairway* to a hole positioned on an area of smooth grass or *green*; additional hazards: trees, bushes, streams, sand-filled *bunkers* and the *rough*, or uncut grass beside the fairway; winner completes the course using the lowest number of strokes. The *par* is the expected number of strokes a good player needs to complete a hole; one stroke above par is called a *bogey*; one stroke below par is a *birdie*; two strokes below an *eagle*; three strokes below an *albatross*; a hole completed in one stroke is a *hole in one*.

Ruling body: Professional Golf Association (PGA), United States Golf Association (USGA), Ladies Professional Golf Association (LPGA), Royal and Ancient Golf Club of St Andrews (R&A)

The Open Championship

First held at Prestwick in 1860; takes place annually; regarded as the world's leading golf tournament.

1981	Bill Rogers (USA)	1994	Nick Price (Zimbabwe)
1982	Tom Watson (USA)	1995	John Daly (USA)
1983	Tom Watson (USA)	1996	Tom Lehman (USA)
1984	Severiano Ballesteros (Spain)	1997	Justin Leonard (USA)
1985	Sandy Lyle (Great Britain)	1998	Mark O'Meara (USA)
1986	Greg Norman (Australia)	1999	Paul Lawrie (Great Britain)
1987	Nick Faldo (Great Britain)	2000	Tiger Woods (USA)
1988	Severiano Ballesteros (Spain)	2001	David Duval (USA)
1989	Mark Calcavecchia (USA)	2002	Ernie Els (South Africa)
1990	Nick Faldo (Great Britain)	2003	Ben Curtis (USA)
1991	Ian Baker-Finch (Australia)	2004	Todd Hamilton (USA)
1992	Nick Faldo (Great Britain)	2005	Tiger Woods (USA)
1993	Greg Norman (Australia)		

US Open

First held at Newport, Rhode Island, in 1895; takes place annually.

1981	David Graham (Australia)	1994	Ernie Els (South Africa)
1982	Tom Watson (USA)	1995	Corey Pavin (USA)
1983	Larry Nelson (USA)	1996	Steve Jones (USA)
1984	Fuzzy Zoeller (USA)	1997	Ernie Els (South Africa)
1985	Andy North (USA)	1998	Lee Janzen (USA)
1986	Raymond Floyd (USA)	1999	Payne Stewart (USA)
1987	Scott Simpson (USA)	2000	Tiger Woods (USA)
1988	Curtis Strange (USA)	2001	Retief Goosen (South Africa)
1989	Curtis Strange (USA)	2002	Tiger Woods (USA)
1990	Hale Irwin (USA)	2003	Jim Furyk (USA)
1991	Payne Stewart (USA)	2004	Retief Goosen (South Africa)
1992	Tom Kite (USA)	2005	Michael Campbell (New Zealand)
1993	Lee Janzen (USA)		

US Masters

First held in 1934; takes place at the Augusta National course in Georgia every Apr.

1981	Tom Watson (USA)	1994	José-María Olazábal (Spain)
1982	Craig Stadler (USA)	1995	Ben Crenshaw (USA)
1983	Severiano Ballesteros (Spain)	1996	Nick Faldo (Great Britain)
1984	Ben Crenshaw (USA)	1997	Tiger Woods (USA)
1985	Bernhard Langer (West Germany)	1998	Mark O'Meara (USA)
1986	Jack Nicklaus (USA)	1999	José-María Olazábal (Spain)
1987	Larry Mize (USA)	2000	Vijay Singh (Fiji)
1988	Sandy Lyle (Great Britain)	2001	Tiger Woods (USA)
1989	Nick Faldo (Great Britain)	2002	Tiger Woods (USA)
1990	Nick Faldo (Great Britain)	2003	Mike Weir (Canada)
1991	Ian Woosnam (Great Britain)	2004	Phil Mickelson (USA)
1992	Fred Couples (USA)	2005	Tiger Woods (USA)
1993	Bernhard Langer (Germany)		

US PGA Championship

The last of the season's four 'Majors'; first held in 1916, and a match-play event until 1958; takes place annually.

1981	Larry Nelson (USA)	1994	Nick Price (Zimbabwe)
1982	Raymond Floyd (USA)	1995	Steve Elkington (Australia)
1983	Hal Sutton (USA)	1996	Mark Brooks (USA)
1984	Lee Trevino (USA)	1997	Davis Love III (USA)
1985	Hubert Green (USA)	1998	Vijay Singh (Fiji)
1986	Bob Tway (USA)	1999	Tiger Woods (USA)
1987	Larry Nelson (USA)	2000	Tiger Woods (USA)
1988	Jeff Sluman (USA)	2001	David Toms (USA)
1989	Payne Stewart (USA)	2002	Rich Beem (USA)
1990	Wayne Grady (Australia)	2003	Shaun Micheel (USA)
1991	John Daly (USA)	2004	Vijay Singh (Fiji)
1992	Nick Price (Zimbabwe)	2005	Phil Mickelson (USA)
1993	Paul Azinger (USA)		

Greenland Golf

Every spring golfers converge from all over the world to compete in the World Ice Golf Championships, held in Uummannaq, Greenland. The green is the 'white', the ball is fluorescent pink or orange, the temperatures drop to −50°C/−58°F and the obstacles are icebergs and polar bears. The shape of the course, which is created anew each year, is dictated by the position of icebergs in the frozen fjord in which the Championships take place; however, the course changes constantly as the pack ice drifts and new icy outcrops are thrown up. It melts completely by May.

Ryder Cup

The leading international team tournament; first held at Worcester, Massachusetts in 1927; takes place every two years between teams from the USA and Europe (Great Britain 1927–71; Great Britain and Ireland 1973–7).

1981	USA	18½–9½	1993	USA	15–13
1983	USA	14½–13½	1995	Europe	14½–13½
1985	Europe	16½–11½	1997	Europe	14½–13½
1987	Europe	15–13	1999	USA	14½–13½
1989	*Drawn*	14–14	2002	Europe	15½–12½
1991	USA	14½–13½	2004	Europe	18½–9½

Kolf, Colf, Gouf and Golf

A similar game to golf was played by the Dutch c.1300, and was known as *kolf* or *colf*. *Gouf* was definitely played in Scotland in the 15c, and the world's first golf club, the Gentleman Golfers of Edinburgh, was formed in 1744.

GYMNASTICS

Physical exercises. Men compete on the parallel bars, pommel horse, high bar, rings, horse vault and floor exercise, and women on the asymmetrical bars, beam, horse vault and floor exercise. Judges award marks out of ten, looking for control, suppleness, balance and ingenuity. The ancient Greeks and Romans performed such exercises for health purposes; modern techniques date from late-18c Germany.

Ruling body: International Gymnastics Federation (FIG; Fédération Internationale de Gymnastique)

World Championships

First contested in 1903; women's championships first held in 1934.

Individual – Men
1981	Yuri Korolev (USSR)
1983	Dmitri Belozerchev (USSR)
1985	Yuri Korolev (USSR)
1987	Dmitri Belozerchev (USSR)
1989	Igor Korobichensky (USSR)
1991	Vitaly Scherbo (USSR)
1993	Vitaly Scherbo (Belarus)
1994	Ivan Ivankov (Belarus)
1995	Li Xiaoshuang (China)
1997	Ivan Ivankov (Belarus)
1999	Nikolay Krukov (Russia)
2001	Jing Feng (China)
2003	Paul Hamm (USA)
2005	Hiroyuki Tomita (Japan)

Individual – Women
1981	Olga Bitscherova (USSR)
1983	Natalia Yurtschenko (USSR)
1985	Yelena Shoushounova (USSR) and Oksana Omeliantchuk (USSR)
1987	Aurelia Dobre (Romania)
1989	Svetlana Boginskaya (USSR)
1991	Kim Zmeskal (USA)
1993	Shannon Miller (USA)
1994	Shannon Miller (USA)
1995	Lilia Podkopayeva (Ukraine)
1997	Svetlana Khorkina (Russia)
1999	Maria Olaru (Romania)
2001	Svetlana Khorkina (Russia)
2003	Svetlana Khorkina (Russia)
2005	Chellsie Memmel (USA)

Team – Men		Team – Women	
1981	USSR	1981	USSR
1983	China	1983	USSR
1985	USSR	1985	USSR
1987	USSR	1987	Romania
1989	USSR	1989	USSR
1991	USSR	1991	USSR
1993	*no team prize*	1993	*no team prize*
1994	China	1994	Romania
1995	China	1995	Romania
1997	China	1997	Romania
1999	China	1999	Romania
2001	Belarus	2001	Romania
2003	China	2003	USA

Perfect Ten

One of the most famous gymnasts of all time is Nadia Comaneci (born 1961) from Romania. At the 1976 Olympic Games, at the age of just 14, Comaneci won gold medals in the parallel bars and beam disciplines, and a bronze in the floor, becoming the first gymnast to obtain a perfect score of 10 for her performance on the bars and beam. She also won a gold medal at the 1978 world championships and gold medals in the 1980 Olympics, later becoming an international judge and coach to the Romanian national team. In 1989 she defected to the USA.

HOCKEY

Stick-and-ball game played by two teams of eleven, the object being to move the ball around with the sticks until a player can score from within the semicircle in front of the opposing side's goal; game is split into two halves of 35 minutes. Also known in North America as *field hockey*.

Ruling body: International Hockey Federation (FIH; Fédération Internationale de Hockey)

Historic Hockey

The ancient Greeks played a game akin to hockey c.2500BC, and the ancient Egyptians are believed to have played an early version of it 4 000 years ago. The Romans, ancient Ethiopians and Aztecs are all thought to have played similar games.

Hockey pitch

World Cup

Men's tournament first held in 1971, and every four years since 1978; women's tournament first held in 1972, and now takes place every three or four years.

Men		Women	
1982	Pakistan	1981	West Germany
1986	Australia	1983	The Netherlands
1990	The Netherlands	1986	The Netherlands
1994	Pakistan	1990	The Netherlands
1998	The Netherlands	1994	Australia
2002	Germany	1998	Australia
		2002	Argentina

Olympic Games

Regarded as hockey's leading competition; first held in 1908; included at every celebration since 1928; women's competition first held in 1980.

Men		Women	
1984	Pakistan	1984	The Netherlands
1988	Great Britain	1988	Australia
1992	Germany	1992	Spain
1996	The Netherlands	1996	Australia
2000	The Netherlands	2000	Australia
2004	Australia	2004	Germany

HORSE RACING

Racing of horses against one another, each ridden by a jockey. Two categories: flat racing for thoroughbred horses on a flat grass or dirt surface over a predetermined distance from 1–4km/5 furlongs–2.5mi, and national hunt racing in which the horses negotiate either movable hurdles or fixed fences over a distance of up to 6.5km/4.5mi. The ancient Egyptians took part in horse races in c.1200BC; popularized in 12c England. Most monarchs have supported the sport, hence the name the 'sport of kings'.

Ruling body (UK): British Horseracing Board (BHB)

The Derby

The 'Blue Riband' of the turf; run at Epsom over 1½ miles; first run in 1780.

	Horse (Jockey)		Horse (Jockey)
1981	Shergar (W Swinburn)	1994	Erhaab (W Carson)
1982	Golden Fleece (P Eddery)	1995	Lammtarra (W Swinburn)
1983	Teenoso (L Piggott)	1996	Shaamit (M Hills)
1984	Secreto (C Roche)	1997	Benny the Dip (W Ryan)
1985	Slip Anchor (S Cauthen)	1998	High Rise (O Peslier)
1986	Shahrastani (W Swinburn)	1999	Oath (K Fallon)
1987	Reference Point (S Cauthen)	2000	Sinndar (J Murtagh)
1988	Kahyasi (R Cochrane)	2001	Galileo (M Kinane)
1989	Nashwan (W Carson)	2002	High Chaparral (J Murtagh)
1990	Quest For Fame (P Eddery)	2003	Kris Kin (K Fallon)
1991	Generous (A Munro)	2004	North Light (K Fallon)
1992	Dr Devious (J Reid)	2005	Motivator (J Murtagh)
1993	Commander in Chief (M Kinane)		

The Oaks

Run at Epsom over 1½ miles; for fillies only; first run in 1779.

	Horse (Jockey)		Horse (Jockey)
1981	Blue Wind (L Piggott)	1994	Balanchine (F Dettori)
1982	Time Charter (W Newnes)	1995	Moonshell (F Dettori)
1983	Sun Princess (W Carson)	1996	Lady Carla (P Eddery)
1984	Circus Plume (L Piggott)	1997	Reams of Verse (K Fallon)
1985	Oh So Sharp (S Cauthen)	1998	Shahtoush (M Kinane)
1986	Midway Lady (R Cochrane)	1999	Ramruma (K Fallon)
1987	Unite (W Swinburn)	2000	Love Divine (R Quinn)
1988	Diminuendo (S Cauthen)	2001	Imagine (M Kinane)
1989	Aliysa (W Swinburn)	2002	Kazzia (F Dettori)
1990	Salsabil (W Carson)	2003	Casual Look (M Dwyer)
1991	Jet Ski Lady (C Roche)	2004	Ouija Board (K Fallon)
1992	User Friendly (G Duffield)	2005	Eswarah (R Hills)
1993	Intrepidity (M Roberts)		

One Thousand Guineas

Run at Newmarket over 1 mile; for fillies only; first run in 1814.

	Horse (Jockey)		Horse (Jockey)
1981	Fairy Footsteps (L Piggott)	1994	Las Meninas (J Reid)
1982	On The House (J Reid)	1995	Harayir (R Hills)
1983	Ma Biche (F Head)	1996	Bosra Sham (P Eddery)
1984	Pebbles (P Robinson)	1997	Sleepytime (K Fallon)
1985	Oh So Sharp (S Cauthen)	1998	Cape Verdi (F Dettori)
1986	Midway Lady (R Cochrane)	1999	Wince (K Fallon)
1987	Miesque (F Head)	2000	Lahan (R Hills)
1988	Ravinella (G Moore)	2001	Ameerat (P Robinson)
1989	Musical Bliss (W Swinburn)	2002	Kazzia (F Dettori)
1990	Salsabil (W Carson)	2003	Russian Rhythm (K Fallon)
1991	Shadayid (W Carson)	2004	Attraction (K Darley)
1992	Hatoof (W Swinburn)	2005	Virginia Waters (K Fallon)
1993	Sayyedati (W Swinburn)		

Charlotte and Wizard

The very first One Thousand Guineas race in 1814 was won by a horse named Charlotte, owned by Christopher Wilson and ridden by Bill Clift. The same team of owner and jockey had also triumphed at the very first Two Thousand Guineas race in 1809 with a horse named Wizard.

Two Thousand Guineas

Run at Newmarket over 1 mile; first run in 1809.

	Horse (Jockey)		Horse (Jockey)
1981	To-Agori-Mou (G Starkey)	1994	Mister Baileys (J Weaver)
1982	Zino (F Head)	1995	Pennekamp (T Jarnet)
1983	Lomond (P Eddery)	1996	Mark of Esteem (F Dettori)
1984	El Gran Senor (P Eddery)	1997	Entrepreneur (M Kinane)
1985	Shadeed (L Piggott)	1998	King of Kings (M Kinane)
1986	Dancing Brave (G Starkey)	1999	Island Sands (F Dettori)
1987	Don't Forget Me (W Carson)	2000	King's Best (K Fallon)
1988	Doyoun (W Swinburn)	2001	Golan (K Fallon)
1989	Nashwan (W Carson)	2002	Rock of Gibraltar (J Murtagh)
1990	Tirol (M Kinane)	2003	Refuse to Bend (P Smullen)
1991	Mystiko (M Roberts)	2004	Haafhd (R Hills)
1992	Rodrigo de Traiano (L Piggott)	2005	Footstepsinthesand (K Fallon)
1993	Zafonic (P Eddery)		

Royal Racing

The One Thousand Guineas and Two Thousand Guineas are raced on the Rowley Mile Racecourse in Newmarket. The course is named after King Charles II (1630–85) – one of whose nicknames was supposedly 'Old Rowley' – who encouraged horse racing in Newmarket in the 17c.

St Leger

The oldest of the five English classics; first run in 1776; run at Doncaster annually over 1 mile 6 furlongs 127 yards.

	Horse (Jockey)		Horse (Jockey)
1981	Cut Above (J Mercer)	1994	Moonax (P Eddery)
1982	Touching Wood (P Cook)	1995	Classic Cliche (F Dettori)
1983	Sun Princess (W Carson)	1996	Shantou (F Dettori)
1984	Commanche Run (L Piggott)	1997	Silver Patriarch (P Eddery)
1985	Oh So Sharp (S Cauthen)	1998	Nedawi (J Reid)
1986	Moon Madness (P Eddery)	1999	Mutafaweq (R Hills)
1987	Reference Point (S Cauthen)	2000	Millenary (R Quinn)
1988	Minster Son (W Carson)	2001	Milan (M Kinane)
1989	Michelozzo (S Cauthen)	2002	Bollin Eric (K Darley)
1990	Snurge (R Quinn)	2003	Brian Boru (J Spencer)
1991	Toulon (P Eddery)	2004	Rule of Law (K McEvoy)
1992	User Friendly (G Duffield)	2005	Scorpion (F Dettori)
1993	Bob's Return (P Robinson)		

Becher's Brook

When the first Grand National was run at Aintree competitors had to jump a stone wall and cross a ploughed field, as well as clearing two final hurdles. Today, the course includes a total of 30 fences (16 jumped on the first circuit and 14 on the second), described by the organizers as being some of 'the most testing fences in the world of jump racing'. The most famous is the sixth, Becher's Brook, renowned for its difficulty because of its average take-off height of just over 1.2m/4ft but steep drop of almost 2.2m/7ft on the landing side. The obstacle is named after one Captain Martin Becher. Becher was thrown from his horse at the fence during the first Aintree Grand National in 1839 and deposited unceremoniously in the water – he famously commented on 'how dreadful water tastes without the benefit of whisky'. It was his first and last Grand National appearance.

Grand National

Steeplechasing's most famous race; first run at Maghull in 1836; at Aintree since 1839; wartime races at Gatwick 1916–18; run over 4½ miles.

	Horse (Jockey)		Horse (Jockey)
1981	Aldaniti (B Champion)	1994	Miinnehoma (R Dunwoody)
1982	Grittar (D Saunders)	1995	Royal Athlete (J Titley)
1983	Corbiere (B de Haan)	1996	Rough Quest (M Fitzgerald)
1984	Hallo Dandy (N Doughty)	1997	Lord Gyllene (T Dobbin)
1985	Last Suspect (H Davies)	1998	Earth Summit (C Llewellyn)
1986	West Tip (R Dunwoody)	1999	Bobbyjo (P Carberry)
1987	Maori Venture (S Knight)	2000	Papillon (R Walsh)
1988	Rhyme 'N' Reason (B Powell)	2001	Red Marauder (R Guest)
1989	Little Polveir (J Frost)	2002	Bindaree (J Culloty)
1990	Mr Frisk (M Armytage)	2003	Monty's Pass (B Geraghty)
1991	Seagram (N Hawke)	2004	Amberleigh House (G Lee)
1992	Party Politics (C Llewellyn)	2005	Hedgehunter (R Walsh)
1993	*race declared void* Esha Ness (J White) first past the post		

Prix de l'Arc de Triomphe

The leading end-of-season race in Europe; raced over 2 400 metres at Longchamp; first run in 1920.

	Horse (Jockey)		**Horse (Jockey)**
1981	Gold River (G Moore)	1994	Carnegie (T Jarnet)
1982	Akiyda (Y Saint-Martin)	1995	Lammtarra (F Dettori)
1983	All Along (W Swinburn)	1996	Helissio (O Peslier)
1984	Sagace (Y Saint-Martin)	1997	Peintre Celebre (O Peslier)
1985	Rainbow Quest (P Eddery)	1998	Sagamix (O Peslier)
1986	Dancing Brave (P Eddery)	1999	Montjeu (M Kinane)
1987	Trempolino (P Eddery)	2000	Sinndar (J Murtagh)
1988	Tony Bin (J Reid)	2001	Sakhee (F Dettori)
1989	Caroll House (M Kinane)	2002	Marienbard (F Dettori)
1990	Suamarez (G Mosse)	2003	Dalakhani (C Soumillon)
1991	Suave Dancer (C Asmussen)	2004	Bago (T Gillet)
1992	Subotica (T Jarnet)	2005	Hurricane Run (K Fallon)
1993	Urban Sea (E Saint-Martin)		

Kentucky Derby

Run at Churchill Downs, Louisville, Kentucky, USA over 1¼ mile; first run in 1875.

	Horse (Jockey)		**Horse (Jockey)**
1981	Pleasant Colony (J Velasquez)	1994	Go for Gin (C McCarron)
1982	Gato Del Sol (E Delahoussaye)	1995	Thunder Gulch (G Stevens)
1983	Sunny's Halo (E Delahoussaye)	1996	Grindstone (J Bailey)
1984	Swale (L Pincay, Jr)	1997	Silver Charm (G Stevens)
1985	Spend a Buck (A Cordero, Jr)	1998	Real Quiet (K Desormeaux)
1986	Ferdinand (W Shoemaker)	1999	Charismatic (C Antley)
1987	Alysheba (C McCarron)	2000	Fusaichi Pegasus (K Desormeaux)
1988	Winning Colors (G Stevens)	2001	Monarchos (J Chavez)
1989	Sunday Silence (P Valenzuela)	2002	War Emblem (V Espinoza)
1990	Unbridled (C Perret)	2003	Funny Cide (J Santos)
1991	Strike the Gold (C Antley)	2004	Smarty Jones (S Elliott)
1992	Lil E Tee (P Day)	2005	Giacomo (M Smith)
1993	Sea Hero (J Bailey)		

You Bet

The 2005 Kentucky Derby was the first time that betting had exceeded $100 million on just one race at a US race. The day's big winners were those who had bet on 50–1 outsider Giacomo, who stormed home to win.

HURLING

Irish 15-a-side field game played with curved sticks (the *hurley* or *camán*) and a ball (the *sliothar*); object to hit ball into opposing team's goal: under the crossbar scores three points; above the crossbar but between the posts scores one.

Ruling body: Gaelic Athletic Association (GAA)

Hurling pitch

Note: Pitch size is approximate (length minimum 130m/426.5ft, maximum 145m/475.7ft; width minimum 80m/262.5ft, maximum 90m/295.3ft). The goalpost height of 7m/23ft is the minimum permitted.

All-Ireland Championship

First contested in 1887; played on the first Sunday in Sep each year.

1981	Offaly	1990	Cork	1999	Cork
1982	Kilkenny	1991	Tipperary	2000	Kilkenny
1983	Kilkenny	1992	Kilkenny	2001	Tipperary
1984	Cork	1993	Kilkenny	2002	Kilkenny
1985	Offaly	1994	Offaly	2003	Kilkenny
1986	Cork	1995	Clare	2004	Cork
1987	Galway	1996	Wexford	2005	Cork
1988	Galway	1997	Clare		
1989	Tipperary	1998	Offaly		

Hurling in History

Hurling is thought to be the oldest field game in Europe. The Gaelic Athletic Association believes that it was brought to Ireland by the Celts, and that the game has been part of Irish culture for 2 000 years.

ICE HOCKEY

Fast game played by two teams of six on an ice rink with sticks and a small rubber puck; aim is to score goals by using the stick to hit the *puck* into the opposing team's goal; players wear ice skates and protective clothing; possibly first played in Canada in the 1850s.

Ruling body: International Ice Hockey Federation (IIHF)

Ice hockey rink

World Championship

First held in 1920; takes place annually (except in the Olympic years 1980, 1984 and 1988); up to 1968 Olympic champions also regarded as world champions.

1981	USSR	1992	Sweden	2001	Czech Republic
1982	USSR	1993	Russia	2002	Slovakia
1983	USSR	1994	Canada	2003	Canada
1985	Czechoslovakia	1995	Finland	2004	Canada
1986	USSR	1996	Czech Republic	2005	Czech Republic
1987	Sweden	1997	Canada		
1989	USSR	1998	Sweden		
1990	USSR	1999	Czech Republic		
1991	Sweden	2000	Czech Republic		

Ouch!

The first ice-hockey goalie to wear a protective mask was one Clint Benedict in 1927. He adopted a leather mask after a shot knocked him unconscious; however, he then couldn't see the game properly, and masks were abandoned until 1959.

Stanley Cup

The most sought-after trophy at club level; the end-of-season meeting between the winners of the two conferences in the National Hockey League (NHL) in the USA and Canada; first held in 1893.

1981	New York Islanders	1990	Edmonton Oilers	1999	Dallas Stars
1982	New York Islanders	1991	Pittsburgh Penguins	2000	New Jersey Devils
1983	New York Islanders	1992	Pittsburgh Penguins	2001	Colorado Avalanche
1984	Edmonton Oilers	1993	Montreal Canadiens	2002	Detroit Red Wings
1985	Edmonton Oilers	1994	New York Rangers	2003	New Jersey Devils
1986	Montreal Canadiens	1995	New Jersey Devils	2004	Tampa Bay Lightning
1987	Edmonton Oilers	1996	Colorado Avalanche	2005	*not held*
1988	Edmonton Oilers	1997	Detroit Red Wings		
1989	Calgary Flames	1998	Detroit Red Wings		

ICE SKATING

Figure skating is artistic dancing on ice for individuals and pairs; first known skating club formed mid-18c London; first artificial rink opened on Baker Street in 1876.

Ruling body: International Skating Union (ISU)

World Championships

First men's championships in 1896; first women's event in 1906; pairs first contested in 1908; Ice Dance officially recognized in 1952.

Men		Women	
1981	Scott Hamilton (USA)	1981	Denise Biellmann (Switzerland)
1982	Scott Hamilton (USA)	1982	Elaine Zayak (USA)
1983	Scott Hamilton (USA)	1983	Rosalynn Sumners (USA)
1984	Scott Hamilton (USA)	1984	Katarina Witt (East Germany)
1985	Alexander Fadeyev (USSR)	1985	Katarina Witt (East Germany)
1986	Brian Boitano (USA)	1986	Debbie Thomas (USA)
1987	Brian Orser (Canada)	1987	Katarina Witt (East Germany)
1988	Brian Boitano (USA)	1988	Katarina Witt (East Germany)
1989	Kurt Browning (Canada)	1989	Midori Ito (Japan)
1990	Kurt Browning (Canada)	1990	Jill Trenary (USA)
1991	Kurt Browning (Canada)	1991	Kristi Yamaguchi (USA)
1992	Viktor Petrenko (CIS)	1992	Kristi Yamaguchi (USA)
1993	Kurt Browning (Canada)	1993	Oksana Baiul (Ukraine)
1994	Elvis Stojko (Canada)	1994	Yuka Sato (Japan)
1995	Elvis Stojko (Canada)	1995	Lu Chen (China)
1996	Todd Eldredge (USA)	1996	Michelle Kwan (USA)
1997	Elvis Stojko (Canada)	1997	Tara Lipinski (USA)
1998	Alexei Yagudin (Russia)	1998	Michelle Kwan (USA)
1999	Alexei Yagudin (Russia)	1999	Maria Butyrskaya (Russia)
2000	Alexei Yagudin (Russia)	2000	Michelle Kwan (USA)
2001	Evgeny Plushenko (Russia)	2001	Michelle Kwan (USA)
2002	Alexei Yagudin (Russia)	2002	Irina Slutskaya (Russia)

Men

2003	Evgeny Plushenko (Russia)		
2004	Evgeny Plushenko (Russia)		
2005	Stephane Lambiel (Switzerland)		

Women

2003	Michelle Kwan (USA)
2004	Shizuka Arakawa (Japan)
2005	Irina Slutskaya (Russia)

Pairs

1981	Irina Vorobieva/Igor Lisovski (USSR)
1982	Sabine Baess/Tassilo Thierbach (East Germany)
1983	Yelena Valova/Oleg Vasiliev (USSR)
1984	Barbara Underhill/Paul Martini (Canada)
1985	Yelena Valova/Oleg Vasiliev (USSR)
1986	Yekaterina Gordeeva/Sergei Grinkov (USSR)
1987	Yekaterina Gordeeva/Sergei Grinkov (USSR)
1988	Yelena Valova/Oleg Vasiliev (USSR)
1989	Yekaterina Gordeeva/Sergei Grinkov (USSR)
1990	Yekaterina Gordeeva/Sergei Grinkov (USSR)
1991	Natalya Mishkutienok/Artur Dmtriev (USSR)
1992	Natalya Mishkutienok/Artur Dmtriev (USSR)
1993	Isabelle Brasseu/Lloyd Eisler (Canada)
1994	Evgenia Shiskova/Vadim Naumov (Russia)
1995	Radka Kovarikova/Rene Novotny (Czech Republic)
1996	Marina Eltsova/Andrei Bushkov (Russia)
1997	Mandy Woetzel/Ingo Steuer (Germany)
1998	Elena Berezhnay/Anton Sikharulidze (Russia)
1999	Elena Berezhnay/Anton Sikharulidze (Russia)
2000	Maria Petrova/Alexei Tikhonov (Russia)
2001	Jamie Sale/David Pelletier (Canada)
2002	Hongbo Zhao/Xue Shen (China)
2003	Hongbo Zhao/Xue Shen (China)
2004	Tatiana Totmianina/Maxim Marinin (Russia)
2005	Tatiana Totmianina/Maxim Marinin (Russia)

Ice Dance

1981	Jayne Torvill/Christopher Dean (Great Britain)
1982	Jayne Torvill/Christopher Dean (Great Britain)
1983	Jayne Torvill/Christopher Dean (Great Britain)
1984	Jayne Torvill/Christopher Dean (Great Britain)
1985	Natalya Bestemianova/Andrei Bukin (USSR)
1986	Natalya Bestemianova/Andrei Bukin (USSR)
1987	Natalya Bestemianova/Andrei Bukin (USSR)
1988	Natalya Bestemianova/Andrei Bukin (USSR)
1989	Marina Klimova/Sergei Ponomarenko (USSR)
1990	Marina Klimova/Sergei Ponomarenko (USSR)
1991	Isabelle and Paul Duchesnay (France)
1992	Marina Klimova/Sergei Ponomarenko (CIS)
1993	Maya Usova/Alexandr Zhulin (Russia)
1994	Oksana Gritschuk/Yevgeni Platov (Russia)
1995	Oksana Gritschuk/Yevgeni Platov (Russia)
1996	Oksana Gritschuk/Yevgeni Platov (Russia)
1997	Oksana Gritschuk/Yevgeni Platov (Russia)
1998	Anjelika Krylova/Oleg Ovsyannikov (Russia)
1999	Anjelika Krylova/Oleg Ovsyannikov (Russia)
2000	Marina Anissina/Gwendal Peizerat (France)

Ice Dance

2001	Barbara Fusar-Poli/Maurizio Margaglio (Italy)
2002	Irina Lobacheva/Ilia Averbukh (Russia)
2003	Shae-Lynn Bourne/Victor Kraatz (Canada)
2004	Tatiana Navka/Roman Kostomarov (Russia)
2005	Tatiana Navka/Roman Kostomarov (Russia)

Skating or Boxing?

US skater Tonya Harding gained notoriety when she won the US Figure Skating Championships in 1994. The favourite, Nancy Kerrigan, was unable to compete having been clubbed on the knee by a hitman while training, and Harding's ex-husband and her bodyguard were later given prison sentences for their role in the attack. Harding herself was later stripped of her skating title, banned for life from the US Figure Skating Association and fined $100 000 when she was found guilty of withholding information concerning Kerrigan's injury. Harding began a new career as a boxer, but lost her first professional fight – a show bout before a Mike Tyson fight in Memphis, Tennessee, USA, in early 2003.

JUDO

Unarmed combat sport of late-19c Japanese origin. Contestants wear a *judogi* or loose-fitting suit and compete on a mat which breaks their falls. When one cannot break a hold, surrender is signalled by slapping the mat; ability is graded from fifth to first Kyu, and then first to 12th Dan – only Dr Jigoro Kano, who devised the sport, has been awarded 12th Dan. Different coloured belts indicate grades; eg white for novice, brown (three degrees) and black (nine degrees).

Ruling body: International Judo Federation (IJF)

World Championships

First held in 1956, now contested every two years; current weight categories established in 1999; women's championship instituted in 1980.

1997

Men

open class	Rafael Kubacki (Poland)
over 95kg	David Douillet (France)
under 95kg	Pawel Nastula (Poland)
under 86kg	Jeon Ki Young (South Korea)
under 78kg	Chul Cho In (South Korea)
under 71kg	Kenzo Nakamura (Japan)
under 65kg	Hyuk Kim (Korea)
under 60kg	Tadahiro Nomura (Japan)

Women

open class	Daina Beltran (Cuba)
over 72kg	Christine Cicot (France)
under 72kg	Noriko Anno (Japan)
under 66kg	Kate Howey (Great Britain)
under 61kg	Servenr Vandenhende (France)
under 56kg	Isabel Fernandez (Spain)
under 52kg	Marie-Claire Restoux (France)
under 48kg	Ryoko Tamura (Japan)

1999

Men

open class	Shinichi Shinohara (Japan)
over 100kg	Shinichi Shinohara (Japan)
under 100kg	Kosei Inoue (Japan)
under 90kg	Hidehiko Yoshida (Japan)
under 81kg	Graeme Randall (Great Britain)
under 73kg	Jimmy Pedro (USA)
under 66kg	Larbi Benboudaoud (France)
under 60kg	Manuelo Poulot (Cuba)

Women

open class	Daina Beltran (Cuba)
over 78kg	Beata Maksymow (Poland)
under 78kg	Noriko Anno (Japan)
under 70kg	Sibelis Veranes (Cuba)
under 63kg	Keiko Maedo (Japan)
under 57kg	Driulis González (Cuba)
under 52kg	Noriko Narasaki (Japan)
under 48kg	Ryoko Tamura (Japan)

2001

Men

open class	Alexandre Mikhaylin (Russia)
over 100kg	Alexandre Mikhaylin (Russia)
under 100kg	Kosei Inoue (Japan)
under 90kg	Frederic Demontfaucon (France)
under 81kg	Chul Cho In (South Korea)
under 73kg	Vital Makarov (Russia)
under 66kg	Arash Miresmaeli (Iran)
under 60kg	Anis Lounifi (Tunisia)

Women

open class	Celine Lebrun (France)
over 78kg	Yuan Hua (China)
under 78kg	Noriko Anno (Japan)
under 70kg	Masae Ueno (Japan)
under 63kg	Gella van de Cayeve (Belgium)
under 57kg	Yourisledes Lupety (Cuba)
under 52kg	Sun Hui Kye (North Korea)
under 48kg	Ryoko Tamura (Japan)

2003

Men

open class	Keiji Suzuki (Japan)
over 100kg	Yauyuki Muneta (Japan)
under 100kg	Kosei Inoue (Japan)
under 90kg	Hee Tae Hwang (South Korea)
under 81kg	Florian Wanner (Germany)
under 73kg	Won Hee Lee (South Korea)
under 66kg	Arash Miresmaeli (Iran)
under 60kg	Min Ho Choi (South Korea)

Women

open class	Wen Tong (China)
over 78kg	Fuming Sun (China)
under 78kg	Noriko Anno (Japan)
under 70kg	Masae Ueno (Japan)
under 63kg	Daniela Krukower (Argentina)
under 57kg	Sun Hui Kye (North Korea)
under 52kg	Amarilis Savon (Cuba)
under 48kg	Ryoko Tamura (Japan)

2005

Men

open class	Dennis van der Geest (The Netherlands)
over 100kg	Alexander Mikhailine (Russia)
under 100kg	Keiji Suzuki (Japan)
under 90kg	Hiroshi Izumi (Japan)
under 81kg	Guillaume Elmont (The Netherlands)
under 73 kg	Akos Braun (Hungary)
under 66kg	Joao Derly Junior (Brazil)
under 60kg	Craig Fallon (Great Britain)

Women

open class	Midori Shintani (Japan)
over 78kg	Tong Wen (China)
under 78kg	Yurisel Laborde (Cuba)
under 70kg	Edith Bosch (The Netherlands)
under 63kg	Lucie Decosse (France)
under 57kg	Sun Hui Kye (North Korea)
under 52kg	Ying Li (China)
under 48kg	Yanet Bermoy (Cuba)

KARATE

Martial art of unarmed combat, dating from 17c; developed Japan 20c; name adopted 1930s; aim is to be in total control of the body's muscular power, so it can be used with great force and accuracy at any instant. Experts may show their mental and physical training by eg breaking various thicknesses of wood, but in fighting an opponent blows do not actually make contact; levels of prowess symbolized by coloured belts.

Ruling body: World Karate Federation (WKF)

World Championships

First held in Tokyo in 1970; has taken place every two years since 1980; today, there are team competitions plus individual competitions at Kumite and Kata.

Kumite

Combined

1982	Great Britain
1984	Great Britain
1986	Great Britain
1988	Great Britain
1990	Great Britain

Men		**Women**	
1992	Spain	1992	Great Britain
1994	France	1994	Spain
1996	France	1996	Great Britain
1998	France	1998	Turkey
2000	France	2000	France
2002	Spain	2002	Spain
2004	France	2004	Turkey

Kata

Men		**Women**	
1986	Japan	1986	Taiwan
1988	Japan	1988	Japan
1990	Italy	1990	Japan
1992	Japan	1992	Japan
1994	Japan	1994	Japan
1996	Japan	1996	Japan
1998	Japan	1998	Japan
2000	Japan	2000	France
2002	Japan	2002	France
2004	Italy	2004	Japan

Empty Hand

Karate means 'empty hand' in Japanese.

MARATHON

Long-distance running race, normally on open roads, over 42km 195m/26mi 385yd. In the 1980s the half marathon over 21km/13mi 194yd also became popular. For World Championship marathon results see **Athletics**.

Ruling body: International Association of Athletics Federations (IAAF)

London Marathon

First run in 1981, when 6 255 people completed the course of 42km 195m/26mi 385yd. To date, over half a million people have completed the London Marathon.

Men		**Women**	
1981	Dick Beardsley (USA)/Inge Simonsen (Norway)	1981	Joyce Smith (Great Britain)
		1982	Joyce Smith (Great Britain)
1982	Hugh Jones (Great Britain)	1983	Grete Waitz (Norway)
1983	Mike Gratton (Great Britain)	1984	Ingrid Kristiansen (Norway)
1984	Charlie Spedding (Great Britain)	1985	Ingrid Kristiansen (Norway)
1985	Steve Jones (Great Britain)	1986	Grete Waitz (Norway)
1986	Toshihiko Seko (Japan)	1987	Ingrid Kristiansen (Norway)
1987	Hiromi Taniguchi (Japan)	1988	Ingrid Kristiansen (Norway)
1988	Henrik Jorgensen (Denmark)	1989	Veronique Marot (Great Britain)
1989	Douglas Wakiihuri (Kenya)	1990	Wanda Panfil (Poland)
1990	Allister Hutton (Great Britain)	1991	Rosa Mota (Portugal)
1991	Yakov Tolstikov (Russia)	1992	Katrin Dorre (Germany)
1992	Antonio Pinto (Portugal)	1993	Katrin Dorre (Germany)
1993	Eamonn Martin (Great Britain)	1994	Katrin Dorre (Germany)
1994	Dionicio Ceron (Mexico)	1995	Malgorzata Sobanska (Poland)
1995	Dionicio Ceron (Mexico)	1996	Liz McColgan (Great Britain)
1996	Dionicio Ceron (Mexico)	1997	Joyce Chepchumba (Kenya)
1997	Antonio Pinto (Portugal)	1998	Catherina McKiernan (Ireland)
1998	Abel Antón (Spain)	1999	Joyce Chepchumba (Kenya)
1999	Abdelkader El Mouaziz (Morocco)	2000	Tegla Loroupe (Kenya)
2000	Antonio Pinto (Portugal)	2001	Derartu Tulu (Ethiopia)
2001	Abdelkader El Mouaziz (Morocco)	2002	Paula Radcliffe (Great Britain)
2002	Khalid Khannouchi (USA)	2003	Paula Radcliffe (Great Britain)
2003	Gezahegne Abera (Ethiopia)	2004	Margaret Okayo (Kenya)
2004	Evans Rutto (Kenya)	2005	Paula Radcliffe (Great Britain)
2005	Martin Lel (Kenya)		

Deciding Distance

The slightly unusual marathon distance of 42km 195m/26mi 385yd was first used at the London Olympics in 1908, so that competitors would finish exactly in front of the royal box. The race was introduced at the 1896 Olympic Games in Athens, Greece, to commemorate the run of the Greek courier (according to legend, Pheidippides) who ran the c.39km/24mi from Marathon to Athens in 490BC with the news of a Greek victory over the Persian army.

MOTOR SPORTS

Motor racing: Racing finely-tuned motor cars, either purpose-built or modified production vehicles; season-long (Mar–Nov) *Formula One* world championship involves usually 16–19 races at different venues worldwide; other popular forms include *stock car racing*, *hill climbing*, *sports car racing* and *rallying*; first race 1894, between Paris and Rouen.

Motorcycle racing: Speed competitions for motorcycles which for the annual season-long grand prix are categorized by the engine sizes *80cc*, *125cc*, *250cc*, *500cc*, *Superbike* and *Sidecar*. Other forms include *speedway*, *moto-cross* and *motorcycle trials* riding.

Ruling body: International Automobile Association (FIA; Fédération Internationale d'Automobile), International Motorcycling Federation (FIM; Fédération Internationale de Motocyclisme)

Formula One World Championship

A Formula One drivers' world championship instituted in 1950; constructors' championship instituted in 1958.

	Drivers	Constructors
1981	Nelson Piquet (Brazil; Brabham)	Williams
1982	Keke Rosberg (Finland; Williams)	Ferrari
1983	Nelson Piquet (Brazil; Brabham)	Ferrari
1984	Niki Lauda (Austria; McLaren)	McLaren
1985	Alain Prost (France; McLaren)	McLaren
1986	Alain Prost (France; McLaren)	Williams
1987	Nelson Piquet (Brazil; Williams)	Williams
1988	Ayrton Senna (Brazil; McLaren)	McLaren
1989	Alain Prost (France; McLaren)	McLaren
1990	Ayrton Senna (Brazil; McLaren)	McLaren
1991	Ayrton Senna (Brazil; McLaren)	McLaren
1992	Nigel Mansell (Great Britain; Williams)	Williams
1993	Alain Prost (France; Williams)	Williams
1994	Michael Schumacher (Germany; Benetton)	Williams
1995	Michael Schumacher (Germany; Benetton)	Benetton
1996	Damon Hill (Great Britain; Williams)	Williams
1997	Jacques Villeneuve (Canada; Williams)	Williams
1998	Mika Hakkinen (Finland; McLaren)	McLaren
1999	Mika Hakkinen (Finland; McLaren)	Ferrari
2000	Michael Schumacher (Germany; Ferrari)	Ferrari
2001	Michael Schumacher (Germany; Ferrari)	Ferrari
2002	Michael Schumacher (Germany; Ferrari)	Ferrari
2003	Michael Schumacher (Germany; Ferrari)	Ferrari
2004	Michael Schumacher (Germany; Ferrari)	Ferrari
2005	Fernando Alonso (Spain; Renault)	Renault

Le Mans 24-Hour Race

The greatest of all endurance races; first held in 1923.

1981 Jacky Ickx (Belgium) Derek Bell (Great Britain)	1994 Yannick Dalmas (France) Hurley Haywood (USA)
1982 Jacky Ickx (Belgium) Derek Bell (Great Britain)	Mauro Baldi (Italy)
1983 Al Holbert (USA) Hurley Haywood (USA) Vern Schuppan (Australia)	1995 Yannick Dalmas (France) J J Lehto (Finland) Masanori Sekiya (Japan)
1984 Henri Pescarolo (France) Klaus Ludwig (West Germany)	1996 Manuel Reuter (Germany) Davy Jones (USA) Alexander Würz (Austria)
1985 Klaus Ludwig (West Germany) 'John Winter' (West Germany) Paolo Barilla (Italy)	1997 Michele Alboreto (Italy) Stefan Johansson (Sweden) Tom Kristensen (Denmark)
1986 Hans Stück (West Germany) Derek Bell (Great Britain) Al Holbert (USA)	1998 Allan McNish (Great Britain) Laurent Aiello (France) Stephane Ortelli (France)
1987 Hans Stück (West Germany) Derek Bell (Great Britain) Al Holbert (USA)	1999 Pierluigi Martini (Italy) Joachim Winkelhock (Germany) Yannick Dalmas (France)
1988 Jan Lammers (Holland) Johnny Dumfries (Great Britain) Andy Wallace (Great Britain)	2000 Frank Biela (Germany) Tom Kristensen (Denmark) Emanuele Pirro (Italy)
1989 Jochen Mass (West Germany) Manuel Reuter (West Germany) Stanley Dickens (Sweden)	2001 Frank Biela (Germany) Tom Kristensen (Denmark) Emanuele Pirro (Italy)
1990 John Nielsen (Denmark) Price Cobb (USA) Martin Brundle (Great Britain)	2002 Frank Biela (Germany) Tom Kristensen (Denmark) Emanuele Pirro (Italy)
1991 Volker Weidler (Germany) Johnny Herbert (Great Britain) Bertrand Gachot (Belgium)	2003 Tom Kristensen (Denmark) Rinaldo Capello (Italy) Guy Smith (Great Britain)
1992 Derek Warwick (Great Britain) Mark Blundell (Great Britain) Yannick Dalmas (France)	2004 Tom Kristensen (Denmark) Rinaldo Capello (Italy) Seiji Ara (Japan)
1993 Geoff Brabham (Australia) Christophe Bouchut (France) Eric Helary (France)	2005 Tom Kristensen (Denmark) J J Lehto (Finland) Marco Werner (Germany)

Driving into History

With his victory in 2005, Tom Kristensen became the first driver to achieve seven Le Mans wins, surpassing the previous recordholder, the Belgian racing driver Jacky Ickx.

Indianapolis 500

Often known as the Indy 500; first held in 1911; raced over the Indianapolis Raceway as part of the Memorial Day celebrations at the end of May each year.

1981	Bobby Unser (USA)	1994	Al Unser (USA)
1982	Gordon Johncock (USA)	1995	Jacques Villeneuve (Canada)
1983	Tom Sneva (USA)	1996	Buddy Lazier (USA)
1984	Rick Mears (USA)	1997	Arie Luyendyk (The Netherlands)
1985	Danny Sullivan (USA)	1998	Eddie Cheever (USA)
1986	Bobby Rahal (USA)	1999	Kenny Brack (Sweden)
1987	Al Unser (USA)	2000	Juan Montoya (Colombia)
1988	Rick Mears (USA)	2001	Helio Castroneves (Brazil)
1989	Emerson Fittipaldi (Brazil)	2002	Helio Castroneves (Brazil)
1990	Arie Luyendyk (The Netherlands)	2003	Gil de Ferran (Brazil)
1991	Rick Mears (USA)	2004	Buddy Rice (USA)
1992	Al Unser (USA)	2005	Dan Wheldon (Great Britain)
1993	Emerson Fittipaldi (Brazil)		

Winning by a Whisker

Some Indy 500 races have been won by the slenderest of margins. The closest ever finish took place in 1992, when Al Unser beat Scott Goodyear by just 0.043 of a second. Other close races have been in 1982 (0.16 of a second separating the winner from the runner up), 1997 (0.57 of a second) and 1996 (0.695 of a second).

World Rally Championship

First held in 1979; comprises a series of races in 16 different countries over a variety of terrains, between Jan and Nov.

1981	Ari Vatanen (Finland)	1994	Didier Auriol (France)
1982	Walter Rohrl (West Germany)	1995	Colin McRae (Great Britain)
1983	Hannu Mikkola (Finland)	1996	Tommi Makinen (Finland)
1984	Stig Blomqvist (Sweden)	1997	Tommi Makinen (Finland)
1985	Timo Salonen (Finland)	1998	Tommi Makinen (Finland)
1986	Juha Kankkunen (Finland)	1999	Tommi Makinen (Finland)
1987	Juha Kankkunen (Finland)	2000	Marcus Gronholm (Finland)
1988	Miki Biasion (Italy)	2001	Richard Burns (Great Britain)
1989	Miki Biasion (Italy)	2002	Marcus Gronholm (Finland)
1990	Carlos Sainz (Spain)	2003	Petter Solberg (Norway)
1991	Juha Kankkunen (Finland)	2004	Sebastien Loeb (France)
1992	Carlos Sainz (Spain)	2005	Sebastien Loeb (France)
1993	Juha Kankkunen (Finland)		

Motorcycling World Championships

First organized in 1949; current titles for Superbike, 500cc, 250cc, 125cc, 80cc and Sidecar; Formula One and Endurance world championships also held annually; the most prestigious title is the 500cc category, known as MotoGP.

500cc

1981	Marco Lucchinelli (Italy)	1993	Kevin Schwantz (USA)
1982	Franco Uncini (Italy)	1994	Michael Doohan (Australia)
1983	Freddie Spencer (USA)	1995	Michael Doohan (Australia)
1984	Eddie Lawson (USA)	1996	Michael Doohan (Australia)
1985	Freddie Spencer (USA)	1997	Michael Doohan (Australia)
1986	Eddie Lawson (USA)	1998	Michael Doohan (Australia)
1987	Wayne Gardner (Australia)	1999	Alex Criville (Spain)
1988	Eddie Lawson (USA)	2000	Kenny Roberts (USA)
1989	Eddie Lawson (USA)	2001	Valentino Rossi (Italy)
1990	Wayne Rainey (USA)	2002	Valentino Rossi (Italy)
1991	Wayne Rainey (USA)	2003	Valentino Rossi (Italy)
1992	Wayne Rainey (USA)	2004	Valentino Rossi (Italy)
		2005	Valentino Rossi (Italy)

Isle of Man TT Races

The most famous of all motorcycle races; take place each Jun; first held 1907; principal race is the Senior TT.

Senior TT

1981	Mick Grant (Great Britain)	1994	Steve Hislop (Great Britain)
1982	Norman Brown (Great Britain)	1995	Joey Dunlop (Northern Ireland)
1983	Rob McElnea (Great Britain)	1996	Phil McCallen (Northern Ireland)
1984	Rob McElnea (Great Britain)	1997	Phil McCallen (Northern Ireland)
1985	Joey Dunlop (Northern Ireland)	1998	Ian Simpson (Great Britain)
1986	Roger Burnett (Great Britain)	1999	David Jefferies (Great Britain)
1987	Joey Dunlop (Northern Ireland)	2000	David Jefferies (Great Britain)
1988	Joey Dunlop (Northern Ireland)	2001	*not held*
1989	Steve Hislop (Great Britain)	2002	David Jefferies (Great Britain)
1990	Carl Fogarty (Great Britain)	2003	Adrian Archibald (Northern Ireland)
1991	Steve Hislop (Great Britain)		
1992	Steve Hislop (Great Britain)	2004	Adrian Archibald (Northern Ireland)
1993	Phil McCallen (Northern Ireland)	2005	John McGuinness (Great Britain)

Road Racing

The TT takes place over temporarily closed public roads in the Isle of Man. The island became the home of road racing in the early 1900s, when racing on public roads in the UK was forbidden by an Act of Parliament, and a strict 20mph/32kph speed limit was enforced. However, the ban did not apply to the Isle of Man, and after a little persuasion by early racing enthusiasts, Tynwald – the island's Parliament – passed a Bill allowing road racing in 1904.

ROWING

Propulsion of a boat by oars; involves two or more rowers, each with an oar, and often with a coxswain; sculling involves one rower with two oars; rowing as an organized sport dates from 1715 (first rowing of the Doggetts Coat and Badge race on the River Thames, London).

Ruling body: International Rowing Federation (FISA; Fédération Internationale des Sociétés d'Aviron)

World Championships

First held for men in 1962 and for women in 1974; Olympic champions assume the role of world champion in Olympic years; principal event is the single sculls.

Single sculls – Men		**Single sculls – Women**	
1981	Peter Michael Kolbe (West Germany)	1981	Toma Sanda (Romania)
		1982	Irina Fetissova (USSR)
1982	Reiche Rüdiger (East Germany)	1983	Jutta Hampe (East Germany)
1983	Peter Michael Kolbe (West Germany)	1984	Valeria Racila (Romania)
		1985	Cornelia Linse (East Germany)
1984	Pertti Karppinen (Finland)	1986	Jutta Hampe (East Germany)
1985	Pertti Karppinen (Finland)	1987	Magdelena Georgieva (Bulgaria)
1986	Peter Michael Kolbe (West Germany)	1988	Jutta Behrendt (East Germany)
		1989	Elisabeta Lipa (Romania)
1987	Thomas Lange (East Germany)	1990	Brigit Peter (East Germany)
1988	Thomas Lange (East Germany)	1991	Silke Laumann (Canada)
1989	Thomas Lange (East Germany)	1992	Elisabeta Lipa (Romania)
1990	Yuri Janson (USSR)	1993	Jana Phieme (Germany)
1991	Thomas Lange (Germany)	1994	Trine Hansen (Denmark)
1992	Thomas Lange (Germany)	1995	Maria Brandin (Sweden)
1993	Derek Porter (Canada)	1996	Ekaterina Khodotovich (Belarus)
1994	Andre Wilms (Germany)	1997	Ekaterina Khodotovich (Belarus)
1995	Iztok Cop (Slovenia)	1998	Irina Fedotova (Russia)
1996	Xeno Müller (Switzerland)	1999	Ekaterina Karsten (Belarus)
1997	Jamie Koven (USA)	2000	Ekaterina Karsten (Belarus)
1998	Rob Waddell (New Zealand)	2001	Katrin Rutschow-Stomporowski (Germany)
1999	Rob Waddell (New Zealand)		
2000	Rob Waddell (New Zealand)	2002	Rumyana Neykova (Bulgaria)
2001	Olaf Tufte (Norway)	2003	Rumyana Neykova (Bulgaria)
2002	Marcel Hacker (Germany)	2004	Katrin Rutschow-Stomporowski (Germany)
2003	Olaf Tufte (Norway)		
2004	Olaf Tufte (Norway)	2005	Ekaterina Karsten (Belarus)
2005	Mahe Drysdale (New Zealand)		

University Boat Race

An annual contest between the crews from the Oxford and Cambridge University rowing clubs; first contested in 1829; not held in some years in the early history of the race; held twice in 1849 (Mar/Dec); the current course is from Putney to Mortlake.

1829	Oxford	1840	Cambridge	1845	Cambridge
1836	Cambridge	1841	Cambridge	1846	Cambridge
1839	Cambridge	1842	Oxford	1849	Cambridge

1849	Oxford	1904	Cambridge	1955	Cambridge
1852	Oxford	1905	Oxford	1956	Cambridge
1854	Oxford	1906	Cambridge	1957	Cambridge
1856	Cambridge	1907	Cambridge	1958	Cambridge
1857	Oxford	1908	Cambridge	1959	Oxford
1858	Cambridge	1909	Oxford	1960	Oxford
1859	Oxford	1910	Oxford	1961	Cambridge
1860	Cambridge	1911	Oxford	1962	Cambridge
1861	Oxford	1912	Oxford	1963	Oxford
1862	Oxford	1913	Oxford	1964	Cambridge
1863	Oxford	1914	Cambridge	1965	Oxford
1864	Oxford	1915	*not held*	1966	Oxford
1865	Oxford	1916	*not held*	1967	Oxford
1866	Oxford	1917	*not held*	1968	Cambridge
1867	Oxford	1918	*not held*	1969	Cambridge
1868	Oxford	1919	*not held*	1970	Cambridge
1869	Oxford	1920	Cambridge	1971	Cambridge
1870	Cambridge	1921	Cambridge	1972	Cambridge
1871	Cambridge	1922	Cambridge	1973	Cambridge
1872	Cambridge	1923	Oxford	1974	Oxford
1873	Cambridge	1924	Cambridge	1975	Cambridge
1874	Cambridge	1925	Cambridge	1976	Oxford
1875	Oxford	1926	Cambridge	1977	Oxford
1876	Cambridge	1927	Cambridge	1978	Oxford
1877	*dead heat*	1928	Cambridge	1979	Oxford
1878	Oxford	1929	Cambridge	1980	Oxford
1879	Cambridge	1930	Cambridge	1981	Oxford
1880	Oxford	1931	Cambridge	1982	Oxford
1881	Oxford	1932	Cambridge	1983	Oxford
1882	Oxford	1933	Cambridge	1984	Oxford
1883	Oxford	1934	Cambridge	1985	Oxford
1884	Cambridge	1935	Cambridge	1986	Cambridge
1885	Oxford	1936	Cambridge	1987	Oxford
1886	Cambridge	1937	Oxford	1988	Oxford
1887	Cambridge	1938	Oxford	1989	Oxford
1888	Cambridge	1939	Cambridge	1990	Oxford
1889	Cambridge	1940	*not held*	1991	Oxford
1890	Oxford	1941	*not held*	1992	Oxford
1891	Oxford	1942	*not held*	1993	Cambridge
1892	Oxford	1943	*not held*	1994	Cambridge
1893	Oxford	1944	*not held*	1995	Cambridge
1894	Oxford	1945	*not held*	1996	Cambridge
1895	Oxford	1946	Oxford	1997	Cambridge
1896	Oxford	1947	Cambridge	1998	Cambridge
1897	Oxford	1948	Cambridge	1999	Cambridge
1898	Oxford	1949	Cambridge	2000	Oxford
1899	Cambridge	1950	Cambridge	2001	Cambridge
1900	Cambridge	1951	Cambridge	2002	Oxford
1901	Oxford	1952	Oxford	2003	Oxford
1902	Cambridge	1953	Cambridge	2004	Cambridge
1903	Cambridge	1954	Oxford	2005	Oxford

RUGBY LEAGUE

Team ball game played with oval ball; developed 1823 from football (supposedly when William Webb Ellis of Rugby school picked up the ball and ran with it); Rugby League was formed by the breakaway Northern Union after a dispute with the Rugby Football Union about pay in 1895; object is to score a *try* by grounding ball in opposing team's scoring area behind goal line. The 13-a-side Rugby League game is now a professional game; scoring: try 4 points, conversion 2 points, penalty 2 points, drop goal 1 point.

Ruling body: Rugby League (RL)

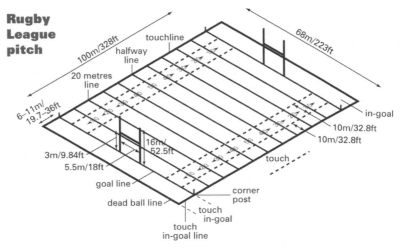

Rugby League pitch

World Cup

First held in 1954 between Great Britain, France, Australia and New Zealand; played intermittently since; will next be held in 2008.

1954	Great Britain	1970	Australia	1988	Australia
1957	Australia	1972	Great Britain	1992	Australia
1960	Great Britain	1975	Australia	1995	Australia
1968	Australia	1977	Australia	2000	Australia

Engage Super League

First held in 1996. The top six teams in the league at the end of the season play off for the title; known as the JJB Super League from 1996 to 1999 and the Tetley's Super League 2000–2004.

1996	St Helens	2000	St Helens	2004	Leeds
1997	Bradford	2001	Bradford	2005	Bradford
1998	Wigan	2002	St Helens		
1999	St Helens	2003	Bradford		

Challenge Cup

First contested in 1897 and won by Batley; first final at Wembley Stadium in 1929.

1981	Widnes	1990	Wigan	1999	Leeds
1982	Hull	1991	Wigan	2000	Bradford
1983	Featherstone	1992	Wigan	2001	St Helens
1984	Widnes	1993	Wigan	2002	Wigan
1985	Wigan	1994	Wigan	2003	Bradford
1986	Castleford	1995	Wigan	2004	St Helens
1987	Halifax	1996	St Helens	2005	Hull
1988	Wigan	1997	St Helens		
1989	Wigan	1998	Sheffield		

RUGBY UNION

Team ball game played with oval ball; developed 1823 from football (supposedly when William Webb Ellis of Rugby school picked up the ball and ran with it); object is to score a *try* by grounding ball in opposing team's scoring area behind goal line. The 15-a-side Rugby Union game is now a professional game; scoring: try 5 points, conversion 2 points, penalty 3 points, drop goal 3 points.

Ruling body: Rugby Football Union (RFU), International Rugby Board (IRB)

Rugby Union pitch

in-goal

22m line

halfway line

22m line

touchline

100m/110yd

68.62m/ 75yd

22.87m/25yd touch in-goal line

World Cup

The first Rugby Union World Cup was staged in 1987 and now takes place every four years.

1987	New Zealand	1995	South Africa	2003	England
1991	Australia	1999	Australia		

Six Nations' Championship

A round robin competition involving England, Ireland, Scotland, Wales, France and, from 2000, Italy; first contested in 1882.

1981	France	1990	Scotland	1999	Scotland
1982	Ireland	1991	England	2000	England
1983	France and Ireland	1992	England	2001	England
1984	Scotland	1993	France	2002	France
1985	Ireland	1994	Wales	2003	England
1986	France and Scotland	1995	England	2004	France
1987	France	1996	England	2005	Wales
1988	France and Wales	1997	France		
1989	France	1998	France		

County Championship

First held in 1889.

1981	Northumberland	1990	Lancashire	1999	Cornwall
1982	Lancashire	1991	Cornwall	2000	Yorkshire
1983	Gloucestershire	1992	Lancashire	2001	*not held*
1984	Gloucestershire	1993	Lancashire	2002	Gloucestershire
1985	Middlesex	1994	Yorkshire	2003	Lancashire
1986	Warwickshire	1995	Warwickshire	2004	Devon
1987	Yorkshire	1996	Gloucestershire	2005	Devon
1988	Lancashire	1997	Cumbria		
1989	Durham	1998	Cheshire		

Powergen Cup

An annual knockout competition for English club sides; first held in the 1971–2 season; known as the John Player Special Cup until 1988, the Pilkington Cup until 1997, and the Tetley's Bitter Cup until 2000.

1981	Leicester Tigers	1990	Bath	1999	London Wasps
1982	Gloucester/Moseley	1991	NEC Harlequins	2000	London Wasps
1983	Bristol	1992	Bath	2001	Newcastle Falcons
1984	Bath	1993	Leicester Tigers	2002	London Irish
1985	Bath	1994	Bath	2003	Gloucester
1986	Bath	1995	Bath	2004	Newcastle Falcons
1987	Bath	1996	Bath	2005	Leeds
1988	NEC Harlequins	1997	Leicester Tigers		
1989	Bath	1998	Saracens		

English League (Guinness Premiership)

Known as the Courage League until 1997, the Allied Dunbar Premier League between 1998 and 2000, and the Zurich Premiership until 2005.

1988	Leicester Tigers	1994	Bath	2000	Leicester Tigers
1989	Bath	1995	Leicester Tigers	2001	Leicester Tigers
1990	Wasps	1996	Bath	2002	Leicester Tigers
1991	Bath	1997	Wasps	2003	Wasps
1992	Bath	1998	Newcastle Falcons	2004	Wasps
1993	Bath	1999	Leicester Tigers	2005	Wasps

Welsh Rugby Union Challenge Cup (Konica Minolta)

The knockout tournament for Welsh clubs; first held in 1971–2; formerly known as the Schweppes Welsh Cup, the Swalec Cup and the Principality Cup.

1981	Cardiff	1990	Neath	1999	Swansea
1982	Cardiff	1991	Llanelli	2000	Llanelli
1983	Pontypool	1992	Llanelli	2001	Newport
1984	Cardiff	1993	Llanelli	2002	Pontypridd
1985	Llanelli	1994	Cardiff	2003	Llanelli
1986	Cardiff	1995	Swansea	2004	Neath
1987	Cardiff	1996	Pontypridd	2005	Llanelli
1988	Llanelli	1997	Cardiff		
1989	Neath	1998	Llanelli		

Welsh Premiership

Premiership begun in 1991 and revived in 1998; from 1992–7 title taken by Division 1 Welsh League champions.

1991	Neath	1996	Neath	2001	Swansea
1992	Swansea	1997	Pontypridd	2002	Llanelli
1993	Llanelli	1998	Swansea	2003	Bridgend
1994	Swansea	1999	Llanelli	2004	Newport
1995	Cardiff	2000	Cardiff	2005	Neath

Scottish Club Championship (BT Premiership)

First held in 1973–4.

1981	Gala	1990	Melrose	1999	Heriot's FP
1982	Hawick	1991	Boroughmuir	2000	Heriot's FP
1983	Gala	1992	Melrose	2001	Hawick
1984	Hawick	1993	Melrose	2002	Hawick
1985	Hawick	1994	Melrose	2003	Boroughmuir
1986	Hawick	1995	Stirling County	2004	Glasgow Hawks
1987	Hawick	1996	Melrose	2005	Glasgow Hawks
1988	Kelso	1997	Melrose		
1989	Kelso	1998	Watsonians		

SAILING

Travelling over water in a suitable craft, usually a small single or double-sided dinghy, often with outboard motor or auxiliary engine for use in no wind; sailing involves racing small, light sailing vessels with crews of one, two or three; large ocean-going yachts may be 25m/80ft or more in length; several classes of racing yacht in Olympic and international competitions – eg the Admiral's Cup and America's Cup.

Ruling body: International Sailing Federation (ISAF); Royal Ocean Racing Club (RORC)

America's Cup

One of sport's famous trophies; first won by the schooner *Magic* in 1870; now held approximately every four years, when challengers compete in a series of races to find which of them races against the holder; all 25 winners up to 1983 were from the USA.

	Winning Yacht (Nation) (Skipper)
1983	Australia II (Australia) (John Bertrand)
1987	Stars & Stripes (USA) (Dennis Conner)
1988	Stars & Stripes (USA) (Dennis Conner)[1]
1992	America (USA) (Bill Koch)
1995	Black Magic (New Zealand) (Russell Coutts)
2000	Black Magic (New Zealand) (Russell Coutts)
2003	Alinghi (Switzerland) (Russell Coutts)

[1] *Stars & Stripes won a special challenge match but on appeal the race was awarded to the New Zealand boat. However, the decision was reversed by the New York Appeals Court in 1989.*

The Auld Mug

Europe secured its first America's Cup victory in 2003 with a win for Switzerland, a landlocked country not usually known for its sailing prowess. However, the win is less surprising given that Alinghi's skipper was Russell Coutts, a Kiwi who had defected to the Swiss attempt with several key New Zealand team members. Coutts's victory also meant that he became the record holder for captaining the most America's Cup race wins, with 14 race victories under his belt. The America's Cup is affectionately known by those in the business as the 'Auld Mug'.

Admiral's Cup

A two-yearly series of races, originally held in the English Channel, around Fastnet rock and at Cowes; originally four national teams of three boats per team, now nine teams of three boats per team; first held in 1957.

1981	Great Britain	1991	France	2001	*not held*
1983	West Germany	1993	Germany	2003	Australia
1985	West Germany	1995	Italy	2005	*not held*
1987	New Zealand	1997	USA		
1989	Great Britain	1999	The Netherlands		

SKIING

Propelling oneself along snow while standing on skis, aided by poles; named from Norwegian *ski*, 'snowshoe'; two forms of competition skiing: *alpine skiing*, consisting of the *downhill*, *slalom* (zigzag courses through markers) and *ski jumping*, and *Nordic skiing* or *langlaufing* (on narrower skis to which only the toe is attached), incorporating cross-country skiing and the biathlon.

Ruling body: International Ski Federation (FIS; Fédération Internationale de Ski)

World Cup

A season-long competition first organized in 1967; champions are declared in downhill, slalom, giant slalom and super-giant slalom, as well as the overall champion; points are obtained for performances in each category.

Overall winners

Men		Women	
1981	Phil Mahre (USA)	1981	Marie-Therese Nadig (Switzerland)
1982	Phil Mahre (USA)		
1983	Phil Mahre (USA)	1982	Erika Hess (Switzerland)
1984	Pirmin Zurbriggen (Switzerland)	1983	Tamara McKinney (USA)
1985	Marc Girardelli (Luxembourg)	1984	Erika Hess (Switzerland)
1986	Marc Girardelli (Luxembourg)	1985	Michela Figini (Switzerland)
1987	Pirmin Zurbriggen (Switzerland)	1986	Maria Walliser (Switzerland)
1988	Pirmin Zurbriggen (Switzerland)	1987	Maria Walliser (Switzerland)
1989	Marc Girardelli (Luxembourg)	1988	Michela Figini (Switzerland)
1990	Pirmin Zurbriggen (Switzerland)	1989	Vreni Schneider (Switzerland)
1991	Marc Girardelli (Luxembourg)	1990	Petra Kronberger (Austria)
1992	Paul Accola (Switzerland)	1991	Petra Kronberger (Austria)
1993	Marc Girardelli (Luxembourg)	1992	Petra Kronberger (Austria)
1994	Kjetil-Andre Aamodt (Norway)	1993	Anita Wachter (Austria)
1995	Alberto Tomba (Italy)	1994	Vreni Schneider (Switzerland)
1996	Lasse Kjus (Norway)	1995	Vreni Schneider (Switzerland)
1997	Luc Alphand (France)	1996	Katja Seizinger (Germany)
1998	Hermann Maier (Austria)	1997	Pernilla Wiberg (Sweden)
1999	Lasse Kjus (Norway)	1998	Katja Seizinger (Germany)
2000	Hermann Maier (Austria)	1999	Alexandra Meissnitzer (Austria)
2001	Hermann Maier (Austria)	2000	Renate Götschl (Austria)
2002	Stephan Eberharter (Austria)	2001	Janica Kostelic (Croatia)
2003	Stephan Eberharter (Austria)	2002	Michaela Dorfmeister (Austria)
2004	Hermann Maier (Austria)	2003	Janica Kostelic (Croatia)
2005	Bode Miller (USA)	2004	Anja Paerson (Sweden)
		2005	Anja Paerson (Sweden)

SNOOKER

Indoor game played on a standard billiard table by two (or occasionally four) players; aim is to *pot* the 21 coloured balls (arranged on the table at the start) by hitting them with the white *cue ball*, itself hit using a tapered pole or *cue*. Fifteen of the balls are red; these must be potted alternately with the coloured ones. This sequence is called a *break* and continues until a mistake is made; reds remain in the pockets but coloured balls are returned to their designated *spots* on the table until no reds are left, when they are potted in ascending order; game ends when the black is finally potted. Points 1–7 relate to the colours, in order: red, yellow, green, brown, blue, pink, black. The maximum break possible is 147.

Ruling body: International Billiards and Snooker Federation (IBSF), World Professional Billiards and Snooker Association (WPBSA)

Snooker table

3.57m/11ft 8½in

1.78m/5ft 10in

Baulk

D

centre spot

Y

R

P

Bl

B

29.2cm/ 11½in

G

Blk

pyramid spot

73.7cm/ 29in

top pocket

centre pocket

Baulk-line

bottom pocket

Note: The snooker table is 85–88cm/2ft 9½in–2ft 10½in high.

Y	yellow	P	pink
G	green	R	red
Br	brown	Blk	black
Bl	blue		

Breaking the Bank

Ronnie O'Sullivan made the fastest ever 147 break (at the 1997 World Championship), pocketing not only the balls but also £165 000 in bonus money. His maximum break took just 5 minutes and 20 seconds – working out at a cool £515 per second!

World Professional Championships

Instituted in the 1926–27 season; a knockout competition open to professional players who are members of the World Professional Billiards and Snooker Association; played at the Crucible Theatre, Sheffield.

1981	Steve Davis	(England)	1994	Stephen Hendry	(Scotland)
1982	Alex Higgins	(Northern Ireland)	1995	Stephen Hendry	(Scotland)
1983	Steve Davis	(England)	1996	Stephen Hendry	(Scotland)
1984	Steve Davis	(England)	1997	Ken Doherty	(Ireland)
1985	Dennis Taylor	(Northern Ireland)	1998	John Higgins	(Scotland)
1986	Joe Johnson	(England)	1999	Stephen Hendry	(Scotland)
1987	Steve Davis	(England)	2000	Mark Williams	(Wales)
1988	Steve Davis	(England)	2001	Ronnie O'Sullivan	(England)
1989	Steve Davis	(England)	2002	Peter Ebdon	(England)
1990	Stephen Hendry	(Scotland)	2003	Mark Williams	(Wales)
1991	John Parrott	(England)	2004	Ronnie O'Sullivan	(England)
1992	Stephen Hendry	(Scotland)	2005	Shaun Murphy	(England)
1993	Stephen Hendry	(Scotland)			

Sinistral Snooker

Lefties everywhere rejoiced when Mark Williams won the Championship in 2000, the first left-hander ever to do so.

SQUASH

Strenuous indoor racket-and-ball game played (in English singles) on an enclosed court; small rubber ball is hit alternately by players against the front wall; object is to play so that the ball cannot be returned; developed 1817 from rackets at Harrow school. Also sometimes known as *squash rackets*.

Ruling body: World Squash Federation (WSF)

Squash Worldwide

The World Squash Federation keeps records of the number of squash courts worldwide; they estimate that there are more than 47 000 courts around the globe. They calculate that there are 6 136 courts in Africa, 6 436 in Asia, 22 973 in Europe, 7 339 in the Americas and 4 443 in Oceania. Squash-playing nations include Antigua (2 courts), Bhutan (1 court), Republic of Congo (2 courts), Kyrgyzstan (2 courts), Moldova (1 court) and Vanuatu (2 courts). Somewhat surprisingly, Papua New Guinea has no fewer than 48 courts.

Squash court

World Open Championship

First held in 1976; takes place annually for men and women; women's event first held 1979; every two years for women until 1989.

Men		Women	
1981	Jahangir Khan (Pakistan)	1981	Rhonda Thorne (Australia)
1982	Jahangir Khan (Pakistan)	1983	Vicki Cardwell (Australia)
1983	Jahangir Khan (Pakistan)	1985	Sue Devoy (New Zealand)
1984	Jahangir Khan (Pakistan)	1987	Sue Devoy (New Zealand)
1985	Jahangir Khan (Pakistan)	1989	Martine Le Moignan (Great
1986	Ross Norman (New Zealand)		Britain)
1987	Jansher Khan (Pakistan)	1990	Sue Devoy (New Zealand)
1988	Jahangir Khan (Pakistan)	1991	*not held*
1989	Jansher Khan (Pakistan)	1992	Sue Devoy (New Zealand)
1990	Jansher Khan (Pakistan)	1993	Michelle Martin (Australia)
1991	Rodney Martin (Australia)	1994	Michelle Martin (Australia)
1992	Jansher Khan (Pakistan)	1995	Michelle Martin (Australia)
1993	Jansher Khan (Pakistan)	1996	Sarah Fitz-Gerald (Australia)
1994	Jansher Khan (Pakistan)	1997	Sarah Fitz-Gerald (Australia)
1995	Jansher Khan (Pakistan)	1998	Sarah Fitz-Gerald (Australia)
1996	Jansher Khan (Pakistan)	1999	Cassie Campion (Great Britain)
1997	Rodney Eyles (Australia)	2000	Carol Owens (Australia)
1998	Jonathon Power (Canada)	2001	Sarah Fitz-Gerald (Australia)
1999	Peter Nicol (Great Britain)	2002	Sarah Fitz-Gerald (Australia)
2000	*not held*	2003	Carol Owens (New Zealand)
2001	*not held*	2004	Vanessa Atkinson (The
2002	David Palmer (Australia)		Netherlands)
2003	Amr Shabana (Egypt)	2005	Nicol David (Malaysia)
2004	Thierry Lincou (France)		
2005	Amr Shabana (Egypt)		

SWIMMING AND DIVING

Swimming: Propelling oneself through water without mechanical aids. Four strokes: *breast stroke*, the slowest stroke, developed in the 16c; *front crawl* or *freestyle*, the fastest stroke; *backstroke*; and *butterfly*, developed in the USA in the 20c. In competitions there are also relays, involving four swimmers, and medley races, combining all four strokes. Olympic-size pool is 50m/55yd long, with eight lanes; race lengths from 50m/55yd to 1 500m/1 640yd; earliest reference to swimming as a sport is 36BC Japan.

Diving: Jumping from an elevated rigid or sprung board into a swimming pool, often performing a variety of twists and somersaults. Style gains marks, as does successfully completing the dive, based on the level of difficulty of each attempt (which is used as a multiplying factor). Springboard events take place from a board 3m/9ft 10in above the water; platform diving from a rigid board 10m/32ft 10in above the water.

Ruling body: International Swimming Federation (FINA; Fédération Internationale de Natation)

World Championships

First held in 1973 and again in 1975; from 1978 held approximately every four years; since 2001 held every two years.

1994

Men

50m freestyle	Alexander Popov (Russia)
100m freestyle	Alexander Popov (Russia)
200m freestyle	Antti Kasvio (Finland)
400m freestyle	Kieren Perkins (Australia)
1 500m freestyle	Kieren Perkins (Australia)
100m backstroke	Martín López-Zubero (Spain)
200m backstroke	Vladimir Selkov (Russia)
100m breaststroke	Norbert Rózsa (Hungary)
200m breaststroke	Norbert Rózsa (Hungary)
100m butterfly	Rafal Szukala (Poland)
200m butterfly	Denis Pankratov (Russia)
200m individual medley	Jani Sievinen (Finalnd)
400m individual medley	Tom Dolan (USA)
4×100m freestyle relay	USA
4×200m freestyle relay	Sweden
4×100m medley relay	USA
1m springboard diving	Evan Stewart (Zimbabwe)
3m springboard diving	Yu Zhuocheng (China)
10m platform diving	Dimitri Sautin (Russia)

Women

50m freestyle	Le Jingyi (China)
100m freestyle	Le Jingyi (China)
200m freestyle	Franziska van Almsick (Germany)
400m freestyle	Yang Aihua (China)
800m freestyle	Janet Evans (USA)

Women

100m backstroke	He Cihong (China)
200m backstroke	He Cihong (China)
100m breaststroke	Sam Riley (Australia)
200m breaststroke	Sam Riley (Australia)
100m butterfly	Liu Limin (China)
200m butterfly	Liu Limin (China)
200m individual medley	Lu Bin (China)
400m individual medley	Dai Guohong (China)
4×100m freestyle relay	China
4×200m freestyle relay	China
4×100m medley relay	China
1m springboard diving	Chen Lixia (China)
3m springboard diving	Tan Shuping (China)
10m platform diving	Fu Mingxia (China)

1998

Men

50m freestyle	Bill Pilczuk (USA)
100m freestyle	Alexander Popov (Russia)
200m freestyle	Michael Klim (Australia)
400m freestyle	Ian Thorpe (Australia)
1 500m freestyle	Grant Hackett (Australia)
100m backstroke	Lenny Krayzelburg (USA)
200m backstroke	Lenny Krayzelburg (USA)
100m breaststroke	Fred Deburghgraeve (Belgium)
200m breaststroke	Kurt Grote (USA)
100m butterfly	Michael Klim (Australia)
200m butterfly	Denys Sylantyev (Ukraine)
200m individual medley	Marcel Wouda (The Netherlands)
400m individual medley	Tom Dolan (USA)
4×100m freestyle relay	USA
4×200m freestyle relay	Australia
4×100m medley relay	Australia
1m springboard diving	Yu Zhuocheng (China)
3m springboard diving	Dimitri Sautin (Russia)
10m platform diving	Dimitri Sautin (Russia)

Women

50m freestyle	Amy Van Dyken (USA)
100m freestyle	Jenny Thompson (USA)
200m freestyle	Claudia Poll (Costa Rica)
400m freestyle	Yan Chen (China)
800m freestyle	Brooke Bennett (USA)
100m backstroke	Lea Maurer (USA)
200m backstroke	Roxanna Maracineanu (France)
100m breaststroke	Kristy Kowal (USA)
200m breaststroke	Agnes Kovacs (Hungary)
100m butterfly	Jenny Thompson (USA)
200m butterfly	Susie O'Neill (Australia)
200m individual medley	Wu Yanyan (China)
400m individual medley	Yan Chen (China)
4×100m freestyle relay	USA
4×200m freestyle relay	Germany

Women
4×100m medley relay   USA
1m springboard diving   Irina Lashko (Russia)
3m springboard diving   Yulia Pakhalina (Russia)
10m platform diving   Olena Zhupyna (Ukraine)

2001

Men
50m freestyle   Anthony Ervin (USA)
100m freestyle   Anthony Ervin (USA)
200m freestyle   Ian Thorpe (Australia)
400m freestyle   Ian Thorpe (Australia)
1 500m freestyle   Grant Hackett (Australia)
100m backstroke   Matt Welsh (Australia)
200m backstroke   Aaron Peirsol (USA)
50m breaststroke   Oleg Lisogor (Ukraine)
100m breaststroke   Roman Sloudnov (Russia)
200m breaststroke   Brendan Hansen (USA)
50m butterfly   Geoff Huegill (Australia)
100m butterfly   Lars Frolander (Sweden)
200m butterfly   Michael Phelps (USA)
200m individual medley   Massimiliano Rosolini (Italy)
400m individual medley   Alessio Boggiatto (Italy)
4×100m freestyle relay   Australia
4×200m freestyle relay   Australia
4×100m medley relay   Australia
1m springboard diving   Feng Wang (China)
3m springboard diving   Dimitri Sautin (Russia)
10m platform diving   Liang Tian (China)

Women
50m freestyle   Inge de Bruijn (The Netherlands)
100m freestyle   Inge de Bruijn (The Netherlands)
200m freestyle   Giaan Rooney (Australia)
400m freestyle   Yana Klochova (Ukraine)
800m freestyle   Hannah Stockbauer (Germany)
1 500m freestyle   Hannah Stockbauer (Germany)
50m backstroke   Haley Cope (USA)
100m backstroke   Natalie Coughlin (USA)
200m backstroke   Diana Iuliana Mocanu (Romania)
50m breaststroke   Luo Xuejuan (China)
100m breaststroke   Luo Xuejuan (China)
200m breaststroke   Agnes Kovacs (Hungary)
50m butterfly   Inge de Bruijn (The Netherlands)
100m butterfly   Petria Thomas (Australia)
200m butterfly   Petria Thomas (Australia)
200m individual medley   Martha Bowen (USA)
400m individual medley   Yana Klochova (Ukraine)
4×100m freestyle relay   Germany
4×200m freestyle relay   Great Britain
4×100m medley relay   Australia
1m springboard diving   Blythe Hartley (Canada)
3m springboard diving   Mian Xu (China)
10m platform diving   Mian Xu (China)

2003

Men

50m freestyle	Alexander Popov (Russia)
100m freestyle	Alexander Popov (Russia)
200m freestyle	Ian Thorpe (Australia)
400m freestyle	Ian Thorpe (Australia)
1 500m freestyle	Grant Hackett (Australia)
100m backstroke	Aaron Peirsol (USA)
200m backstroke	Aaron Peirsol (USA)
50m breaststroke	James Gibson (Great Britain)
100m breaststroke	Kosuke Kitajima (Japan)
200m breaststroke	Kosuke Kitajima (Japan)
50m butterfly	Matthew Welsh (Australia)
100m butterfly	Ian Crocker (USA)
200m butterfly	Michael Phelps (USA)
200m individual medley	Michael Phelps (USA)
400m individual medley	Michael Phelps (USA)
4×100m freestyle relay	Russia
4×200m freestyle relay	Australia
4×100m medley relay	USA
1m springboard diving	Xiang Xu (China)
3m springboard diving	Alexander Dobrosok (Russia)
10m platform diving	Alexandre Despatie (Canada)

Women

50m freestyle	Inge de Bruijn (The Netherlands)
100m freestyle	Hanna-Maria Seppälä (Finland)
200m freestyle	Alena Popchanka (Bulgaria)
400m freestyle	Hannah Stockbauer (Germany)
800m freestyle	Hannah Stockbauer (Germany)
1 500m freestyle	Hannah Stockbauer (Germany)
50m backstroke	Nina Zhivanevskaya (Spain)
100m backstroke	Antje Buschschulte (Germany)
200m backstroke	Katy Sexton (Great Britain)
50m breaststroke	Luo Xuejuan (China)
100m breaststroke	Luo Xuejuan (China)
200m breaststroke	Amanda Beard (USA)
50m butterfly	Inge de Bruijn (The Netherlands)
100m butterfly	Jenny Thompson (USA)
200m butterfly	Otylia Jedrzejczak (Poland)
200m individual medley	Yana Klochova (Ukraine)
400m individual medley	Yana Klochova (Ukraine)
4×100m freestyle relay	USA
4×200m freestyle relay	USA
4×100m medley relay	China
1m springboard diving	Irina Lashko (Australia)
3m springboard diving	Guo Jingjing (China)
10m platform diving	Emilie Heymans (Canada)

2005

Men

50m freestyle	Roland Schoeman (South Africa)
100m freestyle	Filippo Magnini (Italy)
200m freestyle	Michael Phelps (USA)
400m freestyle	Grant Hackett (Australia)

Men

800m freestyle	Grant Hackett (Australia)
1 500m freestyle	Grant Hackett (Australia)
50m backstroke	Aristeidis Grigoriadis (Greece)
100m backstroke	Aaron Peirsol (USA)
200m backstroke	Aaron Peirsol (USA)
50m breaststroke	Mark Warnecke (Germany)
100m breaststroke	Brendan Hansen (USA)
200m breaststroke	Brendan Hansen (USA)
50m butterfly	Roland Schoeman (South Africa)
100m butterfly	Ian Crocker (USA)
200m butterfly	Pawel Korzeniowski (Poland)
200m individual medley	Michael Phelps (USA)
400m individual medley	Laszlo Cseh (Hungary)
4 x 100m freestyle relay	USA
4 x 200m freestyle relay	USA
4 x 100m medley relay	USA
1m springboard diving	Alexandre Despatie (Canada)
3m springboard diving	Alexandre Despatie (Canada)
10m platform diving	Hu Jia (China)
3m springboard synchronized	Wang Feng/He Chong (China)
10m platform synchronized	Dmitry Dobrosok/Glen Galperin (Russia)

Women

50m freestyle	Lisbeth Lenton (Australia)
100m freestyle	Jodie Henry (Australia)
200m freestyle	Solenne Figues (France)
400m freestyle	Laure Manaudou (France)
800m freestyle	Kate Ziegler (USA)
1 500m freestyle	Kate Ziegler (USA)
50m backstroke	Giaan Rooney (Australia)
100m backstroke	Kirsty Coventry (Zimbabwe)
200m backstroke	Kirsty Coventry (Zimbabwe)
50m breaststroke	Jade Edmistone (Australia)
100m breaststroke	Leisel Jones (Australia)
200m breaststroke	Leisel Jones (Australia)
50m butterfly	Danni Miatke (Australia)
100m butterfly	Jessicah Schipper (Australia)
200m butterfly	Otylia Jedrzejczak (Poland)
200m individual medley	Katie Hoff (USA)
400m individual medley	Katie Hoff (USA)
4 x 100m freestyle relay	Australia
4 x 200m freestyle relay	USA
4 x 100m medley relay	Australia
1m springboard diving	Blythe Hartley (Canada)
3m springboard diving	Guo Jingjing (China)
10m platform diving	Laura Ann Wilkinson (USA)
3m springboard synchronized	Li Ting/Guo Jingjing (China)
10m platform synchronized	Tong Jia/Pei Lin Yuan (China)

TENNIS

Properly lawn tennis. Racket-and-ball game for two or four players; net is stretched across centre; rackets have oval heads strung with nylon or gut; playing surface can be grass, clay, shale, concrete, wood, or other man-made materials; object is to play unreturnable strokes, thus scoring points; progression of scoring is 15, 30, 40, deuce if both reach 40, and game; set won by winning six games with a two game lead (or one in a 'short' set); a very close set can be decided using a tie-break. In doubles, players may hit the ball in any order, but must serve in rotation.

Ruling bodies: International Tennis Federation (ITF), Lawn Tennis Association (LTA)

Tennis court

All-England Championships at Wimbledon

The All-England Championships at Wimbledon are lawn tennis's most prestigious championships; first held in 1877.

Men's singles

1981	John McEnroe (USA)
1982	Jimmy Connors (USA)
1983	John McEnroe (USA)
1984	John McEnroe (USA)
1985	Boris Becker (West Germany)
1986	Boris Becker (West Germany)
1987	Pat Cash (Australia)
1988	Stefan Edberg (Sweden)
1989	Boris Becker (West Germany)
1990	Stefan Edberg (Sweden)
1991	Michael Stich (Germany)
1992	André Agassi (USA)
1993	Pete Sampras (USA)

Women's singles

1981	Chris Evert Lloyd (USA)
1982	Martina Navratilova (USA)
1983	Martina Navratilova (USA)
1984	Martina Navratilova (USA)
1985	Martina Navratilova (USA)
1986	Martina Navratilova (USA)
1987	Martina Navratilova (USA)
1988	Steffi Graf (West Germany)
1989	Steffi Graf (West Germany)
1990	Martina Navratilova (USA)
1991	Steffi Graf (Germany)
1992	Steffi Graf (Germany)
1993	Steffi Graf (Germany)

Men's singles

1994	Pete Sampras (USA)
1995	Pete Sampras (USA)
1996	Richard Krajicek (The Netherlands)
1997	Pete Sampras (USA)
1998	Pete Sampras (USA)
1999	Pete Sampras (USA)
2000	Pete Sampras (USA)
2001	Goran Ivanisevic (Croatia)
2002	Lleyton Hewitt (Australia)
2003	Roger Federer (Switzerland)
2004	Roger Federer (Switzerland)
2005	Roger Federer (Switzerland)

Women's singles

1994	Conchita Martínez (Spain)
1995	Steffi Graf (Germany)
1996	Steffi Graf (Germany)
1997	Martina Hingis (Switzerland)
1998	Jana Novotna (Czech Republic)
1999	Lindsay Davenport (USA)
2000	Venus Williams (USA)
2001	Venus Williams (USA)
2002	Serena Williams (USA)
2003	Serena Williams (USA)
2004	Maria Sharapova (Russia)
2005	Venus Williams (USA)

Men's doubles

1981	Peter Fleming/John McEnroe (USA)
1982	Peter McNamara/Paul McNamee (Australia)
1983	Peter Fleming/John McEnroe (USA)
1984	Peter Fleming/John McEnroe (USA)
1985	Heinz Gunthardt (Switzerland)/Balazs Taroczy (Hungary)
1986	Joakim Nystrom/Mats Wilander (Sweden)
1987	Ken Flach/Robert Seguso (USA)
1988	Ken Flach/Robert Seguso (USA)
1989	John Fitzgerald (Australia)/Anders Jarryd (Sweden)
1990	Rick Leach/Jim Pugh (USA)
1991	John Fitzgerald (Australia)/Anders Jarryd (Sweden)
1992	John McEnroe (USA)/Michael Stich (Germany)
1993	Todd Woodbridge/Mark Woodforde (Australia)
1994	Todd Woodbridge/Mark Woodforde (Australia)
1995	Todd Woodbridge/Mark Woodforde (Australia)
1996	Todd Woodbridge/Mark Woodforde (Australia)
1997	Todd Woodbridge/Mark Woodforde (Australia)
1998	Jacco Eltingh/Paul Haarhuis (The Netherlands)
1999	Mahesh Bhupathi/Leander Paes (India)
2000	Todd Woodbridge/Mark Woodforde (Australia)
2001	Donald Johnson/Jared Palmer (USA)
2002	Todd Woodbridge (Australia)/Jonas Bjorkman (Sweden)
2003	Todd Woodbridge (Australia)/Jonas Bjorkman (Sweden)
2004	Todd Woodbridge (Australia)/Jonas Bjorkman (Sweden)
2005	Stephen Huss (Australia)/Wesley Moodie (South Africa)

Women's doubles

1981	Martina Navratilova/Pam Shriver (USA)
1982	Martina Navratilova/Pam Shriver (USA)
1983	Martina Navratilova/Pam Shriver (USA)
1984	Martina Navratilova/Pam Shriver (USA)
1985	Kathy Jordan/Elizabeth Smylie (Australia)
1986	Martina Navratilova/Pam Shriver (USA)
1987	Claudia Kohde-Kilsch (West Germany)/Helena Sukova (Czechoslovakia)
1988	Steffi Graf (West Germany)/Gabriela Sabatini (Argentina)
1989	Jana Novotna/Helena Sukova (Czechoslovakia)
1990	Jana Novotna/Helena Sukova (Czechoslovakia)
1991	Natalya Zvereva/Larissa Savchenko (USSR)
1992	Gigi Fernandez (USA)/Natalya Zvereva (CIS)
1993	Gigi Fernandez (USA)/Natalya Zvereva (CIS)

Women's doubles
1994   Gigi Fernandez (USA)/Natalya Zvereva (CIS)
1995   Arantxa Sanchez Vicario (Spain)/Jana Novotna (Czech Republic)
1996   Helena Sukova (Czech Republic)/Martina Hingis (Switzerland)
1997   Gigi Fernandez (USA)/Natalya Zvereva (Belarus)
1998   Jana Novotna (Czech Republic)/Martina Hingis (Switzerland)
1999   Lindsay Davenport/Corina Morariu (USA)
2000   Serena Williams/Venus Williams (USA)
2001   Lisa Raymond (USA)/Rennae Stubbs (Australia)
2002   Serena Williams/Venus Williams (USA)
2003   Kim Clijsters (Belgium)/Ai Sugiyama (Japan)
2004   Cara Black (Zimbabwe)/Rennae Stubbs (Australia)
2005   Cara Black (Zimbabwe)/Liezel Huber (South Africa)

Mixed doubles
1981   Betty Stove (The Netherlands)/Frew McMillan (South Africa)
1982   Anne Smith (USA)/Kevin Curren (South Africa)
1983   Wendy Turnbull (Australia)/John Lloyd (Great Britain)
1984   Wendy Turnbull (Australia)/John Lloyd (Great Britain)
1985   Martina Navratilova (USA)/Paul McNamee (Australia)
1986   Kathy Jordan/Ken Flach (USA)
1987   Jo Durie/Jeremy Bates (Great Britain)
1988   Zina Garrison/Sherwood Stewart (USA)
1989   Jana Novotna (Czechoslovakia)/Jim Pugh (USA)
1990   Zina Garrison/Rick Leach (USA)
1991   Elizabeth Smylie/John Fitzgerald (Australia)
1992   Larissa Savchenko-Neiland (Latvia)/Cyril Suk (Czechoslovakia)
1993   Martina Navratilova (USA)/Mark Woodforde (Australia)
1994   Helena Sukova (Czech Republic)/Todd Woodbridge (Australia)
1995   Martina Navratilova/Jonathan Stark (USA)
1996   Helena Sukova/Cyril Suk (Czech Republic)
1997   Helena Sukova/Cyril Suk (Czech Republic)
1998   Serena Williams (USA)/Max Mirnyi (Belarus)
1999   Lisa Raymond (USA)/Leander Paes (India)
2000   Kimberly Po/Donald Johnson (USA)
2001   Daniela Hantuchova (Slovakia)/Leos Friedl (Czech Republic)
2002   Elena Likhovtseva (Russia)/Mahesh Bhupathi (India)
2003   Martina Navratilova (USA)/Leander Paes (India)
2004   Cara Black/Wayne Black (Zimbabwe)
2005   Mary Pierce (France)/Mahesh Bhupathi (India)

US Open

First held in 1891 as the United States Championship; became the United States Open in 1968.

Men's singles
1981   John McEnroe (USA)
1982   Jimmy Connors (USA)
1983   Jimmy Connors (USA)
1984   John McEnroe (USA)
1985   Ivan Lendl (Czechoslovakia)
1986   Ivan Lendl (Czechoslovakia)
1987   Ivan Lendl (Czechoslovakia)
1988   Mats Wilander (Sweden)

Women's singles
1981   Tracy Austin (USA)
1982   Chris Evert Lloyd (USA)
1983   Martina Navratilova (USA)
1984   Martina Navratilova (USA)
1985   Hana Mandlikova (Czechoslovakia)
1986   Martina Navratilova (USA)
1987   Martina Navratilova (USA)
1988   Steffi Graf (West Germany)

Men's singles

1989	Boris Becker (West Germany)
1990	Pete Sampras (USA)
1991	Stefan Edberg (Sweden)
1992	Stefan Edberg (Sweden)
1993	Pete Sampras (USA)
1994	André Agassi (USA)
1995	Pete Sampras (USA)
1996	Pete Sampras (USA)
1997	Pat Rafter (Australia)
1998	Pat Rafter (Australia)
1999	André Agassi (USA)
2000	Marat Safin (Russia)
2001	Lleyton Hewitt (Australia)
2002	Pete Sampras (USA)
2003	Andy Roddick (USA)
2004	Roger Federer (Switzerland)
2005	Roger Federer (Switzerland)

Women's singles

1989	Steffi Graf (West Germany)
1990	Gabriela Sabatini (Argentina)
1991	Monica Seles (Yugoslavia)
1992	Monica Seles (Yugoslavia)
1993	Steffi Graf (Germany)
1994	Arantxa Sanchez Vicario (Spain)
1995	Steffi Graf (Germany)
1996	Steffi Graf (Germany)
1997	Martina Hingis (Switzerland)
1998	Lindsay Davenport (USA)
1999	Serena Williams (USA)
2000	Venus Williams (USA)
2001	Venus Williams (USA)
2002	Serena Williams (USA)
2003	Justine Henin-Hardenne (Belgium)
2004	Svetlana Kuznetsova (Russia)
2005	Kim Clijsters (Belgium)

Anyone for Sphairistike?

'Field tennis' was played in the 18c, but a game similar to the modern game was invented in Wales in 1873 by Walter Wingfield, who christened the new game *sphairistike*. He patented the game and it was quite widely known for a time by this name, which comes from the Greek *sphairistike techne* 'the art of playing ball', from *sphaira* 'ball'. The simpler term *tennis* is thought to come from the French word *tenez*, the imperative of *tenir* meaning 'to take or receive'.

French Open

First held in 1891 as the French Championships, became an international competition in 1925, and was renamed the French Open in 1968 when professionals were first allowed to enter.

Men's singles

1981	Bjorn Borg (Sweden)
1982	Mats Wilander (Sweden)
1983	Yannick Noah (France)
1984	Ivan Lendl (Czechoslovakia)
1985	Mats Wilander (Sweden)
1986	Ivan Lendl (Czechoslovakia)
1987	Ivan Lendl (Czechoslovakia)
1988	Mats Wilander (Sweden)
1989	Michael Chang (USA)
1990	Andres Gomez (Ecuador)
1991	Jim Courier (USA)
1992	Jim Courier (USA)
1993	Sergi Bruguera (Spain)
1994	Sergi Bruguera (Spain)
1995	Thomas Muster (Austria)
1996	Yevgeny Kafelnikov (Russia)
1997	Gustavo Kuerten (Brazil)
1998	Carlos Moya (Spain)

Women's singles

1981	Hana Mandlikova (Czechoslovakia)
1982	Martina Navratilova (USA)
1983	Chris Evert Lloyd (USA)
1984	Martina Navratilova (USA)
1985	Chris Evert Lloyd (USA)
1986	Chris Evert Lloyd (USA)
1987	Steffi Graf (West Germany)
1988	Steffi Graf (West Germany)
1989	Arantxa Sanchez Vicario (Spain)
1990	Monica Seles (Yugoslavia)
1991	Monica Seles (Yugoslavia)
1992	Monica Seles (Yugoslavia)
1993	Steffi Graf (Germany)
1994	Arantxa Sanchez Vicario (Spain)
1996	Steffi Graf (Germany)
1997	Iva Majoli (Croatia)
1995	Steffi Graf (Germany)
1998	Arantxa Sanchez Vicario (Spain)

Men's singles		Women's singles	
1999	André Agassi (USA)	1999	Steffi Graf (Germany)
2000	Gustavo Kuerten (Brazil)	2000	Mary Pierce (France)
2001	Gustavo Kuerten (Brazil)	2001	Jennifer Capriati (USA)
2002	Albert Costa (Spain)	2002	Serena Williams (USA)
2003	Juan Carlos Ferrero (Spain)	2003	Justine Henin-Hardenne (Belgium)
2004	Gaston Gaudio (Argentina)	2004	Anastasia Myskina (Russia)
2005	Rafael Nadal (Spain)	2005	Justine Henin-Hardenne (Belgium)

Australian Open

First held in 1905 as the Australasian Tennis Championships; became the Australian Championships in 1927.

Men's singles		Women's singles	
1981	Johan Kriek (South Africa)	1981	Martina Navratilova (USA)
1982	Johan Kriek (South Africa)	1982	Chris Evert Lloyd (USA)
1983	Mats Wilander (Sweden)	1983	Martina Navratilova (USA)
1984	Mats Wilander (Sweden)	1984	Chris Evert Lloyd (USA)
1985	Stefan Edberg (Sweden)	1985	Martina Navratilova (USA)
1986	*not held*	1986	*not held*
1987	Stefan Edberg (Sweden)	1987	Hana Mandlikova (Czechoslovakia)
1988	Mats Wilander (Sweden)	1988	Steffi Graf (West Germany)
1989	Ivan Lendl (Czechoslovakia)	1989	Steffi Graf (West Germany)
1990	Ivan Lendl (Czechoslovakia)	1990	Steffi Graf (Germany)
1991	Boris Becker (Germany)	1991	Monica Seles (Yugoslavia)
1992	Jim Courier (USA)	1992	Monica Seles (Yugoslavia)
1993	Jim Courier (USA)	1993	Monica Seles (Yugoslavia)
1994	Pete Sampras (USA)	1994	Steffi Graf (Germany)
1995	André Agassi (USA)	1995	Mary Pierce (France)
1996	Boris Becker (Germany)	1996	Monica Seles (USA)
1997	Pete Sampras (USA)	1997	Martina Hingis (Switzerland)
1998	Petr Korda (Czech Republic)	1998	Martina Hingis (Switzerland)
1999	Yevgeny Kafelnikov (Russia)	1999	Martina Hingis (Switzerland)
2000	André Agassi (USA)	2000	Lindsay Davenport (USA)
2001	André Agassi (USA)	2001	Jennifer Capriati (USA)
2002	Thomas Johansson (Sweden)	2002	Jennifer Capriati (USA)
2003	André Agassi (USA)	2003	Serena Williams (USA)
2004	Roger Federer (Switzerland)	2004	Justine Henin-Hardenne (Belgium)
2005	Marat Safin (Russia)	2005	Serena Williams (USA)

Davis Cup

International men's team competition organized on a knockout basis; first held in 1900; contested on a challenge basis until 1972.

1981	USA	1990	USA	1999	Australia
1982	USA	1991	France	2000	Spain
1983	Australia	1992	USA	2001	France
1984	Sweden	1993	Germany	2002	Russia
1985	Sweden	1994	Sweden	2003	Australia
1986	Australia	1995	USA	2004	Spain
1987	Sweden	1996	France	2005	Croatia
1988	West Germany	1997	Sweden		
1989	West Germany	1998	Sweden		

Grand Slam winners (singles)

Players who have won the Australian Open, the French Open, Wimbledon and the US Open in the same calendar year.

Men		Women	
1938	Don Budge (USA)	1953	Maureen Connolly (USA)
1962	Rod Laver (Australia)	1970	Margaret Court (Australia)
1969	Rod Laver (Australia)	1988	Steffi Graf (West Germany)

VOLLEYBALL

Indoor court game; two teams of six play on a court which has a raised net stretched across the centre; aim is to score points by grounding the inflated ball on opponent's side after hitting it over net with the arms or hands; ball may not be hit more than three times on one team's side of the net.

Ruling body: International Volleyball Federation (FIVB; Fédération Internationale de Volleyball)

Volleyball court

service area
backline
centre line
attack line
3m/9ft 6in
18m/59ft
9m/29ft 6in
6m/19ft 6in

World Championships

Inaugurated in 1949; first women's championships in 1952; now held every four years, but Olympic champions are also world champions in Olympic years.

Men		Women	
1982	USSR	1982	China
1984	USA	1984	China
1986	USA	1986	China
1988	USA	1988	USSR
1990	Italy	1990	USSR
1992	Brazil	1992	Cuba
1994	Italy	1994	Cuba
1996	The Netherlands	1996	Cuba
1998	Italy	1998	Cuba
2000	Yugoslavia	2000	Cuba
2002	Brazil	2002	Italy

WEIGHTLIFTING

Test of strength by lifting weights attached to both ends of a metal pole or *barbell*. Competitors have to make two successful lifts: the *snatch*, taking the bar to an outstretched position above the head in one movement (held for two seconds), and the *clean and jerk* or *jerk* which is achieved in two movements, first onto the chest, then above the head with outstretched arms; aggregate weight of the two lifts gives a competitor's total, and the weights are gradually increased. Another form is *powerlifting*, which calls for sheer strength rather than technique, and takes three forms: the *squat*, *dead lift* and *bench press*. Weightlifting was part of ancient Olympic Games; introduced as sport c.1850.

Ruling body: International Weightlifting Federation (IWF)

World Championships

First held in 1891; 11 weight divisions; the most prestigious is the 105kg-plus category (formerly known as Super Heavyweight, then 110kg-plus; in 1993 changed to 108kg-plus; in 1998 reduced to current weight); Olympic champions are automatically world champions in Olympic years. Women's World Championships instituted in 1987; the most prestigious of 7 weight divisions is the 75kg-plus category (formerly 82.5kg-plus; in 1993 changed to 83kg-plus; in 1998 reduced to current weight).

Men 105kg-plus

1981	Anatoli Pisarenko (USSR)
1982	Anatoli Pisarenko (USSR)
1983	Anatoli Pisarenko (USSR)
1984	Dean Lukin (Australia)
1985	Antonio Krastev (Bulgaria)
1986	Antonio Krastev (Bulgaria)
1987	Aleksandr Kurlovich (USSR)
1988	Aleksandr Kurlovich (USSR)
1989	Stefan Botev (Bulgaria)
1990	Stefan Botev (Bulgaria)
1991	Aleksandr Kurlovich (USSR)
1992	Aleksandr Kurlovich (UT)
1993	Ronnie Weller (Germany)
1994	Aleksandr Kurlovich (Belarus)
1995	Andrey Chemerkin (Russia)
1996	Andrey Chemerkin (Russia)
1997	Andrey Chemerkin (Russia)
1998	Andrey Chemerkin (Russia)
1999	Andrey Chemerkin (Russia)
2000	Hossein Reza Zadeh (Iran)
2001	Saeed Salem Jaber (Qatar)
2002	Hossein Reza Zadeh (Iran)
2003	Hossein Reza Zadeh (Iran)
2004	Hossein Reza Zadeh (Iran)
2005	Hossein Reza Zadeh (Iran)

Women 75kg-plus

1987	Han Changmei (China)
1988	Han Changmei (China)
1989	Han Changmei (China)
1990	Li Yajuan (China)
1991	Li Yajuan (China)
1992	Li Yajuan (China)
1993	Li Yajuan (China)
1994	Karolina Lundahl (Finland)
1995	Erika Takacs (Hungary)
1996	Ni Wan (China)
1997	Ma Runmei (China)
1998	Tang Gonghong (China)
1999	Ding Meiyuan (China)
2000	Ding Meiyuan (China)
2001	Albina Khomich (Russia)
2002	Agata Wrobel (Poland)
2003	Ding Meiyuan (China)
2004	Tang Gonghong (China)
2005	Mi-Ran Jang (South Korea)

WRESTLING

Fighting person to person without using fists; aim is to throw opponent to the ground; most popular forms are *freestyle*, where the legs can be used to hold and trip, and *Graeco-Roman* where holds below the waist are not allowed. Ten weight divisions, from 55kg to 120kg.

Ruling body: International Federation of Associated Wrestling Styles (FILA; Fédération Internationale de Lutte Amateur)

World Championships

Graeco-Roman world championships first held in 1921; first freestyle championships in 1951; each style contests 10 weight divisions, the heaviest being the 120kg (formerly over 100kg, and until Dec 2001 130kg) category; Olympic champions become world champions in Olympic years.

Super-heavyweight/120kg

Freestyle

1981	Salman Khasimikov (USSR)	1994	Mahmut Demir (Turkey)
1982	Salman Khasimikov (USSR)	1995	Bruce Baumgartner (USA)
1983	Salman Khasimikov (USSR)	1996	Mahmut Demir (Turkey)
1984	Bruce Baumgartner (USA)	1997	Zekeriya Güclü (Turkey)
1985	David Gobedzhishvilli (USSR)	1998	Alexis Rodriguez (Cuba)
1986	Bruce Baumgartner (USA)	1999	Stephen Neal (USA)
1987	Aslam Khadartsev (USSR)	2000	David Moussoulbes (Russia)
1988	David Gobedzhishvilli (USSR)	2001	David Moussoulbes (Russia)
1989	Ali Reiza Soleimani (Iran)	2002	David Moussoulbes (Russia)
1990	David Gobedzhishvilli (USSR)	2003	Artur Taymazov (Uzbekistan)
1991	Andreas Schroder (Germany)	2004	Artur Taymazov (Uzbekistan)
1992	Bruce Baumgartner (USA)	2005	Aydin Polatci (Turkey)
1993	Bruce Baumgartner (USA)		

Graeco-Roman

1981	Refik Memisevic (Yugoslavia)	1994	Aleksandr Karelin (Russia)
1982	Nikola Dinev (Bulgaria)	1995	Aleksandr Karelin (Russia)
1983	Jewgeni Artjuchin (Russia)	1996	Aleksandr Karelin (Russia)
1984	Jeffrey Blatnick (USA)	1997	Aleksandr Karelin (Russia)
1985	Igor Rostorotzki (USSR)	1998	Aleksandr Karelin (Russia)
1986	Thomas Johansson (Sweden)	1999	Aleksandr Karelin (Russia)
1987	Igor Rostorotzki (USSR)	2000	Rulon Gardner (USA)
1988	Aleksandr Karelin (USSR)	2001	Rulon Gardner (USA)
1989	Aleksandr Karelin (USSR)	2002	Dremiel Byers (USA)
1990	Aleksandr Karelin (USSR)	2003	Khassan Baroev (Russia)
1991	Aleksandr Karelin (USSR)	2004	Khassan Baroev (Russia)
1992	Aleksandr Karelin (UT)	2005	Mijain Lopez Nunez (Cuba)
1993	Aleksandr Karelin (Russia)		

Wrestling Around the World

Other forms of wrestling include *sumo*, the national sport in Japan; *sambo* in Russia; *kushti* in Iran; *glima* in Iceland; *Schwingen* in Switzerland; and *yagli*, the national sport in Turkey. There are also variations within the UK, such as *Devon and Cornwall* wrestling and *Cumberland and Westmoreland* wrestling.

CRUFTS WINNERS

Crufts is the world's largest dog show. It is held annually under the auspices of the Kennel Club UK. Named after the show's founder, Charles Cruft (1852–1938); first held in 1891.

Year	Name	Breed
1981	Ch Astley Portia of Rua	Irish Setter
1982	Ch Grayco Hazelnut	Toy Poodle
1983	Ch Montravia Kaskarak Hitari	Afghan Hound
1984	Ch Saxonsprings Hackensack	Lhasa Apso
1985	Ch Montravia Tommy-Gun	Standard Poodle
1986	Ch Ginger Xmas Carol	Airedale Terrier
1987	Ch Viscount Grant	Afghan Hound
1988	Sh Ch Starlite Express at Valsett	English Setter
1989	Ch Potterdale Classic of Moonhill	Bearded Collie
1990	Ch Olac Moon Pilot	West Highland White Terrier
1991	Sh Ch Raycrofts Socialite	Clumber Spaniel
1992	Ch Pencloe Dutch Gold	Whippet
1993	Sh Ch Danaway Debonair	Irish Setter
1994	Ch Purston Hit	Welsh Terrier
1995	Ch Starchelle Chicago Bear	Irish Setter
1996	Sh Ch Canigou Cambrai	Cocker Spaniel
1997	Ch Ozmilion Mystification	Yorkshire Terrier
1998	Ch Saredon Forever Young	Welsh Terrier
1999	Sh Ch Caspians Intrepid	Irish Setter
2000	Ch Torums Scarf Michael	Kerry Blue Terrier
2001	Ch Jethard Cidevant	Basenji
2002	Nord Ch Topscore Contradiction	Standard Poodle
2003	Ch Yakee A Dangerous Liaison	Pekingese
2004	Ch Cobyco Call The Tune	Whippet
2005	Am Ch/Ch Cracknor Cause Celebre	Norfolk Terrier

Note: In the names of pedigree dogs, Ch stands for Champion and Sh Ch for Show Champion.

Popular Pooches

The Kennel Club, organizers of Crufts, report that the labrador retriever has been the most popular breed of dog in the UK and the USA for 15 consecutive years. The labrador is also the most popular dog in Denmark, Germany, the Netherlands and Portugal. In Sweden and Norway, however, the German Shepherd dog was most popular, while Finland has most Finnish hounds and in Spain the Yorkshire terrier tops the list. The UK's other top dogs were the cocker spaniel, English springer spaniel, German shepherd, Staffordshire bull terrier, cavalier King Charles spaniel, golden retriever, West Highland white terrier, boxer and border terrier.

MONOPOLY® PROPERTY VALUES

Property values shown are for the standard British edition of the game.

Property	Value	Colour
Old Kent Road	£60	brown
Whitechapel Road	£60	brown
Kings Cross Station	£200	—
The Angel Islington	£100	light blue
Euston Road	£100	light blue
Pentonville Road	£120	light blue
Pall Mall	£140	pink
Electric Company	£150	—
Whitehall	£140	pink
Northumberland Avenue	£160	pink
Marylebone Station	£200	—
Bow Street	£180	orange
Marlborough Street	£180	orange
Vine Street	£200	orange
Strand	£220	red
Fleet Street	£220	red
Trafalgar Square	£240	red
Fenchurch Street Station	£200	—
Leicester Square	£260	yellow
Coventry Street	£260	yellow
Water Works	£150	—
Piccadilly	£280	yellow
Regent Street	£300	green
Oxford Street	£300	green
Bond Street	£320	green
Liverpool Street Station	£200	—
Park Lane	£350	navy blue/purple
Mayfair	£400	navy blue/purple

Monopoly® Money

The game's makers estimate that more than 160 million copies of Monopoly® have been sold worldwide in 80 countries, and it has been translated into 26 languages. More than 20 million of those copies have been sold in the UK – manufacturers Hasbro estimate that is more than £302.8 billion in Monopoly® money, as a total of £15 140 in Monopoly® money is included in each game. Games have been played in the House of Commons, the London Stock Exchange and the Bank of England – where real money was used for the 1996 UK finals.

BINGO CALLS

A selection of traditional bingo calls is given.

1	Kelly's eye *or* Buttered scone *or* At the beginning
2	One little duck *or* Me and you *or* Little boy blue
3	Cup of tea *or* You and me
4	Knock at the door
5	Man alive
6	Half a dozen *or* Tom's tricks
7	Lucky
8	Garden Gate *or* One fat lady
9	Doctor's orders
10	Tony's Den[1]
11	Legs eleven
12	One dozen
13	Unlucky for some *or* Baker's dozen
14	Valentine's Day
15	Young and keen *or* Rugby Team
16	Sweet sixteen *or* Never been kissed
17	Dancing queen
18	Coming of age *or* Now you can vote
19	Goodbye teens
20	One score
21	Key of the door
22	Two little ducks *or* All the twos
23	Thee and me *or* The Lord's My Shepherd
24	Two dozen
25	Duck and dive
30	Dirty Gertie
40	Naughty forty
50	Half a century
60	Five dozen
70	Three score and ten
80	Eight and blank
90	Top of the shop

[1] *Name changes with the incumbent prime minister; for example, during Margaret Thatcher's time in office it would have been Maggie's Den.*

Bingo Lingo

Other classic bingo calls include *Tweak of the thumb* (51), *Heinz varieties* (57), *Brighton line* (59), *Old age pension* (65), *Clickety click* (66), *Danny la Rue* (72), *Trombones* (76), *Torquay in Devon* (87), *Two fat ladies* (88) and *Nearly there* (89).

INDEX

G

N

O

S